Answers to Every Windows Question...

11 When what you're programming is the registry...

You really need to see Chapter 10, "Programming and the Registry: a Developer's Paradise?"

12 How do you change icons on the Desktop for Outlook, Exchange, Internet Explorer programs, and others?

See Chapter 12, "The Windows XP User Interface: Changing How It Looks."

13 Don't have a tape drive and want to back up the registry?

See Chapter 2, "Readme.1st: Preventing Disaster!"

14 How is the Registry data stored?

In a number of standard data formats. These formats are described briefly in Chapter 1, "What Is a Registry—and Why?" and fully in Appendix B, "Registry Data Types."

15 Find out all about the six main hives in the registry...

In Chapter 1, "What Is a Registry—and Why?"

16 Want to change the Desktop background, even before anyone logs on?

See the section "Backgrounds and Wallpapers" in Chapter 12, "The Windows XP's User Interface: Changing How It Looks."

17 How do you customize Microsoft Office?

Chapter 14, "Microsoft Office Entries," shows you.

18 Need a quick list of all the world's telephone area and country codes?

Check out the section "CurrentVersion\ Telephony" in Chapter 18, "Introduction to HKEY_LOCAL_MACHINE\Software."

19 Where is that Windows XP "Easter egg"?

Windows XP doesn't have an 'Easter egg', but for Windows 2000, check out the "Easter Egg Hunt?" section in Chapter 12.

20 How do you find a particular hive or key?

Take a quick peek at Appendix A, "Common Hives and Keys."

Mastering™
Windows® XP Registry

Peter Hipson

SYBEX® San Francisco   London

Associate Publisher: Joel Fugazzotto

Acquisitions and Developmental Editor: Ellen L. Dendy

Editor: Anamary Ehlen

Production Editor: Elizabeth Campbell

Technical Editor: Donald Fuller

Electronic Publishing Specialist: Maureen Forys, Happenstance Type-O-Rama

Proofreaders: Nanette Duffy, Emily Hsuan, Laurie O'Connell, Yariv Rabinovitch, Nancy Riddiough

Book Designer: Maureen Forys, Happenstance Type-O-Rama

Indexer: Ted Laux

Cover Designer: Design Site

Cover Illustrator: Sergie Loobkoff

This book is dedicated to my students at FPC. Perhaps the hardest part of their education is putting up with me. I expect a lot, and they give it.

Acknowledgments

AN ACKNOWLEDGMENTS SECTION IS always hard to write; there are just so many people who have helped. An author's greatest fear is forgetting someone, so I always start off by saying thanks to everyone. If I didn't list you, please don't hate me!

Thanks go to Ellen Dendy, of course, who served as acquisitions and developmental editor for this book. Ellen Dendy also helped greatly by providing critical direction whenever needed. (Of course, if you don't like this book, the blame falls on me and only me!)

Thanks to the Sybex editorial staff, especially Anamary. Thanks also to Elizabeth Campbell, production editor, for her skillful work and management; to Maureen Forys, electronic publishing specialist, for her expert and speedy layout skills; and to Nanette Duffy, Emily Hsuan, Laurie O'Connell, Yariv Rabinovitch, and Nancy Riddiough, proofreaders, for their proficient proofreading of the pages.

Don Fuller served well as our technical editor. It was Don's job to make sure that I told no lies, made no mistakes.

Jerold Schulman (JSI, Inc.) maintains the web page at `http://www.jsiinc.com/reghack.htm`. He provided a lot of expert hints for this book. If you need assistance with your Windows XP installation, check out Jerold's web pages for his tips, tricks, and registry hacks.

Special thanks to Laura Belt at Adler & Robin Books. Laura is the person who makes this a business and not a hobby.

Thanks to Barry and Marcia Press for their input on the book's contents. Barry asked for a number of things to be covered, and I've covered as many as I could.

Thanks to the ExpertZone (and my team members who put up with my slow responses), and everyone at Microsoft who helped, too.

Of course, I would be remiss if I didn't thank my family, especially my wife, Nang, who has supported me through thick and thin, and the folks at CMC and MCH who made sure that I survived the experience.

Contents at a Glance

Contents

Introduction

THE REGISTRY HAS EVOKED emotions from terror to mystery. Few Windows XP users consider the registry their friend. After all, think of it: The registry is the heart and soul of the Windows XP operating system. The registry is everything—it is the brain of the operating system. Damage the registry, and Windows XP quickly develops brain damage and needs major surgery.

This is it—the only book on the Windows XP registry that you will need. Now, I won't kid you; there are a few other books on the Windows registry. Every current version of Windows uses a similar registry structure, but we do find that there are sufficient differences between them make it difficult for one book to cover everything well.

Will you need another book or tool besides this book? Maybe not. But I do recommend that you get Microsoft's Windows XP Resource Kit, too; it has a lot of good utilities that you will find invaluable. The Windows XP Resource Kit also has a lot of good non-registry stuff.

This book covers the Windows XP registry from A to Z. I've covered the standard stuff, from things that most of us should know to things that are not documented at all and are probably only known by a very few first-rate system administrators.

Who Is This Book For?

This book is valuable to all Windows XP users. Even users of Windows NT 4 and 2000 and Windows 95/98/Me may find good information in this book, though it is primarily oriented toward Windows XP.

This book is intended for:

◆ General users who use Windows XP at their desks and are responsible for their own computer(s). Typically, these users don't have responsibility for other users' computers, though they may help their friends out from time to time.

◆ System administrators who are responsible for an organization's computers (and perhaps thousands of Windows XP installations). Administrators will be presented with virtually every conceivable problem over a given period of time. Whatever can go wrong will; Murphy's Law is applied double to system administrators.

◆ Help desk staff who support users, even if they don't usually administer the system. Help desk staff roam throughout the organization, providing help and assistance as needed. All help desk people are going to find this book very useful.

If you are a user who wants to get the most out of your Windows XP installation (either Home Edition, Professional, or one of the upcoming .NET Server versions), this book is a very good starting point. Think of it this way: If you are a system administrator, this book is one of the tools that you will need to manage and administer your Windows XP network. Manning the help desk? If so, having this book close at hand can save you lots of time and effort.

Overview of the Contents

This book is made up of four major sections.

PART I: REGISTRY BASICS

In Part I, "Registry Basics," I discuss ways to avoid problems, do backups, and restore the registry, and I cover some of the tools that are used with the registry. The first chapter, "What Is a Registry—and Why?," introduces the registry. You'll learn about the registry's major sections, called hives. This chapter also tells you about the registry's history.

TIP   *The fastest way to access the registry is to use* `RegEdit.exe`, *which comes with Windows XP. To access* `RegEdit.exe`, *simply click the Start button, then click Run. Type* **RegEdit** *in the dialog box and press Enter. The RegEdit window will appear.*

Chapter 2 is called "Readme.1st: Preventing Disaster!" It jumps right into one of the most important topics in this book: how to avoid getting into trouble. Most Windows XP disasters are registry related, and they are also preventable. Registry problems often arise because we don't have a good backup of the registry, and something comes along and damages it. Once damaged, the registry can be very difficult to recover.

Chapter 3, "Anatomy of the Registry: The Blood, Gore, and Guts," is an in-depth analysis of what's in the registry. Each major hive is covered in detail. We'll discuss the way the hives relate to each other, along with how Windows XP manages users in the registry.

Tools, tools, and more tools. Chapter 4, "Registry Tools and Tips: Getting the Work Done," takes a close look at the registry tools that are included with Windows XP. The Registry Editor is covered, as well as the Backup utility and the registry software that is included in the Windows XP Resource Kit.

In Chapter 5, "Policies: Good for One, Good for All," you learn all about policies in Windows XP. Policies affect specific computers, users, and groups.

PART II: ADVANCED REGISTRY STUFF

In this second part of the book, I cover OLE (Object Linking and Embedding), some history of the `win.ini` and `system.ini` files, how to remove excess baggage from the registry, registry programming interfaces, and the Performance Monitor entries. Getting into the advanced stuff, we jump right into the issues of OLE, associations, and such. Chapter 6 is called "Associations, Linkages, and OLE: How Confusing Can This Get?" It tries to clear the often muddy water that swirls around the OLE registry components. A major part of the registry is OLE related, with Windows XP using OLE to manage much of the user interface.

Even though the `System.ini` and `Win.ini` files have not been used for some time, we still have them. Chapter 7 is called "Why, Oh Why, Are There System.ini and Win.ini Files?" Here we delve into why these two files are still found under Windows and what makes them necessary.

If you want to get rid of that memo from your boss telling you that your project is due, you toss it into the trash can. Something in the registry that is not needed can be more difficult to get rid of. Chapter 8, "Getting Rid of the Unwanted," introduces the problem of registry clutter and describes some very useful tools to clean up this excess.

By following the advice in Chapter 9, "Recovering from Disaster, or Making the Best of a Bad Situation," you can make sure that disaster doesn't strike. However, sometimes disaster just happens. Recovery, whether from backups or from manually cleaning the registry, is vital.

My name's Peter, and I'm a programmer. Ah, there, I said it, and I feel much better. I felt even better after writing Chapter 10, "Programming and the Registry: A Developer's Paradise?" This is where the programming interface to the registry is unveiled. Examples in C/C++ and a lot of information about Microsoft's MFC registry interface come to light in this chapter.

The Windows XP Performance Monitor allows analysis of the system's performance and the development of performance-enhancement strategies. In Chapter 11, "The Performance Monitor Meets the Registry," you begin to understand how the Windows XP Performance Monitor interacts with the registry and how you can add performance-monitoring technologies to your own applications.

PART III: WINDOWS AND OFFICE REGISTRY ENTRIES

In Part III, I discuss the UI (user interface), networking, and internal Windows XP entries. What we see as users is all stored in the registry. Chapter 12, "The Windows XP User Interface: Changing How It Looks," delves into the various registry entries that control the look and feel of Windows XP. This chapter covers both the graphical Desktop and the Windows command windows.

Under the hood of Windows XP are entries in the registry for both networking and other internal Windows XP components. Chapter 13, "Networking and Registry System Entries," digs into these less visible entries in the registry and explains them to you.

Chapter 14, "Microsoft Office Entries," covers changes that Microsoft Office has made to the registry. Sometimes Microsoft Office components are installed and then removed. Sadly, not all registry entries for these products are removed. How do you get them out of there? Also, how do you create a configuration so those new users of Microsoft Office will get a predefined configuration? Care to program the registry using Visual Basic for Applications? (It's easy, really.) Check this chapter for the answers to these questions.

PART IV: THE REGISTRY INTERFACE

Part IV is a reference to many of the registry entries, arranged by hive. Program associations, OLE associations, and file-type management are all part of HKEY_CLASSES_ROOT. Chapter 15, "Introduction to HKEY_CLASSES_ROOT," covers this hive's contents.

User information that is stored in HKEY_USERS and used in HKEY_CURRENT_USER is the subject of Chapter 16, "Introduction to HKEY_CURRENT_USER and HKEY_USERS." Windows XP keeps only the currently logged-on user and the .DEFAULT user in HKEY_USERS; other users are saved in HKEY_LOCAL_MACHINE's SAM (Security Accounts Manager) sections.

HKEY_LOCAL_MACHINE is the hive that controls the system itself. This topic is so large that three chapters are dedicated to it. Chapter 17, "Introduction to HKEY_LOCAL_MACHINE," covers the major parts of HKEY_LOCAL_MACHINE. Information about installed software is found in Chapter 18, "Introduction to HKEY_LOCAL_ MACHINE\Software." Virtually every installed application or component is found in HKEY_LOCAL_MACHINE\Software. The system configuration is covered in Chapter 19, "Introduction to HKEY_LOCAL_MACHINE\System and HKEY_CURRENT_CONFIG." System entries are critical to the health and welfare of Windows XP.

Typesetting Conventions

This book is typeset so that it is readable. Otherwise the pages would all be blank.

OK, seriously. This book uses various conventions to present information. Notes, Tips, and Warnings, shown below, appear throughout the text in order to call attention to special details.

NOTE   This is a Note. Notes contain additional comments and information related to the discussion.

TIP   This is a Tip. Tips highlight important information that you need to know when working with the registry.

WARNING   This is a Warning. Warnings call attention to trouble spots and things to watch out for. Speaking of which, have you backed up your registry lately?

This book also takes advantage of different font styles. **Bold font** in the text indicates something that the user types. A monospaced font is used for registry objects, program strings, entries, commands, and URLs.

To Contact the Author

If you so desire, you may contact me, the author, via e-mail. My e-mail address is phipson@acm.org. Please do not attempt to telephone, even if you find my phone number; my schedule really doesn't allow for answering the phone!

Sybex Technical Support

If you have questions or comments about this book or other Sybex books, you can contact Sybex directly. The following contact information for Sybex is listed in order of preference from the most preferred method to contact Sybex (e-mail) to the least preferred method (snail mail).

FOR THE FASTEST REPLY

E-mail us or visit the Sybex website! You can contact Sybex through the Web by visiting http://www.sybex.com and clicking Support. You may find the answer you're looking for on this site in the FAQ file, so check there too.

When you reach the support page, click Support@sybex.com to send Sybex an e-mail. You can also e-mail Sybex directly at Support@sybex.com.

It's important that you include all the following information to expedite a reply:

Name   The complete title of the book in question.

ISBN number   The ISBN that appears on the back cover of the book. This number appears at the bottom right corner on the back cover and looks like this:

0-7821-2987-0

Printing The printing of the book. You can find this near the front of the book at the bottom of the copyright page. You should see a line of numbers as in the following:

10 9 8 7 6 5 4 3 2

The lowest number in this line of numbers is the printing. The example here indicates that the book is from the second printing.

The ISBN number and printing are very important for technical support, because they indicate the edition and reprint you have in your hands. Many changes occur between printings and editions. Don't forget to include this information!

Page number or filename Include the page number where you have a problem.

PC details Include the following information:

- Name of your PC (the manufacturer)

- Operating system being used

- The software you have installed that relates to the book (indicate the exact version number)

- Whether your machine has any unique characteristics

Sybex technical support will try to answer your question quickly and accurately.

OTHER WAYS TO REACH SYBEX

The slowest way to contact Sybex is through the mail. If you do not have access to the Internet or a telephone, write Sybex a note and send it to the following address:

SYBEX Inc.
Attention: Technical Support
1151 Marina Village Parkway
Alameda, CA 94501

Part I

Registry Basics

In this section, you will learn how to:
- ◆ Understand the development and organization of the registry
- ◆ Prevent registry disasters before they strike
- ◆ Interpret the anatomy and configuration of the registry
- ◆ Use registry tools and other resources
- ◆ Apply policies to individuals and groups

Chapter 1

What Is a Registry and Why?

SOME USERS OF WINDOWS know exactly what the registry is a system designed to cause users and administrators to lose their hair. I know this is true because I can no longer feel the wind ruffling through my hair. Oh, I feel the wind; I just don't feel the hair.

The registry is a simple, hierarchical database of information that Windows operating systems (and some applications) use to define the configuration of the system. Originally, in the early, simple days of Windows (16-bit Windows versions especially), the same information that is now stored in the registry was stored in text files. Though these text files were simple, their organization made access to the information they contained too slow to keep up with increasingly speedy technology.

Many applications use the registry the same way, though some applications are now moving to separate storage locations for their data—a technique that allows the applications to easily back up and restore their configuration data.

In this chapter, I'll discuss the history of the registry and define it in greater detail. We'll cover the following topics:

◆ The development of the registry

◆ How the registry is organized

◆ How the registry is used

◆ Distinctions in terminology

The Registry: Past and Present

The development of the registry, like Windows, has been evolutionary. The registry was preceded by a pair of flat-text files, called `win.ini` and `system.ini`. While the performance with these files left something to be desired, they formed the basis for today's registry.

In fact, these two files live on today in Windows XP, though they are virtually unchanged from Windows NT version 4. The first registry to appear in Windows was created to solve a number of problems: poor performance (retrieving information from the original flat-text `.ini` files was cumbersome), size limitations (the `.ini` files could be only so large), and maintenance problems (the `.ini` files were organizationally impaired!).

Today, the Windows XP system `.ini` files contain only a few entries used by a few applications. (Most are legacy 16-bit applications, though a few new programs are also placing some items in the `win.ini` file, too!)

These system `.ini` files are of no importance to us, and we may safely ignore them. For Windows XP, it's the registry that is most important to the system, because it contains the heart and soul of Windows XP. Without the registry, Windows XP would be nothing more than a collection of programs, unable to perform even the basic tasks that we expect from an operating system. Every bit of configuration information that Windows XP has is crammed into the registry. Information about the system's hardware, preferences, security, and users—everything that can be set is set in there.

However, times are a-changing. Microsoft now realizes that if every application stores application-specific information in the system registry, then the system registry can grow to an enormous size. That isn't quite what Microsoft had in mind when they created the registry structure. Microsoft's policy now states that applications may (and should) use standalone `.ini` files as needed.

Some advantages to using application-specific `.ini` files include these:

♦ Individual applications sometimes need to be restored from backup. With an application-specific `.ini` file, it is not necessary to back up and restore the entire registry to reinstall any single application. (This eliminates the attendant problem of restoring one part of the registry only to lose another part during the restoration!)

♦ The system registry has a practical limited size. Granted, the size is large, but some applications have lately been adding substantial content to the registry without regard to the fact (sad as it is) that the registry is a *shared* resource that everyone, including the system, must use! Once the registry gets too large, some registry operations may take an excessive amount of time.

NOTE   *Microsoft limits the size of any object that is stored in a registry data key to 1MB. This limit is basically only meaningful for REG_BINARY objects, because strings and such are unlikely to become this large. If you must store more than 1MB in a registry object, then store the information in a file and store a pointer to the file in the registry. Without this limitation, the registry could easily grow to be the largest file on your system.*

FOR WINDOWS BEFORE WINDOWS XP

Windows 2000 and earlier versions set restrictions on registry size. If you approach your registry limit, you'll get a message stating that you are low on registry quota. This indicates that the registry has grown too large for the current size allocation. Unless you change it, the registry size is set to 25 percent of the paged pool size; for most computers, the paged pool size is approximately equal to the amount of installed RAM, up to a maximum of 192MB. The registry can be set to 80 percent of the paged pool size (80 percent of 192MB is just under 154MB, though good sense says to round down to 150MB).

Earlier versions of Windows adjust the registry size based on the currently installed RAM. Several registry entries affect registry size, though most users will find that the defaults are acceptable for their use. To create a very large registry, ensure that the amount of RAM installed is sufficient and set the `RegistrySize-Limit` and `PagedPoolSize` entries.

Organization

The registry is organized into five major sections. These sections are called *hives*, which are analogous to root directories on your hard drive. Each hive, by definition, has its own storage location (a file) and log file. If necessary, a given hive can be restored without affecting the other hives in the registry.

Inside a hive you find both keys (and subkeys, analogous to directories and subdirectories on your hard disk) and values. The term *value* (or data value, as it is sometimes called) refers to the information, or data, assigned to a key, making the key analogous to a file on your hard drive as well.

A key or subkey may have zero, one, or more value entries, a default value, and from zero to many subkeys. Each value entry has a name, data type, and a value:

- The entry's name is stored as a Unicode character string.

- The entry's type is stored as an integer index. The type is returned to the querying application, which must then map this type to the type that the application knows.

- The entry's value is stored as necessary to allow efficient retrieval of the data when needed.

Both the Windows XP operating system and applications store data in the Windows XP registry. This is both good and bad. It is good because the registry makes an efficient, common storage location. Here's the bad part: as I mentioned earlier, as more and more applications and systems store information in the registry, it grows larger, and larger, and larger.

It is most unusual for the registry to get smaller—I'm unaware of any application that does a really complete job of cleaning up all of its own registry entries when the application is uninstalled. Many applications leave tons of stuff in the registry when they are uninstalled, and not many applications clean up unused entries as a routine process. The end result is that the registry will grow, like Jack's magic beanstalk, as time goes on.

NOTE *From time to time in this book I'll refer to hives, keys, subkeys, and values using the generic term* object. *When the term* object *is used, assume that the item could be any valid item in the registry!*

Hives and Their Aliases

There are five main, or top level, hives in the Windows XP registry, and accepted abbreviations for each:

- HKEY_CLASSES_ROOT, a.k.a. HKCR

- HKEY_CURRENT_USER, a.k.a. HKCU

- HKEY_LOCAL_MACHINE, a.k.a. HKLM

- HKEY_USERS, a.k.a. HKU

- HKEY_CURRENT_CONFIG, a.k.a. HKCC

NOTE *The Windows 98 and Windows Me (Millennium Edition)* HKEY_DYN_DATA *hive, which has no abbreviation, does not exist in Windows XP, though Microsoft had originally intended to include information about Plug and Play in this hive. So where is PnP data saved if the* HKEY_DYN_DATA *hive is gone? Windows XP supports PnP, and Microsoft decided to integrate PnP data with the main registry rather than use a separate hive.*

Each hive begins with HKEY_. HKEY is an abbreviation for "hive key," though the significance of this is not terribly important in understanding the registry. The H also signifies that the name is a "handle" for a program to interface with the registry. These handles are defined in the file winreg.h, included with the Windows XP SDK (Software Development Kit).

The registry contains duplication—sort of. For example, you'll notice that everything in HKEY_CURRENT_USER is also contained in the hive HKEY_USERS. But these aren't two different sets of the same information; rather, they're two names for the same set of information. Microsoft needed to make some parts of the registry appear to be in two places at one time. But they didn't want to copy these sections, because that could have created problems with keeping each of the two sections updated. Instead, they created an alias, or another name, for some registry components. The alias points to the original component and is updated whenever the original is. These aliases are created solely by Windows. You, as a user, can't create an alias in the registry no matter how hard you try!

The most common alias is the registry hive HKEY_CURRENT_USER. It is an alias to either the .DEFAULT user or the current user in HKEY_USERS. If you take a quick peek at HKEY_USERS, you will see several keys there: one is .DEFAULT, and the others are named with long strings of characters. These are SIDs (security identifiers), which Windows XP uses to identify users. One of these subkeys for the currently logged-on user consists of just the SID, while the other consists of the SID suffixed with _Classes. For example, on one Windows XP server, the administrator has the two subkeys HKEY_USERS\S-1-5-21-1004336348-842925246-1592369235-500 and HKEY_USERS\S-1-5-21-1004336348-842925246-1592369235-500_Classes. I'll clear up what a SID is and how it is used in Chapter 17.

NOTE *The default user, used when no user is logged on, has only one subkey, named* .DEFAULT. *(How do you edit the registry when no one is logged on? Simply by using remote registry editing, with a different computer.)*

There are also other aliases in the registry. For example, the registry key HKEY_LOCAL_MACHINE\System\CurrentControlSet is an alias to *one* of the other control sets—ControlSet001, ControlSet002, or sometimes ControlSet003. Again, this is that same magic; only one registry object is there it just has two names. Remember, in modifying a specific registry key or subkey; don't be surprised when another registry key or subkey seems to magically change also!

Data Values

A value may contain one or, in some instances, more than one data item. The only type of multiple-item value entry that the registry editor can handle is REG_MULTI_SZ, which may contain zero, one, or more strings.

Data is stored in a number of different formats. Generally the system uses only a few simple formats, while applications, drivers, and so forth may use more complex types defined for a specific purpose. For example, REG_RESOURCE_LIST is a complex registry type used primarily by drivers. Though it would be inefficient, all registry data could be considered to be REG_BINARY data.

Data types for value entries include:

- REG_BINARY
- REG_COLOR_RGB
- REG_DWORD
- REG_DWORD_BIG_ENDIAN
- REG_DWORD_LITTLE_ENDIAN
- REG_EXPAND_SZ
- REG_FILE_NAME
- REG_FILE_TIME
- REG_FULL_RESOURCE_DESCRIPTOR
- REG_LINK
- REG_MULTI_SZ
- REG_NONE
- **REG_QWORD**
- **REG_QWORD_LITTLE_ENDIAN**
- REG_RESOURCE_LIST
- REG_RESOURCE_REQUIREMENTS_LIST
- REG_SZ
- REG_UNKNOWN

NOTE *REG_QWORD was new to Windows 2000 and is a quad-word (64-bit) numeric entry; REG_QWORD_LITTLE_ENDIAN is the same as REG_QWORD.*

Applications may access each of these data types. Additionally, some applications store data in formats that only they understand. Actually, a provision in the registry allows the storing application to assign a specific type to the registry data. Any application or component that doesn't understand the format would simply treat the data as a REG_UNKNOWN type and read the data as binary.

NOTE *Oops, did I say something special? Yes! Don't forget that applications can and do store data in the registry, and that data needn't be one of the established registry data types.*

How the Registry Is Used

How does Windows XP use the registry? When is the registry first opened and used?

WHAT IS WINDOWS XP?

Windows XP comes in a number of versions, including a Home version and a Professional version. Windows XP Home is configured for home users. Windows XP Professional, which is configured to work as a workstation client, is a somewhat more powerful configuration for business users. Throughout this book, I'll point out any differences in usage between the Home and Professional versions.

While not the focus of this book, Windows XP also comes in a number of server versions named Windows XP .NET. Microsoft has planned several server product offerings, including Windows XP .NET Server and Windows XP .NET Advanced Server. We don't expect that there will be major changes in .NET's use of the registry.

The registry is a tree-based hierarchical system that offers quick access to data stored in almost any format. Actually, the registry is a rather flexible database. Registry information comes from a number of sources:

◆ From installing Windows XP

◆ From booting Windows XP

◆ From applications, systems, and user interaction

Every component of Windows XP uses the registry, without exception. A set of APIs allows both Windows XP and other applications to access registry information easily and quickly.

Windows XP starts to use the registry at the very beginning stages of system bootup. The Windows XP boot process is based on which file format is installed, though the important parts are identical in either case. The unimportant parts are the loading of the specific drivers to read the NTFS file system.

NOTE   *Throughout this book, I'm referring to Windows XP installed on an Intel x86 platform. There are differences in the boot process on RISC-based systems (such as the Digital Alpha system), though these differences are not terribly significant, considering how the registry is used. However, it seems that non–Intel systems are becoming very unusual, and they probably will receive little or no support from Microsoft in the future.*

The Windows XP boot process consists of the following steps:

1. The system is powered up, the video is initialized, and the hardware self-tests are performed. The BIOS performs these tests, which are called POSTs (power-on self-tests). Usually, the memory test is the most visible one; its progress is shown on most computer screens.

2. After running POST, the system initializes each adapter. If the adapter has its own built-in BIOS, the adapter's BIOS is called to perform its own initialization. For IDE adapters (most computers have either two or four IDE adapters), each connected drive (there may be up to two drives for each IDE adapter, allowing for a total maximum of eight IDE type drives) is queried for its specifications and access method.

Some adapters, such as Adaptec's SCSI adapters, display messages and allow the user to interact. Some adapters that don't have a BIOS aren't initialized until Windows XP loads their drivers much later in the boot-up process.

3. After all the adapters that have a BIOS have been initialized, the system boot loader reads in the sector located at the very beginning of the first bootable disk drive and passes commands to this code. This sector is called the *boot sector*, or the MBR (Master Boot Record), and it is written by the operating system when the operating system is installed.

4. The code in the MBR then loads the NTLDR file. (This file has no extension, though it is an executable file.) Once loaded, the MBR passes control to the code in NTLDR.

5. NTLDR then switches into 32-bit mode. (Remember, an Intel *x*86 processor always boots into 16-bit real mode.) It then loads a special copy of the necessary file system I/O files and reads in the file `boot.ini`.

6. The file `boot.ini` has information about each operating system that can be loaded. Remember, Windows XP supports multiboot configurations. It is trivial to create a Windows XP installation that can boot Windows NT, Windows XP, and Windows 95 or Windows 98. The boot loader can even boot two different copies of Windows XP with either the same or different version numbers. NTLDR then processes `boot.ini`, displaying boot information that allows the user to select which operating system will be loaded. At this point, let's assume that Windows XP will be loaded.

7. When you select Windows XP to be loaded, NTLDR loads the file `ntdetect.com`. This program then collects information about the currently installed hardware and saves this information for the registry. Most of this information is stored in the `HKEY_LOCAL_MACHINE` hive.

8. Once NTDETECT has detected the hardware, control is passed back to NTLDR, and the boot process continues. At this point, the registry has been substantially updated with the current hardware configuration, which is stored in `HKEY_LOCAL_MACHINE\Hardware`.

9. The prompt to select the configuration is then presented. This prompt, "Press spacebar now to invoke Hardware Profile/Last Known Good menu," allows you to force Windows XP to use a specific configuration as stored in the registry hive `HKEY_LOCAL_MACHINE`.

10. Following the detection of NTDETECT, NTLDR loads and initializes the Windows NT kernel, loads the services, and then starts Windows.

11. When the kernel is loaded, the HAL is also loaded. (The HAL—Hardware Abstraction Layer—is used to manage hardware services.) Next, the registry system subkey `HKEY_LOCAL_MACHINE\System` is loaded into memory. Windows XP scans the registry for all drivers with a start value of zero. This includes those drivers that should be loaded and initialized at boot time.

12. You can see the beginning of the next stage, kernel initialization. The screen switches to a blue background, and you see a message about the Windows XP build number and the number of system processors. Again, the system scans the registry and finds all drivers that must be started at the kernel initialization stage.

13. From this point, Windows XP starts various components and systems. Each component and system reads the registry and performs various tasks and functions. In the final stage, the program that manages the user logon, WinLogon, starts. WinLogon allows the user to log on and use Windows XP.

Once Windows XP is booted, both the operating system and applications use the registry. The registry is dynamic, but usage of the registry may be dynamic or static. That is, some registry items are read one time and never reread until the system is restarted. Other items are read every time they are referenced. There is no fixed rule as to what is read each time it is needed and what is not, but to be on the safe side, follow these guidelines:

◆ Application-related data is probably read when the application starts. If you change application-based data, restart the application. In fact, the best path to follow is this: do not change application-based data while the application is running.

◆ User-interface data is sometimes dynamic, sometimes static. With user-interface data, the way to go is to change the data and wait to see the results of the change. If the change doesn't appear, try logging on again.

◆ System data is usually either static or otherwise buffered. Many system-related registry changes won't become effective until the system is restarted. Some system data is rewritten, or created, at startup time, precluding changes by users. Many of the items in HKEY_LOCAL_MACHINE may be reset at system boot time, especially those items that are hardware related.

A Note on Terminology

The registry is made up of hives, keys, subkeys, and value entries. Well, actually, depending on the source, you may be faced with hives and data keys, or keys and items, or just data keys, or who knows what else.

There is some indication that Microsoft wants to drop the original term for a registry section—the *hive*—and replace this term with the word *key*. In the Windows NT Resource Kit, Microsoft makes the following definition:

The registry is divided into parts called *hives*. A hive is a discrete body of keys, subkeys, and values rooted at the top of the registry hierarchy. Hives are distinguished from other groups of keys in that they are permanent components of the registry; they are not created dynamically when the system starts and deleted when it stops. Thus, HKEY_LOCAL_MACHINE\Hardware, which is built dynamically by the Hardware Recognizer when Windows NT starts, is not a hive.

In the Windows XP documentation, Microsoft says a hive is:

A section of the registry that appears as a file on your hard disk…

These definitions are absolute and state exactly what is a hive and what is not. However, in the real world, no one follows this exact definition. Many authors call all holders of information *hives* (or *subhives*) and call data objects *keys*. Others never refer to hives at all, and instead call all holders *keys*, or *subkeys*, and refer to data objects as *values*.

Virtually every definition leaves something to be desired. To call the thing that holds data a "value entry" sometimes makes it awkward to refer to the contents. Consider these examples:

The value entry named asdf contains the value 1234.

The value called asdf contains the value 1234.

The following example is much more readable:

The value entry `asdf` is a REG_DWORD with a value of `1234`.

Is there a need to distinguish between what Microsoft calls a "hive" (a top-level, permanent, registry component) and what Microsoft calls a "key"? When does a hive become a key, and is this important? I can't think of any context in which anything is gained by making this distinction. Referring to the top-level objects as *hives* certainly frees up the term *key* to be used elsewhere, but why not stick to one term?

Table 1.1 compares registry terminology against the terminology used for the Windows file system—and gives the terminology I'll be using in this book.

TABLE 1.1: REGISTRY TERMINOLOGY EXPLAINED

CONTEXT	ROOT COLLECTIONS	SUBCOLLECTIONS	OBJECTS	DATA
Disks	Root directories		Files	Data
Older registry terminology	Hives	Subhives	Data keys	Data
Newer registry terminology	Hives	Keys/subkeys	Value entry	Data
Registry terminology used in this book	**Hives**	**Keys/subkeys***	**Value entry**	**Data**

Just to keep things easy to read, I'll use the term key to refer to both keys and subkeys.

Chapter 2

Readme.1st: Preventing Disaster!

PREVENTING DISASTER IS AN important thing to do. No one wants a system failure or to have to reinstall Windows XP. Not the least of your problems will be the issues with product authorization, in that Windows XP, when reinstalled, must be reauthorized!

You are reading this chapter for your own particular reason. Perhaps, as I am recommending, you are here because you want to do everything possible to prevent a disaster with your Windows XP installation. Or maybe you really, really want to recover from an existing disaster. If you are recovering from a problem, you may want to skip to the section later in this chapter titled "Restoring the Registry." For those of you who never do anything wrong, read on. You'll find information on the following topics:

- ◆ Locating the registry
- ◆ Making multiple backup copies
- ◆ Using several backup techniques
- ◆ Restoring the registry
- ◆ Recovering from failure with the Recovery Console
- ◆ Using other backup and restore programs

What's the Deal with the Registry, Anyway?

The registry has always been the one part of Windows that virtually every user neither understands nor trusts. Just when things go well, the registry gets corrupted, and it is time to reinstall everything.

NOTE *Office XP (a.k.a. Office 10) saves its registration information in a file. See Chapter 14 for a bit of information about the registration data file.*

The Windows XP operating system is very robust. However, many things can cause problems. For example, a hard drive failure (even a small soft error on the system drive in the registry files), a controller failure, or a more complex memory bit that sometimes doesn't set correctly all can cause many problems with Windows XP and the registry.

WARNING *Windows XP is robust, but our hardware is not. Most Pentium systems do not have memory parity. Though earlier PC systems used memory parity, this feature disappeared quietly a few years back when memory prices skyrocketed and there was a serious effort to keep computer prices to a minimum. Most of the newest computers now do support parity for their memory (though this support may well not be in use); many of the systems still in use do not support parity, and as a result, routine memory errors won't be detected until it is much too late.*

One of the biggest problems with the registry is that Windows uses it constantly. The entire process of backing up and restoring the operating system is much more difficult because Windows must have the registry files open as a restore is being done.

There are several ways to solve this problem: One solution is to use the backup program supplied with Windows XP. Another is to use an after-market backup program. Such a backup program has to contain the code necessary to do registry backups and restores.

TIP *Oh, joy! The backup program that is included with Windows XP (and Windows 2000) allows backing up to media other than tape drives. Now it is possible to back up to other hard drives (a technique that I use), Zip drives, and other storage media.*

However, these backup and restore techniques may not work well under your circumstances. You may already have had a registry failure, and there may be no registry backup to rely on for recovery. Backing up and recovering the registry without a tape backup was excruciatingly difficult using previous versions of the backup program.

Using the ASR (Automated System Recovery) disk is easy, but you cannot simply stick in a diskette, type `restore registry`, and expect it to work! Windows XP does not store any registry information on the ASR disk (Microsoft recognized that the registry was becoming too large to store on a typical diskette). The Windows XP ASR disk contains only three files: `autoexec.nt`, `config.nt`, and `setup.log`. The directory `%SystemRoot%\Repair` (the same location in which they've been stored since Windows NT 4) holds all the registry files that are backed up.

In fact, restoring the registry from the `%SystemRoot%\Repair` directory requires the Windows XP installation program. It's not that bad; you don't have to reinstall Windows, but the installation program will restore the registry from the backup, if necessary.

The menu that is presented when you boot up Windows XP also allows you to restore parts of the registry based on copies of the registry saved from previous sessions.

WARNING *Always, always make sure that you back up the registry whenever you install new software or hardware or remove anything from your computer. If you do not back up the registry, and you restore a previous copy from an old backup, the system will not work as expected!*

Where Exactly *Is* the Registry?

In order to back it up, you need to know where the registry is located. Sometimes you get to the registry as if by magic—the standard registry editors don't tell you where the registry is; they simply load it automatically. However, many times you need to know where to find the registry files. They're not too difficult to find; the registry's files are in the directory %SystemRoot%\System32\Config.

ENVIRONMENT VARIABLES

Every Windows XP installation automatically has some shortcut variables installed that are accessible to the user and the system. These variables are called *environment variables*. One environment variable, %SystemRoot%, contains the drive, path, and directory name for the directory that Windows XP was installed in.

Using these environment variables makes it easy to write batch files and to otherwise locate components of your current Windows XP installation. For example, you might type at a command prompt:

```
CD %SystemRoot%
```

This command would then change to the directory that Windows XP was installed in.

Using the environment variables also can be very useful when writing software that must be run on a number of different Windows XP installations, especially when these installations are made to different drives or directories.

The %SystemRoot%\System32\Config directory includes the following set of files, each of which is a critical component of the registry. These files are backed up to the Repair directory, so that they may be restored as necessary in the event of a registry failure.

autoexec.nt   The file that initializes the MS-DOS environment unless a different startup file is specified in an application's PIF.

config.nt   The file that initializes the MS-DOS environment unless a different startup file is specified in an application's PIF.

Default   The default registry file.

SAM   The SAM (Security Accounts Manager) registry file.

Security   The security registry file.

setup.log   The file that contains a record of all files that were installed with Windows XP. Service packs and other components of Windows XP use the information in this file to update the operating system.

Software   The application software registry file.

System   The system registry file.

Two additional files are used to reconfigure security when the registry must be repaired. These are contained only in the Repair directory and not in the %SystemRoot%\System32\Config directory:

SecDC.inf The default security settings that have been updated for domain controllers.

SecSetup.inf The out-of-the-box default security settings.

In a typical Windows XP installation, the **%SystemRoot%\System32\Config** directory contains these files:

AppEvent.evt The application(s) event log file.

DEF$$$$$.del The default registry recovery file.

Default The default registry file.

Default.sav A backup copy of the information contained in the default registry file.

DnsEvent.evt The DNS server event log.

File Rep.evt One of two File Replication Service event log files.

Netlogon.dnb A NetLogon support file.

Netlogon.dns A NetLogon support file.

NTDS.evt The Windows XP directory service event log.

NtFrs.evt The second of two File Replication Service event log files.

SAM The Security Accounts Manager registry file.

SecEvent.evt The security event log.

Security The security registry file.

SOF$$$$$.del The software registry recovery file.

Software The application software registry file.

Software.sav A backup copy of the information contained in the software registry file.

SYS$$$$$.del The system registry recovery file.

SysEvent.evt The system events log.

System The system registry file.

System.alt A copy of the information contained in the system registry file.

System.sav A backup copy of the information contained in the system registry file.

Userdiff The file that migrates preexisting user profiles from previous versions of Windows NT to Windows XP.

In the registry, the most important files are those with no extensions—these are the current registry files. Another important file is **System.alt**, a duplicate of the **System** registry file.

SIDE TRIP: RESTORING WINDOWS XP

Restoring a copy of Windows XP from a backup can be a difficult process. First, without a working copy of Windows XP, you can't run the backup and restore programs. This means you have to install a new copy of the operating system to be able to run the restore program. You'd then use this copy of Windows XP to restore the original system from the backup. Some users will reformat the drive, reinstall Windows XP into the same directory that the original installation was made to, and restore on top of this new installation. There's nothing wrong with doing this, as long as you remember one critical point: If you installed any Windows XP service packs on your original installation, these service packs must also be installed on the new installation being used to run the restoration program. If you don't install the service packs, Windows XP restores system files from the original installation (with the service pack) on top of the new files (without the service pack); the files will be out of version sync with the existing operating system files and the registry. This will usually cause the restore to crash without much of a warning as to what happened.

To perform a full restore of Windows XP (and everything else on the drive), do the following:

1. Reformat the drive. Remember that you're doing a full restore here, and nothing that was on the drive is considered valuable at this point.

2. Install Windows XP, using your original distribution CD-ROM.

3. Install the service packs that were installed with the version of Windows that is being restored. Remember that the service packs are cumulative, so you need only reinstall the last service pack. For example, if Service Pack 3 was installed, it will not be necessary to install Service Packs 1 and 2. You only need to reinstall Service Pack 3.

4. Reinstall your backup/restore program, if necessary, and begin your restoration process.

The files in the `%SystemRoot%\System32\Config` directory that have the extensions `.log` or `.sav` contain a history that may be viewed with the Event Viewer program. For example, files with the extension `.sav` are saved using the Last Known Good booting process. Files with the `.log` extension are records of changes made to the registry when registry auditing is turned on. Though the `.log` and `.sav` files are not strictly necessary to have a working Windows XP installation, it is best to consider each of these files a member of a complete set.

WARNING   *Be careful not to replace one file in the registry without replacing all the others. It is simply too easy to get one file out of sync with the remaining registry files, and this would spell disaster.*

Are Two Copies Better Than One?

Generally, two of anything is better than one. It's easier to ride a bicycle than a unicycle. However, it is even easier to drive a car—you don't even have to keep your balance. Where the registry is concerned, keeping *at least* two copies of it is a good idea. I'd recommend that you keep at least four:

◆   The copy created by the Windows XP backup program, which is stored in `%SystemRoot%\Repair`. The Windows XP Setup program is able to use this copy to restore the registry.

◆ A backup copy of the registry files found in `%SystemRoot%\Repair`, saved in a safe and convenient location. Consider a Zip drive or some other type of removable storage media for this copy.

◆ One (or more) backup copies, created using a backup technique on a type of media that is compatible with the backup and restore program of your choice. (I'll discuss backup methods to use in the next section.)

◆ A copy of the registry files contained in `%SystemRoot%\System32\Config` stored on separate media, such as a different drive, diskettes, a Zip drive, CD-RW , or some other easily accessible, writeable media. Try to avoid media requiring special drivers and such, because these drivers may not work when you need to restore that pesky registry. This copy may only be made by dual-booting into another copy of Windows XP (or Windows 95/98/Me if the drive is FAT compatible).

NOTE *In Windows NT 4, keep the special copy created by the RDisk utility that is stored in the Windows NT directory* `%SystemRoot%\Repair`. *This copy of the registry can only be used by the Windows NT Setup program to repair an existing copy of Windows NT. Also keep the copy created by the RDisk utility that is stored on the Windows NT ERD. Again, this copy of the registry can only be used by the Windows NT Setup program to repair an existing copy of Windows NT. Windows XP doesn't support RDisk. Instead, the registry backup and ASR disk-creation functionality is incorporated into the finally-useful-for-everyone Backup program.*

Be absolutely sure you keep these copies secure. Lock 'em up, stash 'em away. Oh, and by the way, that lock on your desk drawer is not good enough; use a good fireproof safe or strong box.

DANGER, WILL ROBINSON, DANGER!

Throughout this chapter and this book we talk about backing up the registry to diskettes, other drives, and tapes. That's all well and good. However, you must remember that the registry contains sensitive information, especially if it is for a Windows XP server.

The registry is the heart and soul of the Windows XP operating system. It contains information critical to both the operation and security of Windows XP. There are many ways that someone could use your backup registry files to breach your system's security, perhaps costing you money or (gasp!) your job.

Be absolutely sure you maintain the highest levels of security for any copies of the registry that you make. If saved to external media (diskettes, tapes, or Zip drives, for example), make sure these copies are securely locked up. Why? Someone could, with little effort, completely subvert system security and then use the backup copies of the registry to hide their actions.

I recommend you use a quality fireproof safe or a strong box for storing your registry backup copies. Me, I use a fireproof, locked strong box inside a federal government–rated Mosler safe—and I don't think I'm being overly protective, either.

Backup Techniques

You can choose from several methods to back up your registry, and you can store your backed-up version on a variety of media. Whether you use the Windows XP Backup program or similar utilities,

DOS commands, or the Registry Editor, you should first understand what type of file systems your computer network uses.

Windows XP supports two different file systems. The first file system, called FAT (File Allocation Table), is identical to the file system used with both DOS and Windows 95/98/Me. The FAT file system is not secure and offers no resistance to hackers and others who want to access files improperly. There are several flavors of the FAT file system: FAT12, FAT16, and FAT32. Windows XP fully supports FAT32 and FAT16. This support allows compatibility with Windows 98's large disk support.

NOTE *Windows NT 4 does not support FAT32 except in a very limited, read-only manner. You cannot install Windows NT 4 onto a FAT32 drive. FAT12 is antiquated and is unlikely to be found on Windows NT systems.*

The second file system, NTFS (NT File System), is unique to Windows XP. Though it is possible to read an NTFS drive from DOS or Windows 95 using shareware utilities, it is generally not possible to write to an NTFS drive unless you are using Windows XP. However, System Internals (see their Internet site at `www.sysinternals.com`) has two utilities that allow you to write to an NTFS volume from DOS or Windows 95/98/Me.

Backup Utility—Backing Up to Tape or Other Media

The Windows XP backup program, Backup (`NTBackup.exe`), is one of a whole slew of compatible backup programs that allow backing up the system registry to tape, diskettes, other hard drives, CD-R, CD-RW, or for that matter, any other Windows XP–supported writeable media. The process is straightforward and can be done as part of a regular backup cycle, or whenever desired. Just check System State in the backup tree to back up using Backup (Figure 2.1) or use the Automated System Recovery Wizard on Backup's Welcome tab (See Figure 2.2).

FIGURE 2.1

Windows XP's Backup utility: System State is selected.

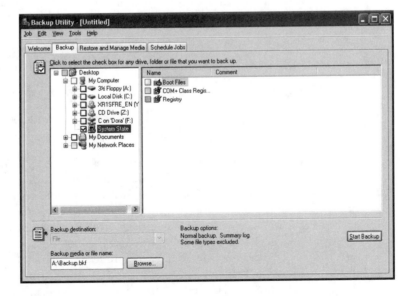

FIGURE 2.2

Use the Automated
System Recovery
Wizard (ASR) to
select System State.

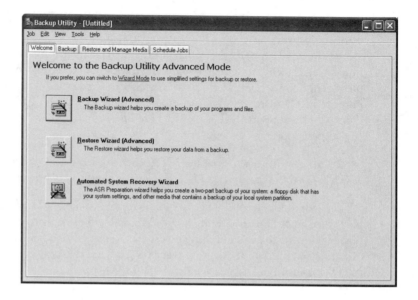

With ASR selected, the wizard creates three backup sets:

- A full backup of the system drive. This backup contains everything that is on the drive. These files are backed up prior to Backup saving the registry to the %SystemRoot%\Repair folder.

- A backup of the %SystemRoot%\Repair folder, after Backup has removed the original backed-up registry components. The only two files contained in this folder are asr.sif and asrpnp.sif.

- A copy of the System State. When Backup stores the System State, it saves the following three items:

  - Boot files: the files used to boot Windows XP

  - COM+ Class Registration database: the COM+ classes' registration

  - Registry: the set of files that comprise the configuration of Windows XP

NOTE   *In Windows 2000, to create an ERD, you use the Backup program. In the Tools menu, simply select Create an Emergency Repair Disk. Backup will prompt for diskettes as needed. Windows XP does not allow separate creation of the ASR disk.*

Using Backup is simple if you are familiar with creating and restoring tape backups. However, you may encounter a few difficulties in using backups of the registry. First, to keep the System State backup easily accessible, it would be wise to place the System State backup on its own media. If the media is inexpensive, this is a viable practice, but if you are paying an arm and a leg for media, this can be costly. Each System State backup includes a full disk backup as part of the backup process.

Second, System State and registry backups must be kept secure, perhaps more secure than standard backups. Everyone's situation is different; just realize that unrestricted access to the registry allows unrestricted, unaudited access to everything else as well. Hacking a backup copy of the registry can reveal information that might seriously compromise your system's security!

Finally, tape backups are sometimes slow. Stick the tape in the drive and the first thing that happens is that the tape gets rewound (to re-tension it). This process alone can take some time—time that is not available when you are working on getting a server up and running. Consider instead backing up the registry to a local hard drive (a drive other than the system drive, however). Backups to networked drives should be approached with caution: unless running a fast network, such a backup might seriously compromise the network performance for an extended period of time. As an example, on a 10BaseT network, backing up 1GB of data would take over 16 minutes!

Backing Up Using copy or xcopy

It is not possible to copy back the current registry while Windows XP is using the registry. Period. Therefore, to restore the registry using either copy or xcopy, it is necessary to shut down Windows XP and start another operating system, such as DOS, Windows 95/98/Me, or a second copy of Windows XP. Which operating system you use depends on which file system is being used on the computer. If the file system is FAT, you should start DOS or Windows 95/98/Me. If the file system is NTFS, you should start a second copy of Windows XP.

NOTE *Microsoft recommends that Windows XP be installed on NTFS partitions. This recommendation is for both performance and security reasons. You can install multiple copies of Windows XP on the same computer, and these installations do not have to be the same "type" (Server and Workstation). As long as the operating system installed has a user with sufficient privilege, you can access files (including the registry) from any of the Windows XP installations.*

Backing up the registry with copy or xcopy is easier than using Backup:

1. Run the Backup program and create an ASR disk (if you do not have a current ASR disk).

2. Copy the backup of the registry found in the %SystemRoot%\Repair directory to another location.

3. Then (this step is optional, but can't hurt), xcopy the current registry files in the %SystemRoot%\ System32\Config directory. Use the /c option to tell xcopy to ignore errors. (This is necessary because the current registry is in use. The xcopy command cannot copy files that are open and will generate an error without the /c option.)

BACKING UP IF YOU'RE USING FAT

Those Windows XP users who are using the FAT file system can simply boot a DOS, or Windows 95/98/Me (if FAT32 is used), diskette formatted with the /sys option. This will give you a DOS command prompt allowing you to read from and write to the hard drive quite easily (of course, accessing output media requires DOS or Windows 95/98/Me support).

To create a bootable FAT-compatible disk, simply use the Windows 95/98/Me or DOS FORMAT command with the /s system option. Then copy xcopy's files (xcopy*.*) to the diskette, too. This disk may then be booted in the Windows XP computer, allowing unrestricted accesses to all FAT-formatted drives installed on the computer. When using Zip, CD-R, or CD-RW drives, it may be necessary to add DOS drivers for these drives to your boot diskette.

NOTE *If the system is already configured for dual-booting, you probably can use the second operating system instead of using a boot diskette. It probably won't matter which alternate operating system is installed (DOS, Windows 95/98/Me, or even variations of Windows NT); all will work fine for the purpose of backing up the registry. There is no need for boot diskettes in this situation.*

After booting into a command prompt, it is a simple task to copy the registry files to a safe location, such as another hard drive, a set of diskettes (the registry won't fit on a single diskette), a Zip drive, a CD-R/CD-RW drive, or other supported media.

NOTE Some computers allow booting from the CD-ROM drive. If this is the case for your computer, then it is also possible, if you have a CD-R/CD-RW drive, to create a bootable CD.

BACKING UP IF YOU'RE USING NTFS

Users with NTFS are presented with a much more difficult problem. The NTFS file system is a secure file system that may not be easily accessed using other operating systems not compatible with NTFS, such as DOS or Windows 95/98/Me. Files on an NTFS drive may only be written by Windows XP and not by other operating systems. Sure, some utilities allow NTFS to be accessed from Windows 95/98/Me. However, the mode of access is typically read-only; there is no chance of a restore that way. Some utilities or drivers do offer write access to NTFS file systems, however I don't recommend using them except as a last resort, because they may not be compatible with future versions of NTFS.

To be able to access the registry files on an NTFS drive, you must install a second copy of Windows XP.

TIP Actually, everyone should have at least two installations of Windows XP: the working copy and an emergency installation to use if the working copy of Windows XP is unable to boot.

Windows XP supports multiple boot configurations quite effectively. To create a multiple boot installation of Windows XP, simply follow these steps:

1. Ensure that you have sufficient space on your hard drive for a second copy of Windows XP. Your second copy of Windows XP only needs to be the basic operating system—only a minimal amount of hard disk space is required. Figure 200MB to 1GB of hard disk space for this backup installation, depending on how much additional software and features you install. (Some users want two virtually identical installations, though this type of installation may consume substantially more disk space than a minimal installation of Windows XP.)

2. Using the Windows XP installation boot diskettes, begin your installation. When prompted for a destination, simply specify a new, different directory than the working installation of Windows XP. If you are farsighted enough, and are doing this before disaster has struck, you can install directly from the distribution CD without using the boot diskettes. To do so, run the Windows XP Setup program to begin the installation process. (You can also install directly from the distribution CD if the hardware supports a boot from the CD drive.)

WARNING Don't install to the same directory that your current working installation of Windows XP is installed into. That won't create a second copy of Windows XP.

3. The Windows XP Setup program will configure the Boot Manager (creating new entries in the boot menu) so that you are able to choose which copy of Windows XP you want to boot.

CUSTOMIZING THE BOOT MENU

Once you install a second copy of Windows XP, your boot menu will list both copies of Windows XP. This can be confusing since the descriptions will be almost identical.

There is a solution: the boot menu can be customized. The boot drive's root directory contains a file called boot.ini. This file includes the boot options for each copy of Windows XP that is installed.

Edit boot.ini by following these steps:

1. Open the Windows XP Control Panel in Classic view.

2. Open System Properties.

3. Click the Advanced tab.

4. In the Startup and Recovery section, click Settings. The Startup and Recovery window opens.

5. In the System Startup section of the Startup and Recovery window, click the Edit button. This launches Notepad, loading the boot.ini file.

6. Edit boot.ini and save the file once you have completed your edits.

7. Close the Startup and Recovery and System Properties windows. (Closing these windows after saving boot.ini ensures that the correct file attributes for boot.ini are preserved.)

When manually editing boot.ini, you need to remove the system, read-only, and hidden attributes by going to a command prompt and typing C:\> **attrib C:\boot.ini -r -s -h**. Don't forget to restore these attributes after you have completed your editing.

The boot.ini file includes quoted text strings that describe the installation:

```
type boot.ini
[boot loader]
timeout=30
default= disk(0)rdisk(0)partition(1)\WINXP
[operating systems]
signature Disk(0)rdisk(0)partition(1)\WINXP="Microsoft Windows XP Server" /fastdetect
multi(0)disk(0)rdisk(0)partition(1)\WINXPBU="Windows NT Server"
multi(0)disk(0)rdisk(0)partition(1)\WINXPBU="Windows NT Server" /basevideo /sos
```

You can modify anything in the quoted strings. I suggest calling your backup installation of Windows XP just that—"Windows XP B/U." For example:

```
multi(0)disk(0)rdisk(0)partition(1)\WINXPBU="Windows XP Server Registry B/U"
multi(0)disk(0)rdisk(0)partition(1)\WINXPBU="Windows XP Server Registry B/U [VGA
mode]" /basevideo /sos
```

Don't forget to use the Control Panel's System applet to change the default boot to the version of Windows XP that normally will be booted by default. After Windows XP is (re)installed, the latest installation is made the default operating system by the installation (Setup) program.

To copy or to xcopy, That Is the Question

Users of FAT file systems can access the registry with a DOS boot disk, and users of either FAT or NTFS may gain access with a second copy of Windows XP as described earlier. Once a method to access the registry has been established, it is a simple task to completely back up the registry.

Typically, I'll use a command window (a "DOS box," or command prompt), because I use NTFS and have a second copy of Windows XP installed. I'll now describe how I back up the registry on my Windows XP server.

Using the md (make directory) or mkdir command, I create a new directory called \RegBU on another drive (my system has at least five hard drives):

```
md D:\RegBu
```

I then use the xcopy command (or copy) to copy the registry files in C:\Winnt\System32\Config directory to the RegBU directory. The Winnt directory is where my main copy of Windows XP is installed.

```
xcopy C:\Winnt\System32\Config\*.* D:\RegBu\*.* /s
```

This example saves a backup to a subdirectory on the D: drive. This is a good solution if the system (C:) drive becomes unreadable, because the backup copy will still be accessible on the other drive. Other alternatives include backing up to a removable (Zip) drive, CD-R/CD-RW drive, or a network drive on a different computer.

If things are going well, I may also use WinZip to back up the registry files to a set of diskettes. In my system, the files in my Config directory are just over 16MB in size. Am I typical? No. I only have a few users in my user database, so my registry is smaller than most. WinZip is able to compress the files down to only two or three diskettes, which is a reasonable number. Of course, if I used a Zip or CD-R/CD-RW drive, I could put these files on a single disk, but in my case that might be a waste of space.

Once you've copied your registry files to a safe location, simply remove the boot diskette (if used) and reboot the computer. This will give you a copy of the registry that is restorable later using an almost identical technique: boot to DOS and restore the files.

TIP   What the heck is a safe location? A safe location typically might be another hard drive, a Zip drive, or perhaps even diskettes. Diskettes present a small problem in that the registry files are typically going to be a total of 10 to 20MB in size. Using a utility such as WinZip allows you to write these large files to a number of diskettes while at the same time compressing them, reducing the number of diskettes required to a minimum. (We won't get into the issues of using off-site backup storage!)

What's on My ASR Disk?

The files found on a typical Windows XP ASR disk include the following:

asr.sif   Not part of the registry, this file is saved on the ASR disk. A SIF file is a file that contains state information (SIF is an acronym for state information file). The **asr.sif** file contains information about Windows XP and the computer hardware.

asrpnp.sif   Not part of the registry, this file is saved on the ASR disk. This SIF file contains information about the computer's Plug and Play hardware.

setup.log   This file contains information about the initial setup of Windows XP.

All of these files are critical when restoring the registry or system using the Setup program's repair function.

Using RegEdit to Back Up the Registry

Using the Windows Registry Editor, you can make an additional copy of the registry and restore it by double-clicking a single icon. The Windows Registry Editor, RegEdit, is included with Windows XP.

New!

NOTE *RegEdt32 and RegEdit have been "combined" into a single program. Actually, the original RegEdit program was removed from Windows XP, and RegEdt32 has replaced it. (You can start the Registry Editor with either RegEdit or RegEdt32 with the same result.)*

If you follow the steps outlined shortly, you can create a copy of the system registry that includes everything except the Security and SAM registry keys. When backing up a Windows XP workstation on a network, RegEdit will usually use this technique to save everything needed. There are other methods to back up the security database, though those methods are awkward and somewhat difficult to manage: it is easier to use the techniques described earlier in the chapter to do a complete registry backup.

NOTE *If you are a system administrator and you have Windows 95/98/Me systems, the technique described below will work for these computers as well. Actually, they work better with Windows 95/98/Me than with Windows XP, but we'll keep that our carefully guarded secret.*

Because the Security and SAM keys are not backed up, this is not a complete backup technique. Rather, this is an interesting technique for backing up the other major parts of the registry—one that is very easy and quick to do.

To use RegEdit to back up the registry:

1. Run RegEdit. Either go to a command window and type the command **RegEdit**, or choose Start ➢ Run to open the Run dialog box, type **RegEdit** in the Open input area, and click the OK button.

2. After RegEdit starts, note that My Computer is highlighted. If My Computer is not highlighted, click it to highlight it. This ensures that the entire registry, not just part of it, is backed up.

3. Select the Registry menu item Export Registry File.

4. RegEdit displays the Export Registry File dialog box. Using the dialog box's toolbar, navigate to the Desktop (or some other location that is convenient for you) and type a name for the file (for example, **RegistrySave**) and click Save.

5. Exit RegEdit.

Notice that the RegEdit version that is supplied with Windows XP writes the registry file out in Unicode format (each character is two bytes long). Editors and utilities that do not understand Unicode character sets will have difficulty working with this file. To convert a Unicode text file to one-byte text format, use the type command, with the output redirected to a new file. For example:

```
type "file in unicode.reg" >"file in text.txt"
```

The new file created will be (within a byte or two) half the size of the original registry file that you saved.

This method of saving the registry is easy and almost painless. Using this technique to back up the registry immediately after installation allows you to restore the system to a known state very easily and quickly.

To restore the registry with the file created with RegEdit, simply double-click the file you created in step 4 above, and this file will be reloaded as the current registry.

NOTE *The saved registry file may be placed anywhere you desire. In some cases, placing a registry restore capability on a user's Desktop is tantamount to courting disaster. Some users will click it just to see what will happen. One solution is to hide the file (that is, set the file's hidden attribute) or save it to an offline or other safe storage location.*

Restoring the Registry

To restore the registry, you must consider how the registry was saved. There are four ways to save a registry, each of which differs in just how much of the registry was saved and where the registry was saved:

- You can use a backup program (such as the one included with Windows XP) to copy the registry to a tape or other online or offline location. The backup program will then restore the registry backup to its original location.

- You can copy the registry (as described earlier), creating identical copies of the registry that can then be recopied back to the original registry locations. This requires that you use a second operating system (such as a second copy of Windows XP) to copy the files back.

- The Windows XP Backup program (also) saves the registry to the `%SystemRoot%\Repair` directory. You can then use the Windows XP Setup program to restore these files.

- You can use RegEdit to save the registry in a text file with an extension of `.reg`. Windows XP knows that this is a registry file (because the `.reg` file type is a registered extension) and will reload the file automatically into the registry if the file is double-clicked in Explorer or from the Desktop. From a command prompt, enter the command **start `filename.reg`**, where *filename* is the name of the registry backup file.

Restoring from Tape

Restoring a tape backup is a simple, though time-consuming, process. When you use a backup and restore program compatible with Windows XP, make sure that you select the option to restore the local registry. You will have to make the decision about restoring other files at this time based upon your circumstances. If you suspect that other system files may be corrupted, or if you are simply not sure of the state of the system, then I would recommend repairing Windows XP (using the Windows XP Setup program), or restoring the entire operating system and the registry at the same time. If you know that the registry is the only damaged component, simply restoring the registry and not other system files may save some time.

Restoring from Other Media Supported by Backup

Restoring backups saved on other media (such as disks, diskettes, Zip drives, CD-R/CD-RW drives, and so forth) is a simple and usually fast process. Use the Windows XP Backup program and select System State from the list of backed up items to restore. System State will contain three items: Boot Files, COM+ Class Registry, and Registry.

NOTE   *It is not possible to restore only part of the System State data; you must restore it all!*

Your ASR backup includes other files in addition to the System State (including a full backup of the system drive), and you may restore those files at any time. You will have to make the decision about restoring these other files based on your circumstances. If you suspect that other system files may be corrupted, or if you are simply not sure of the state of the system, then I would recommend repairing Windows XP or restoring the entire operating system and the registry at the same time. If you know that the registry is the only damaged component, simply restoring the System State and not other system files may save a certain amount of time.

When Active Directory is running, it is not possible to restore the System State. This limitation requires that you stop the Active Directory services by doing the following: Reboot Windows XP and during the boot process select the advanced startup option Directory Services Restore Mode. Once the system has completed the boot, restore the System State. After restoring the System State, perform a normal Windows XP reboot.

If you're using another backup program, then simply follow the instructions provided with the program. The same general cautions about which files to restore (only the System State or the entire operating system) still apply regardless of which restore program you use. The main difference between most backup and restore programs is the user interface and media compatibility. Never forget that tapes usually must be restored using the same program used to create the tape!

NOTE   *When restoring, be especially cautious that you do not restore the wrong, or out-of-date, version of the System State. Generally, you want to make sure that you restore the most current working version of the registry for the system.*

Recovering a Copied Registry

A registry that has been backed up using copy or xcopy is restored in the opposite manner from which it was backed up. For example, if you have the NTFS file system, then you have to restart the system using your backup copy of Windows XP.

FAT AND NTFS

When restoring a registry on a FAT-based file system running Windows XP, it's necessary to boot DOS, Windows 95/98/Me, or a second copy of Windows XP. If you have a dual-boot installed (either DOS or Windows 95/98/Me), you can use the dual-boot to get to the other operating system.

If you are restoring the registry on an NTFS system, then dual-boot into the backup copy of Windows XP that you installed to back up the registry. Avoid dual-booting into a previous version of Windows, as there may be incompatibilities in NTFS support offered by earlier versions of Windows.

WARNING   *Once running the alternate operating system, find your latest working copy of the registry before you lose it in the restore process, and back up the current registry to another, safe, location. Take this precaution just in case the current registry is not the problem (it happens), and the backup copy is actually not quite as good as you thought it was.*

You can follow these steps to restore your registry from a backup you have created:

1. Boot to another operating system: Windows XP/NT, DOS, or Windows 95/98/Me for FAT; use Windows XP/NT for NTFS.

2. Save the current registry to a safe location just in case the registry is not the problem after all.

3. Copy your saved registry (from wherever it was stored) to the correct registry location.

4. Boot the problematic version of Windows XP and test to see if the restore worked. If it didn't, keep reading; more golden tips are coming up soon.

The ASR Disk Strikes Again: Using Setup to Recover

If you have no other acceptable backup copies of the original registry, then you'll have to fall back on the ASR disk and the copy of the registry that is saved in the `Repair` directory. This technique is fraught with peril, including the fact that the registry saved with ASR may not have all the necessary information or be up-to-date.

Properly restoring the system registry from the `Repair` directory and the ASR disk requires running the Windows XP Setup program. When it first starts, Setup examines the hard drive and looks for already-installed copies of Windows XP and their `Repair` directories. Once the examination is complete, Setup gives you some choices, including Press F2 to Run Automated System Recovery (ASR).

WARNING   *Running ASR with Setup will, repeat, will cause Setup to reformat the system hard drive, without further warning! If your backup is on the system drive or a networked drive, be aware that you will either lose the backup or you will probably be unable to access it! This will result in having to do a complete reinstall of the system, and the loss of all user data on the drive. Don't ask how I found this small issue...*

At a later point, if you didn't run ASR, the Windows XP's Setup program gives you three choices:

♦ To set up Windows XP now, press Enter.

♦ To repair a Windows XP installation using Recovery Console, press R.

♦ To quit Setup without installing Windows XP, press F3.

Now, you know that you are in trouble at this point—the only choice is whether it might be possible to recover from your problems without doing a complete reinstallation of Windows XP.

Let's say that you are going to try to repair. First, select the repair option by pressing R. At this stage, the Setup program switches to repair mode and continues. The next screen displays four choices. You may choose any combination or all of them:

Inspect registry files.   This choice allows the repair program to check and repair the registry files. This is the option that most of us will select. The repair program will need either an ASR disk or the files stored in the `%SystemRoot%\Repair` directory.

Inspect startup environment.   The startup environment is the Boot Manager, which is called by the program contained in the boot sector. There are also other supporting files—including `boot.ini`, `ntdetect.com`, and others—that must be validated. The repair program repairs or replaces these files as best as it can, but be prepared for some items to be restored to the state they were in when you installed Windows XP.

Verify Windows XP system files.   Verifying the system files is a process where the repair program will go through the root directory and all the system directories (such as the `Windows` and `System` directories) and verify that each and every file is valid. This process is used when a hard disk error (especially on an NTFS volume) has made one or more system files invalid. Careful! You will lose all service packs installed to this repair process. Reinstall your service packs immediately after choosing this option.

Inspect boot sector.   There are several reasons to inspect (and repair) the boot sector. For example, if you inadvertently install another operating system with boot sector virus infections, this could damage the boot sector, especially with the FAT file system.

All four of these selections are selected by default. You can use the selector bar (use the arrow keys) to highlight and deselect any option that is not desired; use the Enter key to select or clear an option.

Once you have elected to continue, Setup does a device check. This is the same check that is done prior to an installation of Windows XP.

The next stage is to determine where the registry repair information will be coming from. Remember, you can use either the ASR disk or the copy stored in the `Repair` directory. If you have multiple installations of Windows XP, be sure to choose the correct `Repair` directory to repair from.

TIP   *The ASR disk tells Setup which copy of Windows XP you are attempting to repair. You cannot use the ASR disk from one installation of Windows XP to repair another installation of Windows XP. It just won't work.*

If you don't have an ASR disk (or you don't want to use it), then Setup searches your drive for Windows XP. You may have multiple installations of Windows XP; this is common, considering how many times I've recommended installing at least two copies. If this is the case, Setup lists each installation of the operating system that it finds. Select the version of Windows XP you want to repair and press Enter to repair the selected installation.

WARNING   *Careful! Make sure you repair the right Windows XP installation if you have more than one copy of the operating system installed. Nothing is worse than successfully repairing a copy of Windows XP that wasn't broken in the first place; that'll break it for sure.*

Next, Setup does a drive check. The message indicates that drives are being checked, and the status indicator at the bottom of the screen shows the progress. Actually, Setup only checks the boot (C:) drive, but that's probably all that is needed right now.

The next prompt, which is displayed when you have elected to have the registry repaired, is to determine which key or keys are to be repaired:

- System

- ◆ Software

- ◆ Default

- ◆ ntuser.dat

- ◆ Security

- ◆ SAM

Replacing some hives and not others might result in some problems if items in the registry have been updated since the registry was last saved. Typically, it is best to replace all files if possible to avoid any problems with different versions.

Once the registry has been updated, the Setup program prompts you to remove any diskettes from the drives and reboot the computer. If all went well, the computer will reboot and run.

Loading a .reg file

Any .reg file created by RegEdit (discussed earlier) is usually loaded by simply double-clicking the .reg file in Windows Explorer or on the Desktop.

You can also go into RegEdit to load the .reg file. From the RegEdit main menu, select Registry ➤ Import Registry File. Actually, when you double-click a .reg file, Windows XP starts RegEdit to do the registry file load. The main advantage of loading a registry file from the RegEdit menu is that you're able to see the effect of the registry load in RegEdit.

A .reg file, being a text file, may be *carefully* edited. Did I emphasize *carefully* enough? Realize you are making a registry change if you modify the .reg file and then reload it. And make certain that the editor you use understands Unicode. Notepad works fine, just remember not to use Notepad's default .txt file extension when saving the file.

Realize that you will not be able to use this technique if you are unable to boot or run Windows. This is another good reason to have multiple backups of the registry in different formats.

NOTE *When restoring the registry, several errors may be displayed. Some errors will state "System Process – Licensing Violation" and advise the user that the system has detected tampering with the product registration component of the registry. Click OK when these messages appear and also when another error stating that it was not possible to write to the registry shows up. This final error is actually an artifact of the licensing violation errors and does not indicate a failure of the entire process.*

Using the Restored Registry

To make the restored registry active, you must restart Windows XP. (Windows XP caches most of the registry while it is running.) There is no prompt to restart. However, some changes to the registry will not be reloaded until the system is restarted. Select Shut Down from the Start menu and then select Restart the Computer in the Shutdown dialog box.

NOTE *It is not uncommon for applications to update the registry using a .reg file during program installation time. This is one method used by software developers. Why? One simple reason is that this allows the registry to be repaired, restoring the application's default values without having to reinstall the entire program.*

The Recovery Console

The Windows XP Recovery Console is a tool that allows recovery from a number of failures. Previously, all you could do was boot another copy of Windows XP and hack your way around, replacing files, even registry components, in the blind hope that you would somehow fix the problem.

With Windows XP, you have two tools to use: the Recovery Console and the Safe Mode feature. The Recovery Console is a powerful, simple (no, that's not an oxymoron!) feature that is supplied with Windows XP, but it is not installed by default. The Windows XP Safe Mode works in the same manner as the Safe Mode found in other versions of Windows. You can modify a number of system settings using Safe Mode (such as video modes).

Installing the Recovery Console after the system has failed is quite like locking the barn door after the horse has been stolen—it really won't work that well.

Installing the Recovery Console

The Recovery Console must be installed *before* disaster strikes. It will be difficult (maybe even impossible) to install it after a disaster has reared its ugly head. So, let's install the Recovery Console right now.

First, you must use the Windows XP distribution CD (or share containing the appropriate files, if installing from a network device). The Recovery Console is installed using the winnt32.exe program. The winnt32.exe program is the same program that is used to install Windows XP; however, by selecting the correct option, you are able to tell winnt32.exe to not install Windows XP, but to install the Recovery Console instead.

NOTE *It is not possible to install the Recovery Console at the same time as Windows XP. You must first install Windows XP, then install the Recovery Console. If you have multiple copies of Windows XP installed, it is only necessary to install the Recovery Console one time—the Recovery Console will work with as many copies of Windows XP as are installed.*

Follow these steps to install the Recovery Console from the Windows XP distribution CD:

1. Insert the distribution CD and change into the i386 directory.

2. Run winnt32.exe using the /cmdcons option. Typically, no other options are needed, though some users may wish to specify source options, especially if installing from a network share rather than a hard drive.

3. The installation program contacts Microsoft to check for updates to this Windows XP component (see Figure 2.3).

4. The winnt32.exe program opens the dialog box shown in Figure 2.4. This dialog box allows you to cancel the installation if you need to. Note that multiple installations of the Recovery Console will simply overwrite previous installations; in such cases, no error is generated.

5. If there are no errors, the dialog box shown in Figure 2.5 is displayed. The Recovery Console is ready for use at this point.

FIGURE 2.3

Windows XP's Dynamic Update uses the Internet to retrieve the latest files directly from Microsoft.

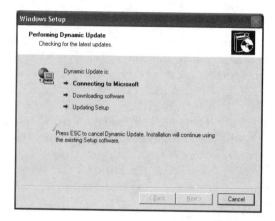

FIGURE 2.4

Setting up the Recovery Console using `winnt32/cmdcons` bypasses all other setup options.

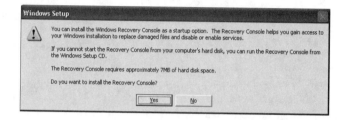

FIGURE 2.5

The Recovery Console has been successfully installed.

What's in the Recovery Console?

The Recovery Console consists of a minor modification to the `boot.ini` file, and the addition of a *hidden* directory on the boot drive. The added directory's name is `cmdcons`. The change to the `boot.ini` file is simply the addition of another line providing for a new boot option:

```
C:\cmdcons\bootsect.dat="Microsoft Windows Recovery Console" /cmdcons
```

This option consists of a fully qualified file name (`C:\cmdcons\bootsect.dat`), a text description (`Microsoft Windows Recovery Console`), and a boot option (`/cmdcons`).

As everyone should be well aware, the Windows XP Boot Manager is able to boot virtually any operating system (assuming that the operating system is compatible with the currently installed file system).

How Windows XP Supports Booting other Operating Systems

Windows XP can be told to "boot" any directory or file location. For example, the Recovery Console is saved in the cmdcons directory. In the cmdcons directory is a 512-byte file named bootsect.dat.

Windows XP will treat a file named bootsect.dat exactly as if it were a hard disk's boot sector. In fact, one could, theoretically, copy the bootsect.dat file to a drive's boot sector location and cause that operating system to be booted directly.

One use for this technology is in a multiple-boot configuration where the other operating system or systems are not compatible with Windows NT (such as Windows 95/98/Me).

The Recovery Console does qualify as an operating system, though it is very simple—and limited. A major question will always be this: is the Recovery Console secure? In most situations, the Recovery Console is actually quite secure. The user, at startup of the Recovery Console, is prompted for two pieces of information:

◆ Which Windows XP installation is to be repaired (assuming that there is more than one Windows XP installation!).

◆ The Administrator's password for that installation. The Recovery Console then uses the installation's SAM to validate this password to ensure the user has the necessary permission to use the system.

A situation comes to mind: if the Administrator's password is lost or otherwise compromised, not only may it be impossible to use the Recovery Console, but anyone with access to the compromised password could modify the system with the Recovery Console. This is not really an issue, though. If the Administrator's password is lost, that's life. It will be difficult, if not impossible, to recover the password. If the security of the Administrator's password is compromised, then it will be necessary to repair the damage—changing the password is mandatory in this case. In either case, the Recovery Console is no less secure than Windows XP is.

The cmdcons directory holds over 100 files. Most of these files are compressed and are uncompressed by the Recovery Console when needed. Here's a list of the uncompressed files found in this directory:

```
C:\cmdcons\autochk.exe
C:\cmdcons\autofmt.exe
C:\cmdcons\biosinfo.inf
C:\cmdcons\bootsect.dat
C:\cmdcons\disk101
C:\cmdcons\disk102
C:\cmdcons\disk103
C:\cmdcons\disk104
C:\cmdcons\drvmain.sdb
C:\cmdcons\KBDAL.dll
C:\cmdcons\KBDBE.dll
C:\cmdcons\KBDBLR.dll
C:\cmdcons\KBDBR.dll
```

```
C:\cmdcons\KBDBU.dll
C:\cmdcons\KBDCA.dll
C:\cmdcons\KBDCR.dll
C:\cmdcons\KBDCZ.dll
C:\cmdcons\KBDCZ1.dll
C:\cmdcons\KBDDA.dll
C:\cmdcons\KBDDV.dll
C:\cmdcons\KBDES.dll
C:\cmdcons\KBDEST.dll
C:\cmdcons\KBDFC.dll
C:\cmdcons\KBDFI.dll
C:\cmdcons\KBDFR.dll
C:\cmdcons\KBDGKL.dll
C:\cmdcons\KBDGR.dll
C:\cmdcons\KBDGR1.dll
C:\cmdcons\KBDHE.dll
C:\cmdcons\KBDHE220.dll
C:\cmdcons\KBDHE319.dll
C:\cmdcons\KBDHELA2.dll
C:\cmdcons\KBDHELA3.dll
C:\cmdcons\KBDHU.dll
C:\cmdcons\KBDHU1.dll
C:\cmdcons\KBDIC.dll
C:\cmdcons\KBDIR.dll
C:\cmdcons\KBDIT.dll
C:\cmdcons\KBDIT142.dll
C:\cmdcons\KBDLA.dll
C:\cmdcons\KBDLT.dll
C:\cmdcons\KBDLV.dll
C:\cmdcons\KBDLV1.dll
C:\cmdcons\KBDNE.dll
C:\cmdcons\KBDNO.dll
C:\cmdcons\KBDPL.dll
C:\cmdcons\KBDPL1.dll
C:\cmdcons\KBDPO.dll
C:\cmdcons\KBDRO.dll
C:\cmdcons\KBDRU.dll
C:\cmdcons\KBDRU1.dll
C:\cmdcons\KBDSF.dll
C:\cmdcons\KBDSG.dll
C:\cmdcons\KBDSL.dll
C:\cmdcons\KBDSL1.dll
C:\cmdcons\KBDSP.dll
C:\cmdcons\KBDSW.dll
C:\cmdcons\KBDTUF.dll
C:\cmdcons\KBDTUQ.dll
C:\cmdcons\KBDUK.dll
C:\cmdcons\KBDUR.dll
```

```
C:\cmdcons\kbdus.dll
C:\cmdcons\KBDUSL.dll
C:\cmdcons\KBDUSR.dll
C:\cmdcons\KBDUSX.dll
C:\cmdcons\KBDYCC.dll
C:\cmdcons\KBDYCL.dll
C:\cmdcons\ksecdd.sys
C:\cmdcons\migrate.inf
C:\cmdcons\ntdetect.com
C:\cmdcons\ntfs.sys
C:\cmdcons\setupldr.bin
C:\cmdcons\setupreg.hiv
C:\cmdcons\spcmdcon.sys
C:\cmdcons\System32
C:\cmdcons\txtsetup.sif
C:\cmdcons\winnt.sif
C:\cmdcons\System32\ntdll.dll
C:\cmdcons\System32\smss.exe
```

The files disk101, disk102, disk103, and disk104 are disk image identifier files, and they contain nothing but a single space and a carriage return/line feed. The bootsect.dat file is the bootable boot sector image file. The migrate.inf file contains information used to update the registry if needed. The setupreg.hiv file is used to update the registry; however, this file is in a special format usable only with certain applications. The cmdcons directory also contains the subdirectory System32. This subdirectory contains two files, ntdll.dll and smss.exe (the Windows XP session manager).

Using the Recovery Console

Once the Recovery Console is installed, it appears in the Start menu as the last item in the list, named "Microsoft Windows Recovery Console."

WARNING   *It is strongly recommend that the Recovery Console not be invoked unless absolutely necessary! The commands available in the Recovery Console are powerful, and if used improperly, they can destroy a Windows XP installation.*

To use the Recovery Console, follow these steps:

1. Boot the system.

2. When the startup screen displays, select Microsoft Windows Recovery Console.

3. Select the installation to be repaired if there are multiple Windows XP installations. (The first installation is number 1. Enter **1**.)

4. Enter the correct Administrator password for the installation to be repaired. (This password is a local or SAM password and not an Active Directory password.)

5. Use any Recovery Console commands (see the later section "Recovery Console Commands and Options") needed to do the repair.

When you're done repairing the installation, simply enter the exit command to restart the computer.

Starting the Recovery Console from the Installation CD-ROM

Follow these steps to start the Recovery Console for computers that either do not have the Recovery Console installed or cannot be booted (perhaps due to errors in the partition table, or MBR):

1. Boot the system, using the CD-ROM (or diskettes) as appropriate.

2. When the initial setup text screen is displayed, select Repair by pressing the R key.

3. At the prompt, select Recovery Console by pressing C.

4. Select the installation to be repaired if there are multiple Windows XP installations.

5. Enter the correct Administrator password for the installation to be repaired.

6. Use any Recovery Console commands (see the next section) needed to do the repair.

When you're done repairing the installation, enter the `exit` command to restart the computer.

Recovery Console Commands and Options

New!

When the computer is started in the Recovery Console mode, a prompt similar to a command prompt is the only interface available to the user. The Recovery Console's functionality is limited, and there is only support for the commands listed in Table 2.1 (`Bootcfg` and `Net Use` are new to Windows XP):

TABLE 2.1: RECOVERY CONSOLE COMMANDS AND OPTIONS

COMMAND	FUNCTION
attrib	Changes file attributes. The read, hidden, and system attributes may be either set or cleared as desired.
batch	Allows execution of a set of Recovery Console commands that have been saved in a text file. Both the filename and extension must be specified for the `batch` command to work. This command allows specifying an output file as well.
bootcfg	Activates the boot file (`boot.ini`) configuration and recovery command utility.
chdir (cd)	Works identically to the command session's `cd` command, changing the current working directory to the directory specified or, if no directory is specified, displaying the current working directory.
chkdsk	Works similarly to a command session's `chkdsk` command. Two options are available: `/p` specifies that the drive is to be checked regardless of whether the dirty flag is set; `/r` specifies that `chkdsk` should repair any bad sectors found.
cls	Works identically to the command session's `cls` command—clears the screen.
copy	Copies a file from a source location to a destination location. The file, if compressed, is uncompressed when copied. No wildcards are permitted with the `copy` command. There are no options to this command.
delete (del)	Works much like a command session's `delete` command. This command deletes the specified file or files. It only works in the system directories of the installation being repaired, in hard drive root directories, and with local installation source files.

Continued on next page

TABLE 2.1: RECOVERY CONSOLE COMMANDS AND OPTIONS *(continued)*

COMMAND	FUNCTION
dir	Works similarly to a command session's dir command. This command displays the names of files and subdirectories in the location specified. The dir command has no options, listing file sizes, modification dates, and attributes.
disable	Disables a service or device driver. The service or device driver to be disabled is marked as SERVICE_DISABLED to prevent it from being started when the system is subsequently restarted.
diskpart	Manages partitions on disk devices. This command is able to add or delete partitions as desired. When adding a partition, a command parameter specifies the size of the partition in megabytes.
enable	Enables a service or device driver. The service or device driver to be enabled is marked with the user specified service type: SERVICE_AUTO_START, SERVICE_DISABLED, SERVICE_DEMAND_START, SERVICE_BOOT-START, or SERVICE_SYSTEM_START.
exit	Ends the Recovery Console session and reboots the computer.
expand	Works similarly to a command session's expand command. This command allows expanding files from a source CAB file. Two options are available: /d displays the contents of the CAB file; /y suppresses any overwrite warnings that may be given.
fixboot	Repairs or replaces the (optional) specified drive's boot sector.
fixmbr	Repairs or replaces the (optional) specified drive's master boot record.
format	Works similarly to a command session's format command. This command allows formatting disks using FAT, FAT32, and NTFS. One option, /q, allows quick formatting without a scan when the drive is known to be good.
help	Lists the available Recovery Console commands.
listsvc	Displays a list of services and drivers that are currently available on the computer.
logon	Logs on to an installation of Windows NT 4 or Windows XP. This command is run automatically when the Recovery Console first starts.
map	Displays a list of all drive mappings. This command's output is very useful for the fixboot, fixmbr, and fdisk commands.
mkdir (md)	Works similarly to the command session's md (mkdir) command. This command allows creating directories within the system directories of the currently logged-on installation, removable disks, root directories of hard disk partitions, and local installation sources.
more	Works like the command session's type command. Displays the file's contents on the screen. There are no parameters for the more command.
net use	Associates a drive letter to an available shared network drive.
rename (ren)	Allows the user to rename a file. This command does not support wildcard specifications.

Continued on next page

TABLE 2.1: RECOVERY CONSOLE COMMANDS AND OPTIONS *(continued)*

COMMAND	FUNCTION
rmdir (rd)	Works similarly to the command session's rd (rmdir) command. This command allows deleting directories within the system directories of the currently logged-on installation, removable disks, root directories of hard disk partitions, and local installation sources.
set	Sets Recovery Console environment variables. The Recovery Console supports a limited set of environment variables. These variables affect Recovery Console commands only.
systemroot	Changes to the current installation's %SystemRoot% directory. Functionally equivalent to cd %SystemRoot% in a normal command session.
type	Works like the command session's type command. This command displays the file's contents on the screen. There are no parameters for the type command.

The Recovery Console may be installed permanently so that whenever the system is booted, there is an option to select the Recovery Console. This works well for installations that will still boot to the Start menu (where one selects the installation or operating system to be booted). The Recovery Console is placed into the cmdcons directory, located on the boot drive.

NOTE   *The* cmdcons *directory is always located on the boot drive, not on the system drive, unless the boot drive is also the system drive.*

Other Backup and Restore Programs

There are other registry backup and restoration programs. One excellent source for them is the Windows XP Resource Kit's REG program, which has backup and restore functionality. Take a look at Chapter 4 for a listing of the registry tools found in the Windows XP Resource Kit.

Chapter 3

Anatomy of the Registry: The Blood, Gore, and Guts

IN CHAPTER 1, WE talked a little about what the registry is and the terminology used for its various components. In Chapter 2, we covered backing up and restoring the registry. In this chapter, we will get into more of the details of what actually is in the registry. If you're only interested in how to use (or recover) the registry, but not *what* the registry is, it's possible to skip this chapter. However, if you're unsure about this, I'd recommend reading it anyway.

In this chapter, I will discuss the following topics:

◆ An overview of the registry

◆ The machine's configuration in HKEY_LOCAL_MACHINE

◆ User settings under HKEY_USERS

◆ Current configuration settings in HKEY_CURRENT_CONFIG

◆ The Performance Monitor settings found in HKEY_PERFORMANCE_DATA

◆ New user profiles in NTUSER

The Registry Structure

Now humor me for just a moment; I think I'm going to back up my registry. In fact, it is a good time for *you* to do a backup as well, since it is entirely possible that at any time you might have some kind of problem (or disaster) with the registry and really need that backup copy to restore it. Start Backup, select the System State option in the Backup tab, and back up to a safe location. Alternatively in the Welcome tab, select Automated System Recovery Wizard.

Next, let some time pass by...

NOTE *When doing a System State backup to a networked location, realize that the selected network location may not be available when attempting to restore! It may be possible (and necessary) to install a minimal Windows XP installation so that you can access the backup location, however.*

Ah, that feels better. I've got a fresh backup copy of my registry (and everything else on the drive) just in case I do something stupid, and so do you—not that we ever do anything stupid, right?

The registry is subdivided into the following five clearly defined sections, called *hives*:

◆ HKEY_CLASSES_ROOT

◆ HKEY_CURRENT_USER

◆ HKEY_LOCAL_MACHINE

◆ HKEY_USERS

◆ HKEY_CURRENT_CONFIG

Some registry objects are less important than others. For example, a damaged Security Accounts Manager key (SAM), can probably be recovered easily without serious, permanent problems—you could restore the SAM without much difficulty. You could possibly lose the entire user database, so no users would be able to log on to the server. However, as long as you can log on as Administrator, the worst case is that you would have to enter the other user information again (just hope that there are not thousands of users on your network!) The default SAM registry will contain at least the initial Administrator user ID and password, which you would have to know.

However, say you lose the system component of the registry without adequate backup. In that case, it is unlikely that you'll be able to recover without reinstalling Windows XP, and that would be a painful experience at best.

Of Hives and Bees—A Registry Overview

As we discussed in Chapter 1, the Windows XP/NT registry is arranged into logical units called *hives*. Though I can't vouch for its truth, legend has it that some unnamed programmer at Microsoft seemed to see a logical relationship between the various keys in the registry and the structure of a beehive. Now me, I just don't see this, so let's consider the two following alternative analogies that make much more sense:

◆ The registry is arranged just like the directories, folders, and files contained on your hard drive. Hives are analogous to root directories, and keys are like subdirectories and files. In fact, this relationship is almost 100 percent parallel: hives are usually shown separated by backslashes (just like directories on the drive) from keys, and keys typically (but not always) have values, or they can be like directories and contain subkeys. Remember, just as a file may be empty, a key may well contain no value.

◆ The registry is arranged as a hierarchical database, nothing more, and nothing less. If you are a database person, this view of the registry might make more sense to you. In truth, the database arrangement is more like the registry's actual, physical, construction.

Specific data is assigned to a key. As I've mentioned, some registry keys don't have a value set; this is also acceptable.

WARNING   *Be careful not to delete empty keys just because they are empty. Even though they don't have a value, their presence in the registry may be necessary for the health and well being of Windows XP, or other applications. Never, ever delete a key unless you know that there will be no adverse side effects, and keep a backup of what you delete so that it may be restored when adverse side effects develop.*

The Registry Hives

The Windows XP registry is divided into five hives, each named using the prefix HKEY_. Each hive embodies a major section of the registry that has a specific functionality. Each hive is separate from the other hives and is typically stored as a file in the directory %SystemRoot%\System32\Config. Hive storage files have no extension or file type, making them easier to find. These hives are discussed next.

HIVES, KEYS, AND VALUES

In this book, I use terminology similar to that used when referring to disk drives, directories, subdirectories, files, and the contents of files. Often Microsoft confuses the issue somewhat. I will try to keep it clear:

Hive   A hive is similar to a root directory on a drive. A hive contains keys (like files and subdirectories). A hive is the highest level; a hive can not be a subhive inside another hive. An example of a hive in the registry is HKEY_LOCAL_MACHINE.

Key   A key is similar to a subdirectory or a file and is found inside a hive. Inside a key there may be other keys (like files) that contain values or other keys (like subdirectories) that contain both keys and values. A key will have either a hive or key as a parent above it, and *zero* or more keys contained within it. Sometimes Microsoft refers to a key as a subhive. An example of a key in the registry is HKEY_LOCAL_MACHINE\SAM.

Value   A value is similar to a file's data. Each key will have one value (though the value may consist of many parts) or no value set at all. There is also something called the *default value* (sometimes called the *unnamed value*), an object that may be assigned a value, or not. It is up to the using application (or the system, if the value is being used by the system) to properly interpret the value's meaning. When a value is requested, the registry simply provides raw data.

HKEY_CLASSES_ROOT

The HKEY_CLASSES_ROOT hive contains information about both OLE and various file associations. The purpose of HKEY_CLASSES_ROOT is to provide for compatibility with the existing Windows 3.x registry. The information contained in HKEY_CLASSES_ROOT is identical to information found in HKEY_LOCAL_MACHINE\Software.

NOTE   *You'll use the Windows XP utility Notepad to print the contents of many files. Notepad supports two command line options for printing: /p, which directs the printout to the default printer, and /pt <printer>, which directs the printout to the specified printer.*

HKEY_CURRENT_USER

The HKEY_CURRENT_USER hive is used to manage specific information about the user who is currently logged on. This information includes:

- The user's Desktop and the appearance and behavior of Windows XP to the user.

- All connections to network devices, such as printers and shared disk resources.

- Desktop program items, application preferences, screen colors, and other personal preferences and security rights. They are stored for later retrieval by the system when the user logs on.

All other environment settings are retained for future use.

By accessing the roaming user profile, Windows XP is able to make any workstation that the user logs on to appear the same to the user. Domain users need not worry about having to set up or customize each workstation that they will be using.

The information contained in HKEY_CURRENT_USER is updated as users make changes to their environments.

HKEY_LOCAL_MACHINE

The HKEY_LOCAL_MACHINE hive contains information about the computer that is running Windows XP. This information includes applications, drivers, and hardware. There are five separate keys contained within HKEY_LOCAL_MACHINE:

Hardware　The key used to save information about the computer's hardware. So that new hardware can be added easily, the Hardware key is always re-created when the system is booted. Changes to this key are not meaningful. Contained within the Hardware key are the following four subkeys:

　Description　Contains information about the system, including the CPU, FPU, and the system bus. Under the system bus is information about I/O, storage, and other devices.

　DeviceMap　Contains information about devices (keyboards, printer ports, pointers, and so on).

　ResourceMap　Contains information about the HAL (Hardware Abstraction Layer). Remember, as we have passed the year 2001, HAL is not a talking computer on a spaceship, HAL is the hardware. Also contained are I/O devices, drivers, SCSI adapters, system resources, and video resources.

　ACPI　Contains information about the ACPI (Advanced Configuration and Power Interface).

SAM　The Security Accounts Manager stores information about users and domains in the SAM key. This information is not accessible using any of the resource editors. Rather, this information is better managed using the administrator's User Manager program.

Security　Contains information about local security and user rights. A copy of the SAM key is found in the Security key. As with SAM, the Security key is not accessible using the resource editors, and the information is best modified using the administrator's tools.

Software　Contains information about installed system and user software, including descriptions. There are generally subkeys for each installed product in which the products store information—

including preferences, configurations, MRU (most recently used files) lists, and other application-modifiable items.

System   Contains information about the system startup, device drivers, services, and the Windows XP configuration.

HKEY_USERS

The HKEY_USERS hive contains information about each active user who has a user profile. In Windows XP, two subkeys in HKEY_USERS key are .DEFAULT and the information for the currently logged-on user.

NOTE   The SID (security identifier) for the currently logged-on user begins with S-1-5-21. The value 21 indicates active users.

The purpose of the .DEFAULT key is to provide information for users who log on without a profile. Information for the current user is stored under the user's SID.

With the Windows Server, you may find more user identifiers that the system uses to create new user accounts.

Personal profiles are contained in either the %SystemRoot%\Profiles folder or the %System-Drive%\Documents and Settings\Default User folder, unless roaming profiles are used, in which case a copy is stored in one of these folders, but the original resides on a server.

HKEY_CURRENT_CONFIG

The HKEY_CURRENT_CONFIG hive contains information about the system's current configuration. This information is typically derived from HKEY_LOCAL_MACHINE\System and HKEY_LOCAL_ MACHINE\Software, though HKEY_CURRENT_CONFIG does not contain all the information that is contained in the source keys.

NOTE   Users migrating from Windows 95/98/Me take note: As I noted in Chapter 1, the HKEY_DYN_DATA hive no longer exists in Windows XP. In Windows NT 4, this hive was intended to contain information about the system's Plug and Play status. However, since Windows NT 4 does not support Plug and Play, this key was empty. Windows XP does not have this hive.

Registry Key Data Types

The keys within hives can contain values that can be edited using the Registry Editor. These values have different data types:

REG_BINARY   Represents binary values. They may be edited or entered as hexadecimal or binary numbers. Figure 3.1 shows the Registry Editor's Edit Binary Value window.

REG_SZ   Used for registry keys containing strings. Editing is easy; just type in the new string. Case is preserved, but realize that the string is initially selected, so be careful not to inadvertently delete it. Strings are of fixed length and are defined when the key is created. Figure 3.2 shows a string being edited in the Edit String window. A string key may be made longer by adding more characters to the string; it will be reallocated if this happens.

FIGURE 3.1

The Edit Binary Value window for the Registry Editor

FIGURE 3.2

The Edit String window for the Registry Editor

REG_EXPAND_SZ Used if the key is to contain an environment variable that must be expanded prior to its use. Some keys need to contain values that reference environment variables, much like a batch file—for example, if a string contains the field %SystemRoot%\System32, and it is necessary to replace the %SystemRoot% part of the string with the value that is assigned to it in the environment. To do this substitution, this string must be defined as a REG_EXPAND_ SZ type string. The result of the expansion is then passed to the requestor. %SystemRoot% is a standard environment variable containing the location, drive, and directory where Windows XP has been installed. The Registry Editor uses the same window as is used for REG_SZ for entering a REG_EXPAND_SZ key, as shown in Figure 3.3.

NOTE   *Any environment variable, created by either the system or the user, may be used in a REG_EXPAND_SZ key.*

FIGURE 3.3

The Edit String window, where you can use an expanded environment variable in the string

REG_DWORD A 32-bit value, entered as decimal or hexadecimal. The Edit DWORD Value window, as Figure 3.4 shows, allows you to enter only valid numeric data to save you from sloppy typing.

FIGURE 3.4

You can enter only numeric data in the Edit DWORD Value window.

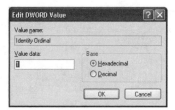

REG_MULTI_SZ   Used to store multiple strings in a single registry key. Normally, a string resource in the registry can contain only one line. However, the multistring type allows a string resource in the registry to hold multiple strings as needed. Figure 3.5 shows multiple strings being edited, with four lines of value data.

FIGURE 3.5

The Edit Multi-String window lets you add multiple values to a string resource.

REG_FULL_RESOURCE_DESCRIPTOR   Used to manage information for hardware resources. No one should edit the items that appear in the Resources window fields. Figure 3.6 shows a resource object displayed in the Registry Editor. However, these objects are never, ever changed manually.

REG_NONE   An identifier used when no data is stored in the key. It doesn't take a rocket scientist to figure out that there is no editor for the REG_NONE type.

REG_UNKNOWN   Used when the key's data type cannot be determined.
Other registry data types not fully supported by the Registry Editor include:

REG_DWORD_BIG_ENDIAN   Like REG_DWORD, but specifies the big endian format, where the four bytes of the DWORD are arranged in opposite order than little endian format (little endian format is the native mode for Intel processors, while noncompatible processors from other companies, such as Apple's Macintosh computers, use big endian).

REG_LINK   Used for a symbolic link between a registry value and either Windows or an application's data. Entries in REG_LINK are in Unicode text.

FIGURE 3.6

A disk resource shown in the Resources window

REG_QWORD A 64-bit integer number.

REG_RESOURCE_LIST Contains entries used by device drivers, including information about the hardware's configuration.

REG_RESOURCE_REQUIREMENTS_LIST Contains a list of resources required by a driver.

In addition to the above types of registry data, applications also have the ability to create custom registry data types as needed. This flexibility allows the application to both save and load the registry data without having to perform complex conversions and translations. Now, let's move on to the various major hives that make up the registry.

HKEY_LOCAL_MACHINE: The Machine's Configuration

The HKEY_LOCAL_MACHINE hive contains information about the current hardware configuration of the local computer. The information stored in this hive is updated using a variety of processes, including the Control Panel, hardware and software installation programs, and administrative tools, and is sometimes automatically updated by Windows XP.

It is important not to make unintended changes to the HKEY_LOCAL_ MACHINE hive. A change here could quite possibly render the entire system unstable.

NOTE *All the settings in the* HKEY_LOCAL_MACHINE *hive are recomputed at boot time. If a change has been made, and the change is causing problems, first try rebooting the system. The Windows XP Boot Manager should rebuild the* HKEY_LOCAL_MACHINE *hive at reboot time, discarding any changes made.*

HKEY_LOCAL_MACHINE\Hardware: The Installed Hardware Key

HKEY_LOCAL_MACHINE\Hardware contains information about the hardware configuration of the local machine. Everything hardware related (and I do mean everything) is found in this hive.

In Windows XP, the HKEY_LOCAL_MACHINE\Hardware key is subdivided into four subkeys:

Description   Contains descriptive information about each device, including a general description, information about basic configurations, and so on.

DeviceMap   Contains information about devices, including the location in the registry where a device's full configuration is saved.

ResourceMap   Contains translation information about each major component that is installed in the system. Most keys contain a set value entries named .Raw and .Translated.

ACPI   Contains information about the ACPI (Advanced Configuration and Power Interface). The ACPI key is only found on systems that support ACPI. Potential ACPI subkeys include the following:

RSDP   Root System Description Pointer

DSDT   Differentiated System Description Table

FADT   Fixed ACPI Description Table

FACS   Firmware ACPI Control Structure

PSDT   Persistent System Description Table

RSDT   Root System Description Table

SSDT   Secondary System Description Table

NOTE   In Windows NT 4, the Hardware *key contains another subkey,* OWNERMAP, *which contains information about removable PCI-type devices. These are devices plugged into the system's PCI bus but generally not permanently installed on the system's motherboard. However, not all PCI-type devices are listed in* OWNERMAP.

DESCRIPTION

Within HKEY_LOCAL_MACHINE\HARDWARE\Description is a wealth of information about the installed hardware. The only subkey, System, fully describes the CPU and I/O. Items in the Description key are always redetected at boot time.

The System subkey contains the following subkeys:

CentralProcessor   Contains information about the CPU. This includes speed, which is an identifier that contains the CPU's model, family, and Stepping. This subkey also contains vendor information; for example, a "real" Intel CPU has the VendorIdentifier string "GenuineIntel", while a CPU from AMD contains the string "AuthenticAMD".

FloatingPointProcessor   Describes the system's FPU (floating point unit) in a set of entries similar to that of the CPU. The fact that the typical CPU has an integral FPU is not considered here; the FPU is listed separately, regardless.

MultiFunctionAdapter Describes the system's bus (PCI), any PnP BIOS installed, and other devices, including the controllers for disk drives, keyboards, parallel and serial ports, and the mouse. For a mouse that is connected to a serial port, the mouse is found under the serial port, while a mouse that is connected to a PS/2 mouse port is shown connected to a pointer controller as a separate device.

ScsiAdapter Describes the system's IDE interfaces, if there are any. Windows XP lists these as SCSI interfaces, and they include the controllers for IDE disk drives, IDE CD-ROM drives, and other supported IDE devices. This key may not be found in all installations. Windows XP does not use this information, though it may be found in legacy installations that have been updated from earlier versions of Windows.

NOTE ScsiAdapter *lists only the devices attached to the IDE controller. The IDE controller itself is described in* HKEY_LOCAL_MACHINE\Hardware\DeviceMap.

Typically, the `Description` key can be used to determine what hardware is installed (and being used) and how the installed hardware is connected. However, some devices, such as storage devices (non-IDE hard drives, SCSI devices, non-IDE CD-ROM drives, video, and network interface cards), are not listed in HKEY_LOCAL_MACHINE\Hardware\Description. Instead, they are listed in HKEY_LOCAL_MACHINE\Hardware\DeviceMap. Why? Because these devices are not detected at the bootup stage; instead, they are detected when they are installed.

DEVICEMAP

The HKEY_LOCAL_MACHINE\Hardware\DeviceMap subkey contains information about devices, arranged in a similar fashion to the HKEY_LOCAL_MACHINE\HARDWARE\Description subkey discussed earlier. Windows XP does not have any changes in the DeviceMap, when compared to earlier versions of Windows. The DeviceMap subkey contains the following subkeys:

KeyboardClass Contains the address of the subkey that manages information about the keyboard.

PARALLEL PORTS Contains the address of the subkey that manages information about the parallel printer ports.

PointerClass Contains the address of the subkey that manages information about the system mouse.

Scsi A complex subkey that contains information about each SCSI interface found on the computer. A note about what is considered a SCSI port is in order. Actually, Windows XP pretends that IDE devices, as well as many CD-ROM devices that are connected to special interface cards, are SCSI devices. This is a management issue. Windows XP is not converting these devices to SCSI, nor is it using SCSI drivers; rather, Windows XP is simply classifying all these devices under a common heading of SCSI.

SERIALCOMM Contains the address of the subkeys that manage information about the available serial ports. In Windows NT 4, if the system mouse is connected to a serial port and not to a PS/2 mouse port, that port is not listed in the SERIALCOMM subkey.

VIDEO   Contains the address of the subkey that manages the video devices. Two devices are typically defined in VIDEO: one is the currently used adapter, and the second is a backup consisting of the previously installed (usually the generic VGA) adapter's settings to use as a backup in the event of a problem with the video system.

NOTE   For those of you still working with, or migrating from, NT 4, it's important to note that DeviceMap in NT 4 includes two additional subkeys which do not appear in Windows XP. KeyboardPort contains the address of the subkey that manages information about the keyboard interface unit, often called the 8042 after the original chip that served as the keyboard controller in the original PC. PointerPort contains the address of the subkey that manages information about the port that the system mouse is connected to. These two additional subkeys do not appear in later versions of Windows.

RESOURCEMAP

All the various hardware device drivers use the ResourceMap subkey to map resources that they will use. Each ResourceMap entry contains the following usage information:

◆ I/O ports

◆ I/O memory addresses

◆ Interrupts

◆ DMA (direct memory access) channels

◆ Physical memory installed

◆ Reserved memory

The ResourceMap subkey is divided into subkeys for each class of device (such as Hardware Abstraction Layer), and under these subkeys lie subkeys for different devices.

Windows XP and Windows 2000 include a new key in ResourceMap called PnPManager. This key contains Plug and Play information.

HKEY_LOCAL_MACHINE\SAM: The Security Access Manager

HKEY_LOCAL_MACHINE\SAM contains information used by all versions of Windows 2000 and Windows XP. It also contains user information (permissions, passwords, and the like). The SAM key is mirrored in HKEY_LOCAL_MACHINE\Security\SAM; making changes to one changes the other.

NOTE   Can't see the SAM or Security key? Use the Registry Editor to select the subkey you cannot see and then select Edit ➤ Permissions from the main menu. Next, change the Type of Access from Special Access to Full Control.

In Windows, this information is set using the Microsoft Management Console (MMC), Local Users and Groups branch. If the Windows system is a domain controller, the SAM is not used (we have the Active Directory services now). The SAM subkeys (both in HKEY_LOCAL_MACHINE\SAM\SAM and HKEY_LOCAL_MACHINE\Security\SAM) should only be modified using the MMC in Windows or the User Manager administrative programs in Windows NT 4.0 and earlier. However, attempts to modify information that is in the SAM subkeys typically result in problems. For example, users will be unable to log on, wrong permissions will be assigned, and so on.

WARNING   *Don't attempt to modify the* SAM *or* Security *key unless you have made a full backup of your registry, including the* SAM *and* Security *keys, as described in Chapter 2.*

HKEY_LOCAL_MACHINE\Security: The Windows Security Manager

The HKEY_LOCAL_MACHINE\Security key contains information relevant to the security of the local machine. This information includes:

◆ User rights

◆ Password policy

◆ Membership of local groups

In Windows XP, you'll set this information using the Active Directory Users and Computers program.

NOTE   *For those of you migrating from NT 4, or still working with NT 4 machines, it's important to note that under Windows NT 4, the* Security *subkeys should only be modified using the User Manager or the User Manager for Domains. With all versions of Windows 2000 and Windows XP Professional, only the Active Directory administrative programs (Active Directory Users and Computers) should be used. Attempts to modify information in the* Security *key typically result in problems. For example, users are unable to log on, wrong permissions are assigned, and so on. The XP Home edition cannot join a domain and therefore has no access to Active Directory.*

HKEY_LOCAL_MACHINE\Software: The Installed Software Information Manager

The HKEY_LOCAL_MACHINE\Software registry key is the storage location for all software installed on the computer. The information contained in HKEY_LOCAL_MACHINE\Software is available to all users and consists of a number of standard subkeys as well as a few subkeys that may be unique to each computer.

One computer on my network, using a beta version of Windows .NET Server (this also applies to Windows XP), has the following subkeys in HKEY_LOCAL_MACHINE\Software. These subkeys correspond to items that I have installed on my computer:

Adobe   Contains information about the copy of Adobe's Acrobat program that was recently installed.

Federal Express   Contains information about the FedEx online access and support I have on my computer. All of my FedEx airbills are produced by computer, making shipments much easier.

INTEL   Contains information about the Intel 3D Scalability Toolkit that I installed at some point. I don't remember when or why, but it's there.

Intuit   Contains information specific to the financial software that is Intuit's specialty.

Qualcomm   Contains information specific to the Eudora e-mail program. The nice thing about Eudora is that there is a free version for private use.

The following are system subkeys probably installed on your computer; however, some of these subkeys, such as ODBC and Clients, may not be present on some minimal installations:

Classes　Contains two types of items. First are file-type association items. For example, a typical association entry might have the name DIB, with a string that associates this name with the application Paint Shop Pro. Second are COM (Common Object Model) associations. For example, the extension .doc is associated with Microsoft Word for Windows or with WordPad, the default viewer for .doc files. Both WordPad and Word may be embedded in other applications. For instance, Outlook, Microsoft's upscale e-mail system, can use Word-formatted documents and embed either Word for Windows or WordPad to display and edit these documents.

Clients　Contains client-server relationships. For example, Microsoft Outlook is a multipurpose program with e-mail, a calendar, contact lists, news, and other features. Each of these parts of Outlook has a complex series of calling protocols that are defined in the Clients subkey.

Gemplus　Stores information for use with GemSAFE Smart Cards. These cards are used for security in Windows XP.

Microsoft　Stores a number of items that pertain to Microsoft products or parts of Windows XP. As few as 20 or as many as 100 entries can be in the Microsoft subkey.

ODBC　Stores items that pertain to Open Database Connectivity, which allows applications to retrieve data from a number of different data sources. Many users install ODBC, either intentionally or as a side effect of installing another product.

Policies　This subkey contains entries for policy enforcement, a feature that has been added to Windows XP Professional. Policies are not used in XP Home.

Program Groups　This subkey contains one value entry, ConvertedToLinks, which is used to indicate whether the program groups were converted. A value of one (0x1) shows that the conversion is complete. Even a system installed on a new computer that didn't require conversion will have this value.

Schlumberger　This subkey contains entries used with Windows XP security management. This group includes both smart cards and terminals.

Secure　If you say so. The Secure subkey is the location in which any application may store "secure" configuration information. Only an Administrator may modify this subkey, so mere mortal users can't change secure configuration information. Not many, if any, applications use the Secure subkey.

Windows 3.1 Migration Status　Used to indicate if the computer was upgraded from Windows 3.x to later versions of Windows NT and Windows XP. Though at one time there were many upgrades, more users today are likely to be doing clean installations—virtually all existing Windows 3.x systems have already been upgraded. This key contains two subkeys: IniFiles and reg.dat. These values show whether the .ini and reg.dat files have been migrated successfully to later formats.

NOTE *For those of you migrating from NT 4, or still working with NT 4 machines, it's important to note that NT 4 has a* Description *subkey that contains names and version numbers for software installed on the local computer. Though any vendor may use this subkey, the author can only see one entry, which is entered during installation of Windows XP. Microsoft RPC (Remote Procedure Call) has several entries in this subkey.*

HKEY_LOCAL_MACHINE\System: The System Information Manager

The HKEY_LOCAL_MACHINE\System subkey holds startup information used by Windows XP when booting. This subkey contains all the data that is stored and not recomputed at boot time.

NOTE *A full copy of the* HKEY_LOCAL_MACHINE\System *information is kept in the* system.alt *file, found in the* %SystemRoot%\System32\Config *directory in versions of Windows prior to Windows XP.*

The HKEY_LOCAL_MACHINE\System key (a.k.a. the System key) is organized into control sets (such as ControlSet001, ControlSet002, and CurrentControlSet) containing parameters for devices and services. (The Clone key, present in prior versions of Windows NT, is not found in Windows XP.)
The main control sets are as follows:

ControlSet001   The current and the default control set used to boot Windows XP normally. Mapped to CurrentControlSet at boot time, ControlSet001 is the most critical component in the registry in the normal bootup process.

ControlSet002   A backup control set from the Last Known Good boot that is used to boot when the default control set (ControlSet001) fails or is unusable for some reason.

ControlSet003   ControlSet003 (and ControlSet00*n*, where *n* is greater than 3) is a backup control set from the Last Known Good boot that may be used to boot from when the default control set (ControlSet001) fails or is unusable for some reason.

CurrentControlSet   The control set Windows XP has booted from. It is usually mapped to ControlSet001.

NOTE *For those of you migrating from NT 4, or still working with NT 4 machines, it's important to note that the* Clone *control set found in NT 4 is the volatile copy of the control set (usually* ControlSet001) *that was used to boot the system. Created by the system kernel during initialization, this key is not accessible from the Registry Editor. Windows XP uses the CurrentControlSet and previous control sets; it does not use the* Clone *control set at all.*

The HKEY_LOCAL_MACHINE\System key contains three or four other items:

MountedDevices   Contains items for each locally attached storage device that is available to the system.

DISK   Found in some systems that have been upgraded from earlier versions of Windows, this subkey contains items for each mapped CD-ROM drive. For example, I map my CD-ROM drives to drive letters after S:—I have three entries in this subkey mapping each CD-ROM drive to a different drive letter. This subkey is updated by the Disk Administrator tool.

Select Contains four subkeys. It also has information on which control set was booted and which subkey is the Last Known Good set. Also, if there is a "failed" control set, the failed control set's identity will be found in the Select subkey.

Setup Contains information used by Setup to configure Windows XP. This information includes locations of drives and directories, the setup command line, and a flag telling if setup is currently in progress.

The HKEY_LOCAL_MACHINE\System key is critical both to the boot process and to the operation of the system. Microsoft has created a number of tools and processes that help protect the HKEY_LOCAL_MACHINE\System key information. These include the Last Known Good boot process, which allows mapping in a known (or so we hope) copy of the control set, which in turn allows the system to boot if the original control set is too damaged to be booted.

WARNING   Do not, I repeat, do not, boot using the Last Known Good control set unless it is necessary! Any changes made to the system during the previous session will be lost, gone, forever and ever!

When modifying the control sets, be aware of the process of booting and creating the control sets. Generally, modifying a backup control set won't affect the system.

WHEN IS THE CURRENT CONTROL SET THE LAST KNOWN GOOD CONTROL SET?

At some point in the boot process, the current control set is copied into the Last Known Good control set. In Windows XP, the process of replacing the Last Known Good control set is done after the initial logon is performed. This allows the system to catch any problems related to the logon process.

HKEY_USERS: Settings for Users

Let's take a closer look at SIDs. No, despite what you may think, SID is not the kid down the street; SID is short for Security Identifier. The SID, which Windows XP uses to identify a user, contains information about user rights and privileges, settings, and any other information that is specific to that particular user.

The Anatomy of a SID

A SID always begins with the letter *S*, which denotes that this object is a SID, followed by long number separated with hyphens. The number consists of three to seven groups of numerals expressed in hexadecimal. For example, a valid SID might be this:

```
S-1-5-21-1234567890-1234567890-1234567890-123
```

This SID consists of eight separate parts separated by hyphens. After the *S*, the next three parts are the version number, authority, and subauthority values. The following three identify the specific installation—each Windows installation has different installation identifiers. The final part indicates the type of SID.

As mentioned, the number immediately following the *S* is a revision (or version) number. Windows XP (and all previous versions of Windows that used SIDs) have a number 1 in this position. Perhaps some day in the future, a version of Windows will have a version number that is not 1; however, it seems that the version number, and SIDs in general, are very stable objects.

THE SID IDENTIFIER AUTHORITY

The field immediately following the S-1 in a SID is the Identifier Authority. The meaning of the Identifier Authority varies somewhat on the following fields (the subauthority values). Table 3.1 shows some typical Identifier Authority values and their modifiers.

TABLE 3.1: SID IDENTIFIER AUTHORITY VALUES AND MODIFIERS

AUTHORITY - SUBAUTHORITY	AUTHORITY NAME	DESCRIPTION
0	Null	The basic Identifier Authority.
0 - 0	Nobody	Used when there is no security.
1	World	The basic Identifier Authority.
1 - 0	Everyone	Everyone: all users, guest, and anonymous users.
2	Local	The basic Identifier Authority.
3	Creator	The basic Identifier Authority.
3 - 0	Creator/Owner	The owner of an object.
3 - 1	Creator/Group	The primary group of the owner.
3 - 2	Creator/Owner Server	Not used after Windows NT 4.
3 - 3	Creator/Group Server	Not used after Windows NT 4.
4	Non-unique	The basic Identifier Authority.
5	NT	The basic Identifier Authority. Most work with Windows XP users will be in the NT authority (that is, the SID will begin with S-1-5).
5 - 0	(undefined)	Not used in Windows XP.
5 -1	Dialup	Used for users who are logged on to the system using a dial-up connection.
5 - 2	Network	Used for users who are logged on to the system using a LAN connection.
5 - 3	Batch	Used for users who are logged on to the system in a batch queue facility.

Continued on next page

TABLE 3.1: SID IDENTIFIER AUTHORITY VALUES AND MODIFIERS *(continued)*

AUTHORITY - SUBAUTHORITY	AUTHORITY NAME	DESCRIPTION
5 - 4	Interactive	Used for users who are logged on to the system interactively (a locally logged on user).
5 - 5 - X - Y	Logon Session	Used for users who are logging on to the system. The X and Y values identify the logon session.
5 - 6	Service	Used for a Windows XP service.
5 - 7	Anonymous	Used for users who are logged on anonymously to the system.
5 - 8	Proxy	Not used after Windows NT 4.
5 - 9	Enterprise Controllers	Used to identify Active Directory domain controllers.
5 - 10	(undefined)	Undefined in Windows XP.
5 - 11	Authenticated Users	Used for users who have been authenticated by the system and are logged on.
5 - 12	Restricted Code	Unknown in Windows XP.
5 - 13	Terminal Server User	Used for users who are logged on to the system using Microsoft Terminal Server.
5 - 18	Local System	The local computer's system account. This subauthority is new to Windows XP.
5 - 19	Local Service	The local computer's service account. This subauthority is new to Windows XP.
5 - 20	Network Service	The computer's network service account.
5 - 21	Non-Unique	A non-unique value to identify specific users.
5 - 32	Domain	Used with domains to identify users. See Table 3.3.

New!   SID Authority values greater than 5 are undefined in Windows XP. Subauthority values greater than 32 are not documented. Note that both Local Service and Network Service Authorities are new to Windows XP.

SIDs Used by Windows XP

Current user configurations are saved in HKEY_USERS, which contains at least three keys. These keys are SIDs. The first key, .DEFAULT, is the default user profile. This profile is used when no user is currently logged on. Once a user logs on, their profile is loaded and stored as the second and third keys found in HKEY_USERS.

The second key, the user profile for the user who is currently logged on, appears as something like this:

```
S-1-5-21-45749729-16073390-2133884337-500
```

This key is a specific user's profile—either the user's own profile or copied from the default user profile (found in %SystemDrive%\Documents and Settings\All Users) if the user has not established his or her own profile.

The third key looks something like this:

```
S-1-5-21-45749729-16073390-2133884337-500_Classes
```

This key contains information about the various classes specifically registered for the current user.

In these keys, or SIDs, the ending three- or four-digit number identifies both the user, and for some users, the type of user. Table 3.2 lists a number of general user types that might be assigned. In this book, the most commonly seen value is 500, which is assigned to me, the system Administrator account.

TABLE 3.2: COMMON SID VALUES

USER GROUP	SID
DOMAINNAME\ADMINISTRATOR	S-1-5-21-*xxxxxxxxx-xxxxxxxxxx-xxxxxxxxxx*-500
DOMAINNAME\GUEST	S-1-5-21-*xxxxxxxxx-xxxxxxxxxx-xxxxxxxxxx*-501
DOMAINNAME\DOMAIN ADMINS	S-1-5-21-*xxxxxxxxx-xxxxxxxxxx-xxxxxxxxxx*-512
DOMAINNAME\DOMAIN USERS	S-1-5-21-*xxxxxxxxx-xxxxxxxxxx-xxxxxxxxxx*-513
DOMAINNAME\DOMAIN GUESTS	S-1-5-21-*xxxxxxxxx-xxxxxxxxxx-xxxxxxxxxx*-514

General users might be assigned SIDs ending in four-digit numbers starting at 1000. My domain has a user called Pixel, whose SID ends in 1003, and another user, Long, whose SID ends in 1006. Get the picture?

There are also a number of built-in and special groups of SIDs, as shown in Tables 3.3 and 3.4.

TABLE 3.3: THE BUILT-IN LOCAL GROUPS

BUILT-IN LOCAL GROUP	SID
BUILTIN\ADMINISTRATORS	S-1-2-32-*xxxxxxxxx-xxxxxxxxxx-xxxxxxxxxx*-544
BUILTIN\USERS	S-1-2-32-*xxxxxxxxx-xxxxxxxxxx-xxxxxxxxxx*-545
BUILTIN\GUESTS	S-1-2-32-*xxxxxxxxx-xxxxxxxxxx-xxxxxxxxxx*-546
BUILTIN\POWER USERS	S-1-2-32-*xxxxxxxxx-xxxxxxxxxx-xxxxxxxxxx*-547

Continued on next page

TABLE 3.3: THE BUILT-IN LOCAL GROUPS *(continued)*

BUILT-IN LOCAL GROUP	SID
BUILTIN\ACCOUNT OPERATORS	S-1-2-32-*xxxxxxxxx-xxxxxxxxxx-xxxxxxxxxx*-548
BUILTIN\SERVER OPERATORS	S-1-2-32-*xxxxxxxxx-xxxxxxxxxx-xxxxxxxxxx*-549
BUILTIN\PRINT OPERATORS	S-1-2-32-*xxxxxxxxx-xxxxxxxxxx-xxxxxxxxxx*-550
BUILTIN\BACKUP OPERATORS	S-1-2-32-*xxxxxxxxx-xxxxxxxxxx-xxxxxxxxxx*-551
BUILTIN\REPLICATOR	S-1-2-32-*xxxxxxxxx-xxxxxxxxxx-xxxxxxxxxx*-552

TABLE 3.4: THE SPECIAL GROUPS

SPECIAL GROUP	SID
\CREATOR OWNER	S-1-1-0*x-xxxxxxxxx-xxxxxxxxxx-xxxxxxxxxx-xxx*
\EVERYONE	S-1-1-0*x-xxxxxxxxx-xxxxxxxxxx-xxxxxxxxxx-xxx*
NT AUTHORITY\NETWORK	S-1-1-2*x-xxxxxxxxx-xxxxxxxxxx-xxxxxxxxxx-xxx*
NT AUTHORITY\INTERACTIVE	S-1-1-4*x-xxxxxxxxx-xxxxxxxxxx-xxxxxxxxxx-xxx*
NT AUTHORITY\SYSTEM	S-1-1-18-*xxxxxxxxx-xxxxxxxxxx-xxxxxxxxxx-xxx*
NT AUTHORITY\LOCALSERVICE	S-1-1-19-*xxxxxxxxx-xxxxxxxxxx-xxxxxxxxxx-xxx*
NT AUTHORITY\NETWORKSERVICE	S-1-1-20-*xxxxxxxxx-xxxxxxxxxx-xxxxxxxxxx-xxx*

Naturally, there are many more SID codes and definitions. Tables 3.2 through 3.4 simply show a few of the more commonly used SIDs.

NOTE *Remember to differentiate between the* HKEY_USERS *hive and the* HKEY_CURRENT_USER *hive.* HKEY_CURRENT_USER *contains a pointer that references the current user in* HKEY_USERS.

The content of a user's profile, as it is found in the HKEY_USERS hive, is interesting. For example, the following keys are present in a typical user's profile (usually, there is nothing to guarantee that they will all be present, or that others might not be added):

AppEvents   Contains information about events (an event is an action like closing, minimizing, restoring, or maximizing) in a key called EventLabels. This information includes a text label for the event, such as the label "Close program" for the event close. These labels are used for a number of purposes, but one that most of us see is in the Control Panel's Sounds applet. A second section in AppEvents is Schemes, which lists labels for each application that uses specific sounds for its own events.

Console   Contains the default command-prompt configuration. This configuration may be customized for each command prompt individually, or it is possible in this key to change the global default, which would be used for all new command prompts that are created. For an example of command-prompt customization, open a command window and select Properties from the System menu. There are more settings that may be configured in the registry than are found in the Properties dialog box.

Control Panel   Contains information saved by many of the Control Panel's applets. Typically, these are default, or standard, values that are saved here, not user settings, which are stored elsewhere.

Environment   Contains the user environment variables for a user. Generally, the System Properties applet, Environment tab, is used to set user and system environment values.

EUDC   Not implemented in Windows XP. Windows 2000 has the EUDC key, which contains the definitions and other information about End User Defined Characters (EUDC). The program eudcedit.exe lets users edit/design characters that are specific to their needs.

Identities   Contains the information to link users and software configurations. Most configurations are Microsoft based, such as Outlook Express.

Keyboard Layout   Contains the keyboard configuration. Most users, at least those in the U.S., will have few or no substitutions. However, users who are using special keyboards or non–U.S. English keyboards will have some substitutions for special characters found in their languages.

Network   Contains mappings for each network drive connected to the computer. Information about the connections includes the host (server), remote path, and username used for the connection. The Network key is not typically found in the .DEFAULT key because users with no user profile are not automatically connected to a remote drive.

Printers   Contains mappings for each remote (network) printer connected to the computer. Information about the printer connection includes the host (server) and the DLL file used to manage the connection. The Printers key is typically not found in the .DEFAULT key because users with no user profile are not automatically connected to a remote printer.

RemoteAccess   Contains the various remote access configurations. The connections are managed using the Control Panel's Network and Dial-up Connections applet.

New!   **SessionInformation**   New to Windows XP, the SessionInformation subkey, ProgramCount, indicates the number of Windows applications that are loaded and running. This count does not include command prompt windows.

Software   Contains information about software installed, including components such as Schedule, Notepad, and so on. Also included in Software is Windows XP itself, with configuration information specific to the currently logged-on user.

System   Contains information about items such as backup configurations and files that are not to be backed up.

UNICODE Program Groups   Contains information about program groups that use Unicode. More commonly found on computers configured for languages other than English, Unicode is the scheme for displaying characters from both English and non-English alphabets on computers.

`Volatile Environment`   Contains information about the logon server that will be placed in the environment. One typical item is the `logonserver` environment variable. All items in `Volatile Environment` are dynamic; that is, they are created each time a user logs on. Other dynamic environment information might be contained in this key as well.

HKEY_CURRENT_CONFIG: The Current Configuration Settings

The registry hive `HKEY_CURRENT_CONFIG` is created from two registry keys, `HKEY_LOCAL_ MACHINE\System` and `HKEY_LOCAL_MACHINE\Software`. As it is created dynamically, there is little value in modifying any of the objects found in the `HKEY_CURRENT_CONFIG` hive.

The `HKEY_CURRENT_CONFIG` hive is composed of two major subkeys:

`Software`   Contains current configurations for some software components. A typical configuration might have keys under `Software` for Microsoft Internet Explorer, for example.

`System`   Contains information about hardware. The most common device found in this key is the video display adapter (found in virtually all configurations) and sometimes information about the default video modes as well. The video mode settings contained here are typical for any video system: resolution, panning, refresh rates (didn't you wonder where refresh rates were saved?), and BitsPerPel (color depth).

Generally, you would modify the source settings for a hardware device in `HKEY_LOCAL_MACHINE\System\ControlSet001\Hardware Profiles\Current\System\CurrentControlSet\Services\<device>\Device0`, where `<device>` is the device being modified. For example, my Matrox Millennium is listed under the device name `MGA64`.

TIP   For more information about the source for `HKEY_CURRENT_CONFIG`, take a look at `HKEY_LOCAL_MACHINE`, described earlier in this chapter.

HKEY_PERFORMANCE_DATA: The Performance Monitor Settings

Ever wonder where the Windows XP Performance Monitor information is contained? There is a final "hidden" registry hive, named `HKEY_PERFORMANCE_DATA`. This hive, which is simply not accessible except to applications written specifically to access performance data, is primarily dynamic in nature. To find the answer to this question, check out Chapter 11.

NTUSER: The New User Profile

Windows XP's installation process creates a default user profile and configuration. This information is located in `%SystemDrive%\Documents and Settings\Default User`. Whenever a new user logs on to a workstation or domain, this default user profile is copied to the user's profile. After that, the user modifies their profile to their own requirements and needs.

NOTE *Windows XP's* `Default User` *folder has the hidden attribute set, making it invisible unless the View All Files option is turned on.*

As an example, Windows XP's default language is typically U.S. English. (There are other language editions of Windows XP; for this example, I'm assuming the U.S. English version.) Whenever a new user logs on, the user will have U.S. English as his or her language, even if the system administrator has selected a different, non-English locale.

The default user profile is saved in the disk directory at `\Documents and Settings\Default User` `[WINNT]`, where `WINNT` is the directory that Windows XP is installed. (In Windows NT 4, the default user information was stored in `%SystemRoot%\Profiles\Default User`.) User information is always saved in a file named `ntuser.dat`. There is an entire configuration for new users in this directory—check out the Start menu, Desktop, and other directories, too. You will find that interesting modifications can be made that enable new users to become proficient quickly without spending too much time customizing their computers.

WARNING *This technique is an advanced use of the Registry Editor, and you must exercise care not to inadvertently modify the wrong registry or the wrong keys. Back up the registry before doing the following.*

First, to make this new user profile accessible to remote users (that is, all users other than those who log on locally), you must copy the `Default User` directory to the share named Netlogon. This share is typically located in the directory at `%SystemRoot%\SysVol\SysVol\`in Windows Server, in a directory that is named for the server. (For Windows NT 4 users, look in `%SystemRoot%\System32\Repl\Import`.) One way to copy these files is to create a new custom profile and copy the new custom profile using the User Profiles tab in the Control Panel's System applet.

If there are BDCs (Backup Domain Controllers), you would actually edit the file in the `Export` directory (same initial path) because this directory is locally replicated to the Import directory and to the other BDC `Import` directories, although it might be located elsewhere. The NetLogon share can be located quickly by typing the following command:

```
net share
```

at a command prompt. The computer's shares will be displayed.

Follow these steps to modify the default new user profile in your new `Default User` directory (remember to create a new `Default User` directory, saving the current `Default User` directory as a backup):

1. Start the Registry Editor using either a command prompt or the Start menu's Run command.

2. Click the title bar of the HKEY_USERS on Local Machine window to make the window active.

3. Choose File ➢ Load Hive from the Registry Editor menu.

4. Open the hive found in `%SystemRoot%\Profiles\Default User` or `%SystemDrive%\Documents and Settings\Default User`. This hive has the filename `ntuser.dat`.

5. The Registry Editor prompts you for a new key name. Type the name **NTUSER**.

6. Change whatever keys in NTUSER need to be modified. There will be a slew of changeable items in the new profile, including AppEvents, Console, Control Panel, Environment, Keyboard Layout, Software, and Unicode Program Groups. When adding new keys, do be careful to ensure that all users have at least read access to the new keys. No read access means that the key won't be accessible to the user.

TIP   To set the permissions for a key, select the key, and then select Edit ➤ Permissions from the Registry Editor menu. Ensure that the group Everyone has at least read access. Resist the urge to give everyone more than read access to this key, too. Too much power can be a dangerous thing!

7. After making all modifications to NTUSER, choose File ➤ Unload Hive from the Registry Editor menu.

8. Exit the Registry Editor.

Once this profile is saved in the NetLogon share location, new users will get this new profile each time they log on.

Chapter 4

Registry Tools and Tips: Getting the Work Done

WINDOWS XP USES ONLY ONE registry editor. Gone are the separate RegEdit and RegEdt32 editors that existed in Windows 2000. No matter which command you enter in Windows XP, `RegEdt32` or `RegEdit`, the same program (RegEdit, which is called the Registry Editor) will run.

Windows XP also has a utility called REG that is included as part of the system installation—no more needing to install a separate Resource Kit. This tool is run at the command prompt. REG allows flexible manipulation of the registry, replacing earlier versions of a number of the other Resource Kit components.

In this chapter, I'll first discuss the registry tools specific to Windows XP. In the second half of the chapter, I'll review the many useful tools available in earlier versions of Windows.

- ◆ Using the Registry Editor
- ◆ Installing remote registry editing on pre-XP machines
- ◆ Backup's Emergency Repair Disk features
- ◆ The tools in the Windows 2000 Resource Kit

Using the Registry Editor

If you have used Windows 2000's RegEdt32, you'll notice some differences in Windows XP's Registry Editor. While RegEdt32 has much more power, the Registry Editor is easier to use. RegEdt32 is an MDI (multiple document interface) application, and it displays each of the main hives in the registry in its own window. RegEdt32 has powerful administrative tools that the Registry Editor doesn't support, including read-only mode (note the following Warning) and a security configuration, which allows you to restrict access to some registry hives, keys, and subkeys.

Using the Registry Editor is as simple as starting it. From a command prompt, type **regedit** to start the program. You can also select Start ➢ Run, type **RegEdit**, and click the OK button to start the Registry Editor. In either case, typing **RegEdt32** will have exactly the same effect in Windows XP.

WARNING   *Registry Changes Are Permanent! All changes made with the Registry Editor are immediate and, for all intents, permanent! Though you can go back and manually undo a change made with the Registry Editor, everything that you change with the Registry Editor affects the current registry. Unlike Windows 2000's RegEdt32, XP's Registry Editor does not have a read-only mode. There is no safety net and nothing to catch your bloopers and booboos, and generally you'll have to clean up your own mess. In other words, you are editing the real, working, live, honest-to-goodness registry—not a copy. There is no Save command in the Registry Editor; you type in a change, and it is saved right then and there. So, make sure you have a backup of the registry files before fiddling with registry.*

Once started, the Registry Editor displays the current registry (see Figure 4.1). By default, this is the local registry. However, you can open a registry on a remote computer by selecting File ➢ Connect Network Registry and entering the name of the computer (see Figure 4.2) whose registry you want to open. If you cannot remember the exact name of the desired computer, the Select Computer window (Figure 4.3) displays a list of all computers found in the domain directory.

FIGURE 4.1

The Registry Editor automatically opens the current, local registry.

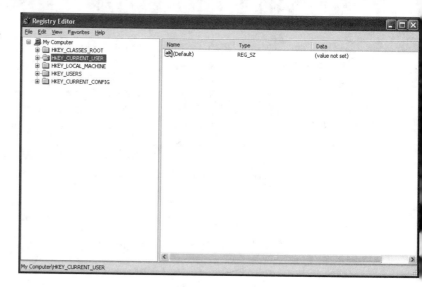

FIGURE 4.2

Use the Registry Editor's standard Select Computer window for remote registry editing.

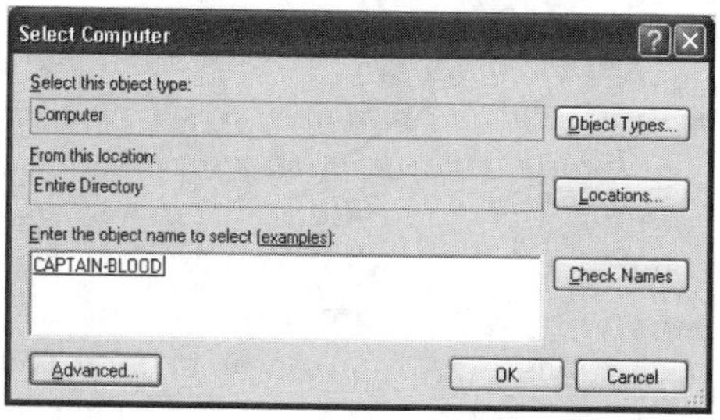

FIGURE 4.3

The Registry Editor's advanced Select Computer window lets you select the name of the computer whose registry you want to edit.

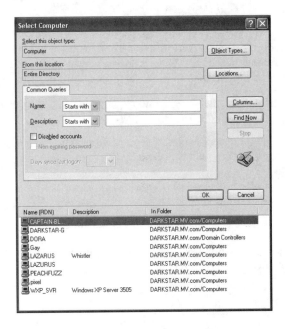

Figure 4.4 shows a remote registry opened in the Registry Editor. Only HKEY_USERS and HKEY_LOCAL_MACHINE may be edited remotely in Windows XP.

FIGURE 4.4

A remote registry is open and ready for editing in the Registry Editor.

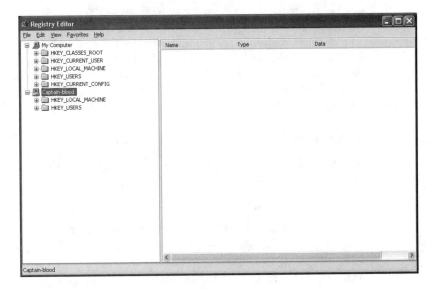

The Registry Editor has a straightforward set of menus. The Edit menu allows you to save and load text-based .reg (registry) files, connect to and disconnect from a network registry, and print the current branch or the entire registry.

MAKING THE REGISTRY EDITOR DO WHAT IT USED TO DO!

Since Windows 2000, the Registry Editor displays the last open key from the previous editing session. Some users like this feature; others do not. There is no easy way to disable this functionality, though perhaps Microsoft will give us the option to do so at a later time. Until that time, try this to disable the feature:

1. Using the Registry Editor, open HKEY_CURRENT_USER\Software\Microsoft\Windows\ CurrentVersion\Applets\Regedit.

2. Edit the LastKey value, and change its contents to an empty string. (If you want to always start in a specified location, you can put that location in this key's value.)

3. Select the RegEdit key.

4. Select Edit ➤ Permissions.

5. Uncheck the Full Control permission for every user in the list.

This prevents the Registry Editor from saving a value in this key. (Note that this also prevents the Registry Editor from saving any defaults or favorites.)

New!

You use the Edit menu to create a new key or value entry. Data types in the Registry Editor are restricted to string, binary, multistring, expandable string, and DWORD. Generally, these types are the only registry data types that you would want to edit. New to the Registry Editor's Edit menu is the Permissions option. Prior versions of the Registry Editor did not allow you to set permissions, but this limitation has been fixed as of Windows XP.

The Edit menu also lets you delete an object, rename a key or subkey, and copy a key name to a new name. At the bottom of the Edit menu are the Find and Find Next options.

Windows 2000 added improvements to the Registry Editor that continue in Windows XP. One improvement is the addition of the Type column in the right-hand display of values and data, which lists each value's type. Although the Registry Editor displays the names of all the data types available to Windows, the user is still restricted to editing the data types listed above.

Another 2000 improvement is the addition of the Favorites menu. This feature lets you place your most commonly accessed subkeys into a list of favorites so you can quickly navigate to a subkey.

NOTE *If you have disabled the Registry Editor's last open key functionality (as described above), then you have essentially disabled the Favorites options as well. You can't have one without the other. . .*

Importing and Exporting Registry Hives and Keys

The ability to export a registry hive or key (or the entire registry, if necessary) is a powerful feature of the Registry Editor. Once a registry is open, select a hive or key (or My Computer to export the entire registry) and choose File ➤ Export to open the Export Registry File window (see Figure 4.5).

NOTE *The typical Windows registry is several thousand to hundreds of thousands of lines long. The registry on my server has over 130,000 lines. At 66 lines per page, the printed report would be at least 2,000 pages. At least, you say? Yes, many registry lines require more than one line to print, so the printout would actually be much more than 2,000 pages.*

FIGURE 4.5

Exporting the currently selected hive or key is easy!

A hive is exported into a Unicode text-based file. This file has no comments; some of the Resource Kit registry tools do comment exported sections of the registry. However, the file may be opened with most any text editor (such as Notepad), searched, and even (carefully) modified. Any changes made to the exported text file may be incorporated into the registry by simply importing the modified file.

Importing a file that the Registry Editor had previously exported is as simple as selecting Registry ➤ Import Registry File and entering the name of the registry file to import.

WHAT IS AN EXPORTED REGISTRY FILE?

A registry file exported by the Registry Editor starts with the line: "Windows Registry Editor Version 5.00." The following line is the first hive exported in a hierarchical format:

```
Windows Registry Editor Version 5.00
[HKEY_LOCAL_MACHINE]
[HKEY_LOCAL_MACHINE\Hardware]
[HKEY_LOCAL_MACHINE\HARDWARE\Description]
```

Generally, a full export of a registry starts with an export of the HKEY_LOCAL_MACHINE hive, as the above example shows.

The contents of an exported registry are arranged in the file as a hive and key combination (fully qualified, enclosed in brackets), with the data key name in quotes and its value following the equal sign. The following example shows the three value entries that the FloatingPointProcessor contains:

```
[HKEY_LOCAL_MACHINE\HARDWARE\DESCRIPTION\System\FloatingPointProcessor\0]
"Component Information"=hex:00,00,00,00,00,00,00,00,00,00,00,00,01,00,00,00
"Identifier"="x86 Family 5 Model 4 Stepping 3"
"Configuration Data"=hex(9):ff,ff,ff,ff,ff,ff,ff,ff,00,00,00,00,00,00,00,00
```

Why export the registry? First, the search capabilities in the Registry Editor are not optimal. (Well, that's my opinion!) Loading an exported registry file into an editor (such as Word, or even Notepad) allows you to quickly search for strings using the editor's search capability.

Another benefit is that it is easy to export the registry before installing an application or system extension. After an installation, it is also a good idea to export the registry. Then, using one of the system comparison tools (such as FC or, if you have it, WinDiff), you can compare the two versions of the registry and see what the installation has changed. Bingo—a quick way to see what's happening to the registry on installations.

Printing the Registry

Printing a registry hive or key is possible in the Registry Editor. As mentioned previously, printing an entire registry is not a swell idea—you'd have to make a major investment in paper and printer supplies. Typically, a registry would require thousands of pages to print.

Printing sections of a registry hive can be very useful if a paper record is needed, or if you need something to take to a meeting, or if you want to jot down some quick notes. The limit of a printed registry hive or key is that searching it might be difficult.

Printing is easily done if you select the hive or subkey to print, then select File ➤ Print from the Registry Editor's main menu. The Print dialog box, shown in Figure 4.6, allows you to edit the branch to be printed (with the currently selected object as the default). The results of printing a registry report are almost identical to exporting, with the exception that a printed report lacks the initial header line that's found in an exported registry file.

FIGURE 4.6

The Registry Editor's Print dialog box is set to print a small part of the hive HKEY_LOCAL_MACHINE.

TIP Is the registry file readable? Generally, the Registry Editor in Windows XP creates a better report than previous versions did. The Registry Editor print facility is basic and simply wraps lines at 80 characters. Any line more than 80 characters wraps and is difficult to read. Complex registry data types (such as REG_FULL_RESOURCE_DESCRIPTOR) are well formatted. Another solution is to print the registry to a file, load the file into a word processor, format it to be readable, and print it from the word processor. To do this, you must define a generic text printer device.

Creating, Renaming, and Deleting Entries

The Registry Editor allows you to quickly create, delete, or rename an entry. Entries may consist of keys, subkeys, or value entries.

CREATING A NEW KEY

You can quickly create a new key by following these steps:

1. Select the hive or key in which the new key is to be created. Either right-click the object or select Edit ➤ New, and then select the type of object to create.

2. The Registry Editor creates the new subkey, giving it a default name of `New Key #n` where *n* is a number beginning with 1. Edit the new subkey's name. Give the subkey a meaningful name or the name that is expected for this subkey. (If you neglect to edit the key's name at this time, you can rename it later.)

Once the new subkey has been created, you can populate it with additional subkeys and value entries.

NOTE   A hive, key, or subkey may contain both value entries and other subkeys at the same time.

New!

WHY CAN'T I CREATE A KEY HERE?

Prior to Windows XP, not all hives allowed you to create keys directly under the hive itself. For example, it was not possible to create a key under HKEY_LOCAL_MACHINE, though you could create a key under HKEY_CURRENT_USER. Now you can create keys virtually anywhere. However...

Why not create an object in those locations? Simply put, the HKEY_LOCAL_MACHINE hive is not "saved" when Windows shuts down. Rather it is re-created anew each time Windows boots—therefore, any key or subkey created is lost at the next boot-up time.

CREATING A VALUE ENTRY, THEN RENAMING IT

You can quickly create a new value entry by following these steps:

1. Select the hive or key in which the new value entry is to be created.

2. Select Edit ➤ New and then select either String Value, Binary Value, DWORD Value, Multi-String Value, or Expandable String Value, depending on the type of data that this value entry will have.

3. The Registry Editor creates the new value entry, giving it a default name of `New Value #n` where *n* is a number beginning with 1. Edit the new value entry's name. Give it a meaningful name or the name that is expected for it. Press the Enter key to save the new name.

TIP   At any point, you may rename a key or value entry by right-clicking the item to be renamed and selecting Rename from the context menu.

4. To enter data into the new entry, double-click the entry. The correct edit box is displayed, allowing you to edit the data. If you right-click, you can choose to edit the object using the binary format (see Figure 4.7).

Once you've created the new value entry, you can enter data as necessary.

NOTE   A key need not have a data value entered. A key is valid without any data, though no-data defaults vary depending on the type of data the key contains: String values have a zero-length string as their default. Binary values have a zero-length binary value (which is different from having a value of zero). DWORD values have a value of zero.

FIGURE 4.7

The Registry Editor after right-clicking on REG_FULL_RESOURCE_DES CRIPTOR, showing the Modify Binary Data selection in the context menu

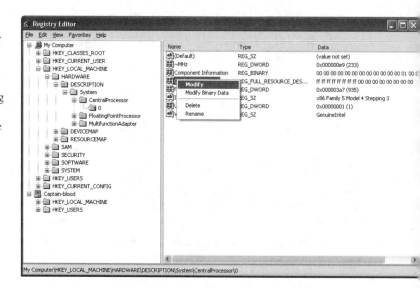

Figure 4.8 shows the Registry Editor with a new subkey containing another subkey, a string value, a binary value, a DWORD value, a multistring value, and an expandable string value, exactly as created by the Registry Editor. Note that I've named the initial subkey Test Key.

In the example, I gave each of the new value entries a name to match the type of data it stores. I created each value using the Edit ➢ New selection in the menu, as shown in Figure 4.9. You can edit value entries at any time, either in their native format or in a raw, binary format. To change the name, select the key or value entry and choose Edit ➢ Rename. To change the value entry's contents, select the value entry and choose Edit ➢ Modify. To change the value entry's contents in binary format, select the value entry and choose Edit ➢ Modify Binary Data. You can also double-click the value entry or right-click (also known as a *context-click*) the item and choose Modify to change the value.

DELETING THE UNWANTED

Getting rid of the unwanted is easy. Select the object, either a key, subkey, or value entry, to be deleted and then either select Edit ➢ Delete or just press the Delete key. The Registry Editor prompts you to confirm that the object is to be deleted, if the Confirm on Delete option is selected.

FIGURE 4.8

The Registry Editor after creating the subkey called Test Key and a further subkey called Test sub-key

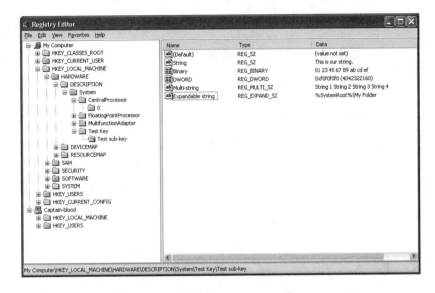

FIGURE 4.9

You create new value entries using the Registry Editor's Edit menu.

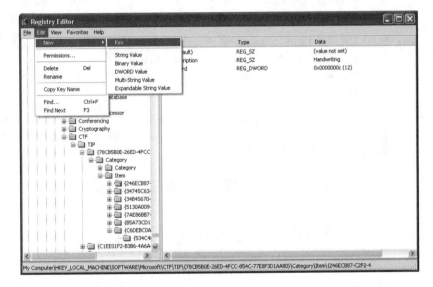

WARNING   *Once deleted, 'tis gone forever! Be careful not to delete anything that you will want later. Prior to deleting, it's appropriate to back up the registry. It also might be a good idea to rename the object, just in case you need to restore it at a later time.*

Copying Key Names

Is this as simple as it seems? A long, convoluted name without having to type it? Yes, it is!

Copy Key Name, found in the Registry Editor's Edit menu (and from the key's context menu if you right-click the key and select Copy Key Name), copies the key's name to the Clipboard. The information is copied in text format and may then be pasted into other applications or word processors as needed. For example, when I copy the new key created in Figure 4.8, the following text is placed into the Clipboard:

    HKEY_LOCAL_MACHINE\Hardware\Description\System\Test Key\Test sub-key

This means it is not necessary to manually type in long registry keys into other applications and documents. This feature, for example, was a great help when writing this book.

TIP   Sadly, we can't copy either value names or their contents in this manner! To copy a key's data, you must edit it and select and copy from the editor.

Searching: Find and Find Next

Searching a registry is one of the most important tasks you'll have to undertake. Before you make a modification, do debugging, or start browsing, it is usually necessary to search for something.

Now, as I've mentioned previously, the Registry Editor's search capabilities are a bit limited.

TIP   The Registry Editor searches downward only. If what you are searching for is located above the current selection, you'll be in for a long wait, as the search will have to scan to the end of the registry and then restart at the beginning to find it. When in doubt, start at My Computer, and you can be assured that the search will include the entire registry. Oh, the Registry Editor's search is deathly slow—a long search, in a large registry, is a sure sign that it's time for a coffee break.

Searching allows you to look at keys, data value names, and data value contents. You may choose to search any or all of these (see Figure 4.10), and you can limit the search to whole strings only, which applies to searching text strings exclusively.

FIGURE 4.10

You can search for any combination of keys, values, and data.

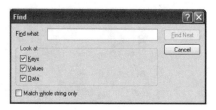

NOTE   The Registry Editor's search is not case specific, so you can enter strings to be searched in lowercase if desired. This is nice, since the case of many registry entries is rather mixed.

Once the search finds the item searched for, it stops on the word(s) found. Use F3 to continue the search or to find subsequent matches.

If the Registry Editor's search is unable to find the string entered, you will see an error dialog box.

Loading and Unloading Hives

The Registry Editor allows a hive to be loaded into the current registry. This hive may be modified and later unloaded. Why?

There are several reasons for loading and unloading hives into the Registry Editor. The following example, configuring a modified new user profile, concerns the file `ntuser.dat`. In `ntuser.dat` is the `HKEY_CURRENT_USER` hive. Within this hive are settings, such as internationalization, colors, schemes, and other items. Windows XP's installation process creates a default user profile—nothing spectacular, a very plain configuration. Whenever a new user logs on to a workstation (or domain), this default user profile is copied to the user's profile. After that, the user may modify this default profile to his or her requirements and needs. Of course, you might want to establish some organizational defaults, such as a company scheme.

WARNING   *The techniques shown next are advanced uses of the Registry Editor. Back up the registry before doing the following.*

The default user profile is saved in the following disk directory:

◆ For new installations: `%SystemDrive%\Documents and Settings\Default User` (this directory may have the hidden attribute set, so that it is not displayed when using either Explorer or a command session)

◆ For Windows NT 4, and Windows 2000 installations that are upgraded from Windows NT 4: `%SystemRoot%\Profiles\Default User\`

The name of the user profile is `ntuser.dat`. There is an entire configuration for new users in the directory `%SystemDrive%\Documents and Settings\Default User`; check out the Start Menu, Desktop, and other directories, too. You will find that interesting modifications can be made that enable new users to become proficient quickly without spending too much time customizing their computers.

First, to make this new user profile accessible to remote users (users other than those who log on locally), you must copy the `Default User` directory to the share named NetLogon. This share is typically located in the directory at `C:\Winnt\SysVol\SysVol` in Windows Server.

Placing files in `Export` (in Windows NT 4) causes replication to copy them locally to `Import`, along with any BDCs (Backup Domain Controllers). Note that the share might be located elsewhere. The NetLogon share can be located quickly by typing the following command at a command prompt:

```
net share
```

The computer's shares will be displayed.

One process to copy these files is to create a new custom profile, and then copy the new custom profile using the System applet's User Profiles tab.

WARNING   *Be smart! Be sure to make a backup copy of the* `ntuser.dat` *file before you make any changes in it!*

Do the following to modify the default new user profile. (Remember to create a new `Default User` directory, saving the current `Default User` directory as a backup.)

1. Start the Registry Editor using either a command prompt or by selecting Start ➢ Run.

2. Click the title bar of the HKEY_USERS on Local Machine window to make it active.

3. Choose File ➤ Load Hive from the Registry Editor menu.

4. Open the hive file in `%SystemDrive%\Documents and Settings\Default User`. (If your system is configured, or installed, with different directory names, choose the correct name.) This hive has a filename of `ntuser.dat`.

5. The Registry Editor prompts you for a new Key Name. Use the name `ntuser`.

6. Change whatever keys in `ntuser` need to be modified. There will be a slew of changeable items in the new profile, including `AppEvents`, `Console`, `Control Panel`, `Environment`, `Keyboard Layout`, `Software`, and `Unicode Program Groups`. When adding new keys, do be careful to ensure that all users have at least read access to the new keys. No read access means that the key won't be accessible to the person named "user."

TIP   To set the permissions for a key, select the key, and then select Security ➤ Permissions from the Registry Editor menu. Ensure that the Everyone group has at least read access. Resist the urge to give everyone more than read access to this key. Too much power can be a dangerous thing!

7. After making all modifications to `NTUSER`, choose File ➤ Unload Hive from the Registry Editor menu. Unload the hive to the file `ntuser.dat`. (You did back up the original file, right?)

8. Exit the Registry Editor.

Once this profile is saved in the Netlogon share location, each time a new user logs on to the network, the user will get this new profile.

CAN'T FIND THE LOCATION FOR NTUSER.DAT?

Remember that the `ntuser.dat` file has the hidden attribute, so it is not normally displayed in either a command window or in Explorer. Either tell Explorer to display hidden files or, at a command prompt, use the `dir` command with the `/ah` option to display hidden files and directories.

If worse comes to worst, open a command window (tough to do this in Explorer) and, in the root of the system drive, use the command:

```
DIR /ah /s ntuser.dat
```

This command lists all copies of the `ntuser.dat` file, allowing you to change the appropriate one. One thought though: don't change the "current user" `ntuser.dat` file—it won't work! Windows will rewrite the file when the user next logs off, causing any changes you made to disappear!

Using the Registry Editor from the Command Line

The Registry Editor may be used from the command line, without user interaction. The commands that the Registry Editor uses include those described below. (Note that not all commands may be available under all operating systems.)

♦ To import a registry file into the Registry Editor:

```
REGEDIT [/L:system] [/R:user] filename1
```

◆ To create a registry object from a file:

    REGEDIT [/L:system] [/R:user] /C `filename2`

◆ To export a registry (or part of the registry):

    REGEDIT [/L:system] [/R:user] /E `filename3` [`regpath1`]

◆ To delete part of a registry:

    REGEDIT [/L:system] [/R:user] /D `regpath2`

In all the above commands, the parameters are as follows:

/L:system	Specifies the location of the system.dat file. Note that there is a colon between the /L and the parameter system.
/R:user	Specifies the location of the user.dat file. Note that there is a colon between the /R and the parameter user.
filename1	Specifies the file(s) to import into the registry.
/C filename2	Specifies the file to create the registry from. Note that there is a space between the /C and the parameter filename2.
/E filename3	Specifies the file to export the registry to. Note that there is a space between the /E and the parameter filename3.
regpath1	Specifies the starting registry key to export from (defaults to exporting the entire registry).
/D regpath2	Specifies the registry key to delete. Note that there is a space between the /D and the parameter regpath2.

WARNING   *Be careful; be very careful. Running the Registry Editor in the command-line mode can be damaging to the registry—it is possible to utterly destroy the registry with a single command.*

Restoring

Restoring is what Joe and Ed on the Learning Channel do to old furniture, right?

Well, maybe so, but it's also possible to restore an object in the registry using the Registry Editor. The process is straightforward, although like everything else, you must have something to restore from. As explained above, using Export (in the File menu), you can save a registry object to a file. The file extension is .reg, and it is a really good idea to keep filenames as descriptive as possible.

A suggestion: If you have a strong desire to play with the import and export functionality of the Registry Editor, install a practice copy of Windows. Don't do this on a working version—at least not a copy of Windows that you, or anyone else, care about.

NOTE   *When an object is restored, the data overwrites the existing object. It becomes permanent, as everything that the Registry Editor does is immediately written to the registry.*

WARNING *More important: When an object is restored, it is written on top of the currently selected object. Make sure that the object you are restoring belongs at the current selection. Again, make sure you name your file well so that you know exactly which object a given file represents. Imagine coming back to a saved file, perhaps weeks later, and trying to restore it without knowing which object it was saved from.*

WARNING *Even* much *more important: Restoring an object may override the read-only mode option—it will write to the registry no matter what! Care to guess how I found that out?*

When an object is restored, the selected object is not renamed, even though the contents of the object are replaced.

Security

Security is paramount in a Windows installation. The registry, just like the NTFS file system, can be protected from unauthorized access. This can be a critical issue, because Windows supports remote registry editing.

NOTE *It is possible to make changes to one computer's registry from another computer without the user of the changed computer even knowing that a change has been made (that is, until they see the results of the change).*

The Registry Editor supports security modifications. If a hive is not accessible to the Registry Editor, the user is unable to view the hive or change it, depending on the level of access granted by the system. However, the Registry Editor's Edit ➤ Permissions menu selection allows you to change the security attributes for a hive and any keys (if you have sufficient authority to do so).

Initially, when you select Edit ➤ Permissions, the Permissions For dialog box is displayed (see Figure 4.11). You set basic security in this dialog box, while you set advanced functionality (permissions, auditing, and owner) in the Advanced Security Settings For dialog box.

FIGURE 4.11

Setting the permissions for an object in the Registry Editor

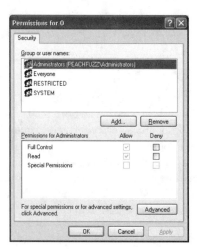

Clicking the Advanced button of the Permissions For dialog box displays the Advanced Security Settings For dialog box, shown in Figure 4.12. The Advanced Security Settings For dialog box has four tabs: Permissions, Auditing, Owner, and Effective Permissions.

FIGURE 4.12

Specific users and administrative units can have their own permissions.

PERMISSIONS

The currently selected object is displayed along with the current permissions granted. Default permissions are typically, but not always, ones that everyone can read; the Administrator accounts and the system both have full control.

The Permissions tab lists the object's name in the dialog box's title bar. To allow the current object to include its parent's permissions, select the check box that says, "Inherit from parent the permission entries that apply to child objects. Include these with entries explicitly defined here." To allow changing permissions for both the selected item and any subkeys it contains, select the check box that says, "Replace permission entries on all child objects with entries shown here that apply to child objects.".

You set detailed permissions by clicking the Edit button in the Permissions tab of the Advanced Security Settings For dialog box. This displays the Permission Entry For dialog box, shown in Figure 4.13. The list box shows the current permissions, organized by name. Select one name (each may be modified separately, or all entries may be cleared using the Clear All button) and set the type of access. The selections include the following:

Full Control   Allows the selected user to have complete, unrestricted access

Query Value   Allows the selected user to have read access

Set Value   Allows the selected user to have write access

Create Subkey   Allows the selected user to create a subkey

Enumerate Subkeys   Allows the selected user to obtain a list of subkeys contained within the object

Notify   Tells Windows XP to notify the owner when the object is modified

Create Link   Allows the selected user to create a link to the object from another object

Delete   Allows the selected user to delete the object

Write DAC   Allows the selected user to modify Discretionary Access Control information

Write Owner   Allows the selected user to modify the owner record information

Read Control   Combines the standard read, Query Value, Enumerate Subkeys, and Notify permissions

FIGURE 4.13

Permissions are customized on a user-by-user basis in the Permission Entry For dialog box.

WARNING   *Of course, the standard warnings apply:* Do not grant more permission than is necessary to do the job. *Understand which permissions are being granted (see the above list) and consider granting permissions temporarily, removing anything granted as soon as it is not necessary.*

AUDITING

The word *auditing*, when mentioned with the words *government* and *taxes*, generally gets us weak in the knees and starts us sweating profusely. However, auditing registry interaction can be somewhat less troublesome and very beneficial to the user.

Auditing, like permissions, is based on users. You set up auditing in the Auditing tab of the Advanced Security Settings For dialog box (see Figure 4.14). For an object that has not had any auditing set, the list will be blank. The first thing to do is to check "Inherit from parent the auditing entries that apply to child objects. Include these with entries explicitly defined here." Next, click the Add button to add new users to the list (see Figure 4.15). In the Select User, Computer, or Group dialog box, you can select both groups and individual users. Select one name in the list box and click the Add button to add that name to the list of names to be audited. Once all names to be audited have been added, click OK. This dialog box also has an Advanced button that provides additional features for specifying an object name.

FIGURE 4.14

The Auditing tab, in which you set auditing permissions

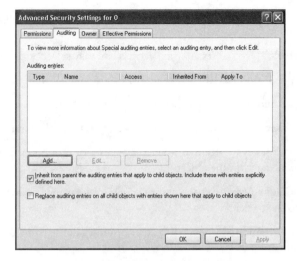

FIGURE 4.15

Add users or administrative units to be audited in the Select User, Computer, or Group dialog box.

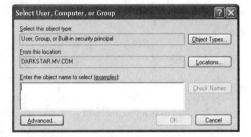

After adding a new user to audit, or selecting Edit in the Advanced Security Settings For dialog box for an existing user, the Auditing Entry For dialog box is displayed (see Figure 4.16).

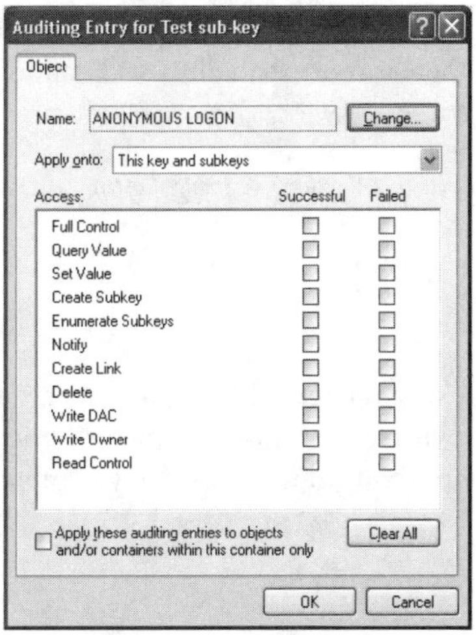

FIGURE 4.16

The Auditing Entry For dialog box is where you set auditing events.

Set specific permissions in the Auditing Entry For dialog box. The following events may be audited:

Full Control   Used to set auditing events (you may select Successful, Failed, or both)

Query Value   Audited whenever the user or group in the name list reads the object

Set Value   Audited whenever the user or group in the name list writes to the object

Create Subkey   Audited whenever the user or group in the name list creates a key

Enumerate Subkeys   Audited whenever the user or group in the name list enumerates a list of keys contained within the object

Notify   Audited whenever the user or group in the name list does anything that generates a notification to the owner

Create Link   Audited whenever the user or group in the name list creates a link to the object from another object

Delete   Audited whenever the user or group in the name list deletes the object

Write DAC   Audited whenever the user or group in the name list modifies the Discretionary Access Control information

Write Owner   Audited whenever the user or group in the name list modifies the owner record information

Read Control   Audited whenever the user or group in the name list does anything that includes the standard read, Query Value, Enumerate Subkeys, or Notify permissions

You can audit for success and/or failure. Either or both may be selected if desired:

Successful   Whenever a successful operation is done, auditing information is saved. This mode is useful when creating a log of information about changes to the registry. Success auditing can help you go back and determine what changes were made to the registry to try to fix the problem.

Failed   Whenever an unsuccessful operation is done, auditing information is saved. Whenever security is an issue (any time there is more than one user), failure auditing can help point to attempts to compromise system security.

TIP   *Select audit success for critical objects that shouldn't be changed often. Select audit failure for any object that is security related.*

OWNER

I own things; you own things. To keep the records straight, we have titles for cars, deeds for property, and other documents that trace ownership of anything that is nontrivial. With computers, especially Windows XP, ownership is an important thing. I "own" my computer, and probably I don't want you messing with it.

When using NTFS, ownership may be set for files. In addition, objects in the registry may have ownership, too. Ownership implies ultimate control: the owner can restrict access, audit, and do whatever he or she wants.

In the Registry Editor, the Owner tab in the Advanced Security Settings For dialog box allows you to take "ownership" of a registry object (see Figure 4.17). An object may have more than one owner, and if there are multiple owners, then they each share owner privilege.

The owner of any object may allow or disallow another user from taking ownership; however, once another user has ownership, the original owner's rights are terminated.

NOTE *Both the current owner and the system administrator may assign ownership of the object to a user or to the system administrator.*

FIGURE 4.17

The Owner tab lists the current owner and allows ownership to be set to the current user.

Tips for Registry Editor Users

Several tips come to mind when using the Registry Editor:

- First, when saving a hive using Save Key (under the Registry menu), make absolutely sure that the filename saved to is descriptive enough to enable the successful restoration of the hive at a later time. The Registry Editor doesn't check whether a hive being restored is the same hive as the one being replaced.

- Second, as with the Registry Editor, be aware that printing can create reports of incredible size. Do not print the entire registry, especially if you are over the age of 22 or so—life is just too short.

- Finally, the Registry Editor Save Subtree As functionality allows saving a detailed text report, identical to the printed report, to a disk file. This report can then be loaded into a text editor or word processor, allowing editing and printing.

Reg.exe

`Reg.exe` is a tool combining the functionality of a number of the other command-line-driven Windows NT 4 Resource Kit registry tools. `Reg.exe` is a standard part of Windows XP, and it is included in the Windows 2000 Resource Kit. It improves the interaction between the command line and the registry and is somewhat easier (and a whole lot more consistent) to use than the handful of other utilities.

NOTE *If you need to administer Windows 2000 machines as well, the Windows 2000 Resource Kit includes* Reg. *If you are still using older Resource Kit components in legacy support systems, there is no urgent need to change or migrate to the newer tools that are contained in the Windows Resource Kits. However, it is not recommended that the older utilities be used when updating support facilities, but that the new tools be integrated wherever possible. Many of the Resource Kit utilities are command-prompt driven. However, being experienced users, we are not afraid of a command prompt, are we?*

`Reg.exe` has the following functions:

- ◆ Add
- ◆ Backup (only found in versions prior to Windows 2000)
- ◆ Compare (only found in Windows 2000 versions and later)
- ◆ Copy
- ◆ Delete
- ◆ Export (only found in Windows 2000 versions and later)
- ◆ Import (only found in Windows 2000 versions and later)
- ◆ Load
- ◆ Query
- ◆ Restore
- ◆ Save
- ◆ Unload
- ◆ Update (only found in versions prior to Windows 2000)

In the following sections, I'll cover each of the functions, showing parameters and results as examples of how to use `Reg.exe`.

ADD

The add function, invoked with the command `reg add <options>`, adds an object (key or value entry) to the registry. Options include the registry object to be added with the object's value, an optional machine name (additions may be made to remote registries), and an optional data type, as described next.

The command line for add is:

```
REG ADD RegistryPath=value [data type][\\Machine]
```

As with other registry tools, the registry path may be a ROOTKEY or a hive (with or without a value entry). The ROOTKEY may be one of the following (HKLM is assumed if none is entered):

◆ HKLM (for HKEY_LOCAL_MACHINE)

◆ HKCU (for HKEY_CURRENT_USER)

◆ HKCR (for HKEY_CLASSES_ROOT)

◆ HKU (for HKEY_USERS)

◆ HKCC (for HKEY_CURRENT_CONFIG)

The hive is further qualified to determine the object to be added.

The data type parameter is one of the following (the default, if the data type is not specified, is to use REG_SZ):

◆ REG_SZ

◆ REG_DWORD

◆ REG_EXPAND_SZ

◆ REG_MULTI_SZ

Here's an example of executing the add command:

```
Windows 8:56:09 C:\
REG ADD HKLM\Software\MyCo\MyApp\Version=1.00
The operation completed successfully.

Windows 9:00:48 C:\
REG query HKLM\Software\MyCo\MyApp\Version
REG_SZ      Version 1.00
Windows 9:00:59 C:\
```

BACKUP

Backup is only found on Windows versions prior to Windows 2000, so this section is of concern only to those working with machines running Windows 95 or 98/Me. On versions of Windows that do not support Backup, including Windows XP, use the Save option instead of Backup. The backup function, invoked with the command reg backup <options>, saves the registry object specified to the file specified. Options include the registry path to be saved, the output filename, and an optional machine name (saves may be made on remote registries).

The command line for backup is:

```
REG BACKUP RegistryPath OutputFileName [\\Machine]
```

As with other registry tools, the registry path to be queried may be a ROOTKEY or a hive, with or without a value entry. The ROOTKEY may consist of one of the following (HKLM is assumed if none is entered):

◆ HKLM

◆ HKCU

◆ HKCR

◆ HKU

◆ HKCC

Only HKLM and HKU may be specified when copying objects to a remote registry.

NOTE *Notice that* reg save *and* reg backup *are identical in functionality.*

An example of executing the backup command is shown below. In this example, I've saved a small key to the file C:\Temp\MyCo.reg:

```
Windows 9:34:19 C:\
REG backup HKLM\Software\MyCo\MyNewApp c:\temp\MyCo
The operation completed successfully.


Windows 9:34:21 C:\
dir c:\temp\myco.*
 Volume in drive C is (c) - Boot drive
 Volume Serial Number is CC56-5631

 Directory of c:\temp

07/17/99 09:34a          8,192          MyCo
        1 File(s)      8,192 bytes
             183,407,104 bytes free

Windows 9:34:27 C:\
```

COMPARE

The compare function, invoked with the command reg compare keyname1 keyname2 <options>, displays the value of an object (key or value entry) in the registry. A required parameter, keyname, specifies the object to be queried. Options include specifying a query for a specific registry, querying for the default value, and specifying that all subkeys and values be displayed.

The command line for query is:

```
REG QUERY Keyname1 Keyname2 [/v valuename or /ve] [/oa | /od | /os | /on] [/s]
```

As with other registry tools, the registry path may be a ROOTKEY or a hive (with or without a value entry). The ROOTKEY may be one of the following (HKLM is assumed if none is entered):

◆ HKLM

◆ HKCU

◆ HKCR

◆ HKU

◆ HKCC

The hive is further qualified to determine the object to be added. Remote registry comparisons may be done; simply specify the keyname as \machine\keyname.

The following output options allow for specifying:

/oa	Output all	Displays both matches and differences
/od	Output differences	Display only differences
/os	Output same	Displays matches
/on	Output none	Displays no output (Use the command's return code to determine if the comparison was successful or not.)

COPY

The copy function, invoked with the command `reg copy <options>`, copies the registry object specified to a new name. Options include the registry path to be copied (the source) and a destination name.

The command line for copy is:

```
REG COPY OldPath [\\Machine] Newpath [\\Machine]
```

As with other registry tools, the registry path to be copied (both the old path and the new path) may be a ROOTKEY or a hive. The path may be specified with or without a value entry. The ROOTKEY may consist of one of the following (HKLM is assumed if none is entered):

◆ HKLM

◆ HKCU

◆ HKCR

◆ HKU

◆ HKCC

Only HKLM and HKU may be specified when copying objects to a remote registry.

NOTE *Consider the case where a registry object is copied from one registry to another registry on a different machine. This command is more powerful than is apparent at first glance.*

The hive may be further qualified to determine the contents of a specific key or value entry. If no value entry is specified, all the value entries in the key will be copied. Here's an example of executing the copy command:

```
Windows 9:10:52 C:\
REG query HKLM\Software\MyCo\MyApp\

Listing of [Software\MyCo\MyApp\]

REG_SZ      Version 1.00

Windows 9:15:18 C:\
REG copy HKLM\Software\MyCo\MyApp\ HKLM\Software\MyCo\MyNewApp
The operation completed successfully.


Windows 9:15:43 C:\
REG query HKLM\Software\MyCo\MyNewApp

Listing of [Software\MyCo\MyNewApp]

REG_SZ      Version 1.00

Windows 9:15:51 C:\
```

DELETE

The delete function, invoked with the command `reg delete <options>`, deletes the specified registry object. Options include the registry path to be deleted, an optional machine name (queries may be made on remote registries), and an optional parameter, `/F`, that forces the deletion without recourse.

The command line for delete is:

```
REG DELETE RegistryPath [\\Machine] [/F]\
```

As with other registry tools, the registry path to be queried may be a ROOTKEY or a hive (with or without a value entry). The ROOTKEY may consist of one of the following (`HKLM` is assumed if none is entered):

- ◆ `HKLM`
- ◆ `HKCU`
- ◆ `HKCR`
- ◆ `HKU`
- ◆ `HKCC`

Only `HKLM` and `HKU` may be specified when deleting objects from a remote registry.

The hive deletion may be forced by using the `/F` option, which forces the deletion without any prompt or confirmation. Microsoft recommends that the `/F` option be used only with extreme care. I agree.

An example of executing the delete command is shown next. Notice that I had to respond with a y to the prompt to delete the specified object.

```
Windows 9:05:30 C:\
REG query HKLM\Software\MyCo\MyApp\Version
REG_SZ     Version 2.00


Windows 9:09:30 C:\
REG delete HKLM\Software\MyCo\MyApp\Version
Permanently delete registry value Version (Y/N)? y
The operation completed successfully.



Windows 9:09:40 C:\
REG query HKLM\Software\MyCo\MyApp\Version
The system was unable to find the specified registry key.

Windows 9:09:43 C:\
```

EXPORT

The export function, invoked with the command reg export, exports the registry object specified to a disk file. The object may be a single-level key, such as HKLM\TEMP. Parameters include the name of the key to export and the name (qualified as necessary) of the file to export to. Export is only allowed on the local machine.

The command line for export is:

```
REG EXPORT keyname filename
```

As with other registry tools, the registry path to be queried may be a ROOTKEY or a hive, with or without a value entry. The ROOTKEY may consist of one of the following (HKLM is assumed if none is entered):

◆ HKLM

◆ HKCU

◆ HKCR

◆ HKU

◆ HKCC

Objects in the key are exported. Here's an example of executing the export command:

```
Windows 9:47:58 C:\
REG export HKLM\TEMP\ myreg.exp
The operation completed successfully.


Windows 9:48:01 C:\
```

IMPORT

The import function, invoked with the command `reg import`, imports the registry object specified from a disk file. The object may be a single-level key, such as `HKLM\TEMP`. Parameters include the name of the key to import and the name (qualified as necessary) of the file to import from. Import is only allowed on the local machine.

The command line for import is:

```
REG IMPORT filename
```

Objects in the exported key are imported. There is no recovery in the event of a user error with this command. Here's an example of executing the import command:

```
Windows 9:47:58 C:\
REG import myreg.exp

The operation completed successfully.


Windows 9:48:01 C:\
```

LOAD

The load function, invoked with the command `reg load <options>`, loads the registry object from the file specified. The object must have been saved using the `reg save` or `reg backup` command. Options include the name of the file to load from, the registry path to be restored, and an optional machine name (restorations may be made to remote registries).

The command line for restore is:

```
REG LOAD FileName keyname [\\Machine]\
```

As with other registry tools, the registry path to be queried may be a ROOTKEY or a hive, with or without a data key. The ROOTKEY may consist of one of the following (`HKLM` is assumed if none is entered):

- HKLM

- HKCU

Only `HKLM` and `HKCU` may be specified in this command.

Objects in the key are loaded, overwriting existing objects if there are any. Here's an example of executing the load command:

```
Windows 9:47:58 C:\
 REG load c:\temp\myco HKLM\TEMP\
The operation completed successfully.

Windows 9:48:01 C:\
reg query HKLM\TEMP /s
Listing of [TEMP\]
REG_SZ      Version 1.00
Windows 9:48:35 C:\
```

QUERY

The query function, invoked with the command `reg query keyname <options>`, displays the value of an object (key or value entry) in the registry. A required parameter, `keyname`, specifies the object to be queried. Options include specifying a query for a specific registry, querying for the default value, and specifying that all subkeys and values be displayed.

The command line for query is:

`REG QUERY Keyname [/v valuename or /ve] [/s]`

As with other registry tools, the registry path may be a ROOTKEY or a hive (with or without a value entry). The ROOTKEY may be one of the following (`HKLM` is assumed if none is entered):

◆ HKLM

◆ HKCU

◆ HKCR

◆ HKU

◆ HKCC

The hive is further qualified to determine the object to be added.

Remote registry query may be done by specifying the keyname to be remotely queried, such as \machine\keyname.

RESTORE

The restore function, invoked with the command `reg restore <options>`, restores the registry object from the file specified. The object must have been saved using the `reg save` or `reg backup` command. Options include the name of the file to restore from, the registry path to be restored, and an optional machine name (restorations may be made to remote registries).

The command line for restore is:

`REG QUERY FileName RegistyPath [\\Machine]`

As with other registry tools, the registry path to be queried may be a ROOTKEY or a hive, with or without a value entry. The ROOTKEY may consist of one of the following (`HKLM` is assumed if none is entered):

◆ HKLM

◆ HKCU

◆ HKCR

◆ HKU

◆ HKCC

Only HKLM and HKU may be specified when copying objects to a remote registry.

Objects in the key are restored and overwritten by the information contained in the specified file. Here's an example of executing the restore command:

```
Windows 9:39:17 C:\
 REG backup HKLM\Software\MyCo\MyNewApp c:\temp\MyCo
The operation completed successfully.


Windows 9:40:20 C:\
 REG restore c:\temp\myco HKLM\Software\MyCo\MyNewApp
Are you sure you want to replace Software\MyCo\MyNewApp (Y/N) y
The operation completed successfully.



Windows 9:40:44 C:\
```

SAVE

The save function, invoked with the command `reg save <options>`, saves the registry object specified to the file specified. Options include the registry path to be saved, the output filename, and an optional machine name (saves may be made on remote registries).

The command line for save is:

```
REG SAVE RegistryPath OutputFileName [\\Machine]
```

As with other registry tools, the registry path to be queried may be a ROOTKEY or a hive (with or without a value entry). The ROOTKEY may consist of one of the following (HKLM is assumed if none is entered):

- HKLM

- HKCU

- HKCR

- HKU

- HKCC

Only HKLM and HKU may be specified when copying objects to a remote registry.

An example of executing the save command is shown next. In this example, I've saved a small key to the file C:\Temp\MyCo.reg:

```
Windows 9:16:27 C:\
REG save HKLM\Software\MyCo\MyNewApp c:\temp\MyCo.reg
The operation completed successfully.

Windows 9:18:35 C:\
dir c:\temp\myco.reg
 Volume in drive C is (c) - Boot drive
 Volume Serial Number is CC56-5631

 Directory of c:\temp
```

```
07/17/99 09:18a          8,192        MyCo.reg
      1 File(s)     8,192 bytes
             183,407,104 bytes free

Windows 9:19:08 C:\
```

UNLOAD

The unload function, invoked with the command `reg unload <options>`, unloads (deletes) the registry object specified. The object must be a single-level key, such as HKLM\TEMP. Options include the name of the key to unload and an optional machine name (objects may be unloaded from remote registries).

The command line for unload is:

```
REG UNLOAD keyname [\\Machine]
```

As with other registry tools, the registry path to be queried may be a ROOTKEY or a hive, with or without a value entry. The ROOTKEY may consist of one of the following (HKLM is assumed if none is entered):

- HKLM

- HKCU

Only HKLM and HKCU may be specified in this command.

Objects in the key are unloaded and are not saved. There is no recovery in the event of a user error with this command. Here's an example of executing the unload command:

```
Windows 9:47:58 C:\
REG unload HKLM\TEMP\
The operation completed successfully.


Windows 9:48:01 C:\
reg query HKLM\TEMP /s

The system was unable to find the specified registry key.

Windows 9:48:35 C:\
```

UPDATE

Update is supported in versions of Windows prior to Windows 2000, so this section is of concern only to those working with machines running Windows 95 or 98/Me. On versions of Windows that do not support Backup, including Windows XP, use the Save option instead of Backup Update is invoked with the command `reg update <options>`, updates an existing object (key or value entry) to the registry. Options include the registry object to be added (with the object's value) and an optional machine name (updates may be made to remote registries).

The command line for update is:

```
REG UPDATE RegistryPath=value [\\Machine]
```

As with other registry tools, the registry path to be queried may be a ROOTKEY or a hive, with or without a value entry. The ROOTKEY may consist of one of the following (HKLM is assumed if none is entered):

- HKLM

- HKCU

- HKCR

- HKU

- HKCC

The hive is further qualified to determine the object to be added.

Below is an example of executing the update command. First I show the original value, then I update the object, and then I show the new value.

```
Windows 9:00:48 C:\
REG query HKLM\Software\MyCo\MyApp\Version
REG_SZ     Version 1.00


Windows 9:01:33 C:\
REG update HKLM\Software\MyCo\MyApp\Version=2.00
The operation completed successfully.


Windows 9:03:47 C:\
REG query HKLM\Software\MyCo\MyApp\Version
REG_SZ     Version 2.00


Windows 9:03:53 C:\
```

Installing Remote Registry Editing on Windows 95, Windows 98, and Windows Me

NOTE   This section addresses the concerns of system administrators working in mixed-networking environments.

Though Windows NT Workstation and Windows 2000 Professional have remote registry editing installed already, Windows 95, 98, and Me do not. The installation process is similar on both operating systems, though the source of the necessary drivers differs with each version.

You have to install a network service to enable remote registry editing. This service, REGSERV, is found in the following location:

- Windows 95: Look on the Windows 95 distribution CD, in the directory \Tools\ResKit\ NetAdmin\RemotReg, for the regserv program files.

- Windows 98/Me: Look on the Windows 98/Me distribution CD, in the directory \Admin\NetTools\RemotReg, for the regserv program files.

In each operating system, the installation is identical:

1. Open the Control Panel.

2. Start the Network applet.

3. Click the Add button in the Configuration tab.

4. Select Service from the list, and click the Add button.

5. Click the Have Disk button, and provide the directory information as given above.

6. Select Microsoft Remote Registry.

7. Install the Remote Registry service, and reboot the computer when prompted.

TIP   The Remote Registry service files are identical in Windows 95 and Windows 98/Me. Either will work with either version of the operating system.

Windows 2000 Backup's Emergency Repair Disk Features

The RDisk utility is not available under Windows 2000 or Windows XP. Windows 2000's Backup program contains the functionality of RDisk. With Windows 2000, the ERD (Emergency Repair Disk) has slightly different contents than under previous versions of Windows NT.

NOTE   Windows XP does not support the ERD disk capability!

The repair disk holds some of the system configuration components. Backup can back up registry files to a location on the hard drive (the `Repair` directory) and configuration files to a diskette (the ERD). The ERD contains files used to help Windows 2000 restore the system to a known state in the event of damage to the working copy of the registry.

Generally, copies of the registry contained in the `Repair` directory are only usable with the Setup program's repair facility. This may seem to limit their usefulness. However, when disaster strikes, anything is better than nothing. Actually, spending half an hour running the Setup repair function is a small price to pay to recover from a damaged registry.

There can be only one `Repair` directory on a Windows 2000 system, always at `%SystemRoot%\Repair`. However, there may be many ERDs in existence at one time. Since an ERD's contents are (generally) matched to the registry, it is best to simply keep one or two copies of the most recent registry backed up.

TIP   Actually, you can copy the files in the `Repair` directory to another safe location, as well, then copy them back to the `Repair` directory if necessary. Make sure that all files are copied or backed up and restored as a set—don't attempt to back up only some of the files in the `Repair` directory. If you copy the `Repair` directory files to another location, also create a copy of the ERD and save that as well.

Creating an Emergency Repair Disk

To create an ERD, follow these steps:

1. Start Backup without any options.

2. Select the Emergency Repair Disk button in the Welcome tab.

3. At the prompt to insert a diskette (see Figure 4.18), insert a diskette containing nothing of value. The diskette must already be formatted.

FIGURE 4.18

Backup will write backup files to the ERD, and optionally to the `Repair` directory.

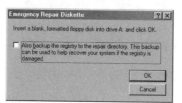

4. Once Backup is done, it will display a dialog box prompting you to label the ERD and place it in safekeeping. You may then create another ERD, update the repair information on the hard disk, perform other backup tasks, or exit.

NOTE   Remember to remove the floppy diskette from the drive once Backup finishes writing the repair information to it. Attempting to boot this diskette won't cause a problem; however, it will have to be removed before the system can be rebooted.

Saving to the Repair Directory

In Windows 2000, Backup can save the entire registry to the `Repair` directory. To update the `%SystemRoot%\Repair` directory, follow these steps:

1. Start Backup without any options.

2. Select the Emergency Repair Disk button in the Welcome tab.

3. At the prompt to insert a diskette, insert a diskette containing nothing of value. The diskette must already be formatted.

4. Select the "Also backup the registry..." check box (see the previous Figure 4.18).

5. Once Backup is done, it displays a dialog box prompting you to label the ERD and place it in safekeeping. You may then create another ERD, perform other backup tasks, or exit.

The Windows 2000 Resource Kit

The Windows 2000 Resource Kit contains a number of very useful tools. Many of these tools run from a command prompt, although one has a Windows-type interface. The Resource Kit changed substantially in Windows 2000. Gone are all the old registry utilities, leaving only the multipurpose `reg.exe` program.

NOTE   *There are two resource kits: one is included with the operating system, on the distribution CD, and has only limited contents. The second version has both a book and a CD with many more utilities and is available from Microsoft Press. Try the URL* `http://www.microsoft.com/mspress/windows/windowsxp/itpros/default.asp` *for more information.*

If nothing else, the Windows 2000 Resource Kit is an excellent source of both information and a whole bunch of really neat utilities and tools for the Windows 2000 user.

NOTE   *While I've got you in support mode, make a link on your Desktop for the URL* `http://support` `.microsoft.com/support/search/c.asp?SPR=`. *This URL links to the online TechNet search support. TechNet contains a vast amount of technical information oriented toward system administrators. I don't know what I'd do without TechNet.*

WARNING   *Many of the earlier versions of the Windows Resource Kit utilities work with both Windows NT 4 and Windows 2000. However, be most cautious when using older utilities with Windows XP, as they may not have been well tested on the Windows XP platform!*

Chapter 5

Policies: Good for One, Good for All

WINDOWS XP PROFESSIONAL STORES CONFIGURATIONS for all users, and computers, as *policies*. (Windows XP Home does not support policies.) By default, no policies are set, but an administrator can easily set policies for a group of users or for the entire system. It's possible to set some policies by manually "hacking" the registry. However, that's the hard way. An easier way to change policies is to use one of the policy tools that Microsoft provides.

The first question on your mind is, "What does this have to do with the registry?" Well, of all things in Windows XP Professional, policies affect (and change) the registry more than anything else. With policy settings, you can change the way hardware and software behave and can be used.

In this chapter we will cover the following topics:

◆ A general overview of policies

◆ Policy configurations

◆ Software, operating system, and administrative policy settings

◆ Microsoft tools for managing policies

◆ Policies in Windows NT

An Introduction to Policies

Policies govern a site, a domain, or an organizational unit (often referred to as an OU) but not a specific user or computer. Policy is applied in a hierarchy, with higher-level policies used where no lower-level policy exists. For example, policy is applied as site (the highest level), then domain, organizational unit, and user. Policies in the domain override those they conflict with in the site, while conflicts between the domain and organizational unit are resolved with the organizational unit taking precedence. Conflicts between nested organizational units are resolved with the lower-level organizational unit taking precedence.

NOTE *Policy objects and settings can be set, unset, or not configured.*

Policy settings are configured in objects called group policy objects (GPOs). GPOs are edited using the Microsoft Management Console (MMC).

THE OFFICIAL ORDER OF POLICY IMPLEMENTATION IS...

When Windows XP Professional (when joined to a domain) implements system policies, the policies are applied in this order:

1. Policies inherited from previous versions of Windows. For example, Windows NT 4 policies are contained in the NTConfig.pol file. Note that Windows NT 4 policies need not exist, and they will not exist on a clean installation of Windows XP Professional.

2. The policies contained in the local group policy object.

3. Site group policy objects, in the order specified by the administrator.

4. Domain group policy objects, in the order specified by the administrator.

5. Organizational unit group policy objects, from higher-level to lower-level organizational unit (parent to child organizational unit), and in administratively specified order at the level of each organizational unit.

Organizational units may be nested. That is, you can have an organizational unit called Students. Within Students, you then might have Freshmen, Sophomores, Juniors, and Seniors, representing the four classes. (You might also have Graduate Students, Master's, or Doctoral.) Nesting can be as simple or as complex as your organization is.

When nesting organizational units, policy may be either inherited or not. You, the administrator, specify inheritance rules, within the following framework:

◆ Inheritance is downward only. In the example above, Freshmen inherit from Students, but Students *never* inherit from Freshmen.

◆ Settings that have not been configured are not inherited.

◆ Settings that are disabled are inherited as disabled.

◆ When a setting is configured in the higher-level organizational unit, and not configured in the lower-level organizational unit, then the lower-level organizational unit inherits the setting from the parent organizational unit.

◆ When settings between the higher-level organizational unit and a lower-level organizational unit don't conflict (are compatible), but are not the same, both are used to form the lower-level organizational unit's policy.

◆ When settings between the higher-level organizational unit and a lower-level organizational unit do conflict (are incompatible), but are not the same, the lower-level organizational unit's policy is used.

NOTE   *Well, almost always... An attribute called No Override, if selected at the higher-level organizational unit, will cause the lower-level organizational unit to always execute the higher-level OU's policy.*

Just More Confusion?

In the previous section, you saw that policies are set for sites, domains, and organizational units. Now, I'm going to confuse things a bit and say that policies are divided into two parts, Computer Configuration and User Configuration. Computer Configuration specifies policies that are applied to a computer without regard to who the user is. User Configuration specifies policies that are applied to a user without regard to which computer the user logs on to.

Both the Computer Configuration and the User Configuration are made up of three sections:

Software Settings Everything in Software Settings deals with software installation policy—for example, what can be installed, what must be uninstalled, and when.

Windows Settings Settings for Windows XP Professional are controlled in this section. There are more items in the Windows Settings section for the User Configuration than for the Computer Configuration.

Administrative Templates The extensible section, almost a catchall for everything that doesn't fall into the other two sections, is the Administrative Templates section. Items are added to Administrative Templates using `.adm` files.

NOTE *Though we are talking about Office throughout this chapter, many other Microsoft components use* `.adm` *files, including Microsoft Internet Explorer.*

Software Settings

The Software Settings section contains policies that deal with software installation and maintenance, such as what applications can be installed, what must be uninstalled and when, what maintenance must be done, and so on.

For example, if you configure Microsoft Word XP under Software Settings, and a user logs on to a computer that doesn't have Microsoft Word XP installed already, the user will still see a Start menu selection (shortcut) for Microsoft Word XP. If the user selects this shortcut, Microsoft Word XP will install itself (from a network share) for the user to use.

Windows Settings

In both Computer Configuration and User Configuration, you'll find a Windows Settings section. For Computer Configuration, the settings are applied to each user who logs on to the computer. For User Configuration, the settings are applied to users who log on regardless of the computer they log on to.

Administrative Templates

The Administrative Templates section contains all registry-based information. Two hives are used:

- `HKEY_CURRENT_USER`, the location where user configuration settings are saved
- `HKEY_LOCAL_MACHINE`, the location where computer configuration information is saved

Both user application policy items and policy for Windows XP Professional are managed in Administrative Templates. Adding policy items to Administrative Templates is simple. Most applications (that support policy) come with .adm files that contain information about which registry settings can be configured. For example, Microsoft Office XP has an .adm file named word10.adm (to Microsoft, Word XP is also known as both Microsoft Word version 10 and Microsoft Word 2002).

You can download the Microsoft Office policy tools from Microsoft's Internet website. They are part of the Microsoft Office Resource Kit located at http://www.microsoft.com/office/tech-info/reskit/default.htm.

A small fraction of the Microsoft Word XP .adm file is:

```
CLASS USER

CATEGORY "Microsoft Word 2002"
KEYNAME Software\Policies\Microsoft\Office\10.0\Word\Options
CATEGORY "Tools | Options..."
KEYNAME Software\Policies\Microsoft\Office\10.0\Word\Options\vpref
CATEGORY "View"
KEYNAME Software\Policies\Microsoft\Office\10.0\Word\Options\vpref
CATEGORY "Show"
KEYNAME Software\Policies\Microsoft\Office\10.0\Word\Options\vpref
POLICY "Startup Task Pane"
KEYNAME Software\Policies\Microsoft\Office\10.0\Word\Options
    PART "Check to enforce setting on; uncheck to enforce setting off" CHECKBOX
    VALUENAME StartupDialog
    VALUEON NUMERIC 1
    VALUEOFF NUMERIC 0
    END PART
    END POLICY
POLICY "Highlight"
    PART "Check to enforce setting on; uncheck to enforce setting off" CHECKBOX
    VALUENAME fShowHighlight_533_1
    VALUEON NUMERIC 1
    VALUEOFF NUMERIC 0
    END PART
    END POLICY
POLICY "Bookmarks"
    PART "Check to enforce setting on; uncheck to enforce setting off" CHECKBOX
    VALUENAME grpfvisi_146_1
    VALUEON NUMERIC 1
    VALUEOFF NUMERIC 0
    END PART
    END POLICY
POLICY "Status bar"
    PART "Check to enforce setting on; uncheck to enforce setting off" CHECKBOX
    VALUENAME fStatusBar_83_1
    VALUEON NUMERIC 1
    VALUEOFF NUMERIC 0
    ACTIONLISTON
    VALUENAME fStatLine_3_1 VALUE NUMERIC 1
    END ACTIONLISTON
```

```
        ACTIONLISTOFF
        VALUENAME fStatLine_3_1 VALUE NUMERIC 0
        END ACTIONLISTOFF
        END PART
        ACTIONLISTOFF
        VALUENAME fStatLine_3_1 VALUE DELETE
        END ACTIONLISTOFF
        END POLICY
      POLICY "ScreenTips"
        PART "Check to enforce setting on; uncheck to enforce setting off" CHECKBOX
        VALUENAME grpfvisi_159_1
        VALUEON NUMERIC 1
        VALUEOFF NUMERIC 0
        END PART
        END POLICY
    <Many deleted lines...>
    POLICY "Tools | Compare and Merge Documents, Legal blackline"
    KEYNAME Software\Policies\Microsoft\Office\10.0\Word\Options\vpref
        PART "Check to enforce setting on; uncheck to enforce setting off" CHECKBOX
        VALUENAME fDefaultToCompare_1848_1
        VALUEON 1
        VALUEOFF 0
        END PART
        PART " " TEXT
        END PART
        PART "When this option is turned on, a comparison between two documents" TEXT
        END PART
        PART "automatically generates a new Legal Blackline document, leaving" TEXT
        END PART
        PART "the originals unchanged." TEXT
        END PART
        END POLICY
    END CATEGORY
    END CATEGORY
```

In this example, we see that the registry section being changed is HKEY_CURRENT_USER. The key being set (or changed) is Software\Policies\Microsoft\Office\10.0\Word\Options\vpref (vpref stands for "view preferences"). The key to be changed is shown in a KEYNAME line in the .adm file.

Checking Microsoft Word XP's menu structure, we see a top-level menu item called Tools, and under Tools is a menu selection called Options. Clicking Options will display Microsoft Word XP's Options dialog box (see Figure 5.1), which has a tab named View. On the View tab is a section called Show. Each of these items correlates to a CATEGORY line in the .adm file, shown partially in the above listing.

Finally, in the .adm file, we have the POLICY lines. The first POLICY line shown is Startup Task Pane.

Figure 5.2 shows the MMC Group Policy window with the Administrative Templates settings opened under User Configuration. The Start Menu & Taskbar settings are being displayed. You can select from a wide variety of options, one of which is to add a logoff command to the Start menu.

FIGURE 5.1

User options in
Microsoft Word XP
are set in the Options
dialog box.

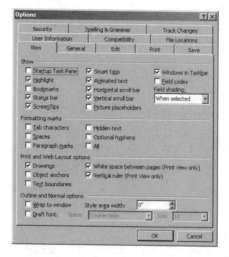

FIGURE 5.2

Microsoft
Windows XP
Professional group
policy for user
configuration

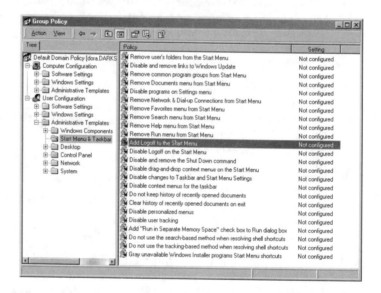

Back to the above listing, under POLICY, there's a PART line with the text "Check to enforce setting on; uncheck to enforce setting off", followed by the keyword CHECKBOX. CHECKBOX specifies that this policy is toggled on and off (that is, checked and unchecked). If on, the value of the key will be 1 (specified with the line VALUEON NUMERIC 1) or 0 (specified by the next line, VALUEOFF NUMERIC 0).

The next two lines end blocks that start at PART (ends at the END PART line) and POLICY (ends at the END POLICY line). Each policy has one or more parts; most policies have only a single part, however.

Armed with this information, you can go out and create policy files for other applications. Granted, if you are not the application's creator, it will be difficult—but not impossible—to set things like defaults using policies.

The changes made under Administrative Templates are saved in two `Registry.pol` files. These files are stored in subdirectories under `%SystemRoot%`, one called `Machine` (which contains the `Registry.pol` file that is used to update `HKEY_LOCAL_MACHINE`) and the other called `User` (which contains the `Registry.pol` file that is used to update `HKEY_CURRENT_USER`).

FINDING REGISTRY.POL FILES

I can't say where the `Registry.pol` files are, except to tell you to use the Windows Find feature, or a command session's `dir` command. Why? Well, each installation is unique in the locations where these files are stored; for example, on my computer, I have the following `Registry.pol` files:

```
G:\WINNT\System32\GroupPolicy\Machine\Registry.pol
G:\WINNT\System32\GroupPolicy\User\Registry.pol
G:\WINNT\SysVol\Domain\Policies\{31B2F340-016D-11D2-945F-
00C04FB984F9}\MACHINE\Registry.pol
G:\WINNT\SysVol\Domain\Policies\{6AC1786C-016F-11D2-945F-
00C04FB984F9}\USER\Registry.pol
G:\WINNT\SysVol\Domain\Policies\{EE520C60-1F3E-11D3-A6E8-
00A024D2DD82}\User\Registry.pol
G:\WINNT\SysVol\SysVol\darkstar.mv.com\Policies\{31B2F340-016D-11D2-945F-
00C04FB984F9}\MACHINE\Registry.pol
G:\WINNT\SysVol\SysVol\darkstar.mv.com\Policies\{6AC1786C-016F-11D2-945F-
00C04FB984F9}\USER\Registry.pol
G:\WINNT\SysVol\SysVol\darkstar.mv.com\Policies\{EE520C60-1F3E-11D3-A6E8-
00A024D2DD82}\User\Registry.pol
```

Notice the use of GUIDs (globally unique identifiers) for some of the directory names—those may be different for each installation.

The Microsoft System Policies for Windows XP

Windows XP Professional supplies several tools for setting policies. The System Policy Editor, which is used to set policy in Windows NT 4, is still included, and may be used, but it is definitely not recommended. Now you use the Active Directory Users and Computers to manage policy. Changes made to policy are made to the registry, either immediately or when a given user or member of an organizational unit logs on, or when the computer starts. Policy is a registry issue, and a complex one at that.

WARNING   *Wait a minute—I know I changed that registry entry! With policies, it is possible to "hack," or change, the registry and have the change go nowhere fast. That's right: the policy will be reapplied automatically, wiping out whatever changes you have made to the registry, all without even telling you it is happening! If you ever find your changes mysteriously disappearing, round up the usual suspects, and make sure that policy is high on the suspect list!*

You can edit policy in a number of different ways:

System Policy Editor   This utility, which is becoming obsolete, is retained for compatibility with Windows NT 4. Neither Microsoft nor I recommend that you use the System Policy Editor.

Microsoft Management Console (MMC)   This program is used to manage many facets of Windows XP. The MMC is able to load whatever functionality you need through the use of a custom extension called a *snap-in*. With Windows XP Professional, Microsoft provides about 40 different snap-ins to use with the MMC. Windows XP Home Edition provides about 20 different snap-ins to use with the MMC.

Active Directory Users and Computers   This administrative tool (select Start ≻ Programs ≻ Administrative Tools) allows management of computers, users, groups, domain controllers, and policy. Actually, this is the MMC, using a snap-in to do Active Directory. When you choose to edit policies, the MMC is used with the policy snap-in.

Active Directory Site and Services   This administrative tool (select Start ≻ Programs ≻ Administrative Tools) allows management of sites (an Active Directory organizational level) and services.

NOTE   *Each of these Windows XP administrative tools actually uses the MMC as a common interface. And each in turn uses the MMC to edit policy. It's not uncommon to have many copies of the MMC open at the same time.*

Each of these tools requires that you select certain objects to enable editing of group policies. The next section describes how to use each policy-editing tool.

System Policy Editor

The System Policy Editor is obsolete, retained only for compatibility with NT 4. Neither Microsoft nor I recommend that you use the System Policy Editor if you can possibly avoid using it. To start the System Policy Editor, from the Start menu's Run command, enter **poledit** and click OK. See "The Microsoft System Policy Editor for Windows NT 4" later in this chapter for information on how to use the Microsoft System Policy Editor.

Microsoft Management Console (MMC)

The MMC is a "universal" management tool that Microsoft has created to manage Windows XP (Home Edition and Professional). Using the MMC is easy, and since the MMC presents a standardized appearance and operating methods, it will become the preferred tool to use for management.

To start the MMC, from the Start menu's Run command, enter **MMC** and click OK. Once started, the MMC is able to load whatever functionality is needed.

Group Policy not yet installed in the MMC? That's easy to fix; just follow these simple steps:

1. Start the MMC. In addition to using the Run command as described above, you can also type **MMC** at a command prompt.

2. In the File menu, select Add/Remove Snap-In (see Figure 5.3).

3. In the Add/Remove Snap-In dialog box, select the Standalone tab (shown in Figure 5.4). Make sure that Console Root is displayed in the Snap-Ins Added To list box, and then click Add. The Add Standalone Snap-In dialog box opens.

4. In the Add Standalone Snap-In dialog box, select Group Policy, as shown in Figure 5.5. Scroll through the list as necessary. Click the Add button to start the Group Policy Wizard.

FIGURE 5.3

Add MMC snap-in components from the MMC File menu selection.

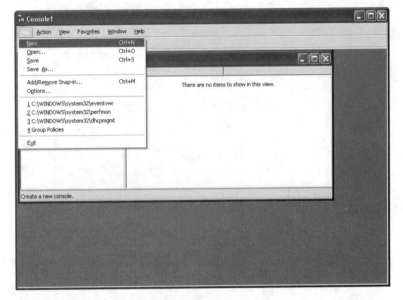

FIGURE 5.4

Use the Add/ Remove Snap-In dialog box to add functionality to the MMC.

5. In the Select Group Policy Object window (see Figure 5.6), select Local Computer for the Group Policy Object. Then click Finish.

NOTE *There is no Group Policy snap-in for XP Home Edition. Once you create a policy using the Group Policy snap-in, you have to link it to the proper level—sites, domains, or organizational units. Otherwise the policy just sits there and does nothing.*

FIGURE 5.5

Scroll until you get to Group Policy.

FIGURE 5.6

The Group Policy Wizard lets you configure the Group Policy Object.

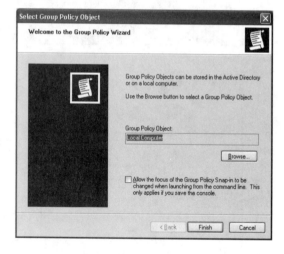

6. Click Close in the Add Standalone Snap-In dialog box, and click OK in the Add/Remove Snap-In dialog box.

Using the MMC to manage group policy is easy! First, it is trivial to create an MMC console file that is configured to display a given GPO policy object. Just follow these steps:

1. Open the administrative tool Active Directory Users and Computers.

2. Right-click the organizational unit that uses the policy to be edited to display its context menu. If you're creating a new policy, select the organizational unit that will use the policy once it is created. If creating policy for a domain, select the domain. Figure 5.7 shows how I've expanded Local Computer Policy, then User Configuration, Windows Settings, and Internet Explorer Maintenance. I then selected Browser User Interface. This shows how simple it is to set options for Microsoft Internet Explorer. You can easily set the title, the static logo, and browser toolbar customizations.

FIGURE 5.7

In the MMC, policies are navigated using a tree structure very similar to Explorer.

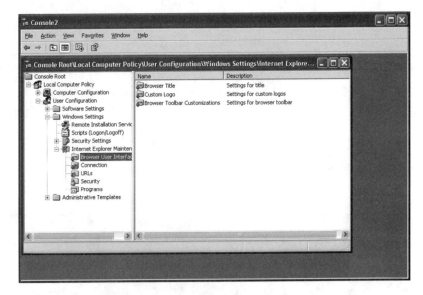

3. Select Properties from the context menu, or select Properties from the Action menu. In Figure 5.8, I selected the Browser Title and then displayed the properties.

4. In the Properties dialog box for the object (display this by double-clicking on the object—Browser Title in this example), make changes as desired. Notice that each object's Properties dialog box is different, and that most have substantial prompting to allow you to easily change the object.

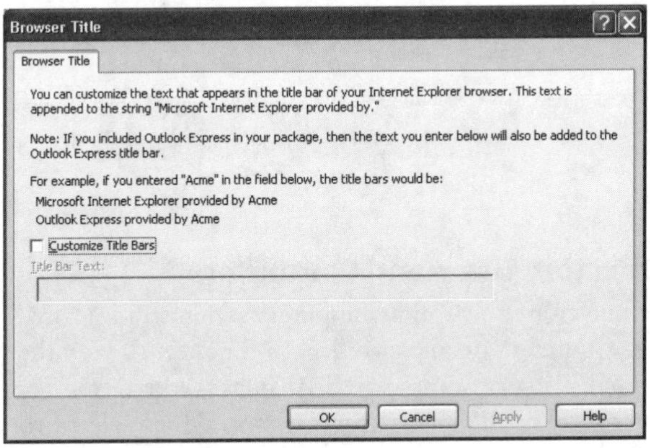

FIGURE 5.8

Use an item's Properties dialog box to set various policy settings. Here I'm setting the Browser Title.

5. Now for the hard part. To create an MMC configuration file (these files have an extension of `.msc`), select File ➤ Save As. Enter a new filename when prompted (I used the name `Group Policies.msc`). Click Save to save this file. You can save the `.msc` file in Administrative Tools, on the Desktop, or on any drive you'd like.

Well, now you have created your policy MMC configuration file; next is what to do with it. (Actually, you have probably saved a bunch of MMC configuration files—one for each group policy object.) My recommendation is to create a folder to hold these files, maybe called `Policy`. Then create a second folder under Administrative Tools, again called `Policy`. Then place shortcuts to each of the MMC configuration files in this folder. This will give you one-click access to each group policy object.

Figure 5.9 shows an example of just this type of policy control. My Start menu is opened to my `Administrative Tools` folder. Notice that I have a shortcut for Group Policies. Easy, fast, and efficient—sure beats threading through Active Directory Users and Computers, properties, and everything else.

FIGURE 5.9

My Start menu's Administrative Tools folder contains a shortcut called Group Policies, where I can start the MMC to manage my policies.

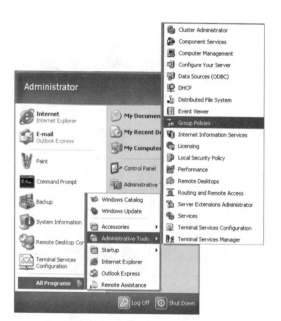

Active Directory Users and Computers

The Active Directory Users and Computers administrative MMC tool allows you to manage computers, users, groups, domain controllers, and policy. To view the Group Policies properties tab, select a computer domain (in Figure 5.10, `darkstar.mv.com` is one domain, while DORA is the domain controller) or an organizational unit, and then select Properties in either the context menu or the Action menu.

FIGURE 5.10

Using the MMC to manage the domain's directory of Users and Computers.

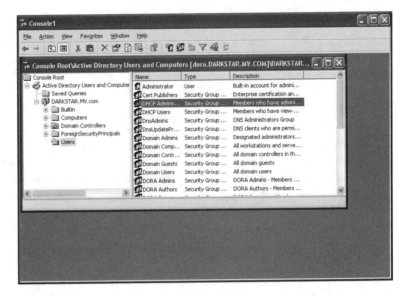

SETTING POLICY FOR A USER

To set policy for a given user, you need the user, an organizational unit to assign the user to, and a policy to apply to the organizational unit. For example, I have students, and some students are seniors (and seniors are much more responsible than freshmen!). This creates two levels of organization. Your organization may have more (or fewer) levels of organization, but the process is similar. In this example, I'll set policy for one student, Marie Theplama, who is a senior.

If I haven't yet set up any policies, then to apply the global policy object to Marie Theplama, I must do the following:

1. I first create an organizational unit called Students.

2. I display the properties for the Students organizational unit, and click the Group Policy tab.

3. I click the New button to create a new policy. The policy is created, and I am placed into rename mode to name the new global policy object.

4. I select the new global policy object and click the Edit button to change whatever policies are applicable.

5. I repeat steps 1 through 3 to create another organizational unit under Students named Seniors.

6. After creating Seniors, I select Properties, and on the Group Policy tab I click New to create a New Group Policy Object.

7. I select the new global policy object and click the Edit button to change whatever policies are applicable so that seniors have appropriate privileges and policies.

8. I then create Freshmen, Sophomores, and Juniors organizational units and global policy objects in the same manner.

9. I create a user for Marie Theplama. She's a senior; nothing else is special about her. I create her user under the organizational unit Seniors.

SETTING POLICY FOR A COMPUTER

To set policy for a given computer, the process is very similar to the process for users, above. You need to create a computer record, an organizational unit to assign the computer to, and a policy to apply to the organizational unit. Here at DarkStar, computers are named after famous science fiction characters. One computer is called Pixel (who is a cat that can walk through walls); another computer is named Lazarus.

Just like for users, computers need their own organizational unit. For this example, I'll use Students for the computers that will be accessible to and used by students.

NOTE *A computer's organizational unit is no different than an organizational unit for a user; in fact the same organizational unit could be used for both if appropriate.*

I create a computer under Students for Lazarus. Once created, as a computer, I can set a description, assign membership into security groups and organizational units, and specify the computer's location and who is responsible for this computer. I can assign membership to the Students organizational unit, any other applicable organizational units, and security groups.

Just like with users, you have a lot of latitude when configuring computers. While users are typically assigned to organizational units based on the administrative hierarchy of the organization, computers are often assigned based on physical location, or how they are to be used.

In Figure 5.11, I'm setting policy for `darkstar.mv.com`, which is managed by the server DORA. I can make changes, and they will be applied to the remote computer—after all, DORA is not the computer where the MMC is running. The MMC is actually running on my other server, PeachFuzz!

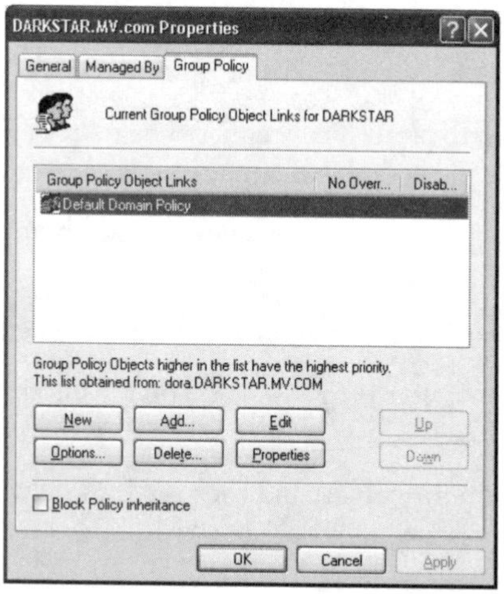

FIGURE 5.11

The MMC, managing the domain `darkstar.mv.com`. This will actually modify policy on the server DORA.

The Microsoft System Policy Editor for Windows NT 4

The System Policy Editor is a tool that allows users to set policy. Even though it is intended for Windows NT 4, it comes as "standard equipment" in Windows XP. As I mentioned earlier in this chapter, I don't recommend that you use the System Policy Editor to set policy in Windows XP. Microsoft included it only for compatibility with Windows NT. That said, if you do work with Windows NT systems, read on.

Many of the changes made by the System Policy Editor are to the registry, so although the System Policy Editor is not thought of as a registry tool, I'll document it here anyway. Actually, modifying the Windows NT 4 registry using the System Policy Editor is a wise move—it will validate your changes, preventing you from doing something that may have seemed logical to you, but actually is not.

The System Policy Editor allows you to open either a policy file (with the extension of `.pol`) or a computer. It uses a simple user interface, as shown in Figure 5.12. When you click an object, the object's Properties dialog box is displayed. In Figure 5.12, Local Computer and Local User are both objects that can be opened.

FIGURE 5.12

The System Policy Editor displays a Properties dialog box when you click an icon. Then you can open the tree to see specific settings.

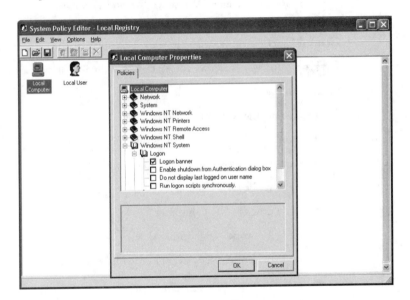

With the System Policy Editor, the Local Computer entry should display eight items, all applicable to a Windows NT system. For a Local User, the Properties dialog box should have six items. In both cases, the items displayed are unique; there is no overlap.

You can use the System Policy Editor for Windows 95/98/Me clients, enabling some remote administration of these machines. However, the System Policy Editor has not been well tested on these three platforms.

WYSIWYG? FROM SYSTEM POLICY EDITOR?

What is displayed in the Properties dialog boxes is dependent on which template(s) are loaded. Windows NT supplies three templates by default:

`common.adm`   Contains user interface options common to both Windows NT and Windows 95/98.

`winnt.adm`   Contains specific settings for Windows NT.

`windows.adm`   Contains specific settings for Windows 95/98.

Two sections in all .adm files, CLASS MACHINE and CLASS USER, define how settings are applied.

The .adm files are text files that can be modified to suit the user's needs. A competent user should be able to write an .adm file, or modify an existing one, without too much trouble. However, those pesky "make sure you have good backup" warnings also apply if you customize your .adm files.

Typically, for all machines (Windows NT and Windows 95/98/Me), you can modify the following categories:

Control Panel   Allows you to restrict the display of the Control Panel.

Desktop   Allows/disallows you to change wallpaper and/or color schemes.

Shell   Allows you to do the following:

- Remove the Run command from the Start menu
- Remove folders from Settings on the Start menu
- Remove the Taskbar from Settings on the Start menu
- Remove the Find command from the Start menu
- Hide drives in My Computer
- Hide Network Neighborhood
- Hide the Entire Network in Network Neighborhood
- Hide all items on the Desktop
- Disable the Shut Down command
- Not save settings at exit

System   Allows you to do the following:

- Disable registry editing tools
- Run only allowed Windows applications

For Windows NT, you can modify the following categories:

Windows NT Shell   Consists of three sections, which allow setting the following:

Custom User Interface	Set custom shell
Custom Folders	Set custom Programs folder
	Hide Start menu subfolders
	Set custom Startup folder
	Set custom Network Neighborhood
	Set custom Start menu
Restrictions	Use only approved shell extensions
	Remove File menu from Explorer
	Remove common program groups from Start menu
	Disable context menus for the Taskbar
	Disable Explorer's default context menu
	Remove the Map Network Drive and Disconnect Network Drive options
	Disable Link File Tracking

Windows NT System   Consists of four choices:

◆ Parse `autoexec.bat`

◆ Run logon scripts synchronously

◆ Disable Task Manager

◆ Show welcome tips at logon

For Windows 95, you can modify the following categories:

Windows 95 Control Panel   Consists of four sections, which allow setting the following:

Network   Restrict Network Control Panel

Printers   Restrict printer settings

Passwords   Restrict Passwords Control Panel

System   Restrict System Control Panel

Windows 95 Shell   Consists of one section, Custom Folders, which allows you to set the following:

◆ Custom Programs folder

◆ Custom Desktop icons

- Hide status of Start menu subfolders
- Custom Startup folder
- Custom Network Neighborhood
- Custom Start menu

Windows 95 System   Consists of one section, Restrictions, which allows you to do the following:

- Disable the MS-DOS prompt
- Disable the single-mode MS-DOS apps

Windows 95 Network   Consists of one section, Sharing, which allows you to do the following:

- Disable file sharing
- Disable print sharing

For any type of machine (Windows NT or Windows 95/98/Me), you can modify the following:

Network   Consists of one choice:

    System Policies Update   Remote update

System   Consists of two sections, SNMP and Run, which allow you to set the following:

    SNMP   Communities

                                  Permitted managers

                                  Traps for Public community

    Run   Items that are executed at startup

For Windows NT-only machines, you can modify the following:

Windows NT Network   Consists of one section, Sharing, which allows you to do the following:

- Create hidden drive shares (workstation)
- Create hidden drive shares (server)

Windows NT Printers   Consists of three choices:

- Disable browse thread on this computer
- Scheduler priority
- Beep for error enabled

Windows NT Remote Access   Consists of four choices:

- Max number of unsuccessful authentication retries
- Max time limit for authentication

◆ Wait interval for callback

◆ Auto Disconnect

Windows NT Shell   Consists of one section, Custom Shared Folders, which contains four choices:

◆ Custom shared Programs folder

◆ Custom shared Desktop icons

◆ Custom shared Start menu

◆ Custom shared Startup folder

Windows NT System   Consists of two sections:

Logon	Allow logon banner
	Enable shutdown from Authentication dialog box
	Do not display last logged on username
	Run logon scripts synchronously
File System	Do not create 8.3 filename for long filenames
	Allow extended characters in 8.3 filenames
	Do not update last access time

Windows NT User Profiles   Consists of four sections:

◆ Delete cached copies of roaming profiles

◆ Automatically detect slow network connections

◆ Slow network connection time-out

◆ Timeout for dialog boxes

For Windows 95 machines, you can modify the following:

Access Control   Consists of one section:

◆ User-level access control

Logon

Consists of three sections:

◆ Custom logon banner

◆ Require validation by network for Windows access

◆ Allow logon without name or password

Passwords   Consists of four sections:

- Hide share passwords with asterisks
- Disable password caching
- Require alphanumeric Windows password
- Min Windows password length

Microsoft Client Service for NetWare Networks   Consists of four sections:

- Preferred server
- Support long filenames
- Search mode
- Disable automatic NetWare login

Microsoft Client for Windows Networks   Consists of three sections:

- Log on to Windows NT
- Workgroup
- Alternate workgroup

File and Printer Sharing   Consists of two sections:

- Disable file sharing
- Disable printer sharing

Dial-up Networking   Consists of one section:

- Disable dial-in

Windows 95 System   Consists of three sections:

SNMP	Enables Internet MIB (RFC1156)
Network Paths	Enables network path for Windows setup
	Enables network path for Windows tour
Profiles	Enables user profiles

For each item, choices may range from a simple disable or enable of the property to setting of text, additional options, and so on. For instance, Figure 5.13 shows the Local User Properties dialog box. I've selected Local User, Control Panel, Display, and Restrict Display. In the Settings for Restrict Display area are five additional settings that I can change for this item.

FIGURE 5.13

Setting hide attributes for the Control Panel's Display applet and tabs.

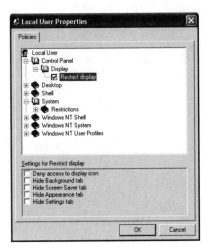

NOTE *Policies for client computers only take effect when they are stored in the NetLogon share: NTConfig.pol for NT and Config.pol for Win9x.*

Part II

Advanced Registry Stuff

In this section, you'll learn how to:
- Use OLE with the registry
- Understand system.ini and win.ini
- Clean up your system
- Recover from system disasters
- Program for the registry
- Manage the Performance Monitor

Chapter 6

Associations, Linkages, and OLE: How Confusing Can This Get?

OLE (OBJECT LINKING AND Embedding) is a technology that allows applications to share data and functionality easily. I like that. Sounds good. It's quick and easy to understand, and it's basically accurate. Using OLE, applications can pass data back and forth, and OLE also allows a server and client to pass programming functionality between them. The server is able to do something that the client wishes done.

OLE works extensively with the registry. But before we get to that, it's important to understand how OLE evolved and how it functions. In this chapter, we'll cover the following topics:

◆ The evolution of OLE

◆ What OLE is all about

◆ Client-server OLE applications

◆ OLE and the registry

◆ Linking between applications

Understanding OLE (or Not)

First, let's start out with a few ground rules:

◆ There is no way to learn all about OLE in one chapter. (I doubt you could learn all about OLE in a single book!)

◆ Even OLE experts are not really experts.

◆ There are a number of good books on OLE, but unless you are programming, avoid them.

◆ If you don't understand everything about OLE after reading this chapter, don't feel bad.

◆ The author takes no responsibility for what happens when you wake up at 2 A.M. and shout, "Now I understand!"

Most programmers don't build their OLE applications from the ground up. Instead, for the difficult parts, they use development systems such as Microsoft's Developer Studio. Today, a programmer can create an OLE application almost as quickly as any other type of application.

Most applications manage their initial OLE setup by themselves. Some applications rely on their installation programs to do the OLE setup. And some applications use the installation program both to set up OLE and, if the configuration becomes damaged, to repair the damage to the extent that they can reconfigure the OLE components.

This brings up some questions. First, how does OLE work? Second, what does OLE have to do with the registry? Moreover, why do we have to worry about it? Do we mention DDE? And where, oh where, does the Clipboard fit into this mess?

OK, stay tuned for answers to all of these questions.

Introduction to OLE

Kraig Brockschmidt of Microsoft is probably the best-known expert on OLE. Here's how he describes its evolution:

> *Windows API (Application Program Interface) evolved into Windows Objects, which eventually became what we know as OLE.*

Kraig admits it's not that simple, but OLE developed by evolution, not by revolution.

Way back in the good old days, Windows was much simpler and easier to understand. In its first incarnation, Windows allowed virtually no interprocess communications. There was the Clipboard (which we still know and love), to which one program could post data that another program could (hopefully) read. However, that exchange required user interaction. The user was required to take steps to put the selected data on the Clipboard and then in the recipient application take steps to retrieve the data stored in the Clipboard.

Problems arose. First, the basic Clipboard supported only a very limited range of data types. Programs could exchange data in various basic formats (text and binary, for the most part), but these formats were sorely lacking the flexibility to express any object that was composed of compound data.

COMPOUND DATA?

Compound data is data that contains information in multiple formats. The easiest type of compound data to envision is a word-processing document that includes some images. At this point in the evolution of the Clipboard, the word-processing program couldn't just toss that document and its images on the Clipboard. After all, how would the program identify the format of that data? If it said binary, no other application would be able to understand or use the data. If it said text, what would happen when an application tried to use the data and encountered the images? Would it delete the images? Sure, that would work, but if the user wanted the complete document, including the images, he or she would be most unhappy about the results.

Microsoft realized quickly that applications needed a direct, application-to-application communication method that didn't rely on the Clipboard. Quickly or slowly, depending on your point of view, the concept of DDE (Dynamic Data Exchange) was born. Actually "conceived" would be a better description, because DDE wasn't viable in its original format. As it grew, DDE did allow applications to communicate data. However, there were still problems. With DDE, there was no way for applications to find out about their partners. Developers created most DDE applications specifically as pairs. For applications from two independent sources, DDE was unlikely to be useful, because the developers would have to cooperate in order to take advantage of DDE.

OLE became the next stage in the development of interapplication communications and data sharing. OLE allowed an application to interact with another one without knowing, in advance, about the other application. Magic, really.

The Clipboard

The Clipboard is the original and most basic method to transfer data between applications. The Clipboard supports both inter-application transfers (between two applications) and intra-application transfers (within the same application).

There is only one object in the Clipboard at any one time. (Microsoft Office uses a multiple document Clipboard interface; however, this interface is created and implemented by Office, and not Windows.) There are some complex rules on the Clipboard, such as the following:

◆ An application cannot assume that an object placed in the Clipboard will remain there after the application releases the Clipboard. Therefore, it is not possible to use the Clipboard as a temporary storage location.

◆ The format of the object in the Clipboard must be in one of the standard formats (listed below), or the application placing the data on the Clipboard must be prepared to render or display the Clipboard's contents.

◆ Some objects in the Clipboard are in a format that is not native to Windows. These objects require the application that places the object to be available to display or render the object if necessary.

Windows XP supports the following types of data in the Clipboard, without creating custom formats:

CF_BITMAP   A bitmap (image)

CF_DIB   A DIB (Device Independent Bitmap)

CF_DIBV5   A version 5 bitmap (available on Windows 2000 and later versions)

CF_DIF   A DIF (Data Interchange Format) object

CF_DSPBITMAP   A private format bitmap

CF_DSPENHMETAFILE   An enhanced metafile display format object

CF_DSPMETAFILEPICT   A metafile-picture display format object

CF_DSPTEXT   A text display format object, with private format

CF_ENHMETAFILE   An enhanced metafile object

CF_GDIOBJFIRST through CF_GDIOBJLAST   A range of integer values for application-defined GDI (Graphical Device Interface) objects

CF_HDROPV   A handle of type HDROP, identifying a list of files

CF_LOCALE   Locale information

CF_METAFILEPICT   A metafile picture object

CF_OEMTEXT   A text format in the OEM (original equipment manufacturer) character set

CF_OWNERDISPLAY   An object of owner display format

CF_PALETTE   A color palette object

CF_PENDATA   An object containing data for the pen extensions to the Microsoft Windows for Pen Computing

CF_PRIVATEFIRST through CF_PRIVATELAST   A range of integer values for private Clipboard formats

CF_RIFF   A sound object too complex for the CF_WAVE format

CF_SYLK   An object in Microsoft Symbolic Link (SYLK) format

CF_TEXT   A plain-text format object

CF_WAVE   An audio object, using PCM (Pulse Code Modulation)

CF_TIFF   A Tagged Image File Format object

CF_UNICODETEXT   A text object using the two-byte Unicode character set

As this list shows, Windows supports many different formats, without any programmer intervention. However, in many situations, these formats are not adequate. In these cases, the application serving (placing) the data on the Clipboard may register a new format with Windows. To enable viewing of the Clipboard data, you must also have code that displays the Clipboard data.

DDE

DDE, or Dynamic Data Exchange, has been part of Windows since the early days. An Excel spreadsheet (the client) for managing stock market information is an example of DDE. A second software application that actually retrieves the stock prices (quotes) is the server. In addition, another application goes to the Internet and gets current stock market quotes (the server). The two programs need to interact dynamically (after all, prices change), so using the Clipboard is not optimal; you want your spreadsheet updated dynamically and efficiently, without any user interaction.

Through a process of broadcasting, Excel (the client) establishes a communications link with the server. Excel broadcasts its request and the server responds that it is able to fulfill this request. A DDE linkage is established, allowing Excel to request information from the server as necessary.

As an example, you may be interested in a particular list of stocks. Excel would tell the server to check these stocks and provide the current quote for them. Excel might also have a timer loop that repeats this process every five minutes, providing you with up-to-date stock quote information.

As another example, you might request a one-time quote on a stock of interest. Maybe you're interested in just how well Microsoft (MSFT) is doing on the stock exchange. Perhaps your spreadsheet has a section where you type in the stock name. You enter the name, and the quote comes back.

Either the client or the server can perform automatic updating. Client-initiated updates might occur on a time-based basis, or when the user makes a change if the data retrieved was relatively static. Servers might initiate an update whenever the server recognizes that the information the user is requesting has become out of date.

OK, no one said DDE was easy. If they did, they didn't tell the truth. DDE is complex and very difficult to understand or use. Programmers exposed to DDE shuddered and desperately searched for better alternatives. Some programmers kludged together broadcast messages to pass simple data, but for many, DDE was still the best (only) method to exchange data between two applications.

WHY IS IT DIFFICULT TO EXCHANGE DATA?

Memory protection causes most of the problems; one application cannot access memory objects belonging to other applications.

When an object is placed in the Clipboard, the memory that the object occupies is given to Windows. From that point onward, Windows owns the object, and the application that placed the object in the Clipboard loses control of the object. This means that whenever an object is placed in the Clipboard, the application will usually make a copy of the object and place the copy in the Clipboard, keeping the original object for the application's use.

The DDE process uses the Clipboard to transfer large blocks of data, too. Typically, the server application places the data on the Clipboard and uses DDE to tell the client application about the data. Server applications are able to pass small data objects to the client application as part of the DDE conversation.

What Is OLE?

OLE means Object Linking and Embedding. That says it all. With DDE, and with the Clipboard, applications only pass data and do not pass any functionality. With OLE, we expand on what the server application can do for the client.

As I mentioned earlier, applications can pass both data and programming functionality back and forth using OLE. The client can request action from the server. However, the client program's developer does not have to develop all this functionality if it exists already.

As an example, take the e-mail client called Outlook. Outlook has a simple, built-in e-mail editor. However, some users want (demand, actually) more functionality in their e-mail editors. They want formatting, macros, even included images, and other nifty stuff. They want the functionality of Microsoft Word to create their e-mail.

Wouldn't it be nice if the Outlook development team could borrow part of Word? Now, it would make little sense for the Outlook development team to sneak into the Word group's office and steal the code for Word. After all, they'd then have to maintain it, and Word's one big puppy—major maintenance blues there.

What's the next best thing? First, let's let the Word developers continue to maintain Word. Second, let's get Word to work for us. We know that the developers on the Word team included OLE server technology into Word; Word has client OLE technology too, in case you wondered. However, we find that the Outlook team can't really expect the Word team to put special stuff into Word for them, so what can they do?

Things are not so bad here: because Word is an OLE-compliant application, all Outlook has to do is to ask Word, "What can you do for me?" Outlook does this by first checking with the server at the most basic OLE level (a level that all OLE applications must support). This level allows the client to ask the server what functionalities are supported.

Realize that when we talk about supported functionalities, we are not talking about "Do you support italic text?" Rather, we are asking such questions as "Do you support embedding?" or "Do you support automation?" The server is then able to tell the client exactly what it is able to do. In the case of Outlook using Word to edit e-mail, Outlook asks, "Can you be embedded?" and Word responds, "Yes, I can."

NOTE   *You might ask, "Peter, why are you are adding yet another term, OLE automation?" This process allows the client application to take control of the server, and it lets the server see the client as a user. The client is able to actually click buttons and otherwise interact with the server application.*

Now read on.

EMBEDDING

With *embedding*, an object (which could be either a data object or server functionality) is embedded into the client application or the client application's data. When you embed Word into Outlook, you create a window, and using OLE, you tell Word to use this window to interact with the user. You also tell Word how it should appear to the user; for example, Outlook customizes Word's toolbars.

This embedding works regardless of whether Word is running or not. If Word is running, anything that Word is currently doing is unaffected by having Word embedded into Outlook's e-mail editing system. In fact, the OLE server treats these as separate instances of the program, and keeps them separate. There are advantages, however. If the server is already running, it is not necessary to load a second copy of the server. Instead, the two instances share the executable code.

With embedded objects, the client owns a private copy of the object. The server may update the client's object, though the server won't change any other instances of the data.

Each time an embedded object is used, there will be a new copy of the object. For complex objects, graphics, and so on, this can consume substantial system resources.

OBJECT LINKING

Object linking is a mysterious technology where one application creates an object used by another application later. A linked object remains the property of the creating application, and there is only one copy of the object.

The server is the creating application. The server links to the client application. When the server updates the object, the client gets a message and updates the object display in the client as necessary. Some objects are not visible, so there is no display update necessary.

The closest thing to showing how linking works is to look at Windows itself. There are a number of icons on your Desktop. Most are called shortcuts, which are denoted by that funny up-pointing arrow image in the lower-left corner. Think of these shortcuts as links. Open the properties for a shortcut and go to the Shortcut tab. In the Target edit box, you will see the name of the file that is associated with this shortcut (link). If you have a dozen shortcuts to the same file, each shortcut will open the same copy of the program. There won't be a dozen copies of the program.

OLE Controls, a.k.a. ActiveX

In the previous examples, the server application was a typical Windows program. Applications like this are native Windows applications. For example, Word for Windows is a server application. Word has a user interface and it runs on its own, without needing any client to embed the Word object.

Sometimes the server application doesn't have a native, stand-alone mode. That is, such an application doesn't have a user interface—no window, no direct way for the user to interact with the program. Applications like this are ActiveX controls; they used to be called OLE controls. ActiveX controls are commonly used with programs such as Internet Explorer and other web browsers; however, many programs can use ActiveX controls.

NOTE   *An ActiveX control must be embedded and may never be run alone.*

A typical user could have a large number of ActiveX controls installed, and the user might never know it. It is common for a user to download ActiveX controls from the Internet without ever realizing that this has happened.

VBX, WHAT'S A VBX?

VBX controls, or Visual Basic controls, were the first generation of ActiveX controls. When VBX controls were first developed, they served in dialog boxes as custom controls, things such as progress bars, and so on.

Generally, a VBX control doesn't handle data, while an ActiveX control might. In addition, only Visual Basic was able to easily create VBX controls. Programmers who developed in C/C++, for example, had difficulty creating their own VBX controls. However, Microsoft eventually developed a system to create VBX controls using development platforms other than Visual Basic.

Microsoft also realized that the concept of VBX (embeddable controls) was a good one, and that these controls were here to stay. In came the OCX (OLE Control) technology; it was development-platform independent, usage-platform independent, and more flexible.

Evolution and the name game reared their heads again. Microsoft moved to ActiveX controls more as a change in name than in function. It is common to see ActiveX controls referred to as OCX controls, and vice versa.

Some ActiveX controls display data. Some don't do anything other than provide some form of user interface. For example, these controls were on one of my computers:

- BtnMenu Object
- CarPointProximityCtrl
- ChatShowClt Object
- DirectAnimation Java Classes
- HHCtrl Object
- Internet Explorer Classes for Java
- IPTDImageControl.SImage
- Label Object
- Microsoft MSChat Control Object
- Microsoft Search Settings Control
- Microsoft XML Parser for Java
- PopupMenu Object
- Win32 Classes

All of these controls were installed in the %SystemRoot%\Occache directory. If you are not using Internet Explorer or are not active on the Internet, you probably won't have many of these controls.

NOTE *If you don't find an* Occache *directory, don't panic. It is probably because you don't have any ActiveX controls installed on your computer!*

LIAR, LIAR, PANTS ON FIRE!

Remember when I said previously that OLE controls don't have a user interface? Well actually, I lied a little. It is possible to use RunDll32 to execute some OLE controls. RunDll32 doesn't have a user interface either, and any control that works with RunDll32 must be written specifically for this type of usage. For example, the OLE Active Movie control will run with the command:

```
%SystemRoot%\System32\rundll32.exe amovie.ocx,RunDll
```

This opens the Active Movie OLE control (RunDll provides a main window for the control), and Active Movie then displays an Open File dialog box. You might select an Active Movie file (try clock.avi in Windows XP's %SystemRoot% directory) and run it using amovie.ocx. This is possible because Active Movie was written to work with RunDll, and as such, it works. Try this trick with most any other OLE control, and you will get the message, "Missing entry point RunDll," which indicates that the entry point passed in the command was not found.

Continued on next page

LIAR, LIAR, PANTS ON FIRE! *(continued)*

Oh, yes, you can also pass parameters to your OLE control with the command:

```
RunDll:%SystemRoot%\System32\rundll32.exe amovie.ocx,RunDll   %SystemRoot%\clock.avi
```

This command loads Active Movie, loads `clock.avi`, and allows the user to interact with the control. Try it. Better yet, try this:

```
%SystemRoot%\System32\rundll32.exe amovie.ocx,RunDll /play /close
%SystemRoot%\clock.avi
```

Don't mistakenly insert spaces between the executable file (`amovie.ocx` in the previous example), the comma, and the entry point (`RunDll` in the previous example). This will break RunDll without telling you why it failed.

Get the hint? I passed a parameter to the Active Movie control to play the `clock.avi` file and then close it when the `.avi` file is finished. Active Movie loaded the file specified, played the file, and closed it—all without user intervention.

Oh, don't blame me if the `clock.avi` file is a bit annoying.

Actually, RunDll will run more than OLE controls—RunDll will (or will at least attempt to) execute any executable file, including DLL (Dynamic Link Library) and EXE (executable) files. This is true as long as you know the file's entry point and the file to be executed follow the RunDll protocol. For more information, see Microsoft Knowledge Base article Q164787, which can be viewed at `http://support.microsoft.com/default.aspx?scid=kb;EN-US;q164787`. Though originally written for Windows 95/98, it has been updated to include support for Windows XP users.

NOTE   Don't have `amovie.ocx`*? This control is part of many versions of Microsoft Internet Explorer. Virtually all Windows 9x or Windows 2000 computer have a copy that you can use. You can download from Microsoft; however, the* `amovie.ocx` *file is combined with an earlier version of Microsoft Internet Explorer.*

Client-Server OLE Applications

Client-server OLE applications make up a substantial number of programs on most Windows computers. Even though the user may not be aware of which client-server OLE applications are installed, there are many.

One of the best-designed and best-integrated sets of applications is Microsoft Office, currently released as Office XP.

NOTE   Office XP is really Office, version 10. Microsoft has not used the version number as part of the product name for some time. However, many of Office's registry entries and file/folder names use the version number. Just remember that Office XP is Office version 10 (and Office 2000 is Office version 9).

Office XP combines word processing (Word XP for Windows), spreadsheets (Excel XP), a database system (Access XP), a presentation program (PowerPoint XP), and a host of utilities (such as Chart). Each of the main applications in Microsoft Office works as both a client and a server application. Some applications—such as the Word Art and Chart utilities—are not designed to run as simple clients. For example, take Word XP (a program that at least I know how to use).

Word, as a client is . . . Word. Open Word and edit a document. Write a short letter to someone—it doesn't matter whom. Create something, about a page long, three or four paragraphs. You have Word's functionality in all these paragraphs; you did everything using Word and nothing else.

Now things start to get exciting. Insert an object. For grins, insert a drawing into a Word document. Click Insert ➤ Object. Word displays the Object dialog box that lists all the embeddable OLE server objects (see Figure 6.1). Actually, OLE uses an API call to display the dialog box.

FIGURE 6.1

Inserting a Media Clip object is as easy as selecting it from the Object dialog box.

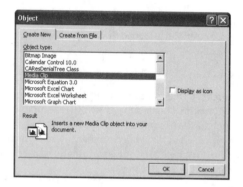

Some servers work by totally embedding themselves into Word. For example, Microsoft Photo Editor is called to edit (or select, if you are creating a new object) the picture you have inserted. With Office XP, Word does not embed the server, rather the server is called as a separate process. Word XP displays the standard picture toolbar, and you may edit the picture either by selecting Edit ➤ Photo Editor Photo Object ➤ Edit or by simply double-clicking the image. (I'm jumping ahead some here, but notice how Figure 6.3 shows Word XP with the image of Figure 6.2 embedded as a Microsoft Photo Editor object.)

It is quite incredible that Microsoft Photo Editor (or any other object server, for that matter) works without Microsoft Word having prior knowledge of it. Actually, select (double-click the object, for example) a Microsoft Photo Editor object, and Word gives control to Microsoft Photo Editor. Microsoft Photo Editor then displays its own window along with Word's window, so that the user can switch between the Word document and the object as necessary—I use this same process while I write.

When the Microsoft Photo Editor object is not selected, Word allows normal operation (see Figure 6.2). You do context-switching between Word and Microsoft Photo Editor whenever you select something in the document. If your selection is a Microsoft Photo Editor object (see Figure 6.3), Microsoft Photo Editor is put in control; otherwise, Word takes control.

A lot of magic goes on behind the scenes here. When saving a complex document containing OLE objects, the objects' servers save the OLE objects when and *where* instructed to do so by Word.

FIGURE 6.2

Microsoft Office XP allows embedding many types of objects, and uses other applications (including Photo Editor) to manipulate these embedded objects.

FIGURE 6.3

Microsoft Word XP with Figure 6.2's image embedded in a Word document. Double-click the image to edit it in Photo Editor.

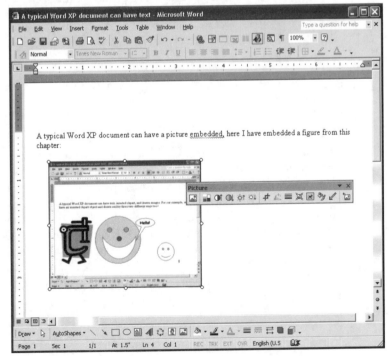

Oops, topic-drift. I'm trying to make everyone an OLE expert. Let's see if I can wrap this up in a nutshell, then connect everything with the registry.

So, in a nutshell:

- ◆ Client applications may have OLE objects embedded into their documents, and/or have OLE server functionality embedded into their basic functionality.

- ◆ This embedding is done at runtime, so the developer knows nothing about what embedding will be done when the program is being written.

- ◆ When a client application wants to embed an OLE object, the client application calls OLE to display the Insert Object dialog box to the user. The user then selects the embedded object.

- ◆ By selecting the object, OLE allows the client's user interface (menus and toolbars, for example) to be turned over to the server application.

- ◆ Server applications may edit the object in place, or may create a special editing window, which may have menu/toolbar support, as appropriate. Usually, complex objects have their own windows for editing just to keep things simpler for the user.

- ◆ OLE uses the registry to learn about embeddable server applications.

- ◆ OLE server and client applications are identified by CLSIDs; call 'em UUIDs, or GUIDs, if you want. A CLSID is a unique long string of numbers.

- ◆ The server application is able to use OLE to tell the client what capabilities the server has. This allows the client to behave in a predictable manner.

NOTE   *It is possible to embed a purely functional OLE object into a document. From time to time with database programming, OLE controls (ActiveX) and OLE applications (without instance-specific data, such as Microsoft Calendar Control 10.0) are used.*

OK, I've prattled on about OLE long enough (is that a wild cheer I hear?), so let's get to the registry component of OLE.

OLE and the Registry

Wow, now we're back to the registry. That was a lot of stuff to cover, just to get a handle of the basics of OLE.

As I've mentioned, OLE works extensively with the registry. When an application registers itself with OLE as a potential server application, this registration process consists of adding a number of entries into the registry. For OLE applications, such as ActiveX controls, these entries are relatively simple and easy to follow. More complex OLE applications—take Microsoft Word as an example— have hundreds of entries in the registry and are typically difficult to understand.

Let's look at a simple OLE control—the ActiveX control called Calendar Control 10.0, which is an application available from Microsoft (as part of Office XP) that allows users to insert a calendar into their document.

Yes, Calendar Control 10.0 is embeddable into a Word document (you can also embed it into many other types of documents). This usage, which is typical, is very useful—think of how many times you needed to include a calendar in a document. Check out Figure 6.4 to see Word and Calendar Control 10.0 working together. In the document that I used for this figure, I actually used the date that I was writing this chapter.

FIGURE 6.4

Embedding a Microsoft Calendar Control adds a new dimension to your Word documents, and makes a normally complex task easy.

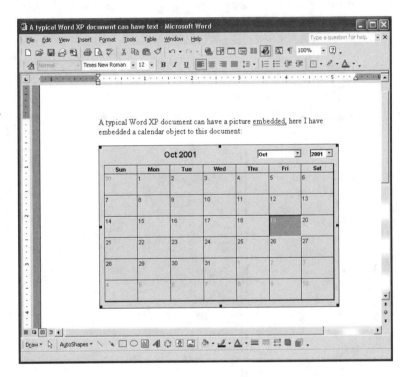

SIZE AND PLACEMENT...

Calendar Control 10.0 allows for easy resizing. However, some versions of ActiveX controls don't work as well when embedded into Word. They may create an underlying window that makes sizing the control's main window difficult. Because of this, the embedded control tends to resize its display in unexpected ways. This is not acceptable behavior, I might add.

If you embed an object that is difficult to resize, try this: First resize the offending control to make it smaller, and then quickly—before Word can resize it—click the underlying base window. This locks the base window so you can resize the control's window as appropriate. A simple double-click anywhere inside the base window restores the normal display.

Microsoft Calendar Control 10.0 allows a lot of interaction with other documents and applications—you can set the month and year as desired using the drop-down list boxes. Nevertheless, why would you, a user, want other interaction? Easy! One classic example is to embed Calendar Control into a Web page, a document whose application is the Web browser. Another example is to embed Calendar Control into an e-mail message. Ding! Did the light go off? E-mail everyone on your team and include in the message the details of a virtual meeting with the calendar showing the appropriate date.

You can modify the properties of embedded objects. There are usually two ways to set the object's properties. The first is to use the programmatic interface (geeky—see Figure 6.5). You can also use the object's *Object* Properties dialog box (see Figure 6.6). The programmatic interface allows access to all possible properties, while the *Object* Properties dialog box allows quick and simple modification of selected object properties.

FIGURE 6.5

You can directly modify the object's properties with the Properties dialog box. This is a standard object properties dialog box, not the one written by the object's author.

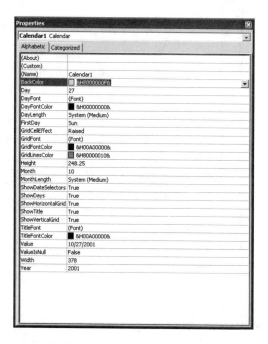

So, we have a Microsoft Calendar Control 10.0 OLE server application implemented as an ActiveX control. Let's look at the registry entries for Calendar Control.

First are the entries in `HKEY_LOCAL_MACHINE\Software\Classes\CLSID`. These entries define much of the OLE interface:

```
{8E27C92B-1264-101C-8A2F-040224009C02}]
@="Calendar Control 10.0"
```

The lines above are the hive (`HKEY_LOCAL_MACHINE`), key (`Software`), and subkeys (`Classes\CLSID`), followed by any values that these keys might contain. A value in the form of `@=data` denotes the default value entry found in every registry key and subkey.

FIGURE 6.6

The *Object* Properties dialog box, created by the object's author, is much easier to use than the interface shown in Figure 6.5.

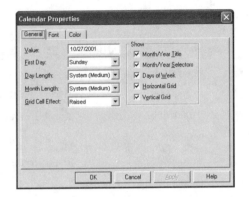

NOTE *The Windows XP CLSID is identical the Windows NT 2000 CLSID. Surprised? Don't be, as the CLSID comes from the application, not the operating system. Also, Calendar Control 10.0 probably has the same CLSID as Calendar Control 9.0.*

The first subkey contains the CLSID for the Calendar Control 10.0 server. This CLSID happens to be 8E27C92B-1264-101C-8A2F-040224009C02, although other versions of Calendar Control (if they were substantially different) might have different CLSIDs. The default data variable contains a string describing the program. Notice that this string is also found in the second section of the registry, HKEY_LOCAL_MACHINE\SOFTWARE\Classes\MSCAL.Calendar.7, described next.

```
{8E27C92B-1264-101C-8A2F-040224009C02}\CLSID
@="8E27C92B-1264-101C-8A2F-040224009C02"
```

Windows uses the AuxUserType subkey for short, people-readable names for the application. Menus, both regular and pop-up, use these short names. Microsoft recommends that the names in AuxUserType be limited to not more than 15 characters.

The entry, InprocHandler32, tells the system what in-process handler will be used.

```
{8E27C92B-1264-101C-8A2F-040224009C02}\InprocServer32
@="C:\Program Files\Microsoft Office\Office10\MSCAL.OCX"
```

Many applications use InprocServer.dll as their in-process handler, although this is not a requirement. Another commonly used in-process handler is MAPI32.DLL, which is used by many mail-enabled objects:

Intended for use with Windows XP, the Insertable entry indicates to the system that the application is listed in the insert list of the Insert New Object dialog box:

```
{8E27C92B-1264-101C-8A2F-040224009C02}\Insertable
@=" "
```

The next entry contains the application's fully qualified path and executable filename. This string is not a REG_EXPAND_SZ, so don't use substitution variables:

```
{8E27C92B-1264-101C-8A2F-040224009C02}\MiscStatus
@="131473"
```

Table 6.1 lists the flag values allowed in MiscStatus.

TABLE 6.1: FLAG VALUES USED IN THE MISCSTATUS OBJECT

FLAG (VALUE) IN DECIMAL	FLAG (VALUE) IN HEX	DESCRIPTION
1	0x00000001	When resizing, the object is recomposed.
2	0x00000002	The object is only available as an icon.
4	0x00000004	The object is used in insert mode, not replace mode.
8	0x00000008	The object is static.
16	0x00000010	The object can't link inside.
32	0x00000020	OLE 1 can link the object.
64	0x00000040	The object is a link object.
128	0x00000080	The object is inside out.
256	0x00000100	Activate the object when it is visible.
512	0x00000200	The object's rendering is device independent.
1024	0x00000400	The object is invisible at runtime.
2048	0x00000800	The object is always run.
4096	0x00001000	The object acts like a button.
8192	0x00002000	The object acts like a label.
16384	0x00004000	The object may not be inactivated.
32768	0x00008000	The object has a simple frame.
131072	0x00010000	The object sets the client site first.
262144	0x00020000	The object runs in IME (Input Method Editor) mode.

NOTE *In* MiscStatus, *combine values using binary or bitwise addition; the easiest way to do a bitwise is to simply add the values. For example, an application with the flags:*

"The object sets the client site first" (131072),
"Activate object when it is visible" (256)
"The Object is inside out" (128)
"The object can't link inside" (16), and
"When resizing, the object is recomposed" (1)

would store a value of (131072 + 256 + 128 + 16 + 1) = 131473 in MiscStatus, *which is exactly the value that is in our Calendar Control object's MiscStatus.*

In some entries, the `Printable` subkey denotes an OLE object that will support the IPrint method (Printable is not found in all objects—only those that are printable using the IPrint method):

```
{8E27C92B-1264-101C-8A2F-040224009C02}\Printable
@=""
```

For an object that may be inserted, there must be an associated `ProgID` value (`ProgID` is shorthand for "programmatic identifier"). This value consists of a short name, a type, and a numeric value (the numeric value is often a version number):

```
{8E27C92B-1264-101C-8A2F-040224009C02}\ProgID
@="MSCAL.Calendar.7"
```

A registry section is created with this name (see the next entry), where more registry values will be stored for this object:

```
{8E27C92B-1264-101C-8A2F-040224009C02}\Verb
@=""
```

Verbs indicate types of action that the object may take. Always numbered consecutively in the registry, there are three components to verb entries, as shown here:

```
{8E27C92B-1264-101C-8A2F-040224009C02}\Verb\0
@="&Edit,0,2"
```

This sample verb, `Edit`, shows three things. First, the text used in the menu, `&Edit`. The `&` indicates that the letter following it will be underscored and used as a hotkey value.

Second, the first number, `0`, is the menu flag's value. Table 6.2 shows the valid values. (Not all are used with OLE menus, such as MF_OWNERDRAW.)

TABLE 6.2: FLAG TYPES ALLOWED

FLAG NAME	VALUE	DESCRIPTION
MF_STRING	0x0000	The menu item is a string.
MF_ENABLE	0x0000	The menu item is enabled.
MF_UNCHECKED	0x0000	The menu item is unchecked.
MF_INSERT	0x0000	The menu item is an inserted item.
MF_BITMAP	0x0004	The menu item is a bitmap.
MF_CHECKED	0x0008	The menu item is checked.
MF_DISABLED	0x0002	The menu item is disabled.
MF_GRAYED	0x0001	The menu item is dimmed.
MF_OWNERDRAW	0x0100	The menu item is an owner-draw item.

Third, the second number, 2, is the verb flag. There are only two possible values for this entry, as shown in Table 6.3.

TABLE 6.3: VERB FLAG NAMES

VERB FLAG NAME	VALUE	DESCRIPTION
OLEVERBATTRIB_NEVERDIRTIES	1	Indicates that the verb does not modify the object, so the object will not require storing in persistent storage.
OLEVERBATTRIB_ONCONTAINERMENU	2	Indicates that the verb should appear on a pop-up menu.

There is a second section of the registry for the Calendar Control 10.0 OLE object. This section, in HKEY_LOCAL_MACHINE\Software\Classes, is called MSCAL.Calendar.7.

In the MSCAL.Calendar subkey, there are two possible value entries. One is shown below:

```
[HKEY_LOCAL_MACHINE\SOFTWARE\Classes\MSCAL.Calendar]
@="Calendar Control 10.0"
```

The first value entry is the default value (@=) that contains the name ("Calendar Control 10.0") used in the insert list of the Insert Object dialog box. A second value that some objects may use is EditFlags, which contains the edit flags, expressed as hex values.

The CLSID subkey contains the object's CLSID:

```
[HKEY_LOCAL_MACHINE\SOFTWARE\Classes\MSCAL.Calendar\CLSID]
@="{8E27C92B-1264-101C-8A2F-040224009C02}"
```

When present, the next subkey (which works with the Microsoft OLE DocObject technology) may contain information about the capabilities of the OLE object:

```
[HKEY_LOCAL_MACHINE\SOFTWARE\Classes\MSCAL.Calendar.7\DocObject]
@="0"
```

Intended for use in Windows 2000 and Windows XP, the following entry indicates to the system that the application should be listed in the insert list of the Insert New Object dialog box:

```
[HKEY_LOCAL_MACHINE\SOFTWARE\Classes\MSCAL.Calendar\Insertable]
@=""
```

The protocol subkey is used for compatibility with OLE 1 container (client) applications:

```
[HKEY_LOCAL_MACHINE\SOFTWARE\Classes\MSCAL.Calendar\protocol]
@=""
```

There is one subkey in protocol, called StdFileEditing. Within StdFileEditing, there are a number of items, as shown here:

```
[HKEY_LOCAL_MACHINE\SOFTWARE\Classes\Word.Document.6\protocol\StdFileEditing]
@=""
```

The default entry in `StdFileEditing` is an empty string.

```
[HKEY_LOCAL_MACHINE\SOFTWARE\Classes\Word.Document.6\protocol\StdFileEditing\server]
@="C:\\PROGRA~1\\MICROS~2\\winword.exe"
```

The first subkey in `StdFileEditing` is the `server` subkey. Inside `server` is the default string containing the fully qualified name of the server executable file. (The Calendar control doesn't have this entry, so I've shown the entry for Word.) Because this string is REG_SZ, do not use any substitutable variables, such as `%SystemRoot%`, in it.

```
[HKEY_LOCAL_MACHINE\SOFTWARE\Classes\MSCAL.Calendar\protocol\StdFileEditing\verb]
@=""
```

The next subkey in `StdFileEditing` is `verb`. Inside `verb` are one or more numbered subkeys; numbers begin with 0 and should be consecutive. Each verb that the OLE application uses in a menu will be included, as shown here:

```
[HKEY_LOCAL_MACHINE\SOFTWARE\Classes\MSCAL.Calendar\protocol\StdFileEditing\verb\0]
@="&Edit"
```

This verb is the Edit menu selection. The text used in the menu is `&Edit`. The `&` indicates that the letter following it will be underscored and used as a hotkey value.

Finally, a version-independent `ProgID` is created. Even when the control is updated, this entry won't change:

```
HKEY_LOCAL_MACHINE\SOFTWARE\Classes\CLSID\{8E27C92B-1264-101C-8A2F-040224009C02}\
VersionIndependentProgId
@="MSCAL.Calendar"
```

Like `ProgID`, this identifies the program, without any version references.

How Linkages Are Made between Applications

OK, now we'll look at a few of the mechanisms that Windows XP uses to manage OLE applications, CLSIDs, and the user interface.

First, let's confuse applications and documents. Considering them identical for now will ease some of the issues here. OLE is one complex puppy, so anything we can do to understand it is OK. Later in this chapter, I'll spend some time pointing out what the differences are between a document and an application.

OK, so the user's application wants to use OLE. There are a couple of ways that applications can use OLE:

♦ Write the application from the get-go to use OLE controls. Some applications do this; however, many do not.

♦ Write the application to allow the user to embed OLE objects into it. Many OLE applications do this.

Neither of these two scenarios is mutually exclusive. For example, an application could have both methods built into it. In either case, it is necessary to register the server of the OLE object that the client will be using.

When registered, the server's basic properties are in the registry, in the `HKEY_LOCAL_MACHINE\Software\Classes` and `HKEY_LOCAL_MACHINE\Software\Classes\CLSID` sections. This information in the registry provides the client with the minimum (got that, *minimum*) amount of information needed to interact with the OLE server.

However, the client application needs to know more about the server. Questions that must be answered include what the server does, expectations of the server, whether support for in-place editing exists, and what information or data is communicated between the server and the application.

An ActiveX control, for example, probably won't have any data that is stored in the client's document. Most ActiveX controls display information for the user. However, the displayed information varies greatly. Some ActiveX controls display contents that vary only in detail. A classic example of this type of ActiveX control is a real-time clock control—the control retrieves the time from the system and displays the time in a specified format. Another controls data changes in content, but not type. For example, the Calendar Control 10.0 control always displays a calendar. However, a Microsoft Photo Editor server's data and type both would change from invocation to invocation. Who knows what the user might try to display in the Microsoft Photo Editor control? The display could be anything from a company logo to a cheery holiday greeting.

Regardless, each server must communicate with the client application. The client always initiates communications between a server and a client; otherwise, how would the server know a client needed it? This communication uses a technique called *querying the interface*. The server will respond with information about exactly what the server can do.

EVERYONE USES OLE

Everyone uses OLE, we just don't realize it. Windows XP uses OLE to perform a number of useful tasks. OLE is a built-in, not an added-on-later, part of Windows.

Explorer, the Windows user interface, relies on OLE for many of its abilities. For example, look at your Desktop. Do you understand what is going on there? Probably not. Do you care? Maybe, and a bit of understanding can help later when you decide to customize it. Explorer is responsible for much of the functionality that you see on your Desktop. Explorer is the program that paints your Desktop background; puts up those icons (such as the pesky Recycle Bin, My Briefcase, and My Computer); and manages aspects of the user interface, such as property sheets and context menus. This is all done with the very valuable assistance of OLE.

Let's give OLE a big hand—it does a lot for us.

Embedded Documents

Embedded documents have references to each OLE object that they have. Unlike when OLE controls are used with an application (remember, we blurred this distinction in the previous section), OLE objects in a document can and do vary greatly. Each document is unique—one document may contain no OLE objects, while the next may contain many different objects.

Transportability is a critical issue. Say I create a chapter for my publisher and embed an OLE object into the document. Then I e-mail that document to my editor. When the editor opens the document and wants to have access to the object, the OLE server application will have to display the object on the computer. It is not necessary that the OLE server be in the same directory, or in any specific directory. OLE uses the registry to take care of locating the server and activating it as necessary. I might have the OLE server installed in a directory on my Q: drive, while my editor might have the same server located on the C: drive, and the executable filename may well be different in each installation, too. Regardless, as long as the `ProgID` value is identical, Windows XP will be able to locate the server and launch it.

Critical items in the registry are those entries shown in the previous sections of this chapter. If you find it necessary to move an OLE server's files from one location to another, it may be possible to edit the registry and change the file locations that are stored in entries, such as shown below in Figure 6.7.

FIGURE 6.7

An object's registry entries shown in the Registry Editor

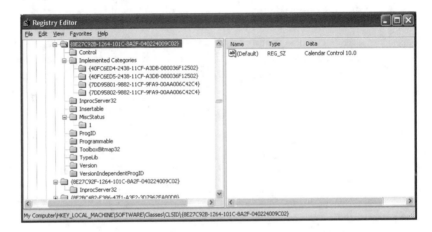

NOTE *Before making any change such as this, be sure your backups are up-to-date.*

WARNING *Don't even consider moving system OLE servers and objects. Leave anything supplied with Windows XP that is related to OLE where it is. There can be references to these objects in places other than the registry.*

Fixing an OLE Disaster

Common OLE problems arise when a user inadvertently deletes the OLE server files, often in an ill-advised attempt to clean up hard disk space, while the OLE registry entries remain in the registry. There are several tricks to recover from this. First, attempt to reinstall a new copy of the OLE server in the original location. This will probably work in most cases. However, if you cannot reinstall—maybe you don't know where the source files are located—consider restoring the files from a backup.

As a last resort, try to remove the registry entries for the OLE server. This probably will result in your registry and system becoming unstable, but if it is unusable anyway, what do you have to lose? Check the sections listed here for entries about the OLE server:

- `HKEY_LOCAL_MACHINE\SOFTWARE\Classes\CLSID\`

- `HKEY_LOCAL_MACHINE\SOFTWARE\Classes\`

Doing this will require some detective work. You will have to search the registry using either the Registry Editor or by exporting the registry to a text file and using a text editor's search. While searching, note all locations listing the OLE server. There will be at least the two mentioned in the previous list, although some OLE components may have more entries.

Disaster typically raises its ugly head when there are multiple dependencies between a number of OLE objects. The fix here is to restore if possible.

Another disaster point is when a new application installs an OLE object that conflicts with an existing one. Typically, the two OLE objects would have different CLSIDs. However, it is possible that the CLSIDs are identical, although in theory this should not happen. Installing a second copy of an OLE object modifies the object's `ProgID`. The user will frequently see two OLE objects in the Insert Object dialog box with the same name. Often, only one of the objects will work correctly.

Chapter 7

Why, Oh Why, Are There system.ini and win.ini Files?

EVEN WITH WINDOWS XP, MICROSOFT'S latest operating system, we still see, as a remnant dragged kicking and screaming, both system.ini and win.ini files. These files do serve a purpose (as I describe below), so we have to live with them.

Okay, so now we have a registry, and that registry was supposed to replace the system.ini and win.ini files that the first 16-bit versions of Windows were plagued with. However, some legacy applications still depend on system.ini and win.ini to run, and Microsoft has wisely retained support for these files in Windows XP. In this chapter, we'll take a look at these topics:

◆ How system and configuration files have evolved

◆ system.ini

◆ win.ini

The Evolution of System and Configuration Files

If you have been a Windows user for more than a few years, you're probably well aware of the issues that have evolved concerning the win.ini and system.ini files. These files contained almost all of the information used to configure earlier versions of Windows; other configuration files, such as protocol.ini (no, there is no protocol.ini file in Windows XP, so don't bother trying to look for it!), were used to store network information as well. When the time to design Windows NT arrived, those wonderful software guys at Microsoft decided that there were some problems with using .ini files. Several problems were apparent:

◆ Users would edit these files, often without regard for the consequences of making changes. Sometimes these changes were totally inadvertent.

◆ Some editors (typically those used to doing word processing) would add, remove, or even change some characters without explicitly telling the user. An example is quotes used around strings, for which the editor would stick in stylized quotes.

◆ The system.ini and win.ini files were growing at an alarming rate. As users added software, fonts, and system components, these files grew. The result was that the primitive search routines employed in the early versions of Windows could not efficiently search for entries in the files.

◆ Applications were able to modify system entries in the win.ini and system.ini files with impunity. A rogue application could butcher these files and no one would be the wiser until the damage caused a failure in the operating system—no protection or security was available.

These problems with win.ini and system.ini prompted Microsoft to move to a more efficient method of storing information that both Windows and user applications could access easily and efficiently. The registry—a binary, tree-oriented database—is quick and easy to work with. Changes to existing products as they were migrated to 32-bit environments, such as Windows NT versions (including Windows 2000 and Windows XP) and Windows 95/98/Me, presented a few problems for programmers to resolve. Moving to the registry-based model also presented a few problems for *legacy applications*, applications that already exist either on the user's computer(s) or as products that are being sold but will not be updated. These problems include:

◆ Existing 16-bit applications must be supported in executable form. That is, an application that expects win.ini and system.ini files to exist must be able to use them.

◆ Some 16-bit applications do not have access to registry manipulation APIs. These applications must be supported using the preexisting win.ini and system.ini files also.

NOTE *Today, there are still many 16-bit applications being sold on the Windows platform. This is over three years after the introduction of Windows 95, a 32-bit platform that supports 32-bit applications very well. In the foreseeable future, there will always be at least one 16-bit application being sold or used somewhere. Old habits, and old software, die hard.*

To handle these problems, Microsoft decided to retain support for both win.ini and system.ini. Windows would no longer use these files, but they would be available to any applications that chose to access or utilize them.

In this chapter, we'll look at the system.ini and win.ini files that Windows XP provides. The default files are not too large, although the win.ini file might become larger when the user installs more 16-bit applications. The system.ini file might also grow as the user adds items that are not designed to work with Windows.

When Windows applications write to the win.ini or system.ini file, and those applications use the Windows XP registry-updating APIs, the information that would have been stored in the .ini file will be stored in the registry. This is subject to the exclusions discussed next.

Any file listed in the HKEY_LOCAL_MACHINE\Software\Microsoft\Windows NT\CurrentVersion\ IniFileMapping section (that is, an .ini file or registry entries) will also be updated using the Windows XP registry-updating APIs. Windows will search the IniFileMapping section for the application's section. If the section is found, it is used. If no application section is found, Windows will search for an .ini file to use.

NOTE *Any application that directly opens an .ini file, perhaps using the 16-bit .ini file-processing APIs or direct file I/O, will bypass the registry file manipulation entirely.*

system.ini

Located in the system.ini file are a few entries that the Windows XP Setup program supplies by default. Here is a typical, basic system.ini file:

```
; for 16-bit app support

[drivers]
wave=mmdrv.dll
timer=timer.drv

[mci]
[driver32]
[386enh]
woafont=dosapp.FON
EGA80WOA.FON=EGA80WOA.FON
EGA40WOA.FON=EGA40WOA.FON
CGA80WOA.FON=CGA80WOA.FON
CGA40WOA.FON=CGA40WOA.FON
```

This file contains four sections—[drivers], [mci], [driver32], and [386enh]—and only a few entries in these sections. Entries are primarily for fonts (in the [386enh] section), as well as two drivers used with Windows XP:

mmdrv.dll   A driver that is used for multimedia (sound) support

timer.drv   A driver that is used to provide timer support

In addition, your system.ini file may contain other entries and other sections if you are using 16-bit-incompatible applications. These applications would use the win.ini file to write application-specific information, typically in sections created for the application.

Most of the Windows XP system entries were moved from the system.ini file to the registry key HKEY_LOCAL_MACHINE\Software\Microsoft\Windows NT\CurrentVersion\WOW. This key contains many entries that would be found in a Windows 3.1x installation.

NOTE   *Windows XP cannot use any 16-bit screen savers because they do not perform correctly when used in the Windows NT environment. Any entry found in the* [BOOT] *section of the* system.ini *file will never be migrated to Windows XP.*

win.ini

Few entries are located in the win.ini file, except for computers that have been used for some time and have had additional software or components installed.

The default win.ini file contains four sections with no entries and two sections—[Mail] and [MAPI]—containing entries:

```
; for 16-bit app support
[fonts]
[extensions]
[mci extensions]
```

```
[files]
[Mail]
MAPI=1
[MCI Extensions.BAK]
aif=MPEGVideo
aifc=MPEGVideo
aiff=MPEGVideo
asf=MPEGVideo2
asx=MPEGVideo2
au=MPEGVideo
ivf=MPEGVideo2
m1v=MPEGVideo
m3u=MPEGVideo2
mp2=MPEGVideo
mp2v=MPEGVideo
mp3=MPEGVideo2
mpa=MPEGVideo
mpe=MPEGVideo
mpeg=MPEGVideo
mpg=MPEGVideo
mpv2=MPEGVideo
snd=MPEGVideo
wax=MPEGVideo2
wm=MPEGVideo2
wma=MPEGVideo2
wmp=MPEGVideo2
wmv=MPEGVideo2
wmx=MPEGVideo2
wvx=MPEGVideo2
```

A computer with a few more miles on it might have additional entries, like these:

```
[WinZip]
Note-1=This section is required only to install the optional WinZip Internet
➥Browser Support build 0231.
Note-2=Removing this section of the win.ini will have no effect except preventing
➥installation of WinZip Internet Browser Support build 0231.
win32_version=6.3-7.0
[SciCalc]
layout=0
```

This computer has some additional applications installed. These applications are a mixture of system components and added-on programs from a variety of sources:

Mail   The entries in the [Mail] section describe the mail interface that is installed on this computer.

WinZip   WinZip is an enhancement to the very popular DOS-based PKZIP program. WinZip adds both a Windows interface and the ability to handle long filenames.

The first application, Mail, is most certainly part of the 32-bit e-mail system. Why does it have entries in the win.ini file? This allows 16-bit applications to know something about the already-installed e-mail interface. Remember: 32-bit applications can use `.ini` files, including `win.ini`, although it is strongly recommended that they do not.

The win.ini system-based settings are stored in the registry in a number of subkeys. Table 7.1 shows some of these settings and their locations. This is mostly of interest to users who are using dual environments, such as Windows NT and Windows XP.

TABLE 7.1: SECTIONS FOUND IN WIN.INI

SECTION IN WIN.INI	REGISTRY PATH	DESCRIPTION
`[extensions]`	`HKEY_CURRENT_USER\Software\Microsoft\` `Windows NT\CurrentVersion\Extensions`	File associations used by Explorer
`[fonts]`	`HKEY_CURRENT_USER\Software\Microsoft\` `Windows NT\CurrentVersion\Fonts`	Fonts used by Windows
`[fontsubstitutes]`	`HKEY_CURRENT_USER\Software\Microsoft\` `Windows NT\CurrentVersion\FontSubstitutes`	Fonts used by Windows
`[mci extensions.bak]`	`HKEY_CURRENT_USER\Software\Microsoft\` `Windows NT\CurrentVersion\MCI Extensions`	The Media Control Interface settings and extensions
`[mci extensions]`	`HKEY_CURRENT_USER\Software\Microsoft\` `Windows NT\CurrentVersion\MCI Extensions`	The Media Control Interface settings and extensions

Some items are never migrated in a dual-environment system. These items are usually not moved to the registry either due to their complexity or for other reasons. Other items are migrated, but not used. Such items include:

♦ `[Ports]`, `[Devices]`, and `[PrinterPorts]` that are migrated during the migration process as part of installation; these settings are not used for any purpose.

♦ Persistent shares and users as used by Windows for Workgroups, but not Windows 3.1x.

♦ The default domain and user ID from Windows for Workgroups or the `LANMAN.ini`.

♦ Individual user profiles that are maintained by WinLogin.

♦ Changes that users make in their copies of the Main, Startup, Games, and Accessories Program Manager groups.

♦ MS-DOS drive letters, which are managed using the Windows Disk Administrator. (Drive letters usually vary between Windows 3.1x, Windows 2000, and Windows XP due to how drives are detected and the possible presence of Windows 3.1x–incompatible drive formatting, such as NTFS drives.)

♦ Auto Arrange, Minimize on Run, and Save Settings on Exit options for Program Manager. These settings are not type compatible. (Program Manager uses strings, while Windows XP uses DWORD values for these settings.)

♦ DOS command window font details.

Chapter 8

Getting Rid of the Unwanted

SOMETIMES WE DON'T HAVE what we want in the registry. Other times, we have too much of what we *don't want* in the registry. This chapter covers the second case. We install software, try it, don't like it, and remove it. Things come and things go, sometimes intentionally, sometimes by accident. But whatever the cause or reason, any computer that has been running Windows XP for more than a few months will probably have a few entries in the registry that do nothing more than clutter it up. Additionally, a few unlucky users will have some entries that are doing something that they really don't want to happen.

For whatever the reason, this chapter covers the very difficult task of trying to remove unwanted things from the registry without having to reinstall Windows XP. I'll discuss the following:

◆ Automated cleaning with RegClean

◆ The interactive interface of RegMaid

◆ Finding files with CleanReg

◆ Using RegView to view the registry

Before You Clean Up

The classic problem is that we are not always good at removing things we install. Many software programs come with uninstall programs, but many others don't. Sometimes we lose track of an application—usually because, in a moment of weakness, we delete the application's directory without properly uninstalling the application. Desperation for even a few more MB of hard disk space will make us do strange things.

Have you ever installed an application on a secondary drive only to later have that secondary drive fail? Maybe you have a good backup, maybe not. Perhaps you just want to do a general housecleaning. Whatever your situation may be, removing unwanted items from the registry should be handled with extreme caution.

WARNING   *Have I already said this? Back up your registry before doing anything described in this chapter. Manually removing items from a registry is perhaps the easiest way to trash everything. Back up, back up, and back up again.*

Using third-party utilities can help make this formidable task easier and help prevent you from unintentionally deleting files you need. In this chapter, I cover three utilities that help clean up the registry: RegClean, RegMaid, and CleanReg. A fourth utility, RegView, lets you easily take a quick look at the registry.

WARNING   *Windows XP is a "new" operating system—utilities specific to Windows XP are only beginning to become widely available. Utilities described in this chapter were originally created for Windows NT and are commonly used successfully with Windows 2000; however, they should be used with caution. I've tested each of the described utilities, but that is no guarantee that these utilities will work with your Windows XP configuration.*

RegClean

Microsoft created a program that automates cleaning the registry. Called RegClean, it is available from several sources; I used to recommend that you retrieve it directly from Microsoft's Internet site at `http://support.microsoft.com/download/support/mslfiles/regclean.exe`. However, Microsoft no longer makes RegClean available! The reason for the discontinuation of RegClean is not documented—one might guess that there were problems with the program.

Since Microsoft does not make RegClean available, your best bet is to use one of the Internet web search sites (such as `http://www.google.com`) and search for `RegClean.exe`. I found many references to the program and several sites offering downloads, such as ZDNet and CNET.

The most recent version of RegClean is RegClean 4.1a. This version was released in early 1998. It is fully compatible with Windows XP, although you may need to update to a later version of the OLE driver `OLEAUT32.dll`. This update is included with the distribution of RegClean. Documentation on how to install the driver is also included in the RegClean readme file.

Using RegClean is simple—just follow these steps:

1. Download the `RegClean.exe` file from an Internet site. Check with Microsoft's website first; they may have restored the files since this chapter was written.

2. Execute the `RegClean.exe` file to start the self-extractor program. Alternatively, you may use either WinZip or PK_UNZIP on the `RegClean.exe` distribution file to extract the program and other files. Files contained in the `RegClean.exe` distribution file include:

   OADIST.exe   The update for `OLEAUT32.dll`, if needed

   Readme.txt   A text file with instructions on how to use RegClean and information about `OADIST.exe`

   RegClean.exe   The real `RegClean.exe` program, which is an executable Windows XP application

3. Execute the extracted `RegClean.exe` program.

NOTE   *RegClean.exe writes a program called `RegClean.exe`. Confused? Well, you should be. The `RegClean.exe` file that you download (about 800KB in size) is a self-extracting zip file. One of the files contained in `RegClean.exe` is `RegClean.exe`—the actual program. In order for both files to coexist, the self-extracting `RegClean.exe` file must write its output to a different directory or drive. `RegClean.exe` cannot extract to its own directory.*

If you receive the message(s):

```
REGCLEAN.EXE is linked to missing export OLEAUT32.DLL:421
```

and/or:

```
A device attached to the system is not correctly functioning
```

it is probable that you will need an updated OLEAUT32.dll file.

OLEAUT32.dll is installed with Internet Explorer 3.x or later, so most of the users who are affected by this problem have earlier versions of Windows, such as Windows NT.

Installing OLEAUT32.dll is a simple process—just execute the OADIST.exe file that was extracted from the RegEdit.exe file (see step 2 in the "RegClean" section).

Running RegClean

Executing RegClean is simple; it doesn't care what directory it is run from. However, RegClean will save undo information to the directory that it has been executed from.

Start RegClean either by choosing Start ➢ Run, by using a command-prompt window, or from Explorer. Once started, RegClean displays a window similar to the one shown in Figure 8.1. In this window, the lower status bar and the descriptive text just above it indicate the progress of RegClean's initial pass through the registry.

FIGURE 8.1

RegClean has just two buttons: Fix Errors and Cancel. The Fix Errors button is initially labeled Start, even though RegClean starts automatically.

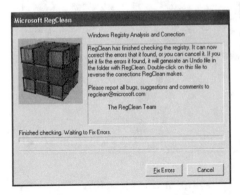

NOTE Though RegClean has a Cancel button, it is disabled (inactive) and cannot be selected while RegClean is running. Once RegClean completes the initial check, the Cancel button's text changes to Exit, and the button is made active. Additionally, RegClean does not appear in the Taskbar or on the Task Manager's Applications tab. To end RegClean, open the Task Manager's Processes tab, select RegClean.exe, and click End Process.

Once RegClean finishes the scan of the registry, it advises the user either that it has not found any registry errors (this usually happens if you run RegClean frequently) or that RegClean can correct the errors found. Clicking the Fix Errors button tells RegClean to clean the registry. Clicking Cancel causes RegClean to exit without doing anything else.

If RegClean doesn't find any errors, the message shown in Figure 8.2 appears. This message tells you that no errors were detected in the registry.

FIGURE 8.2

If RegClean finds no errors, this message is shown. Only the Exit button is active.

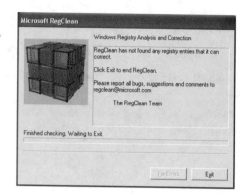

When RegClean finds errors (this happens often, even on a very clean system), the Start button's text changes to Fix Errors, and this button is enabled. You may then click either Fix Errors or Exit, as desired. If you choose to fix the registry errors that RegClean finds, the utility creates a registry backup file of those items changed, as shown in Figure 8.3.

FIGURE 8.3

If RegClean finds errors, this message is shown. Both the Fix Errors and Exit buttons are active.

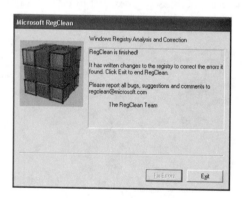

As RegClean cleans the registry, it writes a registry file to the drive that RegClean was run from. This registry file may be used to restore the registry to the same condition that it was in before running RegClean.

The registry save file created by RegClean is named in the following manner:

```
Undo computer yyyymmdd hhmmss.Reg
```

Here, *computer* is the name of the computer whose registry was cleaned; you may keep a single copy of RegClean and then link to and execute it from many other computers. The *yyyymmdd* is the year, month, and day that RegClean was executed; and *hhmmss* is the time of day that RegClean was executed.

For example, my computer's RegClean folder now has a file named Undo PEACHFUZZ 20011022 162809.Reg. This file contains about 1100 lines, all from a relatively recent clean installation of Windows Server.

Undoing RegClean

After RegClean runs, it is important to make sure that all applications and systems are still functioning correctly. If you find that something has broken (this is unlikely, but could happen), it is imperative that you restore the registry to its original state immediately. To do this, simply use Explorer and double-click the Registration Entries backup file created by RegClean (see Figure 8.4).

FIGURE 8.4

RegClean creates the Registration Entries files whose filenames all start with Undo.

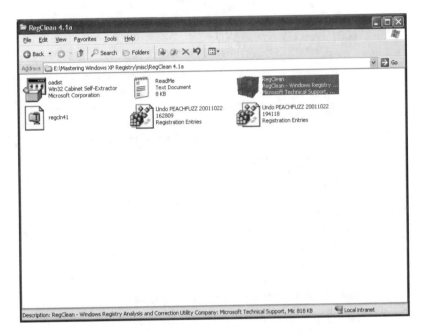

Be careful that you select the correct .reg backup file if there is more than one. Remember, you can tell Explorer to list files in date/time order, making the selection process much simpler.

Sometimes, users find that they are unable to undo the changes. Windows XP will give an error when the registry backup file created by RegClean is double-clicked. The user (that's you) will get one or more errors that indicate a problem has occurred. These errors are caused by a problem with the registry, not with the .reg file.

To fix this problem, follow these steps:

1. Open Explorer and select Tools ➢ Folder Options.

2. In the Folder Options dialog box, select the File Types tab.

3. In the Details for 'REG' Extension area, click the Advanced button.

4. In the Edit File Type dialog box, select Merge in the Actions list box. Then click the Edit button to open the Editing Action for Type: Registration Entries dialog box.

5. In the Application Used to Perform Action box, enter the name **regedit.exe "%1"** (including the double quotes).

6. Click OK (or Close, as appropriate) in all open dialog boxes.

After doing this, you should be able to restore registry entries from a `.reg` registry backup file. It is rare that the Registration Entries configuration becomes corrupted. However, Microsoft mentions that this may be a problem with RegClean.

RegMaid

Like RegClean, RegMaid is a utility that helps users of Windows XP clean up their registries. RegMaid is much more interactive than RegClean; RegMaid actually has a user interface. The RegMaid program is available from several sources. I suggest that you retrieve it directly from Microsoft's Internet site at `ftp://ftp.microsoft.com/Softlib/MSLFILES`. There may be other versions of RegMaid or other products called RegMaid, but I recommend that you use the Microsoft version found at this address. (The RegMaid file was available from Microsoft's FTP site as of early 2002, when this was written.)

The current version of RegMaid, 1.1, was released in 1995. This version is fully compatible with Windows NT 4 and was actually last revised in late 1997. The changes in the revision were slight.

NOTE RegMaid, unlike RegClean, comes with source code. That's right, you can customize RegMaid to do specific cleanups as desired. To rebuild RegMaid, you will need a copy of Microsoft Visual C++. However, to ensure that the correct directory structure for Visual C++ is maintained, be sure to use either the RegMaid self-extractor or the /d PKUNZIP option.

IS REGMAID COMPATIBLE WITH WINDOWS XP?

I am not convinced that RegMaid works correctly under Windows XP.

OK, I'll be honest; I know that RegMaid has problems with Windows XP. One problem that I found is that RegMaid doesn't expand TypeLib entries in REG_EXPAND_SZ format. (It is probable that RegMaid doesn't expand any REG_EXPAND_SZ objects at all.) On my computer, RegMaid won't find the file %SystemRoot%\Speech\Xtel.dll (where %SystemRoot% is set to C:\Windows), but it will find the file C:\Windows\Speech\Xtel.dll!

Since Windows XP stores many TypeLib entries in REG_EXPAND_SZ format, RegMaid fails to find these entries.

If you use RegMaid with Windows XP, I strongly recommend that you back up the registry and have a second copy of XP installed so that you are able to repair any damage to the registry that RegMaid may inflict. Hopefully, Microsoft will introduce a new version of RegMaid after Windows XP is released. Check Microsoft's website for more information on the current release status of RegMaid.

Using RegMaid is simple—just follow these steps:

1. Download the `RegMaid.exe` file from Microsoft's Internet site at `ftp://ftp.microsoft.com/Softlib/MSLFILES`. (If Microsoft moves the file, you can search for it from any point in Microsoft's website.)

2. Execute the `RegMaid.exe` file to start the self-extractor program. Alternatively, you can use WinZip on the `RegMaid.exe` distribution file to extract the program and other files. If you are manually unzipping the file, use the `/d` option to force the creation of subdirectories. I do not recommend manually unzipping these files, but if you do so, make sure that you do not unzip to the same folder that the `RegMaid.exe` archive is stored in—the program name is identical to the archive name, and an error will result.

NOTE *If you manually unzip to extract the RegMaid programs without using the `/d` option, you will receive a message that there are two copies of `RegMaid.hlp`. Select Overwrite to retrieve the correct help file.*

3. Files contained in the `RegMaid.exe` distribution file include an executable copy of `RegMaid.exe` (look in the `Release` directory for the executable program file), help files, and the program's source files. The RegMaid distribution package contains just under 100 files.

4. Execute the `RegMaid.exe` program that is extracted. When RegMaid is extracted properly, you will be provided with a directory called `RegMaid\Release`. RegMaid and the necessary support files are located in the `Release` directory. They may be copied to any location you desire.

RegMaid's primary user interface is the toolbar; like almost all Windows applications, RegMaid has a full function menu, too. The toolbar buttons allow you to quickly navigate through the registry objects that RegMaid has found suspect. You may easily and quickly delete any of these objects.

WARNING *Careful. Unlike RegClean, RegMaid doesn't create a recovery file. Once RegMaid removes a registry entry, it will be difficult to restore it. Before running RegMaid, you would be very wise to fully back up the registry. This will also facilitate recovery from any blunders that RegMaid might make.*

RegMaid contains four views:

◆ CLSID view

◆ ProgID view

◆ TypeLib view

◆ Interface view

These views are discussed next. The views are used in order—CLSID, ProgID, TypeLib, and Interface. There is a Refresh button on RegMaid's toolbar, and it is recommended that you refresh after deleting objects, before moving to a new view, and after moving to a new view.

CLSID View

The first view that RegMaid displays is the CLSID view. This view lists objects, their names, and CLSIDs. The CLSID view looks for CLSIDs (OLE components) that don't have a handler or server or for which the handler or server specified is missing, probably because the file or directory was deleted.

Valid handlers are listed here:

◆ InprocHandler

◆ InprocHandler32

◆ InprocServer

◆ InprocServer32

◆ LocalServer

◆ LocalServer32

NOTE *The missing item is shown in the first column in the CLSID view, Missing. This column has six positions, with five dashes and one X. The position where the X is found is the type of the missing handler. For example, if the Missing column shows - - - X - -, this indicates that the InprocServer32 is missing.*

Notice that each handler or server comes in two flavors, either 16-bit or 32-bit. Generally, Windows XP components will be 32-bit. However, some systems and components do use the 16-bit entries, including some versions of Microsoft Word Basic.

Take a look at Figure 8.5. RegMaid found over 340 items that were not correct in the registry of a relatively stock Windows installation. Some items were the result of installing aftermarket applications, others come with Windows.

Items listed in Figure 8.5 include the following, which are all InprocServer32 objects:

◆ `Window List in Shell Process`

◆ `History`

◆ An unnamed object

◆ `CompositeFolder`

I can tell RegMaid to clean up these entries automatically. To do this, I must select an entry (see Figure 8.6), and then click the Delete button in the toolbar or select Clean Up ➤ Delete Entries.

A second, and perhaps better, way is to simply uninstall the problem application. Start the Add/Remove Programs applet in the Control Panel and select the program, application, component, or whatever it is that you want to remove. Do this only if the product is not in use anymore; if the product is still in use, this won't be an option.

Regardless of what I do, after fixing the problem, I next click the Refresh button in RegMaid and make sure that no new entries show up in the CLSID view. If nothing new shows up, I go on to the next view, ProgID, which is described next. If any new entries appear, I follow this process a second time.

FIGURE 8.5

RegMaid's report for the CLSID view shows some objects that have problems with their handlers.

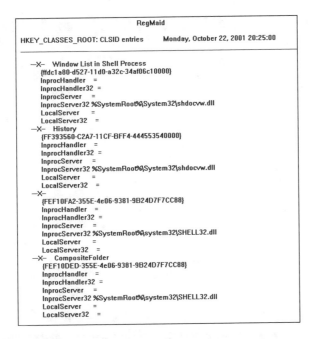

```
                              RegMaid

HKEY_CLASSES_ROOT: CLSID entries       Monday, October 22, 2001 20:25:00


   —X—   Window List in Shell Process
          {ffdc1a80-d527-11d0-a32c-34af06c10000}
          InprocHandler   =
          InprocHandler32 =
          InprocServer    =
          InprocServer32 %SystemRoot%\System32\shdocvw.dll
          LocalServer     =
          LocalServer32   =
   —X—   History
          {FF393560-C2A7-11CF-BFF4-444553540000}
          InprocHandler   =
          InprocHandler32 =
          InprocServer    =
          InprocServer32 %SystemRoot%\System32\shdocvw.dll
          LocalServer     =
          LocalServer32   =
   —X—
          {FEF10FA2-355E-4e06-9381-9B24D7F7CC88}
          InprocHandler   =
          InprocHandler32 =
          InprocServer    =
          InprocServer32 %SystemRoot%\system32\SHELL32.dll
          LocalServer     =
          LocalServer32   =
   —X—   CompositeFolder
          {FEF10DED-355E-4e06-9381-9B24D7F7CC88}
          InprocHandler   =
          InprocHandler32 =
          InprocServer    =
          InprocServer32 %SystemRoot%\system32\SHELL32.dll
          LocalServer     =
          LocalServer32   =
```

FIGURE 8.6

RegMaid's CLSID view showing objects that could be fixed. The first four objects are shown in Figure 8.5 too.

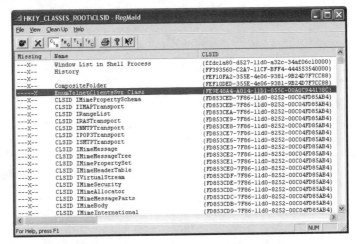

ProgID View

The ProgID view contains items that are associated with the registry's ProgID entries. Entries in ProgID view show a name, a CLSID, and a ProgID name (see Figure 8.7). As with the CLSID view, it is imperative to determine exactly what each entry listed is for and why there is an error. Unlike CLSID problems, the ProgID entries are not simply a matter of a missing file—in this case, we are dealing with registry entries that are corrupt or, more likely, missing. Don't be too surprised if you find that you have no entries in the ProgID view.

FIGURE 8.7

RegMaid's ProgID
view shows those
entries with invalid
ProgID entries.

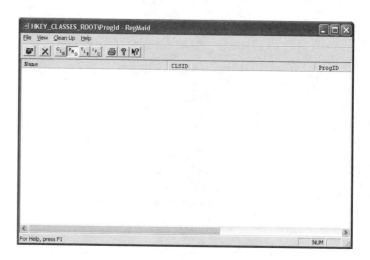

Generally, it is safe to remove these entries. As with any other registry change, back up the registry first.

NOTE   *Windows 2000 users take note: Right from the start, some Windows 2000 systems (those upgraded from Windows NT 4, for example) have several invalid ProgID entries. The* Scheduler Queue Object *and* Scheduler Job Object *entries are found in all Windows 2000 systems. No documentation exists with regard to their use or necessity, other than that they are used to process* .job *or* .que *file types. No actions are specified for either. Also, a clean installation of Windows 2000 typically has one invalid ProgID entry, called* TimeStamp. *There is no documentation on this entry. You may also find similar entries in Windows XP.*

TypeLib View

RegMaid will search all entries in the HKEY_CLASSES_ROOT\Typelib section of the registry to determine if there is an associated .tlb (TypeLib) file. If the file cannot be found based on the entry, RegMaid will report that entry.

Here, I have to disagree with RegMaid's documentation (regarding whether to delete the entry or not). My recommendation is to do the following:

♦ For any TypeLib entry with an entry in one (or more) of the file columns, search for the file on the hard drive. If the file is found, but at a different location from where the registry entry says it should be, you may consider updating the registry manually to show the correct pathname (see Figure 8.8). I've found that about half of the entries flagged as being bad in the TypeLib view are marked this way because the path to the file was incorrect.

♦ For any TypeLib entry that lists two or more versions, it is possible that one version has improper entries, while the other version may be okay. Typically, when a new version of a product is installed, the older version may not be completely removed from the registry. In this situation, I'd recommend leaving these entries in the registry without change, or deleting the version that has incomplete values. RegClean actually does a proper job of cleaning up this type of registry chaff.

WARNING   *Generally, my recommendation is to err on the cautious side. If in doubt, don't use RegMaid to delete the entry. RegClean does a much better job of cleaning and repairing the TypeLib entries than RegMaid does.*

FIGURE 8.8

This TypeLib entry has an erroneous data value of `%System-Root%\System32\dmview.ocx`. Changing the value to `C:\Windows\System32\dmview.ocx` will solve the problem that RegMaid found.

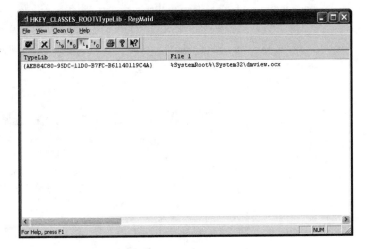

Interface View

The Interface view searches the `HKEY_CLASSES_ROOT\Interface` entries. Each entry that has a `TypeLib` subkey is checked to determine that there is a match between the TypeLib entry's CLSID and a valid OLE object found in the `HKEY_CLASSES_ROOT\Typelib` subkey. If no entry is found in `HKEY_CLASSES_ROOT\Typelib`, RegMaid will flag the line.

RegMaid claims that entries that don't match may be safely deleted. However, I recommend that you don't allow RegMaid to fix this error—RegMaid will delete the entire subkey in `HKEY_CLASSES_ROOT\Interface` instead of deleting the suspect TypeLib entry. RegClean also does not flag this discrepancy as an error. Figure 8.9 shows RegMaid displaying Interface errors.

WARNING   *If you wish to invoke RegMaid's Delete function on an Interface view item, back up the registry or subkey in question before continuing. Blind deleting like this will probably lead to disaster, sooner or later.*

Recommendations for RegMaid

I have several recommendations you should follow when using RegMaid:

◆ Make a full backup of the registry before starting RegMaid.

◆ Be careful about what is removed with RegMaid. RegMaid does not have any methodology to recover from errors, either its own or yours.

◆ The CLSID view entries may be safe to delete, but do review each of them first.

◆ The ProgID view entries are probably safe to delete, although you should review each of them first as well.

◆ The TypeLib and Interface view entries probably should not be deleted unless you are absolutely sure that these entries are not being used.

◆ Run RegClean before running RegMaid. RegClean will clean many problem entries that Reg-Maid would find. RegClean will create a .reg file that allows restoring these entries if desired, so there is an additional recovery path that RegMaid doesn't offer.

◆ Consider rewriting RegMaid to write a recovery file for each item deleted. Since Microsoft supplies the source code file for RegMaid, a recovery file is not difficult to create (if you are a C/C++ programmer).

FIGURE 8.9

This Interface entry has a TypeLib entry value of 1.0. Reg-Maid does not like this entry, because TypeLibs are sup-posed to be in the form of a CLSID.

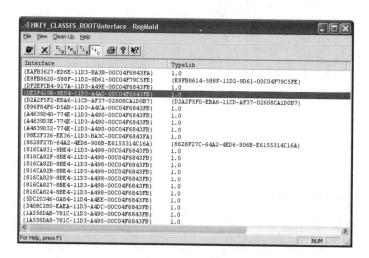

The best course of action with RegMaid is to keep RegEdit open at the same time. For each entry that RegMaid finds suspect, find the entry in the registry. See if you can determine what Reg-Maid is unhappy about. Can you fix the problem? For example, is the path missing or invalid? If either of these is the case, fix it. Is the problem caused by a ProgID or TypeLib entry that has one valid version and another invalid version? If so, consider manually deleting the invalid version while retaining the valid one. RegMaid will attempt to delete all versions when one version is found invalid.

WARNING   *Due to the lack of any restore methodology, always use RegMaid with caution!*

CleanReg

Matt Pietrek, a columnist for *Microsoft Systems Journal* and a developer at Compuware's NuMega Labs, created a program called CleanReg for an article he wrote for *MSJ*. This very clever utility may be obtained from several sources. If you have access to a subscription to MSDN, the source for Clean-Reg is available on the MSDN CD-ROM or in the MSDN Library. Or, if you have a subscription to *MSJ* and still have the September 1996 issue, the source is located on page 77. The source code is also available at http://www.microsoft.com/msj/defaulttop.asp?page=/msj/archive/s358a.htm.

NOTE   Checking out Microsoft's entire MSJ website at `http://www.microsoft.com./msj/` *will reveal lots of good information, especially for programmers. For example, all source code from back issues is available by clicking on the Back Issues link and scrolling to the desired issue.*

NOTE   CleanReg works a bit differently from RegClean and RegMaid. CleanReg looks at registry entries and attempts to find filenames. Whenever CleanReg finds what it thinks is a filename, it searches for the file.

Pietrek had to overcome several difficulties when he wrote CleanReg. For one thing, he had to determine what constitutes a valid filename. With long filenames, Pietrek correctly states that the following is actually a valid filename (try it, I did):

```
foo -p .exe
```

SO YOU SAY CLEANREG WON'T COMPILE RIGHT?

There is a problem with CleanReg and some later versions of Microsoft Visual C++: Microsoft Visual C++ will indicate an error in `clnregui.cpp` with the `WinMain` function. The error indicates that `WinMain` has been either redefined or overloaded. The error is in the types assigned to the parameters of the `WinMain` function. To correct this problem, change the `WinMain` parameter list to what I have shown here. Simply add all characters and lines shown in bold in this listing fragment to your version of `clnregui.cpp` (and don't forget the comment characters, //):

```
    TEXT("CD-ROM) for all documentation questions.");
    // int PASCAL WinMain( HANDLE hInstance, HANDLE hPrevInstance,
    //           PSTR lpszCmdLine, int nCmdShow )
    // Function parameters cleaned 6/8/98 by Peter D. Hipson
    int PASCAL WinMain(
      HINSTANCE hInstance,
      HINSTANCE hPrevInstance,
      LPSTR lpszCmdLine,
      int nCmdShow )
    {
        InitCommonControls();   // Gotta do this for treeview controls
```

Fix the `WinMain` function before correcting any errors, such as an error calling the `DialogBox( )` function a bit later in the `WinMain` function, because these other errors are caused by the incorrect `WinMain` parameters.

I've successfully compiled CleanReg with Microsoft Visual Studio 6.0 after fixing the `WinMain` line.

But, in the registry, what's to differentiate the filename foo -p .exe from the executable foo taking the parameter -p .exe? Is there a standard in the registry? No, not really. Is there a standard anywhere else? Yes, somewhat. For a command passed to the operating system, it is expected that the executable filename will be enclosed in double quotes (" ") if it is not a short (8.3) name. That is, if you have the file foo -p .exe, and you want to execute this file, you must enter the command exactly as:

```
"foo -p .exe"
```

There will be an error if you enter the name like this, without quotes:

```
foo -p .exe
```

In this case, the operating system will assume that the name of the executable file is foo, and will then attempt to pass the parameter(s) -p .exe to that file.

NOTE *Sometimes Windows XP is able to correctly determine the filename even if it is a long name. In these cases, Windows XP usually can figure it out if the name doesn't contain any spaces or other special characters.*

Entries in the registry don't have set, fixed rules. Programmers of applications have been known to code exactly what they expect and not to bother considering any other application or system convention. Now, some programmers have adopted a convention that Microsoft uses for many registry entries. It involves filenames and parameters—don't quote the filename, but instead, quote the parameters, if there are any, such as in this example:

```
foo "-p .exe"
```

This works well, but unless you know this rule is being followed, it is difficult to determine whether the programmer is following this rule or simply being lazy about including quotes in the following string:

```
foo -p .exe
```

This leads us right back to the original problem: what constitutes a valid filename in a registry entry and what does not? In the end, you, the user, will have to determine whether a filename is valid when running CleanReg. Some simple tricks of the trade will be helpful. When given a path, take the name up to the first non-alpha character, append *.* to that name, and try to find the file with the dir command in a command window. (An alpha character is a letter, a number, or one of the allowed special characters.)

For example, when searching for:

```
C:\temp\foo -p .exe
```

take the first part, up to the first invalid character (the space):

```
C:\temp\foo
```

append *.* to this name:

```
C:\temp\foo*.*
```

and do a dir command:

```
dir C:\temp\foo*.*
```

The dir command will list all files beginning with foo, allowing you to determine if the file in question is foo, foo.exe, foo -p.exe, or whatever. Then you may make an educated guess with CleanReg as to whether to remove the file's entry in the registry or not, depending on the search.

CleanReg allows you to remove either a single value or a key. When removing a key, CleanReg will delete all subkeys contained in the subject key. This should raise a note of caution with you—be careful not to delete too much when using CleanReg.

Figure 8.10 shows CleanReg running on a Windows system. CleanReg found almost 200 entries that were suspect. A manual check showed that about 80 percent of these entries were indeed bad. In this figure, there is a file found in the open files common dialog box MRU (most recently used) list. This file was named E:\mas.TIF. I had accidentally saved this file in the wrong place. Later I resaved it in the correct place and deleted the wrong file. Unfortunately, the open files common dialog box's MRU list was not updated.

FIGURE 8.10

CleanReg listing a bad reference to the file E:\mas .TIF. Okay, so I deleted that file on purpose...

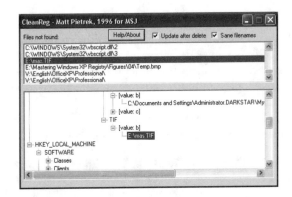

In Figure 8.10, the file that CleanReg thought was missing (E:\mas.TIF) was deleted by another user. It was very hard for Windows to know that the file was intentionally deleted.

CleanReg has two check boxes in the user interface:

Update after Delete   This option tells CleanReg to update the display after the user deletes anything. Checking this option could slow things down a bit when the user's registry is large, so the use of this option is up to the user, based on experience.

Sane Filenames   A "filename" means that there's a :\ near the beginning of the string that CleanReg is checking. If Sane Filenames is checked, CleanReg assumes that characters like / and - aren't part of the filename, although they're technically legal.

Some entries to suspect and delete are those that point to your Temp directory. Often these files are artifacts of checking out a file and having the file appear in a program's MRU (most recently used) list. Or perhaps a program was temporarily installed into the Temp directory to be checked out. My Temp directory is C:\Temp. My rule is that anything in the Temp directory may be deleted at any time. Nothing to be saved should ever be placed in the Temp directory.

Many applications store their MRU in the registry in a subkey called Recent File List. Manually removing entries from such a subkey usually results in few bad side effects. However, using the application to clear the MRU list is the best alternative, if possible; some applications don't have a mechanism to clear the MRU list.

Some applications save work or other files in the Temp directory, too. Generally, these applications are robust enough that they will not fail should these files be deleted. Any critical work file will typically be kept open by the application just so the user is unable to delete the file.

NOTE   *CleanReg doesn't see hidden files or directories. Be careful that you don't mistake a file that is hidden—one that has the hidden attribute—with a file that is truly missing. In a command-prompt window, you can determine a file's attributes with the* attrib *command. In Windows, use Explorer's options to turn on the display of files with the hidden attribute on.*

When Matt Pietrek wrote CleanReg, he wisely decided not to check for files on floppy drives or other drives with removable media, such as CD-ROM drives. CleanReg does check for files on currently accessible network drives. However, be careful of the case where a CD-ROM is accessed over a network.

To use or make changes to Pietrek's program, download the original source from Microsoft and compile it, or see if you can find an executable version of CleanReg on the Internet.

RegView

Microsoft offers a nifty little program named RegView on the site `ftp://ftp.microsoft.com/Softlib/MSLFILES`. This program works somewhat like the Registry Editor; however, the program provided by Microsoft does not allow modification. Only viewing registry items is allowed.

The program is supplied in source code format only. To use it, you must have Visual C++ to build the executable files.

RegView is a Shell Name Space Extension program. That is, once installed, the program will appear in Explorer's Address bar as a selection. Figure 8.11 shows just how RegView is invoked.

FIGURE 8.11

Registry View (RegView's nice friendly name) may be started by simply selecting it in Explorer's Address drop-down list.

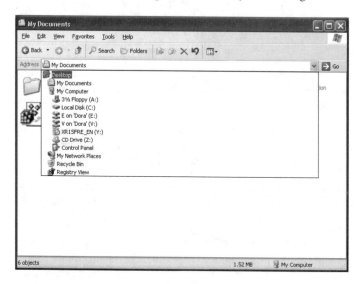

Now Microsoft was also thoughtful in that when RegView is created, an icon is added to the Desktop. Now we all realize that the Windows Desktop is a rather barren place, so this does add a bit of color.

NOTE   *For fun, right-click on the Desktop's Registry View icon. Hum, no properties selection for this one! This is the way that Shell Name Space Extensions work.*

If you start Windows Explorer and select Registry View, you can click through the hierarchy of any of the registry hives. For example, `HKEY_LOCAL_MACHINE` has the following object:

    HKEY_LOCAL_MACHINE\HARDWARE\DESCRIPTION\System

If you click through the `HKEY_LOCAL_MACHINE` hive, you eventually get to `System`, as shown in Figure 8.12.

FIGURE 8.12

Registry View shows the current subkey. `System` has three keys and eight data values.

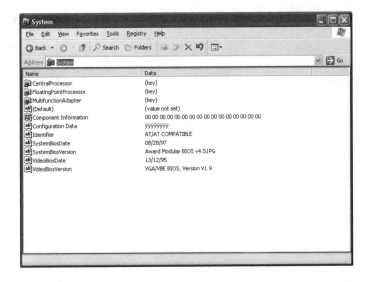

To find out where you are in the registry hierarchy, you must go back to Explorer's Address bar. Open the drop-down list to see the entire path to where you are. You can move up the path by selecting any point in the drop-down list along that path.

The Registry View program has the minimum number of interfaces needed to make it work as a multilevel name space extension. (This multilevel functionality is shown in Figure 8.13.)

NOTE   *RegView is copyright by Microsoft, so don't even think about enhancing and then redistributing it without their permission.*

FIGURE 8.13

Explorer's Address bar shows all levels above the currently displayed one. You can move up to `DESCRIPTION`, `HARDWARE`, or `HKEY_LOCAL_MACHINE` with a single click on the address tree.

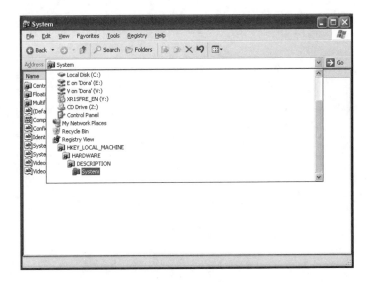

Chapter 9

Recovering from Disaster, or Making the Best of a Bad Situation

DISASTER USUALLY STRIKES WHEN least expected. There it is, usually late at night, just when things are sailing smoothly along, and whammo! A server fails, maybe with an infamous "blue screen of death." (When a system error occurs in Windows that is so severe that the operating system cannot continue, it displays a blue screen with white characters telling you about the error.)

Disaster can also strike when Windows XP boots. Maybe the system starts fine, then mysteriously crashes in any of a thousand ways after a few minutes, a few hours, or even a few days. On the other hand, maybe, just maybe, out of the blue something happens and the system becomes unstable.

In this chapter, we'll look at how to survive when disaster strikes. Rather than panic, I'll show you how to systematically discover the problem and get your system up and running again. I'll cover the following topics:

◆ Deciding whether to repair or replace the operating system

◆ A step-by-step approach to stabilizing your system

◆ Analyzing the problem

◆ Common problems and how to fix them

◆ Manually removing registry entries

When Failure Strikes

One server on my network used to crash on a regular basis. It was easy to blame the operating system or applications. I never could figure out exactly why it crashed, but I do know that when I upgraded the system with a new CPU, motherboard, and memory, those mysterious system crashes became a thing of the past. It is now common for the server to run for weeks without a single problem.

NOTE   *"Bad" memory is probably the single most common problem with computers. Memory failures can (and do) masquerade as many different faults, and they can be very difficult to troubleshoot. Consider using the best memory available and keeping spare memory on hand to swap into an unreliable computer.*

Sometimes you have to figure out what happened. Maybe a hardware problem precipitated the failure. Or perhaps a failing hard drive with a bad sector in an infrequently used section of a system file caused the problem. Maybe, and this one is nasty, there's a bad spot in the registry. When disaster strikes, a methodical approach to recovery is the only reasonable path to follow. You can try the shotgun technique: replace things randomly until something fixes the problem. Or you can use a more logical technique: analyze the problem and apply fixes in a systematic method. I vote for the latter; I've tried shotgun type repairs, and they are so difficult to do that in the end, only the most inexperienced user will try to fix a problem using such a random technique.

WARNING   *Have I already said this? Back up your registry before doing anything described in this chapter. Manually removing items from a registry is perhaps the easiest way to trash everything! Back up, back up, and back up again.*

NOTE   *Remember to check the Event Viewer. The event log can contain valuable information about failures of both applications and system components!*

If I haven't mentioned it, read Chapter 8, "Getting Rid of the Unwanted," as well. Sometimes the unwanted is the root cause of all of our problems.

WHAT FAILS MOST OFTEN?

The things that cause serious problems with Windows XP registries and installations are:

◆ Removing software without using the software's "uninstall" program. If you don't use the uninstall program, entries are left in the registry that point to files that are no longer there.

◆ Improperly or incompletely installed software. Again, the problem is often due to insufficient disk space for the software's files, or an installation program that fails. In this case, the installation program probably updated the registry before the file copy process had completed; it then failed to undo the registry update after the file copy process failed.

◆ Damaged software files, caused by installing either the wrong software or wrong software version into a directory where an existing software program or version exists. Some problems arise when software versions become mixed, or when the installation process cannot properly update one or more files.

To Repair or to Replace?

The Windows XP installation program allows you to repair a broken installation. This is nice. This is good. This can be dangerous, too.

Generally, the repair options in the Windows XP installation program simply allow you to replace the Windows system files with fresh copies from the distribution media. These system files are the same files installed at the original installation. Now how can that be bad? Well, if you have installed a service pack, such as Service Pack 4, you may find that when you refresh the Windows installation, part of your service pack goes away. However, some things, like registry entries, won't go anywhere. This can result in some rather strange problems, to say the least. Sometimes it becomes a catch-22 situation. A service pack is installed, so you can't refresh the Windows installation; you can't remove the service pack (most service packs have an uninstall process) because the system won't run; and if you force a refresh of the system files, the system won't run to allow you to install the service pack. Oops, you're stuck, again.

NOTE *Catch-22 is the title of a popular book by Joseph Heller. This term describes a situation in which two actions are mutually dependent and cannot be done separately. However, they can't be done at the same time, either. Like how you can't reinstall the Windows XP system files and the service pack at the same time, although to run Windows XP, you might need the service pack.*

What do you do? Try refreshing the Windows XP installation using the repair options in the installation program. Immediately after that, install the same or a higher-level service pack as was installed originally on the system. That should refresh the Windows XP installation and the service pack installation. Of course, if you refresh the installation and the system won't run afterwards, you do have a problem; it may be time to reinstall Windows XP from scratch.

NOTE *At least one supplier of Windows backup and restore software noted the following scenario and problem: Let's say you have a system for which the system drive has totally failed. You replace the drive and install a minimum copy of Windows XP to run the restore program to recover the original disk's contents from backup. The original system included a service pack. You will probably find that you can't complete the restore. The problem is that the minimum copy of Windows XP must have the same service pack installed as the original copy of Windows XP; otherwise, you are restoring mismatched files into the system directories.*

Stabilizing the System

Once a disaster has occurred, the first step is to stabilize the system. It is important that you prevent further problems or damage. After stabilizing the system, it will be much easier to fix the problem and get everything performing at its best.

Consider stabilization a systematic analysis. Start with the first step, discussed next. Can you do what this step calls for? If not, go to step 2. If so, does the system work right? If not, go back through step 1 and see if any of the hints and suggestions might apply to your system. I can't list every possible problem or fix, but I'll try to cover the most common ones here in this chapter.

When this chapter doesn't help, consider Microsoft's Internet news server at `msnews.microsoft.com`. This server is accessible using one of the Microsoft news programs, such as Outlook Express or Microsoft New, or an Internet news program, such as Agent from Forte or any of the other Internet news programs available to users.

A few of the newsgroups to check on `msnews.microsoft.com` include (in most cases, you may substitute `windowsnt`, or `win2000` for `windowsxp` to access newsgroups pertaining to those operating system versions):

◆ `microsoft.public.windowsxp.accessibility`

◆ `microsoft.public.windowsxp.basics`

◆ `microsoft.public.windowsxp.customize`

◆ `microsoft.public.windowsxp.device_driver.dev`

◆ `microsoft.public.windowsxp.embedded.techpreview`

◆ `microsoft.public.windowsxp.games`

◆ `microsoft.public.windowsxp.general`

◆ `microsoft.public.windowsxp.hardware`

◆ `microsoft.public.windowsxp.help_and_support`

◆ `microsoft.public.windowsxp.messenger`

◆ `microsoft.public.windowsxp.music`

◆ `microsoft.public.windowsxp.network_web`

◆ `microsoft.public.windowsxp.newusers`

◆ `microsoft.public.windowsxp.perform_maintain`

◆ `microsoft.public.windowsxp.photos`

◆ `microsoft.public.windowsxp.print_fax`

◆ `microsoft.public.windowsxp.security_admin`

◆ `microsoft.public.windowsxp.setup_deployment`

◆ `microsoft.public.windowsxp.video`

◆ `microsoft.public.windowsxp.winlogo`

◆ `microsoft.public.windowsxp.work_remotely`

NOTE *Things change. The above list of newsgroups was current when this chapter was written, but most likely Microsoft has since added new newsgroups to their site! Best bet: get to the site and review all the newsgroups; then subscribe to those that are relevant to your problem!*

Posting a query in one of these newsgroups will certainly create some response. Whether the respondents are able to assist you is something that you won't know until you try. I've posted a number of questions over the years; I've gotten help about half the time, and usually when I did not receive a useful reply, I did get the feeling that people on the newsgroup had at least tried to assist with a solution.

WARNING   *Be careful not to lose your Last Known Good configuration. When Windows XP boots successfully, it overwrites the Last Known Good configuration with the current configuration. This could cause great gnashing of teeth later on. Try very hard to back up the registry and the operating system if possible (discussed next).*

Step 1: Can You Boot into a Spare Operating System?

Can you boot the system into a different operating system or a different copy of Windows XP? If not, go to step 2.

NOTE   *Microsoft's new "product authorization" introduces a new wrinkle in the process of installing a second copy of the operating system. You have 30 days from the installation of Windows XP to authorize it, or it stops working. There are no easy workarounds for installing two copies without seeking two product authorizations. However, since the hardware will be identical in both authorizations, I suspect that Microsoft won't object.*

By booting into a different operating system or a different copy of Windows XP, you will possibly be able to preserve (back up) the existing registry and hard drives and even do tests on the system's hardware. Once you've booted and are running, *back up immediately.*

WARNING   *When backing up, do not back up to existing backup tapes. Use new tapes so that you do not overwrite any existing backups. There is a very high probability that you will be making a backup of information that is not good, while any existing backup (especially older backups) may have valid copies that you will have to restore later. If necessary, go out and buy a new set of backup tapes.*

Once the computer boots another copy of the operating system, do the following:

1. Back up the registry files using the techniques described in Chapter 2. Copy the files from the copy of Windows XP that failed. You will find this copy of the registry in the installation directory, `C:\Windows\System32\Config`, of the failed Windows XP installation. Any process used to back up this directory and its files will be useful. Copy the directory to removable media, such as a Zip drive or a network drive. Using diskettes is a possibility, although the size of many registry files (a total of 30 or more megabytes) will necessitate the use of many diskettes.

2. Back up the entire system. Use the booted operating system's backup program to create a copy of the system exactly as it was when it failed. Don't delete anything, don't rename anything, and don't change anything. Get a backup—just in case you are wrong about the problem and need to restore everything to the state that it was in when it failed. More than one time, I've hacked about on a failing system only to realize after I've done considerable damage that the

problem is somewhere else. When this happens, it is nice to be able to restore the drive to undo your own self-induced damage.

3. Back up any drives used to hold components and applications. This generally means doing a complete backup of all the system's hard drives.

4. Run diagnostic software on the computer. Check the drives fully, including a surface (read) scan if possible, and check the memory and CPU before going any further. Sometimes a system will boot another operating system even when there is a hardware failure—perhaps the other operating system doesn't have any critical components in the area of memory that is bad. (Windows XP pushes the hardware very hard, while earlier versions of Windows are less demanding on the system and memory.) If you suspect bad memory, many computers will allow you to set, in the BIOS, the maximum amount of memory allowed. However, if the bad memory is in the first few megabytes, it is unlikely that there will be enough memory to boot the system. In this case, swapping the bad RAM with good units can help diagnose the problem.

NOTE   *Diagnostic software? Where does one get diagnostic software? There are several good commercial test programs, such as Q&A Plus, that test computer hardware. These programs let you determine if the system is performing correctly. Be careful with any diagnostic software, especially when checking storage media. Some diagnostic program functions may be destructive to data on drives. Be sure to follow all program instructions carefully and heed all warnings.*

Step 2: Can You Boot the System in Normal Mode?

If you can boot the system in its normal mode, go to step 3. Otherwise, read on.

Windows XP has a different bootup manager than Windows NT 4. Differences include only one selection for the initial boot (the option to boot to a VGA mode has been moved) for each installed copy of Windows XP. Figure 9.1 shows the Windows XP boot menu. Compare this menu with the Windows 2000 boot menu (shown in Figure 9.2) and the Windows NT 4 boot menu (shown in Figure 9.3) and note the subtle changes made.

TIP   *In each menu where there is an automatic selection, you will see the message, "Seconds until highlighted choice will be started automatically," and a countdown timer. The countdown timer stops whenever an arrow key (either up or down) is pressed. Even if there is only one selection, pressing an arrow key still stops the timer, giving you time to read the menu's text.*

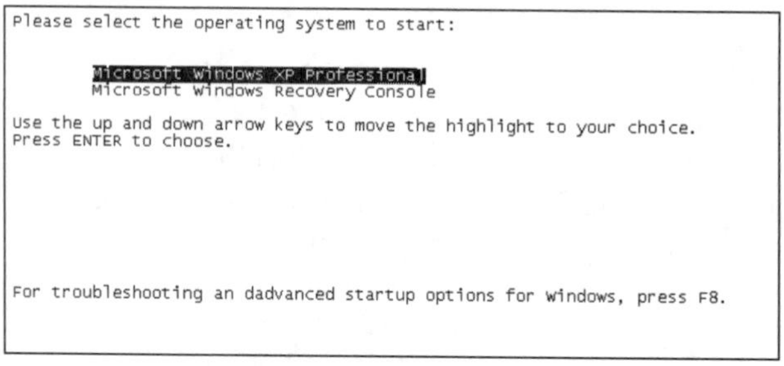

FIGURE 9.1

The Windows XP boot menu is almost the same as the boot screen found in Windows 2000. Booting problems require pressing F8 to get to the debugging screen.

FIGURE 9.2

The Windows 2000 boot menu allows you to boot in one mode only. The only visible changes for Windows XP are small text edits.

```
Please select the operating system to start:

    Microsoft Windows 2000 Server
    Microsoft Windows 2000 Server Backup Install
    Windows NT Server 4.00 DARK_STAR
    Windows NT Server 4.00 DARK_STAR [VGA mode]


Use ↑ and ↓ to move the highlight to your choice.
Press Enter to choose

Seconds until highlighted choice will be started automatically: 30




For trouble shooting and advanced options for Windows 2000, press F8.
```

FIGURE 9.3

The Windows NT 4 boot menu allows you to boot in VGA mode. Later versions of Windows take a more complex route to booting in a straight VGA mode.

```
OS Loader V4.00

Please select the operating system to start:


    Windows NT Workstation Version 4.00
    Windows NT Workstation Version 4.00 [VGA mode]
    Microsoft Windows 98

Use ↑ and ↓ to move the highlight to your choice.
Press Enter to choose

Seconds until highlighted choice will be started automatically: 30
```

If you have a problem and you can boot to the boot menu, you can press F8 and set debugging modes as appropriate (see Figure 9.4).

FIGURE 9.4

The Windows XP Advanced Options menu allows you to choose how Windows will boot.

```
For troubleshooting and advanced startup options for windows, press F8.

windows Advanced Options Menu
Please select an option:


    Safe Mode
    Safe Mode with Networking
    Safe Mode with Command Prompt

    Enable Boot Logging
    Enable VGA Mode
    Last Known Good Configuration (your most recent setting that worked)
    Directory Services Restore Mode (windows domain controllers only)
    Debugging Mode

    Start Windows Normally
    Reboot
    Return to OS Choices Menu


Use the up and down arrow keys to move the highlight to your choice.
```

The Advanced Options menu has 10 choices:

Safe Mode   This mode starts the system with a minimal set of files and drivers. Drivers loaded include only mouse, monitor, keyboard, mass storage, base video, and default system services. There is no network support in this version of Safe mode.

Safe Mode with Networking   This mode adds network support to the standard Safe mode. This is useful when debugging tools reside on a network drive, or when you are confident that there are no networking problems.

Safe Mode with Command Prompt   With the command-prompt mode, the same configuration is loaded as with Safe mode, but instead of starting the GUI, Windows displays a command prompt. Users who are familiar with the command prompt may find this mode more stable and easier to use.

Enable Boot Logging   Using boot logging allows you to determine which drivers and other objects are loaded when Windows XP boots. Listing 9.1 shows part of a typical boot log. The boot log is stored in `%SystemRoot%\ntbtlog.txt`. Use Notepad to display this file, which typically has several hundred entries.

Enable VGA Mode   This starts Windows XP using the default VGA driver, in 640 × 480, 256-color mode. This driver is compatible with all display adapters supported by Windows XP. The default VGA driver is not an optimal driver. It lacks support for higher resolutions, higher color depth, and any high-performance features of the display adapter. However, the default driver will usually work regardless of the hardware installed.

Last Known Good Configuration   This starts Windows using the Last Known Good configuration. `HKEY_LOCAL_MACHINE\System\Select\LastKnownGood` is a pointer to the Last Known Good configuration. This value contains an index to one of the `ControlSetnnn` subkeys. Use the Last Known Good configuration when a bad configuration change (such as improperly adding new hardware) happens. The Last Known Good configuration will not help when system configuration files are missing or damaged.

Directory Services Restore Mode (Windows 2000 or Windows .NET Server edition domain controllers only):   Use this option to restore the Active Directory. The Directory Services Restore Mode is usable on a domain controller, not on Windows XP (Home Edition and Professional) or Windows .NET Server member servers.

Debugging Mode   This mode sends status messages to the default communications port, which is COM1. Connect a terminal or other serial device to the communications port, and configure the device correctly.

Start Windows Normally   This mode essentially is the same boot as if you had not selected advanced startup options.

Reboot   To restart from scratch (perhaps because a device was not ready and that problem has been resolved) by rebooting the computer, select this option.

LISTING 9.1: EXCERPTS FROM A TYPICAL NTBTLOG.TXT BOOT LOG FILE

```
Microsoft (R) Windows (R) "codename" Whistler Version 5.1 (Build 3505)
10 28 2001 19:18:17.500
Loaded driver \WINDOWS\System32\ntoskrnl.exe
Loaded driver \WINDOWS\System32\hal.dll
Loaded driver \WINDOWS\System32\KDCOM.DLL
```

```
Loaded driver \WINDOWS\System32\BOOTVID.dll
Loaded driver pci.sys
Loaded driver isapnp.sys
Loaded driver intelide.sys
Loaded driver \WINDOWS\System32\DRIVERS\PCIIDEX.SYS
Loaded driver MountMgr.sys
Loaded driver ftdisk.sys
Loaded driver \WINDOWS\System32\DRIVERS\WMILIB.SYS
Loaded driver dmload.sys
Loaded driver dmio.sys
Loaded driver PartMgr.sys
Loaded driver VolSnap.sys
Loaded driver atapi.sys
Loaded driver disk.sys
Loaded driver \WINDOWS\System32\DRIVERS\CLASSPNP.SYS
Loaded driver Dfs.sys
Loaded driver Fastfat.sys
Loaded driver KSecDD.sys
Loaded driver NDIS.sys
Loaded driver Mup.sys
Loaded driver \SystemRoot\System32\DRIVERS\audstub.sys
Loaded driver \SystemRoot\System32\DRIVERS\rasl2tp.sys
Loaded driver \SystemRoot\System32\DRIVERS\ndistapi.sys
Loaded driver \SystemRoot\System32\DRIVERS\ndiswan.sys
Loaded driver \SystemRoot\System32\DRIVERS\raspppoe.sys
Loaded driver \SystemRoot\System32\DRIVERS\raspptp.sys
Loaded driver \SystemRoot\System32\DRIVERS\ptilink.sys
Loaded driver \SystemRoot\System32\DRIVERS\raspti.sys
Loaded driver \SystemRoot\System32\DRIVERS\cdrom.sys
Loaded driver \SystemRoot\System32\DRIVERS\redbook.sys
Loaded driver \SystemRoot\System32\DRIVERS\usbuhci.sys
Loaded driver \SystemRoot\System32\DRIVERS\mgaum.sys
Loaded driver \SystemRoot\System32\DRIVERS\el90xnd5.sys
Loaded driver \SystemRoot\System32\DRIVERS\rdpdr.sys
Loaded driver \SystemRoot\System32\DRIVERS\termdd.sys
Loaded driver \SystemRoot\System32\DRIVERS\kbdclass.sys
Loaded driver \SystemRoot\System32\DRIVERS\mouclass.sys
Loaded driver \SystemRoot\System32\DRIVERS\swenum.sys
Loaded driver \SystemRoot\System32\DRIVERS\update.sys
Loaded driver \SystemRoot\System32\DRIVERS\i8042prt.sys
Loaded driver \SystemRoot\System32\DRIVERS\parport.sys
Loaded driver \SystemRoot\System32\DRIVERS\serial.sys
Loaded driver \SystemRoot\System32\DRIVERS\serenum.sys
Loaded driver \SystemRoot\System32\DRIVERS\fdc.sys
Loaded driver \SystemRoot\System32\Drivers\NDProxy.SYS
Did not load driver \SystemRoot\System32\Drivers\NDProxy.SYS
Loaded driver \SystemRoot\System32\DRIVERS\usbhub.sys
```

SAFE MODE

When you experience problems with your Windows XP system, try booting in the Safe mode first. This is the default, and often the most useful, debugging mode. Safe mode is much like Windows 95/98/Me's Safe mode, in that only a minimum system is loaded.

There are three Safe modes in Windows XP. First, there's Safe mode with no networking (the default). This mode loads only the basic files and drivers: the base video (VGA for most systems), basic mouse, monitor, services, and storage.

The next level of Safe mode is Safe mode with networking. In this mode, drivers and files loaded are still the same basic ones loaded with Safe mode without networking. However, Windows XP attempts to load the networking support as well. Using Safe mode with networking allows you to connect to other computers if necessary.

Safe mode with command prompt does not start the Desktop, Start menu, or Taskbar. Instead, you're presented with a command prompt to work from. This final mode is similar to the Recovery Console described in Chapter 2.

Try Safe mode without networking first; if that works, and you need networking, try Safe mode with networking. If Safe mode without networking fails, try Safe mode with command prompt. If Safe mode with command prompt fails, then it will be necessary to fall back to the Recovery Console.

USING THE LAST KNOWN GOOD CONFIGURATION

To use the Last Known Good Configuration menu, choose it from the Advanced Options menu shown earlier in Figure 9.4 and press Enter. The system will continue the boot by displaying the initial boot menu (with the bottom line indicating the selected boot option). Use the arrow keys and press Enter to boot the desired version of the operating system.

Once the system starts, the boot process displays the Hardware Profile/Configuration Recovery menu (shown in Figure 9.5). A Windows XP installation can have multiple hardware configurations. (The most common applications for multiple configurations are a notebook computer, a computer with PCMCIA, or PC, cards, or an active USB or IR bus configuration.) Those of us with standard PC configurations, without easily removable hardware, will have only a single hardware profile (by default named Profile 1), and anyone with removable hardware should have a profile for each configuration that may be used.

FIGURE 9.5

Use the Hardware Profile/Configuration Recovery menu to select the hardware profile and Last Known Good configuration.

```
        Hardware Profile/Configuration Recovery Menu

This menu allow syou to select a hardware profile
to be used when Windows is started.

If you system is not starting correctly, then you may switch to a
previous system configuration, which may overcome startup problems.
IMPORTANT: System configuration changes made since the last successful
startup will be discarded.

    Profile 1
    Backup Profile




Use the up and down arrow keys to move the highlight
to selection you want, then press ENTER.
Tow switch to the Last Known Good configuration, press 'L'.
To Exit this menu and restart your computer, press F3.

Seconds until highlighted choice will be started automatically: 30
```

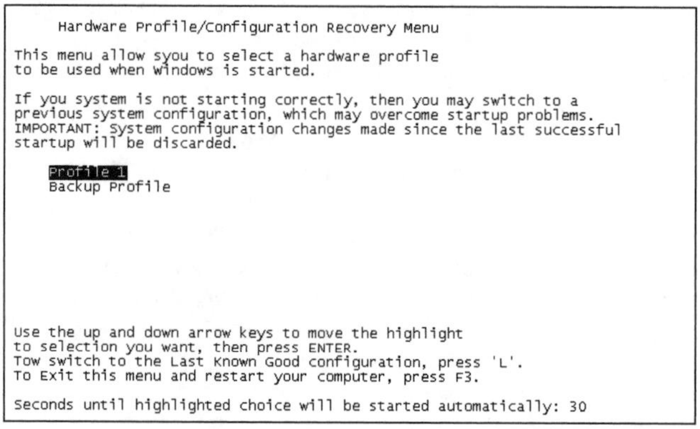

NOTE *It has been suggested that users set their profiles on all machines to indicate that their computers are portable computers with unknown docking states. This is supposed to relax the product authorization requirements substantially, allowing more flexibility in how to manage hardware.*

If it is necessary to change to the default configuration, press D, which turns off the Last Known Good selection. You can re-enable the Last Known Good selection by pressing the L key.

For systems with multiple hardware configurations, select the boot configuration from the list. For a system with one default configuration, the configuration name is Profile 1, and it is automatically selected for you.

The Profile 1 entry, by the way, comes from the System applet in the Control Panel. In that applet, on the Hardware tab, click the Hardware Profiles button to display the dialog box for configuring hardware profiles (shown in Figure 9.6). In this dialog box, you can also set the time delay before taking the default selection. Though many users will have only one hardware configuration, anyone using Windows XP on a dockable portable platform will certainly have at least two profiles, one for when docked, one for when not.

FIGURE 9.6

Configure hardware profiles in the Hardware Profiles dialog box. This is the same dialog box that is found in Windows 2000.

When you need to change to a configuration other than the default one, you must select this configuration using the up and down arrow keys. After you select the Last Known Good configuration (and hardware profile, if necessary), you still have to press Enter to continue the boot process. The boot process for Windows waits indefinitely until Enter is pressed.

WARNING *Remember, once the Last Known Good configuration is booted, it becomes the current configuration (the current control set), and the current configuration that would have been booted is discarded. Anything installed after the previous boot will be lost.*

If you manage to boot the Last Known Good configuration, consider yourself lucky; the system should be stable, although it probably will be missing whatever software and hardware you installed during the last session. However, this should be only a minor problem. In this case, consider everything installed during the last session. Think very carefully as to whether it makes sense to reinstall the same item a second time. Consider setting up a test machine, or another installation of Windows XP, to install the system that caused the problems, and see if this other installation also fails.

If you are successful in using the Last Known Good configuration to boot, it usually will be safe to delete the application's files and directories, because the registry should not have any entries for this application. However, having a backup is vital at this stage.

NOTE *Instead of deleting files and directories, do this: Use either Explorer or the* move *command at a command prompt to rename the directory. I usually prefix the original directory with* delete_, *just to remind me which directory to delete. Then, do nothing for a week or so. If the system displays no odd behavior, back up the directory and delete it from the drive. Did you notice what I said? I said back up the directory before deleting it. Again, a backup is very good insurance.*

CONTROL SETS, CONTROL SETS, AND MORE CONTROL SETS

After booting using the Last Known Good configuration option, your registry "grows" a new control set. This control set is numbered one higher than the currently known highest control set. For example, if your system has ControlSet001 and ControlSet002, a new control set called ControlSet003 will also be created. In this situation, one control set is the one that failed, one is the current control set, and one is the Last Known Good configuration. After booting my system, the Last Known Good configuration had the following control sets:

ControlSet001 Marked as the control set that failed. This control set would have been booted if the Last Known Good configuration had not been chosen.

ControlSet002 Marked as the Last Known Good control set. This control set will be booted if the Last Known Good configuration is selected at the next boot.

ControlSet003 Marked as the current control set—the control set used to boot the system. Prior to booting, this control set was marked as Last Known Good.

Step 3: Does the System Run without Crashing?

Say the system boots in normal mode; or by following step 2, you have the system booted in Safe mode or using the Last Known Good configuration. Now, does the system run without crashing? If yes, go to step 4. Otherwise, read on.

First, since the system boots, it is probably almost right. But "almost" covers a really wide territory. Does the system boot, but then crash almost immediately? Or does the crash come sometime later? Can you cause it to crash by running an application or performing a specific task? Does the crash seem to happen at random times, or does there seem to be some rhyme and reason to the crash? We're in detective mode now.

THE SYSTEM BOOTS, THEN CRASHES ALMOST IMMEDIATELY

This situation is virtually as bad as a system that won't boot. Possibly the cause of the crash is something that is starting up when the system starts. Try this: Start the system, but don't log on. Just sit and watch for at least twice as long as it normally takes to crash. Does it crash? If it does, this is probably due to some system component. You are probably stuck with little or no hope except to reinstall or to restore from a backup.

If the system doesn't crash immediately, the crash is probably due to something that the user is loading. Log on as another user. Does it crash? If it does, the problem is probably something that is common to all users. Check out the common `Startup` directory (`%SystemRoot%\Profiles\All Users\Start Menu\Programs\Startup` or `%SystemDrive%\Documents and Settings\All Users\Start Menu\Programs\Startup`) and clean it out. Try starting the system again. If it fails again, you are probably stuck with either a restore or a reinstallation.

If the system only crashes when you log on as a particular user, you may be saved yet. Check the failing user's Programs ➢ Startup directory in the Start menu. Check all `Programs\Startup` directories for that matter, cleaning out each one; put anything contained in the `Startup` directories into temporary directories. Once you have cleaned out the `Startup` directories, log on again as the user who causes the system to fail.

If the system doesn't fail once you've cleaned out a user's `Startup` directory or the `Startup` directory for all users (you're almost home free now), check the entries that were in the `Startup` directory. Consider manually starting each one; then wait for a reasonable period to see if the system fails or not. This will almost certainly help localize the problem to a single entry in the `Startup` directory.

How do you get to the `Startup` directory if the system keeps failing? Again, you can rely on your old friend, the dual-boot. (You did create a dual-boot system as I described in Chapter 2, right?) Boot the backup operating system and use it to allow you to clear out the `Startup` directories. Just make sure you are deleting the *correct* `Startup` directories.

Some additional locations that items may run from include:

- HKEY_LOCAL_MACHINE\Software\Microsoft\Windows\CurrentVersion\Run

- HKEY_LOCAL_MACHINE\Software\Microsoft\Windows\CurrentVersion\RunOnce

- HKEY_LOCAL_MACHINE\Software\Microsoft\Windows\CurrentVersion\RunOnceEx

- HKEY_LOCAL_MACHINE\Software\Microsoft\Windows\CurrentVersion\RunServices

- HKEY_LOCAL_MACHINE\Software\Microsoft\Windows\CurrentVersion\RunServicesOnce

- HKEY_LOCAL_MACHINE\Software\Microsoft\Windows NT\CurrentVersion\Winlogon\Userinit

- HKEY_CURRENT_USER\Software\Microsoft\Windows\CurrentVersion\Run

- HKEY_CURRENT_USER\Software\Microsoft\Windows\CurrentVersion\RunOnce

- HKEY_CURRENT_USER\Software\Microsoft\Windows\CurrentVersion\RunOnceEx

- HKEY_CURRENT_USER\Software\Microsoft\Windows\CurrentVersion\RunServices

- HKEY_CURRENT_USER\Software\Microsoft\Windows\CurrentVersion\RunServicesOnce

- HKEY_CURRENT_USER\Software\Microsoft\Windows NT\CurrentVersion\Windows\Run

- HKEY_CURRENT_USER\Software\Microsoft\Windows NT\CurrentVersion\Windows\Load

THE CRASH COMES SOMETIME LATER

How much later? Minutes, hours, or days? A crash that comes many hours or days later is probably not related to the registry. A crash that happens a few minutes later is almost identical to the above situation where the crash is virtually immediate. Nevertheless, a crash that happens some minutes or even an hour later could easily be a registry entry gone awry. How does this happen? When Windows XP starts, it starts up many services and devices. Some services are slow to start and other services start but then spend some time initializing.

Try this: In either `%SystemRoot%\Profiles\All Users\Start Menu\Programs\Startup` or `%SystemDrive%\Documents and Settings\All Users\Start Menu\Programs\Startup` (depending on whether the current installation is an upgrade or a clean installation), put in a link to `taskmgr.exe`. This launches the Windows XP Task Manager application. Look at what Task Manager is saying. Sort the entries in the Processes tab by CPU usage. Do you see an application that is jumping up in CPU utilization just before the system crashes? This may be the problem.

OK, let's say you have a suspect. The Task Manager shows a big chunk of CPU utilized by a particular application. Let's call this application `badapp.exe`. (Great name, isn't it?) What do you do? First, it would be nice to simply tell Windows XP not to load or execute `badapp.exe`. However, it may be virtually impossible to do that, since this application may be launched by a registry entry. Remember, there are six places in the registry that function much like the various `Programs\Startup` directories.

What is the next best thing? If you have nothing to lose, consider temporarily renaming the file. Boot into your backup operating system and use it to rename the file, giving it a new temporary filename. I would add the prefix `bad_` to the original filename, making it easy to find later. Just make sure you are renaming the *correct* file.

After renaming the file, restart the original or backup Windows XP installation. You should expect to see at least one message informing you that the file you renamed can't be found, and you can *probably* ignore this. Probably, but not always. If the file is a necessary part of the operating system, Windows XP probably won't start. Arrgggg! Such is life; in this case, an operating system restoration or repair is the only solution.

CAN YOU CAUSE THE SYSTEM TO CRASH?

Sometimes the system will remain stable until you do a specific thing. In this case, there are two possible courses of action. If the application worked at one time and just recently started to fail, something has happened either to the application's files or to the application's registry entries. In either case, a good course of action is to simply try reinstalling the application.

If possible, try removing the application before doing the reinstallation; be sure to back up any user data files first, though. Sometimes installation programs don't write over certain files that already exist.

If the application never worked on your system, again, there is but one alternative: uninstall the application, posthaste. Sadly, some applications are poorly written and don't have an uninstall program. With due caution (make backups), rename the application's directory to something you'll notice, so that in a week or so, if the system remains stable, you can delete the directory.

After renaming the application's directory, restart the system and see if there is any instability. If things are stable after a day or two, use a registry cleanup tool such as RegClean, CleanReg, or Reg-Maid to extract any registry entries for this application. My choice would be to use CleanReg (see Chapter 8), because CleanReg will check more than just the OLE entries.

THE CRASH HAPPENS AT A SPECIFIC TIME OR DATE

If the system always seems to crash after a specific time, check to make sure that there are no time-based applications or commands that run. (The Windows XP AT command is a suspect here.) What other things happen at the time? Is the time absolute or relative to boot? If absolute, suspect that something is being started at the specific time or shortly before. If relative, look for something that is being started with the system bootup, but maybe taking a very long time to initialize because it fails. Note that some systems are timing interdependent, which means that process A must start after process B. Again, beware of any catch-22 situations where two processes are mutually dependent.

Step 4: Do the System Components and Subsystems Run Okay?

If you find that your system will run indefinitely without failing, you may have good reason to suspect that an installed application is the problem. You randomly run applications, and eventually something fails.

At this point, you say, "*Voila!* I've found the problem." Alas, it is not that simple. You may find the problem's trigger, but the odds are high that the problem itself is somewhere else.

Narrow down interdependencies between applications by running only one at a time. Start Windows XP; then start and use one application. (This works well for most applications, but when you have two applications designed to work together, this may not be a viable way to troubleshoot the problem.)

Review your list of recently installed applications. Anything installed just before the system became unstable should be suspect. If an application has never worked on your system, again there is but one alternative: uninstall the application if possible.

NOTE   *A possible test is to create a second, clean installation of Windows XP and install the suspect application under the second copy of the operating system. That is a good indicator as to whether the application can run under Windows XP without problems. Using a clean installation of Windows XP will help minimize unwanted interaction between two applications.*

If your application doesn't have an uninstall program, make a backup and rename the application's directory. Rename the directory to something you'll notice, so that in a week or so, if the system remains stable, you can delete the directory.

After renaming the application's directory, restart the system and see if there is any instability. If things are stable after a day or two, use a registry cleanup tool such as RegClean, CleanReg, or RegMaid to extract any registry entries for this application. My choice would be to use CleanReg (see Chapter 8), because CleanReg will check more than just the OLE entries.

Step 5: Do Installed Applications Run Okay?

If installed applications run okay, go to step 6. Otherwise, read on.

What is happening? Probably something has corrupted the registry, or there is a hardware problem. First, back up the system fully. Then, run sufficient diagnostics to rule out any hardware problems. Finally, try restoring the registry. Start with the most recent backup—not the one you made before running diagnostics, but the most recent regularly scheduled backup. If the most recent backup doesn't solve the problem, continue working back through older backups to see if one of them will restore system stability.

Be aware that by going back through older backups, you only want to restore system files and the registry—for example, you do not want to restore user files.

Step 6: Is the System Generally Stable?

If the system is generally stable, go to step 7. Otherwise, read on.

A system that is unstable—and the instability cannot be traced to a specific application or component—usually points to a hardware problem. In this situation, analysis of the failures is important. These steps may help in diagnosing and fixing the problem:

◆ Run all possible hardware checks and diagnostics.

◆ Swap out whatever hardware parts may be replaced easily.

◆ Install and run a second copy of Windows XP with all the software and components that the failing system uses.

◆ Reinstall (repair) the failing installation of Windows XP.

◆ Reinstall the applications and optional components.

Step 7: Then What Is the Problem?

What is the problem, then, if the system starts, runs, and shuts down okay, and it doesn't crash or otherwise fail? There can be serious problems even when a system doesn't crash.

Take the situation in which the computer's hardware is simply overwhelmed by the demands that the operating system and applications place on it. Running some applications—for example, server components such as SMS, SQL Server, and Exchange Server—will quickly bring a substandard system to its knees.

TIP *Windows XP is even more demanding on hardware performance than earlier versions of Windows! Do not be surprised if, upon upgrading, you find that that the system doesn't run as well as it did prior to the upgrade.*

Use the Windows XP Performance Monitor to analyze system performance problems. This program is able to monitor all Windows XP performance indicators and indicators for a number of add-on components, such as Exchange Server, SQL Server, and others.

Analysis

First, do an analysis. Ask yourself what changed. Analysis of the problem means that you must determine why the computer worked yesterday but doesn't work today. For example, did you:

◆ Remove any software or system components?

◆ Clean up the drive, deleting files that you thought were unneeded?

◆ Install any new applications?

- Upgrade any applications?

- Upgrade the operating system (install any service packs?)

- Change system hardware?

- Experience a power failure or fluctuation?

To keep this chapter from becoming a general system failure analysis tool, I'll limit the effects of these items to what might happen to the registry.

Fixing Things Up

Next, decide if it is better to try to restore things to their original states either by reinstalling the component or application or by removing the offending item.

If there is a backup of the registry and the item in question, restoring to get the system back to a working state will probably be a good starting point. A stable system that is not having trouble is much easier to work on than a system that fails for unexplained reasons.

Once the system is restored, try the established method for removing the component, such as the Add/Remove Programs applet in the Control Panel or the application's uninstall program.

If there is no backup of the registry or component, a different tack must be taken. There are three possible avenues of attack:

- Try reinstalling the component. Typically, the installation program will restore any registry entries that are necessary for the component to run. Often, any customization done since the last installation will be lost, but that's life.

- Try finding an uninstall program. First, check the Add/Remove Programs applet in the Control Panel. If the component is listed, run uninstall from there. If the component is not listed, then check the component's directories. List all the executable (`.exe`) files. If there is one named `uninstall` or `remove`, this may be the program that you need. Don't forget to check the component's documentation regarding uninstall procedures, too.

- If there is no uninstall program, and the application must be removed, and you are going to have to do this manually, read on.

NOTE *Some components, especially those that are system components, make so many changes to the registry that it is impossible to remove them manually. This is especially true for components that have replaced already existing components, as in the case of upgrading to a new version. Though you can remove the entries for the component in question, you cannot restore the entries that the component has changed to their original state; this is especially true if you don't know their original state. Changes to the registry are usually not well logged, so there is typically little to tell you what has changed from time to time.*

Possible Problems, Quick Fixes

Some possible problems that cause the system to fail include those listed next. There are other problems too, so don't consider this list to be exhaustive.

An Application or a System Component Was Deleted

Say an application or a system component was deleted, perhaps in error. In this case, you would do the following:

◆ Try restoring the application's files. Running the application's installation program may be the best way to restore files, though many applications allow a single file to be restored from the distribution media. Be aware that some applications store the files on the distribution media in compressed format, so that the only way to restore a single file may be to reinstall the entire application.

◆ If that fails, try reinstalling the application. Reinstalling the application may be necessary when the application's files are not accessible on the distribution media. Be aware that some installation programs will delete user configurations and other items that either you or other users have modified since the original installation.

◆ If that fails, try removing the application with the application's uninstall program and then reinstalling the application. Some applications try to be smart and only reinstall those files and components that have not already been installed. But you may be trying to replace a file that you suspect has been corrupted or trying to restore registry entries, and the setup program doesn't realize that. It's just trying to save some time! (Some time-saver, huh?) In this case, it will probably be necessary to remove the original application (use its uninstall program, if there is one) before reinstalling it.

Another Application Has Overwritten an Application's Files

A new application has been installed, and this new installation has overwritten a previously installed application's files. Okay, this was probably an error, but you inadvertently installed the new application in the existing application's directory. This sometimes happens when the two applications have the same default installation directory. More often, we simply make a mistake and choose the wrong directory. Most application setup programs won't warn that the path already exists. Major bummer. When you suspect an application's files have been overwritten, here are some things to do:

◆ First, use the new application's uninstall program to uninstall the new application. If the new application has been used, and there are user document or data files, back up these files. However, get rid of that new application; you can reinstall it later. If there is no automated uninstall for the new application that you are removing and you must remove it manually, make certain to clean up as many of the new application's registry entries as possible. If you don't, and you reinstall the new application into a new directory, the setup program may not properly update the registry because it thinks the application has already been installed.

◆ Next, restore the application's files, perhaps from a known good backup. If that fails, try reinstalling the application from the original distribution media.

◆ If that fails, try removing the original application with the application uninstall program and then reinstalling the original application.

There Is an Error Reading the Application's Files

If there is an error reading the application's files, or the application crashes (faults) when executed, the application's files are probably damaged. What happened? There are several possibilities, and some of them are very ugly, by the way.

Maybe a user error caused one or more files to be overwritten. In this case, things don't look too bleak. Generally, a restore of the application's files will allow you to recover from this situation. Use a known good backup or reinstall from the distribution media.

Maybe another application or the operating system overwrote one or more files. This is rare, but it could happen. Check file dates to try to determine when the file overwrites occurred and see if there is a way to determine the culprit. Restore the correct files and consider setting permissions to read/execute for everyone but an administrative userID that you won't use except to manage these files. Using file system permissions allows you to get immediate notification when a file overwrite occurs.

WARNING Permissions are the Windows XP way to protect applications and system files from unauthorized changes. Always set permissions so that most users, other than those who must have higher-level permissions, have read/execute permissions only. Allowing all users to have write permissions for system and application executable files is not a very good move, no matter how trusted the users are. Eventually, someone will unintentionally overwrite something, delete a file, or do some other damage.

There Is an Error Reading the Drive

Well, actually this is the beginning of the end of the world.

First, run chkdsk and determine what Windows XP is able to do to fix the problem. Realize that when Windows XP fixes a file on an NTFS drive, it doesn't fix the file; it only makes the file readable. Windows XP is not able to recover the file's contents—if it could, everything would be all right. Instead, it gives a message that says file so-and-so has been repaired, which is somewhat misleading in this respect. However, you must do this repair to be able to replace the file with the right one.

When chkdsk runs, it will tell you if there are any damaged files. Windows XP is able to recover from minor problems and errors on the drive. Don't worry about these types of errors; it is not unusual to have a drive reported as having minor errors.

After running chkdsk, you must make a decision. A backup at this point can't hurt, but don't back up over any existing backups. Use a fresh tape, or whatever your backup program backs up to, and put this backup to the side. Here are the actions I'd take, in order of preference:

1. Replace the drive and restore to the new drive from the most recent known good backup. Since drives usually fail in stages, a little bit at a time, it is possible that your backups are not going to help as much as you'd like. This is a judgment call—if you are confident that a recent backup is okay, try it. If you are not confident of your more recent backups—often errors develop over time and contaminate all backups long before they are discovered—don't use the backup.

2. Reformat the failing drive and restore from a known good backup.

3. Restore the entire drive from a known good backup without reformatting. This is sometimes necessary if, for some reason, the drive can't be formatted.

4. Try to restore specific files known to be defective, either from backups or from the application's distribution media.

If there is an error reading the application's files, or the application crashes (faults) when executed, the application's files are probably damaged. What happened? There are a few possibilities. Maybe one or more files were overwritten by user error. As I mentioned earlier, a restore of the application's files will generally allow you to recover from this situation.

Maybe another application or the operating system overwrote one or more files. Again, check file dates to try to determine when the file overwrites occurred, and see if there is a way to determine the culprit. Restore the correct files and consider setting permissions to read/execute for everyone but an administrative userID that you won't use except to manage these files. Using file system permissions allows you to get immediate notification when a file is overwritten.

Manually Removing Registry Entries

In Chapter 8, I described three programs that automate the process of registry entry removal. But sometimes when repairing a problem, it is necessary to remove entries manually. Here I'll cover manual removal techniques.

Manual removal techniques are even more dangerous than using a program to clean out entries. Removing things by hand is tedious, and you won't be able to fully check registry integrity this way. Backups are in order before even thinking of starting to manually remove an entry from the registry.

Finding Entries

The first thing that you must do is find all the entries relative to the problem. This means you have to do a search.

Searching the registry with the Registry Editor is possible but not optimal. RegEdit has search capabilities, but rather than using it to search, try the following technique: Launch RegEdit and select My Computer. Next, select Registry ➤ Export Registry File. This writes the entire registry, excluding items such as the security hives, to a text file. Next, use a text editor (I use Notepad, as Notepad's search is reasonably fast, at least compared to RegEdit.) to find your problem application. Sounds too easy, doesn't it? However, finding the application may present a few problems. What do you search for? Try searching for the executable name or directory name. Or try searching for the known name of the application. If none of these work, search for things such as the application's document file extension, if it has one.

There may be entries for applications in HKEY_LOCAL_MACHINE\Software. Many applications install subkeys here, but others do not. If you're looking for a potentially optional component of Windows XP, check the HKEY_LOCAL_MACHINE\Software\Microsoft\Windows\CurrentVersion and HKEY_LOCAL_MACHINE\Software\Microsoft\Windows NT\CurrentVersion subkeys. Virtually everything that is part of the Windows XP operating system and from Microsoft should have entries in these two subkeys.

Still having problems finding your application? Try reading through the registry line by line. Start in the CLSID section, `HKEY_LOCAL_MACHINE\Software\Classes\CLSID` in `HKEY_CLASSES_ROOT`.

Visually scan the registry, starting with `HKEY_CLASSES_ROOT`, then `HKEY_LOCAL_MACHINE`, to see if any entries match anything that you can associate with the errant application. Look at the program's name, its publisher—anything that might be a link. At this point, you are in detective mode.

NOTE *Ever wonder how hackers break into systems? Oftentimes, it's by doing things just like this. They read anything about the system they can find. In short, they do just what you'll be doing.*

Most of the time, the application will have entries grouped together under a subkey. Some applications will have other entries that tend to float, but these are rather unusual. Once you find something that matches what you are looking for, see if there is a CLSID for it. Searching for a CLSID will be helpful in finding other entries in the registry for that application or component.

Removing Entries

Warning: If you are trying to remove entries from the registry, you should have exhausted all other alternatives; removing these entries is your last resort short of reinstalling Windows XP. Got that? The odds are very good that if you start hacking away at the registry, you'll destroy it.

But if you have nothing to lose, and you want to learn about the registry, this can be a way to do so. Back up the registry. I'd recommend having a parallel installation of either Windows NT, Windows XP or Windows Server, or perhaps Windows 95/98/Me (if your drives are formatted using the FAT file system) that you can boot to when you have totally destroyed your installed registry; this will allow you to restore the registry with a minimum of grief. If you don't have a parallel installation of Windows, now would be as good a time as any to install one.

To remove items, use the Registry Editor (RegEdit). Select the entry (key, subkey, or value) to be deleted and remove it. Don't forget that the Registry Editor is editing the actual working registry; once you delete something; there is no easy way to restore it.

With the Registry Editor, you may want to consider saving any major subkeys to disk files before deleting them. By saving these subkeys to the disk, you will be able to restore them should you find that you've deleted the wrong thing. It is possible to delete items from the registry that will make it impossible to start or run Windows XP. Having a complete backup of the registry that is restorable without using the affected copy of Windows XP is a very good idea.

Chapter 10

Programming and the Registry: A Developer's Paradise?

DISCLAIMER # 1: I'M a C/C++ programmer, so this chapter will deal with C/C++ programming. However, to be fair, I've included some Visual Basic for Applications registry programming in Chapter 14, "Microsoft Office Entries." All of the programming techniques discussed in that chapter are usable with virtually any version of Visual Basic.

Disclaimer # 2: I'm a Microsoft Visual C++ programmer. However, any development platform that uses MFC (Microsoft Foundation Classes) will be compatible with this chapter's content. Also, those registry manipulation techniques that are part of the Windows XP (either Home Edition or Professional) API are exposed in all development platforms as standard Windows XP API calls. So, if you are not using Visual C++, don't despair: Your system will be sufficiently similar. You should experience only minor problems in using everything discussed in this chapter with other languages and compilers on your system.

Disclaimer # 3: I could write an entire book on programming for the Windows registry. Remember, programming is an art, not a science, and there are many, many different ways to write your applications. Use MFC, don't use MFC, use C++ and classes, don't use C++ and classes, use a dialog interface, use a window interface, use a command-prompt interface, and so on. I don't spend a lot of time on the interface in this chapter; instead, I work more on the actual calls and functions that you, a programmer, would be using.

In this chapter, I'll cover the following topics:

◆ The registry's API functions

◆ Obsolete functions

◆ Using Microsoft Foundations Classes

A Word on the Registry's History

NOTE   Much of what this chapter covers is directly applicable to Windows XP, Windows 2000/NT, and even Windows 95/98/Me. In Windows 95/98/Me, many registry entries are in slightly different locations, although the basic concepts are identical for the programmer. The operating system does a good job of masking these differences.

Remember the registry's history. You see, the history of the registry is important in understanding how the various registry functions work and the parameters that are passed to these functions. What is now the registry was, once upon a time, a set of .ini files (specifically win.ini and system.ini). In addition, each application had its own .ini file. An application could store information in the win.ini and system.ini files, but that practice didn't gain much acceptance for a number of reasons, including performance and file bloat.

Much of the code that updated .ini files was reworked so that applications could easily work with the registry. In some cases, the applications didn't need to be modified at all; in other cases, there were minor modifications. However, all in all, you will see a lot of excess baggage in some registry functions. In some cases you will see that, even today, the same functions will still work with .ini files if need be.

NOTE   The .ini files of old were divided into sections called profiles. *Typically, a profile section is dedicated to a specific application or module.*

Windows XP Registry API Functions

A program manipulates the registry using a number of registry functions. These functions are prefixed with Reg, and the rest of the function name describes the function's actual purpose in life. Table 10.1 lists the Windows XP registry functions, along with a short description of each one's functionality.

NOTE   Two new functions were added to Windows 2000, and the newer versions of the Windows SDK (Software Development Kit) show the registry hive HKEY_PERFORMANCE_DATA *as a predefined type.*

TABLE 10.1: WINDOWS XP REGISTRY FUNCTIONS

FUNCTION	DESCRIPTION
RegCloseKey	Closes the connection between the application and a specific registry object. The function RegOpenKey opens this connection.
RegConnectRegistry	Allows an application to modify a remote registry. It establishes a connection with the registry on a specified remote computer.
RegCreateKey	Creates a new registry subkey. This simple function allows no options; see RegCreateKeyEx for a more powerful version of this API.
RegCreateKeyEx	Creates a new registry subkey. This function allows setting security, options, and classes.

Continued on next page

TABLE 10.1: WINDOWS XP REGISTRY FUNCTIONS *(continued)*

FUNCTION	DESCRIPTION
RegDeleteKey	Deletes an existing subkey that opened with RegOpenKey.
RegDeleteValue	Deletes an existing data key that opened with RegOpenKey.
RegEnumKey	Enumerates all the subkeys starting with the specified key or subkey. One object is returned for each call to RegEnumKey until the function returns the value ERROR_NO_MORE_ITEMS. This function exists for compatibility with earlier versions of Windows; programmers for Windows XP should use RegEnumKeyEx.
RegEnumKeyEx	Enumerates all the subkeys, starting with the specified key or subkey. One object is returned for each call to RegEnumKeyEx until the function returns the value ERROR_NO_MORE_ITEMS. This function retrieves the class name, the time of last modification, and the object's name.
RegEnumValue	Enumerates all the data keys in the specified key or subkey. One object is returned for each call to RegEnumValue until the function returns the value ERROR_NO_MORE_ITEMS. This function retrieves the name, the value, and the type for the object.
RegFlushKey	Causes any changes made to a registry entry to be written to the actual registry. This implies only simple buffering because, generally, changes to the registry are immediate.
RegGetKeySecurity	Retrieves the security attributes for a given registry object; the security may be set (changed) if the user has sufficient privileges.
RegLoadKey	Creates a new subkey under either HKEY_USERS or HKEY_LOCAL_MACHINE; the information to create the new subkey is contained in a file, the name of which is passed to the function.
RegNotifyChangeKeyValue	Tells the system to inform the caller if the specified object is changed or if the object's attributes are changed. If the object is deleted, no notification is sent. An event handler in the application processes the notification.
RegOpenKey	Opens a registry object. This function is called before many other registry functions. The handle returned by RegOpenKey is then passed to other registry functions that require a registry handle. Microsoft recommends that RegOpenKeyEx be called by Windows XP, Windows 2000, Windows NT, and Windows 95/98/Me applications.
RegOpenKeyEx	Opens a registry object. This function is called before many other registry functions. The handle returned by RegOpenKeyEx is passed to other registry functions that require a registry handle. RegOpenKeyEx handles security and other options that RegOpenKey does not handle.
RegQueryInfoKey	Returns information about the specified object.

Continued on next page

TABLE 10.1: WINDOWS XP REGISTRY FUNCTIONS *(continued)*

FUNCTION	DESCRIPTION
RegQueryMultipleValues	Returns information about the data keys in a specified subkey.
RegQueryValue	Returns the value of the default (unnamed) value entry associated with each key and subkey. Microsoft recommends that RegQueryValueEx be called by Win32 applications.
RegQueryValueEx	Returns the value of the default (unnamed) value entry associated with each key and subkey. RegQueryValueEx handles security and other options that RegQueryValue does not handle.
RegReplaceKey	Tells the operating system to use a different file for this key upon restarting (the registry is stored as a series of files, one file for each of the main keys). Use this function to back up and restore the registry and for disaster recovery.
RegRestoreKey	Restores the key's or subkey's contents from a file. The RegRestoreKey function will restore multiple objects, as many as are contained in the registry file provided.
RegSaveKey	Saves the key's or subkey's contents to a file. The RegSaveKey function will save multiple objects, as many as are specified to the registry file provided.
RegSetKeySecurity	Sets the specified object's security attributes. The user must have sufficient privileges to use this function.
RegSetValue	Sets the value of the default (unnamed) value entry associated with each key and subkey. Microsoft recommends that RegSetValueEx be called by Win32 applications.
RegSetValueEx	Sets the value of the default (unnamed) value entry associated with each key and subkey. RegSetValueEx handles security and other options that RegSetValue does not set.
RegUnLoadKey	Removes from the registry the specified object(s).
RegOpenUserClassesRoot	Retrieves the HKEY_CLASSES_ROOT hive for a specific user. This function is useful when managing one user while not logged on as that user.
RegOverridePredefKey	Allows mapping of a predefined key or hive name (such as HKEY_CLASSES_ROOT) to a different key or hive. For example, you could map HKEY_CLASSES_ROOT to HKEY_CURRENT_USER\Temp\DLL.

A number of different functions that work with the older .ini files are obsolete by Microsoft's standards, although they still allow support for legacy applications. These functions should not be incorporated into new code, although they may be encountered in legacy code. Use the functions described in Table 10.1 for new work. Table 10.2 lists the now obsolete registry functions.

TABLE 10.2: OBSOLETE WIN32 REGISTRY FUNCTIONS

FUNCTION	DESCRIPTION
GetPrivateProfileInt	Returns an integer value entry value from the specified location
GetPrivateProfileSection	Returns an entire section's contents
GetPrivateProfileSectionNames	Returns the names in a section
GetPrivateProfileString	Returns a string value entry value from the specified location
GetPrivateProfileStruct	Fetches a private structure from the specified location, comparing the checksum retrieved with the checksum that was written when the object was saved
GetProfileInt	Returns an integer value entry value from the specified location
GetProfileSection	Returns an entire section's contents
GetProfileString	Returns an integer value entry value from the specified location
WritePrivateProfileSection	Saves or writes to the specified location an entire section's contents
WritePrivateProfileString	Writes to the specified location a value entry string value
WritePrivateProfileStruct	Writes to the specified location, saving a checksum written with the object
WriteProfileSection	Writes an entire section's contents
WriteProfileString	Writes to the specified location a value entry string value

In many cases, these functions will map directly into the registry, in the entry under HKEY_LOCAL_ MACHINE\Software\Microsoft\Windows NT\CurrentVersion\IniFileMapping. This mapping allows many legacy applications that used the win.ini, system.ini, or control.ini files to continue to function correctly. Support for this functionality is available under Windows XP, Windows 2000, and Windows NT only and does not apply to any other version of Windows. However, for new code, do not use these functions: use the newer functions described earlier in Table 10.1.

Writing an application that uses the registry API calls is simple and straightforward. For example, an application that queries the registry for a certain object's value might be as simple as:

1. Open the object.

2. Query the object's contents.

3. Close the object.

Let's try that. In Windows XP (actually, all versions of Windows 2000 and Windows NT, too), we have some advantages in that we can write console applications that interact with the registry. Okay, Windows 95/98/Me has many of these advantages, too. Although console applications are not always the most user friendly, they are very quick and easy to write; and since this is not a programming book, we'll develop our example program as a console application.

To develop any application using Visual C++, use the New Project Wizard. Why not—after all, this wizard saves us a lot of work. Follow these steps:

1. In Visual C++, select File ➤ New.

2. Select the Projects tab in the New dialog box.

3. Select Win32 Console Application in the Project Type list.

4. Provide a name for the project (**Reg1**, say) and a location; then click OK.

5. Open the newly created `Reg1.cpp` file and drop in the code shown in Listing 10.1. It is best if you download the code from www.sybex.com, and cut and paste to save time and to avoid typing errors. However, if you do not have Internet access, you may type in this code directly.

TIP   You can download the entire project from the Sybex website, at www.sybex.com. *Click Catalog, type the name of the book or the reference number from the book's ISBN (2987), and press Enter. From the main page for this book, click Downloads to go to the code. All of the files in the project are zipped into a single file called* reg1.zip.

6. Build the project.

7. Correct your typing errors.

8. Rebuild the project and try out Reg1.

Slight modification of these steps will be necessary if you are not using Visual C++. Regardless, the basics are the same: create a new, empty console application and, in the main source file, add the code from Listing 10.1.

LISTING 10.1: REG1.CPP, A PROGRAM TO ACCESS THE REGISTRY

```cpp
// Reg1.cpp : Defines the entry point for the console application.
//

#include "stdafx.h"
#include "windows.h"
#include "winreg.h"
#include <winerror.h>
#include "stdio.h"


int main(int argc, char* argv[])
{
#define  MAX_VALUE_NAME 4096        // How big things can get.
CHAR      ClassName[MAX_PATH] = ""; // Buffer for class name.
CHAR      KeyName[MAX_PATH];        // Name for the data value entry.
char      *szHive = "HARDWARE\\DESCRIPTION\\System";
char      szBufferReturn[MAX_VALUE_NAME];
char      szData[MAX_VALUE_NAME];           // Data value returned.
DWORD     dwcClassLen = MAX_PATH;   // Length of class string.
```

```
DWORD      dwcMaxClass;              // Longest class string.
DWORD      dwcMaxSubKey;             // Longest sub key size.
DWORD      dwcMaxValueData;          // Longest Value data.
DWORD      dwcMaxValueName;          // Longest Value name.
DWORD      dwcSecDesc;               // Security descriptor.
DWORD      dwcSubKeys;               // Number of sub keys.
DWORD      dwcValues;                // Number of values for this key.
DWORD      dwType = 0;               // Type of data such as REG_SZ;
DWORD      i = 0;
DWORD      nBufferReturnSize = sizeof(szBufferReturn);
DWORD      nDataSize = MAX_PATH;     // Data value buffer size.
DWORD      dwcValueName = MAX_VALUE_NAME;
DWORD      retCode;
FILETIME   ftLastWriteTime;          // Last write time.
HKEY       hKey = NULL; // Handle for the registry key.
HKEY       hKeyResult;
long       nReturnCode = 0;
PHKEY      phkResult = &hKeyResult;  // Result code hole!

    printf("Reg1: version Windows XP/.Net\n");
    hKey = HKEY_LOCAL_MACHINE;
    hKeyResult = HKEY_LOCAL_MACHINE;

    // First open the key specified in szHive:
    if ((nReturnCode = RegOpenKeyEx(hKey,
        0,
        KEY_ENUMERATE_SUB_KEYS|KEY_EXECUTE|KEY_QUERY_VALUE,
        &hKeyResult)) == ERROR_SUCCESS)
    {// Get Class name, Value count. Display for the user.
        retCode = RegQueryInfoKey (hKeyResult,      // Key handle.
            ClassName,          // Buffer for class name.
            &dwcClassLen,       // Length of class string.
            NULL,               // Reserved.
            &dwcSubKeys,        // Number of sub keys.
            &dwcMaxSubKey,      // Longest sub key size.
            &dwcMaxClass,       // Longest class string.
            &dwcValues,         // Number of values for this key.
            &dwcMaxValueName,   // Longest Value name.
            &dwcMaxValueData,   // Longest Value data.
            &dwcSecDesc,        // Security descriptor.
            &ftLastWriteTime); // Last write time.

        printf("\n\nLooking at HKEY_LOCAL_MACHINE\\%s\n\n", szHive);

        printf (
            "ClassName, '%s' \n"
            "dwcClassLen, '%ld'\n"
            "dwcSubKeys, '%ld'\n"
```

```
                    "dwcMaxSubKey, '%ld'\n"
                    "dwcMaxClass, '%ld'\n"
                    "dwcValues, '%ld'\n"
                    "dwcMaxValueName, '%ld'\n"
                    "dwcMaxValueData, '%ld'\n"
                    "dwcSecDesc, '%ld'\n",
                    ClassName,          // Buffer for class name.
                    dwcClassLen,        // Length of class string.
                    dwcSubKeys,         // Number of sub keys.
                    dwcMaxSubKey,       // Longest sub key size.
                    dwcMaxClass,        // Longest class string.
                    dwcValues,          // Number of values for this key.
                    dwcMaxValueName,    // Longest Value name.
                    dwcMaxValueData,    // Longest Value data.
                    dwcSecDesc);        // Security descriptor.

printf("\n\n");

for (i = 0, retCode = ERROR_SUCCESS;
    retCode == ERROR_SUCCESS; i++)
{
    retCode = RegEnumKey (hKeyResult, i,
        KeyName, MAX_PATH);

    if (retCode == (DWORD)ERROR_SUCCESS)
        printf("Sub-key name = '%s'\n", KeyName);
}

retCode = ERROR_SUCCESS;

printf("\n\n");

// Next get the value stored in Identifier:
for (i = 0; i < 100 && nReturnCode == ERROR_SUCCESS; i++)
{
    nBufferReturnSize = sizeof(szBufferReturn);
    szBufferReturn[0] = '\0';
    nDataSize = sizeof(szData);
    szData[0] = '\0';

    if ((nReturnCode = RegEnumValue(
        hKeyResult, i,
        szBufferReturn, &nBufferReturnSize,
        NULL,
        &dwType,
        (LPBYTE)szData, &nDataSize
        )) == ERROR_SUCCESS)
    {
        printf("Identifier is '%s'\n\n", szBufferReturn);
```

```
        nBufferReturnSize = sizeof(szBufferReturn);

        if (dwType == REG_SZ)
        {
            printf("Identifier contains '%s' REG_SZ \n\n",
                szData);
        }
        else
        {
            printf("Identifier contains a non-string'\n\n");
        }
    }
    else
    {// We're done, check for errors now:
        if (nReturnCode != ERROR_NO_MORE_ITEMS)
        {// No need to tell we are at end of list...
            nBufferReturnSize = sizeof(szBufferReturn);

            FormatMessage(FORMAT_MESSAGE_FROM_SYSTEM, NULL,
                nReturnCode, 0, szBufferReturn,
                nBufferReturnSize, NULL);

            printf("RegEnumValue() %ld failed '%s'!\n\n",
                nReturnCode, szBufferReturn);
```

NOTE   *This is when I usually regale the reader with stories about my first Windows program. It took me about six months to get the basics of my first Windows interface displayed on the screen, and there was no functional code in that interface. Today, with Visual C++ and the wizards, I can do that six months of work in about ten minutes. Progress, ah progress—and to think there are those who'd choose to stifle this innovation.*

A programmer is able to write a program that interacts with the registry using only a few lines of source code. Listing 10.1 shows the main source file for just such a program. The program in Listing 10.1 also requires simple stdafx.cpp and stdafx.h files. Listing 10.2 shows the stdafx.cpp file, and Listing 10.3 shows the stdafx.h header (include) file for Reg1.cpp.

LISTING 10.2: STDAFX.CPP, THE SUPPORT PRECOMPILED HEADER FILE FOR REG1

```
// stdafx.cpp : source file that includes just the standard includes
//     Reg1.pch will be the pre-compiled header
//     stdafx.obj will contain the pre-compiled type information

#include "stdafx.h"

// TODO: reference any additional headers you need in STDAFX.H
// and not in this file
```

LISTING 10.3: STDAFX.H, THE SUPPORT PRECOMPILED HEADER FILE FOR REG1

```
// stdafx.h : include file for standard system include files,
//  or project specific include files that are used frequently, but
//      are changed infrequently
//

#if !defined(AFX_STDAFX_H__BD7FBDE9_14B4_11D2_88CB_0060970BB14F__INCLUDED_)
#define AFX_STDAFX_H__BD7FBDE9_14B4_11D2_88CB_0060970BB14F__INCLUDED_

#if _MSC_VER > 1000
#pragma once
#endif // _MSC_VER > 1000


// TODO: reference additional headers your program requires here

//{{AFX_INSERT_LOCATION}}
// Microsoft Visual C++ will insert additional declarations
//      immediately before the previous line.

#endif
//!defined(AFX_STDAFX_H__BD7FBDE9_14B4_11D2_88CB_0060970BB14F__INCLUDED_
```

To create your own Reg1 program, simply plug these files into a project. Output for this program uses simple `printf` statements, because this program doesn't have a Windows user interface.

NOTE *The Reg1 program, though nominally a C++ program, is really a standard C program. Although it would be very easy to include additional C++ (and even MFC) code, I chose to keep this program as simple as possible.*

Now, let's take a closer look at the Reg1 program. The first step after basic program initialization is to open a registry subkey:

```
if ((nReturnCode = RegOpenKeyEx(hKey,
      szHive,
      0,
      KEY_ENUMERATE_SUB_KEYS|KEY_EXECUTE|KEY_QUERY_VALUE,
      &hKeyResult
      )) == ERROR_SUCCESS)
   {// Get Class name, Value count. Display for the user.
```

In this code, I call `RegOpenKeyEx` and save the return code; the error handler will use the return code to display an error message, if appropriate. If `RegOpenKeyEx` returns `ERROR_SUCCESS`, the registry subkey was opened successfully. In `hKey` is the base key given to `RegOpenKeyEx`. We initialize this to `HKEY_LOCAL_MACHINE`. We initialize the desired key to open in `szHive`. The desired key to open is hard-coded as `"HARDWARE\\DESCRIPTION\\System"`. Finally, `hKeyResult` will contain the handle to the key opened if the function is successful.

Once opened, the next step is to get some information about our key:

```
retCode = RegQueryInfoKey (hKeyResult,            // Key handle.
            ClassName,           // Buffer for class name.
            &dwcClassLen,        // Length of class string.
            NULL,                // Reserved.
            &dwcSubKeys,         // Number of sub keys.
            &dwcMaxSubKey,       // Longest sub key size.
            &dwcMaxClass,        // Longest class string.
            &dwcValues,          // Number of values for this key.
            &dwcMaxValueName,    // Longest Value name.
            &dwcMaxValueData,    // Longest Value data.
            &dwcSecDesc,         // Security descriptor.
            &ftLastWriteTime);   // Last write time.
```

The call to `RegQueryInfoKey` returns the information about the key that's shown in Table 10.3.

TABLE 10.3: INFORMATION RETURNED BY REGQUERYINFOKEY()

VARIABLE IN REG1 (THE USER MAY SPECIFY A DIFFERENT NAME)	DESCRIPTION
ClassName	Class name (this field may be blank under Windows 95/98/Me)
dwcClassLen	Length of class string buffer and the returned length of the class string
dwcSubKeys	Number of subkeys in this key
dwcMaxSubKey	Longest object name
dwcMaxClass	Longest class string
dwcValues	Number of value entries in this subkey
dwcMaxValueName	Longest value name
dwcMaxValueData	Longest value data
dwcSecDesc	Security descriptor
ftLastWriteTime	Last write time for Windows XP, Windows 2000, and Windows NT systems

Once we have some information about the subkey, we display this information for the user and carry on.

The next step in our simple program is to display all the subkeys that are contained within our target key. A simple loop that enumerates all the subkeys and prints the results of this enumeration does the job. We monitor the results of the `RegEnumKey` function call until an error is returned. Most loops would check the return value to determine what the error was, in order to build in error recovery; in our simple program, this is unnecessary.

```
for (i = 0, retCode = ERROR_SUCCESS;
    retCode == ERROR_SUCCESS; i++)
{
    retCode = RegEnumKey (hKeyResult, i,
        KeyName, MAX_PATH);

    if (retCode == (DWORD)ERROR_SUCCESS)
        printf("Sub-key name = '%s'\n", KeyName);
}
```

The next step is to get each value entry's name and value. Due to the simple nature of this program, I only display keys that have a data type of REG_SZ and skip other keys. However, adding a more complex case statement would allow displaying all the different data types.

As in code used to enumerate subkeys, the printing of value entry values uses a loop and a test to ensure that the enumeration function, RegEnumValue, returns successfully.

This loop is composed of two steps. The first step is to get the value entry's name; the second step is to get the actual data value contained in the entry. Separate printf statements display this data for the user, as appropriate:

```
for (i = 0; i < 100 && nReturnCode == ERROR_SUCCESS; i++)
{
    nBufferReturnSize = sizeof(szBufferReturn);
    szBufferReturn[0] = '\0';
    nDataSize = sizeof(szData);
    szData[0] = '\0';

    if ((nReturnCode = RegEnumValue(
        hKeyResult, i,
        szBufferReturn, &nBufferReturnSize,
        NULL,
        &dwType,
        (LPBYTE)szData, &nDataSize
        )) == ERROR_SUCCESS)

    {
        printf("Identifier is '%s'\n\n", szBufferReturn);
        nBufferReturnSize = sizeof(szBufferReturn);

        if (dwType == REG_SZ)
        {
            printf("Identifier contains '%s' REG_SZ \n\n",
                szData);
        }
        else
        {
            printf("Identifier contains a non-string'\n\n");
```

```
                }
            }
            else
            {// We're done, check for errors now:
                if (nReturnCode != ERROR_NO_MORE_ITEMS)
                {// No need to tell we are at end of list...
                    nBufferReturnSize = sizeof(szBufferReturn);

                    FormatMessage(FORMAT_MESSAGE_FROM_SYSTEM, NULL,
                        nReturnCode, 0, szBufferReturn,
                        nBufferReturnSize, NULL);

                    printf("RegEnumValue() %ld failed '%s'!\n\n",
                        nReturnCode, szBufferReturn);

                    printf("RegEnumValue() failed!\n\n");
                }
            }
        }
        // When done, always close the key!
        RegCloseKey(hKey);
    }
```

This is error handling at its simplest. We save the return code from a registry function call. If the return is not ERROR_SUCCESS, something went wrong. For such a case, we can use FormatMessage to create a more user-friendly error message, which we can print on the screen for the user:

```
    else
    {// Could not open the registry object!
        nBufferReturnSize = sizeof(szBufferReturn);

        FormatMessage(FORMAT_MESSAGE_FROM_SYSTEM, NULL, nReturnCode,
            0, szBufferReturn, nBufferReturnSize, NULL);

        printf("RegOpenKey() %ld failed '%s'!\n\n",
            nReturnCode, szBufferReturn);
    }
```

A Windows program uses a message box to display the error message text.
Figure 10.1 shows the results of an execution of Reg1.

NOTE   *Even when run under other versions of Windows, Reg1 will provide useful output (although the output is different than Windows XP). This shows the compatibility between the Windows XP registry and the registry found in earlier versions of Windows.*

NOTE   *For complete source code for the Reg1 program, check this book's website at* **www.sybex.com***; click Catalog, enter the book title or reference number from the book's ISBN (2987), and press Enter. From the main page for this book, click Downloads to go to the code.*

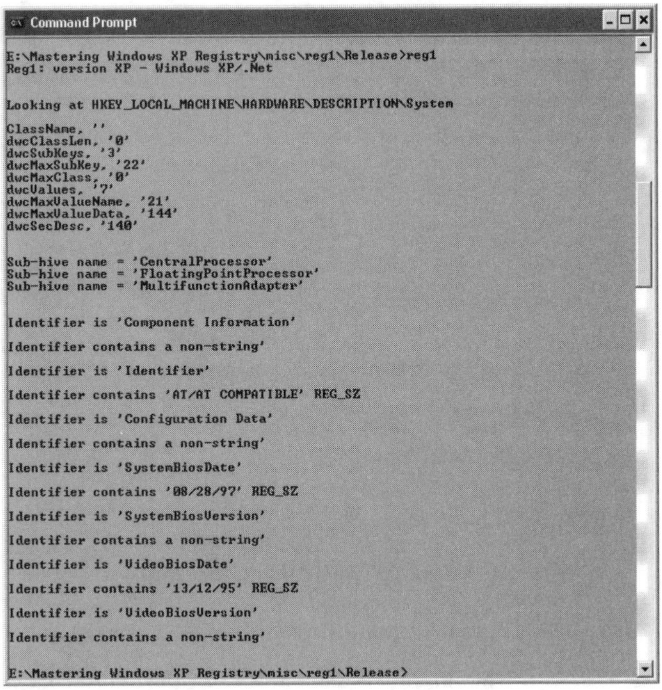

FIGURE 10.1

Reg1, a simple command-prompt application, provides lots of interesting information about a registry subkey.

DOES FORMATMESSAGE ALWAYS RETURN THE BEST MESSAGE?

It probably does, but not always; the problem is exactly as it seems. Regardless, whatever FormatMessage does return is better than just displaying an error code value to the user.

Take this example of an error message:

    "Error number 259 occurred."

Descriptive? No.

Useful? No.

User friendly? No.

The better result comes from FormatMessage, formatted in a string:

    "The Error 'No more data is available.' occurred in the call to RegEnumValue."

This message, though not perfect, is much better and provides useful information to the user of the program. Programmers who display meaningless numbers in their error messages without explanatory text should be banned from ever using a computer again.

One caution, however: The error strings returned by FormatMessage may contain a trailing newline character. It may be necessary to pare these from your error messages.

To Use MFC or Not to Use MFC? That Is the Question

C++, MFC (Microsoft Foundation Classes), and the concept of object-oriented programming (a.k.a. OOP) have all hit the big time. Some programmers actually believe that it is not possible to use old C calls in a C++ program. Actually, it is fully possible to use the Windows API calls in any program, whether the program is C, C++, MFC, or whatever. However, Microsoft did bundle a few of the registry functions into MFC to make programming a bit easier. For example, the `CWinApp` class contains a number of both documented and undocumented registry manipulation functions.

First, the good news: some registry functions are available in `CWinApp`. Now, the bad news: there are not many registry functions available in `CWinApp`. The functions listed in Table 10.4 are available to programmers directly. Don't despair, however—you can just call the plain old Windows API registry functions as well.

TABLE 10.4: REGISTRY FUNCTIONS THAT ARE PART OF `CWinApp`

FUNCTION, WITH PARAMETERS PASSED	DOCUMENTATION	DESCRIPTION
`void SetRegistryKey (LPCTSTR lpszRegistryKey)`	Yes	This overloaded function fills in the `m_pszRegistryKey` variable using the passed string. This string would typically contain the company name. `m_pszRegistryKey` is used to create the necessary key(s) under `HKEY_CURRENT_USER\Software\m_pszRegistryKey\m_pszProfileName`. `m_pszProfile`➥`Name` is set to `m_pszAppName` by `SetRegistryKey`.
`void SetRegistryKey (UINT nIDRegistryKey)`	Yes	This overloaded function fills in the `m_pszRegistryKey` variable from a string contained in the application's string resources. This string would typically contain the company name. `m_pszRegistryKey` is used to create the necessary key(s) under `HKEY_CURRENT_USER\Software\m_pszRegistryKey\m_pszProfileName`. `m_pszProfile`➥`Name` is set to `m_pszAppName` by `SetRegistryKey`.
`HKEY GetSectionKey (LPCTSTR lpszSection)`	No	Returns `hKey` for `HKEY_CURRENT_USER\Software\RegistryKey\AppName\lpszSection`, creating it if it doesn't exist, where `RegistryKey` is the company name as stored in `m_pszRegistryKey`, and AppName is the application name as stored in `m_pszAppName`. The caller must close the `hKey` returned.

Continued on next page

TABLE 10.4: REGISTRY FUNCTIONS THAT ARE PART OF CWINAPP *(continued)*

FUNCTION, WITH PARAMETERS PASSED	DOCUMENTATION	DESCRIPTION
HKEY GetAppRegistryKey()	No	Returns hKey for HKEY_CURRENT_USER\Software\ RegistryKey\AppName, creating it if it doesn't exist, where RegistryKey is the company name as stored in m_pszRegistryKey, and AppName is the application name as stored in m_pszAppName. The caller must close the hKey returned.
UINT GetProfileInt (LPCTSTR lpszSection, LPCTSTR lpszEntry, int nDefault)	Yes	Calls GetSectionKey() to open lpsz ➥Section; then calls RegQueryValue ➥Ex() to get the value for the key specified in lpszEntry. Returns nDefault if the entry is not found. Works on an .ini file if a call to SetRegistryKey() has not previously been made.
BOOL WriteProfileInt (LPCTSTR lpszSection, LPCTSTR lpszEntry, int nValue)	Yes	Calls GetSectionKey() to open lpsz ➥Section; then calls RegSetValueEx() to set the value for the key specified in lpszEntry. Returns FALSE if the entry cannot be set. Works on an .ini file if a call to SetRegistryKey() has not previously been made.
CString GetProfileString (LPCTSTR lpszSection, LPCTSTR lpszEntry, LPCTSTR lpszDefault = NULL)	Yes	Calls GetSectionKey() to open lpszSection; then calls RegQuery-ValueEx() to get the value for the key specified in lpszEntry. Returns lpszDefault if the entry is not found. Works on an .ini file if a call to Set ➥RegistryKey() has not previously been made.
BOOL WriteProfileString (LPCTSTR lpszSection, LPCTSTR lpszEntry, LPCTSTR lpszValue)	Yes	Calls GetSectionKey() to open lpsz ➥Section; then calls RegSetValueEx() to set the value for the key specified in lpszEntry. Returns FALSE if the entry cannot be set. Works on an .ini file if a call to SetRegistryKey() has not previously been made.

Continued on next page

TABLE 10.4: REGISTRY FUNCTIONS THAT ARE PART OF CWINAPP *(continued)*

FUNCTION, WITH PARAMETERS PASSED	DOCUMENTATION	DESCRIPTION
BOOL GetProfileBinary (LPCTSTR lpszSection, LPCTSTR lpszEntry, LPBYTE* ppData, UINT* pBytes)	Yes	Calls GetSectionKey() to open lpszSection; then calls RegQuery ➥ValueEx() to get the value for the key specified in lpszEntry. The size of the buffer to return the data in is specified by pBytes. The parameter pBytes is set to the size of the returned data. Works on an .ini file if a call to SetRegistryKey() has not previously been made.
BOOL WriteProfileBinary (LPCTSTR lpszSection, LPCTSTR lpszEntry, LPBYTE pData, UINT nBytes)	Yes	Calls GetSectionKey() to open lpsz ➥Section; then calls RegSetValueEx() to set the value for the key specified in lpszEntry. The buffer containing the data to save is pData, and the data's size is specified by nBytes. Works on an .ini file if a call to SetRegistryKey() has not previously been made.
LONG DelRegTree(HKEY hParentKey, const CString& strKeyName)	No	Deletes the specified subkey from the specified parent. Since a registry subkey may not be deleted unless it is empty, a helper function is used to recursively delete further subkeys and keys.

NOTE   A bright programmer could write a wrapper around the Windows API registry functions if desired. However, there's a reason that Microsoft didn't already do that: you'd actually gain no additional functionality or usability. On the other hand, it might be possible to improve the registry access, especially searching for and retrieving specific keys, with a C++ registry class. I'll leave it up to you to design your own registry class.

The process for using the CWinApp registry functions is simple:

1. Call CWinApp::SetRegistryKey() to tell MFC that your application is going to work with the registry rather than a separate .ini file.

2. Call the functions to retrieve or set values in the registry.

Closing code is not needed unless a call has been made to one of the following CWinApp functions:

◆   HKEY GetSectionKey(LPCTSTR lpszSection)

◆   HKEY GetAppRegistryKey()

If one of these functions is used, be sure that your application does a proper close of the registry key returned. Of course, check to ensure that the function didn't fail.

Chapter 11

The Performance Monitor Meets the Registry

A PART OF THE registry that we've not discussed yet is `HKEY_PERFORMANCE_DATA`, the registry's performance hive. This registry hive contains the necessary information to allow an application to successfully interact with and display performance data. Hidden from the Registry Editor, it is contained in a place in the registry that is only accessible programmatically; otherwise, it's not visible or editable.

That `HKEY_PERFORMANCE_DATA` does not actually exist is an interesting part of Windows. Windows stores this hive temporarily, mostly in memory. Quick updating of these performance-monitoring counters is necessary to avoid impacting performance. Windows has no need to store, on disk, performance data—this type of information is transient, constantly changing while the system is used.

Although it is somewhat more difficult to access the performance hive than other registry hives, this difficulty can be overcome using the tools provided in the Windows header file, `winperf.h`, distributed with Visual C++. In addition, in this chapter I'll show you a simple program I've created for browsing `HKEY_PERFORMANCE_DATA`. PerfMon1 is a program that views the information in `HKEY_PERFORMANCE_DATA`. Keep in mind that the program as presented in this chapter is only an example and doesn't actually do any useful retrieval of data—you will have to add that functionality. We'll cover the following topics:

- ◆ Using PerfMon1 to access HKEY_PERFORMANCE_DATA

- ◆ Analyzing the code of PerfMon1

- ◆ Adding performance data to the registry

PerfMon1: A Program to Access HKEY_PERFORMANCE_DATA

The PerfMon1 program is a simple console application, displaying its voluminous data using `printf()` statements. To keep this example as simple as possible, I've forgone any semblance of a user interface. The example program's inability to do any real monitoring is for the same reason—simplicity!

There are two methods to access performance data under Windows. The first, the "standard" registry interface, is powerful, but does not focus on performance data. The second, the Performance Data Helper (PDH), is newer and actually easier to use. The PDH is oriented toward single counters, rather than groups of counters. PerfMon1 uses the rather standard interface.

NOTE   *When you're using PerfMon1, I suggest you use I/O redirection and capture the data into a file. Then edit or browse the file. PerfMon1 might typically print over 50,000 lines of output; watching all of this scroll past on the screen won't be any fun.*

The performance data is entirely contained within the `HKEY_PERFORMANCE_DATA` hive, with the exception of the object and counter names and help information, which are contained in the key `HKEY_LOCAL_MACHINE\Software\Microsoft\Windows NT\CurrentVersion\Perflib\009`.

NOTE   *Are the performance data and `HKEY_PERFORMANCE_DATA` part of the registry? Well, that's a good question. It seems obvious that the storage of performance data wasn't part of Microsoft's original conception of the registry. `HKEY_PERFORMANCE_DATA` is an example of Microsoft extending the registry functionality and interface to provide special services.*

There are only two values in this key: `Counter` and `Help`. Both of these values are REG_MULTI_SZ, with many entries in each.

NOTE   *Appendix D lists a typical installation's counters and objects. You can use the information in Appendix D to determine which items are objects and what counters are found in each object.*

An Example Portion of PerfMon1 Output

First, let's take a look at PerfMon1's output:

```
PerfMon1 - Check out HKEY_PERFORMANCE_DATA! Version 2002
+--------------------------------------------------------

Index: 10386
    Counter: 10388
    Counter: 10390
    Counter: 10392
    Counter: 10394
    Counter: 10396
    Counter: 10398
    Counter: 10400
    Counter: 10402
    Counter: 10404
```

```
     Counter: 10406
     Counter: 10408
     Counter: 10410
     Counter: 10412
     Counter: 10414
     Counter: 10416
     Counter: 10418
     Counter: 10420
     Counter: 10422
     Counter: 10424
     Counter: 10426
     Counter: 10428
     Counter: 10430
     Counter: 10432
     Counter: 10434
     Counter: 10436
     Counter: 10438
     Counter: 10440
     Counter: 10442
     Counter: 10444
     Counter: 10446
     Counter: 10448
     Counter: 10450
     Counter: 10452
     Counter: 10454
Index: 10548
     Counter: 10550
     Counter: 10552
     Counter: 10554
Index: 10524
     Counter: 10526
     Counter: 10528
     Counter: 10530
     Counter: 10532
     Counter: 10534
     Counter: 10536
     Counter: 10538
     Counter: 10540
     Counter: 10542
     Counter: 10544
     Counter: 10546
```

PerfMon1's Performance Counters

To make sense of PerfMon1's output, you can look up the object and counter IDs in Appendix D. It'll also help to start off with a good understanding of what counters are. A *counter* is an item that indicates how many times, or at what rate, a given event happens. For example, the counter named

Page Faults/Sec indicates the number of page faults (that is, the number of times the system needed to use virtual memory) that occurred in the previous second. Most, if not all, counters are based on a time interval (that you, the user, may set). A temporary counter is used, and when the time interval expires, the counter in the registry is updated. Then, any performance-monitoring application is able to retrieve and display the updated counter.

And a performance object? A *performance object* is a collection of performance counters used to monitor a specific functionality.

The output begins with the Active Server Pages performance object at index 10386. This object measures various parameters regarding Active Server Pages. Counters in Active Server Pages (see Figure 11.1) include those shown below:

Counter	Name
10388	Debugging Requests
10390	Errors during Script Runtime
10392	Errors from ASP Preprocessor
10394	Errors from Script Compilers
10396	Errors/Sec
10398	Request Bytes in Total
10400	Request Bytes out Total
10402	Request Execution Time
10404	Request Wait Time
10406	Requests Disconnected
10408	Requests Executing
10410	Requests Failed Total
10412	Requests Not Authorized
10414	Requests Not Found
10416	Requests Queued
10418	Requests Rejected
10420	Requests Succeeded
10422	Requests Timed Out
10424	Requests Total
10426	Requests/Sec
10428	Script Engines Cached

Counter	Name
10430	Session Duration
10432	Sessions Current
10434	Sessions Timed Out
10436	Sessions Total
10438	Templates Cached
10440	Template Cache Hit Rate
10444	Template Notifications
10446	Transactions Aborted
10448	Transactions Committed
10450	Transactions Pending
10452	Transactions Total
10454	Transactions/Sec

FIGURE 11.1

The Performance Monitor's Add Counters dialog box showing Active Server Pages and some counters

The next object is number 10548, Indexing Service Filter. This object has only three counters:

Counter	Name
10550	Total Indexing Speed (MB/hr)
10552	Binding Time (msec)
10554	Indexing Speed (MB/hr)

Moving on in the PerfMon1 report, the next index is number 10524, or in more friendly terms, Indexing Service. This object is a bit different from the Indexing Service Filter, but why? It's because the actual indexing service is different from the indexing service filter. The counters in the Indexing Service performance object are shown here:

Counter	Name
10526	Word Lists
10528	Saved Indexes
10530	Index Size (MB)
10532	Files to Be Indexed
10534	Unique Keys
10536	Running Queries
10538	Merge Progress
10540	# Documents Indexed
10542	Total # of Documents
10544	Total # of Queries
10546	Deferred for indexing

The Performance Monitor itself is another example of the MMC (Microsoft Management Console). In Figure 11.2, the Performance Monitor shows the first few counters for the system's CPU usage. In this figure, the bottom lines show various types of usage. The top line graphed shows idle time, which drops whenever the CPU is utilized.

Figure 11.2 also shows how you can customize a performance graph. I've customized both the chart title and the title for the vertical axis. Current data values are shown in the chart's data display area directly below the actual chart. The legend, located below the chart, shows the items being displayed and allows modification of the displayed item's attributes, such as color, line style, and width.

FIGURE 11.2

The Performance Monitor displaying some CPU usage counters.

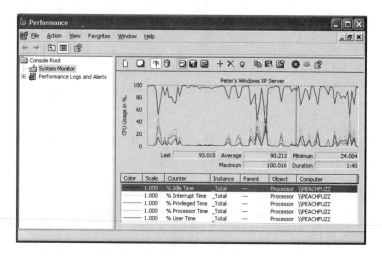

A Look at the Program

Now let's take a look at the PerfMon1 program itself. Listing 11.1 contains the main program, PerfMon1.cpp, a very simple program that accesses performance counters and objects stored in the registry. To create PerfMon1, see the instructions for creating a project in Chapter 10.

NOTE *You may download the PerfMon1 code from the Sybex website at* **www.sybex.com**. *Click Catalog, type the name of the book or the reference number from the book's ISBN (2987), and press Enter. From the main page for this book, click Downloads to go to the code.*

LISTING 11.1: PERFMON1.CPP

```cpp
// PerfMon1.cpp : Defines the entry point for the console
//application.

#define _UNICODE

#include "stdafx.h"

#include <windows.h> // Standard windows header
#include <winperf.h> // Performance monitor definitions
#include <stdio.h> // printf() and other I/O stuff
#include <malloc.h> // memory allocation definitions.

#define BUFFERSIZE 8192 // initial buffer size,

#define INCREMENT 4096 // If too small, increment by 4096

int main(int argc, char* argv[])
{
// These objects are shown in winperf.h:
PPERF_DATA_BLOCK        PerfDataBlock = NULL;
PPERF_OBJECT_TYPE       PerfObjectType;
PPERF_INSTANCE_DEFINITION PerfInstanceDefinition;
PPERF_COUNTER_DEFINITION  PerfCounterDefinition;
PPERF_COUNTER_DEFINITION  PerfCurrentCounter;
PPERF_COUNTER_BLOCK     PerfCounterBlock;

// Program variables:
DWORD BufferSize = BUFFERSIZE; // Size of our buffer.
DWORD nShort;    // If TRUE, display minimal data
DWORD i;       // Index
DWORD j;       // Index
DWORD k;       // Index
char szOutput[512]; // temporary output buffer
```

```c
// Create a reference, and initialize test buffer:
szOutput[0] = '\0';

printf("PerfMon1 - Check out HKEY_PERFORMANCE_DATA! ");
printf("Version 2000\n");

// Check options, /S for short output display!

nShort = FALSE;

if (argc > 1)
{
 if (argv[1][0] == '/' &&
  (argv[1][1] == 'S' || argv[1][1] == 's'))
 {
  nShort = TRUE;
 }
}

// Allocate an initial buffer, which we'll resize later.
PerfDataBlock = (PPERF_DATA_BLOCK) malloc(BufferSize);

printf("+");
while (RegQueryValueEx(HKEY_PERFORMANCE_DATA,
 "Global", NULL, NULL, (LPBYTE) PerfDataBlock,
 &BufferSize) == ERROR_MORE_DATA)
{// The buffer is too small, so expand it!
 printf("-");
 BufferSize += INCREMENT;
 PerfDataBlock = (PPERF_DATA_BLOCK)
  realloc(PerfDataBlock, BufferSize);
}
printf("!\n\n");

// Buffer is sized OK now, let's get the first object!
PerfObjectType = (PPERF_OBJECT_TYPE)
 ((PBYTE)PerfDataBlock + PerfDataBlock->HeaderLength);

// loop through objects in HKEY_PERFORMANCE_DATA
for (i = 0; i < PerfDataBlock->NumObjectTypes; i++)
{
 if (nShort)
 {
  printf("Index: %ld\n",
   PerfObjectType->ObjectNameTitleIndex);
 }
 else
 {
```

```
    printf("\n");
    printf("Index to name in Title Database %ld\n",
     PerfObjectType->ObjectNameTitleIndex);
    printf("Length of this object definition %d\n",
     PerfObjectType->TotalByteLength);
    printf("Length of object definition %ld\n",
     PerfObjectType->DefinitionLength);
    printf("Length of this header structure %ld\n",
     PerfObjectType->HeaderLength);
    printf("use by analysis program to point to "
     "retrieved title string %ld\n",
     PerfObjectType->ObjectNameTitle);
    printf("Index to Help in Title Database %ld\n",
     PerfObjectType->ObjectHelpTitleIndex);
    printf("Used by analysis program to point to "
     "retrieved title string %ld\n",
     PerfObjectType->ObjectHelpTitle);
    printf("Object level of detail %ld \n",
     PerfObjectType->DetailLevel);
    printf("Number of counters in each "
     "counter block %ld \n",
     PerfObjectType->NumCounters);
    printf("Default counter to display %ld \n",
     PerfObjectType->DefaultCounter);
    printf("Number of object instances %ld\n",
     PerfObjectType->NumInstances);
    printf("Instance name Code page, "
     "or 0 if UNICODE %ld\n",
     PerfObjectType->CodePage);
    printf("Sample Time in 'Object' units %ld\n",
     PerfObjectType->PerfTime);
    printf("Frequency of 'Object' units %ld\n\n",
     PerfObjectType->PerfFreq);
}

// next get the counter block,
//  containing counter information!
PerfCounterDefinition = (PPERF_COUNTER_DEFINITION)
 ((PBYTE)PerfObjectType +
 PerfObjectType->HeaderLength);

if (PerfObjectType->NumInstances > 0)
{// first instance:
 PerfInstanceDefinition =
  (PPERF_INSTANCE_DEFINITION)
  ((PBYTE)PerfObjectType +
  PerfObjectType->DefinitionLength);
```

```
// Next instance loop:
for(k = 0;
 k < (DWORD)PerfObjectType->NumInstances; k++)
{
 if (nShort)
 {
  printf("\n\tInstance '%S'\n", (char *)
   ((PBYTE)PerfInstanceDefinition +
   PerfInstanceDefinition->NameOffset));
 }
 else
 {
  printf("\n\tUnicode name of "
   "this instance '%S'\n",
   (char *)((PBYTE)PerfInstanceDefinition +
   PerfInstanceDefinition->NameOffset));
  printf("\tLength including the "
   "subsequent name %ld\n",
   PerfInstanceDefinition->ByteLength);
  printf("\tTitle Index to name "
   "of 'parent' object %ld\n",
   PerfInstanceDefinition->
   ParentObjectTitleIndex);
  printf("\tIndex to instance "
   "of parent object %ld\n",
   PerfInstanceDefinition->
   ParentObjectInstance);
  printf("\tA unique ID used "
   "instead of matching the "
   "name to identify this "
   "instance, -1 = none %ld\n",
   PerfInstanceDefinition->UniqueID);
  printf("\tLength in bytes "
   "of name; 0 = none %ld\n\n",
   PerfInstanceDefinition->NameLength);
 }

 PerfCurrentCounter = PerfCounterDefinition;

 // Get first counter in this instance
 PerfCounterBlock = (PPERF_COUNTER_BLOCK)
  ((PBYTE)PerfInstanceDefinition +
  PerfInstanceDefinition->ByteLength);

 // Then retrieve all counters in this
 //  instance with a loop:
 for(j = 0; j < PerfObjectType->NumCounters; j++)
 {
```

```
  if (nShort)
  {
   printf("\t\tCounter: %ld\n",
    PerfCurrentCounter->
    CounterNameTitleIndex);
  }
  else
  {
   printf("\t\tLength in bytes of this "
    "structure %ld \n",
    PerfCurrentCounter->ByteLength);
   printf("\t\tIndex of Counter name "
    "into Title Database %ld\n",
    PerfCurrentCounter->CounterNameTitleIndex);
   wprintf(L"\t\tretrieved name string '%s'\n",
    PerfCurrentCounter->CounterNameTitle);
   printf("\t\tIndex of Counter Help into "
    "Title Database %ld\n",
    PerfCurrentCounter->CounterHelpTitleIndex);
   wprintf(L"\t\tretrieved help string '%s'\n",
    PerfCurrentCounter->CounterHelpTitle);
   printf("\t\tPower of 10 to scale %ld\n",
    PerfCurrentCounter->DefaultScale);
   printf("\t\tCounter level of detail "
    "(for controlling display complexity %ld\n",
    PerfCurrentCounter->DetailLevel);
   printf("\t\tType of counter %ld\n",
    PerfCurrentCounter->CounterType);
   printf("\t\tSize of counter in bytes %ld\n",
    PerfCurrentCounter->CounterSize);
   printf("\t\tOffset to the first "
    "byte of this counter %ld\n",
    PerfCurrentCounter->CounterOffset);

   printf("\n\n");
  }

  // Get next counter.
  PerfCurrentCounter = (PPERF_COUNTER_DEFINITION)
   ((PBYTE)PerfCurrentCounter +
   PerfCurrentCounter->ByteLength);
 } // for loop

 // next instance, coming up next!
 PerfInstanceDefinition = (PPERF_INSTANCE_DEFINITION)
  ((PBYTE)PerfCounterBlock +
  PerfCounterBlock->ByteLength);
} // for loop
```

```
} // if (PerfObjectType->NumInstances > 0)
else
{// Get the first counter.
 PerfCounterBlock = (PPERF_COUNTER_BLOCK)
  ((PBYTE)PerfObjectType +
  PerfObjectType->DefinitionLength);

 // Get counters in a loop:
 for(j = 0; j < PerfObjectType->NumCounters; j++)
 {
  if (nShort)
  {
   printf("\tCounter: %ld\n",
     PerfCounterDefinition->CounterNameTitleIndex);
  }
  else
  {
   printf("\tLength in bytes of "
     "this structure %ld \n",
     PerfCounterDefinition->ByteLength);
   printf("\tIndex of Counter name "
     "into Title Database %ld\n",
     PerfCounterDefinition->CounterNameTitleIndex);
   printf("\tretrieved title string '%S'\n",
     PerfCounterDefinition->CounterNameTitle);
   printf("\tIndex of Counter Help "
     "into Title Database %ld\n",
     PerfCounterDefinition->CounterHelpTitleIndex);
   printf("\tretrieved help string '%S'\n",
     PerfCounterDefinition->CounterHelpTitle);
   printf("\tPower of 10 by which to scale %ld\n",
     PerfCounterDefinition->DefaultScale);
   printf("\tCounter level of detail (for "
     "controlling display complexity %ld\n",
     PerfCounterDefinition->DetailLevel);
   printf("\tType of counter %ld\n",
     PerfCounterDefinition->CounterType);
   printf("\tSize of counter in bytes %ld\n",
     PerfCounterDefinition->CounterSize);
   printf("\tOffset to the first "
     "byte of this counter %ld\n",
     PerfCounterDefinition->CounterOffset);
   printf("\n\n");
  }

  // Data is (LPVOID)((PBYTE)PerfCounterBlock +
  // PerfCounterDefinition->CounterOffset);
```

```
   PerfCounterDefinition = (PPERF_COUNTER_DEFINITION)
    ((PBYTE)PerfCounterDefinition +
    PerfCounterDefinition->ByteLength);
  } // for loop

 } // else if (PerfObjectType->NumInstances > 0)

 // Get the next object to monitor
 PerfObjectType = (PPERF_OBJECT_TYPE)
  ((PBYTE)PerfObjectType +
  PerfObjectType->TotalByteLength);

 } // Done! Go home and be sweet about it.

 return(0);
}
```

The program includes references to stdafx.cpp and stdafx.h. These two files are very simple. The file stdafx.cpp contains the lines:

```
// stdafx.cpp : source file that includes just the standard includes
//    PerfMon1.pch will be the pre-compiled header
//    stdafx.obj will contain the pre-compiled type information

#include "stdafx.h"

// TODO: reference any additional headers you need in STDAFX.H
// and not in this file
```

The include file stdafx.h contains these lines:

```
// stdafx.h : include file for standard system include files,
// or project specific include files that are used frequently, but
//   are changed infrequently
//

#if !defined(AFX_STDAFX_H__766546C6_18BD_11D2_88CB_0060970BB14F__INCLUDED_)
#define AFX_STDAFX_H__766546C6_18BD_11D2_88CB_0060970BB14F__INCLUDED_

#if _MSC_VER > 1000
#pragma once
#endif // _MSC_VER > 1000

#define WIN32_LEAN_AND_MEAN // Exclude rarely-used
//                 stuff from Windows headers

#include <stdio.h>
```

```
// TODO: reference additional headers your program requires here

//{{AFX_INSERT_LOCATION}}
// Microsoft Visual C++ will insert additional declarations immediately
//  before the previous line.

#endif // !defined(AFX_STDAFX_H__766546C6_ . . .
)
```

The performance information access program is simple and does not do much more than list the counters found in the registry. Of course, most performance-monitoring programs will want the actual performance data values, too.

If you look at the PERF_COUNTER_DEFINITION structure, you will see that the last three items defined in this structure are CounterType, CounterSize, and CounterOffset. These three items represent the specific information needed to access a particular performance counter. Of course, to use the counter in a meaningful way, you'd also have to (at least) scale and format the counter properly, and then display it.

The following code segment shows the definition of the PERF_COUNTER_DEFINITION object:

```
typedef struct _PERF_COUNTER_DEFINITION {
  DWORD       ByteLength;
    // Length in bytes of this structure
  DWORD       CounterNameTitleIndex;
    // Index of Counter name into Title Database
  LPWSTR      CounterNameTitle;
    // Initially NULL, for use by analysis
    // program to point to retrieved title string
  DWORD       CounterHelpTitleIndex;
    // Index of Counter Help into Title Database
  LPWSTR      CounterHelpTitle;
    // Initially NULL, for use by analysis program
    // to point to retrieved title string
  LONG      DefaultScale;
    // Power of 10 by which to scale chart line
    // if vertical axis is 100
    // 0 ==> 1, 1 ==> 10, -1 ==>1/10, etc.
  DWORD       DetailLevel;
    // Counter level of detail (for controlling
    // display complexity)
  DWORD       CounterType;
    // Type of counter
  DWORD       CounterSize;
    // Size of counter in bytes
  DWORD       CounterOffset;
    // Offset from the start of the PERF_COUNTER_BLOCK
    // to the first byte of this counter
} PERF_COUNTER_DEFINITION, *PPERF_COUNTER_DEFINITION;
```

Notice the last item in PERF_COUNTER_DEFINITION: CounterOffset. The offset from the start of the PERF_COUNTER_BLOCK is CounterOffset. This finds the counter in question. The CounterSize variable (just above CounterOffset) tells you how many bytes the counter in question occupies. Many counters are four bytes (a DWORD) in length.

Another important item for the counter is CounterType, a DWORD that describes the counter's type. The CounterType field is bitmapped and contains a lot of valuable information about the counter, as shown in Table 11.1. Figure 11.3 shows a mapping of the bits in CounterType.

FIGURE 11.3

CounterType bits are all significant.

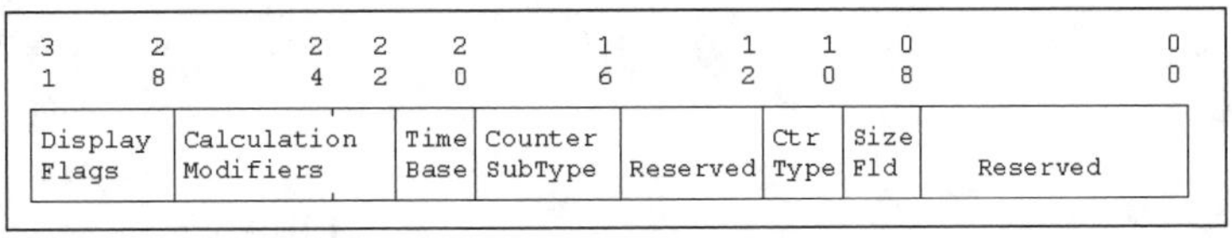

3 1	2 8	2 4	2 2	2 0	1 6	1 2	1 0	0 8	0 0
Display Flags	Calculation Modifiers		Time Base	Counter SubType	Reserved	Ctr Type	Size Fld	Reserved	

TABLE 11.1: THE BITS IN COUNTERTYPE

FIRST BIT	END BIT	DESCRIPTION
0	7	Reserved
8	9	Size field indicating the size, ranging from 0 to variable-length binary
		00 = Displays a DWORD-sized counter (32 bits)
		01 = Displays a large-sized counter
		10 = Displays a zero-length counter
		11 = Displays a variable-length counter
10	11	The counter's type: number, counter, text, or 0
		00 = Displays a number that is not a counter
		01 = Displays a counter that increases as time passes
		10 = Displays a text field
		11 = Displays as a zero
12	15	Reserved
16	19	Subtype, varies depending on the type of counter
		If the counter is number (00) then:
		0000 = Displays as a hexadecimal value
		0001 = Displays as a decimal integer
		0010 = Displays as a decimal integer / 1000
		If the counter is increasing number (01) then:
		0000 = Displays the counter value without modification

Continued on next page

TABLE 11.1: THE BITS IN COUNTERTYPE *(continued)*

FIRST BIT	END BIT	DESCRIPTION
16	19	0001 = Displays the counter divided by the time since the previous counter value
		0010 = Displays the counter divided by a base value
		0011 = Contains the base value used in fractions
		0100 = Displays the counter subtracted from the current time
		0101 = Displays using the Quelen processing function
		0110 = Begins or ends a standard histogram
		0111 = Displays the counter divided by a private clock
		If the counter is text, then:
		0000 = Type of text is in the text field
		0001 = Display the text as ASCII using the CodePage field
20	21	The timer base for the counter: either timer ticks, timer 100 nanoseconds, or an object-based timer
		00 = Uses the system timer tick as the base
		01 = Uses a 100-nanosecond timer base for the counter
		10 = Uses the object timer frequency
22	23	Calculation modifier, used for delta counters
		01 = First computes the difference between the two values
		10 = Shows both the difference and the base difference
24	27	Calculation modifier, used with inverse or multicounters
		01 = Shows as a 1.0 value
		10 = Shows as the cumulative result of multiple values
28	31	Format flag, describing how to display this counter's data
		0000 = Displays no suffix
		0001 = Displays the suffix "/Sec"
		0010 = Displays the suffix "%"
		0011 = Displays the suffix "Secs"
		0100 = Displays no value

The best information on these values is contained in the SDK's `winperf.h`, one of the better-documented header files for Windows XP.

To access a counter, see the section of Listing 11.1 where `PerfCounterBlock` is used. Set this initially to the first counter:

```
PerfCounterBlock = (PPERF_COUNTER_BLOCK)
  ((PBYTE)PerfInstanceDefinition +
  PerfInstanceDefinition->ByteLength);
```

You can access the data using the following line of code:

```
Data = (LPVOID)((PBYTE)PerfCounterBlock +
    PerfCounterDefinition->CounterOffset);
```

When using the code described here, be certain to properly de-reference the pointers.

Adding Performance Data to the Registry

The first part of this chapter delves into accessing preexisting performance data in the registry. It is also possible to add performance data to the registry for your own systems and applications. To do this, you must design your application or system to keep counters and modify the application or system to write these counters into the registry. Use the techniques described in the Microsoft Resource Kit version 3.5, Chapter 13, "Adding Application Performance Counters." This reference is available on the TechNet CD from Microsoft.

The process of adding performance data to the registry involves creating a `.dll` for collecting performance information. This `.dll` must have (at a minimum) a `Collect` entry point function. The entry point names may be determined at the product design phase. When installed, your installation program *must* specify the entry point names. Here are some possible entry points used to support performance monitoring:

Library   The name of the `.dll` file that your application uses to collect performance data. This object is required.

Collect   The routine that is used to report performance data upon request. This function is required.

Open   The function that is used to initialize the performance monitoring; this function is not required if the application is able to update performance counters without requests.

Close   The function that terminates the collection of performance data; as with `Open`, the `Close` function is not strictly required.

Adding counters to the registry is done using the LODCTR function. This function updates the registry and adds performance counters for an application or service as necessary. To use LODCTR, you must write an `.ini` file. The MSDN topic "Adding Counter Names and Descriptions to the Registry" documents this process.

Here is an example of performance counters added to the registry of one Windows XP installation for the IIS Web service:

```
"Library"="w3ctrs.dll"
"Open"="OpenW3PerformanceData"
"Close"="CloseW3PerformanceData"
"Collect"="CollectW3PerformanceData"
"Last Counter"=dword:00002890
"Last Help"=dword:00002891
"First Counter"=dword:000027ee
"First Help"=dword:000027ef
```

In this example, the library to monitor performance data is w3ctrs.dll. There are function entry points defined for Open, Close, and Collect. Your application may add these entries at program installation time or during the first execution of the program.

LODCTR automatically creates the final four entries—Last Counter, Last Help, First Counter, and First Help—when counters are loaded; your application should not modify these four entries.

An example of a LODCTR .ini file follows (all lines that begin with // are comment lines that are ignored by LODCTR):

```
[info]
applicationname=MyApp
symbolfile=symfile.h

// Only English is used by many of us, but there could be
// multiple languages loaded at one time. Just specify
// the language code in addition to (or instead of, if
// English is not used) the definition of 009=English line.
[languages]
009=English

// The object that will be using these counters is defined
// first.
[text]
OBJECT_1_009_NAME=MyApp
OBJECT_1_009_HELP=Monitor performance statistics for MyApp

// Next we define two counters for this object, one called
// Transactions, and another called LostCustomers.
DEVICE_COUNTER_1_009_NAME=Transactions
DEVICE_COUNTER_1_009_HELP=Number of transactions processed/second

DEVICE_COUNTER_2_009_NAME=LostCustomers
DEVICE_COUNTER_2_009_HELP=Number of customers lost due to slow transactions
```

This example is simple. There are two counters with descriptive text and only one language. The strings OBJECT_1, DEVICE_COUNTER_1, and DEVICE_COUNTER_2 are defined in the file symfile.h.

A real application might have many counters, depending on the application's complexity.

In summary, to create performance monitoring, follow these steps:

1. Create the necessary registry entries as described earlier in this section for Library, Open, Close, and Collect.

2. Move or copy the file specified in the Library entry to the %SystemRoot%\System32 directory.

3. Use the LODCTR program to integrate the .ini file's counter entries into the registry.

Part III

Windows and Office Registry Entries

In this section, you'll learn how to:

- ◆ Change the appearance of the Windows XP user interface
- ◆ Make networking and system registry entries
- ◆ Make registry entries that affect Microsoft Office system and user configurations

Chapter 12

The Windows XP User Interface: Changing How It Looks

THE WINDOWS USER INTERFACE IS probably the most modified part of Windows. Virtually all users change some part of the user interface at some time. Regardless of where they are done, many user interface registry modifications are easy to do and are relatively safe. For example, to figure out what is where, I make changes both from the Properties dialog boxes and in the registry, and then I just look at what's changed.

Messing up a registry entry for the user interface will usually not break the operating system; your display may not look like it should, but that's correctable. Typically, it will just make things either less friendly or not so pretty. However, some changes can cause serious damage to the system. Restore a damaged registry from a backup.

In this chapter, I'll cover how to make changes to user interface items, describing each one, its location in the registry, and any tool available to manipulate it.

◆ Manipulating Desktop settings

◆ Adjusting other user interface settings

◆ Setting console and command-prompt options

A New Look for Windows XP

With Windows XP, Microsoft changed how Windows looks and feels, including the Desktop, Explorer, and Internet Explorer. Microsoft has modified the interface that was developed for Windows 2000. For example, for a logged-on user, some Desktop functionality is stored in a different location in the registry than it was in previous versions of Windows.

Why are things different? Well, for one thing, Internet Explorer replaces the Windows Explorer application in most cases.

NOTE   *Notwithstanding any court orders, Windows uses one program for both Windows Explorer and Internet Explorer. While Microsoft was forced to give up packaging Internet Explorer with Windows XP as a browser, it still uses Internet Explorer for the Windows Explorer functionality. Say you install a competitor's browser. . .In reality Windows never removes anything; instead it allows the installed browser to serve the Internet browser needs and uses Explorer for its own needs.*

Now, this is not all bad, as it tends to integrate functions that were originally separate. In addition, Windows uses Internet Explorer for a number of other areas, including the Control Panel, the MMC (Microsoft Management Console), and other minor applications throughout Windows.

The Control Panel is the best tool to use to change the display properties in the registry; open the Display applet in the Control Panel (or right-click an unused place on the Desktop and select Properties). The registry controls everything—the Desktop, how things look, fonts, dialog box styles, colors, and DOS command-prompt windows.

There are some shortcuts for modifying the registry, other than using the Registry Editor. For example, in Windows XP Professional, you can use the MMC Policy Editor snap-in (not available in XP Home Edition) that is part of Computer Management (select Start ➤ Programs ➤ Administrative Tools), the Reg utility in the Resource Kit (see Chapter 4), and a few other tools to implement many of the settings. But the really interesting settings that are often desired, but seldom used, must be set using either very special tools or by direct, manual manipulation of the registry.

When you need to create a new key for setting values, make sure that you choose the correct data type for the key. Many keys are REG_SZ but hold a numeric value. Be careful not to create these keys with the wrong data type, such as REG_DWORD, because Windows XP won't recognize the value. Many of the settings for the user interface won't take effect until you log on the next time.

WARNING   *Do I have to say it? Back up your registry before making changes in it. Admittedly, changing the* HKEY_USERS *hive is less dangerous than changing* HKEY_LOCAL_MACHINE*, but there are hazards in making any changes to the registry.*

Desktop Settings

The Desktop is the single most modified part of the Windows user interface. Users quickly put on a bitmap for their wallpaper, set a background pattern, customize the size and configuration of windows, and change colors—all with wild abandon.

Windows has subkeys in the registry that hold the Desktop settings. Windows XP is a multiuser-enabled operating system, and it adds some complexity to the issue of user interface configuration and customization.

There are, at a minimum, two users to consider: First there's the currently logged-on user. For me, the currently logged-on user is the Administrator; you may have used a different name for your normal logons, but the principles are the same regardless. The second user is the one your computer considers to be the user when no user is actually logged on.

A third user (if you want to consider this a user, which I do) is the user profile used to create a new user's profile. This user is very limited in what they can do. And yes, this user has a name—the user is .DEFAULT. Notice the period, the first character in that user's name; it is significant in that Windows knows that this is the user to use when no other user is logged on. I'll refer to this user as the "default user."

Unfortunately, these two users are somewhat different. For example, the default user does not use Internet Explorer to manage the Desktop. (What management is there, anyway—no icons, only wallpaper, background, and a few color settings.) This means that techniques that are usable on normal users may not work on the default user. However, this is not a major issue, since you configure the default user the same way that you did in prior versions of Windows.

Themes are predefined configurations consisting of Desktop configurations, colors, sounds, icons, cursors, and other visual customizations for the user interface. With earlier versions of Windows, one of the first things to do is load the Microsoft Windows Themes, which are available from Microsoft in their add-on product Plus at `http://www.microsoft.com/windows/plus/`. Themes allows you to load any Windows-compatible theme; this saves time when configuring the Desktop.

Users can create themes themselves or get them from a variety of sources. Many users rely on the themes that come with the various Windows Resource Kits, from Windows 95/98/Me, or from a number of sites on the Internet.

NOTE *I won't get into the issues of copyrights and themes. A number of themes for Windows surely impinge upon the rights of others. For example, Star Trek, Star Wars, Three Stooges, The Simpsons, and a host of other themes are floating around on the Internet. Some are licensed, and most are the creation of the fans that have made these themes available to the public, usually for free. If you use a particular theme, whether you pay for it or not is a value decision that you will have to make. Myself, I'd prefer that everyone respected the intellectual property rights of others.*

Although you can make many of the modifications mentioned in this chapter using various Properties dialog boxes, some modifications can only be done by changing the registry. Of course, I recommend using the easiest method to change things when possible—and that would be the Properties dialog box, in most cases.

The registry key `HKEY_USERS\.DEFAULT\Control Panel\Desktop` contains the settings used by Windows XP when there is no logged-on user. Notice that this subkey includes many settings that probably won't mean much to the system. In the "no user logged on" mode, Windows *normally* doesn't display icons or much of anything else. Notice I said *normally*; there are ways to force Windows to do just this. For example, you can allow services to interact with the Desktop and start services before a user logs on.

The registry key `HKEY_USERS\<SID>\Control Panel` holds settings for the current user.

NOTE *Note that <SID> is a placeholder for a user's SID (security identifier). Usually, finding your SID is easy; just peek at the HKEY_USERS hive. There will be two or three subkeys: .DEFAULT (for use when no user is logged on) and one or more subkeys identified by a SID value—this is your SID.*

Backgrounds and Wallpapers

At some point, every user has probably wondered about the difference between a background and wallpaper. Both are bitmaps. The background bitmap is typically small, consisting of one or two colors. Wallpaper is usually an image that covers some, or all, of the exposed Desktop; this image can be as large as the Desktop, tiled, or stretched to fit.

The background is under everything on the Desktop. When drawing, the first thing that Windows XP does with the Desktop is to draw the background bitmap in the background color(s) selected. The Windows default is pea green—not my favorite color. When there is no background bitmap, Windows by default draws the background as a solid color.

NOTE *We'll talk about changing that pea green background color later; don't worry. Having a solid-color background can improve system performance when compared to having a bitmap for the background.*

Once the background is drawn, Windows draws the wallpaper. Windows draws the wallpaper in one of three modes:

Centered One copy of the wallpaper image is drawn in the center of the screen. If the wallpaper image is too small to fit, then the background will be visible on those areas the wallpaper image does not cover. If the wallpaper image is too large, Windows clips parts to fit.

Tiled The first copy of the wallpaper is drawn in the upper-left corner of the screen; additional copies are drawn below and to the right to fill the entire screen with the wallpaper bitmap. Some bitmaps, by design, fit together well, hiding this seam; other bitmaps present a jagged, clumsy look when tiled.

Stretched This refers to the Windows feature for stretching the Desktop image When enabled, Windows automatically stretches the wallpaper bitmap to fit the screen dimensions. This is the most commonly used mode, and the most inefficient mode.

NOTE *If you primarily use one resolution, you can improve performance by doing the following: Instead of using a bitmap as wallpaper in stretched mode, use a graphics editor to stretch the bitmap to the screen's resolution. Then, select the Centered option to display the wallpaper. Substantial improvements in Desktop-update performance may be achieved by changing the mode.*

After drawing the wallpaper, Windows XP draws objects, such as Desktop icons and other windows. Windows handles icons and their labels in a special manner. Windows draws the icon images over the wallpaper. Next, Windows fills the area under the icon's label with the background color, but not the background pattern; the label's background is a solid color. (Why? Because the labels would be very difficult to read if a pattern were used.) Finally the text for the icon is drawn, so what you see under the text of an icon is not the wallpaper, but the background color.

In addition, there are two sets of background/wallpaper settings. Windows XP maintains one set for the current user and the other set for all users who do not have personalized values. Those users without predefined configurations are supported using the `HKEY_LOCAL_MACHINE\Software\Microsoft\Command Processor` subkey.

WALLPAPER

The `Wallpaper` value entry is a string that must contain the filename of the image file for the wallpaper. The value to modify is in `HKEY_USERS\<SID>\Software\Microsoft\Internet Explorer\Desktop\General`.

Value entry:	`Wallpaper`
Type:	REG_EXPAND_SZ
Typical value:	`" "` (or a fully qualified filename)

The file should be any file that Internet Explorer is able to display, including HTML, HTT (Hypertext Template), JPG, and BMP files. The resolution of the image should be compatible with the current display mode. If the resolution is different from the display mode, it is not the end of the world, but the quality of the display, and system performance, will be compromised.

If you are specifying a file that is not in the `%SystemRoot%` path, be sure to include a fully qualified pathname. Generally, the Display Properties dialog box will include pathname information regardless of where the file is located.

This parameter is compatible with logged-on users only. For the `.DEFAULT` user, the registry value to modify is in `HKEY_USERS\.DEFAULT\Control Panel\Desktop`.

Value entry:	`Wallpaper`
Type:	REG_SZ
Typical value:	`""` (or a fully qualified bitmap image filename)

The file should be a standard (noncompressed) Windows XP bitmap, and the resolution should be compatible with the current display mode. If the resolution is different from the display mode, it is not the end of the world, but the quality of the display, and system performance, will be compromised.

If you are specifying a file that is not in the `%SystemRoot%` path, be sure to include a fully qualified path name. Since this variable is REG_SZ, do not use environment variables to specify the file's path. Alternatively, modify this value with `Reg.exe`.

This parameter is compatible with the default user only. It allows you to configure the Desktop display before any user has logged on. When configuring the Desktop display before a user has logged on, consider placing your company logo there!

NOTE   *For users other than the default user, the image file type for a background is any type that Internet Explorer is able to display. This means that even hypertext files can be used for backgrounds. For the default user, the image type must be a bitmap (`.bmp`) file.*

WALLPAPERSTYLE

The `WallpaperStyle` entry tells Windows XP to stretch or compress a wallpaper bitmap that is different from the Desktop in size or resolution to fit the Desktop fully. For all users except for the default user, this value is located in `HKEY_USERS\<SID>\Software\Microsoft\Internet Explorer\Desktop\General`. For the default user, this value is located in `HKEY_USERS\.DEFAULT\Control Panel\Desktop`.

Value entry:	`WallpaperStyle`
Type:	REG_SZ
Typical value:	`0`

A value of `0` will result in unstretched wallpaper, while a value of `2` will stretch the wallpaper to fit the screen's resolution.

If carried to extremes, this mode can result in an unattractive Desktop. Generally, if the wallpaper image is close to the size of the Desktop, the appearance will be acceptable. Certain bitmaps stretch better than others, so if in doubt, try it.

The WallpaperStyle parameter is compatible with both specific users and the default user subkeys. It allows you to configure the Desktop display before any user has logged on. For the default user configuration, consider stretching either wallpaper that is a different size from the default logon screen or wallpaper designed to be stretched.

TileWallpaper

The TileWallpaper entry tells Windows XP to either tile or center the Desktop's wallpaper. For all users except the default user, this value is located in the subkey HKEY_USERS\<SID>\Software\Microsoft\Internet Explorer\Desktop\General. For the default user this value is located in HKEY_USERS\.DEFAULT\Control Panel\Desktop.

Value entry:	TileWallpaper
Type:	REG_SZ
Typical value:	0

A value of 0 will not tile the wallpaper, while a value of 1 will tile the wallpaper to fit the screen's resolution.

It is possible to have a single copy of the wallpaper that is not centered or located at the upper left of the Desktop; see the next two sections.

This parameter is compatible with both specific users and the default user subkeys. It allows you to configure the Desktop display before any user has logged on. For the default user configuration, when tiling, use either a small bitmap or a tileable bitmap.

WallpaperOriginX

The WallpaperOriginX entry allows you to set the origin for both tiled and untiled wallpaper displays as shown here. Located in HKEY_USERS\.DEFAULT\Control Panel\Desktop, it may be necessary to create the value entry.

Value entry:	WallpaperOriginX
Type:	REG_SZ
Typical value:	0

This entry is useful if, for example, you want to set your wallpaper to be in one of the corners of the Desktop. This parameter works with both centered and tiled wallpapers.

This parameter is compatible with the default user only. It allows you to configure the Desktop display before any user has logged on. For the default user configuration, consider recentering the wallpaper to provide an aesthetically pleasing Desktop. I find that having a small company logo in the lower-right or upper-left corner of the screen can be pleasing!

WALLPAPERORIGINY

The `WallpaperOriginY` entry allows setting the origin for both tiled and untiled wallpaper displays. Located in `HKEY_USERS\.DEFAULT\Control Panel\Desktop`, it may be necessary to create the data value.

Value entry:	`WallpaperOriginY`
Type:	REG_SZ
Typical value:	0

This entry is useful if, for example, you want to set your wallpaper to be in one of the corners of the Desktop. This parameter works with both centered and tiled wallpapers.

This parameter is compatible with the default user only. It allows configuration of the Desktop display before any user has logged on. For the default user configuration, consider recentering the wallpaper to provide an aesthetically pleasing Desktop. I find that having a small company logo in the upper-left or lower-right corner of the screen can be pleasing!

PATTERN

The `Pattern` entry contains a pattern drawn using the background Desktop color. It is stored as a string containing eight numbers. This value is located at `HKEY_USERS\<SID>\Control Panel\Desktop` for all but the default user, and at `HKEY_USERS\.DEFAULT\Control Panel\Desktop` for the default user.

Value entry:	`Pattern`
Type:	REG_SZ
Typical value:	(None)

Internet Explorer converts each number to a line in a bitmap. Each one in the binary number will represent the Desktop color.

The patterns are stored in the key `HKEY_USERS\<SID>\Control Panel\Patterns`. There is a simple editor for modifying (and creating new) patterns. You start this editor in the Background tab of the Display Properties dialog box by clicking the Pattern button.

This parameter is compatible with both specific users and the default user subkeys. This allows you to configure the Desktop display before any user has logged on. For the default user configuration, consider using a pattern when not using stretched or tiled wallpaper.

Task Switching

Most users switch tasks with the keystroke combination Alt+Tab, although some use the Taskbar. You can configure the Task Switch dialog box, displayed when Alt+Tab is pressed, if desired.

Settings for this dialog box are simple to implement. Since there is no task switching before a user logs on, these settings are only meaningful to logged-on users and not the default user. Though the settings can be set for the default user, they will have no useful effect—there is no Task Switch dialog box for the default user!

Each of the task-switching values is located in the registry subkey `HKEY_USERS\<SID>\Control Panel\Desktop`.

CoolSwitch

The `CoolSwitch` entry controls whether Windows displays the task-change window.

Value entry:	`CoolSwitch`
Type:	REG_SZ
Typical value:	1

New!

Prior to Windows NT 4, two styles of task switching were used. In *direct switching*, the system cycles through the running applications as the task-switch keystroke combination is pressed. Usually, only the application's title bar is active until the user releases the task-switch key. The second method of task switching, *CoolSwitch*, is used to display a dialog box, similar to that used in Windows 2000, to allow the user to select the application to switch to. Windows NT 4 and later only support the second method. Therefore, Windows XP does not use the `CoolSwitch`-enabling registry key. Setting this entry to any value other than 1 seems to have no effect. Microsoft recommends not changing this key, so that the key will be compatible with future upgrades.

CoolSwitchColumns

The number of columns in the CoolSwitch dialog box is set using `CoolSwitchColumns`, as shown here.

Value entry:	`CoolSwitchColumns`
Type:	REG_SZ
Typical value:	7

The CoolSwitch dialog box displays icons for each running application that has a displayable window; it displays these icons in rows and columns. The CoolSwitch dialog box does not display applications and components that have no window to display.

This registry key sets the number of columns (the number of icons across) displayed in the CoolSwitch dialog box. The default value, 7, is a reasonable choice for most resolutions. However, users may find that with low-resolution displays, fewer columns may be more appropriate. Users with high-resolution displays, running a large number of applications concurrently, may want more columns displayed.

NOTE *Are more applications running than will fit in the CoolSwitch dialog box? No problem, CoolSwitch will scroll the icons automatically as the user presses the task-switch keystroke combination. However, setting both* `CoolSwitch-Columns` *and* `CoolSwitchRows` *to* 1 *won't create a single-icon CoolSwitch dialog box.*

CoolSwitchRows

The number of rows in the CoolSwitch dialog box is set using `CoolSwitchRows`.

Value entry:	`CoolSwitchRows`
Type:	REG_SZ
Typical value:	3

The CoolSwitch dialog box displays icons for each running application with a displayable window in rows and columns. Windows will not display applications and components without a main window, as they cannot be activated using the task-switch keys.

This registry key sets the number of rows (the number of icons up and down) displayed in the CoolSwitch dialog box. The default value, 3, is a reasonable choice for most resolutions. However, users may find that with low-resolution displays, fewer rows may be more appropriate. Users with high-resolution displays, running a large number of applications concurrently, may want more rows displayed.

Moving Windows

One of the nice things about Windows is that it gives you the ability to drag things. Windows may be moved using a drag operation, and objects may be dragged and dropped. You can move windows either by using the keyboard or by simply clicking the title bar and dragging the window itself.

Both icons and objects can be dragged. This includes selections in documents for those applications that support drag-and-drop. Clicking on the object selects it, and moving the mouse begins a drag-and-drop operation.

There are three registry entries for dragging that are specific to Windows XP: `DragFullWindows`, `DragHeight`, and `DragWidth`. `DragFullWindows` specifies whether a window's contents are displayed (a full-content drag) while moving it, or whether only the window's outline is displayed. The other two entries specify the size the box must be in a drag operation before Windows will actually consider the object as something to be dragged.

Why change the size of the drag box? Some users who have difficulty controlling the amount that they move the mouse may find it preferable to set a larger drag area.

Each of the drag-related values is located in the registry subkey `HKEY_USERS\<SID>\Control Panel\Desktop`. Both logged-on users and the default user can have these values applied to them.

DRAGFULLWINDOWS

Earlier versions of Windows only supported a mode called *outline dragging*. This was necessary primarily due to the incredible lack of performance of early CPUs and video systems. Newer hardware, improvements in video driver technology, and other changes have brought full-window dragging to Windows. `DragFullWindows` allows dragging both a window and the window's contents.

Value entry:	`DragFullWindows`
Type:	REG_SZ
Typical value:	2

To drag the entire window with contents, set this parameter to a nonzero value (I have seen both 1 and 2 used); to drag only a window outline, set this value to 0. This value may also be set by clicking the Effects button on the Appearance tab of the Display Properties dialog box. Look for the check box called Show Windows Contents While Dragging.

There is not much dragging done before a user logs on, so these entries probably won't matter much to the default user's configuration.

DRAGHEIGHT

The `DragHeight` entry determines the height of the rectangle used to detect the start of a drag operation.

Value entry:	DragHeight
Type:	REG_SZ
Typical value:	4

Click an object and move the mouse pointer more than the distance set for `DragHeight` and/or `DragWidth`, and Windows will assume that a drag operation is being performed.

DRAGWIDTH

The `DragWidth` entry determines the width of the rectangle used to detect the start of a drag operation.

Value entry:	DragWidth
Type:	REG_SZ
Typical value:	4

Again, when you click an object and move the mouse pointer more than the `DragWidth` (and/or `DragHeight`), Windows will assume that a drag operation is being performed.

Power Management

New!

There are a number of settings for power management. Two of these are set in the Desktop settings.

LOWPOWERACTIVE

The `LowPowerActive` entry specifies whether an alarm is signaled when the battery power is low. It's found in the subkey `HKEY_USERS\<SID>\Control Panel\Desktop`.

Value entry:	LowPowerActive
Type:	REG_SZ
Typical value:	0

A value of 0 disables the low power warning functionality, while a value of 1 enables the warning.

POWEROFFACTIVE

The `PowerOffActive` entry specifies whether the monitor power-off sequence has been activated. It's found in the subkey `HKEY_USERS\<SID>\Control Panel\Desktop`.

Value entry:	PowerOffActive
Type:	REG_SZ
Typical value:	0

A value of 0 indicates that the system monitor will not enter a power-off state.

POWEROFFTIMEOUT

The `PowerOffTimeOut` entry specifies the amount of time prior to the monitor power-off sequence (as set by the screen saver configuration). It's found in the subkey `HKEY_USERS\<SID>\Control Panel\Desktop`.

Value entry:	PowerOffTimeOut
Type:	REG_SZ
Typical value:	0

A value of 0 indicates that there is no monitor power-off time-out value.

Version Branding

New! A user may select whether the current Windows version is painted in the lower-right corner of the Desktop.

PAINTDESKTOPVERSION

The `PaintDesktopVersion` entry specifies whether Windows will display two lines of product and version identification in the lower-right corner of the Desktop. The first line displayed will be the product identification ("Windows 2000" and "Windows XP Professional" are two examples of product identification). It's found in the subkey `HKEY_USERS\<SID>\Control Panel\Desktop`.

Value entry:	PaintDesktopVersion
Type:	REG_DWORD
Typical value:	0

A value of 0 disables the display of the Windows version on the Desktop, while a value of 1 enables the display. The default value is 1 for beta versions and other special versions of Windows and 0 for standard released products.

User Preferences

New! There is a setting for default user preferences. This value is bitmapped—that is, multiple selections may be included by simply adding the values for each selection.

USERPREFERENCESMASK

The `UserPreferencesMask` entry specifies which user preferences are to be used and which are not allowed. Some preferences are reserved for future use. It's found in the subkey `HKEY_USERS\<SID>\Control Panel\Desktop`.

Value entry:	UserPreferencesMask
Type:	REG_BINARY
Typical value:	Typically 0x80003E9E for Windows 2000 and 0x80071290 for Windows XP installations, but may vary with different installations and types of installations (.NET Server vs. Professional vs. Home Edition)

Table 12.1 lists the various known bits and their meanings.

TABLE 12.1: UserPreferencesMask BIT VALUES AND THEIR MEANINGS

BIT	UI SETTING	DEFAULT VALUE WINDOWS 2000	DEFAULT VALUE WINDOWS XP	MEANING
0	Active window tracking	0	0	Active window tracking is disabled by default; if set, active window tracking is enabled.
1	Menu animation	1	0	When set, menu animations are enabled. Bit 9 controls the effect of the animations.
2	Combo box animation	1	0	When set, the slide-open effect for combo boxes is enabled.
3	List box smooth scrolling	1	0	When set, list boxes have a smooth scrolling effect.
4	Gradient captions	1	1	When set, each window title bar has a gradient effect (changes from one color or shade to another along the length of the title bar).
5	Keyboard cues	0	0	When set, the menu access key letters (those letters that are underlined in a menu) are only visible when the menu is activated using the Alt key on the keyboard.
6	Active window tracking Z order	0	0	When set, a window activated through active window tracking is not brought to the top.
7	Hot tracking	1	1	When set, window hot tracking is enabled.
8	Reserved	0	0	Reserved.
9	Menu fade	1	1	See bit 1 above. Bit 9 allows menu fade animation. If not set, menus use slide animation. This bit is only meaningful if bit 1 is set.
10	Selection fade	1	0	When set, menus fade out after a selection is made.
11	Tool tip animation	1	0	When set, tool tip animation is enabled. The actual effects depend on bit 12.

Continued on next page

TABLE 12.1: UserPreferencesMask BIT VALUES AND THEIR MEANINGS *(continued)*

BIT	UI SETTING	DEFAULT VALUE WINDOWS 2000	DEFAULT VALUE WINDOWS XP	MEANING
12	Tool tip fade	1	1	When set, tool tip fade animation is enabled. When not set, tool tips use slide animation. If bit 11 is not set, this bit is ignored.
13	Cursor shadow	1	0	When set, the cursor has an animated shadow. This bit is not meaningful on systems with fewer than 256 colors.
14		Reserved	0	Used in Windows XP only.
15		Reserved	0	Used in Windows XP only.
16		Reserved	1	Used in Windows XP only.
17		Reserved	1	Used in Windows XP only.
18		Reserved	1	Used in Windows XP only.
19–30	Reserved	0	0	Reserved.
31	UI effects	1	1	When enabled, all user interface effects (combo box animation, cursor shadow, gradient captions, hot tracking, list box smooth scrolling, menu animation, menu underlines, selection fade, tool tip animation) are enabled.

NOTE   *The type of data is REG_BINARY, however this value is actually stored in REG_DWORD format. When edited in the default format, remember that the low-order bits are in the high-order positions. (The default Windows XP value of* 0x80071290 *will show, and be edited, as* 90 12 07 80.*)*

Something Else?

New!   Since Microsoft put this into Windows XP, I'll show it. In the beta test product, users could click a hyperlink in every window's title bar to send comments about that window to Microsoft. The default text was "Comments?" A second key, LameButtonEnabled, turned on the feature. This key is not present in released versions of Windows XP, though you can add it if desired. However, as the name implies, this scheme is rather lame...

LAMEBUTTONENABLED

The `LameButtonEnabled` entry specifies whether the Comments? hyperlink is displayed in each window's title bar. It's found in the subkey `HKEY_USERS\<SID>\Control Panel\Desktop`.

Value entry:	LameButtonEnabled
Type:	REG_SZ
Typical value:	0

Setting this entry to 1 enables the functionality. A value of 0 disables the display of the "Comments?" hyperlink in a window.

LAMEBUTTONTEXT

The `LameButtonText` entry specifies the text in the hyperlink displayed in each window's title bar when LameButtonEnabled is set. It's found in the subkey `HKEY_USERS\<SID>\Control Panel\ Desktop`.

Value entry:	LameButtonText
Type:	REG_SZ
Typical value:	Comments?

An empty string suppresses the display of any text. The text value does not affect the functionality, or action taken by Windows, when this hyperlink is selected.

The Cursor

The cursor can be configured somewhat. The only parameter that can be set for the cursor (sometimes called the *text caret*) is the blink rate. Some video systems, such as portables and video projection systems, don't react well to fast blink rates. Setting the `CursorBlinkRate` entry (discussed next) to a higher value may make the cursor easier to see.

CURSORBLINKRATE

The `CursorBlinkRate` entry specifies, in milliseconds, the blink rate of the cursor. It's found in the subkey `HKEY_USERS\<SID>\Control Panel\Desktop`.

Value entry:	CursorBlinkRate
Type:	REG_SZ
Typical value:	530

A smaller value will make the cursor blink faster, while larger values make it blink slower.

NOTE *Where'd that odd value of 530 milliseconds come from? Why not just use 500 milliseconds, which is half a second? Got me. This is a holdover from the earliest versions of Windows.*

Menus and the Windows User Interface

In the past, the Windows 95/98/Me user interface allowed more user flexibility when selecting menu items. Menu selections follow the cursor better in Windows XP and display cascading menus as the cursor is positioned over them. Try your Start menu for a good example of menu cascading. As an example, the `MenuShowDelay` entry controls cascading-menu delays; I'll cover it next.

MENUSHOWDELAY

The `MenuShowDelay` entry controls how long Windows XP will delay before showing a cascading menu.

Value entry:	`MenuShowDelay`
Type:	REG_SZ
Typical Value:	400

If the user pauses on a menu item that has a cascading menu under it, after the time specified in milliseconds, Windows XP displays the cascading menu automatically.

Slower processors may work better with a smaller value. However, the default of 400 milliseconds works well in most Windows XP installations.

Keyboard Settings

Several value entries are used to configure the keyboard under Windows. For most systems, they will contain default values, though they are all easily modified by the user in the Control Panel's Keyboard applet.

INITIALKEYBOARDINDICATORS

The `InitialKeyboardIndicators` entry is used to set or clear keyboard toggle keys, such as Num Lock and Caps Lock.

Value entry:	`InitialKeyboardIndicators`
Type:	REG_SZ
Typical value:	0

The Num Lock key can be problematic because many users wish to have it turned on at the time they log on. There are two ways to ensure that this happens. One way is to turn on the Num Lock key, then press Ctrl+Alt+Delete and select the Logoff button. Alternately, in the registry, change the user's setting in either HKEY_USERS\<SID>\Control Panel\Keyboard or HKEY_CURRENT_USER\Control Panel\Keyboard. Change the `InitialKeyboardIndicators` entry from whatever value it already has to 2. This will force on the Num Lock key.

NOTE *Other values in the* **Keyboard** *key control the other toggle keys, including the Caps Lock and Scroll Lock keys.*

KEYBOARDDELAY

KeyboardDelay sets the delay before a pressed keyboard key will begin to repeat.

Value entry:	KeyboardDelay
Type:	REG_SZ
Typical value:	1

The auto-repeat function can be very valuable to anyone who needs to draw a line in their word processor, move the cursor with the arrow keys, or repeat the same key a number of times over. With this benefit comes a problem: we sometimes inadvertently hold keys down longer than we should, leading to multipppple characters in our text. Yep, I paused a bit too long on the *p* in that word, trying to decide if my editor would let me do it!

On the other hand, if you are a good typist, then a quickly working key repeat with minimal delay will speed things up. Each has their own value that they'd like to see, and for this one, 0 is about a quarter of a second, and 3 is a full second, more or less.

NOTE *Times are approximate. Though a computer is capable of measuring even very small amounts of time, it cannot accurately repeat such measurements.*

KEYBOARDSPEED

The KeyboardSpeed entry sets how quickly keys will be repeated when a key is held down for longer than KeyboardDelay (above).

Value entry:	KeyboardSpeed
Type:	REG_SZ
Typical value:	31

The repeat rate can be between 2 and 30 characters per second, where the value of KeyboardSpeed ranges from 0 to 31. Too high a repeat rate causes the user to often type more repeating characters than desired, while a low rate causes the user to be frustrated and cranky.

KEYBOARD LAYOUT

Keyboard Layout (notice the space in the name) holds what the user's current keyboard layout is. For example, I can switch to a Thai keyboard layout and type in Thai script, like this: หหดำกญ (no, that word doesn't mean anything). This registry subkey is located at HKEY_USERS\<SID>\Keyboard Layout. Within this subkey are a number of other subkeys, used to hold information about using and customizing keyboards.

TIP *It is easiest to use the Control Panel's Keyboard applet to modify Keyboard Layout objects.*

The Mouse and the Microsoft IntelliMouse

There are a number of settings for the mouse and the Microsoft IntelliMouse, which has a wheel that scrolls windows. As support for Microsoft's IntelliMouse improves, more and more applications will work with the scroll wheel. The scroll wheel has a switch functioning as a separate button. A user may assign functionality to this button.

WheelScrollLines

Only meaningful for the IntelliMouse, the `WheelScrollLines` entry specifies the number of lines to scroll whenever the user uses the mouse wheel. It's found in `HKEY_USERS\<SID>\Control Panel\ Desktop`.

Value entry:	WheelScrollLines
Type:	REG_SZ
Typical value:	3

The wheel has discrete degrees of movement that provide tactile feedback to the user. The default value is to scroll three lines.

TIP   Windows at this point doesn't allow an easy method to modify this value; however, since you have this book, you can change it as needed.

It takes some time to experiment with and get used to using the IntelliMouse's wheel for scrolling. Before long, it can become second nature, and then it can be very fast and easy to use.

NOTE   If you're using Windows NT 4, be sure to get Microsoft's latest drivers for the IntelliMouse. Although there is some native support for wheel mice in Windows NT, the latest drivers offer improved performance.

DoubleClickHeight and DoubleClickWidth

The `DoubleClickHeight` and `DoubleClickWidth` settings in `HKEY_USERS\<SID>\Control Panel\Mouse` control how much the mouse may move before Windows XP won't consider two clicks in quick succession to be a double-click.

Value entry:	DoubleClickHeight or DoubleClickWidth
Type:	REG_SZ
Typical value:	4

For most users, the default values are fine. However, users with notebook computers that don't have good pointer resolution and users with handicaps may wish to make the double-click tolerance higher, especially when working with a high-resolution screen.

Other Mouse Values

Table 12.2 shows some of the other values in the registry that affect mouse performance. Each of these values is located in the `HKEY_USERS\<SID>\Control Panel\Mouse` key. Some are changed using the Control Panel's Mouse applet; others require registry surgery.

TABLE 12.2: MISCELLANEOUS MOUSE VALUES

VALUE ENTRY	TYPE	DEFAULT OR TYPICAL VALUE	DESCRIPTION
ActiveWindowTracking	REG_DWORD	0	Allows the user to bring a window to the top, as can be done in X Windows. Typically turned off, set this value to 1 to turn on this feature.
DoubleClickSpeed	REG_SZ	500	Sets how much time between mouse clicks before Windows won't consider two clicks in succession to be a double-click.
MouseSpeed	REG_SZ	1	Sets the degree of scaling for the mouse-pointer movement. A setting of 1 doubles the speed; 2 quadruples the speed.
MouseThreshold1	REG_SZ	6	Changes the acceleration-to-speed ratio for the mouse.
MouseThreshold2	REG_SZ	10	Changes the acceleration-to-speed ratio for the mouse.
SmoothMouseXCurve	REG_BINARY	00 00 00 00 00 00 00 00 15 6E 00 00 00 00 00 00 00 40 01 00 00 00 00 00 29 DC 03 00 00 00 00 00 00 00 28 00 00 00 00 00	Sets the mouse X coordinate smoothing when a curve is made by the user.
SmoothMouseYCurve	REG_BINARY	00 00 00 00 00 00 00 00 B8 5E 01 00 00 00 00 00 CD 4C 05 00 00 00 00 00 CD 4C 18 00 00 00 00 00 00 00 38 02 00 00 00 00	Sets the mouse Y coordinate smoothing when a curve is made by the user.
SnapToDefaultButton	REG_SZ	0	When set to 1, automatically moves the mouse to the current default button whenever Windows displays a new window.
SwapMouseButtons	REG_SZ	0	When set to 1, swaps the right and left mouse buttons, which is marginally useful for left-handed users (ever seen a left-handed mouse?).

Other User Interface Settings

You can use a few other user interface settings with Windows XP. Some of these just don't fit well in the previous section, so I've given them their own home.

Displaying Your Favorites

With Windows XP, displaying Internet Explorer's Favorites list in the Start menu allows you to quickly jump to an Internet Explorer favorite item. Simply open the Taskbar's Properties dialog box, and in the Advanced tab, turn on Display Favorites. To do the same change in the registry, follow these steps:

1. At a command prompt, create a new directory (using the command MD) named WWW in the following location: "%UserProfile%\Start Menu\WWW". Be sure to include the quotes in this command because this is a long filename.

2. Copy all your favorites, typically in %UserProfile%\Favorites, to your new directory at %UserProfile%\Start Menu\WWW.

3. In the registry, go to HKEY_CURRENT_USER\Software\Microsoft\Windows\CurrentVersion\ Explorer\User Shell Folders.

4. Edit the value entry Favorites, changing its value to "%UserProfile%\Start Menu\WWW". This will force Internet Explorer to use your new Favorites directory instead of your original Favorites.

Hiding Control Panel Applets

New!

You can hide any of the Control Panel applets, thereby not allowing the user to easily change part of the Windows configuration, by modifying the don't load key values. Simply add a data value, whose name is the same as the Control Panel applet that is not to be loaded in the don't load key. Follow these steps:

1. In MyComputer\HKEY_CURRENT_USER\ContorlPanel\don't load, create a new subkey with the same name as the Control Panel applet to be controlled. For example, to force the Control Panel to not display the NCPA.CPL applet, name the new data key ncpa.cpl. Specify a data type of REG_SZ for this key. If this key already exists with the correct data type, then proceed to step 2.

2. Set the data value of this new key to No.

3. In HKEY_CLASSES_ROOT*\openas\command, change the value entry, which is named (default) in RegEdit, to have the following value (if by chance, you do not have an OpenAs subkey, then see the upcoming section "Customizing the Properties Pop-up Menu"):

```
%SystemRoot%\System32\rundll32.exe %SystemRoot%\System32\
shell32.dll ,OpenAs_RunDLL %1
```

Windows XP typically sets both nacp.cpl and odbccp32.cpl to not load when the Control Panel starts.

Setting Your Country

In the registry, you set the country code in International\Geo. A single entry, Nation, is found there. Nation is a REG_SZ data key with a numeric code for the country. For example, the United States has the country code 244, while Canada is 39. This key is under HKEY_CURRENT_USER\Control Panel\ International\Geo.

WARNING   The country codes are not the country/region codes that we normally use. Often country codes are based on the international telephone country prefix. In this case, the country codes used are unique to Windows XP and several other Microsoft applications.

Customizing the Properties Pop-up Menu

You can add functionality to the properties of the pop-up menu that Explorer displays for a file or link. To customize the Windows XP generic properties pop-up menu to add an Open With menu selection, do the following:

1. In HKEY_CLASSES_ROOT*, create a new subkey, called openas.

2. In HKEY_CLASSES_ROOT*\openas, created in step 1, create a subkey called command.

3. In HKEY_CLASSES_ROOT*\openas\command, change the value entry, which is named (default) in RegEdit, to have the value:

    ```
    %SystemRoot%\System32\rundll32.exe %SystemRoot%\System32\
    shell32.dll ,OpenAs_RunDLL %1
    ```

Custom Icons on the Desktop

You can change the icons for certain objects—My Computer, My Network Places, Recycle Bin (full), and Recycle Bin (empty)—using the Display Properties dialog box in the Control Panel. Fine and dandy. Nevertheless, what about changing the other system icons?

The icon that is most often changed is that yellow folder used when Windows XP displays a directory on the Desktop. With all those bright colors and complex icons, the yellow folder icon is just a bit plain. That one's easy to fix; you can change the icon in the Properties dialog box for the specific folder.

Other icons can be more problematic. For example, changing some of the icons on the Desktop can be most intimidating. Table 12.3 lists some of the Windows XPDesktop objects that have icons that are difficult to change.

TABLE 12.3: CLSIDS FOR SOME DESKTOP OBJECTS

NAME	CLSID	WINDOWS 2000 COMPATIBLE	WINDOWS XP COMPATIBLE
Inbox (a.k.a. Outlook)	00020D75-0000-0000-C000-000000000046	✓	✓
Internet Explorer 1.0	0002DF01-0000-0000-C000-000000000046	✓	

Continued on next page

TABLE 12.3: CLSIDs FOR SOME DESKTOP OBJECTS *(continued)*

NAME	CLSID	WINDOWS 2000 COMPATIBLE	WINDOWS XP COMPATIBLE
Internet Explorer 2 or later	FBF23B42-E3F0-101B-8488-00AA003E56F8	✓	✓
Microsoft Outlook	00020D75-0000-0000-C000-000000000046	✓	✓
My Computer	20D04FE0-3AEA-1069-A2D8-08002B30309D	✓	✓
Network Neighborhood	208D2C60-3AEA-1069-A2D7-08002B30309D		
My Network Places	208D2C60-3AEA-1069-A2D7-08002B30309D	✓	✓
Recycle Bin	645FF040-5081-101B-9F08-00AA002F954E	✓	✓
The Internet	3DC7A020-0ACD-11CF-A9BB-00AA004AE837	✓	✓
The Microsoft Network (MSN)	00028B00-0000-0000-C000-000000000046		

To change the name for one of the objects mentioned in Table 12.3, go to HKEY_CLASSES_ROOT\CLSID and scroll down until you find the CLSID for the item that you wish to change. Open the subkey and note that there are by default four values:

(default)   The default registry value for this subkey that contains the title text

InfoTip   A REG_EXPAND_SZ string containing the location of the tip text

IntroText   A REG_EXPAND_SZ string containing the location of the introductory text.

LocalizedString   A REG_SZ string containing a path to shell32.dll, a resource locator, and a second copy of the title text

Modify the (default) and LocalizedString values to include your title rather than the default text. You can also modify the InfoTip text to change the text displayed when the user moves the mouse cursor over the item.

TIP   I always create three new strings, prefixing each original name with Old, and then store the original values. This allows me to restore the original text easily.

To change the Desktop icon for one of these objects, go to HKEY_CLASSES_ROOT\CLSID and scroll down until you find the CLSID (from Table 12.3) for the item that you wish to change. Open the subkey and then under that subkey open the subkey named DefaultIcon.

In the DefaultIcon subkey, there will be a default REG_SZ entry, containing the path to the icon to display. Simply change that path to another icon path.

WANT MORE ICONS?

There are two main sources of icons in Windows XP. The first, `shell32.dll`, contains the icons used by Windows for many components. The icons in `shell32.dll` are numbered starting from 1 (not zero, as was the previous convention). However the icons are not contiguously numbered: rather there are gaps in the numbering sequence, which makes guessing at an icon's ordinal number difficult.

Most program executable files contain icons, too.

Another file that contains only icons is `moricons.dll`. This file is located in the `%SystemRoot%\System32` directory. This file contains hundreds of icons of all different types. If you find that none of the icons in `shell32.dll` are to your liking, check out the `moricons.dll` file.

For fun, I searched my `%SystemRoot%` directory for all files with the word `icon` in them, using the command `dir *icon*.*`. I found about 20 files that had a multitude of icons that I could use for applications on my Desktop. Just be sure that when you use the icon in another file, the file doesn't get uninstalled at some time in the future—it may be a good idea to create a new folder in `System32` called something like `My Icons`, and place a copy of the file in there.

Figure 12.1 shows the registry entry for the Recycle Bin. This entry is the most complex of the Desktop icons, in that the Recycle Bin will automatically switch between an icon representing the full or empty state as necessary. Windows XP always displays the icon that is in the `(default)` entry and doesn't know about any other entries in the `DefaultIcon` subkey. Getting ideas here? You can hide a few icon definitions in the `DefaultIcon` subkey for later manual retrieval if you want.

FIGURE 12.1

The Recycle Bin has two icons, plus the `(default)` entry for icons. You can change both the empty and full icons if you want.

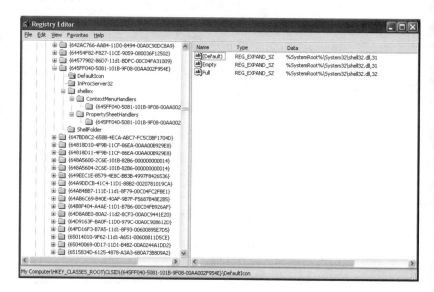

THE RECYCLE BIN'S ICONS

The Recycle Bin is unique; it has two icons: one for empty and one for full. You may change either or both. If you check the Recycle Bin's subkey, you will see their arrangement (see Figure 12.1). Either the empty icon or the full icon will match the icon specified in the default entry. You must maintain this relationship. For example, if the empty icon entry matches the default entry, change both at the same time to the same value. The Recycle Bin automatically changes the default icon depending on its state by copying either the full or empty icon description to the default entry.

Windows XP displays only the icon in the value entry named (default) in RegEdit, because Windows knows nothing about whether the Recycle Bin has anything in it.

If the Recycle Bin's icons get out of sync, drop a file into the Recycle Bin, then empty it. This should force the Recycle Bin to resynchronize the displayed icon.

Enhancing the Start Menu

You may add a number of new entries to the Start menu, such as quick shortcuts to specific Control Panel applets. This process is not really a registry modification; but you do use CLSIDs, so we'll pretend that it is.

A folder named with <any name>.{<CLSID>}, as shown in the following format example, is handled differently from other folders by Windows XP. Explorer will display the part of the name before the period. (Remember, Explorer displays the Start menu, too.) Explorer then uses the part after the period, the CLSID number, to fill in the directory structure.

For example, a directory named Control Panel.{21ec2020-3aea-1069-a2dd-08002b30309d} will display the name "Control Panel" and all the items in the folder in Explorer and in the Start menu. The following Windows XP components support this behavior:

- Control Panel.{21EC2020-3AEA-1069-A2DD-08002B30309D}

- Printers.{2227A280-3AEA-1069-A2DE-08002B30309D}

- Dial-Up Networking.{992CFFA0-F557-101A-88EC-00DD010CCC48}

- Recycle Bin {645FF040-5081-101B-9F08-00AA002F954E}

NOTE   When creating one of these special folders, don't forget to enclose the CLSID in curly braces. It won't work otherwise. The name, the portion before the period, may be any name that you desire.

Sounds Microsoft Never Gave Us

It is possible to add new sounds to Windows XP. For example, every time you start the Registry Editor, you could have ringin.wav play a difficult-to-ignore bell sound.

To add new sounds, follow these steps:

1. Start the Registry Editor and open the subkey HKEY_CURRENT_USER\AppEvents\Schemes\Apps.

NOTE *This process requires setting the* (`default`) *value and works best if done with RegEdit. However, here is another method. Instead of performing step 5 in these instructions, use the Sounds applet in the Control Panel to set the value. The Sounds applet will allow you to fill in the* (`default`) *value.*

2. Create a new subkey named `RegEdit`, or whatever the name is of the program that you are adding sounds to.

3. In your new key, create a subkey called `Open`.

4. In your new `Open` key, create a subkey called `.Current`. Don't forget the leading period.

5. In your `.Current` subkey, set the (`default`) value to `ringin.wav`, or whatever sound file you want.

After completing the entries in steps 2, 3, and 4, modify sounds played using the Control Panel's Sounds applet. The Sounds applet permits browsing and previewing sounds, making setting the sounds easier.

Make .dll Files Show Their Own Icons

Windows displays `.dll` files in Explorer with a generic `.dll` icon. This generic icon conveys no information about the `.dll` file, other than the fact that the file is a `.dll`.

Many `.dll` files have one or more icons. You can force Explorer to display the `.dll`'s first icon, if there is one, or the generic Windows file icon, if there is no icon in the `.dll` file. Change the value contained in `HKEY_CLASSES_ROOT\dllfile\DefaultIcon` to the string `"%1"`. The original value, `"%SystemRoot%\System32\shell32.dll,-154"`, is the generic icon for `.dll` files and won't be used anymore.

NOTE *Some* `.dll` *files have a default icon that is not a reasonable representation of what the* `.dll` *file does. For example, the icon for the* `.dll` *file* `mmcndmgr` *is the same as the generic folder icon.*

Easter Egg Hunt?

As many of us know, Microsoft programmers put little credit screens and other goodies into each Microsoft product. These screens are popularly called Easter Eggs because they are intended to be found by users, perhaps by accident.

The United States government has now forbidden Microsoft from putting Easter Egg type objects in their operating systems, under the guise that programs and products used by the government must not contain undocumented features or functionalities.

Sadly, there is much of Windows XP that is undocumented and only really understood by Microsoft. The only effect that the government's restriction has had is the elimination of the traditional Easter Egg.

Console and Command-Prompt Settings

Windows installations have a subkey under `HKEY_CURRENT_USER` called `Console`. Under `Console`, there is a subkey called `%SystemRoot%_system32_ntvdm.exe`. Windows XP does not, by default, have this subkey, though you may choose to add it. This section describes customizing areas of the user interface specific to a Command Prompt window. As expected, the values discussed in this section affect console and command-prompt windows that do not have a custom configuration created.

All changes to the `Console` subkey will change the default values for all command-prompt windows created after the change takes effect. After opening a window, use the Properties dialog box to change the window's attributes.

The user may create additional subkeys under the `HKEY_CURRENT_USER\Console` key. Name each subkey created with the same name as a console window's title. When Windows creates a console window with the same name as a subkey found in `HKEY_CURRENT_USER\Console`, it will use the setting in this subkey to configure the window's default view. As an example, I have a subkey named `Command Prompt`, which matches the title in several command-prompt windows.

MORE THAN ONE WAY TO SET COMMAND-PROMPT OPTIONS!

In Windows XP, you can have three different values set for many options:

1. The first level, found in the `HKEY_LOCAL_MACHINE\Software\Microsoft\Command Processor` key, affects all users.

2. The next level, found in `HKEY_CURRENT_USER\Software\Microsoft\Command Processor`, affects only the currently logged-on user (and is saved in that user's profile).

3. The final level, where the configuration is entered as a parameter passed to the command processor when it is invoked, affects only that particular session.

For more information about which command-prompt options and parameters may be set in these three ways, enter the command `CMD /?` at any command prompt.

Foreground and Background Colors

You can change a command prompt's foreground and background colors. I prefer a light gray background with black characters, or sometimes dark blue characters. Three areas affect the colors used for a command-prompt window: the color table entries, the command-prompt window colors, and the pop-up window colors.

By modifying the color table entries (`ColorTable00` through `ColorTable15`), you create a custom color palette. Windows XP allows modification of the color palette in the Display Properties dialog box, although some users may be able to use the registry for this.

Setting the foreground and background indexes into the color table entries changes the window colors. Indexes are stored for both foreground and background as a single DWORD entry.

COLORTABLE00 THROUGH COLORTABLE15

The color table entries (see Figure 12.2) allow users to select colors for fonts and backgrounds.

Value entries:	`ColorTable00` through `ColorTable15`
Type:	REG_DWORD
Typical value:	(RGB value, varies)

FIGURE 12.2

The HKEY_CUR-
RENT_USER\Con-
sole key includes
the color entries
used in command
windows.

FIGURE 12.2

The HKEY_CUR-
RENT_USER\Con-
sole key includes
the color entries
used in command
windows.

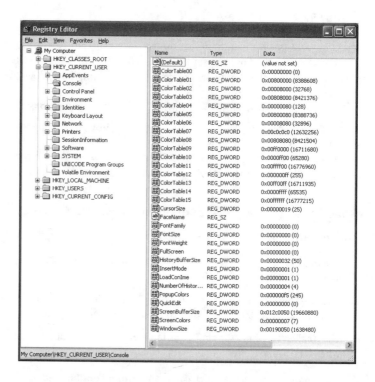

The default colors for a command window are white on a black background. You can display the
command window's properties dialog box from the window's System menu, or you can right-click the
window's title bar and choose Properties.

The Properties dialog box contains four tabs. Choose the final tab, Colors. In this tab, you can
choose the colors for the window or the pop-up window's background and foreground from the
standard 16-color palette (see Figure 12.3).

FIGURE 12.3

The Colors tab
allows setting colors
and color palettes.

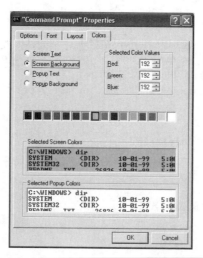

The standard palette allows selecting the rather common and mundane colors. It also allows the user to customize colors using a set of edit controls. Some users will want the custom colors to be available. An alternative to setting these colors manually, one by one, is to change them in HKEY_CURRENT_USER\Console.

Each color index is a DWORD, consisting of red, green, and blue values, for example, 00RRGGBB. Each color value may range from 0 to 255. The initial two digits are always zeros.

PopupColors

Windows uses a pop-up window to inform you of some action or problem. You can set its colors independently from the colors of the command window itself.

Value entry:	PopupColors
Type:	REG_DWORD
Typical value:	0xF5

The DWORD value contains two bytes; one byte is used and the other is ignored. This allows specifying both the foreground and background color indexes. These colors are indexes to the ColorTablenn entries. The first four bits, 5 in the preceding typical value, are the foreground color index. The second four bits, the F in the preceding typical value, are the background color index.

ScreenColors

Command windows may have both foreground and background colors set using ScreenColors.

Value entry:	ScreenColors
Type:	REG_DWORD
Typical value:	0x07

The DWORD value consists of two bytes; one byte is used and the other is ignored. This allows specifying both the foreground and background color indexes. These colors are indexes to the ColorTablenn entries. The first four bits, 7 in the preceding typical value, specify the foreground color index. The second four bits, the 0 in the preceding typical value, specify the background color index.

Memory Used by Command-Prompt Windows

A couple of settings control the memory used by a command-prompt window. This memory is only for the display and does not, for example, affect memory available for applications.

CurrentPage

The CurrentPage entry specifies the current page to use. The user should not reset this system variable.

Value entry:	CurrentPage
Type:	REG_DWORD
Typical value:	0x0

ScreenBufferSize

The ScreenBufferSize entry specifies the size of the screen buffer. The buffer size specifies the height and width value.

Value entry:	ScreenBufferSize
Type:	REG_DWORD
Typical value:	0x012C0050

The DWORD value has two bytes, allowing you to specify both the width and height in characters of the screen buffer. The low-order word (a DWORD consists of two words) specifies the width, while the high-order word specifies the height. For example, 0x012C0050 specifies a screen buffer that is 0 × 12C (300) lines high and 80 characters wide.

Cursors

The cursor attributes allow customizing the cursor size. The standard cursor for a Windows XP command-prompt window is a modified underline cursor that can be set to a block cursor of varying size. I suggest modifying the underline cursor because it is actually a very short block cursor that looks like an underline, and therefore may be difficult to see.

CursorSize

The CursorSize entry specifies the percentage of the character cell that is filled with the cursor.

Value entry:	CursorSize
Type:	REG_DWORD
Typical value:	0x19 (that's 25 in decimal)

The Options tab of the Properties dialog box allows setting the cursor to three sizes: Small, Medium, and Large (see Figure 12.4). Actually, this value may be a number between 0, Windows displays no cursor, and 99, Windows displays a full block cursor.

FIGURE 12.4

The Options tab allows setting many different options, such as three different cursor sizes.

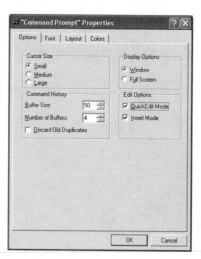

Keep in mind that the cursor consists of discrete lines based on the command-prompt window's font size. As the font size gets larger, the user has more control over the size of the cursor.

NOTE *Windows XP does not have any provision for a nonblinking cursor. Such is life—it just blinks on and on and on.*

Fonts

Font attributes may be set, in a limited fashion, from the Font tab of the command prompt's Properties dialog box (see Figure 12.5). More control of fonts is available in the registry. Setting font values requires an understanding of fonts, especially when using complex ones, such as TrueType.

FIGURE 12.5

The Font tab allows setting some font specifications. You have more flexibility when directly manipulating the registry.

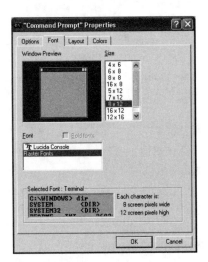

For simple changes, such as font size and so on, use the Properties dialog box. To select fonts that are not available normally, or sizes that the dialog box doesn't allow you to set, direct manipulation of the registry is the way to go.

FACENAME

The FaceName entry specifies the font used to display characters in a command-prompt window and is by default a raster font.

Value entry:	FaceName
Type:	REG_SZ
Typical value:	(None)

Windows creates a *raster font* character in a cell, say 8 dots wide by 12 dots high, producing a moonscape font. Raster fonts are faster for Windows to process, but usually don't have much size flexibility. They are also generally lower in quality due to size constraints. Complex fonts, such as the TrueType fonts, are infinitely variable in size and are typically of higher quality when displayed in larger sizes. However, a complex font, such as a TrueType font, requires more system resources (CPU capacity) to display as the font must be drawn, or rendered, when used.

Most command windows use the default font, which is an undefined raster font. The font size may vary depending on screen resolution, although a default size in most installations is 8 × 12, providing a reasonable, readable display.

FontFamily

The `FontFamily` entry specifies the font family for the window's display font. There are a number of different families, such as TrueType and raster.

Value entry:	`FontFamily`
Type:	REG_DWORD
Typical value:	0

This entry is a DWORD, with values that include:

0	Don't care which is used
10	Roman family
20	Swiss family
30	Modern family
40	Script family
50	Decorative family

As the most flexible font-family specification is 0 or "don't care," most users do not change this value.

WARNING   *Before setting font-family values, be sure to understand what is, and how to specify, a family value. Setting an invalid family value may cause the display to be different from what was expected.*

FontSize

The `FontSize` entry specifies the value for the font displayed.

Value entry:	`FontSize`
Type:	REG_DWORD
Typical value:	0

Windows divides the DWORD value into two halves, allowing both the width and height of the characters to be stored in one value. The low-order word specifies the width, while the high-order word specifies the height. For example, `0x0008000C` specifies a character that is 8 × 12 in size. (Remember, 0x000C in hex is 12 in decimal.)

FONTWEIGHT

The FontWeight value specifies whether a font is bold or light.

Value entry:	FontWeight
Type:	REG_DWORD
Typical value:	0

A default value of zero specifies a default character that is not bold. Values range from 0 to 1000; typical values are shown here:

0	Don't care how bold
100	Thin
200	Extralight
300	Light
400	Normal
500	Medium
600	Semibold
700	Bold
800	Extrabold
900	Heavy

NOTE *The "don't care" (0) value will be equated with the normal level (400) of bolding.*

A generic bold/nonbold may be set from the Font tab in the command prompt's Properties dialog box when displaying a TrueType font. Raster fonts do not support the bold attribute.

What the Window Looks Like

You can change the appearance of the command-prompt window in a number of ways (see Figure 12.6). Direct manipulation is possible; for example, the window location can be set using a simple drag-and-drop procedure. Other window attributes can be set using the registry or the Properties dialog box for the window.

FULLSCREEN

The FullScreen entry specifies whether the console session is full screen or windowed.

Value entry:	FullScreen
Type:	REG_DWORD
Typical value:	0

FIGURE 12.6

The Layout tab allows setting the size, position, and buffer size of the screen.

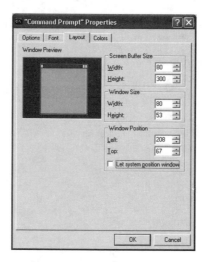

Most users put their command-prompt sessions in a window, and not full screen, for ease of use. The two values allowed for this entry are as follows:

1	Full-screen mode
0	Windowed mode

NOTE   *This option is usable only on Windows running on Intel x86 machines. RISC systems allow only windowed mode.*

WINDOWSIZE

The WindowSize entry specifies the size of the command-prompt window. WindowSize is both a height and a width value, each stored in the same DWORD.

Value entry:	WindowSize
Type:	REG_DWORD
Typical value:	0x190050

Windows splits the WindowSize DWORD into two bytes, allowing you to specify both the width and height of the screen buffer. The low-order word specifies the width, while the high-order word specifies the height. For example, 0x00190050 specifies a screen buffer that is 0×19 (25) lines high and 80 (0×50) characters wide.

WINDOWPOSITION

The WindowPosition entry specifies the Window's location on the Desktop relative to the upper-left corner.

Value entry:	WindowPosition
Type:	REG_DWORD
Typical value:	0x000000000

This position is the number of pixels in the x- and y-axes. Windows splits the DWORD value into two halves, allowing both the x- and y-axes of the window to use the same DWORD. The low-order word specifies the width, while the high-order word specifies the height. For example, 0x00000000 specifies that the command prompt will be located in the upper-left part of the Desktop at screen coordinates 0,0.

NOTE   When setting `WindowPosition` in the Properties dialog box, Windows XP keeps the user from entering a value that would move the window entirely off the Desktop. However, when setting these values manually, there is no safe-guard to prevent placing the window off the screen. This presents some interesting possibilities in hiding a window. (Moving a window off the Desktop hides it; you have to maximize the window from the Taskbar to use it.)

The Command History Buffer

Windows XP maintains a command buffer that allows users to recall previously entered commands for reexecution. You can configure the command history buffer in both the command prompt's Properties dialog box and the registry, setting the buffer size, the number of buffers, whether duplicates are stored, and so on.

Why do we set the number of commands stored in a buffer and the number of buffers as well? I haven't found a satisfactory answer to this question. I am not aware of advantages of having multiple smaller buffers versus having a few large buffers. Microsoft has not clarified this.

DosKey performs the command history management, which is loaded by Windows XP every time a command-prompt session is started. DosKey allows the definition of keys, the creation of macros, and so on.

Windows XP and Windows 2000 have the command history buffer support built into the command processor, while in earlier versions, the buffer support was not as tightly integrated with the command processor. Regardless of where the command history buffer is maintained, the functionality does not change.

For more information on DosKey, enter the command **DosKey /?** at any command prompt. The help screen will assist you in using DosKey.

HISTORYBUFFERSIZE

The command buffer is activated using the up and down arrow keys. The `HistoryBufferSize` entry specifies the number of commands stored.

Value entry:	`HistoryBufferSize`
Type:	REG_DWORD
Typical value:	`0x32` (that's 50 in decimal)

A number of buffers can be set in the command prompt's Properties dialog box, regardless of whether duplicate commands are saved or not.

HISTORYNODUP

The HistoryNoDup entry specifies whether consecutive duplicate entries of a command will be stored in the command history buffer or not.

Value entry:	HistoryNoDup
Type:	REG_DWORD
Typical value:	0x0

This entry controls whether duplicate commands are saved or not. Values allowed in this entry are as follows:

1	Discard duplicates
0	Keep duplicates

NUMBEROFHISTORYBUFFERS

NumberOfHistoryBuffers specifies the size of the Windows XP command buffer.

Value entry:	NumberOfHistoryBuffers
Type:	REG_DWORD
Typical value:	0x4

The command buffer is activated using the up and down arrow keys. This entry allows you to specify how many buffers are used (see also the previous section). The default value, 4, is usually adequate for most users.

Miscellaneous Settings

There are a few settings that don't seem to fit into the other categories I've discussed so far. Settings for the InsertMode, QuickEdit, and CompletionChar entries are helpful to users.

INSERTMODE

A command-prompt window allows a default insert/overwrite mode. (The default may be changed by pressing the Insert key on the keyboard.)

Value entry:	InsertMode
Type:	REG_DWORD
Typical value:	1

Most users set insert on, with a value of 1 (this is my preference), although some users find that overwrite mode is more convenient.

QUICKEDIT

QuickEdit is a mode that allows you to quickly mark information, copy it to the Clipboard, and paste the information from the Clipboard with the mouse.

Value entry:	QuickEdit
Type:	REG_DWORD
Typical value:	0

You can set this mode to QuickEdit disabled, which allows normal editing and is signified with a value of 0, or QuickEdit enabled, which is signified with a value of 1.

COMPLETIONCHAR

CompletionChar is located in HKEY_CURRENT_USER/Software/Microsoft/Command Processor. This value entry tells Windows XP to complete a partially typed filename when the user presses a specified key.

Value entry:	CompletionChar
Type:	REG_DWORD
Typical value:	0

Many users set this key's value to 9, the numeric value for the Tab key. Other keys could be used, but be careful not to select a key that is already used with Windows.

After setting this value and logging on again, open a command window. Next, in the root directory, type the command **dir w**. Next, press the Tab key or whatever key you assigned to the command-completion key. Notice how Windows now cycles through each directory or file that begins with the letter w.

NOTE *The subkey* Command Processor *may not be present for users who have upgraded from previous versions of Windows NT. If this subkey is missing, create it and the* CompletionChar *value entry. Be sure to preserve both case and spaces in these names and to assign the key's data type as REG_DWORD, in order to ensure that they work correctly.*

Chapter 13

Networking and Registry System Entries

FOR A TYPICAL USER, the Windows XP internal registry entries probably occupy about half of the registry. Only after adding many applications does this proportion change much. Many networking and system registry modifications are easy to do, although unlike changes to the user interface, they can be dangerous. Making an improper change can break the operating system, which may prevent you from booting your system. There are many changes that, when done improperly, will cause serious damage to the system, necessitating restoration of the registry from a backup.

You should make most networking changes using the Control Panel's Network applet. The main reason for this is that after making changes, the Network applet will check the registry to ensure that all networking registry entries are valid. This is not an exhaustive, problem-finding check; rather the Network applet just updates some entries if updating is necessary. In other words, don't rely on this updating to detect errors. Windows updates the registry during the binding phase.

Note that many of the settings for networking won't take effect until you restart the system. Simply logging on again isn't sufficient, as Windows reads some network settings only at boot time.

We'll cover these topics:

◆ Where to find system entries

◆ Making networking entries

◆ How to make changes to disk, directory, and related entries

◆ Other hardware support entries

◆ Software configuration entries

System Entries

Many of the other registry hives contain system entries. Most system entries are located in hives HKEY_LOCAL_MACHINE, HKEY_CURRENT_USER (HKEY_USERS), and HKEY_CURRENT_CONFIG. You can ignore HKEY_CURRENT_CONFIG, since it contains only a reference to the CurrentControlSet subkey contained in the HKEY_LOCAL_MACHINE hive. That is, modifying an object in HKEY_CURRENT_CONFIG\System would simply modify the corresponding object in HKEY_LOCAL_MACHINE\System. Ditto for HKEY_USERS, since this information is available in HKEY_CURRENT_USER as well.

So at this point, if you examine the HKEY_LOCAL_MACHINE hive, you'll see most of the configurations that Windows XP uses for the system. Windows divides the entries into a number of major areas, including networking, disk, other hardware support, and other software configuration entries.

DO I ALWAYS HAVE TO REBOOT?

The updating of network settings continues to improve in Windows XP. Generally, it is not necessary to reboot the computer unless prompted to.

Although Windows XP will sometimes work fine without being rebooted following a change made using the Control Panel, I recommend that you always reboot when, and if, the Network applet suggests that you do so. If you have systems or software that slow down the rebooting process, such as Microsoft Exchange Server, consider disabling these systems or software while making changes to the networking registry components.

WARNING   *Do I have to say it repeatedly? Back up your registry before making changes in it! Changing the system and networking sections of the registry is extremely dangerous. These sections are some of the most sensitive and difficult ones to modify.*

Networking Entries

Networking is a major component of Windows XP. Networks connect virtually every Windows user, with many users connected to complex networks.

Often, we use the Control Panel's Network applet to make changes to the network configuration. In fact, I recommend that you use the Network applet whenever possible, because it is much more difficult to make serious, damaging errors using the Network applet.

Many of the network configuration settings are contained in the subkey HKEY_CURRENT_USER\Software\Microsoft\WindowsNT\CurrentVersion\Network. Additionally, other keys that control the networking environment are found in HKEY_LOCAL_MACHINE and elsewhere.

Windows XP handles network issues differently than it handles other components, such as video. For example, the configuration of the network card is separate from any other interface adapter. In addition, the network card configuration process is somewhat different. These differences are due to the deep-rooted nature of networking in Windows.

After initializing the network settings, only certain changes will not necessitate a reboot. Windows XP will advise you, often too frequently, that you must reboot before your changed settings will take effect. Generally, the cautions are accurate—they won't take effect. Sometimes it is necessary to defer rebooting until a later time, particularly when the computer is a vital network server.

NOTE   Sometimes you must make two or three different sets of changes at a given time, and Windows may tell you after each one that it requires a reboot. Now, if you had infinite time (anybody got a few hours to spare?), you could go ahead and reboot every time Windows suggests it. Often, however, you can skip the reboot until you have made the last network-related change. Then when you reboot, you can have all the changes take effect at the same time.

Persistent Connections

Persistent connections are connections to network resources—typically, file- and printer-based resources—that are reconnected each time the user logs on. There are also nonpersistent connections that are lost when the user logs off. Persistence is set at the time of connection creation.

Here is a connection made from a command prompt, using the NET USE command:

```
NET USE * \\computername\sharename /PERSISTENT:YES
```

The NET USE command allows the user to specify persistence, although the default is for the connection to be persistent. The connection would not be persistent had this command been entered as so:

```
NET USE * \\computername\sharename /PERSISTENT:NO
```

When using Explorer to map a network drive, the dialog box used has a check box labeled Reconnect at Logon. When checked, this option creates a persistent connection. Regardless of the method used to create the connection, maintenance of persistence is the same: either Windows restores the connection when the user logs on the next time, generally the default, or the connection is lost when the user logs off.

Other than a value entry named Order, which specifies the order for the shared directory connections (if you edit it, the order in the drop-down changes), the only entry in HKEY_CURRENT_USER\ Software\Microsoft\Windows NT\CurrentVersion\Network\Persistent Connections that seems to do anything significant is SaveConnections. This value entry specifies the default value used with Explorer when mapping a network drive. The setting of the Map Network Drive dialog box's Reconnect at Logon check box is stored in this value entry. If this value is missing, Explorer will assume that the value is yes.

JUST BECAUSE MICROSOFT SAYS IT, DOESN'T MEAN IT'S ALWAYS SO

Concerning persistent connections, the Microsoft Resource Kit for Windows NT 4 stated the following about HKEY_CURRENT_USER\Network:

> This object is no longer used. In previous versions of Windows NT, it stored persistent connections. Persistent connections are now stored in HKEY_CURRENT_USER\Software\Microsoft\Windows NT\ CurrentVersion\Network\Persistent Connections.

However, I've noticed that Windows XP still stores persistent-connection information in HKEY_CURRENT_ USER\Network, and not in the subkey Microsoft identifies in the Resource Kit. This is an example of how you should always check the system itself, rather than simply trusting the documentation.

The main difference is how the share is accessed. If the share is accessed as a drive letter, then the information about that connection seems to be located in HKEY_CURRENT_USER\Network, while shares that are not mapped to a drive letter are stored elsewhere.

RestoreConnection

Ghosted connections are persistent connections that exist when the actual connection to the server has not been reestablished after the user logs on. For example, say user John has persistent connections to 10 network drives. Each time John logs on, Windows XP could restore each network connection, establishing connections with each server. However, when doing this, what happens? First, restoring a number of connections is slow. Second, if one or more servers are unavailable at logon time, John will get some sort of message telling him that Windows could not make the connection. Both situations are problematic because John is always in a hurry. He knows that some of the servers are not available, but he doesn't care, because he won't be using those connections until he knows the server is accessible.

Windows XP uses ghosted connections when a user doesn't need or want an actual connection until there is a need for the connection. Once the user uses the connection, Windows will make the necessary connection. In some instances, this technique can cause problems; for example, there will be a delay the first time that an inactive, ghosted connection is used. To avoid such problems, you can disable ghosting with the following registry value:

Value entry:	`RestoreConnection`
Type:	REG_DWORD
Typical value:	`0`

Values used in this entry are as follows:

`0`	Windows will ghost the connection, restoring each connection as needed.
`1`	Windows restores the connection each time the user logs on.

This value entry is in `HKEY_LOCAL_MACHINE\System\CurrentControlSet\Control\NetworkProvider`. Since this entry doesn't exist by default in any version of Windows, you must create it in order to use it.

OptionalNames

Care to make your server appear as if it had a split personality? With this little-known trick, it is easier to make this change than to tell how to do it. In the registry key `HKEY_LOCAL_MACHINE\System\CurrentControlSet\Services\LanmanServer\parameters`, you can add the following entry:

Value entry:	`OptionalNames`
Type:	REG_SZ or REG_MULTI_SZ
Typical value:	`SPLIT`

You must reboot the system for this change to take effect, but that is a small price to pay to make your network appear to be larger than it really is. (This registry value does not exist by default; you must create it if you are going to use it.)

Why do this? Several reasons. Say you add a new server. Eventually, this new server will replace an old, preexisting server. You know that many users have persistent connections to the old server. You create your new server with the name you choose, which will necessarily be different from the old server, since the old server is still in use on the network. You set up the new server, test it, and all is well.

At some quiet time, like when no clients are logged on, you migrate all resources from the old server to the new server. Then you turn off the existing server. Finally, you just add the `OptionalNames` entry using the name of the existing server. Tell users that you are migrating to the new server and that they should use the new server's name, not the old name, whenever they make new connections.

Users will eventually migrate to the new server's name, or you can change them manually without disrupting the system.

Improving Network Performance

Several networking settings will improve performance. Increasing buffering usually improves performance if sufficient memory is available. The following registry values, found in the subkey `HKEY_LOCAL_MACHINE\System\CurrentControlSet\Services\LanmanWorkstation\parameters`, can help improve network performance. Some of these entries may not exist on your system. If they don't exist, you will need to create them.

First, modify or add a `MaxCmds` value:

Value entry:	MaxCmds
Type:	REG_DWORD
Typical value:	15

This registry entry may contain a value between 0 and 255. Since the default value is only 15, my recommendation is to increase it by steps of five, monitoring performance with each change.

Both `MaxThreads` and `MaxCollectionCount` also affect network performance:

Value entry:	MaxThreads
Type:	REG_DWORD
Typical value:	15

This registry entry should contain the same value as `MaxCmds`, shown in the previous example.

Value entry:	MaxCollectionCount
Type:	REG_DWORD
Typical value:	16

Specify the buffer used for the "character-mode named pipe" writes. You may choose a value up to 65535.

Disk, Directory, and Related Entries

There are probably a thousand different registry entries that affect disk drives. Unfortunately, many are specific to a given hardware configuration. The odds that any two computers would have the same hardware configuration are somewhat remote, unless you bought them all on the same day from the same vendor and had since made all changes yourself. In addition, the number of different permutations of hardware makes it difficult to localize common entries that would be significant to the majority of us. However, even with these staggering obstacles, I've plowed ahead and found as many generic disk registry entries as I could. Let's hope that these will answer most of your questions.

Moving Windows to a New Directory

This section is written for those who administer systems both with Windows XP and with multiple versions of Windows. In Knowledge Base article Q154129, Microsoft outlines how to change the name of the Windows NT 4 installation (root) directory. Microsoft has not given (at the time this book was written) a process to move Windows XP; however, the techniques in this article should be useful for anyone who must move Windows XP to a new directory.

This is not an everyday action. However, for users who have upgraded earlier versions of Windows NT that were installed in a directory with the version number as part of the directory name, this process may make the installation look cleaner. For example, let's say you upgraded an installation of Windows NT 4.0 installed in the directory WINNT. You'd like to rename this directory WNTXP to reflect the current version number. Another example involves installing the new version of the operating system into a temporary directory, such as NewWNT, so that you have both versions of Windows installed at the same time.

NOTE   *No one has tested these renaming techniques with Windows XP. Similar to moving Windows NT 4, moving Windows XP is probably possible, though the process will be just as difficult.*

There are two distinct possibilities here. If you have installed Windows NT or XP on an NTFS partition, you follow a slightly complicated process that's described a little later. If Windows NT is on a FAT partition, you can change the name using another somewhat simpler process, described next.

FAT SYSTEM PARTITIONS: FIRST STEPS

Users who have installed Windows on a FAT partition have a somewhat simple task. FAT doesn't support file security but is compatible with DOS and Windows 95/98/Me. It is a simple process to use a boot diskette made on a DOS or Windows 95/98/Me computer to access the files on the hard drive.

MICROSOFT SAYS "NO" TO BE SAFE

Microsoft doesn't recommend or support renaming the Windows system directory. (Can we blame them?) This means that if something goes wrong, you could be up the creek without a paddle. For this reason, before doing this, do a full backup to ensure that you are able to restore the original configuration just in case something goes wrong.

My own precaution is to carefully check installed applications to ensure that none are expecting Windows to install them in a fixed location.

One test to perform first is to dump the registry and search for the installation directory, such as C:\WINDOWS, in the registry. The Registry Editor could also do this search, but a dump edited with a good text editor may work better. It is *not* necessary to search for the environment variable %SystemRoot% in the registry—this variable will be updated automatically.

Users of NTFS have to install a second copy of Windows to change the installation directory. Luckily, users of FAT partitions don't have to do this. For FAT-based systems, perform the following steps:

I recommend that you have sufficient disk space to hold at least two copies of the operating system temporarily. This allows you to retain your original installation until you are able to ensure that the change in directory names is working correctly. If you retain two copies, be sure to rename the original so that the system won't see it.

TIP   If your system is on a FAT32 partition, then you must use a later release of Windows 95 or any release of Windows 98/Me. The initial release of Windows 95 is not compatible with FAT32.

1.   Open a command-prompt window. Type the command `attrib -r-s c:\boot.ini`.

2.   Create a bootable diskette, either from DOS or from Windows 95/98/Me. Copy the `xcopy`, `edit`, and `move` command files to this diskette. Make sure they are compatible with the operating system version on the diskette.

TIP   It is not necessary to use an ERD (Emergency Repair Disk) to boot a Windows 95/98/Me system. Windows 95/98/Me is capable of creating bootable diskettes with the `format` command, using the `/s` (for system) option. Windows XP does not support formatting diskettes with the system option.

3.   Boot your computer from the bootable disk. Test to ensure that the `xcopy`, `edit`, and `move` commands are functioning correctly. If they aren't, correct this problem before continuing.

4.   After ensuring that the necessary commands work, make a directory, using the `MD` command, with the new name that you wish to run Windows from—for example, type `MD WinNew`.

WARNING   An alternative technique would be to use the DOS command `move` to rename the directory. This is dangerous since you would then have no backup to be able to go back to. I really do recommend making a full copy, just in case!

5.   Use the `xcopy` command to copy all the files and subdirectories from the original Windows system directory to your new Windows system directory.

NOTE   Use the `xcopy` command option `/e` to ensure that even empty subdirectories are copied. Some empty subdirectories may be necessary for the system to work correctly.

6.   Using the `edit` command, change the `boot.ini` file. Edit and change the lines with the original directory name to reflect the new directory name:

    `multi(0)disk(0)rdisk(0)partition(2)\Windows="Windows Server"`

    Both lines contain a directory reference, in our example, it is `Windows`. Change both to read:

    `multi(0)disk(0)rdisk(0)partition(2)\WinNew="Windows Server (new)"`

    In both cases, changing the text in quotes is a good idea. This is the prompt telling the user to select the operating system.

NOTE   It is not necessary, but may be desirable, to change the attributes in the `boot.ini` *file back to System and Read Only. If you do reset the attributes to System and Read Only, do so after everything is working correctly.*

7. Remove your boot diskette and attempt to reboot the system. If the system reboots and runs correctly, continue.

8. Follow the steps outlined later under "Completing the Move." When done with these steps, continue with the next step.

9. Again, reboot the system. If the system reboots and runs correctly, rename the original directory, `WINDOWS` in our example, to a different name (say, `Win_OLD`).

WARNING   Do not delete this directory yet—wait until you have tested the change.

10. Now set the attributes back on `boot.ini`; use the command `attrib c:\boot.ini +r +s`.

11. After a suitable test period with no problems, typically several weeks, back up and then delete the original installation directory that you renamed in step 9.

NTFS SYSTEM PARTITIONS: FIRST STEPS

Users who have installed Windows XP on an NTFS partition have a somewhat more difficult task. NTFS is not accessible from DOS or Windows 95/98/Me, at least not easily accessible in a read/write mode. Because of this limitation, you need to install a second operating system that is compatible with NTFS—Windows XP or a version of Windows Server.

NOTE   I recommend that you have sufficient disk space to hold two copies of the original operating system temporarily, as well as a third, basic installation of the operating system. This allows you to retain your original installation until you are able to ensure that the change in directory names is working correctly. If you retain two copies, be sure to rename the original so that the system won't see it.

To change the system directory name for Windows XP, follow these steps:

1. Install a new, maintenance copy of Windows XP or Server into a new directory. (If you don't already have one installed, that is.) It is not necessary to install this copy of Windows on the boot drive. However, doing so will make things slightly easier.

2. Open a command-prompt window. Type the command `attrib -r-s c:\boot.ini`.

3. Restart the computer, and boot your new maintenance copy of Windows XP/Server.

4. Log on as Administrator and open a command window.

5. Make a directory, using the `MD` command, with the new name that you wish to run Windows from; for example, type `MD WinNew`.

WARNING   An alternative technique would be to use the command `move` *to rename the directory. This is dangerous since you would then have no backup to be able to go back to. I recommend doing a full copy, just in case!*

6. Use the `xcopy` command to copy all the files and subdirectories from the original system directory to your new system directory.

NOTE   Use the `xcopy` command option `/e` to ensure that even empty subdirectories are copied. Some empty subdirectories may be necessary for the system to work correctly.

7. Using the `edit` command, change the `boot.ini` file. Edit the following line, where `Windows` is the original installation directory:

   ```
   multi(0)disk(0)rdisk(0)partition(2)\Windows="Windows Server"
   ```

   This line contains a directory reference; in our example, it is `Windows`. Change it to read:

   ```
   multi(0)disk(0)rdisk(0)partition(2)\WinNew="Windows Server (new)"
   ```

   In both cases, changing the text in quotes is a good idea. This is the prompt telling the user to select the operating system.

NOTE   It is not necessary, but may be desirable, to change the attributes on the `boot.ini` file. If you do not immediately reset the attributes to System and Read Only, remember to do so after everything is working correctly.

8. Attempt to reboot the system, selecting your original installation of Windows XP. If the system reboots OK, continue.

9. Follow the steps outlined under the next section, "Completing the Move." When done with these steps, continue with step 10.

10. Again, attempt to reboot the system, selecting your original installation of Windows XP. If the original version of Windows XP reboots and runs correctly, rename the original Windows XP directory, `WINDOWS` in our example, to a different name (say, `Win_OLD`).

WARNING   Do not delete this directory yet—test the system thoroughly first!

11. Now, set the attributes back on `boot.ini`, using the command **attrib c:\boot.ini +r +s**.

12. After a suitable test period with no problems, *typically several weeks*, back up and then delete the original installation directory that you renamed in step 10.

COMPLETING THE MOVE

Regardless of whether you have an NTFS or a FAT partition, it is necessary to perform the following steps. You must modify a file called `setup.log`. With some versions of Windows, the Backup program's registry restoration and Windows's Setup and Service Pack Setup programs use `setup.log`. Additionally, the registry itself will have many hard-coded references to the Windows system directory. You must modify these references, as well.

Perform the following steps on your FAT or NTFS system to complete the renaming process:

1. Back up the file `setup.log` to `setup.bak` using the `copy` command.

2. Open the file `setup.log` in the `%SystemRoot%\Repair` directory with a text editor, such as the command prompt's `edit` command or Notepad.

3. Globally change all references to the original installation directory with the new name that you have chosen.

WARNING   *Be careful not to change anything other than the installation directory name in this file, or the setup repair process will not be able to repair the system later.*

A short section of a typical `setup.log` file is shown below. Assume that the original installation directory is `WINDOWS`. As an example, I've used underlines here to highlight the lines that would have to be changed:

```
[Paths]
TargetDirectory = "\WINDOWS"
TargetDevice = "\Device\Harddisk0\Partition1"
SystemPartitionDirectory = "\"
SystemPartition = "\Device\Harddisk1\Partition1"
[Signature]
Version = "WinNt5.0"
[Files.SystemPartition]
NTBOOTDD.SYS = "ataboot.sys","ad03"
NTDETECT.COM = "NTDETECT.COM","11f1b"
ntldr = "ntldr","3aae6"
arcsetup.exe = "arcsetup.exe","3036c"
arcldr.exe = "arcldr.exe","33a86"
[Files.WinNt]
\WINDOWS\system32\drivers\kbdclass.sys = "kbdclass.sys","8a28"
\WINDOWS\system32\drivers\mouclass.sys = "mouclass.sys","98d7"
\WINDOWS\system32\drivers\uhcd.sys = "uhcd.sys","d727"
\WINDOWS\system32\drivers\usbd.sys = "usbd.sys","9c73"
\WINDOWS\system32\drivers\hidparse.sys = "hidparse.sys","6230"
\WINDOWS\system32\drivers\hidclass.sys = "hidclass.sys","13b9c"
\WINDOWS\system32\drivers\usbhub.sys = "usbhub.sys","b54b"
\WINDOWS\system32\drivers\intelide.sys = "intelide.sys","4ae2"
\WINDOWS\system32\drivers\pci.sys = "pci.sys","14ec5"
\WINDOWS\system32\drivers\isapnp.sys = "isapnp.sys","12889"
\WINDOWS\system32\drivers\aic78xx.sys = "aic78xx.sys","1ce69"
\WINDOWS\system32\drivers\i8042prt.sys = "i8042prt.sys","c5b9"
```

NOTE   *There are typically about 3000 lines in a* `setup.log` *file. If your file is considerably shorter, or does not start as the above example shows, make sure you are changing the correct file!*

You will need to scan the system registry to ensure that there are no hard-coded references to the installation directory. I found that there were almost 2,000 hard-coded references to the installation directory in a well-used installation. Each of these references would have to be manually changed. Follow these steps to determine all hard-coded references to the installation directory for Windows:

1. Using the Registry Editor, export the entire registry to a file called `orig.reg`. To do so, select My Computer in the registry tree display.

2. Use a text editor's Search and Replace commands to change all occurrences of the original installation directory name to the new directory name.

3. Reintegrate your edited registry into the original registry; either double-click the exported registry in Explorer or type the command **START orig.reg** at a command prompt.

NOTE   This process is somewhat complex. There is an excellent chance that when you've finished, the system will not work correctly. (Yes, you read that right—it may not work correctly!) Always make sure you have a good backup for restoring in case the change fails.

Upgrade Blues

Windows XP comes in two flavors: upgrade and full installation. You can usually get an upgrade for an existing product at a considerable discount over the cost of an entire new product license. Generally, the product is identical in both versions, but in the upgrade version, the Setup program will confirm that you actually have the original product.

The test to see if there is an original product to upgrade is relatively simple, but not flawless. The upgrade version of Windows XP will check the hard drive for a qualifying version of Windows. If Setup finds no prior installation of Windows, it will prompt you to insert a disk for the original product to prove you have a product that can be upgraded.

One problem comes about when you install the Windows XP upgrade on a system and you later need to reinstall a new copy of Windows XP in the same directory. It is possible that the Windows XP upgrade setup program won't work correctly, because it may think that you don't have a product that is included in the upgrade offer when it only finds Windows XP on the drive.

NOTE   If you are installing a second copy of Windows XP, the upgrade program will work. It only fails when reinstalling over the original installation.

Here is a quick workaround for this problem:

1. Edit the registry subkey `HKEY_LOCAL_MACHINE\Software\Microsoft\Windows NT\Current-Version`. Change the value for `CurrentVersion` to 4.0, 5.0, 5.1 or whatever version you need.

2. In the registry subkey `HKEY_LOCAL_MACHINE\System\Setup`, check the value entry `System-SetupInProgress`. If necessary, reset its value to 0.

3. In the registry subkey `HKEY_LOCAL_MACHINE\System\Setup`, check the value entry `Upgrade-InProgress`. If necessary, reset its value to 0. If this value does not exist, don't worry about it; it is not necessary to add it.

4. If Windows has an installed service pack, it would be a very wise move to remove it before reinstalling Windows XP. Otherwise, problems with the TCP/IP drivers may result in system

instability. After reinstalling Windows XP, reinstall the last service pack. Remember, service packs are cumulative, so you only need to install the highest numbered service pack. Finally, reinstall any hotfixes that were applied to the original system.

5. With some earlier versions of Windows, if you have RAS (Remote Access Service) on this computer, it is imperative to uninstall the service packs. (Service packs can substantially change RAS.) However, some users are unable to remove the service packs without breaking other critical parts of Windows XP. In that case, restore the file `%SystemRoot%\System32\Drivers\tcpip.sys` from the original distribution CD-ROM or from the service pack uninstall directory `%SystemRoot%\$NtServicePackUninstall$`.

NOTE *To recover a file from the distribution CD-ROM, you must use the* **expand** *command from a command prompt. Typing* **expand /?** *gives you more information on using* **expand.**

Where Was Windows XP Installed From?

Many of us change the drive letters assigned to the CD-ROM drives after the Windows installation is completed. It is a simple process and helps provide order in the system, especially if you are like me and add or remove drives frequently.

On my computers, I assign all CD-ROM drives to drive letters ranging from S: to Z:. I have four servers with between one and three CD-ROM drives each. Shares have the same drive letters on each networked computer. This way, a reference to S: on any computer on the network will always access the same CD-ROM drive and usually the same CD-ROM, too.

Reassigning the CD-ROM drive letters makes the system more manageable, but there is one problem. Every time you want to make a setup change to Windows XP and the Windows XP Setup or Configuration programs need to access the original Windows XP CD-ROM, the prompt will be for the Windows XP installation CD-ROM drive letter used. This drive letter will be different from the new, reassigned CD-ROM drive letter.

The location of the original installation source CD-ROM is stored in the registry subkey `HKEY_LOCAL_MACHINE\Software\Microsoft\Windows NT\CurrentVersion` in the value entry `SourcePath`. In addition, check the registry subkey `HKEY_LOCAL_MACHINE\Software\Microsoft\Windows\CurrentVersion\Setup`, in the value entries `SourcePath` and `Installation Sources`. The value entry `Installation Sources` is a binary value, so edit this one with caution. Change both instances of `SourcePath` to `X:\I386`, where `X` is the CD-ROM drive letter.

I'm Full, Burp

Windows XP will give a warning when the amount of free space on the drive falls to less than 10 percent. This percentage works well with smaller 1 or 2GB hard drives, but when the drive is large (20GB or more), the amount of free space can be several gigabytes when the warning is given.

To fix this problem, you can alter the percentage-free parameter, changing it from 10 percent to a more reasonable value. Edit the key `HKEY_LOCAL_MACHINE\System\CurrentControlSet\Services\LanmanServer\parameters`. Add a new REG_DWORD data value named `DiskSpaceThreshold`. Edit this data value and set its value to the percentage of free space at which you want the warning given. For example, set the value to 5 to give a warning when there is less than 5 percent free space remaining.

NOTE `DiskSpaceThreshold` *will affect all drives. Consider the effect when your system has a mix of small and large drives.*

Why Is Windows Asking for a Disk in the Drive?

From time to time, we get into a situation with Windows XP in which there is no disk or CD-ROM in the disk drive. This might happen when we start an application or a service or at some other time. After checking whether the drive specified is missing from the path statement, check something less obvious. Check `HKEY_LOCAL_MACHINE\System\Setup`. If it contains a value entry named `WinntPath`, delete this entry and restart Windows.

NOTE *How does a CD-ROM or diskette drive get into the path? Most often, this happens due to either a user error or an application installation that has gone awry. Some applications allow execution from the CD-ROM drive, but don't realize that the application, or a disk, isn't always going to be available in the drive. If inserting any disk satisfies the message from Windows that no disk is in the drive, the message is not significant, and you should try the fix just discussed.*

Removing Context Menu Items

It is easy to remove both the Map Network Drive and Disconnect Network Drive selections in the Explorer context menu (and the Tools menu). You might want to do this to make the context menus simpler and easier to use.

A simple change to the registry tells Explorer not to display either of these entries. In the registry key `HKEY_CURRENT_USER\Software\Microsoft\Windows\CurrentVersion\Policies\Explorer`, change (or add, if it doesn't exist) the following entry:

Value entry:	`NoNetConnectDisconnect`
Type:	REG_DWORD
Typical value:	`1`

This registry entry supports two values. When the value is `1`, then the Map Network Drive and Disconnect Network Drive menu selections are available. When the value is `0`, the Map Network Drive and Disconnect Network Drive menu selections are not available. The policy-editing tools, as described in Chapter 5, are able to make this change.

Using More Than Two IDE Controllers

Most computers now come with two built-in IDE controllers. The hardware may map one controller to the PCI bus and one to the IDE bus. (The PCI bus IDE controller may exhibit better performance.) Windows XP is able to access both IDE controllers, if desired, without any modifications.

More modern motherboards (and computers...) may have two additional IDE controllers (allowing a total of eight IDE drives). Typically, the third and fourth controllers are special purpose, such as RAID (Redundant Array of Independent Disks) enabled. For example, a RAID controller is built in to the main motherboard of my main server.

WARNING   *These techniques have not been well tested with Windows XP. If you need to attempt these procedures, back up critical data before proceeding!*

Several configurations are possible with the two IDE controllers. One configuration is to have four hard drives. Today, IDE drives are available in sizes that rival SCSI drives. (My server, DORA, has an 18GB IDE hard drive, in addition to the SCSI drives.) You can create a very reasonable configuration with as much as several hundred gigabytes (or more, depending on when you read this) of hard disk space using all four IDE drives.

NOTE   *IDE and ESDI drives are basically the same to Windows XP, so actually it's possible to add additional ESDI controllers with the techniques discussed in this section. Of course, ESDI drives and ESDI controllers are scarcer than hen's teeth, but that's not the issue here.*

Another popular configuration is one or two hard drives on the PCI IDE controller (this allows maximum performance with the hard drives) and one or two CD-ROM drives on the second IDE controller. Due to the inherent low performance of CD-ROM drives, it is best to connect the CD-ROM drives to the slower of the two IDE controllers.

Windows XP will support up to two standard IDE controllers. However, it is possible to add a third or fourth IDE controller to many systems. I'm not going to comment on the availability of hardware to do this type of configuration, other than to say that many IDE controller cards are available, some of which offer substantial performance capabilities, and some motherboards are equipped with two additional IDE ports.

NOTE   *One hard drive and one CD-ROM drive? Resist the urge to connect these two devices to a single IDE controller. Some systems will limit the hard drive's performance to the slowest device on the IDE controller—and this device will always be the CD-ROM drive. So, unless you want your hard drive to perform like a CD-ROM drive, keep these two devices on different controllers.*

NOTE   *Only perform this procedure if your computer is an Intel x86 system or if you are only using two IDE controllers. The changes described below only work with x86 systems; Windows XP supports two IDE systems without any modifications. Some motherboards with four IDE port may require drivers from the board manufacturer. In the event that you are installing Windows XP on a system that has four IDE ports located on the motherboard, first check with the manufacturer to determine their support for Windows XP.*

Each IDE controller is numbered. The primary IDE controller is numbered 0 and the secondary IDE controller is numbered 1. An added third IDE controller would be numbered 2, a fourth would be numbered 3, and so forth. Keep this concept in mind as you go about adding a third or fourth (or fifth…) IDE controller:

1. In the Registry Editor, open the subkey `HKEY_LOCAL_MACHINE\System\CurrentControlSet\Services\Atdisk` and add a new subkey named `PARAMETERS`.

2. Open this newly created `PARAMETERS` key and create a subkey named with the number for the added controller. For example, create a subkey named 2 if you are adding a third new IDE controller, or 3 for a fourth new IDE controller.

3. Open the subkey that you named in step 2 and create the following three data values:

Value Entry	Type	Typical Value
BaseAddress	REG_DWORD	Use the physical address of the IDE controller's data register. Configure the controller so that this address does not conflict with any existing IDE controllers or other installed devices.
DriveControl	REG_DWORD	Use the physical address of the IDE controller's drive control register. Configure the controller so that this address does not conflict with any existing IDE controllers or any other installed devices. Typically, this address is at BaseAddress + 0xE.
Interrupt	REG_DWORD	Use the IDE controller's IRQ (interrupt request) address. Configure the controller so that this address does not conflict with any existing IDE controllers or any other installed devices.

Saving Share Information

Many people use Windows XP shares, which may be lost when making a clean installation. You might clean-install for a number of reasons. Perhaps your system is unstable. And since you can't determine the starting date of the problems, you cannot depend on backups. In addition, sometimes the system hardware configuration changes (for example, a new server or disk assembly is installed), which necessitates a clean installation.

For servers with a large number of shares, reentering each share manually can be a time-consuming process. The following registry trick is easier.

WARNING *Before following these steps, realize that the process described may overwrite any existing shares.*

1. Start the Registry Editor (RegEdit).

2. Open the subkey HKEY_LOCAL_MACHINE\System\CurrentControlSet\Services\LanmanServer\ Shares.

3. Select Registry ➢ Export Registry File.

4. Enter a filename for saving the Shares subkey. Preferably, you should save this file to a floppy disk or another nonvolatile location. Click the Selected Branch button, and the saved branch should read
HKEY_LOCAL_MACHINE\System\CurrentControlSet\Services\LanmanServer\Shares.

5. After reinstalling Windows XP, insert the diskette with the file saved in step 4 and type the command **START** *filename***.REG** at the command prompt. Use the filename you saved in step 4.

6. Check to ensure Windows XP has properly incorporated these shares into the registry.

NOTE *Macintosh shared volumes will not be saved using these techniques.*

When using this technique at upgrade time, check that the new version of Windows saves share information in the same location as the previous version; otherwise the changes won't have the desired effect. At the time of this book's writing, this technique works with both Windows NT 4 and Windows XP.

Other Hardware Support Entries

There are thousands of other hardware support entries. The key HKEY_LOCAL_MACHINE\Software\ Microsoft\Windows NT\CurrentVersion\Ports contains default information for each port on the system. A typical system has the following ports:

COM1, COM2, COM3, COM4   These are communications (serial) ports used with mice, modems, and other serial devices.

FILE   These ports, typically used for printer driver output when no matching physical device is attached to the computer, redirect output to a disk file.

LPT1, LPT2, LPT3, LPT4   These are printer (parallel) ports used with printers, some other devices, special modems, and so on.

Ne00, Ne01, Ne02   These ports are used with printers directly connected to the network. Some higher-performance printers include a built-in Ethernet port.

NOTE   *AppleTalk devices connected to the network do not have ports as described above.*

I've gathered a few to describe in this chapter and grouped them by major components—serial ports and printer ports.

Serial Ports

In Windows XP, the serial ports are contained in the subkey HKEY_LOCAL_MACHINE\Software\ Microsoft\Windows NT\CurrentVersion\Ports. In addition, the key HKEY_LOCAL_MACHINE\System\ ControlSet001\Enum\Root*PNP0501 holds port information. Neither of these keys exists in versions earlier than Windows 2000. As Windows XP spreads the information throughout the registry, manual modification is more difficult!

Each communications port entry consists of a REG_SZ string containing the port's speed, parity, bits, and stop bits. The default values for these entries are given below:

Value Entry	Value
COM1:	"9600,n,8,1"
COM2:	"9600,n,8,1"
COM3:	"9600,n,8,1"
COM4:	"9600,n,8,1"

The PnP (Plug and Play) subkeys contain settings for virtually all hardware installed on a Windows XP system. For example, *PNP0501 is the identifier for serial ports (also see Appendix E, "Plug and Play Identifiers").

The key HKEY_LOCAL_MACHINE\System\CurrentControlSet\Enum\Root*PNP0501 on my machine, DORA, consists of two subkeys, one for each of the two serial ports installed on the system. Inside this key are additional subkeys, one for each port. The names of these subkeys may vary, but could be PnPBIOS_14 and PnPBIOS_11. Inside these subkeys are three additional subkeys, Control, Device Parameters, and LogConf.

In the Control subkey, you'll find a number of values that deal with device setup—for example, whether firmware (software on the device) is used or not and how resources are allocated. Modifying this subkey can be very tricky.

In the subkey Device Parameters, you'll find the values shown below (a given Windows XP installation may not have all the values described):

Value Entry	Value
PortName	A string such as COM1.
PollingPeriod	A REG_DWORD with a default value of 0.
ForceFifoEnable	A REG_DWORD with a value of 0 if the FIFO buffers are not used.
RxFIFO	A REG_DWORD with the receive FIFO value set by the user. The value will range from 1 to 14.
TxFIFO	A REG_DWORD with the transmit FIFO value set by the user. The value will range from 1 to 16.

Windows XP seriously limits the user's ability to alter items such as IRQ addresses, I/O addresses, and DMA channels. This limitation is necessary to comply with the PnP requirements.

These settings are contained in a REG_RESOURCE_LIST value in the registry key HKEY_LOCAL_MACHINE\ Hardware\ResourceMap\PnP Manager\PnPManager. Every port (actually every device that is installed on the computer) has a REG_RESOURCE_LIST value. The device driver uses the REG_RESOURCE_LIST (a device driver resource list) to "find" the hardware.

Printer (Parallel) Ports

HKEY_LOCAL_MACHINE\System\CurrentControlSet\Services\Parport contains parameters that help control the system's utilization of the basic parallel or printer ports. Many Windows XP computers use one of these parallel ports connected to a standard printer. An Intel x86 system may have between zero and two parallel ports, although most systems have only one parallel, or printer, port.

Ports on virtually all Windows XP systems utilize a standard printer driver chip as the hardware interface. This chip is configurable in the BIOS, and may allow either one-way (to the printer) or two-way (both to the printer and from the printer to the computer) communications. Additionally, printer port configurations allow for high-speed communications, which are important when you are printing complex images (bitmaps, for example) and transferring a large amount of data between the computer and the printer. Some printers also have a scanning mode. These printers require both high-speed printer ports and ports that support bidirectional data transfers. Many of the parallel port's settings are configurable with the Control Panel's Ports applet.

Other Software Configuration Entries

Some settings affect the user interface and the system equally. Where do we place these entries? `WinLogon` is a section in the registry that holds settings used for things like the users log.

Password Expires in *n* Days

Windows displays a password expiration message to the user a certain number of days before the user's password expires. Configure this message in Windows XP at the client by following these steps:

1. Start the Registry Editor.

2. Open the subkey `HKEY_LOCAL_MACHINE\Software\Microsoft\Windows NT\CurrentVersion\ WinLogon`.

3. Add this value entry, or modify it if it already exists:

Value entry:	`PasswordExpiryWarning`
Type:	REG_DWORD
Typical value:	14

4. This entry holds the number of days Windows XP will display the "password expires" warning.

Domain Refresh Interval

Windows refreshes the domain list whenever the workstation is unlocked, providing that the workstation has been locked for more than 120 seconds. (A user can lock their workstation by pressing Ctrl+Alt+Delete.) On many networks, refreshing the domain list can result in a significant delay before the user regains control of their system.

This problem may be somewhat alleviated by increasing the minimum "locked time" setting (in essence, gambling that the domain list won't have changed during that time), which you do by modifying the following value entry (found in `HKEY_LOCAL_MACHINE\SOFTWARE\Microsoft\Windows NT\ CurrentVersion\Winlogon`):

Value entry:	`DcacheMinInterval`
Type:	REG_DWORD
Typical value:	120

This entry contains the number of seconds that the system must have been locked before the registry will force the system to refresh the domain list. Values range from a minimum of 120 seconds, the default, to a maximum of 86,400 seconds

Chapter 14

Microsoft Office Entries

IN THIS CHAPTER, I'LL tell you how to repair your Office XP registry entries. If Microsoft Office is not running correctly, the problem may be more involved than just a damaged or missing registry entry. For example, it is entirely possible that *files* are either corrupted or missing. For this reason, don't look at this chapter as being a save-all. Rather, try fixing the registry, but if that doesn't have the desired effect, try reinstalling the malfunctioning Office components.

I'll cover the following topics in this chapter:

- ◆ How Microsoft Office shared components are interlinked

- ◆ Changes made by Microsoft Office Setup to the registry

- ◆ Updating the registry with the .reg files

- ◆ Modifying Microsoft Office system configuration information

- ◆ Customizing Office user configuration information

- ◆ Using Office's VBA to program the registry

A Few Words about Office XP

This chapter is a bit different from some of the others. Although I could just list every registry entry for Microsoft Office, the chapter would quickly become boring, and it would be excessively long. Instead, I'm going to focus on particular Office-related topics that affect the registry:

- ◆ Microsoft Office shared components and how they are interlinked to form a cohesive product. Microsoft Office consists of many programs that interact with each other. In addition, some optional Office programs can be installed if the user wants them. And to confuse the issue even more, some programs are automatically installed on "first use"!

- ◆ Changes made by the Microsoft Office Setup program to the registry, which can be extensive in a typical system. Even one Microsoft Office program can result in hundreds of registry changes.

- The `.reg` files that come with Microsoft Office. These files are used to update the registry, making changes that are standardized for all Microsoft Office installations.

- How to modify Microsoft Office configuration information. Each configuration of Microsoft Office is unique. During the installation process, a user may select options and components to install.

- How to customize and copy user information between users. Many organizations choose to install Microsoft Office on an organization-wide basis. Usually this is done by installing one copy, then using cloning techniques to duplicate the installation across a network.

- Programming the registry using Microsoft Office's VBA (Visual Basic for Applications.) VBA offers a lot of power to the typical Office user. For example, it is capable of much of the power that Visual Basic provides. Moreover, all VBA applications are capable of registry interaction.

NOTE *The information in this chapter refers to the Microsoft Office XP Professional Edition, the release that is current at the time of this book's writing. Later versions of Office will be released every year or so, perhaps even in 2003. Hopefully, much of this chapter's information will be usable with these future releases.*

If you're having problems with your installation of Office, I'd never suggest that you try to restore the Office products by first restoring a backup of the files and then adding registry entries. Though this might work, you could expect the need for other subtle things, such as adding critical shared `.dll` files to the Windows XP `System32` directory.

WARNING *Never, under any circumstances, install any beta editions of Office XP on Windows XP. This is virtually guaranteed to cause you substantial grief—you will learn about things in Product Authorization (PA) that you really don't want to know. Resist the urge to "try out" beta copies of Office XP!*

One of two processes performs most of Microsoft Office's registry modifications. The first process is the Setup program. This program will add, subtract, and otherwise modify a number of registry entries, all of which are critical to the running of Microsoft Office. The second process is a group of registry modification files, with the extension of `.reg`. These files are contained in directories on the Microsoft Office distribution CD-ROM.

Repairs to Microsoft Office are relatively easy. On the one hand, some components reinstall well. Reinstalling Microsoft Word, on the other hand, may overwrite your `normal.dot` file. I suggest, therefore, that you save or otherwise back up user-modified Microsoft Office files, such as the document templates like `normal.dot`, before reinstalling Microsoft Office.

NOTE *Notice that there are components listed in this registry section that are not part of the basic Microsoft Office package, such as a listing for Microsoft Publisher.*

Microsoft Office Shared Components

Microsoft Office consists of a number of components. We all know about the big ones—Word, Excel, Access, and PowerPoint. Nevertheless, a number of small helper applications that we don't always see or know about are also included with Office. For example, there is Microsoft Graph (which is also called Microsoft Chart), a graphing program used with Word, Excel, and Access. The Microsoft Office shared components are listed here:

Equation Editor	Used to create visually appealing equations.
WordArt	Used to embed simple drawings into documents. Microsoft Word integrates the WordArt capability, although the original WordArt application, if previously installed, is retained for compatibility.
Graph	A basic graphing tool; used to graphically display data.
Organization Chart	Used for the drawing and maintenance of basic organizational charts.
Media Player	An embeddable media player; most useful for embedding video clips into PowerPoint presentations.
ClipArt Gallery	A collection of clip art from Microsoft PowerPoint that may be used to improve the visual appeal of documents.
Draw	A basic drawing package that can be used to create effects such as 3-D. In Microsoft Word, drawing is integrated into Word itself.

With the possible exception of the ClipArt Gallery, which consists mostly of images, the shared components are usually ActiveX embeddable components. Embedding uses CLSIDs inserted into the registry by the Microsoft Office installation process. Appendix F, "Office XP CLSIDs," lists the significant Microsoft Office CLSIDs.

NOTE   *Office does not install all of the CLSIDs listed in Appendix F. Most of us install only parts of Microsoft Office, and therefore only some of the CLSIDs will be present in the registry. A missing CLSID doesn't signify an error or problem in itself.*

Changes Made by Microsoft Office Setup

Unlike some earlier versions of Office, Microsoft Office XP uses the newer Microsoft installer named MSI, or Microsoft Installer. The Microsoft Office Setup program first adds and sometimes removes a number of registry entries; actually, a full installation process could modify over a thousand registry entries. (Now you see why I don't just list them all!) Each entry modified, deleted, or added by the Setup program is modified because the entry is based on information specific to the current installation. For example, Setup must handle the entry that has the installation directory, which the user may change at setup time. The .reg files cannot do this, because the .reg file technique cannot take into account user preferences.

The main controlling file for the Microsoft Office Setup program, for Microsoft Office XP Professional, is PRORET.msi.

NOTE   *There are many versions of Microsoft Office, and other versions will have a different installation (.msi) filename. The Microsoft Office CD's root directory typically holds two .msi files: the main installation .msi file and a second, smaller one, named OWC10.msi. OWC is for Microsoft Office Web Components.*

PRORET.msi is located in the root directory of the Microsoft Office CD-ROM. This file is binary so that users may not alter it in any way. There is also a setup initialization file, SETUP.ini, which Setup uses to initialize itself. The .msi file contains entries that control which files are copied and where; which registry entries to delete, add, and modify; and everything else that must be done to install Microsoft Office.

The Microsoft Office XP installation .msi file includes:

- 19 registry searches

- 53 retrievals of pathnames

- 1,418 additions to the registry

- 2 checks of the registry

- 28 checks for registry equality

- 9 registrations of type libraries

- 29 self-registrations

- 21 retrievals of the Windows path

- 73 creations of strings of REG_SZ type

- 6 creations of REG_DWORD type objects

- 35 registry entry removals

- 9 registry tree deletions

- 3 copies of registry key values

- 6 items that are specifically not removed if encountered

- 1 copy of .ini file values for the registry

Microsoft Office System Configuration Information

Microsoft Office XP stores information about common configuration settings in the registry key at HKEY_LOCAL_MACHINE\Software\Microsoft\Office (I'll refer to this location as the "system keys"). This key contains a subkey called 10.0 (for the version number of Microsoft Office XP). The next version of Office will probably be stored in a subkey named 11.0. There is also a subkey called 9.0 (and one called 8.0), each with a single object: Outlook, which contains information on registration and setup.

Noncommon configuration information, specific to a given user, is stored in the user's configuration at HKEY_CURRENT_USER\Software\Microsoft\Office (I'll refer to this location as the "user keys"). These settings are modifiable by users and are kept separate from one another, as each user will have their own configuration and defaults.

The structure of these two locations for Microsoft Office is virtually identical. Under Microsoft is the Office subkey. Under Office are one or more subkeys for each version of Microsoft Office installed. For example, many installations have a subkey, 8.0, for Office 97, a subkey, 9.0, for

Microsoft Office 2000, and `10.0` for Microsoft Office XP. Under the version subkey are one or more product keys and a few support keys.

Don't be surprised if there are subkeys for Microsoft Office components that aren't installed. Some components set items for other components regardless of whether they're installed or not. For example, on my computer, in the user keys, I have the following major subkeys. (Throughout this chapter, assume that an unqualified key is a user key, as I will fully qualify, or annotate, any system keys.)

Access   Microsoft Access, a full-featured desktop database system.

Common   Items common to more than one Microsoft Office component.

Excel   Microsoft Excel, a spreadsheet program.

Outlook   Microsoft's advanced e-mail client.

Registration   Microsoft's Office XP user-registration system. The first time a user installs Microsoft Office XP, the registration program will contact Microsoft, relaying user and product statistics.

Word   Microsoft's well-known word processor, used to write this book.

Each of these keys contains more keys and information. For example, I don't actually have Access installed, but Microsoft Office Setup included the **Access** subkey, regardless. The **Access** subkey has entries for the following items:

◆ `Clipboard Formats`

◆ `InstallRoot`

◆ `Jet`

◆ `Menu Add-Ins`

◆ `Options`

◆ `Report Formats`

◆ `Speller`

◆ `Wizards`

I'll describe each of these subkeys in detail in the next section.

In the system keys, we find the subkeys listed below. Generally, at this level the system keys closely parallel the user keys.

Access   Microsoft Access, a full-featured desktop database system

Common   Items common to more than one Microsoft Office component

Excel   Microsoft Excel, a spreadsheet program

Outlook   Microsoft's advanced e-mail client

Shortcut Bar   The Office XP shortcut bar configuration information

Word   Microsoft's well-known word processor, used to write this book (didn't I already say that?)

Like the user keys, each of the system keys contains more keys and information. For example, the `Access` subkey has entries for the following items:

CustomizableAlerts Access gives an alert whenever a certain event occurs.

Settings Access uses an MRU list to allow the user to quickly open a previous file. The MRU file list is contained in this subkey.

The Access Entries

The Microsoft Access database program is Microsoft's main entry into desktop database systems. Though Microsoft also offers a product called FoxPro (and more appropriately, Visual FoxPro), Fox-Pro is not part of the Office suite. We'll look into some subkeys of the `Access` key in the following sections.

CLIPBOARD FORMATS

The entries in the `Clipboard Formats` subkey describe special formats that Microsoft Access is able to process. These entries include formats and descriptive information on the handler for each format. A typical entry might be:

Value entry: HTML (*.html)

Type: REG_SZ

Typical value: soa.dll,30,html,HTML,HTML(*.html),1

This entry indicates that Access will use `soa.dll` to read this type of data. The entry also provides information to Access about requirements necessary to invoke the code in the `.dll` file. A typical installation might define six or more Clipboard formats.

INSTALLROOT

The `InstallRoot` subkey has a single data value, named `Path`. `Path`, a REG_SZ object, contains the fully qualified path to the Microsoft Access program files. A typical entry might be `C:\Program Files\Microsoft Office\Office`, where C: is the drive that Microsoft Office was installed on.

JET

Microsoft Jet is the engine that Microsoft Access uses to access the actual database files. Microsoft has opened the interface to the Jet engine to other application software, allowing developers to create programs. These programs are able to create, read, and write Access-compatible databases.

Microsoft Jet is a complex, high-performance database engine. There are several additional interfaces in the Jet engine, allowing programming interoperability between Access-compatible software and other database systems, including these (there can be others that are not found in this list):

◆ dBase 5.0

◆ dBase III

◆ dBase IV

- Excel 3.0
- Excel 4.0
- Excel 5.0
- Excel 8.0
- Exchange 4.0
- HTML Export
- HTML Import
- Jet 2.*x*
- Jet 3.*x*
- Lotus WJ2
- Lotus WJ3
- Lotus WK1
- Lotus WK3
- Lotus WK4
- Microsoft Access
- Microsoft Access Data Access Page
- Microsoft Active Server Pages (ASP)
- Microsoft IIS
- Microsoft IIS (Internet Information Server)
- Outlook 9.0
- Paradox 3.*X*
- Paradox 4.*X*
- Paradox 5.*X*
- Paradox 7.*X*
- Rich Text Format (RTF)
- Snapshot Format
- SQL Database
- Text
- Word for Windows Merge

MENU ADD-INS

Access may be expanded or enhanced using menu add-in programs. Some menu add-ins supported by Microsoft Access include these:

- Add-In Manager
- Database Splitter
- Linked Table Manager
- Switchboard Manager

A registry subkey defines each add-in in the `Access\Menu Add-Ins` subkey.

OPTIONS

The states of certain Access options are stored in the `Options` subkey. These options can vary greatly from installation to installation. An example value entry is `AttachIndexWarning`.

REPORT FORMATS

The `Report Formats` subkey stores the formats that Access is able to write reports in. Formats typically supported by most installations include the following:

- HTML
- Microsoft Excel
- MS-DOS Text
- Rich Text Format (RTF)
- Snapshot Format

SPELLER

Like the other members of the Microsoft Office family, Access supports a spell-checking mode. Spell checking is important if you or other users are as fumble-fingered as I am. Without a spelling checker, this book would be unreadable, and the editor, who had to work hard enough anyway, would have probably done nasty things to me.

Settings for spell checking include the following:

- Custom Dictionary
- Ignore All Caps
- Ignore Mixed Digits
- Language ID (information about the current language being used)
- Suggest Always
- Suggest Main Dictionary Only

WIZARDS

Access uses wizards to perform a number of the more complex setup and processing tasks. Wizards allow inexperienced users to quickly become proficient and to get the maximum amount of use from Access without spending a great deal of time learning the product.

Each wizard has a unique set of objects. The main categories of wizards are these:

◆ Control wizards

◆ Data Access Page wizards

◆ Form wizards

◆ Preferences

◆ Property wizards

◆ Query wizards

◆ Report wizards

◆ Table wizards

The Common Entries

In Microsoft Office, many of the applications share parts or components. For example, that funny and entertaining Office Assistant (see Figure 14.1) allows a user to get help quickly and easily in any application. Entries for these components are found in the Common subkey. Other common information—such as Default Save, New, Templates, and so on—is stored in this section as well.

FIGURE 14.1

The Office Assistant is always there to provide help. A single click displays the Help balloon, as shown.

Microsoft Office shares the following items among multiple Office applications:

Assistant   This subkey manages the configuration and customization of the Microsoft Office Assistant. Me, I like that cute cat figure. Several settings for the assistant are available, such as whether the assistant works with wizards.

General   This subkey holds a number of miscellaneous objects. General configuration items include installation information and setup data.

HelpViewer   This subkey is where you define the help viewer defaults for small and large help panes and pane position.

Internet   This subkey stores Internet locations, such as where components are downloaded from.

LanguageResources   This subkey stores the language ID (U.S. English is 409).

NOTE   Wait a minute…Isn't U.S. English 1033? What's this 409 number? Okay, use the Windows calculator program, and convert 0x409 from hexadecimal to decimal. If you did it right, you got 1033. That's the secret; the language ID in this object is in hexadecimal!

Migration   This object holds information about migration from one version to a newer version. Applications in this subkey include Excel, Office, Outlook, and Word.

Open Find   This object contains subkeys for each product. Within each subkey are settings specific to the application.

Toolbars   This subkey stores settings such as adaptive menus, whether menus auto-expand, and so on.

UserInfo   This subkey holds the user's name, company, ID, initials, and user information. This information is stored in Unicode format.

INSTALLROOT

InstallRoot contains the Microsoft Office installation directory.

LV

When used, LV describes the installation type, product ID, product name, and so forth.

The Excel Entries

The Excel key, for the Microsoft Excel spreadsheet program, contains a couple of subkeys: Options and Recent Files. The Options subkey contains various optional values for Excel. The Recent Files subkey contains information about files that were recently opened.

The Outlook Entries

The Outlook key contains the settings for the Outlook e-mail client, available as part of the Microsoft Office package. I'll admit a preference for Outlook 2002. It's a tool that I use every day for e-mail, calendar, and contact management tasks. It offers substantial improvements over earlier versions of Outlook. I recommend that if you are considering Outlook, you get the latest version from Microsoft.

The Outlook subkey contains information on the following Outlook 2002 functions:

Dataviz   This subkey holds a flag indicating whether public folders are hidden or not.

InstallRoot   This object holds the fully qualified name of the directory that Outlook 2002 has been installed in.

NameSpaces   A namespace represents a data source, such as the MAPI message store, or file and directory names. This subkey holds namespace information for Outlook.

OMI   This subkey holds the Outlook Internet e-mail system configuration.

Operations   This subkey contains configurations of various operations that Outlook will perform, such as file import, file export, data link export, VCard import, Accounts import, Calendar import, and Eudora import.

SchedulingInformation   This subkey contains options and configuration information for the Outlook Schedule functionality.

SearchTypes   This is the table of CLSID entries for each search type.

Setup   This subkey lists options chosen during setup.

UpgradePath   This is the path to be used for upgrade.

Outlook is one of the most complex components of Microsoft Office. It can be difficult to configure; but once it's set up, it provides flexibility and power, making it a valuable tool for any busy computer user.

The PowerPoint Entries

Microsoft PowerPoint is a tool used to create presentations for display on media, such as video screens, printed handouts, and slides. PowerPoint is capable of such tricks as animation, sounds, and special effects, making it a good presentation and training tool. Many users are familiar with PowerPoint, but most do not use this program to its fullest. Look at the supported features discussed in this section for some ideas of what can be done with this versatile program.

The following list contains subkeys that are specific to PowerPoint:

Addins   Microsoft PowerPoint supports a number of add-in product functionalities. This object contains information about add-ins, including auto-content and PowerPoint tools.

Answer Wizard   This subkey contains settings used with the supplementary help system that assists users in searching for additional help on problems they are having.

AutoContent Wizard   This subkey assists users in designing a presentation and developing content.

DLL Addins   This subkey contains add-in .dll files used by PowerPoint.

Document Routing   This subkey contains a flag to tell Microsoft PowerPoint whether or not to track status.

Export Modules   This subkey contains the names of modules used to export presentations to other formats, such as for an offline publishing or printing system.

InstallRoot   This subkey holds the root directory that Microsoft PowerPoint has been installed in.

OLE Play Options   This object contains any OLE multimedia support that is included. Typically, items in this subkey include sound and video support.

PPCentral   This object consists of basic Microsoft PowerPoint options, many of which are configurable by the user.

Sound   This subkey is concerned with sound formats, such as WAV, that are supported by Microsoft PowerPoint.

Sound Effects   This object contains information about sound effects. The user can use these included sound effects (like Typewriter, Whoosh, Laser, Camera, and Drive By) in a presentation.

Translators   This subkey contains information about import and export support for other versions of Microsoft PowerPoint. The tools include Export to Microsoft PowerPoint 7, and Import from Microsoft PowerPoint 7 and Microsoft PowerPoint 4.

ValuPack   This object specifies the location of the Microsoft Office ValuPack directory. Run `Valupk8.hlp` to find out more about the ValuPack.

Viewer   This object specifies the location for the Microsoft PowerPoint viewer, a stand-alone Microsoft PowerPoint display program.

The Publisher Entries

Microsoft Publisher is a midrange page-layout program that is well integrated with other Microsoft Office products. Using Microsoft Publisher is easy; the application allows you to create professional documents that may be printed locally or sent to a printer/typesetter for duplication. The following list contains subkeys specific to Microsoft Publisher:

ColorSchemes   This subkey contains the definition of the Microsoft Publisher color schemes. Microsoft Publisher allows users to switch color schemes at any point using a four-color palette.

Envelopes   This subkey contains information on any envelopes defined.

HTML   This subkey contains the filter to process HTML documents. Microsoft Publisher will publish in HTML if desired, allowing you to create Web pages from other existing documents with a minimum of effort.

HTMLCharacterEncodings   This subkey holds character encoding for foreign languages.

Mail Merge   This subkey contains information on mail merge. Using the Microsoft Access Jet database engine, Microsoft Publisher is able to merge database information, creating custom documents as necessary.

Page Size   This subkey defines custom page sizes, such as those required for business cards.

Printing   This subkey contains information used by Microsoft Publisher to print user documents.

ProPrint   This subkey contains information used by Microsoft Publisher to print using a high-end image-processing system.

PubBackground   This subkey contains the directory path to the Microsoft Publisher backgrounds that can be used with publications.

PubClipart   This subkey contains the directory path to the Microsoft Publisher clip art that can be used with publications.

Recent File List   This subkey holds the Microsoft Publisher MRU file list.

Spelling   This subkey contains spell-checking options.

Version   This subkey is where version information is saved.

WizType   This subkey contains the Microsoft Publisher wizards that are used to create basic publications with a minimum of effort.

The Registration Entries

The `Registration` subkey contains the Microsoft Office XP product ID value.

The Word Entries

The `Word` subkey contains information about the Microsoft Word installation directory. All of the remaining Word options are set in the user's configuration.

Microsoft Office User Configuration Information

The best way to get to the Office user configuration registry entries is through HKEY_CURRENT_USER\ Software\Microsoft\Office\10.0. Although they are also available in the HKEY_USERS hive, accessing them through HKEY_CURRENT_USER instead will ensure that the correct set of entries (those for the currently logged-on user) is always modified.

Some ways to use these keys include:

◆ Backing up the key and saving it for another user ID. This second user ID could be a different user ID for the same user. This allows a user to recover their entire configuration without changes.

◆ Modifying a specific user's entries. Maybe the organization name changes—you could rely on users to update their systems, or you could go in and make the necessary changes for them.

◆ Implementing a specific backup and restore for whatever reason.

NOTE   *Sometimes we just want to start over and redo our user settings from scratch. So, we uninstall Microsoft Office and do a new clean install. Bang! There are all our old settings back again—we can't seem to get rid of them. The reason for this is simple: Uninstalling doesn't remove these user configuration settings. Uninstalling only removes the system settings. It is actually not even necessary to uninstall to change the user configuration settings; simply delete the user's configuration.*

In the next sections, you'll find some of the common user configuration settings. These may be altered, following standard precautions about backing up, and will only affect the current user. Other users will not see any changes made to the HKEY_CURRENT_USER configuration.

Access User Configurations

Microsoft Access user configurations are stored in subkeys under the Access key. The items found in this key will vary greatly depending on the user's configuration and use of Access.

Binder User Configurations

Any user-specific Binder settings are saved in the Binder subkey.

What's Binder? It is surprising just how many experienced Microsoft Office users don't know what Binder is or how to use it. Microsoft Binder is a program that makes it possible to group all of your documents, spreadsheets, and presentations for a project into a single master document. A typical use for Binder is to create a project proposal and presentation.

Common User Configurations

Items in the Common subkey are shared between more than one of the Microsoft Office applications. For example, the Microsoft Office Assistant is used by all the Microsoft Office products.

Commonly, any user-installed items, such as those from Visual Basic for Applications, will be stored in the Common subkey as well. See "Using the Registry from Microsoft Office Applications," later in this chapter.

Most Common subkeys contain:

Assistant This subkey contains the settings for the Microsoft Office Assistant, including who the assistant is and other Office Assistant configurations. To change these settings, context-click the Microsoft Office Assistant and select an item to change.

AutoCorrect AutoCorrect is mostly used in Microsoft Word. It allows a word that is misspelled to be automatically corrected. Users of Excel, PowerPoint, and Access will also find use for this functionality.

Cursors This subkey is where you can configure cursors displayed by Microsoft Office. I've been unable to find any way other than registry manipulation to change Office's cursor selections.

FileNew This subkey contains the configurations for the File New dialog box.

General This subkey contains the general settings for all Microsoft Office applications.

InstallRoot This subkey contains a count of the number of installations and the path of the basic Office installation.

Internet This subkey contains the Internet settings for all Microsoft Office applications.

LanguageResources This subkey contains the language settings for all Microsoft Office applications.

Open Find This subkey contains the settings for the Open dialog box.

ProductVersion   This subkey contains the product version that is currently installed. A typical product version consists of four parts, separated with periods.

Toolbars   This subkey contains the toolbar configurations and settings.

UserInfo   This subkey contains information about the current user.

W2KMigrationFeatures   This subkey contains information about migration from prior versions of Microsoft Office.

WMEMigrationFeatures   This subkey contains information about migration from prior versions of Microsoft Office.

Draw User Configurations

Microsoft Draw is a helper application that is used to edit and draw within Office documents. Primarily an OLE server application, Draw is not designed or intended to be used as a stand-alone application.

Excel User Configurations

The user's entire Excel configuration is contained in the Excel subkey. Keys in this subkey include:

Init Commands   This subkey contains the commands used to initialize Excel.

Init Menus   This subkey contains information used to initialize Excel's menu.

InstallRoot   This subkey contains the path of the Excel installation.

Line Print   This subkey contains Lotus macro line-printing settings.

Microsoft Excel   This subkey contains basic configuration settings.

Recent File List   This subkey contains the list of the most recently used files.

Spell Checker   This subkey contains the options for configuration of the spelling checker.

WK? Settings   This subkey contains the settings for the Lotus open-and-save feature.

Graph User Configurations

Microsoft Graph is a helper application that is used to edit and include simple graphs and tables within Office documents. Primarily an OLE server application, Graph is not designed or intended to be used as a stand-alone application.

Outlook User Configurations

Outlook's configuration settings are contained in this subkey. Settings for the following areas are included:

Appointment   This subkey contains the appointment book configuration information.

AutoNameCheck   This subkey contains the setting that indicates whether to automatically check names in the Send and CC lines of messages.

Categories   This subkey contains the message categories.

Contact   This subkey contains the contact (names) list management configuration and options.

Dataviz   This subkey contains the interface with external data sources such as the PAB (Personal Address Book) and other data sources.

Item Toolbars   This subkey contains the toolbar configurations.

Journal   This subkey contains the Outlook Journal, used to track items.

Journal Entry   This subkey contains the Outlook Journal configuration.

Message   This subkey contains the message box configuration.

Note   This subkey contains the note configuration.

Office Explorer   This subkey contains the configuration of the Office Explorer.

Office Finder   This subkey contains the Office Finder configuration and settings.

OMI Account Manager   This subkey contains the Outlook Internet e-mail system configuration.

Options   This subkey contains various miscellaneous settings.

Printing   This subkey contains the printing options and configuration.

Report   This subkey contains the reporting options and configuration.

Scripting   This subkey contains the scripting driver's CLSID.

Security   This subkey contains the security settings.

Setup   This subkey contains the setup options and settings.

Task   This subkey contains the task options and settings.

Today   This subkey contains the Outlook Today settings.

WAB   This subkey contains the settings for the Windows Address Book.

Wizards   This subkey contains the wizard settings.

PowerPoint User Configurations

Microsoft PowerPoint user settings are saved in the **PowerPoint** subkey.

Publisher User Configurations

Microsoft Publisher user settings are saved in the **Publisher** subkey. They include the following:

Preferences   This subkey contains the user preferences and settings.

Tracking Data   This subkey contains the tracking items.

UserInfo   This subkey contains the information specific to the current user, including the following entries:

- OtherOrganization

- Personal

- PrimaryBusiness

- SecondaryBusiness

Query User Configurations

The `Query` subkey contains information about the Microsoft Query (`msqry32.exe`) program, if installed and used. Microsoft Query is useful for peeking at various data sources, such as database files created by any ODBC-compliant application.

Word User Configurations

Microsoft Word user configurations are saved in this subkey. Items saved here include the following:

Custom Labels   This subkey holds information that is used when printing on labels. Users may create their own custom label to match their label stock.

Data   This subkey includes the Word MRU file list. This list is hidden in another object and is not editable.

Default Save   This subkey contains the default save format.

Help   This subkey contains the Help file information.

InstallRoot   This subkey contains a count of the number of installations and the path of the basic Office installation.

List Gallery Presets   This subkey contains binary information about presets for the list gallery.

Options   This subkey holds various Microsoft Word options and settings.

Stationery   This subkey contains information used primarily when Microsoft Word is the e-mail editor.

Text Converters   This subkey contains the filters used to convert documents saved as text files into Word. Entries include:

Import\MSPAB   Filter for importing from the Microsoft Personal Address Book

Import\OUTLOOK   Filter for importing from Microsoft Outlook

Import\SPLUS   Filter for importing from Microsoft Schedule Plus

Wizards   This subkey contains configurations for the various Word wizards.

WordMail   This subkey contains WordMail settings used when Word is used as the e-mail editor.

Using the Registry from Microsoft Office Applications

Okay, in the final section of this chapter, let's figure out how to manipulate the registry from a Microsoft Office application. That's right, if you wanted to, you could write an entire registry editor using Microsoft Word.

Most Microsoft Office users won't have a great need to save items in the registry. However, if you find that you need to save information that must be persistent between sessions, saving this information in the registry can be an excellent method.

The example I'll use here is a simple system for saving a string to the registry. This macro is written in VBA (Visual Basic for Applications), and the techniques are portable not only among the Microsoft Office applications, but also to any other application that uses VBA as its scripting language.

In this example, the user enters some information into a single edit control in a basic VBA form. The information is then written into the registry, in the user's section, under the key HKEY_CURRENT_USER\Software\Microsoft\Office\Common\UserOptions. You would use a different name than UserOptions for your application, of course.

Figure 14.2 shows the UserOptions key and the data values saved in it (I used a variable named Text). These values, once saved, can be modified from various places in Word and even in other Microsoft Office applications.

FIGURE 14.2

The UserOptions subkey has a single data object, named Text.

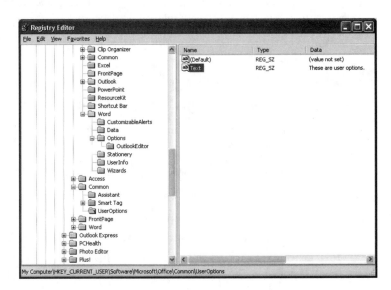

The Set User Options Here dialog box is used to modify the Text data object, stored in the UserOptions subkey. This dialog box (see Figure 14.3) is a simple form that allows easy data entry.

NOTE *Many of Word's options are set in a single REG_BINARY variable named* Settings. *This makes it difficult to "hack" these items as individual things, since it is necessary to find the exact location within* Settings *of a specific functionality.*

FIGURE 14.3

The Set User
Options Here
form sets and resets
a string that is saved
in the registry.

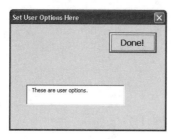

I'm going to show some of the code used to create this form here. Yours does not need to be this complex. A simple form without tabs can be very effective in getting a user interface together; add tabs as needed later on.

First is the main function that displays (shows) the form itself:

```
Sub DisplayPublisherOptionsDialogBox()
   frmUserOptions.Show
End Sub
```

This code shows the form frmUserOptions and then exits. The form takes care of actually initializing itself by reading the various registry entries and updating itself appropriately. This initialization is done in the form's initialization code:

```
Private Sub UserForm_Initialize()

UserOptions = "HKEY_CURRENT_USER\Software\Microsoft\Office\Common\UserOptions"

If System.PrivateProfileString("", UserOptions, "Text") <> "" Then
    frmUserOptions.TextBox1.Text = System.PrivateProfileString("", UserOptions,
"Text")
End If

End Sub
```

First, we initialize the global string variable, named UserOptions. This string contains the name of the registry key that will hold our information. By saving this location in a variable, we can use the variable without worrying about whether a name has changed—if we need to change the registry key, we need only change it in one place.

Next we know the form has been shown and has been initialized. Our variable UserOptions has also been initialized. Note that any line that begins with a leading single quote (') is a comment line. Comments are only there for our own information, and the system ignores them. ActiveWindow tells the system to work with the active window. An example of conditional processing follows:

```
Private Sub CommandButton1_Click()

Dim myString As String

With ActiveWindow
```

```
If frmUserOptions.TextBox1.Text <> "" Then
    System.PrivateProfileString("", UserOptions, "Text") =
frmUserOptions.TextBox1.Text
End If

frmUserOptions.Hide

End With

End Sub
```

This code is executed when the user clicks the Done! Button. We have two things to do.

First we must process the information that the user has provided. We check to see if the text box contains any text, and if it does, we save that information. We test for the presence of entered text using an `If` statement.

An `If` statement allows what is called *conditional processing*. When the subject of the `If` statement is true, the statement after the `Then` is executed. (You can also have an `Else` clause, which is executed if the result of the `If` statement is false.) Conditional processing is the cornerstone of computer programming. Without conditional processing, programs as we know them could not exist.

In the previous example, if the following function:

```
frmUserOptions.TextBox1.Text <> ""
```

returns a value of `"True"`, we set the registry variable to the text contained in the edit box.

NOTE `PrivateProfileString()` *returns the value that the value entry contains if it exists. If the entry doesn't exist,* `System.PrivateProfileString()` *returns the default, an empty string.*

The following code is very similar. We check to see if the data value `"Wrap"` exists and what its value is. If the value is `"True"`, we set the variable `View.WrapToWindow` to `True`. Otherwise, we set the variable `View.WrapToWindow` to `False`.

```
If System.PrivateProfileString("",UserOptions , "Wrap") = "True" Then
  .View.WrapToWindow = True
Else
  .View.WrapToWindow = False
End If
```

This same process—of checking a registry entry for its value, setting a local variable to reflect the registry entry's value, and checking the next registry entry in the list—is performed by checking each of the relevant entries.

After the user finishes with the form and clicks the Done! button, the registry is updated. If the user clicks the Cancel button instead of OK, Visual Basic for Applications discards everything without making any changes in the registry.

TIP *Need a quick way to start a Visual Basic for Applications function? Simply create a macro and edit the macro's code to include the functionality that you need.*

CONFUSED ABOUT SYSTEM.PRIVATEPROFILESTRING?

The first example in this section retrieved a value from the registry. This value was used to initialize the form controls. In the second example, we set a registry data value with the same function. How does it know the difference?

The magic is that the context of how the call is made tells Visual Basic for Applications how to use it. In the first instance, the call was within an If statement. In the second use, the call was part of an assignment statement. Visual Basic for Applications knows the difference.

The entire source code and form definitions for this example are shown in Listing 14.1.

LISTING 14.1: FRMUSEROPTIONS.FRM

```
VERSION 5.00
Begin {C62A69F0-16DC-11CE-9E98-00AA00574A4F} frmUserOptions
    Caption         =    "Set User Options Here"
    ClientHeight    =    3120
    ClientLeft      =    45
    ClientTop       =    435
    ClientWidth     =    4710
    OleObjectBlob   =    "frmUserOptions.frx":0000
    StartUpPosition =    1  'CenterOwner
End
Attribute VB_Name = "frmUserOptions"
Attribute VB_GlobalNameSpace = False
Attribute VB_Creatable = False
Attribute VB_PredeclaredId = True
Attribute VB_Exposed = False
Dim UserOptions As String


Private Sub CommandButton1_Click()

Dim myString As String

With ActiveWindow

If frmUserOptions.TextBox1.Text <> "" Then
    System.PrivateProfileString("", UserOptions, "Text") = _
        frmUserOptions.TextBox1.Text
End If

frmUserOptions.Hide
```

```
    End With

    End Sub


    Private Sub UserForm_Initialize()

    UserOptions = _
        "HKEY_CURRENT_USER\Software\Microsoft\Office\Common\UserOptions"

    If System.PrivateProfileString("", UserOptions, "Text") <> "" Then
        frmUserOptions.TextBox1.Text = _
            System.PrivateProfileString("", UserOptions, "Text")
    End If

    End Sub
```

Part IV

The Registry Reference

In this section, you'll learn how to:

◆ **Understand unique IDs and manage the** HKEY_CLASSES_ROOT **hive**

◆ **Manage the** HKEY_CURRENT_USER **and** HKEY_USERS **hives**

◆ **Understand the five keys in** HKEY_LOCAL_MACHINE

◆ **Find installed software configurations in**
   HKEY_LOCAL_MACHINE\Software

◆ **Work with and tune** HKEY_LOCAL_MACHINE\System **and**
   HKEY_CURRENT_CONFIG

Chapter 15

Introduction to HKEY_CLASSES_ROOT

MANY OF THE REGISTRY'S entries deal with the Windows XP system. These entries comprise a substantial portion of a new installation's registry, although as more and more applications are installed, this percentage will drop.

Is there anything to fear in the registry's system components? Absolutely! A wrong entry in some system entries will make the system unstable, unbootable, or just plain dead. In these remaining chapters, we'll cover the registry, hive by hive, pointing out some of the more important entries, some values, and some cautions to consider.

The HKEY_CLASSES_ROOT branch contains information about both OLE and various file associations. The purpose of HKEY_CLASSES_ROOT is to provide compatibility with the existing Windows 3.*x* registry. The information contained in HKEY_CLASSES_ROOT is identical to information found in HKEY_LOCAL_MACHINE\Software\Classes.

Before we talk too much about HKEY_CLASSES_ROOT, we'll delve into things like GUIDs, UUIDs, and all those other funny registry numbers. Don't let this scare you—it is good (not absolutely necessary, just good) to understand what these numbers *really* are.

Knowing that you have backed up your registry *before* starting this chapter, let's dig in and see what's there.

- ◆ Understanding GUIDs, UUIDs, and other registry numbers
- ◆ Looking at HKEY_CLASSES_ROOT

GUIDs, UUIDs, and Other Funny Numbers in Windows

All versions of Windows are just chock full of strange, long numbers. One type of number is the GUID (globally unique ID), a.k.a. the UUID (universally unique ID). Regardless of which term is used, a GUID is *always* a unique number assigned to an application or component. Controls, applications, parts of Windows, software and components, tools, compilers—everything today has one or more GUIDs. Used primarily with OLE (Object Linking and Embedding), GUIDs link components and the operating system. GUIDs are used as a linkage between applications, file types, embedding, OLE, objects, and the operating system.

NOTE *Though I say that every program has a unique GUID, actually different versions of the same program may share the same GUID. This allows the program to be compatible with earlier versions of itself. Regardless, two different programs should never have the same GUID.*

For example, Microsoft Word has a GUID of {000209FF-0000-0000-C000-000000000046}. This is unique enough that we can be sure that a request for this GUID will always match Microsoft Word, and not some other application. How can we say that? After all, although a GUID is long (it's a number with 16 bytes, or 128 bits), what mechanisms are there to make sure that each programmer uses a unique GUID?

The process of obtaining a GUID is simple and, in most cases, doesn't even require any direct interaction with Microsoft. Does that make you rather nervous? Fear not, Microsoft provides a tool to generate a GUID, and that tool takes some rather interesting steps to attempt to make each GUID unique.

NOTE *Why even bother with these GUIDs? Say two programmers working for different companies create a program with the executable file name of* xyz.exe. *There's nothing wrong with that; a program's filename typically doesn't represent the actual product name or the program's functionality. However, without GUIDs it would be rather difficult for Windows to distinguish between these two programs.*

First, a bit of history (just what you wanted, a history lesson). All Ethernet network interface cards (NICs) have a unique identifying number built into them. That's right, the NIC in your computer is different from the NIC of the computer in the office next door. This means that each computer with a NIC actually has a form of a unique serial number.

NOTE *This unique number is actually the MAC (Media Access Control) address, used by the networking hardware to manage the various resources found on the network.*

The NIC's serial number (the MAC address) allows the hardware layer of the network to distinguish between different computers on the network. An overseeing organization assigns unique identifiers to each NIC manufacturer (which forms the first part of the MAC address), and the manufacturer assigns the second part of the identifier to each NIC at assembly time (usually sequentially). Most NICs have their ID number written on a small sticker on the card, though in today's world, users and administrators have virtually no need for the NIC's MAC address. Figure 15.1 shows a Windows XP computer NIC configuration. Notice the line called Physical Address—that is the NIC's MAC address.

The Microsoft GUID program takes the NIC's identifier number, which is unique; the current time and date information (which is relatively unique), hashed a bit; and a random number for good measure and uses these to create the GUID. To have two identical GUIDs, it would be necessary to have two computers with the same NIC MAC addresses, at the same time (*exactly*, to the millisecond), and with the same random number.

In short, it is unlikely that two GUIDs would be the same. Even if a programmer were to get the command to run at *exactly* the same time on both computers, it is not reasonable that the random number would be the same on both runs. This is because the random number is not based on time or any other factor that a programmer might be able to influence. Hence, you can be reasonably sure that the GUID for each application will be unique.

FIGURE 15.1

A typical NIC's MAC address, as displayed using the IPCONFIG /ALL command

The NIC's MAC address

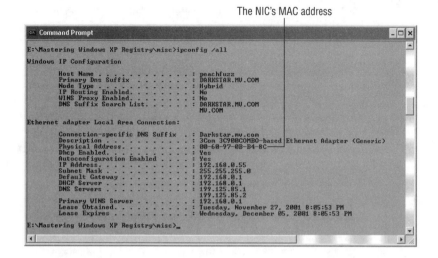

There is actually one instance where a GUID might not be unique: when a programmer intentionally copies the GUID for one program into another program. This could be unintentional; but more likely, the program would do this by design. I can't think of any valid reason why a programmer might create two *different* applications with the same GUID, but I'm sure that someone will write and tell me why this could, or would, happen.

A GUID consists of five groups of digits in hexadecimal. Hyphens separate each group. These groups display four bytes, two bytes, two bytes, two bytes, and six bytes—in that order—as the following GUID shows:

{000209FF-0000-0000-C000-000000000046}

It is common, although not specifically required, that braces enclose a GUID. However, whenever you encounter a number with the above arrangement of digits (8, 4, 4, 4, 12), you can generally assume that the number is a GUID.

A ROSE BY ANY OTHER NAME

UUID and GUID are just different names for the same thing. Ditto for CLSID (class ID). CLSIDs, GUIDs, and UUIDs all identify a specific class of objects. Treat a CLSID the same as you would treat a GUID or a UUID, and all will be well.

HKEY_CLASSES_ROOT

The HKEY_CLASSES_ROOT hive contains information about both OLE and various file associations.

WARNING *A little later in this chapter, we'll start fiddling with the registry. You are an intelligent person; therefore, you know that you should back up your registry before you start. Please, do not change the registry without having a good, easily restored backup.*

HKEY_CLASSES_ROOT provides compatibility with the existing Windows 3.*x* registry; some applications and systems expect HKEY_CLASSES_ROOT to exist. The information contained in HKEY_CLASSES_ROOT is identical to information found in the subkey HKEY_LOCAL_MACHINE\Software\Classes. Actually, these two objects are physically the same. A change made in one will automatically modify the other. Think of HKEY_CLASSES_ROOT as a house on the corner of an intersection. The house might have two addresses, one on each street. Remember: HKEY_CLASSES_ROOT is HKEY_LOCAL_MACHINE\Software\Classes and HKEY_LOCAL_MACHINE\Software\Classes is HKEY_CLASSES_ROOT.

Managing File Types and File Extensions

The HKEY_CLASSES_ROOT hive consists of a list of all file extensions (file types) known to your installation of Windows XP. Each time you install a new application, the application should add or modify one or more extensions. The application's setup program does this, and this process tells Windows XP that the application will handle (open, print, and so on) that type of file when users select it.

For example, the HKEY_CLASSES_ROOT key for an Excel spreadsheet file (any file that ends in .xls) is as follows:

```
HKEY_CLASSES_ROOT\.xls
HKEY_CLASSES_ROOT\.xls\Excel.Sheet.5
HKEY_CLASSES_ROOT\.xls\Excel.Sheet.5\ShellNew
HKEY_CLASSES_ROOT\.xls\Excel.Sheet.5\ShellNew\FileName = excel.xls

HKEY_CLASSES_ROOT\.xls\ExcelWorksheet
HKEY_CLASSES_ROOT\.xls\ExcelWorksheet\ShellNew
HKEY_CLASSES_ROOT\.xls\ExcelWorksheet\ShellNew\FileName = excel4.xls

HKEY_CLASSES_ROOT\.xls\ShellEx
HKEY_CLASSES_ROOT\.xls\ShellEx\{00021500-0000-0000-C000-000000000046}
HKEY_CLASSES_ROOT\.xls\ShellEx\{00021500-0000-0000-C000-000000000046}
    \(Default) = {83799FE0-1F5A-11d1-95C7-00609797EA4F}

HKEY_CLASSES_ROOT\.xls\ShellEx\{BB2E617C-0920-11d1-9A0B-00C04FC2D6C1}
HKEY_CLASSES_ROOT\.xls\ShellEx\{BB2E617C-0920-11d1-9A0B-00C04FC2D6C1}
    \(Default) = {9DBD2C50-62AD-11d0-B806-00C04FD706EC}
```

This complex group of registry entries results from the complexity of the Microsoft Office product; after all, we pay a lot for those Office products.

Another example is for batch files with the extension of .bat. The entry we find for batch files is as follows:

```
HKEY_CLASSES_ROOT\.bat
HKEY_CLASSES_ROOT\.bat\(Default) = batfile
```

We also see a subkey named `PersistentHandler` that contains a GUID. This GUID (`5e941d80-bf96-11cd-b579-08002b30bfeb`) is the plain-text persistent handler, and it is used for many other `HKEY_CLASSES_ROOT` entries as well.

We see an identifier, which has no name, with a data value of `batfile`. Looking a bit further down the line (or down `HKEY_CLASSES_ROOT`, so to speak), we find an entry called `batfile`. Coincidence? Luck? Secret conspiracy? Here are the facts for `batfile`:

```
HKEY_CLASSES_ROOT\batfile
HKEY_CLASSES_ROOT\batfile\(Default) = MS-DOS Batch File
HKEY_CLASSES_ROOT\batfile\EditFlags =  30 04 00 00

HKEY_CLASSES_ROOT\batfile\DefaultIcon
HKEY_CLASSES_ROOT\batfile\DefaultIcon\(Default) =
   %SystemRoot%\System32\shell32.dll,-153

HKEY_CLASSES_ROOT\batfile\shell
HKEY_CLASSES_ROOT\batfile\shell\edit
HKEY_CLASSES_ROOT\batfile\shell\edit\(Default) = &Edit

HKEY_CLASSES_ROOT\batfile\shell\edit\command
HKEY_CLASSES_ROOT\batfile\shell\edit\command\(Default) =
   %SystemRoot%\System32\NOTEPAD.EXE %1

HKEY_CLASSES_ROOT\batfile\shell\open
HKEY_CLASSES_ROOT\batfile\shell\open\EditFlags = 0x00000000
HKEY_CLASSES_ROOT\batfile\shell\open\command
HKEY_CLASSES_ROOT\batfile\shell\open\command\(Default) = "%1" %*

HKEY_CLASSES_ROOT\batfile\shell\print
HKEY_CLASSES_ROOT\batfile\shell\print\command
HKEY_CLASSES_ROOT\batfile\shell\print\command\(Default) =
   %SystemRoot%\System32\NOTEPAD.EXE /p %1

HKEY_CLASSES_ROOT\batfile\shellex\batfile\shellex\PropertySheetHandlers
HKEY_CLASSES_ROOT\batfile\shellex\PropertySheetHandlers\PifProps
HKEY_CLASSES_ROOT\batfile\shellex\PropertySheetHandlers\PifProps\(Default)
   = {86F19A00-42A0-1069-A2E9-08002B30309D}
```

Now, the preceding set of entries tell us and Windows XP everything needed to handle a `.bat` file—the icon to display, how to edit it, how to open it, how to print it, and how to process (execute) it. Let's look at each section of this entry. We'll begin with the first section:

```
HKEY_CLASSES_ROOT\batfile
HKEY_CLASSES_ROOT\batfile\(Default) = MS-DOS Batch File
HKEY_CLASSES_ROOT\batfile\EditFlags = 30 04 00 00
```

Initial handling for batch files includes (in an unnamed variable) the text string used both in Explorer for the file's Properties dialog box and in the Type column of Explorer's detailed list view.

Modifying this string changes the behavior of Explorer and Windows for the properties displayed for a batch file.

The `EditFlags` variable controls how Windows processes the command.

EDITFLAGS AND BITMAPPED VARIABLES

`EditFlags` variables are bitmapped, with a few apparent bits. Flags are combined by ANDing them together. For example, 00 08 00 00 ANDed with 00 01 00 00 would result in the value 00 09 00 00. Use the Windows calculator program and simply add the values; the result will be identical.

NOTE *EditFlags are stored in binary format, so that the bytes in the value are not in the same order that a DWORD value would have. If modifying EditFlags values, be cautious to correctly order the bytes!*

`EditFlags` variables affect the way that Windows XP and its components, such as Internet Explorer, handle receiving certain files, as well as how files are processed.

Table 15.1 shows the bit values defined for `EditFlags`.

TABLE 15.1: BIT VALUES FOR *EDITFLAGS*

NAME	VALUE (IN HEXADECIMAL)	VALUE (IN BINARY)	DESCRIPTION OR EFFECT
Exclude	0x00000001	01 00 00 00	Excludes the file class; suppresses the display of the file type in the file types list
Show	0x00000002	02 00 00 00	Shows extensions for nonfile objects (such as a folder that aren't associated with a filename extension)
HasExtension	0x00000004	04 00 00 00	Shows that the file class has a name extension
NoEdit	0x00000008	08 00 00 00	Does not allow editing registry entries associated with this file class
NoRemove	0x00000010	10 00 00 00	Disables the Remove button in the File Types tab
NoNewVerb	0x00000020	20 00 00 00	Disables the Actions ➢ New command in the File Types tab
NoEditVerb	0x00000040	40 00 00 00	Disables the Edit button in the Edit File Type dialog box
NoRemoveVerb	0x00000080	80 00 00 00	Disables the Remove button in the Edit File Type dialog box
NoEditDesc	0x00000100	00 01 00 00	Disables the Edit Name button in the Edit File Type dialog box

Continued on next page

TABLE 15.1: BIT VALUES FOR *EDITFLAGS (continued)*

NAME	VALUE (IN HEXADECIMAL)	VALUE (IN BINARY)	DESCRIPTION OR EFFECT
NoEditIcon	0x00000200	00 02 00 00	Disables the Change Icon button in the Edit File Type dialog box
NoEditDflt	0x00000400	00 04 00 00	Disables the Set Default button in the Edit File Type dialog box
NoEditVerbCmd	0x00000800	00 08 00 00	Disables modification of commands associated with verbs
NoEditVerbExe	0x00001000	00 10 00 00	Disables modification of command actions
NoDDE	0x00002000	00 20 00 00	Disables changing the DDE settings
NoEditMIME	0x00008000	00 80 00 00	Disables modification or deletion of the content type and default extension entries
OpenIsSafe	0x00010000	00 00 01 00	Specifies that the file class's open verb can be invoked for downloaded files
AlwaysUnsafe	0x00020000	00 00 02 00	Disables the "Never ask me" check box
AlwaysShowExt	0x00040000	00 00 04 00	Ensures that a class extension is always to be shown
NoRecentDocs	0x00100000	00 00 10 00	Disables automatic adding of these files or objects to the Recent Documents folder
ConfirmOpen	0x10000000	00 00 00 01	Confirms open after download in Internet Explorer

COMMON EDITFLAG VALUES

Some commonly used flag combination values are these:

EditFlag 0xD2010000   For drives, directories, folders, and so on. Disables Edit File Type, Remove, Description, and Edit Name in the Edit dialog box. Also adds the file type to the list if this isn't a real file.

EditFlag 0x30040000   For batch files, disables Set Default, Remove, and New.

EditFlag 0x38070000   For applications, disables Edit, Set Default, Change Icon, and Edit Description.

The next section for batch files is as follows:

```
HKEY_CLASSES_ROOT\batfile\DefaultIcon
HKEY_CLASSES_ROOT\batfile\DefaultIcon\(Default) =
   %SystemRoot%\System32\shell132.dll,-153
```

The `DefaultIcon` entry specifies which icon Explorer displays in the Explorer program or on the Desktop, as appropriate. Notice that Explorer won't allow you to use the Explorer Properties dialog box to change the icon for a batch file. Here is where it is changed:

```
%SystemRoot%\System32\shell132.dll,-153
```

What does that magic line mean? The file named `%SystemRoot%\System32\shell132.dll` is a `.dll` file that has, in addition to other things, a whole bunch of icons. The second number is a bit of a mystery, right? First, it is negative; just how do you find a negative icon, anyway? Second, there doesn't seem to be any simple program or method to find which icon matches this magic number.

The negative number isn't so difficult. Icons are stored as resources in executable files; `.exe` and `.dll` files are both executable, but other extensions are also executable and can have icons in them. Each resource has a unique signed number from 0 to 65535 (a two-byte value) assigned. These *resources* (icons, dialog boxes, and strings) use this number to identify themselves to Windows. Programmers, and programmers' tools, ignore the fact that these resources are stored with signed numbers and simply ignore the signs. A programmer sets the icon's identifier to 65382, and Windows, to make things easy for all of us, displays it as −153. So icon number −153 is actually icon number 65382.

Some `.dll` files with lots of icons in them are `pifmgr.dll`, `moricons.dll`, and `shell132.dll`. There are other files containing icons, too.

Let's look at the next section:

```
HKEY_CLASSES_ROOT\batfile\shell
HKEY_CLASSES_ROOT\batfile\shell\edit
HKEY_CLASSES_ROOT\batfile\shell\edit\(Default) = &Edit

HKEY_CLASSES_ROOT\batfile\shell\edit\command
HKEY_CLASSES_ROOT\batfile\shell\edit\command\(Default) =
   %SystemRoot%\System32\NOTEPAD.EXE %1
```

The `shell\edit` section describes how to edit the subject file. The name of the context-menu selection to edit is in the variable having no name. (Right-click the file in Explorer to see the context menu.) The default variable name for most programs is `&Edit`, which displays the word E̲dit. (The letter preceded with an ampersand is the accelerator key's letter and will be underscored.)

The section `shell\edit\command` contains a single, unnamed entry listing the editor to edit the file. In the case of a batch file, the default editor is Notepad. If you have a favorite editor, you can plug it into this location to have it edit the file. Just remember that the editor must be able to open and save the file in the correct format. Fortunately for batch files, this is not difficult; they are plain-text files with no special editing requirements. When the editor is called, the argument `%1` will be substituted with the batch file's name, as shown here:

```
HKEY_CLASSES_ROOT\batfile\shell\open
HKEY_CLASSES_ROOT\batfile\shell\open\EditFlags = 0x00000000
```

```
HKEY_CLASSES_ROOT\batfile\shell\open\command
HKEY_CLASSES_ROOT\batfile\shell\open\command\(Default) = "%1" %*
```

The `shell\open` section contains the code to execute the file. In the case of a batch file, the `Edit-Flags` value is 0x00000000. Notice the format of this command, especially the placement of the quotes: `"%1" %*`. This command string will have the initial (quoted) `%1` substituted with the batch file's name and the second `%*` substituted with any parameters that the user passed to the command. If editing the data, be very careful not to place the quotes in the wrong place; don't quote the entire string, for example.

The next section handles printing requests:

```
HKEY_CLASSES_ROOT\batfile\shell\print
HKEY_CLASSES_ROOT\batfile\shell\print\command
HKEY_CLASSES_ROOT\batfile\shell\print\command\(Default) = %SystemRoot%\
      System32\NOTEPAD.EXE /p %1
```

Printing, managed by the `shell\print` section, contains only one working entry under `HKEY_CLASSES_ROOT\batfile\shell\print\command` with a single, unnamed entry. This entry tells Explorer to print using Notepad, passing the filename and the `/p` option. The option `/p` is a relatively standard option telling the program to open the file, print it to the default printer, and then exit. Generally, Windows prints the entire file, although it is possible that some applications will provide options for the print process. (Notepad is not silent or hidden; you will see it open, see the print dialog, and see Notepad close.)

Entries for property sheets for this object are next:

```
HKEY_CLASSES_ROOT\batfile\shellex
HKEY_CLASSES_ROOT\batfile\shellex\PropertySheetHandlers
HKEY_CLASSES_ROOT\batfile\shellex\PropertySheetHandlers\PifProps
HKEY_CLASSES_ROOT\batfile\shellex\PropertySheetHandlers\PifProps\
      (Default) = {86F19A00-42A0-1069-A2E9-08002B30309D}
```

Mappings to programs for all CLSIDs are in the `CLSID` part of `HKEY_CLASSES_ROOT`. Looking up our magic CLSID, {86F19A00-42A0-1069-A2E9-08002B30309D}, we find it is registered for `shell32.dll`, along with a few other settings. This tells us that the PIF (Program Interface File) manager is actually part of `shell32.dll`, used to display the property sheet for batch files:

```
HKEY_CLASSES_ROOT\CLSID\{86F19A00-42A0-1069-A2E9-08002B30309D}
HKEY_CLASSES_ROOT\CLSID\{86F19A00-42A0-1069-A2E9-08002B30309D}\
      (Default) = .PIF file (handler) property pages
HKEY_CLASSES_ROOT\CLSID\{86F19A00-42A0-1069-A2E9-08002B30309D}\
      InProcServer32
HKEY_CLASSES_ROOT\CLSID\{86F19A00-42A0-1069-A2E9-08002B30309D}\
      InProcServer32\(Default) = shell32.dll
HKEY_CLASSES_ROOT\CLSID\{86F19A00-42A0-1069-A2E9-08002B30309D}\
      InProcServer32\ThreadingModel = Apartment
```

Several items in the `CLSID` section are worth noting. First, `InProcServer32` is the name for a section dealing with in-process servers. In this case, we are working with a 32-bit in-process server, but that's not important right now.

We get the name of the server, shell32.dll, from the variable with no name; and we get the threading model, Apartment, from the ThreadingModel entry. These are important, since specifying the wrong ThreadingModel can cause data corruption. Other possible values for ThreadingModel are Single and Both, although it is unlikely that you will see Single specified.

One picture is worth a thousand words. Or so they say. Figure 15.2 shows the entries for a batch file (.bat) a bit more graphically.

FIGURE 15.2

The entries for .bat (batfile) type files in HKEY_CLASSES_ ROOT, showing their relationships

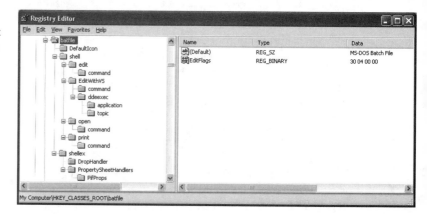

As shown in Figure 15.2, batch files are a relatively more complex example of how a particular file type is processed. Some other types of files are simpler—for example, they may not support context menus—while some are much more complex. Each system will be different for optional components, although Windows components typically are similar regardless of the installation.

Okay, what have we learned? First, for virtually any object that relates to a file (except My Computer, My Network Places, Recycle Bin, and so on), we can set the text description, change the icon, set an editor to edit, set a printer to print, and control how the object is executed or opened, as appropriate. In fact, we can add almost any functionality to the context menu we might want to. For instance, we can set a second editor for batch files; we'll use the command prompt's editor.

This example uses the Registry Editor. I'm going to start right from the beginning since this is our first registry hack, I mean "fix."

1. Open the Registry Editor (RegEdit). The current local registry will be displayed.

2. Make HKEY_CLASSES_ROOT the top window either by selecting it in the Window menu or by clicking it.

3. A batch file's extension is .bat, so find .bat in the list of extensions.

4. Open the .bat key, which holds one unnamed entry with a value of batfile. Figure 15.3 shows this entry. An additional subkey, called PersistentHandler, contains the GUID for the handler for a batch file.

5. Find the entry batfile in HKEY_CLASSES_ROOT and expand the shell subkey. The original shell subkey contains three entries: edit, open, and print.

FIGURE 15.3

Most extension entries have a single entry referring to a subsequent entry in HKEY_CLASSES_ROOT.

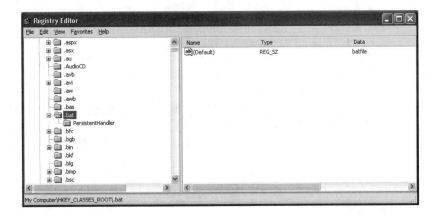

6. Create a new subkey under shell and call this new subkey NewEdit. (Sure, you can call this new subkey anything you want.)

7. In your NewEdit subkey, there is an unnamed entry with a data type of REG_SZ. In this entry, put the text of the new command you are adding. In this example, we are adding the command-level editor (the editor displayed when you type edit at a command prompt), so I'm adding the string Edit with DOS Editor. Take a gander at Figure 15.4 to see what we've done so far!

FIGURE 15.4

The Registry Editor with NewEdit open, showing the unnamed key with the command's menu text

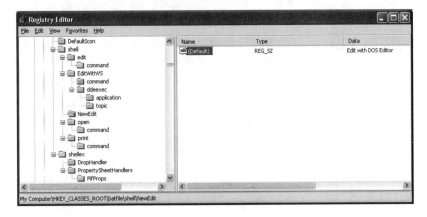

8. Under the NewEdit subkey, create a second subkey called command.

9. In the subkey command, create a new, unnamed value with a data type of REG_EXPAND_SZ. Make sure you use REG_EXPAND_SZ, and not REG_SZ, because this string will have an expansion variable embedded in it.

10. The string value for this new variable is the command itself. In our case, we are going to use the command editor, edit.com, which is located in %SystemRoot%\System32. Add this string like so:

```
%SystemRoot%\System32\edit.com %1
```

The %1 is a substitution variable, much like substitution variables in batch files, where Windows will substitute the name of the file to load into the editor. Figure 15.5 shows this change.

11.   We are done adding a new context-menu selection. Close the Registry Editor and restart Windows.

FIGURE 15.5

The Registry Editor with the new command added

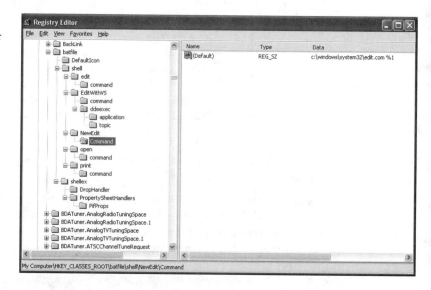

NOTE   *Although not always necessary, I recommend that you restart Windows XP after each registry modification. Windows XP caches some parts of the registry, and changes won't become visible until after restarting. Actually, much of* HKEY_CLASSES_ROOT *is cached, so a reboot is an especially good idea here.*

Figure 15.6 shows the new context menu in action. When the user clicks the menu selection Edit with DOS Editor, the command-prompt editor will open in its own window, and the selected file will be loaded, as shown in Figure 15.7.

Editing with the command editor may be easier for some users, or maybe you have a favorite editor you would like to substitute.

You can modify all context menus in Explorer (which includes the Desktop) using this technique. You can add selections for different file types, new actions to take, new editors, new print options, whatever.

Managing OLE and Embedding

The second function of HKEY_CLASSES_ROOT is to manage OLE. It is perhaps well beyond the scope of this book to really delve into the intricacies of OLE. But a quick review is in order.

OLE (Object Linking and Embedding) is a basic functionality that Microsoft has been working on for the last 8 to 10 years. The origins of OLE, or at least the concepts surrounding OLE, are vague. Some of these techniques and functions can be traced back to the beginnings of Windows and something called DDE (Dynamic Data Exchange). DDE was one hell of a difficult thing to work with, and Microsoft quickly expanded it to make it more flexible.

FIGURE 15.6

The new, modified context menu. Look—we now have a new editor to choose from.

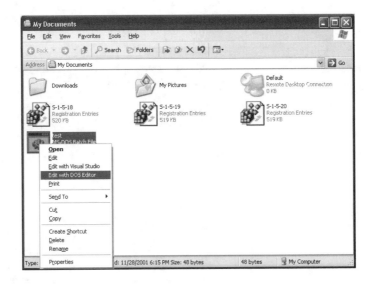

FIGURE 15.7

Using a different editor may be just the trick for some users.

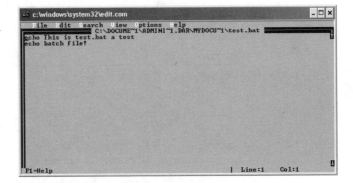

OLE consists of a whole slew of features, but the main one we'll worry about today is the concept of embedding. *Embedding* is the process of using one application inside another application. Many of Microsoft's applications rely heavily on embedding. Outlook is one example; it's the Microsoft Desktop information management system that many of us use for e-mail. Outlook can use Microsoft Word as the preferred e-mail editor by embedding Word into Outlook's e-mail editor window. When this is done, Word's menus, toolbars, and other functions are all available to the user.

Figure 15.8 shows Word as the e-mail editor, running and editing a message to my editor. An invisible Word window exists with this chapter open. Using Word to edit an e-mail message doesn't affect Word's ability to be a word processor, although I do save my work before using Outlook.

There is nothing that would prevent you from writing an application that allowed embedding Word. For that matter, embedding into a client application is possible for virtually all server applications. There are established mechanisms to determine the server's capabilities, what is needed to embed, and so on, although it is well beyond the scope of this book to get into that topic. They say there are only about two programmers who really understand embedding and OLE, and they both work for Microsoft.

FIGURE 15.8

Outlook's e-mail editor with Word embedded

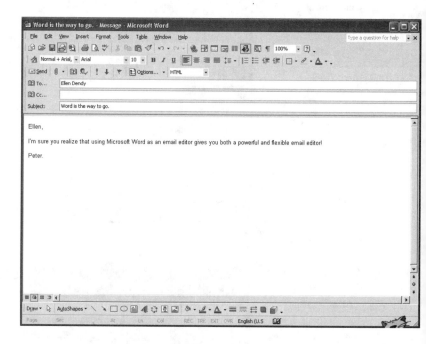

THE DEFAULT CLIENT—IT'S A DIRTY JOB BUT SOMEONE HAS TO DO IT

Windows XP offers what amounts to a default client application. It gives a server application that is incapable of running on its own a way to execute. This default client application is called RunDLL32.exe.

When RunDLL32 is executed, it is passed the name of the server, typically an ActiveX control (a.k.a. an OLE control), some actions, and the name of the subject object, typically a file of some sort.

For example, the entry for amovie.ocx, an ActiveX control used to display MPEG (video) files, is as follows:

```
%SystemRoot%\System32\RunDLL32.exe
%SystemRoot%\System32\amovie.ocx,RunDll /play /close %1
```

In this example, RunDLL32 will load amovie.ocx, passing these four parameters:

RunDll   Tells amovie.ocx who the client is.

/play   Tells amovie.ocx to play the specified object; in this case the object is a file.

/close   Tells amovie.ocx to close after playing the specified object.

%1   Tells amovie.ocx which file contains the object to be played.

Delving into the Unknown

Regardless of how many viewer controls, applications, and whatever else you install under Windows XP, there are going to be unknown file types. Windows refers to these files as *unknown*. When Windows opens an unknown file, a dialog box is displayed that is named Open With. This dialog box, shown in Figure 15.9, allows you to select an application to open files whose file type is currently not defined.

FIGURE 15.9

Open With allows both opening a specific file of an unknown type and setting a new default action for other files at the same time.

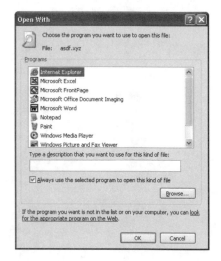

The Open With dialog box allows you to select the application used to open the file. Also, if the "Always use the selected program to open this kind of file" box is checked, Open With will create a new default handler for the file type.

Default handlers include most applications installed under Windows XP that are properly registered in the registry—that is, installed correctly. In addition, several system components are used as handlers, including RunDLL32 (which allows running ActiveX controls), WinHlp32 (to open standard Windows help files), and Internet Explorer.

Whenever a selection does not appear within the list of programs in the Open With dialog box, clicking the Browse button allows you to select any other executable program.

When the box labeled "Always use the selected program to open this kind of file" is checked, new entries in HKEY_CLASSES_ROOT are created for this file type. These entries may then be edited or modified by the user, using the techniques previously shown, to change or enhance the behavior of the context menu.

Chapter 16

Introduction to HKEY_CURRENT_USER and HKEY_USERS

HKEY_CURRENT_USER AND HKEY_USERS ARE HIVES that deal with users and user profiles. When first installed, Windows XP systems have two profiles configured: the default user, used by the system when no user is logged on, and a profile for the currently logged-on user.

HKEY_CURRENT_USER is the profile for the currently logged-on user. HKEY_CURRENT_USER is actually just a link to the user's profile that is stored in HKEY_USERS. Changes made in HKEY_CURRENT_USER are also going to appear in HKEY_USERS and be saved when the user logs off (if the user doesn't have a mandatory profile). HKEY_USERS contains the profile for the currently logged-on user and the default profile.

In this chapter, we'll take an in-depth look at the major subkeys that make up the profile of the currently logged-on user.

◆ Storing and loading user profiles

◆ The major subkeys of HKEY_CURRENT_USER

◆ A brief look at HKEY_USERS

Looking at User Profiles

All user profiles are stored as separate profile files and are loaded as needed. They are saved in the %SystemRoot%\Profiles\<userid> directory. The registry components of the user's profile are contained in the ntuser.dat files.

For example, consider our fictional user, Pixel:

1. The user Pixel logs on to the system.

2. Windows XP validates the user ID and password with the Active Directory server or the local machine's security manager if the user is not logging on to a domain.

3. The logon checks the user's profile status.

4. If the profile is local, or if the user is not logging on to a domain, the profile is loaded from the local machine.

5. If the user's profile is not local, and the user is logging on to a domain and has a roaming or mandatory profile, the correct profile is loaded from the appropriate network share. The user's `ntuser.dat` file is loaded into the registry's HKEY_USERS hive with a subkey name equal to the user's SID (security identifier).

6. The user's profile is read from the server and updated as necessary to reflect the user's preferences. The user uses the same profile when logging on at any computer in the domain.

NOTE Pixel, who's Pixel? Try Robert A. Heinlein's book, The Cat Who Walked Through Walls *(ISBN 0-441-09499-6), to learn about the cat, Pixel.*

In the process of loading the user's profile, the user's `ntuser.dat` file is loaded into HKEY_USERS. This hive contains the user's registry settings, everything that will later appear in the HKEY_CURRENT_USER hive. This becomes a hive with a name equal to the user's SID. Windows XP unloads and saves to the original location the profile of the previously logged-on user. This leaves HKEY_USERS with only two user profiles loaded at any given time, for the default user and the current user. (Actually, if no user logs on, then only one profile is present: the default profile.)

WARNING Careful—backing up a server's registry doesn't back up each user's profile. It is necessary to completely back up the server's Profiles *directory, which contains information for each user who is defined on that machine and who has a profile stored there.*

Users who don't have authority to modify their profile because they are using a mandatory profile may make changes. However, these changes will be lost when the user logs off.

NOTE What happens when the same user ID, with a roaming profile, is used concurrently on two different computers? This situation is not well defined. It is not an error; however, only one of these multiple logged sessions will actually save the user's profile. The session that is the last to log off will overwrite all other saves by other sessions.

The major user components in the registry are:

HKEY_CURRENT_USER The HKEY_CURRENT_USER hive manages specific information about the currently logged-on user. Remember, Windows XP automatically reflects changes made in HKEY_CLASSES_ROOT to the user's information contained in HKEY_USERS.

HKEY_USERS The HKEY_USERS hive also contains information about a pseudo user (named .DEFAULT) that is used when no user is logged on. (It also contains information about the user currently logged-on user and other users as well.)

Remember that HKEY_CURRENT_USER is an alias for the actual user's information that is contained in the HKEY_USERS hive. Modifying one will always modify both. Generally it is easier to make changes to the HKEY_CURRENT_USER hive, as there is no ambiguity as to who's information is being modified.

Again, a backup is vital. I have to do one myself, so while I'm busy, why don't you do a registry backup, too.

HKEY_CURRENT_USER

The HKEY_CURRENT_USER branch manages specific information about the currently logged-on user. This hive contains a complete profile of how Windows will look and behave for the user.

NOTE   If at any time you want to modify the look and feel (the profile) of Windows XP when no user is logged on, then modify the entries in the HKEY_USERS\.DEFAULT subkey. There are parallel entries in this subkey for virtually every entry found in HKEY_CURRENT_USER. Realize that some changes won't be meaningful because they represent parts of the system that are quite inaccessible when no user is logged on.

Major subkeys in HKEY_CURRENT_USER include the following:

AppEvents   This subkey includes information about labels for events, such as the default beep. Other information includes the sounds (such as the beeps, dings, and bongs) that Windows emits when things happen. It is not common to edit label entries, but it is possible. Use the Control Panel's Sounds applet to change event sounds, although some sounds must be changed directly in the registry.

Console   The colors, font, and other command-window metrics are stored in this subkey. These settings apply to console windows only; other windows have their metrics stored elsewhere.

Control Panel   This subkey holds settings for some of the Control Panel's applets. Examples of settings saved here include those for the Accessibility, Appearance, Mouse, and Keyboard applets.

Environment   The system environment strings are saved in this subkey.

EUDC   Information regarding End User Defined Characters is stored in this subkey. (This subkey is not found on all Windows installations.)

Identities   This subkey holds settings for user-specific configurations of certain software.

Keyboard Layout   The keyboard layout can be modified from this subkey, typically when a special-purpose keyboard is used.

Network   All drives to which drive letters are mapped are managed in this subkey. Explorer primarily manages drive mapping of network shares.

Printers   All printers, local and remote, are managed in this subkey. Printer information is accessible in the system's Printer applet.

RemoteAccess   The wizard for dial-up networking services that allows connecting to remote computers and networks stores information in this subkey. (This subkey is not found in all Windows installations.)

SessionInformation   This subkey contains dynamic information about the current session.

Software   Information about all installed software is stored in this subkey. The vendor typically arranges this information, although some applications may be in their own subkeys.

System   This subkey contains information used by the backup and restore process.

Unicode Program Groups   This subkey contains information used by Program Manager. (Is anyone using Program Manager anymore?) The subkeys found in Unicode Program Groups are in a binary format that is difficult to edit. (Have I ever seen entries in the Unicode Program Groups subkey? No, not yet.) Actually, users who upgraded from Windows NT 3.*x* may have entries in this subkey. However, Windows NT version 4 or later will not use this subkey, even though it is found in all versions of Windows, including Windows XP.

Volatile Environment   Typically, this subkey contains a number of entries. For example, a value called LOGONSERVER contains a string with the logon server (the server the user is currently logged on to). For example, my logon server is \\DORA. There are a number of other interesting items found in this subkey.

AppEvents

The AppEvents subkey contains all the information that Windows XP uses to play sounds and make other events happen, whenever a given event happens. Additionally, the AppEvents subkey contains definitions of what sounds to play when an event occurs. Finally, AppEvents also contains sound schemes for both default sounds and no sounds. Users may create new schemes, as desired, using the Control Panel's Sounds applet—more on that later.

First, AppEvents is divided into two parts. The first part, named EventLabels, consists of a list of events and the labels to be used for these events. These labels are hard-coded in mmsys.cpl as string resources. For events that are not part of Windows by default, and therefore do not have any label(s) defined in mmsys.cpl, there will be a display string in the appropriate EventLabels entry. In Windows XP, the standard labels from 5824 to 5856 are currently defined (a total of 32 EventLabels), as shown in Table 16.1.

These strings can be viewed using Microsoft Visual C++ (Visual Studio). Load mmsys.cpl as a resource file and open the string table.

TABLE 16.1: AppEvents LABELS FOR WINDOWS XP

ACTION NAME	ACTION LABEL STRING RESOURCE NUMBER
Default Beep	5824
Program Error	5825
Close Program	5826
Critical Battery Alarm	5827
Device Connect	5828
Device Disconnect	5829
Device Failed to Connect	5830
Empty Recycle Bin	5831

Continued on next page

TABLE 16.1: AppEvents LABELS FOR WINDOWS XP *(continued)*

ACTION NAME	ACTION LABEL STRING RESOURCE NUMBER
Low Battery Alarm	5832
Maximize	5833
Menu Command	5834
Menu Popup	5835
Minimize	5836
New Mail Notification	5837
Start Navigation	5838
Open Program	5839
Print Complete	5840
Restore Down	5841
Restore Up	5842
Asterisk	5843
Default Sound	5844
Exclamation	5845
Exit Windows	5846
Critical Stop	5847
System Notification	5848
Question	5849
Start Windows	5850
Start Menu	5851
Windows Logoff	5852
Windows Logon	5853
Windows Explorer	5854
Hardware	5855
Windows	5856

The next part of AppEvents is a subkey named Schemes. Found in Schemes are two subkeys: Apps and Names. In Apps, we first find a subkey named .Default, which contains subkeys for each of the items listed in EventLabels (see Table 16.1, above). Each item will then have a set of subkeys, .Current and .Default, where .Current contains the currently defined sound, and .Default contains the default sound. Figure 16.1 shows the LowBatteryAlarm sound (which has its own sound in Windows XP).

We previously discussed labels for events. Next, we need a table of sounds to "play" when the event happens. These events are located in `HKEY_CURRENT_USER\AppEvents\Schemes\Apps\.Default`. This subkey contains entries to match each entry in the `EventLabels` subkey (listed in Table 16.1). Each subkey has at least two subkeys, including `.Current` and `.Default`. For example, `HKEY_CURRENT_USER\AppEvents\Schemes\Apps\.Default\.Default\` contains the following:

.Current   This subkey contains one unnamed entry with the value of `ding.wav`, unless the user has changed the sound to be played. That is, when a default event (an event that doesn't have its own sound defined) occurs, Windows will play the `ding.wav` file.

.Default   This subkey contains one unnamed value with the value of `Windows\Media\ding.wav`. Windows will actually hard-code the directory to the Windows installation directory. If at some time the user selects the default sound in the Control Panel's Sounds applet, this one is used.

FIGURE 16.1

When a portable computer's power management reports that the battery is low, the user will hear this sound.

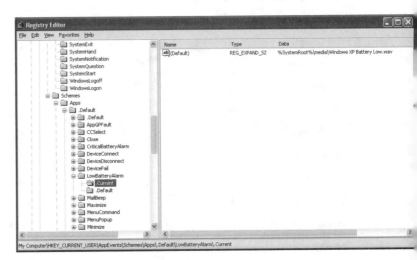

When a sound is not defined (either by default or by user action), the string contained will be empty. Not all sounds are defined!

There are event labels for a number of events, as Table 16.2 shows. This table lists sounds found in virtually all Windows systems right from the first installation, along with some used by Microsoft Visual Studio.

TABLE 16.2: SOUNDS FOUND ON MOST WINDOWS SYSTEMS

SUBKEY	DEFAULT TEXT	DESCRIPTION
.Default	Default Beep	Default sound used when a sound is needed, but no specifi sound has been defined
ActivatingDocument	Complete Navigation	Sound played when the navigation of an object is complete
AppGPFault	Program Error	Sound played when a program returns an error
CCSelect	Select	Sound played when an object is selected

Continued on next page

TABLE 16.2: SOUNDS FOUND ON MOST WINDOWS SYSTEMS *(continued)*

SUBKEY	DEFAULT TEXT	DESCRIPTION
Close	Close Program	Sound played when a program closes
EmptyRecycleBin	Empty Recycle Bin	Sound played when the Recycle Bin is emptied
MailBeep	New Mail Notification	Sound played when a new e-mail arrives
Maximize	Maximize	Sound played whenever a window is maximized
MenuCommand	Menu Command	Sound played whenever a menu item is selected
MenuPopup	Menu Pop-up	Sound played whenever a pop-up (context) menu item is selected
Minimize	Minimize	Sound played whenever a window is minimized
MoveMenuItem	Move Menu Item	Sound played whenever a menu item is moved
MSVC_HitBP	Breakpoint Hit	Sound played when a breakpoint in Microsoft Visual C++ has been reached (may not be present if Microsoft Visual C++ is not installed)
MSVC_OutputError	Error in Output	Sound played when an error in Microsoft Visual C++ has been detected (may not be present if Microsoft Visual C++ is not installed)
MSVC_OutputWarning	Warning in Output	Sound played when a warning in Microsoft Visual C++ has been detected (may not be present if Microsoft Visual C++ is not installed)
Navigating	Start Navigation	Sound played when navigation begins
Open	Open Program	Sound played when a program starts or opens
RestoreDown	Restore Down	Sound played when a window is restored from the maximized size to the normal size
RestoreUp	Restore Up	Sound played when a window is restored from the minimized size to the normal size
RingIn	Incoming Call	Sound played when an incoming telephony call is received
RingOut	Outgoing Call	Sound played when an outgoing telephony call is made
ShowBand	Show Toolbar Band	Sound played when the toolbar band is shown
SystemAsterisk	Asterisk	Sound played as the standard Windows asterisk sound
SystemExclamation	Exclamation	Sound played as the standard Windows exclamation sound
SystemExit	Exit Windows	Sound played when Windows is exited
SystemHand	Critical Stop	Sound played as the standard Windows critical stop sound
SystemQuestion	Question	Sound played as the standard Windows question sound
SystemStart	Start Windows	Sound played when Windows starts

Sounds based on events are set in the Control Panel's Sounds applet. Figure 16.2 shows this simple program. Each event can have one sound assigned, and users can create and save event sound schemes.

FIGURE 16.2

The Control Panel's Sounds applet sets sounds and sound schemes.

All sounds are rather meaningless unless the computer supports audio. Windows systems without sound compatibility will display these labels, and the user may set system sounds, but Windows cannot play these sounds. After all, how can Windows play a sound without a sound system? (Experiments at the Dilbert facility using Elbonionans to make the appropriate sounds did not succeed!)

Maybe, just maybe, there will be systems that don't have all of the above event labels. This is typically the case when a system administrator has substantially customized the installation and has deleted these objects. Although there may seem to be good reasons to delete event labels, it rarely is a good idea—more likely, it is a case of someone trying to generate work for themselves.

Once a system has more software applications and perhaps hardware too, these products may add events. These events will require labels and (probably, although not necessarily) sounds.

Microsoft Office, for example, adds about 40 event labels; that's more than the default version of Windows. Microsoft's Developer Studio consists of a myriad of development tools, including Visual C/C++, Visual BASIC, Visual FoxPro, and others. It will also add many new events. Events and event labels can become overwhelming if lots of applications are installed.

Additionally, if the user has defined one or more schemes, there will be an entry for each user-defined scheme. The name that is used is a system-generated hash of the user's scheme name. For example, I created a scheme called Peter's Scheme, and Windows XP named the relevant subkeys `Peter'0`.

Scheme names are contained in the `HKEY_CURRENT_USER\AppEvents\Schemes\Names` subkey. There will be one subkey for each scheme created by users, plus the two default ones: `.Default` and `.None`. The `.Default` subkey is the scheme used to restore the sounds to their default values. The `.None` subkey is a scheme used to turn off all sounds, which in some situations may be a really good move. There have been times when I wanted to use a really big hammer on someone's speakers. Oh, and by the way, each of these scheme subkeys contains the username for the scheme.

Already we see the possibility to modify the default sounds so that there could be a standard set of sounds for an organization. After all, a company with specialized sounds (for example, any company in the entertainment business) might really want their sounds to be the default sounds.

In the Control Panel's Sounds applet, you can select default sounds in the Schemes section (see Figure 16.2). Select the Windows Default scheme to restore the defaults. In the Sounds applet, you can also select No Sounds to remove all sounds from events.

NOTE   *Before selecting a scheme and making massive changes, it may be a good idea to save the current settings in a new scheme so that you can back out of an undesired change with only a little work. You can delete schemes that you no longer need in the Sounds applet using the Delete button. Better safe than sorry.*

Console

The `Console` subkey contains information used to configure the default sessions. Each entry sets parameters used for character-based applications; those with their own PIF files will use the PIF file settings rather than the settings in this subkey.

In Table 16.3, we are actually dealing with two-digit values (four of them in each `ColorTable` entry). A two-digit hex value can represent a value between 0 and 255 (that's 0 and 0xFF in hex). Table 16.3 shows each value entry, a typical value, and what the value entry means.

TABLE 16.3: CONSOLE SETTINGS FOUND ON MOST WINDOWS SYSTEMS

VALUE ENTRY	TYPICAL VALUE	DESCRIPTION
ColorTable00	0x00000000	An RGB color value that is black as night. RGB is additive, getting lighter as the values increase.
ColorTable01	0x00800000	Dark red.
ColorTable02	0x00008000	Dark green.
ColorTable03	0x00808000	Pea-green color (or a dark yellow, you decide).
ColorTable04	0x00000080	Dark blue.
ColorTable05	0x00800080	Violet.
ColorTable06	0x00008080	Dark cyan.
ColorTable07	0x00c0c0c0	Light gray.
ColorTable08	0x00808080	Darker gray.
ColorTable09	0x00ff0000	Bright red.
ColorTable10	0x0000ff00	Bright green.
ColorTable11	0x00ffff00	Yellow—or a really, really bright pea green.
ColorTable12	0x000000ff	Bright blue.
ColorTable13	0x00ff00ff	Bright violet.

Continued on next page

TABLE 16.3: CONSOLE SETTINGS FOUND ON MOST WINDOWS SYSTEMS *(continued)*

VALUE ENTRY	TYPICAL VALUE	DESCRIPTION
ColorTable14	0x0000ffff	Cyan.
ColorTable15	00x0ffffff	White.
CurrentPage	0x00000000	Page zero is the current page.
CursorSize	0x00000019	The cursor is 25 percent of the character cell in size.
FaceName	(None)	The name of the console font, if defined. A default font is selected if none is defined.
FontFamily	0x00000000	The console font family, if defined. The default family for the selected font is used if none is defined; typical values include TrueType and Raster.
FontSize	0x00000000	The font size; the low word contains the character width; the high word contains the character height. For example, a font 8 × 16 would be 0x00080010.
FontWeight	0x00000000	The weight (bolding) of the font; larger numbers are bolder.
FullScreen	0x00000000	A value of 0x00000001 is set if this window is full screen; a value of 0x00000000 is set if the window is not full screen.
HistoryBufferSize	0x00000032	The size of the history buffer in commands; the hex value of 32 indicates that 50 commands may be stored in each command history buffer.
InsertMode	0x00000000	A value of 0x00000001 is to use insert mode; 0x00000000 is to use overwrite mode.
NumberOfHistoryBuffers	0x00000004	The number of history buffers used for this command session. The size of the history buffers are set using HistoryBufferSize.
PopupColors	0x000000f5	The color used for a pop-up window, if displayed. The first four bits (f in the typical value) are the characters; the next four bits (5 in the typical value) are the foreground color. These values are indexes to the color values defined in this table.
QuickEdit	0x00000000	Setting the value to 0x00000001 enables QuickEdit; setting it to 0x00000000 disables QuickEdit. QuickEdit allows quick cut and paste to the Clipboard.
ScreenBufferSize	0x00190050	The screen buffer size. In the example, 0x0019 equals 25 in decimal and 0x0050 equals 80 in decimal; therefore, the default screen buffer size is 25 × 80 in size. Other common sizes are 50 × 80 (0x00320050) or 43 × 80 (0x002b0050). Windows XP does not restrict you to a width of 80 characters in a command session—line widths are essentially unlimited.

Continued on next page

TABLE 16.3: CONSOLE SETTINGS FOUND ON MOST WINDOWS SYSTEMS *(continued)*

VALUE ENTRY	TYPICAL VALUE	DESCRIPTION
ScreenColors	0x00000007	The index to colors for the screen. The next-to-last digit is the index for characters, and the last digit is the index for the background.
WindowSize	0x00190050	The window size. In the example, 0x0019 equals 25 in decimal and 0x0050 equals 80 in decimal; therefore, the default screen buffer size is 25 × 80 in size. Other common sizes are 50 × 80 (0x00320050) or 43 × 80 (0x002b0050).

Colors are in RGB, stored as a four-byte value. Windows ignores the first byte (actually, Windows uses it internally, and it should always be set to zero). The second byte is red, the third byte is green, and the fourth and final byte is blue. For example, a color value of 0x00AA2020 is a dusky red, the same color as the windbreaker that I wear in the spring. I left the jacket in a restaurant the other day and called them to check to see if it was there. I described the color as an RGB color 170, 32, 32; the person who owned the restaurant told me without any hesitation that it was there. Could the fact that I was the only one to leave a jacket there in weeks have anything to do with it?

TIP   Lazy and don't want to convert between hex and decimal using your fingers and toes—or just can't take off your shoes? The Windows Calculator program will convert between hex and decimal with ease. Just start Calculator and select View ➤ Scientific.

HEXADECIMAL AND COLORS

What the heck is hex? Hexadecimal numbers, usually just called hex for short, are expressed in base 16. To show a hex number, we use the numeric digits 0 through 9 and the letters A through F.

Computers are binary. They know only two number values: either 1 (on) or 0 (off). A single datum of computer data is called a bit, which represents either 0 or 1, and no other value in between.

In computers, numbers are stored in bytes, each comprising 8 bits. A byte's value may range from 0 to 255. In hex, that value range is 0x00 to 0xFF. The prefix 0x precedes hexadecimal numbers, and the letters may be either uppercase or lowercase (case doesn't matter).

Two bytes together (16 bits) form what is called a "WORD" (usually, but not always, written in uppercase). A WORD, if unsigned, may represent a value from 0 to 65535. A signed WORD value represents a value of −32767 to 32767.

Four bytes together (32 bits) form what's called a "DWORD," short for double word. A double WORD, if unsigned, may represent a value from 0 to 4294967295. A signed double WORD represents a value from 2147483647 to −2147483647.

Oftentimes programmers try to fit as much information as possible into a WORD or DWORD value. History has shown how this can backfire, but for some data, this technique works well. Color values are a case where three sets of values (one each for red, green, and blue) fit within the DWORD's four bytes.

Oh, and one more bit of confusion: Half a byte, 4 bits, is called a nibble. A nibble can hold a value between 0 and 15. Several registry entries use 4-bit nibble values.

Control Panel

The `Control Panel` subkey in the registry is where many of the Control Panel applets store settings and defaults. The number of sections may vary depending on installed components. Things that affect the number of sections include special mouse support, screen savers, and installed optional components. There may be some differences between a Windows Server and a Windows workstation installation. This subkey also includes data stored in the `win.ini` and `system.ini` files on Windows 3.*x* and earlier.

The sections that show up in many registries include:

`Accessibility`   Contains Windows XP's features for users who require special support due to physical limitations—items such as a special keyboard, mouse, or sounds, and general support.

`Appearance`   Holds settings for Windows XP's appearance and the schemes used for display configuration.

`Cache`   Appears to control how Control Panel applets are cached—don't you just hate it when there is a component that is both undocumented and apparently unused? I checked every system I could, and the Cache subkey was empty on all systems—both XP Professional and Server.

`Colors`   Contains the colors for buttons, text—just about everything displayed to the user.

`Current`   Contains the currently loaded color scheme.

`Cursors`   Contains a value that indicates where the current cursor source is.

`Custom Colors`   Contains any user-defined color schemes.

`Desktop`   Holds the Desktop configuration, colors, spacing metrics—everything about what the screen displays.

`don't load`   Holds the names of any `.cpl` files that are not to be loaded if found on the system. These `.cpl` files are usually not loaded as they are incompatible with either Windows XP or another component, or they are not desired.

`Input Method`   Contains information about the user's hotkey definitions.

`International`   Contains items dealing with the computer's location (country), including sorting orders.

`IOProcs`   Holds the Media View File System control.

`Keyboard`   Contains configurations for the keyboard, such as initial state of the toggle keys for Caps Lock, Num Lock, and Scroll Lock; and delay and repeat rates.

`Microsoft Input Devices`   Contains information about the interaction between input devices (such as the system mouse) and Windows XP components.

`MMCPL`   Contains Multimedia Control Panel settings.

`Mouse`   Contains mouse settings, such as speed, tracking, and other settings.

`Patterns`   Contains Windows XP's patterns used to create backgrounds, such as Boxes, Critters, Diamonds, and so on.

Powercfg   Contains information about the power configuration settings, including definitions of the various power configuration policies.

Screen Saver.3DflyingObj   Contains configurations for this screen saver.

Screen Saver.3Dpipes   Contains configurations for this screen saver.

Screen Saver.Bezier   Contains configurations for this screen saver.

Screen Saver.Marquee   Contains configurations for this screen saver.

Screen Saver.Mystify   Contains configurations for this screen saver.

Screen Saver.Stars   Contains configurations for this screen saver.

Sound   Contains information about sounds. Contains one entry for something called System-Default or Default. This object was named Sounds in earlier versions of Windows.

In the remainder of this section, we'll look at some of these entries that either seem interesting or can set data that cannot be set elsewhere. Most entries can be set using the Control Panel.

ACCESSIBILITY

The concept of allowing Windows to be accessible to users who have special needs is relatively new. Windows 95 was the first version of Windows to offer accessibility configurations. Windows NT 4, released after Windows 95, followed suit.

The Accessibility key is subdivided into a number of subkeys:

Blind Access   Entries include the following:

On   This entry has a default value of 0, indicating that the blind access functionality of Windows XP is not enabled.

High Contrast   Entries include the following:

Flags   This entry has a value of 126 on my system.

High Contrast Scheme   This entry contains the name of the default high contrast scheme.

Keyboard Preference   Entries include the following:

On   This entry has a value of 0 or 1. When set to 1, the system understands that the user is using the keyboard rather than a mouse. This should allow applications to show keyboard interfaces that might otherwise be hidden on a normally configured system.

Keyboard Response   Entries include the following:

AutoRepeatDelay   This entry has a default value of 1000, or one second. Increasing this value increases the wait time before the keyboard auto-repeat kicks in.

AutoRepeatRate   This entry has a default value of 500. Increasing this value increases the repeat rate.

BounceTime   This entry has a default value of 0. This value specifies the amount of time to ignore a keystroke after pressing and releasing a key. This helps eliminate false double keystrokes.

DelayBeforeAcceptance   This entry has a default value of 1000. Increasing it increases the amount of time that a key must be pressed before it registers as being pressed. Changing the default here is useful if a user has a tendency to hit keys by mistake.

Flags   This is a character field containing a default value of 82 for Windows 2000 and 126 for Windows XP. This object enables or disables the previously discussed flags.

MouseKeys   Entries include the following:

MaximumSpeed   This entry has a default value of 80. It limits the maximum speed, in pixels per second, that the mouse cursor will move when a mouse-movement key is pressed.

TimeToMaximumSpeed   This entry has a default value of 3000, three seconds, and is used to determine the amount of time required for the mouse pointer to reach full speed (specified in MaximumSpeed) when a mouse-movement key is held down.

Flags   This is a character field containing a default value of 18 for Windows 2000 and 62 for Windows XP. This object is used to disable and enable the previously discussed flags.

SerialKeys   This subkey holds settings for a special input device connected to a serial port that emulates the keyboard and mouse on the computer. Note that all versions of Windows support SerialKeys. Typically, people who are unable to use standard keyboards take advantage of these devices. Each device has a unique configuration, and registry entries will be specific to the device. For systems that do not have serial keyboard/mouse emulation devices configured, SerialKeys will have no entries. Otherwise, it has the following objects:

ActivePort   This entry sets the COM port used and has a default of COM1.

Baud   This entry sets the serial speed, in baud, displayed as a hexadecimal number by default.

Port   This entry defines the COM port supported.

Flags   This entry contains a default value of 3, indicating that the feature is supported.

ShowSounds   Entries include the following:

On   This entry indicates (when set to a nonzero value) that rather than using a sound, a pop-up window should be used to notify the user that an event has occurred.

SoundSentry   Entries include the following:

Flags   This entry has three bitmapped values:

1 indicates that SoundSentry is on.

2 indicates that SoundSentry is available.

4 indicates the state of the indicator and is not user settable.

FSTextEffect   There are four values for this object:

0 shows no text effect.

1 flashes characters to draw the user's attention.

2 flashes the window's border to draw the user's attention.

3 flashes the entire display to draw the user's attention.

WindowsEffect   This object has five values:

0 shows no window effect.

1 flashes the window's title bar to draw the user's attention.

2 flashes the entire window to draw the user's attention.

3 flashes the entire display to draw the user's attention.

4 performs a custom action, as defined in the `SoundSentryProc` routine that is exported in `iFSWindowsEffectDLL`.

StickyKeys   With the StickyKeys feature, a key (such as Ctrl, Shift, or Alt) that normally is pressed at the same time as another key to modify the second key's meaning can be set to "stick" on until the next key is pressed. This avoids having to press two keys at the same time, a process that is difficult for some users. There is a single entry in `StickyKeys` called `Flags`, a REG_SZ variable that contains a decimal number that represents the `Flags` value. Table 16.4 shows the known bits.

HOW'S THAT NUMBER AGAIN?

The value stored in the Windows XP registry is a text string containing a number. This number is in decimal. The default value, 510, indicates that the flags at 0x1FE are turned on (plug in 510 into the Windows calculator, then convert it to hexadecimal). Looking at Table 16.4, and the default value of 510 (0x000001FE), we see that the set flags are:

2 (0x00000002)   StickyKeys is available (cannot be changed from the StickyKeys dialog box).

4 (0x00000004)   The StickyKeys hotkey is available.

8 (0x00000008)   A confirmation dialog box is displayed when activating StickyKeys using the hotkey (cannot be changed from the StickyKeys dialog box).

16 (0x00000010)   Windows plays a siren sound when the hotkey turns on or off the StickyKeys feature.

32 (0x00000020)   An indicator is displayed when StickyKeys is enabled.

64 (0x00000040)   Windows plays a sound when a StickyKeys modifier is pressed.

128 (0x00000080)   Pressing the modifier key twice locks it; a third press unlocks it (normally Windows automatically releases the modifier key after one use).

256 (0x00000100)   Windows turns off StickyKeys when a modifier key and another key are pressed simultaneously (cannot be changed from the StickyKeys dialog box).

TABLE 16.4: STICKYKEYS FLAGS BITS DEFINED

Flags Bits	Flags (in Decimal)	Windows XP Compatible	Windows 2000 Compatible	Can Be Set?	Description
0x00000001	1	✔	✔	✔	StickyKeys is turned on.
0x00000002	2	✔	✔	✔	StickyKeys is available. (This setting cannot be changed from the StickyKeys dialog box.)
0x00000004	4	✔	✔	✔	The StickyKeys hotkey is available.
0x00000008	8	✔	✔	✔	A confirmation dialog box is displayed when StickyKeys is activated using the hotkey. (This setting cannot be changed from the StickyKeys dialog box.)
0x00000010	16	✔	✔	✔	Windows plays a siren sound when the hotkey is used to turn on or off the StickyKeys feature.
0x00000020	32	✔	✔	✔	When enabled, StickyKeys displays an indicator.
0x00000040	64	✔	✔	✔	Windows plays a sound when a StickyKeys modifier is pressed.
0x00000080	128	✔	✔	✔	Pressing twice locks the modifier key. Normally the modifier key is automatically released after use. A third press unlocks the modifier key.
0x00000100	256	✔	✔	✔	Whenever a modifier key is pressed simultaneously with a another key, StickyKeys is turned off. (This setting cannot be changed from the StickyKeys dialog box.)
0x00000200	512	✔	✔	✔	Unknown.
0x00000400	1024	✔	✔	✔	Unknown.
0x00000800	2048	✔	✔	✔	Unknown.
0x00001000	4096	✔	✔	✔	Unknown.
0x00002000	8192	✔	✔	✔	Unknown.
0x00004000	16384	✔	✔	✔	Unknown.

Continued on next page

TABLE 16.4: STICKYKEYS FLAGS BITS DEFINED *(continued)*

FLAGS BITS	FLAGS (IN DECIMAL)	WINDOWS XP COMPATIBLE	WINDOWS 2000 COMPATIBLE	CAN BE SET?	DESCRIPTION
0x00008000	32768	✔	✔	✔	Unknown.
0x00010000	65536	✔	✔		Left Shift key is currently locked.
0x00020000	131072	✔	✔		Right Shift key is currently locked.
0x00040000	262144	✔	✔		Left Ctrl key is currently locked.
0x00080000	524288	✔	✔		Right Ctrl key is currently locked.
0x00100000	1048576	✔	✔		Left Alt key is currently locked.
0x00200000	20971520	✔	✔		Right Alt key is currently locked.
0x00400000	4194304	✔	✔		Left Windows key is currently locked.
0x00800000	8388608	✔	✔		Right Windows key is currently locked.
0x01000000	16777216	✔	✔		Left Shift key is currently latched.
0x02000000	33554432	✔	✔		Right Shift key is currently latched.
0x04000000	67108864	✔	✔		Left Ctrl key is currently latched.
0x08000000	34217728	✔	✔		Right Ctrl key is currently latched.
0x10000000	68435456	✔	✔		Left Alt key is currently latched.
0x20000000	536870912	✔	✔		Right Alt key is currently latched.
0x40000000	1073741824	✔	✔		Left Windows key is currently latched.
0x80000000	2147483648	✔	✔		Right Windows key is currently latched.

NOTE   *As time goes on, each new version of Windows adds a number of new values for StickyKeys. A total of seven values are currently unknown, and probably not used.*

TimeOut   There are two entries in `TimeOut` that control when the accessibility options are turned off. They are based on nonuse for a certain period of time.

Flags   A value of 1 is on; a value of 3 indicates that Windows plays a siren sound when the time-out period expires.

TimeToWait   This entry sets the time, in milliseconds, that the computer is idle before accessibility options are turned off. Five minutes is 300000.

ToggleKeys There is a single value in `ToggleKeys` called `Flags`. ToggleKeys is a feature that works like StickyKeys (described above). Unlike with StickyKeys, toggled keys must be manually reset, as they do not reset after the next keystroke. A bitmapped value is used that has six bits defined (see Table 16.5).

TABLE 16.5: ToggleKeys Flags Bits Defined

Flags Bits	Windows XP Compatible	Windows 2000 Compatible	Description
0x00000001	✔	✔	If set, then the ToggleKeys feature is turned on.
0x00000002	✔	✔	If set, then the ToggleKeys feature is available.
0x00000004	✔	✔	If set, the user is able to turn on and off the ToggleKeys feature by pressing the Num Lock key for eight seconds.
0x00000008	✔	✔	Windows displays a dialog box to confirm activation using the hotkey.
0x00000010	✔	✔	Windows plays a siren sound when ToggleKeys turns on or off.
0x00000020	✔		This feature provides a visual indicator of the ToggleKeys state.

APPEARANCE

What Windows XP looks like is contained in the `Appearance` subkey. There are two subkeys called `New Schemes` and `Schemes`. (`Schemes` appears to be retained for compatibility, and may not be included with future versions of Windows.)

`New Schemes` contains the definitions for the schemes defined for Windows XP. These definitions are used by the `themeui.dll` file's routines to manage the themes. Unlike earlier versions of Windows, the values contained in `New Schemes` are easily modified.

In `Schemes`, there are keys (all of which are REG_BINARY data types) containing definitions of the Windows standard color schemes, such as Lilac, Maple, Wheat, Windows Standard, and so on.

Each scheme in this subkey is loaded in the Control Panel's Display applet, which is also accessible from the Desktop's properties menu. Looking in the Appearance tab, there is a drop-down list to select a scheme from.

It is quite possible to hack a scheme from the registry, although many of the parts of the scheme may be modified more easily in the Display Properties dialog box. Once modified, a new scheme may be saved for later reloading as needed.

CACHE

The `Cache` subkey seems to control how the Control Panel displays its icons. Many Windows XP users do not have any entries in this subkey, while others do. An example of the `Cache` subkey is shown in Microsoft's Knowledge Base article Q150541, which you'll find at `http://support` `.microsoft.com/default.aspx?scid=kb;en-us;Q150541`.

COLORS

The `Colors` subkey contains the colors for buttons, text, and just about everything displayed to the user. Keep in mind that more colors may be defined as more applications and components are installed on Windows XP.

Each entry listed in this subkey has a string containing three numbers representing the red, green, and blue color levels, as shown in Table 16.6. As the color value increases, the color becomes lighter, so that a value of `127 0 0` is a dark red, and a value of `255 0 0` is a bright red.

TABLE 16.6: COLOR OBJECTS IN A TYPICAL WINDOWS XP INSTALLATION

ITEM	OBJECT NAME	RED VALUE	GREEN VALUE	BLUE VALUE
Active Window Border	ActiveBorder	212	208	200
Active Window's Title	ActiveTitle	0	84	227
Application Work Space	AppWorkSpace	128	128	128
Background	Background	0	78	152
Button Alternate Face	ButtonAlternateFace	181	181	181
Button Dark Shadow	ButtonDkShadow	113	111	100
Button Face	ButtonFace	236	233	216
Button Hilight	ButtonHilight	255	255	255
Button Light	ButtonLight	241	239	226
Button Shadow	ButtonShadow	172	168	153
Button Text	ButtonText	0	0	0
Gradient Active Title	GradientActiveTitle	61	149	255
Gradient Inactive Title	GradientInactiveTitle	157	185	235
Gray Text	GrayText	172	168	153
Hilight	Hilight	49	106	197
Hilight Text	HilightText	255	255	255
Hot Tracking Color	HotTrackingColor	0	0	128
Inactive Border	InactiveBorder	212	208	200
Inactive Title	InactiveTitle	122	150	223
Inactive Title Text	InactiveTitleText	216	228	248

Continued on next page

TABLE 16.6: COLOR OBJECTS IN A TYPICAL WINDOWS XP INSTALLATION *(continued)*

ITEM	OBJECT NAME	RED VALUE	GREEN VALUE	BLUE VALUE
Info Text	InfoText	0	0	0
Info Window	InfoWindow	255	255	225
Menu	Menu	255	255	255
Menu Text	MenuText	0	0	0
Scrollbar	Scrollbar	212	208	200
Title Text	TitleText	255	255	255
Window	Window	255	255	255
Window Frame	WindowFrame	0	0	0
Window Text	WindowText	0	0	0
Menu Hilight	MenuHilight	49	106	197
Menu Bar	MenuBar	236	233	216

CURRENT

The Current subkey contains the currently loaded color scheme. One key, called Color Schemes, contains the name of the color scheme. Also check HKEY_CURRENT_USER\ControlPanel\Appearance\ Schemes for a list of schemes installed on the computer.

CURSORS

The Cursors subkey contains the currently loaded cursor scheme. One key, called Schemes Source, contains the name of the cursor scheme. Also check HKEY_CURRENT_USER\ControlPanel\Appearance\ Schemes for a list of schemes installed on the computer.

CUSTOM COLORS

The Windows XP common dialog box called Colors allows you to define and save up to 16 custom color definitions. These custom colors are stored in the subkey Custom Colors, in entries named ColorA through ColorP. Each entry contains a six-digit string, in hexadecimal, nominally in RGB, for each custom color. The default value for each color entry is FFFFFF, or white.

DESKTOP

The configuration of the user's Desktop is contained in the Desktop subkey. This key contains between 25 and 50 different entries. Many of these items (see Table 16.7) are adjusted in the various Properties dialog boxes, but some must be changed directly from the registry.

TABLE 16.7: DESKTOP SETTINGS FOUND ON MOST WINDOWS SYSTEMS

ENTRY	TYPICAL VALUE	DESCRIPTION
ActiveWndTrkTimeout	dword:00000000	This value is currently undefined.
AutoEndTasks	0	Sets the automatic task-ending mode that controls whether the system automatically ends a timed-out task without displaying a warning or prompt dialog box.
CaretWidth	dword:00000001	This value is currently undefined.
CoolSwitch	1	The fast task-switching mode; set to 0 to disable. In Windows NT 4 and higher, the feature is always enabled.
CoolSwitchColumns	7	Sets the number of columns of icons in the Alt+Tab dialog box.
CoolSwitchRows	3	Sets the number of rows of icons in the Alt+Tab dialog box.
CursorBlinkRate	530	Sets the time between blinks of the cursor, in milliseconds; the default value is 530 milliseconds.
DragFullWindows	0	The drag mode in Windows XP that supports either full-window dragging or outline dragging; a value of 1 indicates that full-window dragging is enabled.
DragHeight	4 (2 in earlier versions)	Sets the vertical size of the dragging box required before the mouse detects a drag operation.
DragWidth	4 (2 in earlier versions)	Sets the horizontal size of the dragging box required before the mouse detects a drag operation.
FontSmoothing	2	Font smoothing makes certain fonts easier to read on high-resolution color adapters. It is set in the Plus tab of the Display Properties dialog box, under Smooth Edges of Screen Fonts.
FontSmoothingType	1	Set to 0 for no font smoothing, 1 for normal smoothing, and 2 for cleartype (best on digital LCD displays) smoothing.
ForegroundFlashCount	dword:00000003	This value indicates the number of times that the Taskbar icons will flash when user intervention is required.
ForegroundLockTimeout	dword:00030d40	This value indicates the amount of time that an application will not be allowed to move to the foreground following user input.
GridGranularity	0	A grid that helps align objects on the Desktop may be enabled by setting this to any nonzero value.

Continued on next page

TABLE 16.7: DESKTOP SETTINGS FOUND ON MOST WINDOWS SYSTEMS *(continued)*

ENTRY	TYPICAL VALUE	DESCRIPTION
HungAppTimeout	5000	Sets the time, in milliseconds, before a hung application (one that does not respond) will cause Windows XP to display a dialog box to prompt the user to either wait or kill the application.
IconSpacing	75	Sets the icon spacing granularity for the Desktop. (Not present on Windows XP systems by default.)
IconTitleFaceName	MS Sans Serif	Sets the icon font name. (Not present on Windows XP systems by default.)
IconTitleSize	9	Sets the size of icon titles. (Not present on Windows XP systems by default.)
IconTitleStyle	0	Sets the icon title style. (Not present on Windows XP systems by default.)
IconTitleWrap	1	Sets the entry that controls whether icon titles will wrap or be displayed on only one line. (Not present on Windows XP systems by default.)
LameButtonText	Comments	New to Windows XP, this is text, displayed next to the title bar's minimize button, that a tester may click to send comments to Microsoft. Changing the text does not change the functionality of this button, which is only available on beta-released products.
LowPowerActive	0	This value is currently undefined.
LowPowerTimeOut	0	This value is currently undefined.
MenuShowDelay	400	The delay time set before showing a cascading menu; typical values are from 0 to 400, although values can be higher.
PaintDesktopVersion	dword:00000001	This value, when 0, tells Windows to display version information on the desktop (in the lower-right corner).
Pattern Upgrade	TRUE	The pattern used under icon labels or exposed areas of the Desktop that the Desktop wallpaper doesn't cover; set in the Background tab of the Display Properties dialog box.
PowerOffActive	0	This value indicates whether the power off phase of the screen saver is enabled.
PowerOffTimeOut	0	This value is the number of seconds that the power off counter is set to. When zero, the feature is disabled.

Continued on next page

TABLE 16.7: DESKTOP SETTINGS FOUND ON MOST WINDOWS SYSTEMS *(continued)*

ENTRY	TYPICAL VALUE	DESCRIPTION
ScreenSaveActive	1	If this value is set at 1, the screen saver will be displayed when the system has been inactive for a longer amount of time than is specified in ScreenSaveTimeOut.
ScreenSaverIsSecure	0	If this value is set at 1, the screen saver will prompt for a password.
ScreenSaveTimeOut	1500	Sets the amount of time the computer is inactive, in seconds, before displaying the screen saver.
SCRNSAVE.EXE	(NONE)	The fully qualified name of the current screen saver.
TileWallpaper	0	The wallpapering mode. If the value is set at 0, the wallpaper is centered using only a single copy. If the value is 1, the wallpaper is tiled starting in the upper left corner.
UserPreferencesMask	hex:9e,3e,00,80	This value is currently undefined.
WaitToKillAppTimeout	20000	Sets the amount of time that elapses, in milliseconds, before notifying users of any applications that are not responding properly when a logoff or shut-down command is received.
Wallpaper	(None)	Sets the name of the wallpaper file; a bitmap file.
WallpaperStyle	0	This value is currently undefined.
WheelScrollLines	3	The number of lines that the Microsoft wheel mouse will scroll when the wheel is turned; the default value of 3 may be too much for some applications.

As the installation of Windows XP ages and more optional components are added, the number of entries in the Desktop subkey will increase. Many of the possible entries are self-explanatory. Generally, modifying a value won't cause a computer to crash, although the results may be unpleasant.

A subkey under Desktop, named WindowMetrics, contains entries that define the physical attributes for a number of the components that make up the Desktop. The values shown in Table 16.8 are default values, and your values may differ depending on your settings.

TABLE 16.8: DEFAULT VALUES FOR WindowMetrics

ENTRY	TYPICAL CONTENTS	DESCRIPTION
AppliedDPI	96	Sets the visual display DPI (dots per inch) value for the screen
BorderWidth	1	Sets the width of a resizable window's border

Continued on next page

TABLE 16.8: DEFAULT VALUES FOR WindowMetrics *(continued)*

ENTRY	TYPICAL CONTENTS	DESCRIPTION
CaptionFont	A logical font structure defining a font to be used	Sets the font used for captions
CaptionHeight	-270	Sets the height of the characters, varies with display parameters
CaptionWidth	-270	Sets the width of the characters, varies with display parameters
IconFont	A logical font structure defining a font to be used	Sets the font used for icons
IconSpacing	75	Sets the space between each icon
IconTitleWrap	1	Sets whether an icon's title wraps (nonzero) or not
IconVerticalspacing	-1125	Sets the spacing between rows of icons
MenuFont	A logical font structure defining a font to be used	Sets the font used for menus
MenuHeight	-270	Sets the height of the characters
MenuWidth	-270	Sets the width of the characters
MessageFont	A logical font structure defining a font to be used	Sets the font used for messages
MinAnimate	0	Sets whether windows will be animated when being resized (such as minimized, restored, or maximized)
ScrollHeight	-240	Sets the height of the characters
ScrollWidth	-240	Sets the width of the characters
Shell Icon BPP	16	Sets the number of bit planes for icons
ShellIconSize	32	Sets the size of icons in the shell
SmCaptionFont	A logical font structure defining a font to be used	Sets the font used for small captions
SmCaptionHeight	-180	Sets the height of the characters
SmCaptionWidth	-180	Sets the width of the characters
StatusFont	A logical font structure defining a font to be used	Defines the status bar font

INTERNATIONAL

The International subkey stores items dealing with the computer's location (country), including sorting orders. Most of these entries are set in the Control Panel using the Regional Settings Properties applet.

New!

New to Windows XP is the subkey Geo. Contained in Geo is a data value named Nation, which contains a code for the user's country. This code is not based on the international country telephone prefix, but rather on a much less widely used system (which appears to be part of the Microsoft MapPoint mapping system). Table 16.9 lists the country codes which are currently defined:

TABLE 16.9: MICROSOFT MAPPOINT COUNTRY CODES, AS USED BY WINDOWS XP

COUNTRY CODE	COUNTRY
0	LocaleID of the user's computer (not used by Windows XP)
6	Albania
11	Argentina
12	Australia
14	Austria
21	Belgium
23	Bangladesh
26	Bolivia
29	Belarus
32	Brazil
35	Bulgaria
39	Canada
45	China
46	Chile
51	Colombia
61	Denmark
66	Ecuador
68	Ireland
70	Estonia
75	Czech Republic
76	French Guiana
77	Finland

Continued on next page

TABLE 16.9: MICROSOFT MAPPOINT COUNTRY CODES, AS USED BY WINDOWS XP *(continued)*

COUNTRY CODE	COUNTRY
84	France
88	Georgia
94	Germany
98	Greece
109	Hungary
110	Iceland
111	Indonesia
113	India
118	Italy
122	Japan
131	North Korea
134	Korea
140	Latvia
141	Lithuania
143	Slovakia
145	Liechtenstein
147	Luxembourg
166	Mexico
167	Malaysia
176	The Netherlands
177	Norway
181	Suriname
185	Paraguay
187	Peru
191	Poland
193	Portugal
200	Romania
203	Russia

Continued on next page

TABLE 16.9: MICROSOFT MAPPOINT COUNTRY CODES, AS USED BY WINDOWS XP *(continued)*

COUNTRY CODE	COUNTRY
209	South Africa
212	Slovenia
217	Spain
221	Sweden
223	Switzerland
235	Turkey
241	Ukraine
242	United Kingdom
244	United States
246	Uruguay
249	Venezuela
39070	Multiple countries and regions, or countries or regions that do not have a country value defined

Generally, there is little need to manually set anything in International. The Regional Settings Properties dialog box covers each entry fully and includes error checking.

IOPROCS

The IOProcs subkey contains a reference to a single file, mvfs32.dll, which is not found on any system that I have checked. mvfs32.dll is the Media View File System .dll used by some applications to view media files. There is a strong probability that this file system and IOProcs are not used by more recent applications. There are two Media View File System .dlls supplied with Windows XP: mvfs13n.dll and mvfs14n.dll. Like the Cache subkey mentioned earlier in this chapter, this is almost a mystery key. One Microsoft Knowledge Base entry does document a fix for a problem with Encarta 95 and Windows NT 3.5 that requires an entry in IOProcs for M12 = mvfs1232.dll; this is the only information available. Windows XP has the single data value, MVB = mvfs32.dll.

KEYBOARD

The Keyboard subkey stores configurations for the keyboard, such as the initial state of the toggle keys—Caps Lock, Num Lock, and Scroll Lock—and the delay and repeat rates.

A typical system will have these three entries:

InitialKeyboardIndicators This is automatically set by Windows XP when users log off or when the system is shut down. It preserves the previous state of the Num Lock key. 0 turns off Num Lock when the user logs on, and 2 turns on Num Lock when the user logs on.

KeyboardDelay   This is the delay, when a key is held down, before the key auto-repeats. Values from 0 to 3 are accepted, with 0 being a delay of 250 milliseconds, and 3 being a delay of 1 second. (These times are approximate.)

KeyboardSpeed   This is the speed at which a key auto-repeats. Choose a value from 0, which repeats at two characters per second, to 31, which repeats at 30 characters per second.

MMCPL

Some ODBC (Open Database Connectivity) and Multimedia Control Panel settings are stored in the MMCPL subkey. Many computers do not have any entries in MMCPL. Typical entries might include the following:

```
mlcfg32.cpl=G:\\PROGRA~1\\COMMON~1\\System\\MAPI\\1033\\nt\\mlcfg32.cpl
mlcfq32.cpl=G:\PROGRA~1\COMMON~1\System\MAPI\1033\nt\mlcfg32.cpl
NumApps=20
H=230
W=442
X=88
Y=84
```

It is possible to have Control Panel multimedia settings in other directories, with the exception of %SystemRoot%\System32, by specifying their names and paths in the MMCPL subkey.

MOUSE

Mouse settings, such as speed and tracking, are set in the Mouse subkey. Typical settings include those shown in Table 16.10.

TABLE 16.10: MOUSE SETTINGS FOUND ON MOST WINDOWS SYSTEMS

ENTRY	TYPICAL VALUE	DESCRIPTION
ActiveWindowTracking	0x00000000	When this value is set to 0x00000001, the active window will always be the one the mouse is positioned on.
DoubleClickSpeed	500	Sets the amount of time between consecutive clicks of the mouse button for it to be considered a double-click.
DoubleClickHeight	4	Sets the amount of movement allowed (vertical) for a double-click to be valid.
DoubleClickWidth	4	Sets the amount of movement allowed (horizontal) for a double-click to be valid.
MouseThreshold1	6	Sets the motion factor that, when factored with MouseSpeed, controls the motion of the mouse.

Continued on next page

TABLE 16.10: MOUSE SETTINGS FOUND ON MOST WINDOWS SYSTEMS *(continued)*

ENTRY	TYPICAL VALUE	DESCRIPTION
MouseThreshold2	10	Sets the motion factor that, when factored with MouseSpeed, controls the motion of the mouse.
MouseSpeed	1	Sets the speed of the mouse pointer relative to the movement of the mouse.
MouseTrails	0	If zero, no mouse trails, if 1 (or greater) there are mouse trails. The higher the number, the more trails displayed.
SmoothMouseXCurve	(large binary data block)	Defines the x curve parameters for mouse movement smoothing.
SmoothMouseYCurve	(large binary data block)	Defines the y curve parameters for mouse movement smoothing.
SnapToDefaultButton	0	When this value is set to 1, the mouse will snap to the default button in dialog boxes.
SwapMouseButton	0	When nonzero, the functionality of the two outside mouse buttons is swapped—useful for left handed users.

PATTERNS

The `Patterns` subkey is where patterns used to create backgrounds, such as Boxes, Critters, and Diamonds, are set. For Windows XP, a pattern is expressed as an 8 × 8 box of color, black for each 1 bit and the background color for each 0 bit. The first number represents the first, topmost, line in the pattern; the second number represents the second line in the pattern, and so forth.

Each line is a binary representation; for example, the Boxes pattern is:

```
127, 65, 65, 65, 65, 65, 127, 0
```

These values are binary numbers, stored in decimal format, as shown below:

Decimal	Binary
127	0111 1111
65	0100 0001
65	0100 0001
65	0100 0001
65	0100 0001
65	0100 0001

Decimal	Binary
127	0111 1111
0	0000 0000

You can compare these binary numbers with the Boxes pattern. To do so, use the Edit Pattern button (in the Pattern dialog box) to view the pattern in the pattern editor. This fully shows the relationship between the bits and the pattern.

Be creative; you can cook up new patterns using the pattern editor. Enter a new pattern name, click the Add button, and *wola*, there is your new pattern. Just remember: it can be hard to be creative using an 8 × 8 cell.

The standard patterns defined in Windows XP are shown in Table 16.11. Note that the actual text in the (None) entry's value is the same as the name!

TABLE 16.11: DEFAULT PATTERNS DEFINED IN A TYPICAL WINDOWS XP INSTALLATION

NAME	DEFINITION TEXT
(None)	(None)
50% Gray	170 85 170 85 170 85 170 85
Boxes	127 65 65 65 65 65 127 0
Critters	0 80 114 32 0 5 39 2
Diamonds	32 80 136 80 32 0 0 0
Paisley	2 7 7 2 32 80 80 32
Pattern	224 128 142 136 234 10 14 0
Quilt	130 68 40 17 40 68 130 1
Scottie	64 192 200 120 120 72 0 0
Spinner	20 12 200 121 158 19 48 40
Thatches	248 116 34 71 143 23 34 113
Tulip	0 0 84 124 124 56 146 124
Waffle	0 0 0 0 128 128 128 240
Weave	136 84 34 69 136 21 34 81

POWERCFG

Windows XP supports power configuration and power savings. Power configurations are set in the Control Panel's Power Options applet. Each of the five supplied power schemes has a default name, and each scheme can be modified and saved by the user.

A default set of power policies is stored in `GlobalPowerPolicy`, a subkey in the key `PowerCfg`. Another subkey in `PowerCfg`, `PowerPolicies`, contains subkeys for each power configuration, both Microsoft and user created. The Microsoft power policies are:

Name	Description
Home/Office Desk	A Desktop scheme, this is useful when the computer is connected to the power source permanently.
Portable/Laptop	This scheme is useful for notebook and laptop computers for which maximum battery life is important.
Presentation	When performing presentations, this scheme will not allow blanking (turning off) the monitor.
Always On	Typically for network servers, this scheme keeps everything running, without standby. This allows network access to the computer, regardless of whether it is currently being used or not.
Minimal Power Management	Another scheme designed for servers, this one keeps the computer on and at the highest performance level.
Max Battery	For notebooks and laptop computers, using Max Battery will maximize the battery's life.

SCREEN SAVER.3DFLYINGOBJ

The `Screen Saver.3DFlyingObj` key holds configurations for the 3D Flying Objects (OpenGL) screen saver. Actually, you are able to access these settings from the Screen Saver tab in the Display Properties dialog box. Select the 3D Flying Objects (OpenGL) screen saver and click the Settings button to configure these settings.

SCREEN SAVER.3DPIPES

The `Screen Saver.3DPipes` key holds configurations for the 3DPipes (OpenGL) screen saver.

SCREEN SAVER.BEZIER

The `Screen Saver.Bezier` key holds configurations for the Bezier (OpenGL) screen saver.

SCREEN SAVER.MARQUEE

The `Screen Saver.Marquee` key holds configurations for the Marquee (OpenGL) screen saver.

SCREEN SAVER.MYSTIFY

The `Screen Saver.Mystify` key holds configurations for the Mystify (OpenGL) screen saver.

SCREEN SAVER.STARS

The `Screen Saver.Stars` key holds configurations for the Stars (OpenGL) screen saver.

SOUND

Information about basic sounds is contained in the Sound subkey. I've found two entries in this subkey, Beep=yes and ExtendedSounds=yes, with the former seemingly present on all systems. Beep=yes is used to indicate whether Windows XP will make a warning beep when the user attempts to do something that is not allowed.

SOUNDS

The Sounds subkey, when present, contains one value entry called SystemDefault that typically has a value of , (that is just a comma, nothing else). Other entries you might find in the Sounds subkey include the following:

- Enable=1

- SystemAsterisk=chord.wav,Asterisk

- SystemDefault=ding.wav,Default Beep

- SystemExclamation=chord.wav,Exclamation

- SystemExit=chimes.wav,Windows Logoff

- SystemHand=chord.wav,Critical Stop

- SystemQuestion=chord.wav,Question

- SystemStart=tada.wav,Windows Logon

The Sounds key contains information used by legacy systems and will usually be found only in systems that have been upgraded. Windows defines each of these sounds for use elsewhere in the registry.

Environment

The Control Panel's System Properties applet contains a tab called Advanced that is subdivided into three sections (Performance, Environment Variables, and Startup and Recovery). Clicking the Environment Variables button displays the Environment Variables dialog box. This dialog box is subdivided into System Variables and User Variables for <user>, where <user> is the currently logged-on user (see Figure 16.3). Any environment variable defined in System Variables will be available to all users, while environment variables defined in User Variables for <user> will only be available to the currently logged-on user.

Notice in Figure 16.3 that the current user is Administrator. When the next user logs on, they will get a different user environment (all users have an identical set of System variables.)

There is little need to modify the HKEY_CURRENT_USER\Environment section directly. The Control Panel's System Properties applet does a better job of modifying entries in Environment, and using System Properties is much safer than manually editing the registry.

WARNING   Avoid the urge to modify existing system variables unless you understand the ramifications of making such a change. For instance, changing the entry NUMBER_OF_PROCESSORS from 1 to 2 won't give you an extra CPU.

FIGURE 16.3

The Environment Variables dialog box. Environment variables for each user are contained in HKEY_CURRENT_USER\ Environment.

EUDC

EUDC, for End User Defined Characters, contains information about special characters users have created for their specific needs. This feature is supported in the Japanese, Chinese, Hangeul, and Johab character sets. This object is not on all Windows installations.

Identities

Configuration for some software, specific to the user, is stored in the Identities subkey. This subkey contains, on a typical system, information for Outlook Express (stationary lists, username, and so on).

Keyboard Layout

The Keyboard Layout subkey allows users to change keyboard configurations. Since different languages may have different layouts (usually for special symbols, such as currency), Windows XP allows users to change the keyboard layout using the Control Panel's Keyboard and Regional Options applets.

Configuring Windows XP for multiple languages is easy. Open the Control Panel's Regional Options applet, and use the General tab to change language settings.

NOTE *You can have more than two input locales, although it is unusual to have many different locales defined.*

You can define a hotkey to switch locales (in the Input Locales tab). The default hotkey is Left Alt+Shift, although you also can use Ctrl+Shift as an alternative hotkey. If you do not desire a hotkey, uncheck Enable Key Sequence. If you select the "no hotkey" option, it would be a good idea to check the Enable Indicator on Taskbar option so that you can use the Taskbar to switch input locales.

Now, back to our currently scheduled programming . . .

In HKEY_CURRENT_USER\Keyboard Layout, you'll find the following three subkeys:

Preload This subkey contains the keyboard layouts preloaded by Windows. Use the Control Panel's Regional Options applet, a hotkey, or the Taskbar to select the layout.

Substitutes   Any key substitutes will be defined in the Substitutes subkey. Key substitutes typically use the Dvorak keyboard layout. In Substitutes, a key named with the original locale will be substituted with the value of the substituting layout. For instance, the Unites States English locale is 409. In addition, 00000409 = 00000809 substitutes British English on the United States English locale.

Toggle   This subkey contains a single key whose data value will be 0 if no hotkey is defined, 1 if Left Alt+Shift is defined as the hotkey, and 2 if Ctrl+Shift is defined as the hotkey.

TIP   Tired of QWERTY? A different keyboard layout can be most useful if QWERTY is not your thing. One type of keyboard layout is the Dvorak layout. Said to improve typing proficiency by a great deal, Dvorak has a slowly growing band of supporters. To select the Dvorak layout, select an input locale in Regional Options, and click on Properties to modify the layout.

Generally, all modifications to HKEY_CURRENT_USER\Keyboard Layout should be done using the Input Locales tab of either the Regional Options applet or the Keyboard applet.

Network

HKEY_CURRENT_USER\Network contains configuration information for each network drive that the user has permanently mapped. Under Network you will find a subkey for each mapped drive letter.

For instance, if a user in My Network Places selects a server, then selects a share, right-clicks that share, and selects Map Network Drive in the pop-up context menu, the Map Network Drive dialog box (see Figure 16.4) will appear. This allows the user to select which drive letter is mapped to the network share. This dialog box also contains the following:

◆ The folder that is being linked to (this item is for reference only, and cannot be changed)

◆ A selection named Different User Name, allowing access to the drive as another user

◆ A check box called Reconnect at Logon, important because unchecking it will mean that the share is available only for the current session

FIGURE 16.4

The Map Network Drive dialog box

NOTE   Drives mapped without the Reconnect at Logon attribute enabled will not be loaded into the HKEY_CURRENT_USER\Network subkey.

You may map any unused drive letter to a network drive, using either the current user ID or another user ID.

Once you select a drive (H: in our next example) and click the OK button, the registry's HKEY_CURRENT_USER\Network subkey will have F as the new subkey. The F subkey contains six value variables:

ConnectionType   The value of 0x1 is for drives; 0x2 is for printers.

DeferFlags   Indicates whether the connection will be either reestablished whenever the system is restarted, or only be reestablished when there is a need to use the connection.

ProviderName   The network provider, typically Microsoft Windows Network (for Microsoft networking).

ProviderType   The network provider's type is 0x20000 for Microsoft Windows (LanMan) networking.

RemotePath   The UNC path to the network share; \\Dora\F is the share named F on the server whose name is Dora.

UserName   The name of the user for whom the share is established; it is either zero or the name specified in the Map Network Drive dialog box (see Figure 16.4). The username syntax consists of *domain\user*, where *domain* is the user's domain and *user* is the user ID.

Again, as with many other HKEY_CURRENT_USER entries, it is easy to manipulate the entries in Network without using the Registry Editor. If you have problems deleting a connection, one fix would be to delete the subkey from the HKEY_CURRENT_USER\Registry subkey.

Shares can be established quickly from a command-line prompt by using the command-line syntax:

```
net use H: \\Dora\G
```

Here, H: is the drive letter to be mapped and \\Dora\G is the share name. To get the full syntax of the net use command, type **net use /?** at a command-line prompt.

Printers

The HKEY_CURRENT_USER\Printers subkey contains information about printers—both local and remote. Locally attached printers typically use four subkeys in Printers:

Connections   This subkey contains subkeys for each remotely connected printer. Each subkey is named for the printer and contains two objects: Provider, a variable that contains the name of the driving .dll file (often win32spl.dll); and Server, a variable that contains the name of the server that the printer is attached to.

DevModePerUser   The user configurations for the printer, regardless of whether the printer is local or remotely attached, are stored in this subkey. Each printer has a key entry, named for the printer, with a binary data value following it. This way, multiple users may have different printer configurations for the same printer.

DevModes2 The configurations for the printer, regardless of whether the printer is local or remotely attached, are stored in this subkey. Each printer has a value entry, named for the printer, with a binary data value following it.

Settings This subkey contains binary objects for each attached printer. The Printer Wizard also stores its settings in a subkey named **Wizard**.

RemoteAccess

The **RemoteAccess** subkey contains connectoids for RAS (Remote Access Service). *Connectoids?* What the heck is a connectoid? A connectoid consists of all the information needed to implement a connection, typically to a remote computer.

The **RemoteAccess** subkey may include one value variable, called **InternetProfile**. Typically, the **InternetProfile** entry contains a null (empty) string.

RemoteAccess is not found on all systems or configurations. If RemoteAccess is not installed, then this object will probably not exist.

SessionInformation

The **SystemInformation** subkey contains dynamic information about the current session. This data includes a data value named **ProgramCount** that is an indicator of the number of active, running programs.

Software

Information about all installed software is stored in the **Software** subkey. This information is typically arranged by vendor, although some applications may be in their own subkeys.

In a typical installation of Windows XP, the **Software** key has at least the following subkey:

Microsoft Information about many of the components that are part of Windows XP is found in this subkey. On a typical installation, we see about 30 entries. A better-equipped installation could have twice the number of entries. Below is a list of objects found in a typical system:

- ◆ Active Setup
- ◆ Advanced INF Setup
- ◆ Clock
- ◆ Command Processor
- ◆ Conferencing
- ◆ DataEnvironment Designer
- ◆ DevStudio
- ◆ Disk Administrator
- ◆ File Manager
- ◆ Full-Text-System

- IEAK

- Internet Explorer

- Java VM

- Microsoft Setup (ACME)

- Multimedia

- NetDDE

- Notepad

- NTBackup

- Outlook Express

- Protected Storage System Provider

- RegEdt32

- Schedule+

- SystemCertificates

- User Location Service

- Visual Basic

- WAB

- WebPost

- Windows

- Windows Help

- Windows NT

- ODBC

- Policies

- VDO

On more mature installations with more installed software, the Software key expands to cover different product lines. Notice that products are arranged by the company that has produced the product or the product's functionality, such as ODBC, rather than by specific product. For example, if there were two Adobe products installed on the computer, the Adobe key would have information about both products. Here is a list of subkeys found on a mature installation:

- Adobe

- Canon

- Dragon Systems

- Federal Express

- Forte

- Inetstp

- Microsoft

- Netscape

- ODBC

- Policies

- Qualcomm

- VDO

- Wang

System

The System subkey contains information used by the backup/restore program. This information is mapped to the Current Control set.

Unicode Program Groups

The Unicode Program Groups subkey contains information used by Program Manager. The question is, of course, who uses Program Manager anymore?

The subkeys found in Unicode Program Groups are in a binary format that is difficult to edit. Have I ever seen entries in the Unicode Program Groups subkey? No, not yet. Wait a minute, I've never actually run Program Manager with Windows XP, either. Maybe I'll give it a try…

After running Program Manager and creating a couple of personal groups and a few common groups, I now have entries in the Unicode Program Groups key. As mentioned before, these entries are in binary format and are complex structures. As Microsoft recommends, it is best to edit these entries using Program Manager.

NOTE Actually, users who upgraded from Windows NT 3.x may have entries in the Unicode Program Groups *subkey; however, this subkey is unused by Windows NT versions 4 and later unless the user has configured or run Program Manager (*ProgMan.exe*).*

Windows 3.1 Migrations Status

The Windows 3.1 Migration Status subkey is contained only in systems upgraded from Windows NT 3.x. (There may be a few of these installations remaining.) The subkey contains keys that are used to show the status of conversion of the Program Manager Group (.grp) files and associated initialization (.ini) files that have been converted to Windows NT 4 or later format. Deleting this value, and not the Windows 3.1 Migration Status subkey, causes Windows to attempt to convert the Program Manager Group files when Windows restarts. This reconversion may change the Start menu substantially, but should not cause serious damage.

Volatile Environment

Typically, the `Volatile Environment` subkey contains a number of entries:

APPDATA   A fully qualified string indicating the name and location of the user's `Application Data` folder.

CLIENTNAME   The name of the client; this entry is often empty.

HOMEDRIVE   The home drive, typically `C:`.

HOMEPATH   The path to the user's home folder. Typically found in the `Documents and Settings` folder.

HOMESHARE   The UNC path to the user's home folder location. Typically found on a network server. This value might be set using a logon script.

LOGONSERVER   A string with the logon server's name (the server the user is currently logged on to). For example, my logon server is `\\DORA`.

SESSIONNAME   The text Console, typically.

USERDNSDOMAIN   The name of the `DNS` for this computer. For example, my system has the value `DARKSTAR.MV.COM`.

HKEY_USERS

The `HKEY_USERS` hive contains information about each active user who has a user profile. There are a minimum of two keys in the `HKEY_USERS` hive: `.DEFAULT` and the ID for the currently logged-on user.

Chapter 17

Introduction to HKEY_LOCAL_MACHINE

THE HKEY_LOCAL_MACHINE hive contains information about the computer system's configuration as it is currently running. This hive also holds information about users, groups, security, and installed software.

You've backed up your registry before starting this chapter, right? Let's dig in and see what's there. In this chapter, I'll discuss the five subkeys in HKEY_LOCAL_MACHINE:

- ◆ Hardware, which stores information about currently used hardware

- ◆ SAM, which defines all users who may use the computer (and domain information if the computer is a PDC/BDC)

- ◆ Security, which contains information about cached logons, policy, special accounts, and RXACT (registry transaction package), as well as a copy of the SAM

- ◆ Software, which holds software information, a superset of the information contained in HKEY_CURRENT_USER

- ◆ System, the system definitions, control sets, information about removable media (CD-ROMs), and information about Windows XP setup

HKEY_LOCAL_MACHINE

As I mentioned above, HKEY_LOCAL_MACHINE has five sections. Each section is separate, and we'll deal with each separately. Remember that SAM (the Security Accounts Manager) and Security actually cover different aspects of security, so don't confuse 'em. Many parts of the HKEY_LOCAL_MACHINE hive are aliased to other registry locations.

WARNING   *If you change anything in the HKEY_LOCAL_MACHINE hive, there's a good chance you'll trash your system registry. Really: HKEY_LOCAL_MACHINE is probably the most critical part of the registry, so back up before you touch it—before you even browse it!*

Hardware

The Hardware subkey describes the system's hardware. Most everything in the Hardware subkey is set during bootup by the ntdetect.com program or by the ARC (Advanced RISC Computer) database for users running Windows XP on RISC computers.

The Hardware subkey contains three subkeys:

Description   This subkey contains information about the processor, math coprocessor, and multifunction adapters (devices such as the PCI bus, Plug and Play BIOS, and ISA bus).

DeviceMap   This subkey holds subkeys for most devices, such as the keyboard, mouse, serial ports, and video.

ResourceMap   This subkey contains items such as HAL (Hardware Abstraction Layer), keyboard and pointer port(s), serial and parallel ports, SCSI devices (including IDE drives, too), and video information.

NOTE   Early versions of Windows had some problems dealing with the PCI bus, as PCI is designed to work integrally with Plug and Play, which those early versions of Windows did not support. Since the advent of Windows 95, the operating system is much better behaved in supporting PnP.

I'll cover these subkeys fully a little later. If you are having problems with your hardware (no, nothing here will help fix a broken keyboard!) interfacing with Windows XP, it is possible that something in the Hardware key can help you fix the problem.

Before fiddling with registry values in HKEY_LOCAL_MACHINE\Hardware directly, first try Windows XP's Computer Management tool (shown in Figure 17.1), which manages devices, storage, services, and applications.

NOTE   Many times you will see subkeys with numbers for names, starting at 0. Often there is only one of these subkeys, but if multiple objects of the type are described by a key, you will see multiple subkeys numbered from 0 to n, where n is the number of objects minus 1. For example, a computer with five drives on a SCSI bus would have subkeys named 0, 1, 2, 3, and 4 in the key HKEY_LOCAL_MACHINE\Hardware\Description\System\MultifunctionAdapter\3\ DiskController\0\DiskPeripheral\.

FIGURE 17.1

The Computer Management tool, showing disk defragmentation— it checked and decided my drive was still okay.

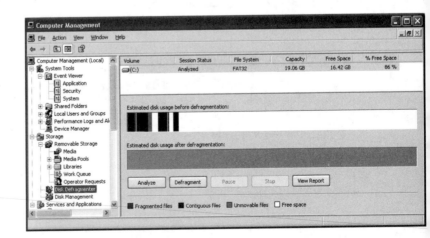

HARDWARE PROFILES, OR HOW CAN I MAKE WINDOWS XP MORE HARDWARE-FRIENDLY?

Windows XP is capable of supporting multiple hardware configurations. This functionality is most useful for notebooks and other portable computers. For instance, in the Control Panel's System Properties applet, the Hardware Profiles tab allows a user to create multiple hardware profiles. To create a new configuration, select an existing configuration and click the Copy button. Enter a new name for the configuration (I used the name Backup Profile in my example), then click OK. Select the new configuration you just created, and then click the Properties button to display the dialog box shown in Figure 17.2; this dialog box's title will vary depending on what you named your new configuration.

NOTE *Don't confuse hardware profiles with user profiles. They are very different animals (goodness—is he referring to users as animals?), dealing with completely different areas.*

For each configuration, it is possible to define the computer as portable, which is useful when there is docking support. When the option This Is a Portable Computer is checked, the docking state can be set as one of the following:

◆ The docking state is unknown.

◆ The computer is docked.

◆ The computer is undocked.

Windows XP also allows making the profile an option when starting the operating system. This is useful when you change hardware configurations frequently.

FIGURE 17.2

The Properties dialog box for the new hardware configuration named Backup Profile.

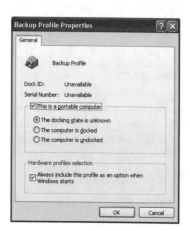

When creating a hardware profile, simply name it to reflect the configuration. For example, if you create a profile for the computer when docked in the docking station, name the profile Docked and make sure you select both This Is a Portable Computer and The Computer Is Docked. When creating a profile for the computer when not docked, name this profile UN-Docked and select This Is a Portable Computer and The Computer Is Undocked.

TIP   *Remember, with Microsoft's Product Authorization, if you change more than a trivial amount of hardware, you must "reauthorize" your Windows XP installation. However, if you set up your hardware profiles to indicate that the computer is a portable, you are allowed more latitude in hardware changes prior to Windows requiring reauthorization.*

Sometimes it is necessary to create a profile for when the portable computer is either docked or undocked. Two scenarios can be envisioned: one where the docking state is not important and another where the docking state is important. When the docking state is not important, you can create a single profile with The Docking State Is Unknown option checked. In configurations where the docking state is important, simply create two profiles, one for each state.

DESCRIPTION

Okay, first, the standard warning: be very careful about making any changes in the `Description` subkey. Everything in this subkey is set during bootup by the `ntdetect.com` program or by the ARC database. As this information is volatile (it is regenerated each time Windows XP starts by the bootup process), it is neither practical nor meaningful to modify the data. You can use a program called System Information to view information in these subkeys. Start System Information by selecting Start ➤ All Programs ➤ Accessories ➤ System Tools ➤ System Information.

NOTE   *In earlier versions of Windows, the System Information program was called WinMSD. System Information replaces both the WinMSD and MSInfo32 programs. If you attempt to execute either of these utilities in Windows XP, System Information will start.*

There is a single subkey in `Description` called `System`. The subkeys inside `System` are described in the following sections.

CentralProcessor

The `CentralProcessor` subkey contains subkeys describing each processor found. For uniprocessor systems, a single subkey named 0 contains information about the processor. Multiprocessor computers will have subkeys named from 0 to *n*, where *n* is the number of processors minus 1. The following list shows the configuration of an Intel Pentium system. Users with other processors or processors from other suppliers will see some different information, although the keys will be identical.

Component Information   This data value identifies information about the processor.

Configuration Data   This is a REG_FULL_RESOURCE_DESCRIPTOR data object containing data about the processor.

Feature Set   This is a REG_DWORD value describing the computer's feature set.

~MHz   A DWORD value containing the CPU speed, this field may not be present or contain a value designating speed for some processors.

Update Status   This is a DWORD value containing a flag indicating the update status for this system.

VendorIdentifier   This is the name of the company that manufactured the CPU, as a text string; for example, an Intel Pentium will have "GenuineIntel", and an AMD system will have "AuthenticAMD".

Identifier   This is the CPU model and other CPU-specific identifying information; for example, an Intel Pentium might have the string "x86 Family 5 Model 4 Stepping 3", or perhaps "x86 Family 6 Model 4 Stepping 2" as the identifier. This string can be used to selectively apply patches to correct known flaws in certain CPUs, for example. All compatible processors will have a similar string.

FloatingPointProcessor

The FloatingPointProcessor key holds subkeys describing each floating-point math coprocessor found. For uniprocessor systems, a single subkey named 0 contains information about the coprocessor. Multiprocessor computers will have subkeys named from 0 to *n*, where *n* is the number of processors minus 1. The following list shows an Intel Pentium system. Users with other processors or processors from other suppliers will see some different information, although the keys will be identical:

Component Information   This data value identifies information about the processor.

Configuration Data   This is a REG_FULL_RESOURCE_DESCRIPTOR data object containing data about the processor.

Identifier   This is the CPU model and other CPU-specific identifying information; for example, an Intel Pentium might have the string "x86 Family 5 Model 4 Stepping 3" as the identifier. This string can be used to selectively apply patches to correct known flaws in certain CPUs, for example, as noted above.

MultifunctionAdapter

As with the entries in the keys CentralProcessor and FloatingPointProcessor, the entries in MultifunctionAdapter are created either by the hardware recognizer (ntdetect.com) for Intel-based systems or by the ARC database found on RISC computers. Inside the MultifunctionAdapter key are subkeys describing the internal structure of the computer, bus structure, PnP (Plug and Play), BIOS (if PnP is installed), and devices installed on these buses.

NOTE   Instead of the MultifunctionAdapter key used with ISA, MCA (Micro-Channel Architecture), and some PCI bus machines, you may find EisaAdapter if your computer uses the EISA bus, or TcAdapter if your computer uses the TURBOChannel bus architecture. Entries for both EisaAdapter and TcAdapter are similar to those in MultifunctionAdapter; they vary based on what components are installed rather than on bus type.

It would not be practical to describe all subkeys found for every different type of computer in the MultifunctionAdapter subkey. Instead, let's look at a typical system: an Intel motherboard, a PCI bus, an IDE hard drive, and typical peripherals.

The MultifunctionAdapter key contains one or more subkeys. There is one subkey for each bus controller (PnP is counted as a bus and is included, though no devices are assigned to PnP). A typical PCI bus computer (virtually all PCI-based computers also have ISA bus support to allow using legacy interface cards) has three, or more, subkeys explained next.

0   The PCI BIOS, this object contains the key `RealModeIrqRoutingTable`, containing data values for `Component Information`, `Configuration Data`, and `Identifier`.

1   The PnP BIOS doesn't have a physical bus as such. PnP works with the ISA bus and the PCI bus in the computer. There are keys for `Component Information`, `Configuration Data`, and `Identifier`.

2   `APM`, or Advanced Power Management, is present in those systems that support APM.

3   The PnP BIOS supports docking, and this subkey provides information about docking. There are keys for `Component Information`, `Configuration Data`, and `Identifier`.

4   The ISA bus, with keys for `Component Information`, `Configuration Data`, and `Identifier`. The ISA bus key contains subkeys for other devices such as disk controllers, keyboards, and printer and serial ports.

Rather than describing all possible entries for the `MultifunctionAdapter` key, I'm going to suggest that you use the Registry Editor (RegEdit) and peruse this key. Figure 17.3 shows most of the `MultifunctionAdapter` key expanded on a typical PCI bus computer.

FIGURE 17.3

RegEdit shows the contents of the `Multifunction-Adapter` subkey.

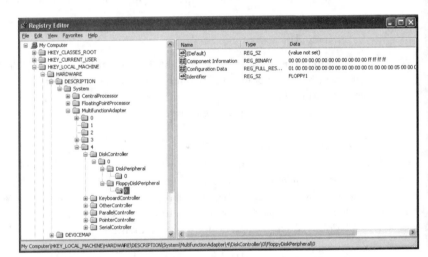

DEVICEMAP

The `DeviceMap` subkey contains subkeys for devices such as the keyboard, mouse (or pointer), serial ports, SCSI, and video. As with other parts of the `HKEY_LOCAL_MACHINE\Hardware` key, `DeviceMap` is generated at boot time, and making modifications to this subkey is ill advised. We can look, however, at several parts of `DeviceMap` that are typical in a Windows XP installation.

One subkey always found in `DeviceMap` is `KeyboardClass`. This subkey has a value entry called "`\Device\KeyboardClass0`" (yes, this entry's name does contain backslashes). The data in this entry is `\REGISTRY\Machine\System\ControlSet001\Services\Kbdclass`. This is a reference to

`HKEY_LOCAL_MACHINE\SYSTEM\ControlSet001\Services\Kbdclass`, where the current keyboard configuration and settings are located.

Another `DeviceMap` subkey, `Scsi`, holds information pertaining to SCSI hard drives and IDE (ATAPI) hard drives. Windows blurs the line between IDE drives and SCSI drives by listing both under the same registry objects.

The keys for a Windows system with one IDE drive are as follows:

```
Scsi
Scsi\Scsi Port 3
Scsi\Scsi Port 3\Scsi Bus 0\
Scsi\Scsi Port 3\Scsi Bus 0\Target Id 0
Scsi\Scsi Port 3\Scsi Bus 0\Target Id 0\Logical Unit Id 0
  Identifier = "QUANTUM FIREBALL_TM2110S300X"
  Type = "DiskPeripheral"
```

These keys identify a QUANTUM FIREBALL 2GB SCSI hard drive.

Now let's look at another system, a Windows server working as a file server (it serves four hard drives and three CD-ROM drives). For a system with two IDE CD-ROM drives, an IDE hard disk drive, a SCSI bus with four SCSI hard drives, and one SCSI CD-ROM drive, the subkeys look like this:

```
Scsi

Scsi\Scsi Port 0
  "FirstBusScanTimeInMs"=dword:000009ef
  "DMAEnabled"=dword:00000001
  "Driver"="atapi"

  Scsi\Scsi Port 0\Scsi Bus 0

  Scsi\Scsi Port 0\Scsi Bus 0\Initiator Id 255

  Scsi\Scsi Port 0\Scsi Bus 0\Target Id 0

    Scsi\Scsi Port 0\Scsi Bus 0\Target Id 0\Logical Unit Id 0
      "Identifier"="Maxtor 91728D8"
      "Type"="DiskPeripheral"

Scsi\Scsi Port 1
  "FirstBusScanTimeInMs"=dword:00000014
  "DMAEnabled"=dword:00000000
  "Driver"="atapi"

  Scsi\Scsi Port 1\Scsi Bus 0

  Scsi\Scsi Port 1\Scsi Bus 0\Initiator Id 255

  Scsi\Scsi Port 1\Scsi Bus 0\Target Id 0
```

```
Scsi\Scsi Port 1\Scsi Bus 0\Target Id 0\Logical Unit Id 0
  "Identifier"="MATSHITA CD-ROM CR-581-M"
  "Type"="CdRomPeripheral"
  "DeviceName"="CdRom0"

Scsi\Scsi Port 1\Scsi Bus 0\Target Id 1

  Scsi\Scsi Port 1\Scsi Bus 0\Target Id 1\Logical Unit Id 0
    "Identifier"="MATSHITA CD-ROM CR-581-M"
    "Type"="CdRomPeripheral"
    "DeviceName"="CdRom1"

Scsi\Scsi Port 2
  "Interrupt"=dword:0000000a
  "IOAddress"=dword:00006300
  "Driver"="aic78xx"

Scsi\Scsi Port 2\Scsi Bus 0

Scsi\Scsi Port 2\Scsi Bus 0\Initiator Id 7

Scsi\Scsi Port 2\Scsi Bus 0\Target Id 0

  Scsi\Scsi Port 2\Scsi Bus 0\Target Id 0\Logical Unit Id 0
    "Identifier"="QUANTUM FIREBALL_TM2110S300X"
    "Type"="DiskPeripheral"
    "InquiryData"=hex:00,00,02. . .

Scsi\Scsi Port 2\Scsi Bus 0\Target Id 2

  Scsi\Scsi Port 2\Scsi Bus 0\Target Id 2\Logical Unit Id 0
    "Identifier"="MICROP 2112-15MZ1001905HQ30"
    "Type"="DiskPeripheral"
    "InquiryData"=hex:00,00,02. . .

Scsi\Scsi Port 2\Scsi Bus 0\Target Id 4

  Scsi\Scsi Port 2\Scsi Bus 0\Target Id 4\Logical Unit Id 0
    "Identifier"="TOSHIBA CD-ROM XM-3301TA2342"
    "Type"="CdRomPeripheral"
    "InquiryData"=hex:05,80,02. . .

Scsi\Scsi Port 2\Scsi Bus 0\Target Id 5

  Scsi\Scsi Port 2\Scsi Bus 0\Target Id 5\Logical Unit Id 0
    "Identifier"="QUANTUM XP34301      1071"
    "Type"="DiskPeripheral"
```

```
    "InquiryData"=hex:00,00,02. . .

  Scsi\Scsi Port 2\Scsi Bus 0\Target Id 6

    Scsi\Scsi Port 2\Scsi Bus 0\Target Id 6\Logical Unit Id 0
      "Identifier"="TOSHIBA MK537FB     6262"
      "Type"="DiskPeripheral"
      "InquiryData"=hex:00,00,02. . .
```

In this example, there is one IDE hard drive and two IDE CD-ROM drives. Both CD-ROM drives are identical MATSHITA CR-581s. There is also one SCSI CD-ROM drive, a Toshiba XM-3301. And there are four SCSI hard drives:

◆   `Identifier = "QUANTUM FIREBALL_TM2110S300X"`

◆   `Identifier = "MICROP 2112-15MZ1001905HQ30"`

◆   `Identifier = "QUANTUM XP34301     1071"`

◆   `Identifier = "TOSHIBA MK537FB     6262"`

In addition to the two IDE CD-ROM drives, there is a single 18GB IDE hard drive:

◆   `Identifier = "Maxtor 91728D8"`

If all drives are listed as SCSI, how do we tell the difference between different drive types? Well, actually, that's easy. Take a look at the different keys defined in the subkey `Scsi Port n`, such as in this example:

```
Scsi\Scsi Port 0
  "FirstBusScanTimeInMs"=dword:000009ef
  "DMAEnabled"=dword:00000001
  "Driver"="atapi"
```

In this example, the driver, ATAPI, tells us that the drive is an IDE drive. (ATAPI is short for AT Attachment Peripheral Interface; IDE is short for Integrated Drive Electronics.)

DRIVES AND BUSES!

Windows changes the way IDE devices are handled by the operating system. Under Windows NT version 4, the atapi.sys file handles I/O for all PCI-connected IDE devices. When the device connects to an ISA bus controller, a different driver, atdisk.sys, manages the I/O.

RESOURCEMAP

ResourceMap includes items such as HAL, keyboard and pointer port(s), serial and parallel ports, SCSI devices (which include IDE drives), and video information. This subkey also includes data about I/O channels, I/O ports and addresses, IRQs, and DMA channels. Everything in ResourceMap is generated at boot time, so changes are transient at best.

ResourceMap entries are based on class, then device, as Figure 17.4 shows. In this figure, notice that the `System Resources` subkey has been opened to show three entries: `Loader Reserved`, `Physical Memory` and `Reserved`. The `Physical Memory` entry describes the memory that exists in the system, while `Reserved` describes the parts of memory reserved for special uses. In the system in this example, there is 256MB of RAM, with some sections reserved for special use (check out Figure 17.5). Notice that both RAM and ROM (typically where the computer's BIOS is stored) are listed. (I've sorted the memory usage by device, to make this figure more readable.)

FIGURE 17.4

The `ResourceMap` key with the `System Resources` subkey opened

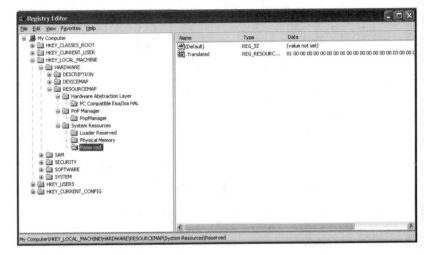

FIGURE 17.5

Reserved memory on this computer is made up of 10 blocks of memory, each block having its own attributes.

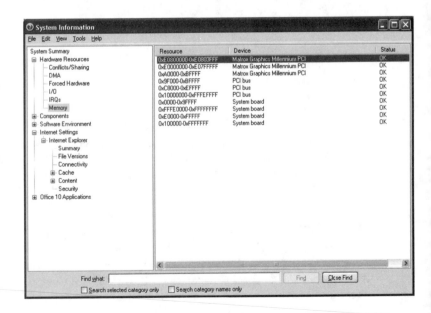

Each subkey in `ResourceMap` consists of one or more subkeys, typically containing two entries: `.Raw` and `.Translated`. These entries hold information about the device resources in a special variable type called REG_RESOURCE_LIST. To edit or view device resources, open the object (use the Registry Editor) to display the Resource Lists edit box (shown in Figure 17.6). In the Resource Lists edit box, select a resource and click the Display button to display the Resources dialog box (see Figure 17.7). The Display button will be disabled until a resource in the resource list is selected. In the Resources dialog box, you can see a myriad of information, including DMA channel, interrupt (IRQ), memory used (commonly with video cards and some network cards), port used, and device-specific data.

SAM

Generally, a Windows XP system configured as a domain controller will use Active Directory to manage users. Earlier versions of Windows NT, and Windows servers that are not part of a domain, use SAM, the Security Accounts Manager, to manage user accounts on the computer. Although Windows domain controllers use Active Directory, the SAM sections of the registry still exist and are updated by Windows installations that are not part of a domain.

NOTE   To view the contents of the SAM keys, you will probably have to give yourself appropriate permissions. Select Edit ➢ Permissions from the RegEdit menu to change permissions.

FIGURE 17.6

In the Resource Lists box, you select a resource and click the Display button. This resource is reserved memory in system resources.

FIGURE 17.7

The Resources dialog box displays information about the reserved memory resource.

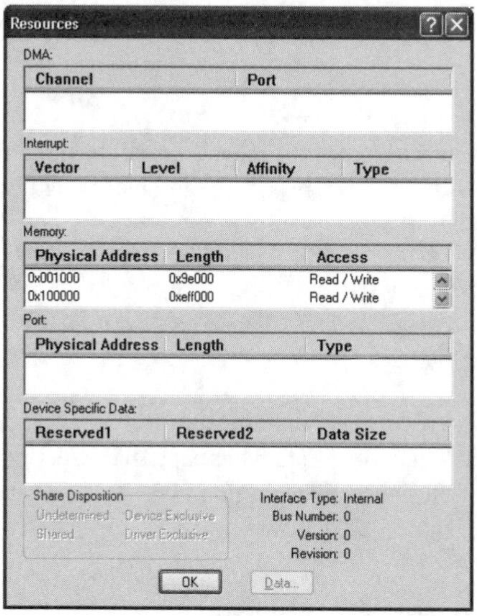

Normally, Windows protects SAM against any viewing or tampering by users. This is good; after all, who wants the typical user going in and monkeying about with the user security database? In Windows XP domain controllers, the Active Directory tools maintain the user information. In Windows NT 4, changes to SAM are made with either the User Manager or User Manager for Domains tools found in the Administrative Tools section of the Start menu.

WARNING   *Again, standard warnings: any playing with the* SAM *section may prevent one, more than one, or all, users from being able to log on. The ultimate result could be that the system may need to be restored from backup or be reinstalled. Be most cautious in making any changes in* SAM.

SAM consists of a single subkey, called (strangely enough) SAM. Inside the SAM subkey are two subkeys. The first subkey, called `Domains`, contains several objects (we'll cover these in a minute, don't panic). The second subkey, called RXACT, contains, as far as I can determine, absolutely nothing useful to the average registry hacker. RXACT is the registry transaction package, used by Windows to manage the registry on servers that are not domain controllers. (However, my experience with Microsoft has indicated that when one thinks that some component of the registry is empty, one is not looking at it correctly.)

Okay, back to the `Domains` subkey. Inside `Domains` are two subkeys, `Account` and `Builtin`.

NOTE   *Much of the data in the* SAM *keys is stored in a format that cannot be displayed or edited by the Registry Editor. Therefore, there is little possibility that you can edit these fields.*

DOMAINS\ACCOUNT

In Windows XP, the `Account` subkey contains virtually everything regarding the users and groups. Three subkeys, `Aliases`, `Groups`, and `Users`, hold information about aliases, groups, and users.

NOTE   *For information on user IDs, see Chapter 3. The section entitled "HKEY_USERS, Settings for Users" contains a full reference to SIDs (security identifiers), present throughout the* SAM *key of the registry. The descriptions below apply to Windows XP and 2000 servers that aren't domain controllers and to Windows NT 4.*

Aliases

The `Aliases` subkey contains information on local groups defined in the registry by the system administrator. Local groups defined by the system are maintained in the `Builtin` subkey.

NOTE   *Windows XP and Active Directory substantially alter the configuration of* SAM *and* Security *in the registry. Do not expect to see all the items found in Windows NT 4 domain controllers in Windows XP domain controllers. All of the below illustrations are for Windows XP and 2000 servers that are not configured as domain controllers and for Windows NT 4 (and earlier) servers.*

Under `Aliases`, there are subkeys for each local group. (The example in Figure 17.8 has seven aliases.) `Aliases` also contains a subkey called `Members` that lists the user IDs of each of the aliases. Each is identified by a DWORD hexadecimal number (see the next section). Another subkey, called `Names`, lists the names for each of the aliases.

FIGURE 17.8

Seven objects, each identified with a hexadecimal number, are found in the `Aliases` subkey on my computer.

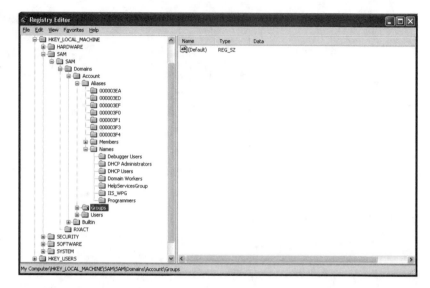

If you have created additional groups, they are found with similar identifiers, such as the following (remember—this is an example; my computer has many such objects):

000003F3 This subkey, expressed as decimal 1011, relates to the global group called Programmers. I created Programmers to cover users working in the R&D division who needed to access the entire domain to do their work.

000003F4 This subkey, expressed as decimal 1012, relates to the global group called Domain Workers. I created Domain Workers to cover a number of users who needed to access the entire domain to do certain work.

Groups

The `Groups` subkey typically has one subkey (see Figure 17.9), pertaining to local user groups. On a Windows XP computer, the subkey found is:

00000201 This subkey, expressed as decimal 513, relates to the None group, which contains ordinary users.

Users

The final subkey within `Domains\Account` is `Users`. This subkey contains one entry for each user defined in the SAM. For large networks, the number of users could be large. It is not uncommon for a large network to have hundreds, if not thousands, of users defined. At the college where I teach, our network has about 2500 users defined. In some networks, such a network would be considered to be small! (But we won't tell our systems administrators that their system is small...)

Fortunately, this author has a small network at home, so there are only a few users defined, making things a bit less cluttered.

FIGURE 17.9

Only one object, named None, is found in the **Groups** subkey on my computer.

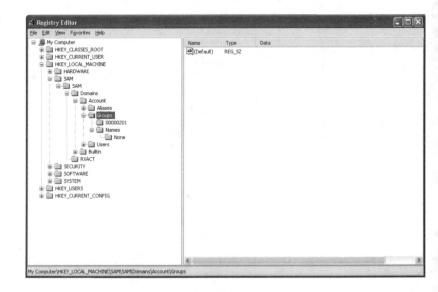

As with groups, system-created users have numbers less than 3F5 (that's 1013) and users created by the system administrator will have numbers greater than or equal to 3F5.

NOTE   There will probably be gaps in the numbers, or your numbers will not match mine. This is normal (as normal as things get, that is) as each installation may have different users defined by default. Also, once a user ID has been deleted, Windows will not reuse the number. After all, there are lots of numbers for Windows to use, millions and millions of them to be exact.

Rather than list every user ID and name on my system (you can see that I have 10 users defined: 2 defined by the system, and 8 defined by the system administrator), let's just talk about a few of them. First, directly under **Users** (see Figure 17.10) are some numbered subkeys. The first two subkeys are predefined by the system:

000001F4   The system administrator account has a SID ending in 500 (which is 0x1F4 in hexadecimal; funny how that worked out).

000001F5   The system guest account has a SID ending in 501 (which is 0x1F5 in hexadecimal; just as funny how that worked out, too).

Looking at Table 17.1, note the ending digits in the SIDs in the table and the above keys. This is much too scary to be coincidence.

TABLE 17.1: SOME COMMON SID VALUES FOR A WINDOWS NETWORKING DOMAIN

SUBKEY NAME	GLOBAL GROUP	SID
000001F4	Domain Administrators	S-1-5-21-xxxxxxxxx-xxxxxxxxx-xxxxxxxxx-500
000001F5	Domain Guests	S-1-5-21-xxxxxxxxx-xxxxxxxxx-xxxxxxxxx-501
000001F6	Domain Users	S-1-5-21-xxxxxxxxx-xxxxxxxxx-xxxxxxxxx-502

FIGURE 17.10

Users and their attributes are contained within the `Users` and `Users\Names` subkeys.

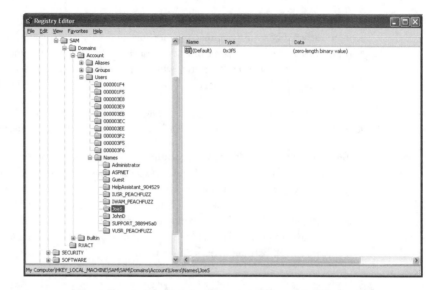

The next subkeys (starting with `000003E8`, which is 1000 in decimal, and ending with `000003F6`, or 1014) have been created for each administrator-created user ID. (Remember, the numbers in your system will likely vary a bit from these values.) Each of these subkeys contains two named keys, called `F` and `V`. Feel free to guess as to the meanings of these names and what the data contained within each is. Some assumptions can be made; for instance, there must be an index between the subkeys and their counterparts found in the `Names` subkey. Information such as group membership, privileges, passwords, and all other data specified by the administrator must be contained in these variables, too.

In the `Names` subkey (refer again to Figure 17.10), you can see a number of user names found on my system. For example:

Administrator The system-created system administrator account.

ASPNET A user ID used by ASP.NET worker processes.

IUSR_PEACHFUZZ A user ID used for anonymous access to Internet Information Services (IIS).

IWAM_PEACHFUZZ A user ID used by IIS to run out of processes.

GUEST Any user may log on without a password using this user ID, but they get only very limited privileges.

SUPPORT_388945a0 The account used by Microsoft to help support your computer. This account is disabled by default; you must enable it to allow Microsoft to use this account.

JohnD The account for a rather fictitious user, who only works here when I am not around. Main purpose of this employee is to collect a paycheck.

The remaining entries (`VUSR_PEACHFUZZ`, `JoeS`, and so forth) are similar. There is nothing unusual about them.

Any name ending in a **$** is a machine (a computer) account, not a user ID. There is always confusion about what constitutes a machine account and what constitutes a user account. To connect a computer to a server, the server must have both the computer's account and the user's account. Got that? Both must exist! The computer, when started, automatically "logs on" to the network, giving its computer name to the logon server.

NOTE   *Most networks today are configured to automatically add a machine account whenever a new computer is attached to the network. This allows adding new hardware with a minimum amount of administrative overhead.*

Generally, when you create a new computer configuration, you create the computer name on that computer. The dialog box used to create the computer name has a section called "Create a computer account in the domain," which when checked will create the computer account. Sometimes, however, it is necessary to create a computer account in a domain, and some documentation says to use the User Manager for Domains program without telling you about this neat trick. No one mentions the ending **$**, and computer accounts aren't visible in User Manager for Domains.

Holy mackerel! Batman, what's a user to do?

COMPUTER ACCOUNTS FOR EVERYDAY ADMINISTRATORS

There are, it seems, two ways to create a computer account.

First, in the User Manager for Domains, you can create a user account with a trailing $. This seems to create a valid computer account, although this is undocumented. Computer accounts created this way remain visible to the User Manager for Domains program.

A second method (a more approved method, I might add!) is to use the command-prompt NET command. Use NET COMPUTER \\<name> /ADD, where <name> is the name of the computer to be added. Use NET COMPUTER \\<name> /DEL, where <name> is the name of the computer to be deleted.

Though Windows 2000/NT/XP computers require a computer account on the server, Windows 95/98/Me computers do not seem to need one. Other computers, including Windows CE machines, have been known to require a computer account in addition to the user account. Try working without a computer account, and if the user is unable to log on, add a computer account to the user database and try again.

Well, we've covered global users and groups that are created by default by the system. Next, we'll cover local users and groups.

DOMAINS\BUILTIN

Under SAM\Domains\Builtin, there are three subkeys. These subkeys perform a similar task to those in Domains\Account.

Aliases

In Aliases, we find the group numbers for each of the local groups. For example, the local group 00000220, when viewed as a decimal number, is 544, which is the local Administrators group. Figure 17.11 shows the Builtin subkey, with most subkeys expanded.

Each of these local groups is used to maintain and use the local machine. There are domain groups to perform remote maintenance. Table 17.2 shows the default groups found in Builtin (your configuration may not have all groups listed).

FIGURE 17.11

Expanding Aliases shows nine built-in groups.

TABLE 17.2: THE BUILTIN LOCAL GROUPS

SUBKEY NAME	BUILTIN LOCAL GROUPS	SID
00000220	Builtin\Administrators	S-1-2-32-xxxxxxxxx-xxxxxxxxxx-xxxxxxxxxx-544
00000221	Builtin\Users	S-1-2-32-xxxxxxxxx-xxxxxxxxxx-xxxxxxxxxx-545
00000222	Builtin\Guests	S-1-2-32-xxxxxxxxx-xxxxxxxxxx-xxxxxxxxxx-546
00000223*	Builtin\Power Users	S-1-2-32-xxxxxxxxx-xxxxxxxxxx-xxxxxxxxxx-547
00000224*	Builtin\Account Operators	S-1-2-32-xxxxxxxxx-xxxxxxxxxx-xxxxxxxxxx-548
00000225*	Builtin\Server Operators	S-1-2-32-xxxxxxxxx-xxxxxxxxxx-xxxxxxxxxx-549
00000226*	Builtin\Print Operators	S-1-2-32-xxxxxxxxx-xxxxxxxxxx-xxxxxxxxxx-550
00000227*	Builtin\Backup Operators	S-1-2-32-xxxxxxxxx-xxxxxxxxxx-xxxxxxxxxx-551
00000228*	Builtin\Replicator	S-1-2-32-xxxxxxxxx-xxxxxxxxxx-xxxxxxxxxx-552
0000022B*	Builtin\Remote Desktop Users	S-1-2-32-xxxxxxxxx-xxxxxxxxxx-xxxxxxxxxx-555
0000022C*	Builtin\Network Configuration Operators	S-1-2-32-xxxxxxxxx-xxxxxxxxxx-xxxxxxxxxx-556

* Available only in Windows XP Professional, .NET Server, and Windows 2000.

Also present in `Aliases` is a subkey called `Members`. This subkey contains users and global groups that are members of local groups, identified by their SID suffixes. Another subkey called `Names` lists the names that match with the various numeric identifiers described above.

NOTE   Remember: Global groups may be members of local groups, but local groups may not be members of global groups. Oh, and yes, local users may be members of global groups, too. Confused? Good, then I am not alone! Basically, the only member relationship not allowed is local groups as members of global groups; other than that, anything goes.

Groups

In `Groups`, we find a single subkey called `Names`. There appears to be no information stored in these subkeys.

Users

In `Users`, we find a single subkey called `Names`. There appears to be no information stored in these subkeys.

RXACT

The key `HKEY_LOCAL_MACHINE\SAM\SAM\RXACT` is undocumented except that it is listed as belonging to the registry transaction package. The `RXACT` subkey contains a single, unnamed, REG_NONE type variable. This variable contains a set of three DWORD values, one of which seems to change between installations, the other two of which don't seem to change. The function of these values is unknown, although a guess is that the password-encryption algorithm uses them. Maybe and maybe not.

TRACKING PASSWORD CHANGES...

Sometimes you'll need to determine who has changed a password. This can be useful for managing security. The following steps are used on a standard Windows XP server to determine who changed a specific password. In this example, we wish to track the system administrator's password modifications, but these same techniques can be applied to any user by substituting the user's SID value for 000001F4 in the following example. The following example pertains to Windows 2000 Server, Windows 2000 Professional, XP Professional, and .NET Server.

1. In Administrative Tools, select Local Security Policy. Then select Security Settings ➤ Local Policies ➤ Audit Policy on the left side of the Security Settings tree. Set Audit Object Access in the Policy list on the right to Audit the Attempts: Success and Failure.

2. Using RegEdit, select the SAM key in HKEY_LOCAL_MACHINE and use Edit ➤ Permissions to set Full Control for the Administrators local group (this may already be set in Windows XP). Check Change Permissions on Existing Subkeys.

3. Navigate to HKEY_LOCAL_MACHINE\SAM\SAM\Domains\Account\Users\000001F4 (or go to the subkey for the desired user.) Select Edit ➤ Permissions, then click the Advanced button and add the Administrators local group to the list. Enable both Successful and Failed auditing for Set Value. Also check the "Replace auditing entries on all child objects with entries shown here that apply to child objects" option.

Once you've made these changes, whenever a change is made to the Administrator account, the change will be placed in the audit log.

Security

Security? What is security? First, it is not something to depend on in your old age, that's assured!

In the HKEY_LOCAL_MACHINE\Security key, we find another key that normally only the system has access to. As with the SAM, discussed previously, you can change the access rights to the Security subkey to allow you (the administrator) to browse and (if you are daring, stupid, or both) modify items.

To change the access rights to Security, select it in RegEdit and click the Edit menu's Permissions selection. In the Registry Key Permissions dialog box, select your user account. In the Type of Access list, select Full Control, and then click OK. It is imperative to be careful: changing something improperly can lead to disaster.

CACHE

Windows XP is able to cache from 0 to 50 previous successful logons locally. This is typically done on systems where a domain controller is used to validate logons and security. Sometimes (it happens to all of us) a domain controller is not available, and then it is still possible to provisionally log on the user, using locally stored logon credentials.

NOTE   *The number of cached logons defaults to 10; however, it may be set to any number between 0 and 50.*

When the domain controller is unavailable and the user can be logged on using the cache, the following message appears:

A domain controller for your domain could not be contacted. You have been logged on using cached account information. Changes to your profile since you last logged on may not be available.

If caching has been disabled or a user's logon information is not in the cache, this message is displayed:

The system cannot log you on now because the domain <*name of domain*> is not available.

The Cache subkey (which is not found in Windows XP Home Edition) holds 11 cache entries (or more, or fewer). One of these entries is NL$Control, which contains the cached entry of the currently logged-on user.

NOTE   *With RegEdit, you are able to see both the hexadecimal values and an ANSI character representation, which is readable even with UNICODE characters.*

The other entries in the Cache key are named NL$1 through NL$10. Each entry contains logon information for one of the previous 10 people who logged on to the computer.

NOTE   *The 10 previous logged-on users are unique users. If a user logs on twice, there will be only one entry in the cache—each entry in the cache is for a unique user account. Any entry that has not been used will contain zeros.*

POLICY

Psst, hey buddy, you want to buy some insurance?

No, not that type of policy! The Policy subkey contains security settings for users, groups, and other components.

A number of subkeys are located under the `Policy` key. In Windows XP, these subkeys include the following (again, your system may not possess all of these objects):

Accounts	DefQuota
Domains	KerLogoff
KerMaxR	KerMaxT
KerMinT	KerOpts
KerProxy	PolAcDmN
PolAcDmS	PolAdtEv
PolAdtFL	PolAdtLg
PolDnDDN	PolDnDmG
PolDnTrN	PolEfDat
PolMod	PolPrDmN
PolPrDmS	PolRevision
PolSecretEncryptionKey	PolState
QuAbsMax	QuAbsMin
SecDesc	Secrets

Each subkey (excluding `Accounts`, `Domains`, and `Secrets`) is constructed in virtually the same manner: a single, unnamed data variable of type REG_NONE. This data variable will contain a binary value, the length of which depends on the entry's purpose.

The `Accounts` subkey will contain information on perhaps six or more different SIDs. Most of these SIDs are listed in Table 17.3 (although each system's entries may vary), along with their descriptions. Note the changes to security and the introduction of the SID S-1-5-11 with Windows NT 4 Service Pack 3.

NOTE   *The S-1-2-32 entries are not found in Windows XP Home Edition.*

TABLE 17.3: SOME USERS LISTED IN THE ACCOUNTS SUBKEY

SUBKEY	PRESENT IN WINDOWS 2000	PRESENT IN WINDOWS XP	DESCRIPTION
S-1-1-0	✓	✓	(Everyone)
S-1-5-11	✓	✓	Authenticated users; only found in Windows NT 4 with Windows NT Service Pack 3 and later
S-1-5-19		✓	The local computer's service account

Continued on next page

TABLE 17.3: SOME USERS LISTED IN THE ACCOUNTS SUBKEY

SUBKEY	PRESENT IN WINDOWS 2000	PRESENT IN WINDOWS XP	DESCRIPTION
S-1-5-20		✓	The computer's network service account
S-1-5-21...		✓	One for each user account that has been defined
S-1-2-32-544	✓	✓	BUILTIN\ADMINISTRATORS
S-1-2-32-545	✓	✓	BUILTIN\USERS
S-1-2-32-546	✓	✓	BUILTIN\GUESTS
S-1-2-32-547	✓	✓	BUILTIN\POWER USERS
S-1-2-32-548	✓	✓	BUILTIN\ACCOUNT OPERATORS
S-1-2-32-549	✓	✓	BUILTIN\SERVER OPERATORS
S-1-2-32-550	✓	✓	BUILTIN\PRINT OPERATORS
S-1-2-32-551	✓	✓	BUILTIN\BACKUP OPERATORS
S-1-2-32-552			BUILTIN\REPLICATOR

The following information is contained in most subkeys described in Table 17.3:

ActSysAc   A DWORD value, stored as binary (REG_BINARY) data; values range from 0x00000001 to an undetermined maximum. This field seems to be bitmapped, though no explanation of its use or possible values has yet to be found. Not found in all Policy\Accounts subkeys.

Privilgs   A variable-length binary value, not found in all Policy\Accounts subkeys.

SecDesc   A variable-length binary value, serving as the object's security descriptor.

Sid   A binary representation of the SID value for the subkey.

In some versions of Windows, the Domains subkey will contain information on typically only one domain. The Domains key will have a subkey for the domain that the computer belongs to, named with the domain server's SID. Other versions may contain zero-length data.

In server versions of Windows, this subkey typically contains four subkeys:

SecDesc   A binary value, probably variable length.

Sid   A binary representation of the SID value for the subkey; the SID value is also used as the subkey name.

TrDmName   A binary value containing both binary data and the name of the domain.

TrDmPxOf   A DWORD value.

NOTE   A computer that is the domain server (for example, a PDC in NT 4) will not have an entry in the Domains *subkey.*

HOW DO I IDENTIFY DYNAMIC REGISTRY KEYS IN THE REGISTRY?

Permanent keys, those not created at boot, are identified in the key at HKEY_LOCAL_MACHINE\System\ CurrentControlSet\Control\hivelist. The one exception is HKEY_CURRENT_USER, which is located at %SystemRoot%\Profiles\UserName.

The value entries identify the registry keys. All are type REG_SZ. The following list shows the HKEY_LOCAL_MACHINE keys.

Permanent Key	Typical Default Value	Comment
\REGISTRY\MACHINE\HARDWARE	(None)	The HKEY_LOCAL_ MACHINE\ Hardware key, re-created upon boot
\REGISTRY\MACHINE\SAM	\Device\Harddisk 0\ Partition1\WINNT\ System32\Config\SAM	HKEY_LOCAL_MACHINE\SAM
\REGISTRY\MACHINE\SECURITY	\Device\Harddisk 0\ Partition1\WINNT\ System32\Config\Security	HKEY_LOCAL_MACHINE\Security
\REGISTRY\MACHINE\SOFTWARE	\Device\Harddisk 0\ Partition1\WINNT\ System32\Config\Software	HKEY_LOCAL_MACHINE\Software
\REGISTRY\MACHINE\SYSTEM	\Device\Harddisk 0\ Partition1\WINNT\ System32\Config\System	HKEY_LOCAL_MACHINE\System
\REGISTRY\USER\.DEFAULT	\Device\Harddisk 0\ Partition1\WINNT\ System32\Config\Default	HKEY_USERS\.DEFAULT
\REGISTRY\USER\Security ID (SID)	\Device\Harddisk 0\Par- tition1\WINNT\Profiles\ Username\ntuser.dat	The current user profile; also holds entries for services running under user accounts
\REGISTRY\USER\Security ID (SID)_ Classes	\Device\HarddiskVolume1\ WINNT\Profiles\Username\ Local Settings\Applica- tion Data\Microsoft\ Windows\UsrClass.dat	The current user's classes defini- tion (see Chapter 15, on HKEY_CLASSES_ROOT, for more information)

Note that in Windows XP Home Edition, the path is similar to those listed above, but you must replace Harddisk 0 with HarddiskVolume1 and replace WINNT with Windows.

The Secrets subkey will contain secret information. (Quiet, someone may be listening to this.) There are a number of subkeys in Secrets. Big users of the Secrets subkey include Windows and IIS.

Due to the nature of the data (no, not that it is secret, just that it is meaningless except to the application or system that is using it), I won't cover it.

NOTE   Secret data is specific to the application that has stored the data there, and generally it is not meaningful to users.

RXACT

The RXACT subkey seems to contain an un-initialized value of RXACT that is stored in SAM. This implies that the information stored in the SAM's version RXACT is dynamic in nature.

SAM

SECURITY\SAM is an alias to the SAM\SAM subkey, which I covered previously.

Software

The HKEY_LOCAL_MACHINE\Software key contains a collection of subkeys for various installed components and applications. Any application can create its own subkey (most do so when they install and store items such as file pointers, user initialization, and so forth), although most often subkeys are based on the organization producing the software, with further subkeys for different applications. For example, Microsoft's subkeys might look like this (actually they are much more complex):

```
HKEY_LOCAL_MACHINE\Software\Microsoft
HKEY_LOCAL_MACHINE\Software\Microsoft\DrWatson
HKEY_LOCAL_MACHINE\Software\Microsoft\Exchange
HKEY_LOCAL_MACHINE\Software\Microsoft\IE4
HKEY_LOCAL_MACHINE\Software\Microsoft\Internet Audio
```

Each of these subkeys will have one or more entries. (DrWatson has 12 entries with data values for different user settings and filenames, set using DRWTSN32.exe.)

Figure 17.12 shows the HKEY_LOCAL_MACHINE\Software key on a computer that has been running Windows XP for several months and has a number of software packages installed.

FIGURE 17.12

The HKEY_LOCAL_
MACHINE\Software
key can become large
if there are many
installed applications
and system compo-
nents.

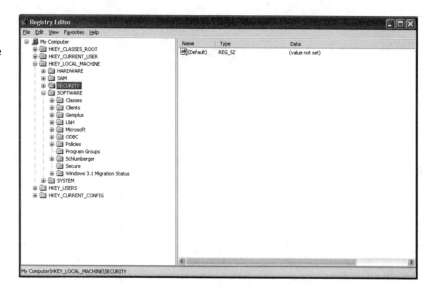

Now, you may think that I should say more about the HKEY_LOCAL_MACHINE\Software key here in this chapter; but no, I won't. There is just too much really good stuff in HKEY_LOCAL_MACHINE\Software to not devote a complete chapter to it, so I've dedicated the next chapter (Chapter 18) to this key.

System

HKEY_LOCAL_MACHINE\System contains the system configurations. Subkeys include:

ControlSet001   A copy of the current control set.

ControlSet002   The Last Known Good control set used to boot from if there is a problem booting from the current control set.

CurrentControlSet   The control set used to boot from.

LastKnownGoodRecovery   The control set used for a recovery.

DISK   Contains information about drive letters, volume sets, RAID (mirrored, stripe, and stripe with parity), and CD-ROM and drive mapping. Windows XP does not use or have this object.

MountedDevices   Contains information about currently available virtual devices (another way of looking at drives!) and drives, including CD-ROM, hard, and floppy disks.

Select   Contains information about which control set is used for what purpose.

Setup   Contains information about Windows XP's installation.

As with HKEY_LOCAL_MACHINE\Software, HKEY_LOCAL_MACHINE\System is a very important key, and therefore I'll cover it fully in Chapter 19. No sense in overdoing it here.

Chapter 18

Introduction to HKEY_LOCAL_MACHINE\ Software

THE HKEY_LOCAL_MACHINE\Software key contains information about installed software on your system. It also contains information about Windows XP although the HKEY_LOCAL_MACHINE\System key contains Windows XP information as well.

HKEY_LOCAL_MACHINE\Software has at least 11 sections. Each of the sections varies in size from small (Secure usually has nothing in it at all!) to huge (Microsoft has settings for every Microsoft application installed, and for some components of Windows also.)

In this chapter, I have tried to cover as many keys, values, and objects as possible. To cover *everything* would make this chapter totally unmanageable.

◆ Classes

◆ Clients

◆ Microsoft

◆ ODBC

◆ Policies

◆ Program Groups

◆ Secure

◆ Voice

Looking inside HKEY_LOCAL_MACHINE\Software

As I mentioned, in a typical installation, HKEY_LOCAL_MACHINE\Software has 11 or 12 different subkeys:

NOTE   *The contents of your* HKEY_LOCAL_MACHINE\Software *hive will vary greatly depending on what software is installed on your computer. On the machine used while writing this book, Windows XP Advanced Server, Microsoft Office XP, and Developer's Studio were installed.*

- Classes

- Clients

- Gemplus

- L&H

- Microsoft

- ODBC

- Policies

- Program Groups

- Schlumberger

- Secure

- Voice

- Windows 3.1 Migration Status

For many installations, there will be additional subkeys under HKEY_LOCAL_MACHINE\Software. For example:

- 3Com, or the supplier of the computer's NIC

- Adobe, for users of Adobe's software, such as Acrobat Reader and PageMaker

- Symantec, for anyone who uses Symantec antivirus software

- INTEL, for software such as the Intel 3D Scalability Toolkit

- Intuit, if you use their accounting or tax software

- Qualcomm, if you use one of their e-mail or communications products

Of course, only the number and types of software packages installed on the target computer limit the number of subkeys. Go hog wild, install tons of stuff, and you'll have a big HKEY_LOCAL_MACHINE\Software subkey.

WARNING   *You have backed up your registry before starting this chapter, right?*

Be cautious! Blow a subkey or value, and you probably will have to reinstall the affected product. If you're really unlucky, you might also have to reinstall Windows XP, if the application's install program doesn't properly repair the registry. If you find you have to reinstall because you didn't have a good registry backup, follow these steps:

1. Reinstall the product without uninstalling the original installation. If this works, you may be able to recover your user settings, profiles, and such. If this doesn't work, try step 2.

2. Uninstall the product and then reinstall. This probably will cause you to lose the user settings, profiles, and such, but that's life. If this doesn't work, try step 3.

3. Install a second copy of Windows XP, and install the application on the second copy of Windows XP into the product's original directory. If the product works on the second copy of Windows XP, try the first copy again. If the product still doesn't work on the first copy but does work on the second copy, you'll have to restore everything from backups or reinstall everything from scratch. Either way, you are in for a long, long night.

Classes

The `HKEY_LOCAL_MACHINE\Software\Classes` subkey is a mapping of the `HKEY_CLASSES_ROOT` registry hive. This ensures that both have the same entries.

The `HKEY_CLASSES_ROOT` hive is described in Chapter 3 and in Chapter 15 (which is devoted entirely to this hive). The information in these chapters applies to all entries in `HKEY_LOCAL_MACHINE\Software\Classes`.

Clients

The `HKEY_LOCAL_MACHINE\Software\Clients` subkey contains information used by Windows for e-mail and related services. Users who have not installed any additional e-mail services will find the Microsoft Exchange client defined as their mail provider—Exchange is a default component of Windows XP.

A Microsoft Internet Explorer installation includes features such as:

Contacts   An integral component of Outlook Express and Outlook, Contacts provides a powerful tool for managing contacts and names. Contacts manages names, addresses (including e-mail addresses), phone numbers, and so on.

EnvelopeHost   Installed by Office, EnvelopeHost is a utility to create envelopes from each of the Office products.

Mail   Internet Explorer 5 installs a product called Outlook Express, which is a scaled-down version of Microsoft's e-mail client, Outlook.

Media   The Media feature includes some settings for the Windows media player program.

News   The News client is a component in Outlook Express. Newsgroups are public (and private) forums on the Internet where users are able to speak their minds on various topics.

StartMenuInternet   This is Internet Explorer's startup command and icon definition.

A full installation of Microsoft's Outlook would include even more components, including:

Calendar   A component of Microsoft Outlook, the Calendar provides a powerful tool for managing time and appointments. Correctly configured, meetings can be scheduled, resources may be reserved, and so on.

Internet Call   NetMeeting is a tool used to hold online, interactive meetings.

Typical subkeys found in HKEY_LOCAL_MACHINE\Software\Clients might include those shown in Figure 18.1, which shows a computer that has Hotmail, the full version of Outlook, and the default Outlook Express.

FIGURE 18.1

Clients can include products from more than one software vendor.

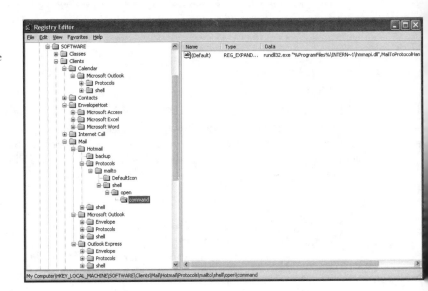

Gemplus

Windows XP supports Gemplus SmartCards. For more information on these devices, visit www.gemplus.com.

L&H

Windows XP supports text-to-speech services. The L&H TTS3000 system may be installed. This software is available from Microsoft at http://www.microsoft.com/msagent/downloads.htm. This functionality is very useful for seeing-impaired users.

Microsoft

The `Microsoft` subkey in `HKEY_LOCAL_MACHINE\Software` is the largest of the subkeys in the Software key. One typical installation of a Windows XP server, with a number of applications from Microsoft installed, has the following subkeys under `HKEY_LOCAL_MACHINE\Software\Microsoft`.

NOTE *Note that some of these entries are only available on servers such as DhcpServer and WINS. Protocol entries are only available when the protocol is installed.*

`.NetFramework` Microsoft's .NET Framework is their attempt to create a better development environment for applications that run in the distributed environment that the Internet offers.

`Access Runtime` Contains information about Microsoft Access.

`ACS` Found in Windows 2000 and later versions, this object contains information about SNMP's ACS functionality.

`Active Accessibility` Contains support for Microsoft Active Accessibility (MSAA). MSAA improves the access of command bars.

Active Setup   Currently used with Internet Explorer as well as many other Windows components, Active Setup is the installation process for applications distributed by the Internet.

AD7Metrics   Contains information about Microsoft Scripting and debugging.

Ads   Found in Windows 2000 and later versions, this object contains information about the Active Directory server functions.

Advanced INF Setup   Contains support for setups based on .inf files, used with Internet Explorer and some Internet Explorer components, such as Java.

ALG   Contains information about Microsoft's FTP Client/Server Protocol. ALG is application-level gateway.

ASP.NET   Contains information about Microsoft's ASP (Active Server Pages) .NET facilities.

AsyncMac   Also known as AsyMAC, this object contains an NDIS 3.0 MAC (Media Access Control) driver used with serial communications (RAS).

AudioCompressionManager   Contains support for the Microsoft Audio Compression Manager system.

BOOTPMibAgent   Found only in later versions of Windows, this object contains information about support for the BootP MIB (Management Information Base) Agent.

Browser   Contains the configuration for the Computer Browser Service.

Catalog42   Contains information about Microsoft's IIS web browser configuration.

ClipArt Gallery   Contains information about clip art objects installed. Typically, but not always, installed with products such as Microsoft Office.

Code Store Database   Used with objects such as Java.

COM3   Found only in later versions of Windows, this object contains information about COM (Common Object Model) version 3 and the Active Template Library.

Command Processor   Found only in later versions of Windows, this object contains initialization parameters for all command-prompt sessions.

Conferencing   Supports Microsoft NetMeeting, a virtual conferencing/meeting system.

Connection Manager Administration Kit   Found only in later versions of Windows, this object contains information about the Connection Manager Administration Kit (CMAK), used to manage RAS connections.

CRS   Contains the configuration for the Content Replication System.

Cryptography   Found only in later versions of Windows, this object contains information about each of the installed cryptography services. It contains the management for the Microsoft CryptoAPI (Cryptographic Application Program Interface).

CTF   This object contains information about Microsoft's Component Testing Facility (CTF). This system is used by developers and software testers to automate COM/DCOM components testing.

DataAccess Found only in later versions of Windows, this object contains information about data access providers for HTTP, HTTPS, IIS, LDAP, and others.

DataFactory Found in Windows 2000 and later versions, this object contains information about OLE data factory handlers.

DeviceManager Found in Windows 2000 and later versions, this object supports information about bus types (not fully implemented in Windows 2000) and troubleshooters.

Dfrg Found in Windows 2000 and later versions, this object contains information about the disk defragmenter, a standard Windows feature.

DFS This object contains information about Microsoft's Distributed File System, installed under Windows 2000 Server and a component that may be installed under Windows XP.

DfsHost This object contains information about Microsoft's Distributed File System, installed under Windows 2000 Server and a component that may be installed under Windows XP.

DhcpServer Found in Windows 2000 and later versions, this object supports the DHCP (Dynamic Host Configuration Protocol) server functionality.

DhcpMibAgent Found in Windows 2000 and later versions, this object supports DHCP MIB.

DHCPServer Contains the support and configuration for DHCP (Dynamic Host Configuration Protocol), which, in a nutshell, allows dynamic (automatic) allocation of IP addresses in a TCP/IP network.

Direct3D Contains Microsoft's high-performance 3-D drawing API.

DirectDraw Found in Windows 2000 and later versions, this object contains information about the high-speed Direct3D support.

DirectInput Found in Windows 2000 and later versions, this object contains information about high-speed input interfaces.

DirectMusic Found in Windows 2000 and later versions, this object contains information about the high-performance music player.

DirectPlay Contains Microsoft's high-performance engine that provides a way for multiplayer games to communicate using networks.

DirectPlay8 Contains Microsoft's high-performance engine that provides a way for multiplayer games to communicate using networks.

DirectPlayNATHelp Contains Microsoft's high-performance engine that provides a way for multiplayer games to provide help.

DirectX Contains Microsoft's I/O system.

DownloadManager Contains a system that allows files being transferred by Internet Explorer to be downloaded in background mode and to be suspended and resumed as desired.

Driver Signing   Found in Windows 2000 and later versions, this object contains information about drivers and driver authentication.

DrWatson   Contains a system for providing information on application and system faults.

DRM   Contains a system for providing support for DRM (Digital Rights Management).

EAPOL   Contains a system for providing support for EAPOL (Extensible Authentication Control Protocol over LANs).

EnterpriseCertificates   Found in Windows 2000 and later versions, this object contains information about various enterprise certificate authorities.

ESENT   Found in Windows 2000 and later versions, this object contains information for the ESENT (Extensible Storage Engine).

EventSystem   Found in Windows 2000 and later versions, this object contains information for the event management system.

Exchange   Contains Microsoft's default e-mail client.

Fax   Found in Windows 2000 and later versions, this object contains information about the built-in Windows fax system.

FrontPage   Contains Microsoft's application to develop and manage Internet Web pages.

Home Publishing   Found in Windows 2000 and later versions, this object contains information about Microsoft Home Publishing.

HostMIB   Found in Windows 2000 and later versions, this object contains information for the Host MIB.

HTML Help Collections   Found in Windows 2000 and later versions, this object contains information about HTML help.

IASAgent   Found in Windows 2000 and later versions, this object contains information about the Internet Authentication Services agent.

IE Setup   Found in Windows 2000 and later versions, this object contains information about setup for Internet Explorer.

IE4   Contains Microsoft's Internet Explorer 4.

IGMPMibAgent   Found in Windows 2000 and later versions, this object contains information about the Internet Group Management Protocol.

InetMgr   The Internet Service Manager, used to manage Microsoft IIS.

Inetsrv   Contains Microsoft IIS.

InetStp   Contains configuration information for Microsoft IIS.

InfoViewer   Contains Microsoft Information Viewer, a data and information retrieval system, typically used with Microsoft TechNet and MSDN.

Intelligent Search   Contains support for the Microsoft Intelligent Search, part of Microsoft Office XP.

IntelliPoint   Contains support for the Microsoft IntelliMouse, an enhanced pointing device.

InteractiveMusic   No, not karaoke. Microsoft Interactive Music is a system used to deliver music over the Internet.

Internet Account Manager   Used to manage e-mail accounts.

Internet Audio   Audio may be sent to clients on the Internet using a number of different compression techniques, such as CCITT, Lernout & Hauspie, and Microsoft's encoding.

Internet Connection Wizard   The Internet Connection Wizard automates the steps used to connect a new user to the Internet.

Internet Domains   Found in Windows 2000 and later versions, this object contains information about special domains. A typical default entry in this object consists of a number of data items for the Hotmail e-mail system.

Internet Explorer   Contains Microsoft Internet Explorer, currently version 6.

Internet Mail and News   Contains Internet Mail and News settings.

Internet Shopper   Contains Microsoft's client Internet commerce system.

IpInIp   Found in Windows 2000 and later versions, this object contains information about IpInIp.

IPMulticastMibAgent   Found in Windows 2000 and later versions, this object contains information about the IP Multicast MIB agent.

IPSec   Feature support for IP Security.

IPXMibAgent   Found in Windows 2000 and later versions, this object contains information about the IPX MIB agent.

Java VM   Contains the Java virtual machine configuration.

Jet   Contains the Microsoft Access database access engine, used by Microsoft Office and other applications.

KeyRing   Contains a small, usually metal, often lost, object used to hold keys. Or contains IIS's Key Manager program.

Languages   Used with Microsoft's Internet browser and server support, used to define file types (such as HTM, HTML, STM, STML, and ALX).

LANManagerMIB2Agent   Found in Windows 2000 and later versions, this object contains information about the LAN Manager MIB agent.

LanmanServer   Manages server support for the SMB (Server Message Block) protocol, the core of Microsoft networking.

LanmanWorkstation   Manages client support for the SMB protocol.

Machine Debug Manager   Works to help define which processes should be debugged and which should be ignored.

MediaPlayer   Found in Windows 2000 and later versions, this object contains information about Microsoft Media Player.

Microsoft Chat Character Editor   Contains an add-on graphics editor for Microsoft Chat characters.

Microsoft Comic Chat   Contains Internet Chat, an interactive conferencing system with a graphic interface (using comic characters).

Microsoft Expedia   Contains Pocket Streets 98, Microsoft's road atlas program.

Microsoft FrontPage   Contains Microsoft's Internet web page publishing utility.

Microsoft Image Composer   Contains Microsoft's graphic- and image-editing application.

Microsoft Reference   Contains a component of Microsoft office that provides a complete reference section.

MMC   Found in Windows 2000 and later versions, this object contains information about the Microsoft Management Console.

MMCtlsForIE   Contains multimedia controls for Internet Explorer.

Mobile   Found in Windows 2000 and later versions, this object contains information about mobile or portable operations.

MOS   Contains configurations for Microsoft Office's Outlook and MSNAudio.

MosTrace   Found in Windows 2000 and later versions, this object contains support for gathering debug information.

Mr. Enigma   Function is unknown. Only found on Windows XP systems.

MSDAIPP   Found in Windows 2000 and later versions, this object contains information for the Microsoft Internet Publishing Provider feature.

MSDTC   Found in Windows 2000 and later versions, this object contains information about Microsoft DTC.

MSE   Found in Windows 2000 and later versions, this object contains information about the Microsoft Script Editor.

MSFTPSVC   Found in Windows 2000 and later versions, this object contains information about the Microsoft FTP service.

MSLicensing   Found in Windows 2000 and later versions, this object contains information used by Microsoft Terminal Services licensing.

MSMQ   Found in Windows 2000 and later versions, this object contains information about Microsoft Message Queue Server.

MSTTS   Found in Windows 2000 and later versions, this object contains information about the Microsoft speech engine (TTS is short for text-to-speech).

Multimedia   Contains the configurations for Active Movie and DirectX components.

Ncpa   Contains the configuration information for the Network Control Panel applet.

NdisWan   Contains the Network Device Interface Standard, used with a WAN (wide area network), such as the Internet.

NetBIOS   Contains the Network Basic Input/Output System, used to control basic network communications, including the software interface and naming conventions.

NetBT   Contains the configuration for NetBIOS when implemented over TCP/IP.

NetDDE   Contains the configuration for Network Dynamic Data Exchange.

NetSh   Found in Windows 2000 and later versions, this object contains information about performance managing for the networking scheduler.

NetShow   Found in Windows 2000 and later versions, this object contains information about the Microsoft Net Show feature.

Non-Driver Signing   Found in Windows 2000 and later versions, this object contains information about signing of non-driver files.

NTDebuggers   Found in Windows 2000 and later versions, this object contains information about the Windows NT debuggers.

NTDS   Found in Windows 2000 and later versions, this object contains information for the Windows NT directory service.

NwlnkIpx   Contains support for the Novell NetWare IPX protocol.

NwlnkNb   Contains the configuration for the NetWare network browser.

NwlnkSpx   Contains the configuration for the NetWare SPX protocol.

Office   Contains support for Microsoft Office (whichever version is installed), typically Office 2000 (version 9.0) or Office XP (version 10.0).

Ole   Contains basic configuration information for Object Linking and Embedding.

OS/2 Subsystem for NT   Contains basic support for OS/2 standards.

OSPFMibAgent   Found in Windows 2000 and later versions, this object contains information about the OSPF MIB agent.

Outlook Express   Contains Microsoft's basic e-mail system, installed by default with Internet Explorer.

Pegasus   Contains winged horse of Greek mythology, or support for Windows CE 2.x.

Protected Storage System Provider   Contains an inaccessible subkey used to protect user security.

RasAuto or **RasAutoDial**   Contains configurations for the Remote Access Service AutoDial facility, used to automatically connect to a remote network.

RAS   Contains configurations for the Remote Access Service, the dial-in component of Windows Server.

RasMan   Contains the Remote Access Service manager program.

ReferenceTitles   Contains Microsoft Bookshelf (part of Microsoft Office).

RemoteAccess   Contains some settings for RAS (Remote Access Service).

ResKit   The basic setup settings for the Windows XP Resource Kit (either for server or workstation).

Resource Kit   Contains the component settings for the Windows XP Resource Kit.

RFC1156Agent   Found in Windows 2000 and later versions, this object contains information about the MIB for use with network management protocols in TCP/IP-based networks.

RIPMibAgent   Found in Windows 2000 and later versions, this object contains information about the Routing Information Protocol MIB agent.

Router   Found in Windows 2000 and later versions, this object contains information about IP routing.

Rpc   Contains the configuration for Remote Procedure Calls.

RPCLOCATOR   Used to enable RPC applications to perform procedures on multiple remote computers.

Schedule+   Contains settings for Schedule+ or a substitute, such as Outlook or Exchange.

SchedulingAgent   Found in Windows 2000 and later versions, this object contains information about Windows scheduling.

ScrptDbg   Contains Microsoft Office's script debugger settings.

Secure   Found in Windows 2000 and later versions, this object contains information about security.

Shared Tools Location   Found in Windows 2000 and later versions, this object contains information about the location of tools that are shared between more than one application.

Shared Tools   Lists and describes relationships with various Microsoft tools that may be "shared" using OLE.

SNMP_EVENTS   Found in Windows 2000 and later versions, this object contains information about SNMP (Simple Network Management Protocol) events.

SNMPMIB Found in Windows 2000 and later versions, this object contains information about the SNMP MIB.

SpeechAPI or Speech Found in Windows 2000 and later versions, this object contains information about the built-in speech API.

SystemCertificates Contains information about security certificates (used primarily with Internet Explorer).

Tcpip Stores system configurations for TCP/IP. Computer-specific configuration information is stored elsewhere.

TelnetServer Found in Windows 2000 and later versions, this object contains information about the Windows Telnet server.

Tracing Found in Windows 2000 and later versions, this object contains information about event tracing.

Transaction Server Found in Windows 2000 and later versions, this object contains information about Transaction Services.

Tshoot Found in Windows 2000 and later versions, this object contains information about troubleshooting.

User information This object contains information for the Microsoft Office user.

VBA This is where Microsoft Visual Basic for Applications, used with a number of Microsoft products, is configured.

Visual Basic This object contains information about Visual Basic.

VisualScriptEditor This object contains information about the Visual Basic script editor.

VisualStudio Contains the configuration for Microsoft's Visual Studio, the development platform.

W3SVC Found in Windows 2000 and later versions, this object contains information about IIS's web server.

WAB Not "Windows Always Breaks;" this is where the WAB (Windows Address Book), used to manage addresses (different from Outlook's Contacts functionality), is configured.

WBEM Found in Windows 2000 and later versions, this object contains information about Web-Based Enterprise Management.

Windows This is where a number of Windows configuration parameters are set. See the second part of this section for more information on this subkey.

Windows Messaging Subsystem Contains configurations for e-mail.

Windows NT This is where a number of Windows configuration parameters are set. The second part of this section documents this subkey.

`Windows Scripting Host`   Found in Windows 2000 and later versions, this object contains information about scripting (JavaScript or Visual Basic Script).

`Wins`   The Windows Internet Name Service, or WINS, saves configuration information in this subkey.

`WZCSVC`   The Windows WZC Service.

Looking at the previous list, you should realize that there are many more possible subkeys under `Software`—so many possibilities, in fact, that no single source could hope to document them all. Each installed application or component can and often does create a subkey in the `HKEY_LOCAL_MACHINE\Software` key.

Even more interesting and unexplainable is the fact that there are both `Windows` and `Windows NT` sections in `HKEY_LOCAL_MACHINE\Software`. Microsoft came up with `Windows`, then later developed `Windows NT`, and chose to group items whichever way they wanted. Were I to tell you that old stuff was in `Windows` and new stuff was in `Windows NT`, I'd be accused of making it all up (and rightly, I might add). There is little rhyme or reason to the organization and contents of these two subkeys.

Now, let's take a detailed peek into a few of the subkeys found on virtually every Windows XP system.

NOTE   *Some items below are specific to server installations, others are specific to workstation installations, and most are applicable to both servers and workstations. If known, I've indicated which ones are specific to which type of installation.*

Windows

First, I know the questions you are asking right now: Why is configuration for parts of Windows XP included in `HKEY_LOCAL_MACHINE\Software`, and other parts included in other sections of the registry? Why isn't it all consolidated? Why spread it out? Why, oh why, is this so hard to understand?

Well, I can't answer the last question, but I may be able to shed a bit of light on a few of the others. Many of the components included in `HKEY_LOCAL_MACHINE\Software` are components that are or were separate from Windows. For example, Internet Explorer, Font support, and even Explorer are separate from the base operating system. Yes, dear friends, you can run Windows XP without using Explorer—Program Manager is still part of Windows. (No, I'm not going to comment on Windows XP's support for this antiquated user-interface component!)

CURRENTVERSION

Under `HKEY_LOCAL_MACHINE\Software\Microsoft\Windows` is a subkey called `CurrentVersion`. This subkey contains a number of keys defining information about the current installation of Windows. It also contains a large number of subkeys (which I've documented below, in separate sections) for various components of Windows XP.

NOTE   *Many of the settings that were originally found in* `CurrentVersion` *in Windows NT 4 are now found in the subkey* `HKEY_CURRENT_USER\<sid>\Software\Microsoft\Windows\CurrentVersion`. *This move allows customization on a user-by-user basis.*

CURRENTVERSION\ADMINDEBUG

Found in Windows 2000 and later versions, the `AdminDebug` subkey contains information that Windows uses to manage debugging.

CURRENTVERSION\APP MANAGEMENT

Found in Windows 2000 and later versions, the `App Management` subkey contains information that Windows uses to manage various applications. You'll find subkeys for many of the installed programs on the computer here.

CURRENTVERSION\APP PATHS

In a typical installation of Windows XP, you might find as many as 30 or 40 objects in the `App Paths` subkey. A clean installation of Windows XP might have fewer than 10 objects; for example:

- `DIALER.exe`

- `HYPERTRM.exe`

- `PINBALL.exe`

- `WORDPAD.exe`

Even this "minimum" list could be smaller if Hyperterm or Pinball were not installed on the computer.

Each subkey in `App Paths` contains one required entry:

`<No Name>` An unnamed value with a data value containing a string with the fully qualified path of the application, including the application's name and extension, typically `.exe`.
Each subkey may contain one additional entry:

Path An entry with a data value containing a string with the fully qualified path of the application, typically used to locate supporting files, if necessary. Not all `App Paths` subkeys have the `Path` value.

If you must move an application component, check `App Paths` to see if the application is listed. If it is, when moving the component, make sure that the `App Paths` entries are updated to reflect the application's new location.

CURRENTVERSION\APPLETS

Found in Windows 2000 and later versions, the `Applets` subkey contains information that Windows uses to manage installed applets.

CURRENTVERSION\CONTROL PANEL

Found in Windows 2000 and later versions, the `Control Panel` subkey contains information that Windows uses to manage the system Control Panel.

CURRENTVERSION\CONTROLS FOLDER

The `Controls Folder` subkey holds a single binary value. The Control Panel uses information from this value to configure the display of Control Panel applets, including title information.

A number of Control Panel applets may also include subkeys in the `Controls Folder` subkey. For instance, when applets use special handlers, typically done with OLE, a mapping of tabs in the Control Panel applet to OLE server is found in `Controls Folder`.

Here is an example of the subkey for the Display Control Panel applet:

Display   Might contain an entry to manage optional components in the Display applet's main window.

In addition to the above example, other Control Panel applets, such as Desk and Device, can and do use the `Controls Folder` subkey.

CURRENTVERSION\CSCSETTINGS

Found in Windows 2000 and later versions, the `CSCSettings` subkey contains information that Windows uses to manage CSC (Client Side Caching) settings.

CURRENTVERSION\DYNAMIC DIRECTORY

Found in Windows 2000 and later versions, the `Dynamic Directory` subkey contains information that Windows uses to manage the Dynamic Directory Service.

CURRENTVERSION\EXPLORER

Microsoft Explorer, which functions as the user interface for Windows XP, has a number of configuration options. Some options are set with various configuration dialog boxes; others must be set using the Registry Editor.

AlwaysUnloadDLL   Contains a single, unnamed string value, with a value of either 1 or 0.

AutoComplete   Contains a single string value, named `UseAutoComplete`. The default value is Yes.

BrowseNewProcess   Contains a single string value, named `BrowseNewProcess`. The default value is Yes.

CSSFilters   Contains a number of entries primarily for Internet Explorer. These entries are for OLE controls used for visual effects, such as Blur, Invert, Glow, and Shadow.

Desktop   Typically contains three entries, for `Inbox`, `Recycle Bin`, and `The Internet`. These are default items on the Desktop.

FileTypesPropertySheetHook   Used by Internet Explorer, the entries in this subkey are used to display files, often containing MIME-encoded objects.

FindExtensions   Used by Internet Explorer, Outlook, and the Windows Address Book to manage their find functionality.

MyComputer   Used with the Start menu (and elsewhere). Other entries found on some computers include dial-up networking and mobile devices.

    NameSpace\Controls   Contains the Control Panel.

    NameSpace\Printers   Contains the Printers Panel.

NewShortcutHandlers   Used to manage items, such as property sheets.

RemoteComputer   Contains a subkey called `NameSpace`, which includes information on remote printers.

Shell Folders   Used by the system to configure part of a user's profile. User profiles consist of two parts: the user's private items and a second common profile called All Users. The `Shell Folders` subkey contains four keys:

Common Desktop   Contains a pathname to the profiles directory. On many systems this will be `C:\Documents and Settings\All Users\Desktop`.

Common Programs   Contains a pathname to the common programs directory. On many systems, this will be `C:\Documents and Settings\All Users\Start Menu\Programs`.

Common Start Menu   Contains a pathname to the Start menu. On many systems, this will be `C:\Documents and Settings\All Users\Start Menu`.

Common Startup   Contains a pathname to the `Start menu\Programs` directory. On many systems, this will be `C:\Documents and Settings\ All Users\Start Menu\Programs\Startup`.

ShellExecuteHooks   Used by Internet Explorer to manage the execution of shell extensions.

SmallIcons   On the Plus tab of the Display Properties dialog box, the Use Large Icons check box state. String values allowed are `YES` and `NO`.

Streams   Could be small rivers, seasonally may be dry. More likely, contains the Taskbar and toolbar and only one subkey:

Desktop   Two entries, `Default Taskbar` and `Default Toolbars`, are found in this subkey.

Thumbnail View   Contains one entry, called `AutoExtract`. The value will be either `0x1` or `0x0`.

Tips   Contains money or value given to a person who serves you, or words of advice. Okay, really. Windows displays tips on a dialog box when a user logs on, although most users turn off the tips as their second or third action after installing Windows. Fifty tips exist in Windows XP by default, but you could add more. And a tip for you: If you add more, Windows won't know about them; Windows expects 50, and uses 50.

User Shell Folders   Contains the folders used for users. Four keys exist in this subkey:

Common Desktop   Contains the path `%SystemRoot%\Profiles\All Users\Desktop`. This provides a path to the common Desktop for users.

Common Programs   Contains the path `%SystemRoot%\Profiles\All Users\Start Menu\Programs`. This provides a path to the common `Start Menu\Programs` directory for users.

Common Start Menu   Contains the path `%SystemRoot%\Profiles\All Users\Start Menu`. This provides a path to the common `Start Menu` directory for users.

Common Startup   Contains the path `%SystemRoot%\Profiles\All Users\Start Menu\Programs\Startup`. This provides a path to the common `Start Menu\Programs\Startup` directory for users.

User Shell Folders\New   Usually empty; contains a location for new common objects for users.

VolumeCaches   Empty, except for the following subkeys:

Active Setup Temp Folders   The description reads: "These files should no longer be needed. They were originally created by a setup program that is no longer running."

Downloaded Program Files   The description reads: "Downloaded Program Files are ActiveX controls and Java applets downloaded automatically from the Internet when you view certain pages. They are temporarily stored in the Downloaded Program Files folder on your hard disk."

Internet Cache Files   The description reads: "The Temporary Internet Files folder contains web pages stored on your hard disk for quick viewing. Your personalized settings for web pages will be left intact."

WindowsUpdate   Contains a single entry called **UpdateURL**, which contains a reference to the Windows Internet Connection Wizard.

CURRENTVERSION\EXTENSIONS

The **Extensions** subkey contains keys that define what program opens a specific file type. Similar to the **Classes** subkeys found elsewhere in the registry, **Extensions** is only for added-on, non-Microsoft applications. The **Extensions** subkey shows, in File Manager, the application that a user prefers to open a certain file with—for example, "Open .rtf files with Word for Windows." Explorer, Windows NT 4, Windows 2000, and Windows XP do not appear to use this subkey.

NOTE   Why have this in the registry if it is not used? Simple: Many legacy (older) applications will attempt to update the subkey even though it is not used. Also, since it is possible to use Program Manager with Windows XP (yes, progman.exe *is still part of Windows XP!), there actually is a potential use for these entries.*

CURRENTVERSION\EXTSHELLVIEWS

Found in Windows 2000 and later versions, the **ExtShellViews** subkey contains information that Windows uses to manage how a view is presented to the user: as either a web view or a thumbnail view.

CURRENTVERSION\GROUP POLICY

Found in Windows 2000 and later versions, the **Group Policy** subkey contains information that Windows uses to manage groups. Some of the Windows Active Directory information about groups is stored in this location. Not available in Windows XP Home Edition.

CURRENTVERSION\H323TSP

Found in Windows 2000 and later versions, the **H323TSP** subkey contains information that Windows uses to manage H323 teleconferencing.

CurrentVersion\Installer

Found in Windows 2000 and later versions, the `Installer` subkey contains information that Windows uses to manage the Microsoft Office installer program. Typically the value is the Windows path `C:\Windows\System32`.

CurrentVersion\Internet Settings

The `Internet Settings` subkey consists of settings used with the Internet, primarily with Internet Explorer. Two keys present in this key include `ActiveXCache`, which points to a directory where Internet Explorer may cache ActiveX (OLE) controls; and `CodeBaseSearchPath`, which points to a Microsoft site where common code is downloadable.

In addition to these two keys, `Internet Settings` also contains these subkeys:

Accepted Documents   Some documents are accepted as safe. These include Word, Excel, and PowerPoint documents. (No, there is no need to tell me about all those nasty Word viruses. I know.) Also considered safe are the GIF, bitmap, and JPEG image types.

ActiveX Cache   A second set of ActiveX control cache directories. Two entries in this subkey provide two locations to store ActiveX controls installed on the user's system.

Cache   Contains Internet Explorer's cache parameters: cleanup factor, interval and time, a debug flag, freshness, and persistence. These factors are set in Internet Explorer's Settings dialog box, on the General tab.

Cache\Paths   Internet Explorer stores web pages and objects in a series of cache directories. The default is to have four cache directories, though the number of cache directories can be modified if necessary. For each cache directory, a subkey named `pathn` (where n is the number of cache directories) is created. Each of the path subkeys contains a pathname and a size limit.

Cache\Special Paths   Two special directories are used by Internet Explorer. These are for cookies (small files stored on the computer by a website), and for the Internet Explorer history list.

> **Cookies**   Contains keys to limit the size of the cookies directory, the cache prefix (cookie:), and the directory path. Cookies track a user's usage of a particular site, monitor favorite selections, establish user-based defaults, and sometimes hold information about the user. Virtually all cookie use is benign, intended to optimize the website's presentation to the user or to cache user-specific information for reuse at a later time.

NOTE   *Don't like cookies? Don't accept them, and clean out your cookies directory. Nothing evil will happen—a few Internet sites will deny access to clients who don't allow cookies, but this is rare. Much of the paranoia about cookies is unfounded; cookies cannot dig into your system and gather information about you.*

> **History**   Internet Explorer keeps a (limited) history of sites visited by the user (URL History). This list is in the directory named by the unnamed value in this subkey.

Last Update   This subkey contains information about the last version of Internet Explorer components installed. Information may consist of a product's date or a version number.

Cryptography\AUTH2UPD   Contains the version number of the currently installed cryptography component.

IEXPLOREV2   Contains the product date for Internet Explorer 2.

IEXPLOREV3   Contains the product date for Internet Explorer 3.

IEXPLOREV4   Contains the product date for Internet Explorer 4.

NOTE   With the Internet Explorer Last Update *information, it is not possible to determine which, if any, versions are installed. It is safe to assume, however, that the latest version is probably the currently installed version. Of course, a user might have gone back to an earlier version—if so, it would not be possible to determine this from the* Last Update *subkey.*

SO   SO is short for security options. To get to these options, go to the Security tab of the Internet Options dialog box in Internet Explorer, then click the Settings button to display the Security Settings dialog box. Here you will find security-based options, subkeys for which include:

ACTIVE_CONTENT\ACTIVEX   Runs ActiveX controls and plug-ins.

ACTIVE_CONTENT\ENABLE   Downloads signed ActiveX objects.

ACTIVE_CONTENT\SAFETY   Initializes and scripts any ActiveX controls that have not been marked as safe.

ACTIVE_CONTENT\SCRIPTSAFE   Scripts any ActiveX controls that have been marked as safe.

ACTIVE_CONTENT\UNSIGNEDACTIVEX   Downloads unsigned ActiveX controls.

AUTH\LOGON   Sets how to handle logon credentials.

DOWNLOAD\FILEDOWNLOAD   Sets whether to download files or not.

DOWNLOAD\FONTDOWNLOAD   Sets whether to download and install fonts or not.

JAVAPER\JAVA   Sets Java permissions.

MISC\DRAGDROP   Sets whether to allow drag-and-drop or cut-and-paste of files.

MISC\FORMDATA   Sets submission of unencrypted form data.

MISC\INSTALLDT   Sets whether to allow installation of Desktop items.

MISC\LAUNCHING   Sets whether to allow launching a file or application in an <IFRAME>.

MISC\SOFTDIST   Sets software channel permissions.

SCRIPTING\SCRIPT   Sets whether to allow active scripting.

SCRIPTING\SCRIPTJAVA   Sets whether to allow Java scripting.

SOIEAK   Contains security options for IEAK (Internet Explorer Administration Kit). With IEAK, you can customize the setup of Internet Explorer, presetting preferences and options to suit a particular set of circumstances. As with the SO options, previously listed, these settings will appear in the Security Settings dialog box in Internet Explorer 6.

NOTE *These are not the only options or settings that may be configured with IEAK. IEAK allows customization of the installation for an ISP, for example, where the user's default home page will be the ISP's page.*

ACTIVE_CONTENT\ACTIVEX Runs ActiveX controls and plug-ins.

ACTIVE_CONTENT\ENABLE Downloads signed ActiveX objects.

ACTIVE_CONTENT\SAFETY Initializes and scripts any ActiveX controls that have not been marked as safe.

ACTIVE_CONTENT\SCRIPTSAFE Scripts any ActiveX controls that have been marked as safe.

ACTIVE_CONTENT\UNSIGNEDACTIVEX Downloads unsigned ActiveX controls.

AUTH\LOGON Sets how to handle logon credentials.

DOWNLOAD\FILEDOWNLOAD Sets whether or not to download files.

DOWNLOAD\FONTDOWNLOAD Sets whether or not to download and install fonts.

JAVAPER\JAVA Sets Java permissions.

MISC\DRAGDROP Sets whether or not to allow drag-and-drop or cut-and-paste of files.

MISC\FORMDATA Sets submission of unencrypted form data.

MISC\INSTALLDT Sets whether or not to allow installation of Desktop items.

MISC\LAUNCHING Sets whether or not to allow launching a file or application in an <IFRAME>.

MISC\SOFTDIST Sets software channel permissions.

SCRIPTING\SCRIPT Sets whether or not to allow active scripting.

SCRIPTING\SCRIPTJAVA Sets whether or not to allow Java scripting.

Subscription Folder Holds certain subscribed objects.

TemplatePolicies These settings initialize (and reset) the SO (security options) for Internet Explorer. The original factory default is Medium, which provides a reasonable medium between excessive safety and minimal safety.

High Typically these settings will keep your system as safe as possible.

Low These settings offer little safety to your system.

Medium These settings offer a compromise between safety and ease of use.

MedLow These settings offer a compromise between safety and ease of use.

Url History Four entries in Url History manage the history list, including the cache limit (number of entries in the history list), the number of days to keep the cache (20 days is the default), and the directory where the history cache is kept.

User Agent   Contains a subkey used to manage MSN entries.

UA Tokens   Two entries for MSN (Microsoft Network) exist in this subkey, one for each version (2.0 and 2.5) of MSN.

ZoneMap   Four predefined zones, which are groupings of Internet sites based on security issues, are contained in Internet Explorer 6. The user is able to set zone attributes (see S0, above) for each zone and assign sites to a specific zone as desired. **ZoneMap** contains subkeys that define which sites fit within a specific zone (local sites not in other zones, sites that bypass the proxy server, and all UNC paths).

Domains   Typically contains an empty subkey.

ProtocolDefaults   Contains the various protocols allowed, such as **file**, **ftp**, and **http**.

Ranges   Contains a place where the buffalo roam, and also entries (if any) for zone ranges.

Zones   Contains definitions of the four default zones, plus the local computer (included but not a zone, as such).

0   The first zone is not a zone at all. Just your computer.

1   The local intranet zone is for sites within your own organization. Generally, all the local intranet sites can be trusted.

2   The trusted sites zone is for intranet and Internet sites that you trust to have safe content (for your computer, but not necessarily for you).

3   The everyone else zone is for sites that you have not placed in any other zone. This is the default zone.

4   The "I really don't trust this site" zone is for sites that have content that is not tested, not known, or otherwise considered to be unsafe for your computer. Maybe call this the *Twilight Zone?*

CurrentVersion\IPConfMSP

Found in Windows 2000 and later versions, the **IPConfMSP** subkey contains information that Windows uses to manage Media Stream Providers.

CurrentVersion\IPConfTSP

Found in Windows 2000 and later versions, the **IPConfTSP** subkey contains information that Windows uses to manage Telephony Service Providers.

CurrentVersion\MCD

MCD is the OpenGL mini-client driver. In this model, the driver is responsible for hardware-accelerated features and handler software for all other features. The **MCD** subkey typically contains about six settings for MCD functionality. Most users only use OpenGL for screen savers. The Pipes screen saver is an example of an OpenGL program.

CurrentVersion\ModuleUsage

The `ModuleUsage` subkey contains a listing of modules, typically ActiveX controls and UUIDs. In the subkeys within `ModuleUsage`, there is information such as the module's owner (if known).

CurrentVersion\MS-DOS Emulation

If you're opening an MS-DOS application, and the application does not have its own PIF file, settings for the application's display are found in the `MS-DOS Emulation` subkey. In `MS-DOS Emulation`, a single subkey named `Font` controls the display's attributes:

Font   Contains the name of the font used for MS-DOS applications. The default is Lucida Console.

CurrentVersion\netcache

Found in Windows 2000 and later versions, the `netcache` subkey contains information that Windows uses to manage whether to enable the network cache, the size of the network cache, and whether the entire network cache is encrypted.

CurrentVersion\Nls

NLS (National Language Support) provides the support to manage and display characters using the Unicode character sets. With Unicode, it is possible to display characters from multiple languages at one time. The `Nls` subkey contains the following:

LocaleMapIDs   Contains a table of lookup values for NLS languages.

CurrentVersion\Policies

The `Policies` subkey manages RSAC (Recreational Software Advisory Council) ratings. The Internet, Internet Explorer, and some games use these settings. This key contains a subkey called `Explorer` as well as other subkeys:

Explorer   Contains one entry by default. `FileName0` contains the name of the RSAC ratings definition file; this file is text and is editable with Notepad. The second entry, called `Key`, contains a binary value.

ShowSuperHidden   A flag that tells Explorer whether it should show files and directories that have the super-hidden attributes applied to them. Super-hidden files/folders have both the system and hidden attributes set. These files are not visible through the GUI by default. You can still get to them through the command prompt or by disabling this in the View tab of Folder Options by unchecking Hide Protected Operating System Files. (They will not be visible unless you have the Show Hidden Files and Folders option selected also.)

NonEnum   Information about non-enumerated objects. One value is present by default:

{BDEADF00-C265-11D0-BCED-00A0C90AB50F}   The handler for web folders.

Ratings   May contain two value entries and two subkeys. The value entry `FileName0` contains the name of the RSAC ratings definition file. The second entry, `Key`, contains a binary value. The subkeys that may exist in `Ratings` are:

.Default   Contains three ratings-oriented keys: `Allow_Unknowns`, `Enabled`, and `PleaseMom`. Each is a binary value.

.Default\http://www.rsac.org/ratingsv01.html   Contains four DWORD values: `1`, `n`, `s`, and `v`.

System   Contains a number of useful keys:

disablecad   Disabling the key combination Ctrl+Alt+Delete is useful for some environments.

DisableNT4Policy   Windows NT 4 policy can be enforced on Windows users, if desired.

dontdisplaylastusername   Controls whether the logon screen will display the user ID of the last user to log on.

legalnoticecaption   The legal notice is a message that is displayed before a user is allowed to log on. The user must click OK to dismiss this message, allowing management to enforce rules or policy.

legalnoticetext   The text in the legal notice message box.

shutdownwithoutlogon   Controls whether Windows can be shut down without logging on first. The default is `true` for nonserver installations and `false` for servers. I often turn this option on when setting up servers, because if a user wanted to shut down the server, they could simply use the power switch.

Undockwithoutlogon   Allows the user to undock without logging on.

CURRENTVERSION\RENAMEFILES

In Windows XP, sometimes an application, when it is being installed, must remove a file for some reason. (The reasons would be specific to the application.) Rather than deleting these files, which the user might need later should the application need to be removed, a common technique is to rename the files. Then, if necessary, they can be renamed back to their original names.

A few of the applications that rename files are:

◆ Sa

◆ Win

◆ WinMail

◆ WinNews

◆ WordPadAttribSet

CurrentVersion\Run

Here is one of those areas in the registry that you want to find, but never seem to be able to. The Run subkey contains the name of executables that will be run each time the system is started.

In one system that I have, the following are included in the Run subkey:

BrowserWebCheck   Contains Internet Explorer's application that uses pull technology to check the currency of subscribed web pages.

H/PC Connection Agent   Contains a program that checks for an HPC (handheld PC) to be connected. If the program detects the HPC, it will automatically initiate logon for the HPC.

POINTER   Contains an enhanced mouse system, part of the Microsoft IntelliPoint program.

SystemTray   Contains the system tray.

TIPS   Contains the Mouse Tips program.

Most Windows XP systems only have an entry for SystemTray in Run. This subkey is much like the Start Menu\Programs\Startup directory—anything there will be run when a user logs on.

NOTE   By putting items in CurrentVersion\Run, *then protecting the registry key from modification, you can force users to open or run certain applications. They will be unable to change this behavior.*

CurrentVersion\RunOnce

Once? When?

The RunOnce subkey allows executing a program the first time a user (any user) logs on, and it does not allow the user to continue until they have exited the program(s). Once the program has completed execution, Windows XP will delete it from the RunOnce key.

To run a program one time, in RunOnce enter an arbitrary name as a value (the program's common name will work fine here); the string data for the program should be the program's fully qualified file name. For example:

```
JobRun = C:\Jobs\JobRun.exe
```

The value's data type should be REG_STRING.

The application runs after the next user logs on. It will not be necessary to restart the computer.

CurrentVersion\RunOnceEx

The RunOnceEx subkey is used by system components and Internet Explorer to run setup and configuration components. Works much like the RunOnce subkey.

CurrentVersion\Setup

The Setup subkey contains information including the boot directory (typically C:\), the installation source directory (often the drive letter of your CD-ROM drive), and the source path (often the same as the source directory).

WHY DOES WINDOWS RUN AN UNKNOWN JOB AT LOGON OR BOOTUP?

If you can't find it in the startup groups (looking under the Documents and Settings folder), do the following:

1. Check HKEY_CURRENT_USER\Software\Microsoft\Windows NT\CurrentVersion\Windows.

2. Load and/or run keys.

3. Remove the offending program.

A program can also be loaded at startup in Windows XP in the Startup folder for the current user and all users and in the following registry locations:

◆ HKEY_LOCAL_MACHINE\Software\Microsoft\Windows\CurrentVersion\Run

◆ HKEY_LOCAL_MACHINE\Software\Microsoft\Windows\CurrentVersion\RunOnce

◆ HKEY_LOCAL_MACHINE\Software\Microsoft\Windows\CurrentVersion\RunServices

◆ HKEY_LOCAL_MACHINE\Software\Microsoft\Windows\CurrentVersion\RunServicesOnce

◆ HKEY_CURRENT_USER\Software\Microsoft\Windows\CurrentVersion\RunOnce

◆ HKEY_CURRENT_USER\Software\Microsoft\Windows\CurrentVersion\RunServices

◆ HKEY_CURRENT_USER\Software\Microsoft\Windows\CurrentVersion\RunServicesOnce

After installing Windows, you may find that you want to change the CD-ROM's drive letter. (I use drive letters after S: for CD-ROM drives, for example.) If you don't tell Windows XP (in Setup) every time you attempt to change the installation (for instance, installing a new component or option), the Windows XP Setup program will prompt you to insert the disk in the wrong drive, making the installation process more complicated. A simple change to the entries in this section will make the process much easier.

BaseWinOptions May contain a number of subcomponents, all controlled by .inf files.

OC Manager The master list of installed options and accessories.

OptionalComponents Provides the status for each optional component installable with Windows XP. This subkey contains a list of optional components and a set of corresponding subkeys, one for each optional component.

CURRENTVERSION\SHAREDDLLS

The SharedDlls subkey contains .dll files shared between multiple applications. Windows maintains a list of all shared .dll files and a count of the number of applications using each shared file.

When removing an application using a shared .dll file, the uninstall program decreases the count by one. If the count becomes zero, Windows will prompt you to remove the shared .dll file.

NOTE   Although this section implies that it is for .dll files only, actually any shared file may be included in the list.

UNINSTALLING APPLICATIONS WHICH DO NOT HAVE AN ADD/REMOVE OR UNINSTALL PROGRAM

All programs for Windows are supposed to have both an installation program and an uninstallation program. Now, in a perfect world, I'd be rich and happy, and you'd never have any problems with Windows. Neither is the case, however.

So we have programs that don't have uninstallation programs. Because these rogue programs have no established removal method, they are rarely listed in the Control Panel's Add/Remove Programs applet. (Or if they are listed, selecting uninstall does nothing...)

To remove these programs you must do several things:

1. Back up the program's folder(s) (a backup is *always* a very good idea). If they were reasonably well behaved when installing, these programs should have created their folder in the Program Files folder. However, rogue programs typically install themselves in either the C: drive's root or under the Windows folder. (Bad choices in either case!)

2. In HKEY_LOCAL_MACHINE\Software and HKEY_CURRENT_USER\Software, search for any registry subkeys, back them up, and then delete them. (Back them up using RegEdit's Export features.)

3. Remove these programs that no longer exist from your Start menu. With Windows XP, the Start menu is a combination of the user's Start menu items and items from the configuration named All Users. Look under %SystemDrive%\Documents and Settings\[username | All Users]\Start Menu\... (search the entire directory structure under these locations).

4. Back up and then delete references to the program that you are attempting to remove.

If your application is listed in the Add/Remove Programs list (but it doesn't really support removal), then look in the registry location HKEY_LOCAL_MACHINE\Software\Microsoft\Windows\CurrentVersion\Uninstall. Back up the objects for this application, then delete them (and their contents).

Some applications may have an entry in the registry at HKEY_LOCAL_MACHINE\System\CurrentControlSet\Services. If you find an entry, back up the entry, and then delete the entry, with any objects contained in it.

If the program starts automatically whenever Windows boots, check the entries described in the sidebar titled "Why Does Windows Run an Unknown Job at Logon or Bootup?" earlier in this chapter.

CURRENTVERSION\SHELL EXTENSIONS

Shell extensions are used to extend and expand the Windows user interface and capabilities. The Shell Extensions key contains a subkey, named Approved, where all shell extensions are stored.

NOTE *For more information on shell extensions, check out Jeff Prosise's March 1995 Microsoft Systems Journal article titled "Writing Windows 95 Shell Extensions."*

CURRENTVERSION\SHELLSCRAP

The ShellScrap subkey, on most systems, holds one subkey, PriorityCacheFormats. In PriorityCacheFormats is a single value entry, named #3, that contains an empty string.

CURRENTVERSION\SHELLSERVICEOBJECTDELAYLOAD

The `ShellServiceObjectDelayLoad` subkey loads objects subject to a delay. The delay allows the operating system to finish initializing, establish connections, and so on. Most systems with Internet Explorer 5 installed load WebCheck. WebCheck is responsible for subscription maintenance. Other items in this subkey are `Network.ConnectionTray` and `SysTray`.

CURRENTVERSION\STILLIMAGE

Found in Windows 2000 and later versions, the `StillImage` subkey contains information that Windows uses to manage the Kodak or third-party imaging system.

CURRENTVERSION\SYNCMGR

Found in Windows 2000 and later versions, the `Syncmgr` subkey contains information that Windows uses to manage the synchronization of folders.

CURRENTVERSION\TELEPHONY

Windows XP works with telecommunications. Modems and telephones establish remote connections (and voice calls, at times). Within the `Telephony` key, there are a number of subkeys:

Country List   This subkey contains about 240 subkeys, one for each country defined. A typical country code is one to four digits and matches the telephone company's country code. For example, the country code for Thailand is 66. (To make a long distance telephone call to Thailand, I'd dial 001-66, where the 001 is the overseas access code and 66 is the country code.) Information in each country subkey includes:

CountryCode   Contains a DWORD value that should be equal to the country code. (Remember that this value is displayed in hexadecimal format.) This code would have to be changed if a country's country code were to change, although this is unlikely.

Name   Contains a string with the country's name, such as `Thailand`.

InternationalRule   Contains the rules used to dial numbers in this country. (See the next sidebar for more on rules.)

LongDistanceRule   Contains the rules used to dial long distance in this country. (See the sidebar for more on rules.)

SameAreaRule   Contains the rules used to dial local numbers in this country. (See the sidebar for more on rules.)

TIP   Need a list of all the countries in the world? Here they are, along with the applicable telephone country codes. Export this subkey of the registry to a text file, and use an editor to clean up the list!

Locations   Each user may have zero, one, or more locations defined. (Actually, each user should have one location: the user's current or home location.) Each location defined is stored in the `Locations` subkey, as `Location0`, `Location1`, and so on.

RULES, RULES, AND MORE RULES

Look in the `InternationalRule`, `LongDistanceRule`, and `SameAreaRule` subkeys given above; you'll see a jumble of letters and numbers. Each has meaning. For example:

0-9	Indicates a number that is to be dialed as entered.
ABCD	Indicates touch-tone characters to be dialed, only usable on tone dial systems. (This produces the special tones named A, B, C, and D.)
E	Dials the country code.
F	Dials the area code or city code.
G	Dials the local number.
H	Dials the card number.
*	Dials a * tone.
#	Dials a # tone.
T	Indicates subsequent numbers dialed as tone dial.
P	Indicates subsequent numbers dialed as pulse dial.
,	Pauses for a fixed period of time (typically 1 second).
!	Flashes the hook (1/2 second on-hook, 1/2 second off-hook).
W	Waits for second dial tone (outside line dial tone).
@	Waits for silent answer (ringback followed by silence for 5 seconds).
$	Waits for calling-card prompt tone.
?	Pauses for user input.

Using Thailand as our example:

    InternationalRule = 001EFG

(Dial 001, the country code, the city code, the local number.)

    LongDistanceRule = 0FG

(Dial 0, the city code, the local number.)

    SameAreaRule = G

(Dial the local number.)

That's all folks, an easy set of rules! With these rules it's easy to add new countries (they pop up all the time, right?) if necessary. What with the sometimes major changes to area codes, which are equivalent to city codes in other countries, it is sometimes necessary to modify the United States entry. You can set rules in the Change Calling Card dialog box by clicking the Rules button.

Providers   Providers are the connections between Windows XP and the modem or other telecommunications device. The most common provider is the Unimodem driver, though there are also other drivers, including the TAPI interface.

CURRENTVERSION\UNIMODEM

The Unimodem driver is a universal modem driver (see, now Unimodem makes sense) used to control virtually all industry-compatible AT-command modems, also known as Hayes-compatible modems. If this subkey is not present, you do not have a modem installed. Most standard modems must be connected to a POTS (plain old telephone service) line. In other words, lines that are not digital are controlled by the Unimodem driver.

The Unimodem driver also controls direct connections between two computers connected via a serial cable. Though good speed performance is impossible, serial cable connections are used when connecting some notebooks and most PDAs (personal digital assistants) and HPCs (handheld PCs). Note that some systems use an IR (infrared) link for these devices, too.

NOTE   Please note that Windows XP/2000/NT 4 and Windows CE version 1 are not compatible. It will be necessary to upgrade to Windows CE version 2.x or later to connect an HPC to your Windows system.

DeviceSpecific   Contains subkeys for each connection. For example, a typical system will have a subkey under `DeviceSpecific` for each modem type installed and one for direct serial cable connections if installed. Each entry contains information that the device, modem, or connection might send to the host computer.

CURRENTVERSION\UNINSTALL

The Control Panel's Add/Remove Programs applet has a list of applications to remove automatically. Using this feature, the removal will be smooth and will not cause problems with system stability.

WARNING   This assumes that the applications designer did a credible job of creating his remove system. If the application does not have a good uninstaller, you may still have problems. No one, other than the supplier of an application, can assure you that the uninstall will go smoothly. Before uninstalling anything, make sure you have a backup of the system, the application (all of it), and the registry. With good backups, it is possible (although nothing is guaranteed) that you may be able to recover from an uninstall gone awry.

The `Uninstall` subkey contains a subkey for each component that is automatically uninstallable. For example, in the `Uninstall\IntelliPoint` subkey, you'll find the following:

DisplayName   Contains a REG_SZ value that holds the string `Microsoft IntelliPoint`.

UninstallString   Contains a value that holds the string `C:\progra~1\MICROS~2\Mouse\UNINSTALL.exe`.

When you select Microsoft IntelliPoint in the Add/Remove Programs applet, the program or object in the `UninstallString` entry is executed, performing the uninstallation. Typically, for a system component such as the IntelliPoint mouse driver being uninstalled, it must reinstall the original component.

TIP   *Ever manually uninstalled a program and then realized that the Add/Remove Programs list had an uninstall for the program? Easy fix: delete the applicable subkey from the* `CurrentVersion\Uninstall` *key. Careful, don't remove the wrong one.*

CURRENTVERSION\URL

Used with Internet Explorer, the `URL` subkey provides a default prefix for a URL when the user does not enter one. For example, I'm in the habit of accessing my web page by typing in the following:

```
www.mv.net/ipusers/darkstar
```

When, in fact, the full URL is:

```
http://www.mv.net/ipusers/darkstar
```

Internet Explorer, using information stored in `CurrentVersion\URL`, determines that the default prefix should actually be `http://`.

DefaultPrefix   Contains the default prefix (usually `http://`) used when the user does not enter a prefix and the initial characters of the URL do not tell Internet Explorer what prefix from the prefixes list (below) to use. The default prefix can be changed if the user is primarily using FTP or Gopher, for example.

Prefixes   Contains a list of all valid prefixes, based on the initial part of the URL. For example, if the URL starts with www, or www., the prefix would be `http://`. If the URL starts with ftp, or ftp., then the prefix would be `ftp://`. The prefixes defined by default (you may add more if you wish) are:

Beginning of URL	Prefix
ftp	ftp://
ftp.	ftp://
gopher	gopher://
gopher.	gopher://
home	http://
home.	http://
mosaic	http://
mosaic.	http://
www	http://
www.	http://

CURRENTVERSION\WEBCHECK

Found in Windows 2000 and later versions, the `WebCheck` subkey contains information that Windows uses to manage Internet Explorer's customization on a per-user basis.

CURRENTVERSION\WELCOME

Found in Windows 2000 and later versions, the `Welcome` subkey contains information that Windows uses to manage the Internet Connection Wizard. The single subkey in this key is called `ICW`; it contains a flag indicating whether the Internet Connection Wizard has been run or not.

CURRENTVERSION\WINDOWSUPDATE

Found in Windows 2000 and later versions, the `WindowsUpdate` subkey contains information that Windows uses to manage OEM installations.

CURRENTVERSION\WINLOGON

Found in Windows 2000 and later versions, the `WinLogon` subkey contains information that Windows uses to manage logon options. One object, `DisableLockWorkstation`, has a REG_DWORD value. With this object, the LockWorkstation feature can be enabled and disabled as needed.

HELP

The `Help` subkey contains a list of help files and their locations. These are used when, inside an application, the user either presses F1 (for help), or selects the What's This button and clicks on a control or object in the application's user interface.

It is possible to remove entries from this section, if desired, when you know for sure that the help file is either no longer used or has been removed.

TIP   If you find that pressing F1 or selecting What's This brings up a WinHelp error, indicating that WinHelp cannot find the help file, search for the file; if you can find it, WinHelp will update this subkey to indicate this file's location.

ITSTORAGE

The `ITStorage` subkey is used with the Microsoft HTML Help control (an ActiveX control) to display help for HTML documents in Internet Explorer.

> **Finders**   For each type of HTML help file, an entry is created. Each entry has a name equal to the extension of the help file. For instance, the CHM HTML help files are listed as being serviced by a specific control, identified by a UUID.

Windows Messaging Subsystem

Another subkey you'll find under `HKEY_LOCAL_MACHINE\Software\Microsoft` on most Windows systems is `Windows Messaging Subsystem`. MAPI (Microsoft Outlook) uses this subkey, which contains a list of all MAPI-enabled applications.

Windows NT

Under `HKEY_LOCAL_MACHINE\Software\Microsoft`, you'll also find a `Windows NT` subkey. Much like the `Windows` subkey (described earlier), the `Windows NT` subkey sets `Windows` operating parameters. Microsoft did not rename this (preexisting) key when Windows NT 5.1 was renamed "Windows XP."

There is only one subkey in the `Windows NT` key. This subkey, `CurrentVersion`, contains about 30 subkeys and perhaps 15 value entries in a typical installation. Unlike the `Windows` subkey, the number of entries in `Windows NT` is relatively constant between different installations.

CurrentVersion

`CurrentVersion` contains a number of value entries. These entries hold information about the installation:

CSDVersion Contains the level of the system. By level, I mean which service packs have been installed (if any). Remember, service packs are cumulative—installing Service Pack 3 automatically installs both Service Pack 1 and Service Pack 2. A system for which there is no installed service pack may not have a `CSDVersion` object.

CurrentBuild Contains an obsolete data value containing old version and build information. Do not use this value; use `CurrentBuildNumber` to determine the build of Windows that is running.

CurrentBuildNumber Contains a number that indicates which build of Windows is running. A higher number indicates a later operating system build. During the development process, build numbers are incremented each time the developers create a complete operating system, sometimes daily.

CurrentType Contains information on whether the installation is uniprocessor or multiprocessor.

CurrentVersion Contains the Windows NT version number, such as 4.0. Microsoft sometimes uses subversion numbers, such as 3.11 or 3.51. The Windows XP version of NT is 5.1.

DigitalProductID The Windows product ID and other binary information are stored here.

HWID Contains a value of `not used`.

InstallDate Contains information on the Windows installation date. This value is the number of seconds since January 1, 1970, and these dates remain valid until early 2038—not much of a problem there.

PathName Contains information on the Windows installation path.

ProductID Contains the Windows product ID. If Windows is installed from something other than OEM media, the product ID will consist of a total of twenty digits: five lead digits, the first three digits of the user's CD key, the last seven digits of the user's CD key, and five trailing digits. The leading and trailing digit numbers will vary from installation to installation. For OEM media installations, the product ID will be equal to the OEM CD key. In both cases, the CD key is written on a small yellow sticker on the back of the CD jewel case.

ProductName The actual name of the operating system—for example, `Microsoft Windows XP`.

RegDone In Windows versions prior to Windows XP, tells if the user has registered the copy of Windows. In Windows XP, Product Authorization is used for this purpose.

RegisteredOrganization Contains the name of your company or organization, as you entered it during setup. If your company or organization name changes, you can edit this value.

RegisteredOwner Contains the name as you entered it during setup. If your name changes (maybe you inherited the computer from your predecessor?), you can edit this value.

Software Type Contains the string SYSTEM.

SourcePath Contains the source path you used to install Windows. If you reassign CD-ROM drive letters (I do, to keep all CD-ROM drives at the end of the alphabet, using letters S through Z), you can edit this value to change the installation source path. This path could be a network path, if the installation is from a shared resource.

SystemRoot Contains information used to create the %SystemRoot% environment variable, the base directory that Windows XP is installed in. Be cautious about changing this value and realize that Windows, when booting, will update this registry entry anyway. There may be other locations where the Windows directory is coded without using the %SystemRoot% variable.

CHANGING YOUR INSTALLATION LOCATION

As mentioned above, the location that you used to install Windows is stored in the SourcePath subkey. If you re-arrange your CD-ROM drive letters (like I do) after installing Windows XP, every time you need to update, or install a feature, Windows will search the original location, and then prompt you for the location of the necessary files.

To make things smoother, you can modify the source path data object found in HKEY_LOCAL_MACHINE\ SOFTWARE\Microsoft\Windows\CurrentVersion\Setup\Sourcepath. Also check to see if SourcePath is found in HKEY_LOCAL_MACHINE\Software\Microsoft\Windows NT\CurrentVersion\Sourcepath and change that occurrence as well. (There is no need to add this object if it is not present in your registry.)

For example, suppose you installed from the default CD-ROM location D:, then later changed the CD-ROM's drive letter to S:. You would modify SourcePath from D:\ to S:\. Of course, you could copy the entire installation CD to a folder on your hard drive (I do this frequently). Then simply update SourcePath to reflect the fully qualified location for the source files.

CURRENTVERSION\AEDEBUG

Windows XP will launch a debugger when there is an application or system failure. A debugger is a program that will either save information about the failure or allow interactive debugging. Most users who are not developers will simply use Dr. Watson as their debugger. Dr. Watson is a simple program that saves vital information about what failed and why there was a failure to a debugging file.

For Dr. Watson users, the typical entries in AeDebug are as follows:

Auto Contains a string value of 1 if automatic debugging is to be done, or 0 if no automatic debugging is to be done.

Debugger Contains the name of the default debugger. If you have a debugger installed other than Dr. Watson, your debugger is listed here.

UserDebuggingHotKey Allows a user to launch the debugger using a keystroke combination. Useful for developers, but the average user will find little use for this functionality.

DR. WATSON'S OPTIONS

Dr. Watson, DRWTSN32.exe, takes a number of command-line options when launched:

◆ Use the −i option to (re)install Dr. Watson as the default debugger. Use this option if a different debugger was installed in the past and you want to use Dr. Watson again.

◆ The −g option is ignored, but no error is generated. This option maintains compatibility with 16-bit (Windows 95 and Windows 3.x) versions of Dr. Watson.

◆ The −p <pid> option tells Dr. Watson to debug the process ID specified.

◆ The −e <event> option tells Dr. Watson to debug the event specified.

◆ Use −? to display a simple help screen of options.

CURRENTVERSION\COMPATIBILITY
CURRENTVERSION\COMPATIBILITY2
CURRENTVERSION\COMPATIBILITY32

Within the three Compatibility objects are value entries for a number of legacy (older, preexisting) applications that are not very compatible with Windows XP. A flag value (a hexadecimal number, expressed as a string) tells Windows about the incompatibility and allows Windows to modify the operating system's behavior to compensate for the application's incompatibility.

What does Compatibility do? During beta testing of the operating system, testers inform Microsoft of applications that do not perform correctly. Microsoft may contact the application's supplier and work with them to make the program work correctly. For some applications, especially for applications where there is a large installed base of users, Microsoft will make patches to the operating system to allow that application to function correctly. Usually these patches consist of doing things that make the new version of the operating system look like the original version for that application. These patches are turned on and off with a set of binary switches—when the application is loaded, Compatibility is checked, and the necessary patches are turned on for that application.

NOTE   *Realize that these patches will be only visible to the offending application and not to any others.*

CURRENTVERSION\CONSOLE

Found in Windows 2000 and later versions, the Console subkey contains information that Windows uses to manage the appearance of console applications.

CURRENTVERSION\DRIVERS

Some drivers use the CurrentVersion\Drivers section of the registry. In certain Windows XP installations, two drivers—timer.drv and mmdrv.dll—are installed. The timer.drv driver creates certain timer functions on PC-compatible systems, and mmdrv.dll is the low-level wave, MIDI, and AUX support driver.

CURRENTVERSION\DRIVERS.DESC

The `drivers.desc` subkey contains descriptions of certain drivers installed under Windows XP. The descriptions are text, intended to be people readable.

CURRENTVERSION\DRIVERS32

Driver mapping for certain virtual devices, such as multimedia, is done in the `Drivers32` subkey. For instance, the value entry named `midi` contains the default value `mmdrv.dll`.

CURRENTVERSION\EFS

Found in Windows 2000 and later versions, the `EFS` subkey contains information used to manage the encrypted file system. This subkey is not used in Windows XP Home Edition.

CURRENTVERSION\EMBEDDING

Embeddable applications (such as PaintBrush and Sound Recorder) are listed in value entries in the `Embedding` subkey.

CURRENTVERSION\FILE MANAGER

The `File Manager` subkey contains one subkey:

AddOns   Contains a subkey containing information on add-on software products for File Manager. WinZip is an add-on software product that fits into this category.

CURRENTVERSION\FONT DRIVERS

The `Font Drivers` subkey contains any needed drivers used to display fonts. The increased usage of TrueType fonts has minimized the use of this subkey.

CURRENTVERSION\FONTCACHE

In Windows, the management of fonts is critical to system performance. Using a cache allows much better performance when displaying frequently used fonts. Windows creates bitmaps of the TrueType fonts, and then caches these bitmaps so that they do not have to be re-created.

The `FontCache` subkey (not used in Windows XP) contains three value entries:

MaxSize   The maximum size of the font cache.

MinIncreSize   The minimum increment size for the font cache.

MinInitSize   The minimum initial size for the font cache.

The `CurrentVersion\FontCache\LastFontSweep` subkey contains one variable:

LastSweepTime   A binary value indicating the last time the font cache was cleaned.

CURRENTVERSION\FONT DRIVERS

Found in Windows 2000 and later versions, the `Font Drivers` subkey contains information that Windows uses to manage non-TrueType fonts, such as Adobe type fonts.

CurrentVersion\FontDPI

Found in Windows 2000 and later versions, the FontDPI subkey contains information that Windows uses to manage the sizing of fonts, based on pixels.

CurrentVersion\FontMapper

Font mapping is an internal component of Windows XP that compares the attributes for a requested but not available font, and then matches these attributes with available physical fonts.

In FontMapper, attribute modifiers are supplied for the font mapper in Windows XP.

CurrentVersion\Fonts

The Fonts subkey contains a list of currently installed fonts. The list is made up of keys in the form:

```
Font display name = fontfile
```

where Font display name is the display name, such as Arial (TrueType), and fontfile is the actual font file—arial.ttf, for Arial (TrueType).

The Font applet in Control Panel and other applications (indirectly, through the operating system) use the information in Fonts. It is possible to manually manipulate the font information; however, using the Fonts applet will make the process much easier.

CurrentVersion\FontSubstitutes

Some fonts that are commonly called for by applications are not supplied with Windows XP. These fonts are older, bitmapped fonts commonly used with early versions of Windows and Windows NT but no longer supplied or directly supported. These fonts are simply mapped to newer TrueType fonts.

The following are font substitutions:

Old font	New font
Helv	MS Sans Serif
Helvetica	Arial
MS Shell Dlg	MS Sans Serif
Times	Times New Roman
Tms Rmn	MS Serif

CurrentVersion\GRE_Initialize

The subkey GRE_Initialize contains objects used by the GRE (Graphics Rendering Engine), which displays a few fonts that Windows XP supports. These fonts are bitmapped fonts (not TrueType). Fonts handled or remapped by GRE are:

FIXEDFON.FON	vgafix.fon
FONTS.FON	vgasys.fon
OEMFONT.FON	vgaoem.fon

CURRENTVERSION\HOTFIX

The HotFix subkey contains information that Windows XP uses to manage whether any hotfixes have been applied. Each applied hotfix will have its own subkey, named with the fix's Q number. This object may not exist if no hotfixes have been applied.

CURRENTVERSION\ICM

Found in Windows 2000 and later versions, the ICM subkey contains information used to manage image color matching.

CURRENTVERSION\IMAGE FILE EXECUTION OPTIONS

Used for debugging objects such as services or DCOM, the Image File Execution Options subkey specifies what debugger to use for a specific service or DCOM object.

NOTE   Notice that the term image file *refers to an executable image file, not a graphics file.*

Your Image File Name Here without a path   In this example subkey, value entries show how to configure the debugger. More information on image file debugging is available from NuMega Lab's website at http://www.compuware.com/products/numega/.

CURRENTVERSION\INIFILEMAPPING

The IniFileMapping subkey maps .ini files (as they were used with early versions of Windows) to registry keys. In all cases, the entries in IniFileMapping point to other registry entries.

CURRENTVERSION\LANGUAGEPACK

Found in Windows 2000 and later versions, the LanguagePack subkey contains information that Windows uses to manage installed second languages.

CURRENTVERSION\LASTFONTSWEEP

Found in Windows 2000 and later versions, the LastFontSweep subkey contains information that Windows uses to record the last time that the font cache was cleaned.

CURRENTVERSION\MCI

The MCI subkey contains the MCI (Media Control Interface) drivers. Most systems with an audio card will have four entries:

AVIVideo   Contains the AVI (video files) driver, mciavi.drv.

CDAudio   Contains the CD audio (music) player driver, mcicda.drv.

Sequencer   Contains the MIDI (sequencer) driver, mciseq.drv.

WaveAudio   Contains the wave file (audio files) driver, mciwave.drv.

CurrentVersion\MCI Extensions

The subkey `MCI Extensions` holds multimedia file extensions and the driver used to handle these objects. For example, the following entry:

```
mpeg = MPEGVideo
```

denotes that Windows XP should use the MPEGVideo driver to process MPEG files.

CurrentVersion\MCI32

The `MCI32` subkey contains 32-bit MCI (Media Control Interface) drivers. Most systems with an audio card will have five entries:

AVIVideo   Contains the AVI (video files) driver, `mciavi32.dll`.

CDAudio   Contains the CD audio (music) player driver, `mcicda.dll`.

MPEGVideo   Contains the MPEG (video) driver, `mciqtz32.dll`.

Sequencer   Contains the MIDI (sequencer) driver, `mciseq.dll`.

WaveAudio   Contains the wave file (audio files) driver, `mciwave.dll`.

NOTE   In `MCI32`, some drivers are common with CurrentVersion\MCI.

CurrentVersion\Midimap

MIDI (Musical Instrument Digital Interface) configuration is saved in the `Midimap` subkey. MIDI creates music using sound (instrument musical note) definitions, combined with the music's score. The score (in a special format) tells the computer how to "play" each instrument. As might be expected, the computer does not make many mistakes, assuming the score has been properly entered into the MIDI file.

Better-quality sound systems use actual recordings of instruments playing specific notes to create a very high-quality sound.

CurrentVersion\ModuleCompatibility

In the `ModuleCompatibility` subkey, you will find entries much like those in `CurrentVersion\ Compatibility`. A flag value (a hexadecimal number, expressed as a string) tells Windows XP about the incompatibility and allows Windows to modify the operating system's behavior to compensate for the application's incompatibility.

Each entry lists a module and a compatibility flag. For example:

```
MYST = 0x8000
```

CurrentVersion\Network

In the `Network` subkey (only in `HKEY_LOCAL_MACHINE`), there are four subkeys. There is some disagreement between what Microsoft documents should be in each subkey and what experience shows is actually there.

Shared Parameters Documented to hold the single value entry Slow Mode, this object lists which servers and domains are accessed over a slow (typically dial-up or modem) connection. Using additional caching on these connections compensates for slow connections.

SMAddOns Contains a pointer to Server Manager extension .dlls used to augment RAS.

UMAddOns Contains a pointer to User Manager extension .dlls used to augment RAS.

World Full Access Shared Parameters Documented to hold the value entry ExpandLogon-Domain, this contains a value (yes or no) that defines whether Windows expands the Shared Directories list in the Connect Network Drive dialog box. Experience shows that the value entry named Slow Mode, used to list which servers and domains will be accessed over a slow connection (typically dial-up or modem), is also present in this subkey, as is the entry RAS Mode.

CurrentVersion\NetworkCards

For each network card installed (remember, servers can have multiple cards) and for remote access (RAS and/or DUN), there will be one subkey in NetworkCards. Subkeys are named with numbers, beginning with 1. In each is a subkey called NetRules. An example, using a 3Com 3C-590 PCI Ethernet card, is shown here:

1 Contains six entries, plus the subkey NetRules. The entries are:
```
Description : REG_SZ : 3Com Etherlink III Bus-Master Adapter (3C590)
InstallDate : REG_DWORD : <a date, expressed as the number of seconds since
➥January 1, 1970>
Manufacturer : REG_SZ : 3Com
ProductName : REG_SZ : E159X
ServiceName : REG_SZ : E159x1
Title : REG_SZ : [1] 3Com Etherlink III PCI Buss-Master Adapter (3C590)
```

1\NetRules Contains the following entries:
```
bindform : REG_SZ : "Ei59x1" yes yes container
class : REG_MULTI_SZ : Ei59xAdapter basic
InfName : REG_SZ : oemnad0.inf
InfOption : REG_SZ : 3C590
type : REG_SZ : ei59x ei59xAdapter
```

CurrentVersion\NTVersionOfLastBackup

Found in Windows 2000 and later versions, the NTVersionOfLastBackup subkey contains information that Windows uses to manage information on the operating system version.

CurrentVersion\OpenGLDrivers

Found in Windows 2000 and later versions, the OpenGLDrivers subkey contains information that Windows uses to manage OpenGL drivers.

CurrentVersion\Perflib

Monitoring system performance is a critical part of managing a Windows XP server. Performance monitoring allows the graphing of between 500 and 800 different parameters. The number of parameters, which may be monitored, varies depending on system components, packages, and configurations. There will be one or more subkeys in the `Perflib` key, one for each installed language. In this example, `009` is the subkey for U.S. English, the language that is installed on my computer:

CurrentVersion\Perflib\009 Contains the performance item names and descriptions. Each is listed in the Performance Monitor's Add Counters dialog box. A REG_MULTI_SZ string contains the item name, and a second REG_MULTI_SZ string contains the item description.

Running the Performance Monitor can be very instructional, especially for Windows servers. With the Performance Monitor, it is possible to see which applications are "hogging" resources, making pigs of themselves, and so forth. Also, the Performance Monitor is able to show usage for optional components such as Exchange Server, SQL Server, and IIS, to name a few.

CURRENTVERSION\PORTS

Ports (serial, printer, file, and network ports) are configured in the `Ports` subkey. For most ports, no entries are needed. For serial ports, the default settings (typically `9600`, `n`, `8`, `1` as set by the Control Panel's Ports applet) for some options are stored here.

CURRENTVERSION\PRINT

Found in Windows 2000 and later versions, the `Print` subkey contains information that Windows uses to manage all printer resources. Each printer will have a subkey.

CURRENTVERSION\PROFILEGUID

A list of user GUIDs, mapped to the user's SID.

CURRENTVERSION\PROFILELIST

User profiles for all users who use the computer are listed in the `ProfileList` subkey. A subkey is created for each user, named with the user's SID. Inside each of these subkeys are five variables:

CentralProfile Contains the location of the user's central profile, if the profile is not stored on the local machine. This location will be specified as a UNC pathname.

Flags Contains a DWORD value, typically `0x2`.

ProfileImagePath Contains the location of the user's local profile. For users with a central profile, a local copy is kept in case the central profile is unavailable.

Sid Contains the user's SID, as a binary object.

State Contains a DWORD value indicating the user's current state.

CURRENTVERSION\RELATED.DESC

The `related.desc` subkey contains descriptions (if any) for items such as `wave`, `wave1`, `wave2`, and `wave3`.

CURRENTVERSION\SECEDIT

Found in Windows 2000 and later versions, the `SeCEdit` subkey contains information that Windows uses to manage the Security Configuration Editor.

CURRENTVERSION\SRVWIZ

Found in Windows 2000 and later versions, the `SrvWiz` subkey contains information that Windows uses to manage the Server Wizard program. Information in this object includes the name of the server and the NetBIOS name for the server. Available on server products only.

CURRENTVERSION\SVCHOST

Found in Windows 2000 and later versions, the `Svchost` subkey contains information that Windows uses to manage the Services Host features.

CURRENTVERSION\TERMINAL SERVER

Found in Windows 2000 and later versions, the `Terminal Server` subkey contains information that Windows uses to configure the Terminal Services features of Windows.

CURRENTVERSION\TIME ZONES

Windows XP is able to compensate for various time zones, and for DST (daylight saving time) in those areas where there is support for DST. Though technically there can only be 24 time zones (if we assumed even hours), actually there are several time zones where the time difference is only 30 minutes, and some time zones have different names depending on the country. Windows supports about 47 different time zones, spanning the entire world. The Control Panel's Date/Time applet uses these settings, and they are passed to other applications as data.

In the `Time Zones` key are subkeys for each possible time zone. Each time zone has information that includes the following:

Display   Contains a string describing the time zone, such as `'Eastern Time (US & Canada)'`.

Dlt   Contains a string describing the daylight time, such as `'Eastern Daylight Time'`.

MapID   Contains a string containing coordinates for the world map displayed by the Control Panel's Date/Time applet. Allows scrolling of the map, although unlike some versions of Windows 95, individual time zones are not highlighted.

TZI   Contains time zone information, a structure documented in KB article Q115231.

CURRENTVERSION\TRACING

Found in Windows 2000 and later versions, the `Tracing` subkey contains information that Windows uses to manage IIS tracing of certain events.

CURRENTVERSION\TYPE 1 INSTALLER

Adobe Illustrator Type1 fonts may be used with Windows XP by converting these fonts to TrueType fonts using the Control Panel's Fonts applet. The `Type 1 Installer` key contains up to four subkeys:

Copyrights   Contains encoded copyright information for Type1 fonts.

LastType1Sweep   Contains the time of the last Type1 font sweep, if there was one.

Type 1 Fonts   Lists any Type1 fonts installed.

Upgraded Type1   Lists any upgraded Type1 fonts installed.

CurrentVersion\Userinstallable.drivers

Any user-installed drivers are listed in the `Userinstallable.drivers` subkey. An example of a user-installed driver might be the Sound Blaster driver. This driver is not installed automatically by Windows XP.

In Windows XP, the generic sound driver, `wdmaud.drv`, is listed as the following:

```
Wave : REG_SZ : wdmaud.drv
```

CurrentVersion\Windows

The `CurrentVersion\Windows` subkey (remember we are still in `HKEY_LOCAL_MACHINE\Software\Microsoft\Windows NT`) contains five value entries. Entries in this section are used to support both Windows XP as it currently runs (`AppInit_DLLs`) and legacy applications (the other entries):

`AppInit_DLLs` Tells Windows XP to attach the specified `.dll`s to all Windows applications. Loading any Windows application will, after restarting the system, load the specified `.dll`s. This feature is used for debugging and performance monitoring, for example.

`Swapdisk` Specifies the location where Windows for MS-DOS in standard mode will swap non-Windows applications. Not terribly useful for Windows XP, and this entry's value is not specified in a default installation of Windows XP.

`Spooler` Tells any applications that might check the `win.ini` file whether to use the spooler. A string (`yes` or `no`) tells the application whether the spooler will or will not be used.

`DeviceNotSelectedTimeout` Sets the time frame, in seconds, that the system waits for an external device to be turned on. Specific printers may have their own values, set in the Printer Manager.

`TransmissionRetryTimeout` Sets the system default time frame for the Printer Manger to attempt to send characters to a printer. Specific printers may have their own values, set in the Printer Manager.

CurrentVersion\Winlogon

Ah, we've come to an important part of the registry. 'Bout time, you say? `WinLogon` contains the configuration for the logon portion of Windows XP. Many logon defaults are stored in this subkey. Each important entry is covered in detail below. The first list shows those entries present on all Windows XP installations. A list of optional components comes next.

`AutoRestartShell` A value of `0x1` indicates that if the shell (usually Explorer) crashes, then Windows XP will automatically restart it. A value of `0x0` tells Windows to not restart the shell (the user will have to log off and log back on to restart the shell).

`CachedLogonsCount` Contains the number of cached logons. If Windows XP is unable to find an authenticating domain controller, Windows authenticates the user's logon using the information cache. The default value is 10 cached entries.

`CachePrimaryDomain` Contains the name of the current domain. If no domain is established, the value will be `NEWDOMAIN`. Not available in Windows XP Home Edition.

DcacheUpdate   Listed by some sources as not used by Windows NT 4, this entry does have a value, which may be a date/time variable.

DebugServerCommand   Used with the internal Microsoft debug tool used to debug CSRSS.exe, a Windows Executive subsystem used to display graphics for text-mode applications. The default value of this string is no.

DefaultDomainName   Contains the default domain name, usually the domain the user last logged on to. The default value is NEWDOMAIN. If the computer cannot log on to a domain such as an XP Home client, the default value is the computer name.

DefaultUserName   Contains the name of the last user who logged on successfully. Displayed if DontDisplayLastUserName has a value of 0.

DontDisplayLastUserName   If this REG_STRING value is 0, the name of the last user to successfully log on will automatically be displayed in the system logon dialog box. Setting this value to 1 will force users to enter both a username and a password to log on. If using automatic logon, make sure this value is set to 0.

LegalNoticeCaption   An optional dialog box may be displayed prior to logging on a user. This value contains the dialog box's title. Typical usage of this dialog box is to advise users of organizational policy (such as a policy that a user may not install software without management approval). It is used with the value LegalNoticeText.

LegalNoticeText   A dialog box may optionally be displayed prior to logging on a user. This value contains the dialog box's text. Typical usage of this dialog box is to advise users of organizational policy (such as a policy that a user may not install software without management approval). Used with LegalNoticeTitle.

PowerdownAfterShutdown   For computers that support automatic power-down, Windows XP is able to perform a power-down. Some computers (such as those with the ATX-style motherboards and many notebooks) support automatic power-down. Set this string value to 1 to enable automatic power-down.

ReportBootOk   Used to enable or disable automatic startup acceptance. This happens after the first successful logon. Use a value of 0 when using alternative settings in BootVerification or BootVerificationProgram.

Shell   Sets the shell or user interface displayed by Windows XP once a user has successfully logged on. The default value is Explorer.exe, though for users who insist, Program Manager, File Manager, or another shell program can be substituted. For users not using Explorer, entries in Shell might be: taskman, progman, wowexec. If the shell cannot be executed, then Windows will execute the programs found in the shell directory.

ShutdownWithoutLogon   The Windows XP logon dialog box has a button to shut down the system. For Windows XP Professional users, this button is enabled, and for Windows Server users, this button is disabled. When ShutdownWithoutLogon is equal to 1, the button is enabled. Changing this button for a server allows a user who's not logged on to shut down the server—but then so does the power switch.

System   The default entry is lsass.exe, the Local Security Authority system. The lsass.exe program is the one that displays the logon dialog box (displayed when the user presses Ctrl+Alt+Delete), and it uses many of the entries in this subkey. Not available in Windows XP Home Edition.

Userinit   Specifies which executable(s) run when the user logs on. Typically, userinit.exe starts the shell program (see Shell, previously discussed), and nddeagnt.exe starts NetDDE (Network DDE).

VmApplet   Runs the Control Panel's System Properties applet.

There are a number of entries that don't exist by default in WinLogon. These entries may be added to modify the logon behavior of the system. The list below shows those optional WinLogon entries that I am aware of:

AllocateCDRoms   This value entry is used to restrict access to the CDs in the CD-ROM drives to the currently logged-on user only. Otherwise, if not restricted, CD-ROM contents and drives are accessible to all processes on the system.

AllocateFloppies   This value entry is used to restrict access to the floppy disks in the floppy drives to the currently logged-on user only. Otherwise, if not restricted, floppy contents and drives are accessible to all processes on the system.

AutoAdminLogon   When used with DefaultPassword and DefaultUserName, and when DontDisplayLastUserName is false (0), AutoAdminLogon logs on a user automatically without displaying the logon dialog box.

CacheLastUpdate   Used internally by WinLogon and should not be modified.

CacheValid   Used internally by WinLogon and should not be modified. The typical value is 1.

DcacheMinInterval   Contains a value, in seconds, that specifies the minimum time period before the domain list cache is refreshed. Since refreshing the domain list cache may be a lengthy process and because the cache is refreshed when a workstation is unlocked, it may be wise to change this value to a longer period of time. The range of this value is from 120 seconds to 86,400 seconds (that's one day).

DefaultPassword   Used with AutoAdminLogon to provide password information for an automatic logon.

WARNING   Be careful of both DefaultPassword and AutoAdminLogon because they can create security problems if misused. Do not automatically log on a user with special privileges, and resist the urge to automatically log on the system administrator for servers. The password stored in DefaultPassword is not encrypted, and AutoAdminLogon doesn't know or care who is sitting in front of the machine when it starts up and logs on the user.

DeleteRoamingCache   To conserve disk space, locally cached profiles may be deleted when the user logs off using this value. Set DeleteRoamingCache to 1, and when the user logs off, their cached profile will be deleted. Computers used by many users who have roaming profiles can create cached profiles that consume a substantial amount of disk space.

KeepRasConnections Normally when a user logs off, all RAS sessions are canceled. By setting KeepRasConnections to 1, the system will keep these RAS sessions active through logons and logoffs. This is useful when there is a permanent connection to a WAN (such as the Internet) that must be maintained.

LogonPrompt Placing a string (up to 255 characters) in this value allows displaying an additional message to users when they log on. This value is similar to the LegalNoticeText value in that it provides a method to advise all users who log on of something.

PasswordExpiryWarning Provides a warning, in days, to users when their password is going to expire. The default is 14 days, though a shorter period—typically 5 days—is often used.

ProfileDlgTimeOut Contains the amount of time, in seconds, in which a user must respond to the choice of using a local or a roaming (remote) profile. The default time-out period is 30 seconds.

RASForce Used to force checking of the Logon Using Dial-up Networking check box in the logon dialog box. If RASForce is set to 1, then it is checked; if 0, it is unchecked. This is meaningful only if RAS is installed and the computer is a member of a domain. Not available in Windows XP Home Edition.

RunLogonScriptSync Windows XP is able to run both the logon script (if there is one) and the initialization of the Program Manager shell at the same time. If RunLogonScriptSync is set to 1, the logon script will finish before Windows starts to run Program Manager.

SlowLinkDetectEnabled Determines if slow link detection is enabled. Used with roaming (remote) profiles to help minimize the amount of time a user might have to wait before a local profile is used.

SlowLinkTimeOut Sets the amount of time (in milliseconds) that the system will wait for a slow connection when loading a user's profile.

Taskman When the name of an alternative task manager is specified, Windows will use the specified program. The default task manager is taskmgr.exe.

Welcome Allows you to specify the text displayed in the title of the logon and lock/unlocked screens. Include a leading space in this text to separate your text from the default title, which is retained.

You can use the MMC with the Policy Editor snap-in to modify many of these settings.

CURRENTVERSION\WOW

WOW, or Win16 on Win32, is a system where legacy 16-bit Windows applications may be run on newer 32-bit Windows systems. WOW emulates Windows 3.1 in standard (not enhanced) mode.

The WOW key contains eight subkeys:

boot Contains drivers (communications, display, mouse, keyboard, and so on) used to emulate the Windows 3.1 mode.

boot.description   Contains a description of the computer system (hardware) such as display, keyboard, and mouse. This subkey also includes the language support requirement—for instance, English (American).

Compatibility   The concept of compatibility and applying minor patches to the operating system to allow legacy applications that are not directly compatible with the newer version is an old one. In this case, compatibility is maintained between the 3.1 emulation and earlier versions of Windows.

keyboard   Holds the keyboard driver .dll file and the keyboard type and subtype.

NonWindowsApp   Could contain two entries, **ScreenLines** and **SwapDisk**. Generally, this section is not used in WOW unless these lines existed in the previous installation of Windows 3.*x*.

SetupPrograms   Contains a list of commonly known installation and setup programs.

standard   Contains entries from the standard-mode settings of **System.Ini**. If Windows XP upgraded a Windows 3.*x* installation, and **system.ini** had modifications affecting standard mode (the mode that WOW runs in), these entries are moved to this subkey.

WowFax   Contains only the subkey **SupportedFaxDrivers**.

> **WowFax\SupportedFaxDrivers**   Contains the name of the supported fax drivers. The only entries, by default, are for WinFax, E-FAX, MAXFAXP, Quick Link II Fax, Quick Link Gold, and ProComm Plus.

ODBC

ODBC (Open Database Connectivity) is a system for Windows (both Windows XP/2000/NT and Windows 95/98/Me) used by applications to share data stored in databases. With ODBC, an application is able to open a database written by another application and read (and sometimes update) data in the database using a set of common API calls.

ODBC, having been around for a while, originally worked using a setup file called **ODBCINST.ini**. Today that file's contents have been moved to the registry as a subkey under **ODBC**, called (guess!) **ODBCINST.ini**. In the **ODBCINST.ini** subkey, there will be information about each installed driver. Drivers commonly installed include Access, Oracle, SQL Server, FoxPro, dBASE, and text files.

NOTE   To learn more about ODBC, I recommend one of my programming books for database programmers, such as Database Developer's Guide with Visual C++ 4 (Que, ISBN 0-672-30913-0). Though this book is out of print, copies are still available from some sources and libraries.

Policies

The Policies subkey contains settings used for network conferencing and system certificates. Most systems will have only a few data values within Policies.

Program Groups

`Program Groups` contains Program Manager's program groups. If a user runs Program Manager and creates any groups, then these groups will appear in the `Program Groups` key.

The `Program Groups` key also contains a single value:

ConvertedToLinks   This value indicates that program groups were converted to Explorer links. If this value is equal to `0x0` or does not exist, Windows will attempt to convert program groups to links.

Secure

There's no documentation on the `HKEY_LOCAL_MACHINE\Software\Secure` subkey. No entries seem to exist in this key.

Voice

Information about the Windows XP text-to-voice engine is contained in the `Voice` subkey. This functionality is not available on all Windows systems.

Windows 3.1 Migration Status

The `HKEY_LOCAL_MACHINE\Software\Windows 3.1 Migration Status` subkey is used to tell Windows XP that the system has migrated the existing Windows 3.*x* `.ini` and `Reg.dat` files to Windows.

Deleting the `Windows 3.1 Migration Status` key causes Windows XP, on the next boot, to prompt the user to migrate. Afterwards, Windows XP will re-create the value and subkeys as needed.

Chapter 19

Introduction to HKEY_LOCAL_MACHINE\System and HKEY_CURRENT_CONFIG

THE HKEY_LOCAL_MACHINE\System key contains information about the system and system configuration. The hive HKEY_CURRENT_CONFIG is a partial mapping of HKEY_LOCAL_MACHINE\System\ CurrentControlSet and information from HKEY_LOCAL_MACHINE\Software. We'll discuss these hives and keys in this final chapter of the book.

- ◆ The control set, beginning with CurrentControlSet
- ◆ The Mounted Devices key
- ◆ The Select key
- ◆ The Setup key
- ◆ The HKEY_CURRENT_CONFIG hive

HKEY_LOCAL_MACHINE\System

In a typical installation, seven subkeys exist in HKEY_LOCAL_MACHINE\System:

CurrentControlSet   Windows XP boots from this control set. It is typically a mapping of ControlSet001 or ControlSet002.

ControlSet001   This is the primary control set, used by default to boot Windows XP.

ControlSet002   This is the backup control set, used to boot in the event that ControlSet001 fails.

LastKnownGoodRecovery   This key shows which configuration was used when the last known good startup option was selected.

MountedDevices   This key shows disk drives that are available to the system.

Select   This small subkey contains information about which control set is used to boot the computer.

Setup   This is a small subkey with information about the initial setup (installation) of Windows XP.

Prior to Windows XP, HKEY_LOCAL_MACHINE\System also contained the DISK key. This object contains parameters used by the Disk Administrator program. Under Windows NT 4, it includes CD-ROM mappings and other binary information. Windows 2000 uses this object differently, in that the Disk Administrator functionality is now part of MMC (Microsoft Management Console). Windows XP does not have this subkey.

Some systems will have slightly different names for the two numbered control sets. Some computers won't have a ControlSet002. For example, your computer might have the following subkeys:

◆ ControlSet001

◆ ControlSet003

It is also possible, but unlikely, that there may be more than two numbered control sets. Each control set key contains four objects:

◆ Control

◆ Enum

◆ Hardware Profiles

◆ Services

The Enum subkey was new as of Windows 2000 and was added to support Plug and Play.

WHAT ARE MAPPED REGISTRY SUBKEYS?

Sometimes more than one name refers to a single registry subkey (control sets in particular do this, as does HKEY_CLASSES_ROOT). The process is simple. Consider the mythical Fizbin Company, the proud maker of Fizzits. (You do use Fizzits, don't you?) Fizbin found that with a high-tech product such as Fizzits, it was necessary to have a high-tech company. They also wanted to make it seem as if they were more international than they really were.

However, Fizbin has a number of stodgy stockholders, most of whom have never seen or used a Fizzit and have only a vague idea of what a Fizzit is or does. These stockholders were dead set against renaming the company for any reason.

As a compromise, the company would still be called the Fizbin Company. However, when doing business, they would use the name International Fizbin. Regardless of the name used, it's the same company. A letter written to the president of International Fizbin still goes to the president of Fizbin Company—one company, two names. Therefore, when the president of Fizbin Company hires a new marketing manager, she automatically becomes the marketing manager of International Fizbin, too.

CurrentControlSet

The current control set is the control set used to boot the computer. It is copied from `Control-Set001` or from one of the other numbered control sets if `ControlSet001` failed to boot, and it is the main control set. Except for the contents of keys that may be different, `ControlSet002` (or `Control-Set003`, if that is what your computer has) has a structure identical to `CurrentControlSet`.

`CurrentControlSet` consists of four subkeys:

Control   Consists of information used to control how Windows XP operates. This information controls everything from bootup to networking parameters to Windows to WOW (Windows on Windows).

Enum   Contains information about hardware, the hardware state, legacy devices, and so on.

Hardware Profiles   You use Hardware Profiles to configure Windows XP for hardware platforms that change frequently. This is common when dealing with notebook computers, for example, as they may be either docked or undocked. An installation of Windows will have one or more hardware profiles. The use of hardware profiles is most helpful when running Windows on portable computers, particularly those with docking stations.

Services   Manages services, such as support for hardware. `Services` are changed using the Control Panel's Services applet.

Control

The `Control` subkey has a number of data values used for booting and system initialization. `Control` also contains about 30 subkeys.

`Control`'s value entries are:

CurrentUser   The name of the currently logged-on user. Actually, this entry always has the default value `USERNAME` because Windows XP does not update it. Client Services for NetWare will store user specific configuration code in this value.

RegistrySizeLimit   Found only on Windows systems prior to Windows XP. If you change the registry size limit from the default value of 8MB, `RegistrySizeLimit` will contain the maximum registry size in bytes. Though users are only able to set the registry size limit in MB, Windows will store the value as a DWORD containing the maximum registry size in bytes. Windows XP does not have the limitations on registry size that earlier versions of Windows had.

SystemStartOptions   This entry contains startup options passed from firmware or the startup contained in `boot.ini`. Options could include debugging information (such as a debugging port and the debugging port parameters) and perhaps information on the system root directory. Changing this value is useless—the system will restore it from the `boot.ini` file at the next reboot.

WaitToKillServiceTimeout   This entry contains the time, in milliseconds, to wait before killing a service when Windows XP is shutting down. If this value is too small, Windows may kill a service before it has finished writing its data; if too large, a hung service will delay shutdown. It is best to leave the `WaitToKillServiceTimeout` value at its default value of 20000 (which is 20 seconds) unless you know you are having a problem.

AGP

The AGP (Advanced Graphics Port) subkey contains a number of values used to configure AGP graphics adapters.

APMACTIVE

The ApmActive object holds information about APM (Advanced Power Management). One value entry, named Active, has a REG_DWORD value of either 1 (APM is active) or 0 (APM is not active). Use of APM requires that the hardware support this function. Most newer desktop and notebook computers support APM. If your computer doesn't support APM, or you are not using APM, then this subkey may be missing from your registry. Information about ApmActive can be found at http://www.microsoft.com/hwdev/archive/onnow/apm.asp.

APMLEGALHAL

New as of Windows 2000, the ApmLegalHal object holds information about whether the hardware actually supports APM. Generally, Windows queries the BIOS to determine APM support. If your BIOS does not have support for APM, then this subkey may be missing from your computer. When the HAL implementation is Halx86.dll, this object will be present and have a value of 1. This object is not found on all versions of Windows.

ARBITERS

New as of Windows 2000, the Arbiters object holds information about bus arbitration. This is part of the support for Plug and Play that has been added to Windows. At least two subkeys exist in Windows XP in Arbiters: AllocationOrder and ReservedResources. The ReservedResources subkey contains the following data values:

- BrokentMemAtF8
- BrokenVideo
- Gateway9500Workaround
- Pci
- PCStandard
- Root

These data values contain either REG_RESOURCE_REQUIREMENTS_LIST objects or REG_SZ strings, as necessary.

BACKUPRESTORE

New as of Windows 2000, the BackupRestore object holds settable configuration information for the backup program that comes with Windows. Included in this object are AsrKeysNotToRestore, DllPaths, FilesNotToBackup, and KeysNotToRestore. AsrKeysNotToRestore is new to Windows XP and indicates which Automated System Recovery keys are not to be restored.

BIOSINFO

New as of Windows 2000, the `Biosinfo` object supports Plug and Play. Entries in this object include date codes for the BIOS and `FullDecodeChipsetOverride`, a value that indicates support for extended address decoding.

BOOTVERIFICATIONPROGRAM

One entry in `BootVerificationProgram`, `ImagePath`, is a data value with a string variable that the boot verification program uses. This value will contain the filename of the boot verification program. Enter an empty string, or delete this value if no boot verification program is used.

   The program used to verify the boot must be supplied by the user.

   To enable boot verification, it is also necessary to set `ReportBootOk` to 1 in `HKEY_LOCAL_MACHINE\` `Software\Microsoft\Windows NT\CurrentVersion\WinLogon`. If `ReportBootOk` is 0, automatic (default) start-up acceptance is disabled. This happens after the first logon that is successful. (`ReportBootOK` is defined in Chapter 18.)

CLASS

The `Class` subkey contains a number of GUIDs, one for each of the following labels. Notice that though later versions of Windows rename some items slightly (making them plural), the functionality of the object is the same despite renaming.

- ◆ `Batteries` (new as of Windows 2000)
- ◆ `Computer` (new as of Windows 2000)
- ◆ `Disk drives` (new as of Windows 2000)
- ◆ `Display adapters`
- ◆ `DVD/CD-ROM drives` (new as of Windows 2000)
- ◆ `Floppy disk controllers` (new as of Windows 2000)
- ◆ `Floppy disk drives` (new as of Windows 2000)
- ◆ `Human Interface Devices` (new as of Windows 2000)
- ◆ `IBM Digital Signal Processors` (new as of Windows 2000)
- ◆ `IDE ATA/ATAPI controllers` (new as of Windows 2000)
- ◆ `IEEE 1394 Bus host controllers` (new as of Windows 2000)
- ◆ `Imaging devices` (new as of Windows 2000)
- ◆ `Infrared devices` (new as of Windows 2000)
- ◆ `Keyboard` (new as of Windows NT 4)
- ◆ `Keyboards` (new as of Windows 2000)

◆ Medium Changers (new as of Windows 2000)

◆ Memory technology driver (new as of Windows 2000)

◆ Mice and other pointing devices (new as of Windows 2000)

◆ Modem (new as of Windows NT 4)

◆ Modems (new as of Windows 2000)

◆ Monitors (new as of Windows 2000)

◆ Mouse (new as of Windows NT 4)

◆ Multifunction adapters (new as of Windows 2000)

◆ Multiport serial adapters (new as of Windows 2000)

◆ Network adapters

◆ Network Client (new as of Windows 2000)

◆ Network Protocol (new as of Windows 2000)

◆ Network Service (new as of Windows 2000)

◆ Non-Plug-and-Play drivers (new as of Windows 2000)

◆ NT Apm/Legacy Support (new as of Windows 2000)

◆ Other devices

◆ PCMCIA adapters (new as of Windows 2000)

◆ Ports (COM & LPT)

◆ Printer (new as of Windows NT 4)

◆ Printers (new as of Windows 2000)

◆ SCSI and RAID controllers (new as of Windows 2000)

◆ SCSI controllers (new as of Windows NT 4)

◆ Smart card readers (new as of Windows 2000)

◆ Sound, video, and game controllers

◆ Storage volumes (new as of Windows 2000)

◆ System devices (new as of Windows 2000)

◆ Tape drives

◆ Universal Serial Bus controllers (new as of Windows 2000)

Each of these subkeys contains one or more of the following value entries:

(Default)   The default name as a string; for example, Mouse or Mice and other pointing devices. When using RegEdit, the name (Default) displays as (Default) with the parentheses.

Class   The device's class as a single word with no embedded spaces. It is a string that is similar to the default entry. For mice and other pointing devices, the value is Mouse.

Default Service   A string defining the default service, usually the same as the Class entry.

Icon   An index to the object's icon.

Installer32   A string pointing to the program or system to install this type of device. The Control Panel, or the SysSetup.dll, installs many devices.

LegacyInfOption   A string with information about legacy support. It is usually a string name for the device, similar to the Class entry.

NoDisplayClass   A flag, 1 or 0, indicating whether to display the class.

NoInstallClass   Contains information as to whether the device is installable.

TroubleShooter-0   Contains information used for the interactive troubleshooter application in Windows XP.

UpperFilters   A filter designed for the specific device.

SilentInstall   A flag value that indicates that this object's installation driver should send no messages or pop-up windows that require user response.

Subkeys do not have all possible entries. The entries (Default) and Class are universal to all subkeys, while Icon, Installer32, and others exist in many (but not all) subkeys.

CoDeviceInstaller(s)

New as of Windows 2000, the CoDeviceInstaller(s) object holds the CLSIDs of handlers for installations from removable media such as CD-ROM drives.

Com Name Arbiter

New as of Windows 2000, Com Name Arbiter manages COM (Common Object Model) DB services. The two values contained in this key include ComDB and ComDBMerge, each of which contain a REG_BINARY value.

ComputerName

ComputerName contains two subkeys and no value entries:

ActiveComputerName   This subkey includes a single value entry, ComputerName, with a string containing the computer's name.

ComputerName   This subkey contains a single value entry, ComputerName, with a string containing the computer's name.

And, yes, both subkeys contain exactly the same thing. Changing ComputerName will cause Windows, on the next reboot, to copy this string to ActiveComputerName.

CONTENTINDEX

New as of Windows 2000, the ContentIndex object works with the management of content indexing. It contains a number of subkeys for both catalogs and languages. Values stored under this subkey include those shown in Table 19.1.

TABLE 19.1: ContentIndex DATA VALUES

ENTRY NAME	DESCRIPTION
CiCatalogFlags	Controls file-modification scanning. Valid values are either (or both): 0x00000001: Disable notification processing for all remote UNC paths. 0x00000002: Disable notification processing for all local paths.
DaemonResponseTimeout	Time-out, in minutes, used by CiDaemon.exe, when an attempt is made to index a corrupt file.
DefaultColumnFile	Fully qualified filename for the file containing column definitions for .asp and .idq files.
DelayedFilterRetries	Number of times (default is 240) the Indexing Service will attempt to reindex a document when a failure occurs.
DelayUsnReadOnLowResource	If this value is set to 1, the USN (Update Sequence Number) is not read while there is a high demand on resources.
DLLsToRegister	A REG_SZ list of DLL files called by the Indexing Service when it starts.
EventLogFlags	If 0, then do not log events; if 2, then log when one or more embedded objects could not be filtered by the Indexing Service. A value of 1 is reserved and should not be specified.
FilterBufferSize	In kilobytes, the size of the buffer used by the Indexing Service filter.
FilterDelayInterval	The delay, in seconds, to suspend indexing when there are more than the specified number of documents in the filter buffer.
FilterDirectories	If 0, then system properties for directories are not indexed; if non-0, then they are indexed.
FilterFilesWithUnknownExtensions	If 0, then files with unknown (unregistered) extensions are not indexed; if non-0, then they are indexed.
FilterIdleTimeout	The amount of time, in milliseconds, that the Indexing Service holds loaded IFilter DLL files that are no longer being used.

Continued on next page

TABLE 19.1: ContentIndex DATA VALUES *(continued)*

ENTRY NAME	DESCRIPTION
FilterRemainingThreshold	Specifies the Indexing Service will wait until this value (in files, the default is 32) in the buffer is exceeded before reindexing.
FilterRetries	The Indexing Service will attempt to retry indexing this many times. The default is 4, and any value between 0 and 10 may be specified.
FilterRetryInterval	Specifies, in minutes, the amount of time that the Indexing Service waits to index a file that is not accessible because the file is in use by another process.
ForcedNetPathScanInterval	Specifies, in minutes, the amount of time that the Indexing Service waits between forced indexing on paths that do not have file notifications.
ForcePathAlias	A value of 1 forces path aliasing.
GenerateCharacterization	A value of 1 generates abstracts.
IMAPSvcInstance	Internet Mail Access instance number.
IsapiDateTimeFormatting	A value of 0 uses the current user's local, 1 uses the default local, and 2 forces use of the format YYYY/MM/DD HH:MM:SS.
IsapiDateTimeLocal	A value of 0 displays time in UTC (Coordinated Universal Time); 1 uses the local time format for display.
IsapiDefaultCatalogDirectory	The catalog directory (the default is System).
IsapiMaxEntriesInQueryCache	The maximum number of queries that may be cached. The default is 2; any value between 0 and 100 may be specified.
IsapiMaxRecordsInResultSet	Specifies the maximum (default is 5000) rows in the result set. Any value between 0 and 1,000,000 may be specified.
IsapiQueryCachePurgeInterval	Specifies, in minutes, the cache purge interval.
IsapiRequestQueueSize	Specifies, in requests, the request queue size. Values may range from 0 to 100,000.
IsapiRequestThresholdFactor	This value, times the number of processors located in the system, sets the number of Indexing Service threads.
IsAutoAlias	A value of 0 does not create aliases; 1 sets aliases.
IsEnumAllowed	A value of 0 does not allow enumeration; 1 allows enumeration. Enumeration, if allowed, can seriously impact server performance.
IsIndexingIMAPSvc	If 0, then does not index IMAP mail; 1 indexes IMAP mail.
IsIndexingNNTPSvc	If 0, then does not index NNTP messages; 1 indexes NNTP Messages.

Continued on next page

TABLE 19.1: ContentIndex DATA VALUES *(continued)*

ENTRY NAME	DESCRIPTION
IsIndexingW3SVC	If 0, then does not index IIS server files; 1 indexes IIS server files.
IsReadOnly	If 0, then the catalog is not updated; 1 updates the catalog.
LeaveCorruptCatalog	If 0, then does not repair errors in the catalog; 1 repairs errors in the catalog.
LowResourceCheckInterval	In seconds (the default is 60), the time interval to check for low resources when creating word lists.
LowResourceSleep	In seconds (the default is 180), the time interval to wait when low resources are detected. Valid values range from 5 to 1200.
MajorVersion	Indexing Service major version number. Typically a value of 3 is found in Windows XP system.
MasterMergeCheckpointInterval	Number of kilobytes (default is 2048, valid values range from 256 to 4096) of memory used when a merge must be restarted.
MasterMergeTime	The time, in minutes since midnight, that a merge will occur. Valid values are 0 to 1439, the default is 60 minutes (1 A.M.).
MaxActiveQueryThreads	The maximum number of threads used for a query.
MaxActiveRequestThreads	The maximum number of threads used for a request.
MaxAutoAliasRefresh	Time, in minutes, that the Indexing Service will wait prior to refreshing aliases. Default is 15 minutes, though this value may range from 0 to 10,080 (7 days).
MaxCachedPipes	Specifies the maximum number (default is 3, though this value may range from 0 to 1000) for cached pipes.
MaxCatalogs	The number of catalogs (default is 32; valid values are 0 to 1000) that may be open at any given time.
MaxCharacterization	The maximum size for an abstract, in characters. The default is 160 characters, with a maximum of 500 allowed.
MaxDaemonVmUse	The amount of paged memory (in kilobytes) allocated to an Indexing Service daemon. Values between 10,240 and 419,303 may be specified.
MaxFilesizeFiltered	Actual content in files that exceed this value (specified in kilobytes) are not indexed; instead only the file properties are. The default is 256 kilobytes.
MaxFilesizeMultiplier	Allows the Indexing Service to recover from corrupt files by specifying how many times larger the indexing data may be compared to the actual file size.

Continued on next page

TABLE 19.1: ContentIndex DATA VALUES *(continued)*

ENTRY NAME	DESCRIPTION
MaxFreshCount	When this number of un-indexed, in the master index, files is reached, the Indexing Service starts a new master merge. The default value is 20,000, and may be any valid number greater than 1000.
MaxFreshDeletes	When this number of files are deleted, the Indexing Service starts an update to the master index. The default value is 320 and may be any valid number greater than 10.
MaxIdealIndexes	Specifies the maximum number of indexes that the system will have. The default is 5, and valid values range from 2 to 100.
MaxIndexes	This value specifies the maximum number of persistent indexes that a catalog may contain. The default is 25, and must range from 10 to 150.
MaxMergeInterval	The time, in minutes, that must pass between consecutive merges. The default is 10, but any value between 1 and 60 may be specified.
MaxPendingDocuments	The number of documents that must be waiting prior to the index being determined to be out of date.
MaxQueryExecutionTime	The time, in milliseconds, for processing a query. Any valid positive value may be specified. The default is 10,000, which is 10 seconds.
MaxQueryTimeslice	Specifies the time, in milliseconds, for a query. Time values range from 1 to 1000, the default is 50 milliseconds.
MaxQueueChunks	The number of buffers used to track unfiltered documents. The range is 10 to 30, and the default is 20.
MaxRestrictionNodes	The maximum number of notes created in a single query by the Indexing Service. The default is 5000, and the value may be any nonzero positive number.
MaxRunningWebhits	Specifies the number of instances of the object module webhits .dll that are in use. The default is 20, and the range may be any nonzero value less than or equal to 200.
MaxShadowFreeForceMerge	When this percentage of available disk space is used by shadow indexes, a new master merge is performed. Though the documented values are listed as being 5 to 100 percent, most installations seem to have a value of 500 (0x1F4) in this object.
MaxShadowIndexSize	When this percentage of total disk space is used by shadow indexes, a new master merge is performed. Values range from 5 to 25 percent, with the default being 15 percent.

Continued on next page

TABLE 19.1: ContentIndex DATA VALUES *(continued)*

ENTRY NAME	DESCRIPTION
MaxSimultaneousRequests	Specifies the maximum number of simultaneous query requests via named pipes that the Indexing Service will support. The default is 50 requests, and this value may range from 1 to 20,000.
MaxTextFilterBytes	The amount of data processed from a given file with a "well known" extension. Specified in bytes, any nonzero value may be specified. The default value is 26,214,400 bytes.
MaxUsnLogSize	The maximum allowed size (the default is 8,388,608 bytes) for the USN (Unique Synchronization Number log file). Any nonzero positive value is valid for this object's value.
MaxWebhitsCpuTime	The amount of time, in seconds, that webhits.dll waits prior to timing out. Values range from 5 to 7200.
MaxWordlistIo	When I/O reaches this threshold, the Indexing Service will wait. Expressed in kilobytes per second, the default is 410, and must be greater than 100.
MaxWordListIoDiskPerf	If you have enabled performance counters, the Indexing Service will wait whenever the threshold specified is reached. Specified as a nonzero percent, the default is 10.
MaxWordLists	Specifies the maximum number of word lists that may exist before the Indexing Service merges them into the master index. The default is 20, and values between 10 and 30 may be specified.
MaxWordlistSize	Maximum amount of memory, in 128-kilobyte blocks, that may be used for a word list. The default is 20 (2,560,000 bytes) and may range between 10 (1,280,000 bytes) and 30 (3,840,000 bytes).
MinClientIdleTime	Time, in seconds, that the query client is idle before it can be dropped. The default is 600.
MinDiskFreeForceMerge	The minimum free disk space that must be available prior to a master merge being processed. The default is 15, and the range is 5 to 25.
MinDiskSpaceToLeave	The minimum amount of free space, in megabytes, that the Indexing Service will leave free on a disk. The default is 20, and any positive value may be specified.
MinIdleQueryThreads	The number of threads that must be kept idle to process incoming queries. The default is 1, and any value up to and including 1000 may be specified.
MinIdleRequestThreads	The number of threads that must be kept idle to process incoming requests to the Indexing Service. The default is 1, and any value up to and including 1000 may be specified.

Continued on next page

TABLE 19.1: ContentIndex DATA VALUES *(continued)*

ENTRY NAME	DESCRIPTION
MinimizeWorkingSet	Set to 0 to maximize the Indexing Service working set, or set to 1 (the default) to minimize the working set size.
MinMergeIdleTime	In percent, the time the CPU must be idle prior to performing an annealing merge. The default is 90, and values range from 10 to 100 percent.
MinorVersion	The Indexing Service's minor revision number. For Windows XP, this value is 1; for earlier versions, this value is 0.
MinSizeMergeWordlists	The word list must exceed this value (in kilobytes) to force a shadow merge. The default is 256.
MinWordlistBattery	On battery-operated computers, the battery life must exceed this value to allow the Indexing Service to run. If the default of 100 is specified, the Indexing Service will not run while on batteries.
MinWordlistMemory	Specifies, in megabytes, the memory for word list creation. The default is 5, and values may range from 1 to 100.
NNTPSvcInstance	The NNTP server's instance number. Typically 1.
PropertyStoreBackupSize	The number of system pages on disk that are used to back up the primary property cache. The default is 1024, and may range from 32 to 500,000.
PropertyStoreMappedCache	The property store cached page count. The default is 4 pages, and may be any integer value.
RequestTimeout	Time, in milliseconds, for a client to wait for a named pipe connection to the Indexing Service.
ScanBackoff	The Indexing Service use of system resources. Range is 0 to 20, with a default of 3. Microsoft notes that you should not specify values between 11 and 20 as these are reserved for future use.
SecPropertyStoreBackupSize	The number of system pages on disk that are used to back up the secondary property cache. The default is 1024, and may range from 32 to 500,000.
SecPropertyStoreMappedCache	The number of pages in memory for the property cache. The default is 4, and any positive value may be specified.
StartupDelay	The Indexing system will delay this number of milliseconds prior to starting any actual work. This allows the system to properly start up without dealing with the overhead of the Indexing Service. Specify a positive value; the default is 480,000 (8 minutes).
StompLastAccessDelay	Files newer than this number (in days) will have their last accessed date updated by the Indexing Service. The default is 7 days, and a value between 0 and 1,000,000,000 is required.

Continued on next page

TABLE 19.1: ContentIndex DATA VALUES *(continued)*

ENTRY NAME	DESCRIPTION
ThreadClassFilter	CiDaemon.exe's priority class filter. Values include: 0x20 (normal priority) 0x40 (idle priority, the default) 0x80 (high priority)
ThreadPriorityFilter	CiDaemon.exe's priority filter. Values include: -2 (lowest priority) -1 (lower priority) 0 (normal priority) 1 (higher priority, the default) 2 (highest priority)
ThreadPriorityMerge	The Indexing Service's merge thread priority filter. Values include: -2 (lowest priority, the default. RegEdit will show this value as 4294967294.) -1 (lower priority) 0 (normal priority) 1 (higher priority) 2 (highest priority)
UsnLogAllocationDelta	When the USN log is full, this amount (in bytes) is removed to make space for additional new entries. Any positive value may be specified; the default is 1048576.
UsnReadMinSize	The minimum size (in bytes) for the USN log before change notifications are processed. The default is 4096, and must be within the range of 1 and 524,288.
UsnReadTimeout	The time (in seconds) to wait prior to processing notifications to the USN log. The default is 300, and the value must greater than 0 and less than or equal to 43,200.
W3SvcInstance	The instance number of the web server (IIS) being indexed. Any nonzero positive value may be specified, which must match an existing web server's instance number.
WebhitsDisplayScript	When 0, the Indexing Service will not return hit highlights. A value of 1 will return highlights in known script files, and a value of 2 will search and return highlights in all script files.
WordlistUserIdle	The time, in seconds, to wait until filtering is resumed.

Two additional subkeys are present: `Catalogs` and `Language`. `Catalogs` defines the catalog folders. `Language` specifies language specific items, including noise filters and so on.

CONTENTINDEXCOMMON

New as of Windows 2000, `ContentIndexCommon` contains the column file entry.

CRASHCONTROL

`CrashControl` brings to mind all kinds of marvelous things. However, the subkey `CrashControl` is actually a basic function for Windows XP when it fails at the system level. `CrashControl` options are generally set using the System applet's Startup and Recovery dialog box (see Figure 19.1). The Startup and Recovery dialog box is activated from the Advanced tab of the Control Panel's System Properties applet.

FIGURE 19.1

The Startup and Recovery system properties

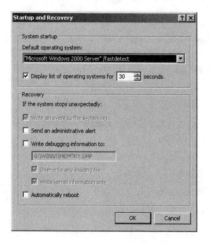

`CrashControl` options are set in the System Failure section at the bottom of the dialog box. Windows XP has seven value entries in `CrashControl`:

AutoReboot   The Automatically Restart control state is set to 0 if there is no automatic reboot after a STOP error.

CrashDumpEnabled   This is the Write Debugging Information control state. It is set to 0 if no dump is required after a STOP error. A value of 1 indicates that a full dump is requested. A value of 2 indicates that a kernel dump is requested, and a value of 3 indicates a minidump (64KB only) is requested.

DumpFile   This is the text control under the Write Debugging Information control. It contains the path to the dump file, by default `%SystemRoot%\memory.dmp`. This file will be as large as (or slightly larger than) the physical memory installed in the computer. Make sure the device to receive this file is large enough to hold the file.

LogEvent   This is the Write an Event to the System Log control state and indicates that the crash event should be logged. When set to 0, Windows will not make an event log entry after a STOP error. This flag cannot be set in Windows XP server versions except by using direct registry manipulation.

MinidumpDir   Found only in Windows XP, this value indicates where (a folder location) to save the minidump (a partial dump of 64KB in size). This object is a REG_EXPAND_SZ string, and defaults to %SystemRoot%\Minidump.

Overwrite   This is the Overwrite Any Existing File control state. It is set to 0 if there is no automatic reboot after a STOP error. If this value is set, Windows XP will create a new debugging file with a new name.

SendAlert   This is the Send an Administrative Alert control state. When set to 0, Windows XP will not send an administrative alert after a STOP error.

Windows 2000 contains an entry, KernelDumpOnly, whose value indicates whether to save all memory or only the Windows 2000 kernel in the dump file. All entries in CrashControl are REG_DWORD except for MinidumpDir and DumpFile, which are REG_EXPAND_SZ. Some references indicate that these values are REG_SZ; this information is incorrect.

CRITICALDEVICEDATABASE

New as of Windows 2000, the CriticalDeviceDatabase object contains the list of devices critical to the operation of Windows. This list is PnP-based.

DEVICECLASSES

New as of Windows 2000, the DeviceClasses object contains CLSID listings of all devices installed on the system.

FILESYSTEM

Entries in FileSystem vary based on the installed file system(s). These are the value entries in FileSystem:

Win31FileSystem   When this value is 1, LFNs (long filenames) are disabled. This maintains compatibility with older operating systems, such as Windows 3.1. However, using this option may create compatibility issues with Windows NT 4 or Windows 95/98/Me, and it should be set only if absolutely necessary. Also, do not set this option except immediately after installing Windows. If you do, it may cause existing, installed applications to fail.

Win95TruncatedExtensions   The following behavior will take place depending on the setting of this option: Say you have two files, smith.htm and jones.html. If Win95TruncatedExtensions is equal to 1 (the default), the command DEL *.htm will delete both files. The command DEL *.html will delete only jones.html. When Win95TruncatedExtensions is equal to 0, the command DEL *.htm will delete only smith.htm. The command DEL *.html will delete only jones.html.

NtfsDisable8dot3NameCreation   If set to 1, Windows XP will not automatically generate standard 8.3 filenames. Without 8.3 filenames, any legacy DOS or Windows 3.*x* applications lacking LFN support will fail. They will not be able to open or otherwise use any file that has an LFN unless the file is renamed to a valid 8.3 filename.

NtfsEncryptionService   This value holds the name of the service used to encrypt files under the NTFS file system. This object may not exist if there are no NTFS volumes present on the system.

NOTE   Some applications, including Microsoft Office, will not even install if NtfsDisable8dot3NameCreation *is set.*

WARNING   Be careful about changing these options. Once installed, some systems do not expect that the state of the FileSystem *entries will change, or that support for LFNs will change, either. This is especially true when changing from allowing LFNs to not allowing them.*

GRAPHICSDRIVERS

By default, the GraphicsDrivers subkey contains subkeys called DCI (Display Control Interface) and UseNewKey. The DCI subkey contains a value entry named Timeout, which has a default value of 7. The UseNewKey object is not populated.

NOTE   Microsoft dropped DCI support for Windows NT 4, and yet DCI remains in Windows XP. Go figure.

One optional entry can be found in GraphicsDrivers: DisableUSWC. With certain higher-performance video cards, Uncached Speculative Write Combining (USWC) memory is not cached. In addition, certain computers have a memory conflict with USWC that may cause the user interface to fail to respond after certain drag-and-drop operations. The DisableUSWC entry does not have a value; its presence in the registry is sufficient to turn off USWC. This type of error is rare.

GROUPORDERLIST

Each service in HKEY_LOCAL_MACHINE\System\CurrentControlSet\Services is listed in the GroupOrderList subkey along with a binary value indicating the order in which the group is to be loaded at system startup time. Systems typically have the following groups:

- ◆ Base
- ◆ Boot Bus Extender (supported in Windows 2000 and later versions only)
- ◆ Extended base
- ◆ ExtendedBase (supported in Windows 2000 and later versions only)
- ◆ Filter

New!   *NOTE   The* FSFilter *entries are new to Windows XP and are part of the file system filters.*

- ◆ FSFilter Activity Monitor
- ◆ FSFilter Anti-Virus
- ◆ FSFilter Bottom
- ◆ FSFilter Cluster File System
- ◆ FSFilter Compression
- ◆ FSFilter Content Screener
- ◆ FSFilter Continuous Backup
- ◆ FSFilter Copy Protection
- ◆ FSFilter Encryption
- ◆ FSFilter HSM
- ◆ FSFilter Infrastructure
- ◆ FSFilter Open File
- ◆ FSFilter Physical Quota Management
- ◆ FSFilter Quota Management
- ◆ FSFilter Replication
- ◆ FSFilter Security Enhancer
- ◆ FSFilter System
- ◆ FSFilter System Recovery
- ◆ FSFilter Top
- ◆ FSFilter Undelete
- ◆ Keyboard Class
- ◆ Keyboard Port
- ◆ Ndis
- ◆ NetBIOSGroup (supported in Windows 2000 and later versions only)
- ◆ Network (supported in Windows 2000 and later versions only)
- ◆ Parallel Arbitrator
- ◆ Pnp Filter (supported in Windows 2000 and later versions only)
- ◆ PNP_TDI (supported in Windows 2000 and later versions only)
- ◆ Pointer Class

- Pointer Port

- Primary Disk

- SCSI CDROM Class

- SCSI Class

- SCSI Miniport

- SpoolerGroup

- Streams Drivers (supported in Windows 2000 and later versions only)

- System Bus Extender

- Video

- Video Init

- Video Save

HIVELIST

Hivelist contains the following value entries listing registry keys and their source files. \REGISTRY\ MACHINE\HARDWARE does not have a source file because Windows creates this key dynamically at boot time. Specific user information (those items that include a SID) will vary based on the currently logged-on user and Windows installation.

- \REGISTRY\MACHINE\HARDWARE =

- \REGISTRY\MACHINE\SECURITY = \Device\Harddisk0\Partition1\WINNTWS\System32\ Config\SECURITY

- \REGISTRY\MACHINE\SOFTWARE = \Device\Harddisk0\Partition1\WINNTWS\System32\ Config\SOFTWARE

- \REGISTRY\MACHINE\SYSTEM = \Device\Harddisk0\Partition1\WINNTWS\System32\Config\ SYSTEM

- \REGISTRY\MACHINE\SAM = \Device\Harddisk0\Partition1\WINNTWS\System32\Config\SAM

- \REGISTRY\USER\.DEFAULT = \Device\Harddisk0\Partition1\WINNTWS\System32\Config\ DEFAULT

- \REGISTRY\USER\S-1-5-21-45749729-16073390-2133884337-500 = \Device\Harddisk0\ Partition1\WINNTWS\Profiles\Administrator.000\ntuser.dat

Here is some further information about the preceding names:

\REGISTRY: The name for the registry itself

\MACHINE: HKEY_LOCAL_MACHINE

\USER: HKEY_USERS

Windows dynamically creates HKEY_CURRENT_CONFIG at boot time. Windows creates HKEY_CLASSES_ ROOT from other registry entries at boot time. Windows creates HKEY_CURRENT_USER when a user logs on.

IDConfigDB

The IDConfigDB subkey is the identification for the current configuration. This key contains four value entries:

CurrentConfig   Indicates which control set is being used.

IsPortable   A value of 1 indicates that this computer is defined as a portable computer.

PropertyProviders   Specifies the name of the .dll file used to display property sheets under Windows XP. The default is profext.dll; however, this object may not be found in all installations.

UserWaitInterval   Specifies the period of time a user waits. In the bootup Hardware Profile/Configuration Recovery menu, Windows takes the default choice after the user waits the time specified in UserWaitInterval. The value is in seconds; the default value is 30 seconds. IDConfigDB also contains the hardware profiles in the Hardware Profiles subkey.

The Windows XP installation process will create one configuration for the user. This default configuration is Original Configuration. Any additional configurations that users create will also appear in the Hardware Profiles subkey.

NOTE   See the Hardware Profiles tab in the System applet of the Control Panel to get more information about setting up multiple hardware profiles.

IDConfigDB also contains the Alias and CurrentDockInfo subkeys, in which Windows XP saves the docking status.

KEYBOARD LAYOUT

There are two subkeys in Keyboard Layout; each deal with supporting MS-DOS applications to use languages other than U.S. English:

DosKeybCodes   Contains a list of keyboard layouts and a two-letter (MS-DOS-compatible) country code.

DosKeybIDs   Contains a list of keyboard layouts and keyboard ID values.

NOTE   See the Knowledge Base article Q117850, titled "MS-DOS 6.22 COUNTRY.TXT File," for more information about support for MS-DOS applications.

KEYBOARD LAYOUTS

Keyboard Layouts contains a subkey for each keyboard layout that Windows XP supports for Windows applications. Each layout subkey contains two, or more, entries:

Layout File   The name of the .dll file that manages the keyboard using that character set; for example, the Icelandic keyboard layout .dll file is named kbdic.dll.

Layout Text   A string identifying the keyboard layout; for example, for Iceland, the string is `Icelandic`.

Layout ID   A string, containing a number, identifying the keyboard layout.

Layout Display Name   A string identifying a resource string with the display name for this keyboard layout. The default layout display names are located in the `input.dll` file.

It is possible, though difficult, to create custom keyboard layouts.

Support is available to Windows XP users who wish to use the Dvorak keyboard layouts. Use the Regional Settings applet in the Control Panel to select either the Dvorak right- or left-hand layout. No special hardware is required, though the markings on the standard keyboard will be incorrect. This is because the Dvorak keyboard has a different keyboard layout with letters arranged based on how often they are used.

LSA

LSA, the Local Security Authority, locally validates security for user rights, secret objects, and trusted domain objects. LSA uses the `msv1_0.dll` file to do the actual validation of security. Within the LSA key is a subkey called `msv1_0` that contains items for `msv1_0`.

WARNING   *Microsoft strongly recommends that you do not touch anything in the LSA subkey. An incorrect entry or change could send the system into a state where no users are able to log on, and the system would have to be completely restored.*

Data objects contained in LSA include:

- Authentication Packages
- Bounds
- Notification Packages
- Security Packages
- LsaPid
- SecureBoot
- auditbaseobjects
- crashonauditfail
- disabledomaincreds
- everyoneincludesanonymous
- fipsalgorithmpolicy
- forceguest
- fullprivilegeauditing
- limitblankpassworduse
- lmcompatibilitylevel

- ◆ nodefaultadminowner
- ◆ nolmhash
- ◆ restrictanonymous
- ◆ restrictanonymoussam

There are also a number of subkeys in LSA, including:

- ◆ AccessProviders
- ◆ Data
- ◆ GBG
- ◆ JD
- ◆ Kerberos
- ◆ MSV1_0
- ◆ Skew1
- ◆ SppiCache

MEDIACATEGORIES

MediaCategories is a key used primarily to describe multimedia controls and objects. Each item is a CLSID-named key containing two value entries. The first entry is Display, a REG_BINARY that indicates to Windows to display this object. The second entry is Name, a REG_SZ containing the name of the object.

MEDIAINTERFACES

MediaInterfaces is a key used to describe multimedia interfaces.

MEDIAPROPERTIES

MediaProperties is a key used primarily to describe MIDI and other device properties. This key contains subkeys to describe any MIDI schemes (custom configurations in the Control Panel's Multimedia Properties applet) that a user has created.

Contained in the MediaProperties key is a subkey named PrivateProperties. In PrivateProperties are three subkeys: DirectInput, Joystick, and Midi (if a MIDI-compatible sound board exists).

The DirectInput key contains subkeys for a number of devices. Each device has a single data object named Flags2. If Flags2 exists with a value, then DirectInput internally maps device axes to logical axes. This prevents the user from remapping the axes.

The Joystick key contains a number of subkeys, each containing data objects. The following data objects can be defined in Joystick, though not all may be present in all configurations:

- ◆ Flags1
- ◆ OEMData

◆ OEMHardwareID

◆ OEMName

The Midi key contains two subkeys, each containing MIDI ports and emulated ports.

MEDIARESOURCES

MediaResources is a key used to describe the resources available for multimedia (specifically for MIDI) on the computer.

Two to six subkeys exist in this section:

DirectSound   Contains information about Windows XP's support for DirectSound, including information about compatibility issues between specific applications and patches implemented to resolve these compatibility issues.

Joystick   Contains information about the driver used to interface with joystick type devices.

msvideo   Contains information about direct video drivers.

MCI   Contains information about MCI (Media Control Interface) devices.

MIDI   Contains subkeys for each installed physical and virtual device. The device subkeys contain definitions for instruments that the user has defined.

NonGeneralMIDIDriverList   Contains resource definitions (including instrumentation) for users with nongeneral MIDI hardware.

MEDIASETS

MediaSets is a key used to describe resources available for multimedia on the computer. This object may not be found on all systems. See "Custom Property Sets and Interfaces" in the Windows DDK for more information on MediaSets.

MSPAPER

This key is for the Microsoft document imaging system, part of Microsoft Office. There are a number of objects in MSPaper, including:

AutoRotation   A REG_DWORD value, controlling whether an image is to be rotated or not.

LocaleID   A REG_DWORD value, specifying the locale identifier (used to determine the language). This object may not be set in all systems.

MaxImageSize   A REG_DWORD value, specifying the maximum scanned image size.

PerformOCR   A REG_DWORD value, controlling whether an image is to be processed using OCR (Optical Character Recognition) to convert the image to text.

NETWORK

The Windows XP Network key houses much of Windows XP's network configuration information. This information includes Connections, NcQueue, RefNames, and several CLSID-named objects.

NetworkProvider

The `NetworkProvider` key contains two objects, `HwOrder` and `Order`, which indicate the specific order of network providers. Both usually contain the same contents. There is a single value entry in each, `ProviderOrder`, a REG_SZ string containing a comma-separated list of providers. The default value is `RDPNP, LanmanWorkstation WebClient`.

If you're using RAS (Remote Access Service), there is an option to disable automatic (ghosted) restoration of network connections at logon. Most users prefer to have connections restored automatically at logon. If RAS is not installed, you can enable ghosted connections by putting the `RestoreConnection` value entry in the `NetworkProvider` key. This REG_DWORD entry may contain a value of either `0x1` or `0x0`. If the value is `0x0`, Windows XP will ghost connections.

NLS

The `NLS` subkey holds Windows XP's National Language Support functionality. There are three or four possible subkeys in `NLS`. However, the `OEMLocale` subkey is not present in installations of Windows unless an OEM has customized Windows for a specific locale.

CodePage `CodePage` contains a series of value entries. Each value's name matches a code page ID. The value will contain a REG_SZ value equal to the filename for that code page. For code pages with no supporting file, the value entry's value will be an empty string. `CodePage` also includes the following additional value entries and subkeys (some of these subkeys may not be found on all systems):

ACP This value is the active (or default) code page used by Windows.

MACCP This value is the Macintosh active code page.

OEMCP This value is the OEM code page to translate ANSI characters.

OEMHAL This value is the OEM display of extended characters at a command prompt.

EUDCCodeRange This subkey holds information for fonts classified as End User Defined Characters. The information is in value entries that indicate ranges of the double-byte character set that are usable for EUDC.

Language The `Language` subkey contains entries used to identify files that support different languages. Each value entry's name matches the ID for a language. The entry contains a REG_SZ data value equal to the name of the file to support that language. If there is no support for the language (the support files have not been installed), the value entry's contents will be an empty string.

Locale The `Locale` subkey contains entries used to identify files that support different locations. Each value entry's name matches the ID for a location. The entry contains a REG_SZ data value equal to a numeric 1 if there is support for the locale. The value has an empty string if there is no support for the locale.

OEMLocale Not normally present on systems, OEMs add the `OEMLocale` subkey to support systems in their specific locale. Entries in `OEMLocale` are similar to those in the `CodePage` subkey.

OEMLocale contains a series of value entries. Each value's name matches a code page ID. Each entry contains a REG_SZ value equal to the filename for that code page. For code pages with no supporting file, the entry's value will be an empty string.

NOTE *Windows will only check the* OEMLocale *subkey if a specific locale ID is not found in the default locale file* (locale.nls).

NTMS

New as of Windows 2000, the NTMS object supports the Windows NT Media Services. Support includes OMID (On-Media Identifiers).

Under NTMS is an object, OMID (Original Manufacturer ID), which in a typical installation contains the object named Tape. In Tape are these objects:

HP   Contains information for the HP Media Label Library.

MTF   Contains information for the MTF (Microsoft Tape Format) Media Label Library.

QIC   Contains information for the QIC (QIC113 Format) Media Label Library.

PNP

New as of Windows 2000, the PnP object manages the Windows Plug and Play capabilities. Much of this information is specific to certain computers and devices. This object includes the following subkeys:

BusInformation   Contains information about the presence and status of various bus types.

Pci   Contains PCI device information.

PciIrqRouting   Contains information about the actual handling of the PCI bus's IRQ routing. Remember, PnP/PCI supports sharing IRQs.

PRINT

The Print key contains all the information accessed by Windows XP when a printer is being used. In addition to the subkeys documented next, there are also a few value entries in the Print key (not all installations will have all of these entries):

BeepEnabled   Enables or disables a beep when a printer error is detected. Set to 0x1 to turn on beeps.

MajorVersion   The version number's high digit(s); for a product with a version number of 4.3, the major version is 4.

MinorVersion   The version number's low digit(s); for a product with a version number of 4.3, the minor version is 3.

NoRemotePrinterDrivers   Contains the name of print drivers incompatible with remote connections. This entry typically has Windows NT Fax Driver as a value.

PortThreadPriority The Windows XP kernel priority for the printer driver. A value of 0 indicates normal priority, –1 indicates lower than normal priority, and 1 indicates a higher than normal priority.

PriorityClass Used to set the priority class for the print spooler. A value of 0 (or no value) indicates a default priority class will be used. The default priority class is 7 for Windows XP Professional, 0 for Windows XP Home Edition, and 9 for Windows servers. Coding any other value will be translated to the priority class for servers, 9.

RouterCacheSize The size of the router cache, in pages.

SchedulerThreadPriority Sets the priority for the scheduler. Setting SchedulerThreadPriority to 1 sets the priority to above normal, 0 sets the priority to normal, and –1 (0xFFFFFFFF) sets the priority to below normal.

Upgrade A flag to indicate the upgrade status.
The Print key contains five or six subkeys, discussed next.

Environments

The Environments key contains subkeys for each possible platform. Each platform key contains two subkeys: Drivers and Print Processors. The platform subkeys are:

Windows 4.0 For Windows 95 drivers.

Windows IA64 Provides support for Intel 64-bit systems.

Windows NT Alpha_AXP Provides support for Alpha systems.

Windows NT x86 Provides support for Intel-based systems.

Each platform subkey contains:

Drivers Contains the driver information for each installed printer driver. Each installed printer has a separate subkey named for the printer. Printer driver configuration subkeys are contained in a subkey named Version-0 for Windows NT 3.1, Version-1 for Windows NT 3.5, Version-2 for Windows NT 4, or Version-3 for Windows 2000 and Windows XP. Each printer driver subkey contains the following value entries:

Attributes Driver attributes; a typical value for attributes might be 0x00000002.

Configuration file The .dll file that holds the printer configuration.

Data file The .ppd or .dll file containing printer data.

Datatype The data type, such as RAW; most printers leave this field blank.

Dependent files Any files that the printer driver is dependent on.

Driver The name of the printer driver .dll file.

DriverDate The date the driver was developed or released.

DriverVersion The version of the printer driver .dll file.

HardwareID   An identifying string for the hardware (an example might be `Apple Laser-writer53b1`).

Help File   The name of the printer driver's help file.

Manufacturer   The name of the printer's manufacturer (`Apple`, for example).

Monitor   If there is a print monitor, the print processor will direct its output to the print monitor.

OEM URL   The URL for the manufacturer of the printer.

Previous Names   The original name of the printer (for example, `Apple LaserWriter Iig`).

Provider   The name of the printer driver's origin (for example, `Microsoft Windows 2000`).

TempDir   A flag that indicates that the printer driver will use a special temporary directory for work files.

Version   Holds the printer's driver version number. It is a value of 0 for Windows NT 3.1, 1 for Windows NT 3.5, 2 for Windows NT 4, and 3 for Windows 2000 or Windows XP.

Print Processors   There are one or more print processors with Windows XP. The default processor is WinPrint (`winprint.dll`).

Forms

By default, forms used when printing documents are defined in the `Forms` subkey. However, a user may also specify a custom form. In most installations of Windows, the following forms will exist:

- `A2 420.0 x 594.0 mm`
- `B3 364.0 x 515.0 mm`
- `Foolscap 13.50 x 17.00in`
- `#10 Env. 9.50 x 4.12 in`
- `DL Env. 220.0 x 110.0 mm`
- `Fanfold 9.50 x 11.00 in`
- `Fanfold 12.00 x 8.50 in`
- `Fanfold 14.50 x 11.00 in`
- `Letter+ 9.00 x 13.30 in`
- `A4+ 223.5 x 355.6 mm`

Create custom forms using the Printers applet in the Control Panel. To do this, follow these steps:

1. Select File ➤ Server Properties. The Forms tab includes a section to create a new form.

2. Click Create a New Form.

3. Change the name in Form Description to a name that describes the new form.

4. Change the sizes and margins to match your form.

5. Click Save Form.

The Metric/English Units control is for display—you may display forms in either metric or English units.

Monitors

No, not that big thing on your desk. A monitor for printing is a program that receives messages from printers and displays information about print jobs to the user. The printer may be either locally connected to a computer or connected directly to the network with a network card installed inside the printer. When working with a network-connected printer, the management of the printer is a bit more difficult. In this case, a printer monitor program receives messages from the printer and then process these messages for the user.

Each type of networked printer is different, and there are different monitors designed to work with each printer. Monitors exist for Hewlett Packard, Lexmark, Digital, and other network printers. There are also monitors for locally connected printers that are more generic in nature—they work with any printer connected to the printer port. Default monitors include PJL (Printer Job Language), USB, and Local Port.

PendingUpgrades

Any pending upgrades are located in the `PendingUpgrades` subkey.

Printers

Each printer installed has a subkey under the `Printers` key. The printer's key name is the same as the printer's description; by default, this is also the system name for the printer.

A printer's subkey is made up of one subkey and the following value entries:

`Attributes`   The printer attributes—for example, those set in the Scheduling tab of the printer's property page.

`ChangeID`   A funny number that is not documented anywhere. Every time you change something on the printer, `ChangeID` changes, too. It is used to track changes.

`Datatype`   The type of data passed to the printer, such as RAW.

`Default DevMode`   The printer's default DevMode structure.

`Default Priority`   The default priority.

`Description`   A printer description provided by the user.

`DnsTimeout`   The amount of time to wait before a DNS timeout, in milliseconds; the default is 15 seconds.

`Location`   User-supplied text describing the printer's location.

Name   The name of the printer.

Parameters   Any printer parameters.

Port   The port the printer connects to.

Print Processor   The print processor; WinPrint is the default.

Printer Driver   The .dll file used to drive the printer.

Priority   The printer's priority: 1 is lowest, 99 is highest.

Security   Security attributes.

Separator File   The name of the job separator file.

Share Name   If the printer is shared, this is the share name.

SpoolDirectory   The directory used to spool, if not the default spool directory.

StartTime   Sets the earliest time the printer is available (see UntilTime). If StartTime = 0 and UntilTime = 0, the printer is always available.

Status   The current printer status.

TotalBytes   The total number of bytes in the print queue.

TotalJobs   The total number of jobs in the print queue.

TotalPages   The total pages to be printed.

txTimeout   The amount of time to wait before the printer times out, in milliseconds; the default is 45 seconds.

UntilTime   Sets the latest time the printer is available (see StartTime); this is set in the Scheduling tab of the printer's property page.

The subkey, PrinterDriverData, has information about the printer's paper sources, permissions, and more. Information in PrinterDriverData is specific to each driver.

Providers

The default provider for printing in Windows XP networking is LanMan Print Services Internet Print Provider. Another provider is Microsoft Windows Network. However, specifying the Microsoft Windows Network provider may cause problems in some installations.

There are a number of value entries in the Providers key:

EventLog   A DWORD value that specifies the event log status.

LogonTime   A REG_BINARY value that specifies the time of logon.

NetPopup   A DWORD value that specifies the NetPopup service status. It is set to 1 to display a pop-up message for remote print jobs.

NetPopupToComputer   A DWORD value that specifies the NetPopup service status. It is set to 1 to display a pop-up message for remote print jobs.

Order A REG_MULTI_SZ multiple string that specifies the order of providers. Generally, Windows XP networks should list LanMan Print Services Internet Print Provider first in the Order value. If you find that you are unable to browse printers, check the Order value and ensure that it contains only LanMan Print Services Internet Print Provider and not Microsoft Windows Network.

RestartJobOnPoolEnabled A DWORD value that specifies whether print jobs are restarted.

RestartJobOnPoolError A DWORD value that specifies the time waited to restart a job (default is 600 seconds).

RetryPopup A DWORD value that specifies whether a pop-up message is displayed if a print job fails.

Under the Providers key, you'll also find a subkey for each provider; I'll use the LanMan Print Services Internet Print Provider as an example. The following entries may be present for each provider:

DisplayName A string that contains the name of the provider. For our example, it is LanMan Print Services Internet Print Provider.

Name A string that contains the name of the driver .dll. For our example, it is win32spl.dll.

LoadTrustedDrivers An optional data value that is a DWORD value. If it is set to 1, drivers will not be installed from a remote print server, but may only be taken from the path specified in TrustedDriverPath.

TrustedDriverPath An optional data value that is a string containing the path to load trusted printer drivers. Both this data value and LoadTrustedDrivers must be set to 1 to restrict the loading of drivers.

The provider key may also contain a subkey named Servers. This subkey may contain an entry called AddPrinterDrivers, a DWORD value that specifies who is allowed to add printer drivers using the Printer applet in the Control Panel. When set to 1, only administrators and print operators (if on a server) or power users (if on a workstation or member server) may add printer drivers.

PRIORITYCONTROL

The PriorityControl key contains a single value entry: Win32PrioritySeparation. It is a DWORD value containing a value between 0 and 32. (Note that Windows NT 4 uses values between 0 and 2.) The Advanced tab of the System applet in the Control Panel includes a section called Performance. Click the Performance Options button to display the Performance Options dialog box, where you'll find a set of buttons that allows you to optimize performance for applications or background services. When set to Applications, Win32PrioritySeparation is 18; otherwise it is 26. Windows XP Professional sets this value to 0; XP Home Edition sets this value to 2.

WARNING   Microsoft cautions that the only way to successfully set the Win32PrioritySeparation value is to use the System applet in the Control Panel. Do not attempt to change this value manually.

PRODUCTOPTIONS

ProductOptions has a single value entry that describes the type of product installed; Windows XP has several different versions.

ProductType   Contains a string with one of the following values:

LANMANNT   A Windows NT Advanced Server (3.1), a Windows NT 4 PDC or BDC configuration, or a Windows server that is running Active Directory.

SERVERNT   Windows NT Server 3.5 or later that is running in stand-alone (not a domain) mode.

WinNT   Windows NT Workstation, Windows 2000 Professional, or Windows XP (nonserver versions).

SAFEBOOT

New!

This object contains two subkeys, Minimal and Network. Each subkey contains definitions of what product options are available for each safeboot mode. This key is new to Windows XP.

SCSIPORT

New!

This object is used to manage some special SCSI devices. These devices include certain disk drives, scanners, and so forth. Note that not all SCSI devices are listed in this section—only those that require special handling. This key is new to Windows XP.

SECUREPIPESERVERS

Pipes—long, hollow objects used to transport fluid materials. Or a virtual connection between two computers using a network. A secure pipe is a virtual pipe that has encryption and other security features to enhance the security of data being moved in the pipe.

In most Windows XP systems, there's an object entry in the SecurePipeServers subkey: winreg, for the remote Windows registry editing facility. The winreg subkey contains one value entry and one subkey. The value entry, named Description, has the value Registry Server.

The winreg\AllowedPaths subkey contains a single value entry, Machine, a REG_MULTI_SZ string containing the registry keys that may be edited remotely using the Registry Editor. Modify this string to add or remove keys that you wish to edit remotely. The default values in the Machine entry are:

- System\CurrentControlSet\Control\ProductOptions
- System\CurrentControlSet\Control\Print\Printers
- System\CurrentControlSet\Services\Eventlog
- Software\Microsoft\Windows NT\CurrentVersion
- System\CurrentControlSet\Services\Replicator

SECURITYPROVIDERS

Security and privacy are important buzzwords in cyberspace today. Governments are working hard at limiting privacy and, essentially, security. It is also the keen intent of users to keep what is private to them private from the prying eyes of their governments. This all makes security a hot, hot topic.

Windows XP includes support for security in the `SecurityProviders` subkey. `SecurityProviders` contains five subkeys, discussed next.

NOTE *The abbreviation* `CA` *in the entries in* `SecurityProviders` *doesn't stand for California; it stands for Certificate Authority.*

CertificationAuthorities

The `CertificationAuthorities` subkey contains the names of a number of different organizations that issue certificates and their products. A typical installation might contain the following values:

- AT&T Certificate Services
- AT&T Directory Services
- AT&T Prototype Research CA
- GTE Cybertrust ROOT
- internetMCI Mall
- Keywitness Canada Inc.
- Thawte Premium Server CA
- Thawte Server CA
- Verisign Class 1 Public Primary CA
- Verisign Class 2 Public Primary CA
- Verisign Class 3 Public Primary CA
- Verisign Class 4 Public Primary CA
- Verisign/RSA Commercial
- Verisign/RSA Secure Server

Ciphers

A *cipher* is a code or key used to encrypt or encode an object. Generally, the term *ciphers* includes the methodology in addition to the actual key. The `Ciphers` subkey contains information relating to a number of cipher technologies. Some of these technologies are more secure than others, although all are satisfactory for most routine work. Ciphers supported in Windows XP include the following:

- DES 40/56
- DES 56/56
- NULL
- RC2 128/128
- RC2 40/128

- RC4 128/128

- RC4 40/128

- RC4 64/128

- Skipjack

- Triple DES 168/168

Hashes

A hash is a form of cipher. Typically thought of as weak encryption, hashes can serve well when small amounts of data are being transmitted; some hash algorithms are quite secure. Windows XP includes the ability to support the following hashes:

- MD5

- SHA

KeyExchangeAlgorithms

Key exchange is the process in which users are able to pass keys among themselves. An encryption algorithm, called a *public-key algorithm*, is used to send the key using plain text. This is possible because the key used to encrypt the message is not the same key used to decrypt it. The encryption key, called the *public key*, is given to everyone who is to send you encrypted messages. You keep the secure decryption key to read your encrypted messages.

WARNING   *Improperly designed public-key encryption schemes have a great potential for back-door type flaws. A back door is a way to decrypt a message without actually having the decryption (or private) key. Many governments argue that they should have the ability to decrypt messages to promote law and order. However, that policy has yet to be shown as valid.*

Key exchange algorithms supported by Windows XP include the following:

- Diffie-Hellman

- Fortezza

- PKCS

Protocols

Protocols are the methodologies used to transmit information. Five security protocols are supported in Windows XP. The most common protocol that computer users are aware of is SSL (Secure Sockets Layer), which is used to transmit secure information over TCP/IP networks such as the Internet.

Secure protocols that Windows XP supports include:

- Protocols\Multi-Protocol Unified Hello

- Protocols\PCT 1.0

- Protocols\SSL 2.0

◆ `Protocols\SSL 3.0`

◆ `Protocols\TLS 1.0`

ServiceGroupOrder

The `ServiceGroupOrder` subkey has a single value entry named `List`. The `List` entry includes a REG_MULTI_SZ string containing the names, in load order, for the services.

When Windows XP starts the services, it will start them in the order given in `ServiceGroupOrder\List`. Services within each group then start in accordance with the values contained in the `Current-ControlSet\Control\GroupOrderList` key.

Drivers are loaded into memory in the order specified in `ServiceGroupOrder\List`; the default for most servers is the following:

◆ `System Bus Extender`

◆ `SCSI miniport`

◆ `port`

◆ `Primary disk`

◆ `SCSI class`

◆ `SCSI CDROM class`

◆ `filter`

◆ `boot file system`

◆ `Base`

◆ `Pointer Port`

◆ `Keyboard Port`

◆ `Pointer Class`

◆ `Keyboard Class`

◆ `Video Init`

◆ `Video`

◆ `Video Save`

◆ `file system`

◆ `Event log`

◆ `Streams Drivers`

◆ `PNP_TDI`

◆ `NDIS`

- NDISWAN

- TDI

- NetBIOSGroup

- SpoolerGroup

- NetDDEGroup

- Parallel arbitrator

- extended base

- RemoteValidation

- PCI Configuration

Notice that service groups may be different in different computers. Don't expect your system to have entries in the same order, or even to always have the same entries.

NOTE *Generally, it would not be prudent to change the load order for services. Some services expect that other services are already loaded.*

SERVICEPROVIDER

The ServiceProvider subkey works with the Winsock RNR (Resolution and Registration) Service APIs. ServiceProvider contains the subkeys Order and ServiceTypes. The entries in this subkey are pointers to other registry keys and entries.

NOTE *Microsoft recommends that you do not manually change these entries.*

The subkey ServiceProvider\Order contains two value entries:

ExcludedProviders A REG_MULTI_SZ string consisting of numbers indicating service providers. Most Windows XP systems do not have any entries in this list. To add an excluded provider, enter the service provider's identifier from Table 19.2.

TABLE 19.2: SERVICE PROVIDERS AND THEIR IDENTIFIERS

SERVICE PROVIDER	IDENTIFIER
NS_SAP	1
NS_NDS	2
NS_TCPIP_LOCAL	10
NS_TCPIP_HOSTS	11
NS_DNS	12

Continued on next page

TABLE 19.2: SERVICE PROVIDERS AND THEIR IDENTIFIERS *(continued)*

SERVICE PROVIDER	IDENTIFIER
NS_NETBT	13
NS_WINS	14
NS_NBP	20
NS_MS	30
NS_STDA	31
NS_CAIRO	32
NS_X500	40
NS_NIS	41

ProviderOrder   A REG_MULTI_SZ value entry containing zero, one, or more values. The number of values varies with the number of installed protocols. Systems might have `Tcpip`, `NwlnkIpx`, or other values in this entry. These values correspond to `CurrentControlSet\Services` values.

A second subkey under `ServiceProvider` is `ServiceTypes`. IIS uses this subkey. `ServiceTypes` typically contains four subkeys (there may be fewer or more, depending on what IIS components you have installed):

GOPHERSVC   Contains the Gopher service configuration. Information includes the GUID for the handler for Gopher requests and the TCP/IP port number (**70** by default). GOPHERSVC is not valid with Windows XP.

Microsoft Internet Information Server   Microsoft's IIS is capable of serving remotely as a service. That is, you can remotely administer IIS.

MSFTPCVC   The FTP service configuration is in this subkey. The information contained here includes the GUID for the handler for FTP requests and the TCP/IP port number (**21** by default).

W3SVC   The Web (WWW) service configuration is in this subkey. The information contained here includes the GUID for the handler for web requests and the TCP/IP port number (**80** by default).

Users may modify the TCP ports for these services; see the Windows Server Resource Kit for more information. When modifying ports, use a port number greater than 1023 to avoid conflict with any existing assigned ports.

SESSION MANAGER

`Session Manager` is a complex subkey used to manage the user's session and basic Windows startup. `Session Manager` contains a number of value entries and subkeys.

The value entries in `Session Manager` are relatively constant between different installations of Windows:

BootExecute   Specifies programs started when the system boots. The default is `autocheck autochk *` and `dfsInit`. `Autochk` is the auto-check utility that is included with Windows XP. `DfsInit` is the distributed file system initializer.

CriticalSectionTimeout   Specifies the time, in seconds, to wait for critical sections to time out. Since Windows XP (retail product) does not wait for critical sections to time out, the default value is about 30 days. Anyone care to wait that long? Not me!

EnableMCA   MCA (Machine Check Architecture) is used in some systems; some Pentium Pro processors support MCA. The default value is enabled (`1`).

EnableMCE   MCE (Machine Check Exception) is supported by some Pentium processors. By default, support for MCE is disabled.

ExcludeFromKnownDlls   Windows NT will use entries in the `KnownDLLs` key to search for `.dlls` when loading them. `ExcludeFromKnownDlls` is used to exclude a `.dll` from the `KnownDLLs` search.

GlobalFlag   Controls various Windows NT internal operations using a bitmapped flag. Table 19.3 shows some common `GlobalFlag` bit values. `GFLAGS.exe` (see Figure 19.2) is a useful tool to set `GlobalFlag`. It is a component of the Windows NT Server Resource Kit Supplement 2. There are indications that Windows XP has no support for `GlobalFlag`.

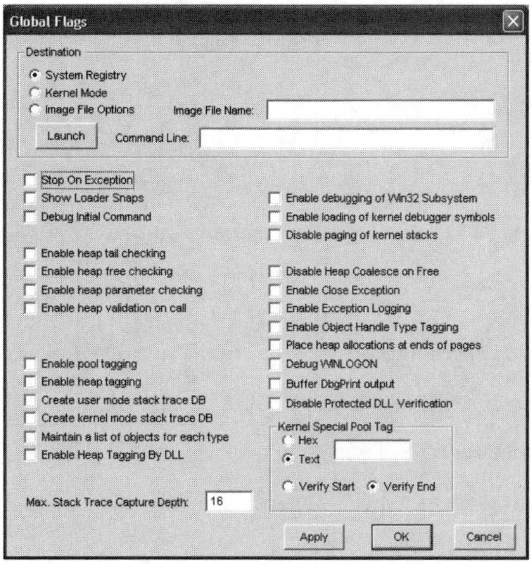

FIGURE 19.2

The GFLAGS program makes it easy to set the `Global-Flag` value. Just click and select a value to be set.

TABLE 19.3: GlobalFlag Bit Values

Value (Bit)	Description
0x00000001	Stop when there is an exception.
0x00000002	Show loader snaps.
0x00000004	Debug initial command.
0x00000008	Stop on hung GUI.
0x00000010	Enable heap tail check.
0x00000020	Enable heap free check.
0x00000040	Check heap validate parameters.
0x00000080	Validate all heap allocations.
0x00000100	Enable pool tail check.
0x00000200	Enable pool free check.
0x00000400	Set up memory tagging.
0x00000800	Enable heap tagging.
0x00001000	Create user mode stack trace DB.
0x00002000	Create kernel mode stack trace DB.
0x00004000	Maintain a list of objects for each type.
0x00008000	Enable heap tags by DLL.
0x00010000	Ignore debug privilege.
0x00020000	Enable csrdebug.
0x00040000	Enable kernel debug symbol loading.
0x00080000	Disable page kernel stacks.
0x00100000	Enable heap call tracing.
0x00200000	Enable heap coalescing.

HeapDeCommitFreeBlockThreshold   Has a default of zero.

HeapDeCommitTotalFreeThreshold   Has a default of zero.

HeapSegmentCommit   Has a default of zero.

HeapSegmentReserve   Has a default of zero.

LicensedProcessors   Specifies the maximum number of processors that are allowed. The standard retail version of Windows 2000 Server allows a maximum of four processors in a multiprocessor server environment and two processors in a workstation environment.

ObjectDirectories   Contains a list of object directories to create during startup.

ProcessorControl   An undocumented DWORD variable. The default value is 0x2.

ProtectionMode   When this value is set to 1, security is increased on shared base objects. The default of 0 reflects a weaker security level.

NOTE   *For more information on making Windows secure, see* `http://www.rl.af.mil/tech/programs/winNT/downloads/NTAG_devguide.doc`.

RegisteredProcessors   Specifies the number of processors allowed. The standard retail version of Windows 2000 Server allows a maximum of four processors in a multiprocessor server environment and two processors in a workstation environment. Standard Windows products such as Windows 95/98/Me and Windows XP Home Edition support one processor.

ResourceTimeoutCount   Specifies the number of four-second ticks allowed before a resource will time out. Windows does not normally time out on resources, and the default value is 30 days. There are also a number of subkeys in `Session Manager`, discussed next.

AppCompatibility   The `AppCompatibility` subkey contains information about the compatibility of a number of applications.

AppPatches   The `AppPatches` subkey contains patches for a number of applications. Typical installations include patches for the following:

- CWD
- MYST
- •PALED40
- USA
- VB
- VB40016

CheckBadApps and **CheckBadApps400**   These two subkeys are interrelated:

CheckBadApps   Contains applications that may be incompatible with earlier versions of Windows NT, such as Windows NT 3.51. There are only a few applications listed in this section.

CheckBadApps400   Contains applications that may be incompatible with Windows NT 4 and Windows 2000. This section has more applications listed then `CheckBadApps`.

When executing a listed application in one of these two subkeys, Windows displays a message for the user. This message tells the user about the possible problems encountered. The system does not prevent the user from running the application after displaying the warning message. This object is not found on Windows XP.

DOS Devices The DOS Devices subkey contains symbolic names and their corresponding logical names. Most systems have the following default entries in DOS Devices:

- advapi32 = advapi32.dll

- comdlg32 = comdlg32.dll

- crtdll = crtdll.dll

- DllDirectory = %SystemRoot%\System32

- gdi32 = gdi32.dll

- kernel32 = kernel32.dll

- lz32 = lz32.dll

- olecli32 = olecli32.dll

- olesvr32 = olesvr32.dll

- rpcrt4 = rpcrt4.dll

- shell32 = shell32.dll

- user32 = user32.dll

- version = version.dll

Environment The Environment subkey holds the Windows system environment variables. User environment variables are stored in the user's profile.

Executive The Executive subkey holds the Windows system executive configuration.

FileRenameOperations The FileRenameOperations subkey holds the list of files that must be renamed, but cannot be renamed at the time.

Kernel The single object, obcaseinsensitive, is a REG_DWORD flag typically set to 1, indicating that case is not considered.

KnownDLLs The KnownDLLs subkey holds the .dll files that Windows knows about and searches first during a system startup. This improves the search time in finding a specified .dll file object.

Memory Management

Memory Management controls the system's virtual memory, paging files, and so on. To define the paging file parameters, use the System applet in the Control Panel and choose the Advanced tab's Performance Options. Other entries include the following:

ClearPageFileAtShutdown If set to a value of 1, the paging file's contents (not the file, just its contents) will be cleared at shutdown. This option is useful for Windows installations that require a high degree of security. The default of 0 causes the paging file's contents to be left on the disk.

DisablePagingExecutive   Setting this value to 1 disables the Windows automatic paging system. The default of 0 allows the paging executive to run normally. Do not change this option unless you understand exactly what the effects of disabling paging are.

IoPageLockLimit   Specifies the number of lockable bytes available for an I/O operation. The default is 0, which is equal to 512K. This object is not typically found on Windows XP systems.

LargeSystemCache   Specifies that the system will favor the system cache working set rather than the processes working set. Server installations typically set this to 1, while workstations will set it to 0.

NonPagedPoolQuota   The maximum space allocated by one process in a nonpaged pool.

NonPagedPoolSize   The nonpaged pool size. The default value of 0 indicates a default size based on the system's physical memory size. The maximum value allowed is 80 percent of the physical memory size.

PagedPoolQuota   The maximum space allocated by one process in a paged pool.

PagedPoolSize   The paged pool size. The default value of 0 specifies that the value will be 32MB. This value affects the maximum registry size.

PagingFiles   The name, path, initial size, and maximum size for the system paging file(s). Set this information using the Change button in the Performance tab of the System applet in the Control Panel.

SecondLevelDataCache   Specifies the size of the second-level data cache.

SystemPages   Specifies the number of page table entries. The default value of 0 denotes that the default number of entries is to be used.

WriteWatch   Specifies that memory writes should be watched for access violations.

Power   The power management policies for both battery and nonbattery operation are defined in the Power subkey.

SFC   The System File Checker (SFC) settings are held here. Two data objects, CommonFilesDir and ProgramFilesDir (which designate paths), are found in this object.

SubSystems   The SubSystems subkey contains subsystem settings established at startup time. There is a subkey named CSRSS (short for client-server runtime subsystem). Most systems have the following entries:

Debug   The debug path, if used; most installations do not have Debug set.

Kmode   The path to the Win32 driver; the default is win32k.sys.

Optional   Defines optional components that are only loaded when the user runs an application that requires them. Typical values include Os2 and Posix.

Os2   The path and filename of the optional Windows NT OS/2 1.*x* emulator. This object may not be found on Windows XP systems.

Posix   The path and filename of the optional POSIX subsystem. This is the only POSIX entry in the registry.

Required   The default entry, `Debug Windows`, is required.

Windows   The path and name of the executable used to start the Win32 subsystem. The default value is:

```
%SystemRoot%\System32\csrss.exe ObjectDirectory=\Windows SharedSection=
1024,3072 Windows=On SubSystemType=Windows ServerDll=basesrv,1 ServerDll=
winsrv:UserServerDllInitialization,3
ServerDll=winsrv:ConServerDllInitialization,2 ProfileControl=Off
MaxRequestThreads=16
```

WPA   The `WPA` subkey contains settings for the Windows Product Authorization system. This system requires that the user "authorize" the use of their product with Microsoft. `WPA` contains three objects:

PnP   Contains a single `REG_DWORD` value named `seed`. This value contains a large number.

SigningHash-   This object, which contains additional characters after the hyphen, contains a single data object, `SigningHashData`, a `REG_BINARY` value.

SessionManager

Found only in Windows NT 4, `SessionManager` is different from `Session Manager` with a space, discussed earlier in this chapter. `SessionManager` contains lists of applications that may not run correctly with Windows NT 4. This object is not found in Windows XP.

Setup

The `Setup` key contains three value entries:

Keyboard   The default value, `STANDARD` (indicating a standard keyboard), is found in virtually all systems.

Pointer   The value `msser` indicates that the standard Microsoft serial mouse is the default choice for setup. The value `msps2` indicates that a Microsoft-compatible PS/2 mouse is connected.

Video   The default value, `VGA`, indicates that VGA is the default video choice for setup.

StillImage

The `StillImage` subkey holds information about the still-image monitoring process. Five items may be found in this object: `Debug`, `DeviceNameStore`, `Events`, `Logging`, and `Twain`.

SYSTEMRESOURCES

The SystemResources subkey holds information about various system resources, generally related to the computer's bus architecture. SystemResources contains three subkeys, discussed next.

AssignmentOrdering   The AssignmentOrdering subkey contains entries for each possible bus type. Each entry specifies either an entry (the default is PCFlat) or a REG_RESOURCE_ REQUIREMENTS_LIST object. Value entries in AssignmentOrdering include the following:

Eisa   Contains the string PCFlat.

Isa   Contains the string PCFlat.

MCA   Contains the string PCFlat.

PCFlat   Contains a REG_RESOURCE_REQUIREMENTS_LIST object.

PCI   Contains a REG_RESOURCE_REQUIREMENTS_LIST object.

PCMCIA   Contains the string PCFlat.

BusValues   Value entries in BusValues order each bus structure using a REG_BINARY object. This object also contains a second field, the use for which is unknown. Table 19.4 shows each entry and the two values stored in each.

TABLE 19.4: BUSVALUE ENTRIES

BUS TYPE	ORDER NUMBER	UNKNOWN NUMBER
CBus	9	0
Eisa	2	1
Internal	0	0
Isa	1	0
MCA (not used in Windows XP)	3	1
MPI	10	0
MPSA	11	0
NuBus	7	0
PCI	5	1
PCMCIA	8	1
TurboChannel	4	0
VME	6	0

NOTE   *Did you realize that there were that many different buses available for microcomputers? Actually, we do not use many of these buses anymore, or they are rather uncommon.*

ReservedResources   The ReservedResources subkey may contain two entries: Isa and Eisa. The Isa entry contains a REG_RESOURCE_LIST object that lists the ISA bus's reserved resource as being bus number 0. The Eisa entry, if present, contains a REG_SZ object with an empty string.

TERMINAL SERVER

The Windows Terminal Server enhances accessibility to Windows. There are about 10 entries in the Terminal Server subkey:

DeleteTempDirsOnExit   Holds a REG_DWORD value, with a default of 1.

FirstCountMsgQPeeksSleepBadApp   Holds a REG_DWORD value, with a default of 15.

IdleWinStationPoolCount   Holds a REG_DWORD value, with a default of 0.

Modems With Bad DSR   Holds a REG_MULTI_STRING value.

MsgQBadAppSleepTimeInMillisec   Holds a REG_DWORD value, with a default of 1.

NthCountMsgQPeeksSleepBadApp   Holds a REG_DWORD value, with a default of 5.

PerSessionTempDir   Holds a REG_DWORD value, with a default of 1.

ProductVersion   Holds a REG_SZ string, with a typical value of 5.0, 5.1 in XP.

TSAppCompat   Holds a REG_DWORD value, with a default of 0.

TSEnabled   Holds a REG_DWORD value, with a default of 0 or 1 in XP.

One of the subkeys found in Terminal Server is AddIns, which contains the keys Clip Redirector, Sound Redirector, and Terminal Server Redirector. In Clip Redirector, you'll find these values entries:

Name   Holds a REG_SZ string, with a typical value of RDPClip.

Type   Holds a REG_DWORD value, with a default of 3.
In the subkey Sound Redirector, you'll find these entries:

Name   Holds a REG_SZ string, with a typical value of RDPSound.

Type   Holds a REG_DWORD value, with a default of 3.
In the subkey Terminal Server Redirector, you'll find these entries:

Name   Holds a REG_SZ string, with a typical value of \\Device\\RdpDr.

Type   Holds a REG_DWORD value, with a default of 0.

The Terminal Server subkey AuthorizedApplications contains the following item:

<default>: This default value entry holds a value of a blank string.

The Terminal Server subkey DefaultUserConfiguration contains the following value entries:

CallbackNumber   Holds a REG_SZ string, with a typical value of an empty string.

Callback   Holds a REG_DWORD value, with a default of 0.

Domain   Holds a REG_SZ string, with a typical value of an empty string.

FInheritAutoLogon   Holds a REG_DWORD value, with a default of 1.

FInheritCallbackNumber   Holds a REG_DWORD value, with a default of 0.

FInheritCallback   Holds a REG_DWORD value, with a default of 0.

FInheritInitialProgram   Holds a REG_DWORD value, with a default of 1.

FInheritMaxDisconnectionTime   Holds a REG_DWORD value, with a default of 0.

FInheritMaxIdleTime   Holds a REG_DWORD value, with a default of 0.

FInheritMaxSessionTime   Holds a REG_DWORD value, with a default of 0.

FInheritReconnectSame   Holds a REG_DWORD value, with a default of 0.

FInheritResetBroken   Holds a REG_DWORD value, with a default of 0.

FInheritShadow   Holds a REG_DWORD value, with a default of 0.

FLogonDisabled   Holds a REG_DWORD value, with a default of 0.

FPromptForPassword   Holds a REG_DWORD value, with a default of 0.

FReconnectSame   Holds a REG_DWORD value, with a default of 0.

FResetBroken   Holds a REG_DWORD value, with a default of 0.

InitialProgram   Holds a REG_SZ string, with a typical value of an empty string.

KbdIdleBusymsAllowed   Holds a REG_DWORD value, with a default of 60.

KbdIdleDetectAbsolute   Holds a REG_DWORD value, with a default of 1.

KbdIdleDetectProbationCount   Holds a REG_DWORD value, with a default of 80.

KbdIdleInProbationCount   Holds a REG_DWORD value, with a default of 35.

KbdIdlemsAllowed   Holds a REG_DWORD value, with a default of 0.

KbdIdlemsGoodProbationEnd   Holds a REG_DWORD value, with a default of 2500.

KbdIdlemsProbationTrial   Holds a REG_DWORD value, with a default of 2500.

KbdIdlemsSleep   Holds a REG_DWORD value, with a default of 100.

KeyboardLayout   Holds a REG_DWORD value, with a default of 0.

MaxConnectionTime   Holds a REG_DWORD value, with a default of 0.

MaxDisconnectionTime   Holds a REG_DWORD value, with a default of 0.

MaxIdleTime   Holds a REG_DWORD value, with a default of 0.

NWLogonServer   Holds a REG_SZ string, with a typical value of an empty string.

Password   Holds a REG_SZ string, with a typical value of an empty string.

Shadow   Holds a REG_DWORD value, with a default of 1.

The Terminal Server subkey Dos contains these value entries:

UserName   Holds a REG_SZ string, with a typical value of an empty string.

WorkDirectory   Holds a REG_SZ string, with a typical value of an empty string.

The Terminal Server subkey KeyboardType Mapping contains two subkeys. The first, JPN, is for Japanese keyboard mapping:

000000000017   Holds a REG_SZ string, with a typical value of kbdlk41a.dll.

00000000   Holds a REG_SZ string, with a typical value of kbd101.dll.

00000001   Holds a REG_SZ string, with a typical value of kbdax2.dll.

000000020015   Holds a REG_SZ string, with a typical value of kbdnecAT.dll.

000000020017   Holds a REG_SZ string, with a typical value of kbdlk41j.dll.

00000002   Holds a REG_SZ string, with a typical value of kbd106.dll.

00000003   Holds a REG_SZ string, with a typical value of kbdibm02.dll.

00000D01   Holds a REG_SZ string, with a typical value of kbdnecNT.dll.

00000D04   Holds a REG_SZ string, with a typical value of kbdnecNT.dll.

00010002   Holds a REG_SZ string, with a typical value of kbd106n.dll.

00010D01   Holds a REG_SZ string, with a typical value of kbdnec95.dll.

00010D04   Holds a REG_SZ string, with a typical value of kbdnec95.dll.

00020002   Holds a REG_SZ string, with a typical value of f3ahvoas.dll.

00020D01   Holds a REG_SZ string, with a typical value of kbdnecAT.dll.

00020D04   Holds a REG_SZ string, with a typical value of kbdnecAT.dll.

The other subkey under KeyboardType Mapping is KOR, for Korean keyboard mapping:

00000003   Holds a REG_SZ string, with a typical value of kbd101a.dll.

00000004   Holds a REG_SZ string, with a typical value of kbd101b.dll.

00000005   Holds a REG_SZ string, with a typical value of kbd101c.dll.

00000006   Holds a REG_SZ string, with a typical value of kbd103.dll.

The Terminal Server subkey Utilities has three subkeys, change, query, and reset. The change subkey contains these value entries:

Logon   Holds a REG_MULTI_STRING value.

Port   Holds a REG_MULTI_STRING value.

User   Holds a REG_MULTI_STRING value.

Winsta   Holds a REG_MULTI_STRING value.

The second `Utilities` subkey, `query`, contains:

Appserver   Holds a REG_MULTI_STRING value.

Process   Holds a REG_MULTI_STRING value.

Session   Holds a REG_MULTI_STRING value.

User   Holds a REG_MULTI_STRING value.

Winsta   Holds a REG_MULTI_STRING value.

The final `Utilities` subkey, `reset`, contains:

Session   Holds a REG_MULTI_STRING value.

Winsta   Holds a REG_MULTI_STRING value.

The `Terminal Server` subkey `VIDEO` contains a single subkey, `rdpdd`. In this subkey, you'll find the following value entries:

\\Device\\Video0   Holds a REG_SZ string, with a typical value of \\REGISTRY\\ Machine\\ System\\ControlSet001\\Services\\RDPDD\\Device0.

VgaCompatible   Holds a REG_SZ string, with a typical value of \\Device\\Video0.

The `Terminal Server` key `Wds` contains the subkey `rdpwd`, which contains these value entries:

BaudRate   Holds a REG_DWORD value, with a default of 57600.

ByteSize   Holds a REG_DWORD value, with a default of 8.

CfgDll   Holds a REG_SZ string, with a typical value of RDPCFGEX.dll.

ConnectType   Holds a REG_DWORD value, with a default of 1.

DeviceName   Holds a REG_SZ string, with a typical value of an empty string.

FAutoClientDrives   Holds a REG_DWORD value, with a default of 0.

FAutoClientLpts   Holds a REG_DWORD value, with a default of 1.

FDisableCam   Holds a REG_DWORD value, with a default of 0 in XP.

FDisableCcm   Holds a REG_DWORD value, with a default of 0 in Windows XP.

FDisableCdm   Holds a REG_DWORD value, with a default of 0 in Windows XP.

FDisableClip   Holds a REG_DWORD value, with a default of 0.

FDisableCpm   Holds a REG_DWORD value, with a default of 0.

FDisableEncryption   Holds a REG_DWORD value, with a default of 1.

FDisableLPT   Holds a REG_DWORD value, with a default of 0.

FEnableBreakDisconnect   Holds a REG_DWORD value, with a default of 0.

FEnableDsrSensitivity   Holds a REG_DWORD value, with a default of 0.

FEnableDTR   Holds a REG_DWORD value, with a default of 1.

FEnableRTS   Holds a REG_DWORD value, with a default of 1.

FFlowSoftwareRx   Holds a REG_DWORD value, with a default of 1.

FFlowSoftwareTx   Holds a REG_DWORD value, with a default of 1.

FForceClientLptDef   Holds a REG_DWORD value, with a default of 1.

FInheritAutoClient   Holds a REG_DWORD value, with a default of 1.

FlowHardwareRx   Holds a REG_DWORD value, with a default of 1.

FlowHardwareTx   Holds a REG_DWORD value, with a default of 1.

FlowType   Holds a REG_DWORD value, with a default of 1.

The subkey rdpwd contains the subkey Tds. This subkey contains the subkey tcp:

InputBufferLength   Holds a REG_DWORD value, with a default of 2048.

InteractiveDelay   Holds a REG_DWORD value, with a default of 10.

MinEncryptionLevel   Holds a REG_DWORD value, with a default of 1.

OutBufCount   Holds a REG_DWORD value, with a default of 6.

OutBufDelay   Holds a REG_DWORD value, with a default of 100.

OutBufLength   Holds a REG_DWORD value, with a default of 530.

Parity   Holds a REG_DWORD value, with a default of 0.

PdClass   Holds a REG_DWORD value, with a default of 2.

PdDLL   Holds a REG_SZ string, with a typical value of tdtcp.

PdFlag   Holds a REG_DWORD value, with a default of 78.

PdName   Holds a REG_SZ string, with a typical value of tcp.

PortNumber   Holds a REG_DWORD value, with a default of 3389.

ServiceName   Holds a REG_SZ string, with a typical value of tcpip.

StartupPrograms   Holds a REG_SZ string, with a typical value of rdpclip.

StopBits   Holds a REG_DWORD value, with a default of 0.

WdDLL   Holds a REG_SZ string, with a typical value of rdpwd.

WdFlag   Holds a REG_DWORD value, with a default of 54.

WdName Holds a REG_SZ string, with a typical value of Microsoft RDP 5.0.

WdPrefix Holds a REG_SZ string, with a typical value of RDP.

WsxDLL Holds a REG_SZ string, with a typical value of rdpwsx.

XoffChar Holds a REG_DWORD value, with a default of 19.

XonChar Holds a REG_DWORD value, with a default of 17.

The Terminal Server key contains the subkey WinStations. WinStations contains a number of data values and nested keys. The data values contained in WinStations include:

Anonymous A REG_BINARY value.

AppServer A REG_BINARY value.

CallbackNumber Holds a REG_SZ string, with a typical value of an empty string.

Callback Holds a REG_DWORD value, with a default of 0.

Comment Holds a REG_SZ string, with a typical value of System Console.

DefaultSecurity A REG_BINARY value.

Domain Holds a REG_SZ string, with a typical value of an empty string.

FEnableWinStation Holds a REG_DWORD value, with a default of 1.

FInheritAutoLogon Holds a REG_DWORD value, with a default of 0.

FInheritCallbackNumber Holds a REG_DWORD value, with a default of 0.

FInheritCallback Holds a REG_DWORD value, with a default of 0.

FInheritInitialProgram Holds a REG_DWORD value, with a default of 0.

FInheritMaxDisconnectionTime Holds a REG_DWORD value, with a default of 0.

FInheritMaxIdleTime Holds a REG_DWORD value, with a default of 0.

FInheritMaxSessionTime Holds a REG_DWORD value, with a default of 0.

FInheritReconnectSame Holds a REG_DWORD value, with a default of 0.

FInheritResetBroken Holds a REG_DWORD value, with a default of 0.

FInheritShadow Holds a REG_DWORD value, with a default of 0.

FLogonDisabled Holds a REG_DWORD value, with a default of 0.

FPromptForPassword Holds a REG_DWORD value, with a default of 0.

FReconnectSame Holds a REG_DWORD value, with a default of 0.

FResetBroken Holds a REG_DWORD value, with a default of 0.

FUseDefaultGina Holds a REG_DWORD value, with a default of 0.

InitialProgram   Holds a REG_SZ string, with a typical value of an empty string.

InputBufferLength   Holds a REG_DWORD value, with a default of 0.

KeyboardLayout   Holds a REG_DWORD value, with a default of 0.

KeyboardName   Holds a REG_SZ string, with a typical value of \\REGISTRY\\Machine\\System\\CurrentControlSet\\Services\\Kbdclass.

MaxConnectionTime   Holds a REG_DWORD value, with a default of 0.

MaxDisconnectionTime   Holds a REG_DWORD value, with a default of 0.

MaxIdleTime   Holds a REG_DWORD value, with a default of 0.

MouseName   Holds a REG_SZ string, with a typical value of \\REGISTRY\\Machine\\System\\CurrentControlSet\\Services\\Mouclass.

OutBufCount   Holds a REG_DWORD value, with a default of 0.

OutBufDelay   Holds a REG_DWORD value, with a default of 0.

OutBufLength   Holds a REG_DWORD value, with a default of 0.

Password   Holds a REG_SZ string, with a typical value of an empty string.

PdClass   Holds a REG_DWORD value, with a default of 1.

PdDll   Holds a REG_SZ string, with a typical value of an empty string.

PdFlag   Holds a REG_DWORD value, with a default of 30.

PdName   Holds a REG_SZ string, with a typical value of console.

RemoteAdmin   A REG_BINARY value.

Shadow   Holds a REG_DWORD value, with a default of 0.

The WinStations key also contains the subkey Console:

UserName   Holds a REG_SZ string, with a typical value of an empty string.

WdDll   Holds a REG_SZ string, with a typical value of wdcon.

WdFlag   Holds a REG_DWORD value, with a default of 36.

WdName   Holds a REG_SZ string, with a typical value of Console.

WorkDirectory   Holds a REG_SZ string, with a typical value of an empty string.

Also found in WinStations is the subkey RDP-Tcp. This subkey contains these values:

CallbackNumber   Holds a REG_SZ string, with a typical value of an empty string.

Callback   Holds a REG_DWORD value, with a default of 0.

CdClass   Holds a REG_DWORD value, with a default of 0.

CdDLL   Holds a REG_SZ string, with a typical value of an empty string.

CdFlag   Holds a REG_DWORD value, with a default of 0.

CdName   Holds a REG_SZ string, with a typical value of an empty string.

CfgDll   Holds a REG_SZ string, with a typical value of RDPCFGEX.dll.

Comment   Holds a REG_SZ string, with a typical value of an empty string.

Domain   Holds a REG_SZ string, with a typical value of an empty string.

fAutoClientDrives   Holds a REG_DWORD value, with a default of 1.

fAutoClientLpts   Holds a REG_DWORD value, with a default of 0.

fDisableCam   Holds a REG_DWORD value, with a default of 0.

FDisableCcm   Holds a REG_DWORD value, with a default of 0.

fDisableCdm   Holds a REG_DWORD value, with a default of 0.

fDisableClip   Holds a REG_DWORD value, with a default of 0.

fDisableCpm   Holds a REG_DWORD value, with a default of 0.

fDisableEncryption   Holds a REG_DWORD value, with a default of 1.

fDisableExe   Holds a REG_DWORD value, with a default of 0.

fDisableLPT   Holds a REG_DWORD value, with a default of 0.

fEnableWinStation   Holds a REG_DWORD value, with a default of 1.

fForceClientLptDef   Holds a REG_DWORD value, with a default of 1.

fHomeDirectoryMapRoot   Holds a REG_DWORD value, with a default of 0.

fInheritAutoClient   Holds a REG_DWORD value, with a default of 1.

fInheritAutoLogon   Holds a REG_DWORD value, with a default of 1.

fInheritCallback   Holds a REG_DWORD value, with a default of 1.

fInheritInitialProgram   Holds a REG_DWORD value, with a default of 1.

fInheritMaxDisconnectionTime   Holds a REG_DWORD value, with a default of 1.

fInheritMaxIdleTime   Holds a REG_DWORD value, with a default of 1.

fInheritMaxSessionTime   Holds a REG_DWORD value, with a default of 1.

fInheritReconnectSame   Holds a REG_DWORD value, with a default of 1.

fInheritResetBroken   Holds a REG_DWORD value, with a default of 1.

fInheritSecurity   Holds a REG_DWORD value, with a default of 0.

fInheritShadow   Holds a REG_DWORD value, with a default of 1.

fLogonDisabled   Holds a REG_DWORD value, with a default of 0.

fPromptForPassword   Holds a REG_DWORD value, with a default of 0.

fReconnectSame   Holds a REG_DWORD value, with a default of 0.

fResetBroken   Holds a REG_DWORD value, with a default of 0.

fUseDefaultGina   Holds a REG_DWORD value, with a default of 0.

InitialProgram   Holds a REG_SZ string, with a typical value of an empty string.

InputBufferLength   Holds a REG_DWORD value, with a default of 2048.

InteractiveDelay   Holds a REG_DWORD value, with a default of 50.

KeepAliveTimeout   Holds a REG_DWORD value, with a default of 0.

KeyboardLayout   Holds a REG_DWORD value, with a default of 0.

LanAdapter   Holds a REG_DWORD value, with a default of 0.

MaxConnectionTime   Holds a REG_DWORD value, with a default of 0.

MaxDisconnectionTime   Holds a REG_DWORD value, with a default of 0.

MaxIdleTime   Holds a REG_DWORD value, with a default of 0.

MaxInstanceCount   Holds a REG_DWORD value, with a default of −1.

MinEncryptionLevel   Holds a REG_DWORD value, with a default of 2.

NWLogonServer   Holds a REG_SZ string, with a typical value of an empty string.

OutBufCount   Holds a REG_DWORD value, with a default of 6.

OutBufDelay   Holds a REG_DWORD value, with a default of 100.

OutBufLength   Holds a REG_DWORD value, with a default of 530.

Password   Holds a REG_SZ string, with a typical value of an empty string.

PdClass   Holds a REG_DWORD value, with a default of 2.

PdDLL   Holds a REG_SZ string, with a typical value of tdtcp.

PdFlag   Holds a REG_DWORD value, with a default of 78.

PdName   Holds a REG_SZ string, with a typical value of tcp.

PortNumber   Holds a REG_DWORD value, with a default of 3389.

Shadow   Holds a REG_DWORD value, with a default of 1.

TraceClass   Holds a REG_DWORD value, with a default of 0.

TraceDebugger Holds a REG_DWORD value, with a default of 0.

TraceEnable Holds a REG_DWORD value, with a default of 0.

Username Holds a REG_SZ string, with a typical value of an empty string.

WdDLL Holds a REG_SZ string, with a typical value of rdpwd.

WdFlag Holds a REG_DWORD value, with a default of 54.

WdName Holds a REG_SZ string, with a typical value of Microsoft RDP 5.0 (for versions prior to Windows XP) and 5.1 for Windows XP.

WdPrefix Holds a REG_SZ string, with a typical value of RDP.

WFProfilePath Holds a REG_SZ string, with a typical value of an empty string.

WorkDirectory Holds a REG_SZ string, with a typical value of an empty string.

WsxDLL Holds a REG_SZ string, with a typical value of rdpwsx.

The RDP-Tcp subkey also contains the subkey UserOverride. This subkey contains the subkey Control Panel, which contains the subkey Desktop, which contains one value entry:

Wallpaper Holds a REG_SZ string, with a typical value of an empty string.

TimeZoneInformation

The TimeZoneInformation subkey contains information used to manage time, time zones, and daylight time. Each entry is filled in from the time zone table contained in the subkey HKEY_LOCAL_MACHINE\Software\Microsoft\Windows NT\CurrentVersion\Time Zones.

Value entries contained in this subkey include:

ActiveTimeBias Specifies the number of minutes that local time is currently offset from GMT (UTC) time. This includes DST (daylight saving time). Divide this value by 60 to convert to hours.

Bias Specifies the number of minutes that local time is nominally offset from GMT (UTC) time, ignoring DST. Divide this value by 60 to convert to hours.

DaylightBias Specifies the amount to change Bias to achieve ActiveTimeBias when DST is in effect.

DaylightName Specifies the name of the time zone when DST is active; for example, eastern daylight time.

DaylightStart A SYSTEMTIME structure indicating the start date for DST.

StandardBias Specifies the amount to change Bias to achieve ActiveTimeBias when DST is not in effect. This value is typically 0.

StandardName Specifies the name of the time zone when DST is not active; for example, eastern standard time.

StandardStart A SYSTEMTIME structure indicating the end date for DST.

UPDATE

Update contains information about how to update policies, which are set using the Active Directory system and MMC. Policies update the file config.pol, and this file's path is known. When a user logs on, the user's computer policies are automatically updated.

The Update subkey contains up to four value entries:

NetworkPath   Contains an empty string if UpdateMode is 1, or the network path to the location of the update files if UpdateMode is 2.

UpdateMode   Contains a DWORD value indicating the update mode. There are three values allowed in UpdateMode:

0   Do not use policies for updates.

1   Automatic policy mode is in effect after validating the user on the domain.

2   Manual policy mode is in effect. The NetworkPath variable is required when using this mode

Verbose   Allows the system to display error messages if Verbose = 1. The default does not display error messages. The Verbose data value is not set by default.

LoadBalance   Allows the system to balance loads if LoadBalance = 1. The default does not display error messages. The LoadBalance data value is not set by default.

USBFLAGS

Windows XP fully supports USB, and this object contains information about the current USB configuration.

VIRTUALDEVICEDRIVERS

Windows XP does not support VDDs (virtual device drivers). The subkey VirtualDeviceDrivers contains any VDDs that are loaded in the VDM (Virtual DOS Machine) when initialized. This sub key is for IHVs (independent hardware vendors) who find it necessary to supply drivers for their hardware products.

There is a single value entry in VirtualDeviceDrivers: VDD, which contains a REG_MULTI_SZ string. This string contains the names of any VDDs used by the VDM. By default, this value is empty because there are no VDDs for Windows XP.

NOTE   Windows XP does not support any 16-bit virtual device drivers. Applications that rely on 16-bit virtual device drivers will fail.

WATCHDOG

A WatchDog is a method to determine whether a system has failed to respond. There is one subobject in WatchDog, Display. Contained in Display are three data values, DisableBugcheck, Shutdown, and ShutdownCount.

WINDOWS

The Windows subkey contains some configuration information for Windows. Value entries included in this subkey are:

CSDVersion The CSD (Microsoft's nomenclature for their service packs) status can be determined from this subkey. In earlier versions of Windows NT (other than Windows NT 3.1 Advanced Server), CSDVersion was a string. However, Windows NT 4 used a DWORD value. Windows 2000 changed back from REG_DWORD to REG_SZ, and it remains this way in Windows XP. This object may not be found if no service packs have been applied.

Directory Includes a REG_EXPAND_SZ string containing the value %SystemRoot%.

ErrorMode May contain a value between 0 and 2:

0 The default mode that serializes errors and waits for a user response.

1 Nonsystem errors are considered normal and are not reported. The event log logs the system errors. The user is given no error message.

2 Errors are logged to the event log, and no error message is given to the user.

NoInteractiveServices If set to 1, no interactive services are allowed.

ShellErrorMode Specifies the mode (see ErrorMode, above) for the shell.

ShutdownTime Specifies the time of the last shutdown.

SystemDirectory Includes a REG_EXPAND_SZ string containing the value %SystemRoot%\System32.

WMI

WMI (Windows Management Instrumentation) provides kernel-level debugging instrumentation to Windows XP. A single subkey exists in WMI. This subkey, Security, contains a REG_BINARY value with a name that is a CLSID.

WOW

WOW, or Windows on Windows, is the mode that allows legacy 16-bit applications to run on 32-bit versions of Windows. It uses a simple emulation of the Windows 3.x standard mode. There are eight value entries in the WOW subkey:

cmdline Contains the command line used to start the WOW system.

DefaultSeparateVDM Specifies whether WOW is to allocate a default separate VDM (Virtual DOS Machine).

KnownDLLs Contains a list of DLLs that the WOW VDM will load to provide compatibility for non-Win32 applications.

LPT_timeout Specifies the time-out period for the printer port.

SharedWowTimeout Contains the time-out value of 3600.

size Contains the memory size allocated. A value of 0 means that the system used the default size.

Wowcmdline Contains the command line used to start the WOW system, including any parameters.

wowsize Specifies the amount of memory supplied to WOW applications. Released versions of Windows automate this value, and changes should not be necessary. The default value is 16.

Enum

The Enum subkey represents the beginning of the hardware tree. Through the Enum key, any subkey named Root (regardless of case) will represent enumerated devices.

Subkeys in this key include those discussed next.

DISPLAY

The DISPLAY subkey represents the display device, a.k.a. the monitor, attached to the system. Generally, a generic monitor setting is all that is required.

FDC

The FDC subkey represents the floppy disk drive installed on the system. As with monitors, floppy disk drives are rather generic.

HTREE

In Windows NT 4, HTREE was a complex object. In Windows 2000 and XP, HTREE contains no data values and only a single subkey: ROOT. Within the ROOT key, again there are no data values, only a single subkey named 0. This subkey contains one data value:

ConfigFlags Holds a REG_DWORD value of 32 (0x00000020).

IDE

New as of Windows 2000, the IDE object contains information about all IDE devices. For example, on the machine I am using, there are two IDE CD-ROM drives and a single 18GB IDE hard drive. There is information in the IDE key for each of these three devices. Information is arranged with a key for each basic device and a subkey for each specific device within the basic device.

For example, my two Matshita CD-ROM drives are attached to one of my IDE channels. Under IDE, there is a subkey named CdRomMATSHITA_CD-ROM_CR-581-M_____1.05____. Quite a name, isn't it? Under this subkey, there are two additional subkeys, one for each drive:

- 4&13b4afd&0&0.0.0

- 4&13b4afd&0&0.1.0

Notice that the only difference between those two subkeys is a single character.

ISAPNP

New as of Windows 2000, the ISAPNP object manages the ISA bus's PnP functionality. ISA systems have a single key named ReadDataPort, used to receive information from the system about PnP.

PCI

New as of Windows 2000, PCI is a subkey with information on each of the PCI bus adapters. For example, one computer here has built-in PCI disk controllers, PCI-to-ISA and PCI-to-USB bridges, a PCI SCSI adapter, a PCI network interface card, and a PCI video adapter. Each PCI device has a subkey containing information about the device.

PCI_HAL

New as of Windows 2000, the PCI_HAL object contains information about the actual PCI bus. A computer could have more than one PCI bus; however, most will have one, documented in this key.

PCIIDE

New as of Windows 2000, the PCIIDE object contains information about all IDE controllers. Most modern computers have two IDE controllers (a primary and a secondary). Although many times these devices are listed as one being attached to the ISA bus and one to the PCI bus, oftentimes both are routed through the PCI bus (this allows for higher performance).

ROOT

The Root subkeys represent enumerators that Windows uses to hold information about the device(s). Each device listed in AttachedComponents receives a subkey under the Root key.

On one of my Windows systems, this object contains the following entries. These entries vary depending on the installed hardware.

- ◆ Root*PNP0000
- ◆ Root*PNP0100
- ◆ Root*PNP0200
- ◆ Root*PNP030b
- ◆ Root*PNP0400
- ◆ Root*PNP0501
- ◆ Root*PNP0700
- ◆ Root*PNP0800
- ◆ Root*PNP0B00
- ◆ Root*PNP0C01
- ◆ Root*PNP0C02
- ◆ Root*PNP0C04

- Root*PNP0F03

- Root*PNPB003

- Root*PNPB02F

- Root\dmio

- Root\ftdisk

- Root\LEGACY_CDFS

- Root\LEGACY_DMBOOT

- Root\LEGACY_DMLOAD

- Root\LEGACY_FASTFAT

- Root\LEGACY_MOUNTMGR

- Root\LEGACY_NTFS

- Root\LEGACY_PARTMGR

- Root\LEGACY_REMOTEREGISTRY

- Root\LEGACY_SNMP

- Root\LEGACY_SNMPTRAP

- Root\LEGACY_SYSMONLOG

- Root\LEGACY_VGA

- Root\MS_NDISWANBH

- Root\PCI_HAL

Notice that not all devices are really hardware. Items such as virtual drivers are included in the list.

These subkeys include information about each device. Devices that receive support from Windows NT have additional information in the form of an extra subkey. An example, the NIC (network interface card) in the computer is a 3Com 3C900 series, which is a PCI device (actually, Plug and Play) that Windows NT is able to support.

Under Windows XP, the subkey for the 3C900 is Enum\Root\LEGACY_EL90X. Where'd the EL90X come from? EL is short for EtherLink (3Com's terminology for their Ethernet cards). The 90X is the designator for the 3C900 series, which contains a number of different devices with varying speeds (10Mbps and 100Mbps) and connection form factors.

The LEGACY_EL90X subkey contains the following entries:

- HKEY_CURRENT_CONFIG

- HKEY_LOCAL_MACHINE\System\CurrentControlSet\Hardware Profiles\Current

- HKEY_LOCAL_MACHINE\System\CurrentControlSet\Hardware Profiles\0001

That's a mouthful, but it really says that there are three names for the same piece of information.

NOTE   Changes made in the Current *subkey change the corresponding subkey in the currently used configuration and vice versa.*

SCSI

New as of Windows 2000, SCSI is a subkey with information on each of the SCSI devices attached to the system. Some systems (many perhaps) do not have any SCSI devices. There is a subkey for each attached SCSI device.

STORAGE

New as of Windows 2000, storage volumes allow Windows to very efficiently manage disk resources. Each writeable storage device (hard disk drive) will have a subkey in the STORAGE key. Within a device's key, there are two subkeys: Control and LogConf.

SW

New as of Windows 2000, SW is used with support for streaming protocols. Items in this subkey could include:

- Microsoft Streaming Clock Proxy
- Microsoft Streaming File System I/O
- File System Reader
- File System Writer
- Microsoft Streaming Quality Manager Proxy
- Microsoft Streaming RIFF Wave File Parser
- RIFF Wave File Parser
- Microsoft Streaming Service Proxy
- Microsoft Streaming Tee/Sink-to-Sink Converter
- Tee/Sink-to-Sink Converter
- Microsoft Streaming Network Raw Channel Access
- Raw Channel Access Capture/Render
- WDM Streaming IOverlay Property Set Interface Handler
- RAS Async Adapter

USB

New as of Windows 2000, USB (Universal Serial Bus) allows connecting, daisy-chain fashion, various devices. Though acceptance of USB has been slow, it appears that the next few years will bring a proliferation of USB devices, including keyboard, pointer, joystick, and output devices.

Hardware Profiles

In Windows XP, the `Hardware Profiles` key contains information about the computer. This information is used in HKEY_CURRENT_CONFIG. In the `Hardware Profiles` key, there may be one or more subkeys, each named with a number; there is also a subkey named `Current`. For a further view of both this key and HKEY_CURRENT_CONFIG, see the sections on HKEY_CURRENT_CONFIG later in this chapter.

Windows maps the `Current` key to the currently used key, typically 0001. The HKEY_CURRENT_CONFIG hive maps to the `Current` key. Changes made in `Current` are reflected in the key it is mapped to and to HKEY_CURRENT_CONFIG. The converse is also true: changing HKEY_CURRENT_CONFIG will change both `Current` and the hive `Current` maps to.

NOTE   *We can assume that Microsoft has other plans for this key in the future. The naming of the key is odd, but then again, we are dealing with Microsoft on this one.*

A decidedly nonhardware object is also contained in the `Hardware Profiles` key: `Software`. A single entry resides in the `Software` subkey: `Internet Settings`. The `Internet Settings` key contains two value entries for controlling how the system connects to the Internet:

`EnableAutodial`   Contains a DWORD value. If the value is 0x0, the system will not attempt to auto-dial to connect to the Internet (or other remote host). If the value is 0x1, the system will attempt to auto-dial when this is necessary to connect to the remote network.

`ProxyEnable`   Contains a DWORD value. If the value is 0x0, the system *will not* use a proxy server to connect to the Internet. If the value is 0x1, the system *will* use a proxy server to connect to the Internet.

Services

The `Services` subkey contains information about the Windows XP services. The Services applet in Administrative Tools manages the `Services` subkey.

A service is any Windows service, such as a device driver, the file system drivers, and so on. Services can be started in several ways:

`Automatic`   The service starts automatically when Windows starts.

`Manual`   The service starts manually and not when Windows starts.

`Disabled`   The service is disabled. The service cannot be started.

The `Services` subkey also contains devices listed in the Devices applet of the Control Panel. Similar to a service, a device may have a number of different startup states:

`Boot`   The device starts when the system boots, before any other devices.

`System`   The device starts when the system boots, after the boot devices.

`Automatic`   The device starts when the system boots, after the boot and system devices.

`Manual`   The device starts manually; the system will not attempt to start the device automatically.

Disabled   A user cannot start the device.

Boot   The device starts when the system boots.

When a service runs, it often must log on as a user. Choices for a service include logging on as the system account or as a specific account. When logging on as a specific account, the service is configured with the account name and password information.

WARNING   *Be careful not to compromise system security by allowing a service to log on as a privileged account and interact with the Desktop.*

ControlSet001

ControlSet001 is the control set used to boot the computer during normal operations. If it fails to boot for some reason, then ControlSet002 (or ControlSet003) will be used instead.

ControlSet002

Though object content may vary, ControlSet002 (or ControlSet003, if that is what your computer has) is identical in structure to ControlSet001.

ControlSet002 is the backup control set and the Last Known Good control set.

DISK

While this key no longer exists in Windows XP, you'll find it in Windows 2000 and earlier versions. The DISK key contains information about specific types of drives, such as CD-ROM drive letter mappings. In Windows 2000, the DISK key contains information about disk configurations, such as fault-tolerant configurations (consisting of mirroring, stripe sets, stripe sets with parity, and so on). DISK contains a single value entry, named Information, which contains an undocumented REG_BINARY value.

Disk Administrator manages the information in the DISK key. In fact, this key doesn't even exist until the first time a user runs Disk Administrator. Disk Administrator also makes backups of this key. Start Disk Administrator and select Partition ➢ Configuration Save. Disk Administrator will then write the DISK key information to a floppy disk. It will not write to any other device, such as a hard drive.

Disk Administrator writes the entire HKEY_LOCAL_MACHINE\System key to a registry export file. However, do not try reloading this file using anything other than Disk Administrator, because another program may restore keys and values that are not up to date.

Mounted Devices

The Mounted Devices key contains information about drives, such as CD-ROM drive letter mappings. In Windows XP, the Mounted Devices key contains information about volume configurations and identifiers, as well as DOS configurations.

Select

The Select key contains information about which control set has been loaded by the system. The following four value entries reside in this key:

Current   Defines the currently used control set.

Default   Defines the currently used control set, which is typically also the current control set.

Failed   Lists a control set that has failed when the system was attempting to start.

LastKnownGood   Specifies the control set that is accessed when a user requests the Last Known Good control set from Windows at boot time.

WARNING   When Windows XP shuts down, Windows copies the current control set to the Last Known Good control set. Be careful when attempting to boot the system that you do not inadvertently overwrite your Last Known Good copy of the control set with a copy that does not work correctly.

Setup

Setup contains information used by the system during the setup stage. This information is contained in a number of value entries:

CmdLine   Contains the command string to set up Windows. Typically, this command is setup –newsetup.

NetcardDlls   Contains the names for the drivers for the NIC.

OsLoaderPath   Contains the path for the OS loader.

SetupType   Has a value of 0, 1, or 4. These values indicate the following:

　　0   Setup has completed.

　　1   Windows is doing a new full install.

　　4   Windows is doing an upgrade.

SystemPartition   A pointer to the system installation device. Typically, for SCSI systems, this string will be \\Device\\Harddisk0\\Partition1. In Windows XP, the string is \\Device\\HarddiskVolume.

SystemPrefix   Used to determine the system type.

SystemSetupInProgress   If the setup has not completed, the value in this entry is 0x1. Once setup has completed, it contains the value 0x0.

uniqueid   A unique directory name used during setup.

UpgradeInProgress   This value is 0 unless an upgrade is in progress.

HKEY_CURRENT_CONFIG

The HKEY_CURRENT_CONFIG hive is nothing more than an alias (or pointer) to the HKEY_LOCAL_ MACHINE\System\CurrentControlSet\Hardware Profiles\Current key. HKEY_CURRENT_CONFIG stores only items changed from the standard configuration contained in HKEY_LOCAL_MACHINE\System\ CurrentControlSet. The most common entries found in HKEY_CURRENT_CONFIG are the entries under Services for the video display. Windows 95 and Windows NT 4 introduced this object.

HKEY_CURRENT_CONFIG contains two subkeys, Software and System, discussed in the next two sections.

HKEY_CURRENT_CONFIG\Software

The HKEY_CURRENT_CONFIG\Software key contains some settings that you may want to configure. Notice that there is no built-in methodology to edit or modify items in the Software key—each application or system must manage these entries and provide the method for the user to modify entries.

Under the Software key, Microsoft applications include a subkey named Microsoft. This subkey contains only one entry on most systems: Windows. The Windows subkey includes a subkey named CurrentVersion. Get the drift here? This structure (HKEY_CURRENT_CONFIG\Software\Microsoft\ Windows\CurrentVersion) is exactly the same structure you find in HKEY_LOCAL_MACHINE\System\ CurrentControlSet\Hardware Profiles\Current\Software\Microsoft\Windows\CurrentVersion. Both subkeys have Microsoft\Windows\CurrentVersion. However, it is possible that other applications will have subkeys under this key, as well. Do not count on the Microsoft subkey being the only one present in HKEY_CURRENT_CONFIG\Software; there may be others some day.

The Software key also contains a subkey called Internet Settings. In Windows XP, the path is Software\Microsoft\windows\CurrentVersion\Internet Settings. There are two value entries in this key:

EnableAutodial   Contains a DWORD value. If the value is 0x0, then the system will not attempt to auto-dial to connect to the Internet or any other remote host. If the value is 0x1, then the system will attempt to auto-dial if necessary to connect to the remote network. This object is only found on systems that use dial-up networking.

ProxyEnable   Contains a DWORD value. If the value is 0x0, then the system will not use a proxy server to connect to the Internet. If the value is 0x1, then the system will use a proxy server to connect to the Internet.

HKEY_CURRENT_CONFIG\System

The HKEY_CURRENT_CONFIG\System key contains objects that temporarily modify the current control set. Microsoft chose to implement multiple hardware configurations this way, rather than allowing users to modify the current control set on-the-fly, for reliability reasons. Regardless of what happens to the system, Windows can be sure that the current control set is representative for all users and configurations, and if changes must be implemented for a specific configuration, these changes will be pointed to by HKEY_CURRENT_CONFIG.

CurrentControlSet

The System key contains a subkey called CurrentControlSet. This subkey matches the HKEY_LOCAL_MACHINE\System\CurrentControlSet key in function. Remember: only modifiers are present in HKEY_CURRENT_CONFIG; therefore, if nothing in the HKEY_LOCAL_MACHINE\System\CurrentControlSet subkey needs modification, the HKEY_CURRENT_CONFIG\System\CurrentControlSet classes will be empty.

The HKEY_CURRENT_CONFIG\System\CurrentControlSet key contains three subkeys: Control, Enum, and Services.

CONTROL

In HKEY_LOCAL_MACHINE\System\CurrentControlSet, the Control subkey has a number of value entries used for booting and system initialization, as well as about 30 subkeys. In HKEY_CURRENT_CONFIG, the Control subkey is typically empty, unless it is necessary to modify HKEY_LOCAL_MACHINE\System\CurrentControlSet\Control based on a particular configuration.

In HKEY_CURRENT_CONFIG, the Control key may contain the following value entries:

RegistrySizeLimit   If the user changes the registry size limit from the default value of 8MB, RegistrySizeLimit will contain the maximum registry size, in bytes. Though users are only able to set the registry size limit in megabytes, Windows will store the value as a DWORD containing the maximum registry size in bytes.

SystemStartOptions   This value contains options used during startup, passed from firmware or the startup process (contained in boot.ini). Options might include debugging information (such as a debugging port and the debugging port parameters) and perhaps information on the system root directory.

WaitToKillService   This value specifies the amount of time, in milliseconds, to wait before killing a service when Windows is shutting down. If this value is too small, Windows may kill the service before it has finished writing its data; if this value is too large, a hung service will delay shutdown. It is best to leave the WaitToKillService value at its default value of 20000, unless you know you are having a problem.

Control could also contain any of the subkeys found in HKEY_LOCAL_MACHINE\System\CurrentControlSet\Control.

ENUM

The Enum subkeys represent the beginning of the hardware tree. Through the Enum key, any subkey named Root (regardless of case) will represent devices enumerated using non-PnP services.

Though HKEY_CURRENT_CONFIG\System\CurrentControlSet\Enum is typically empty, it could contain the two subkeys HTREE and Root.

HTREE   The HTREE subkey represents the hardware devices. There is a subkey under HTREE called ROOT, and within ROOT, there is a subkey called 0. HTREE\ROOT\0 includes any devices that may be transient, such as a device contained within a docking station. Similar to HKEY_LOCAL_MACHINE\

System\CurrentControlSet\Control\Enum, notice that not all devices are really hardware. The list includes items such as virtual drivers and so on.

Root   The Root subkeys represent enumerators used by Windows to hold information about the device(s). Each device listed in AttachedComponents receives a subkey under the Root key.

These subkeys contain information about each device. Devices that receive support from Windows XP have extra information in the form of an additional subkey. For example, the NIC (network interface card) in the computer is a 3Com 3C900, which is a PCI device (actually, Plug and Play) that Windows is able to support.

Again, because HKEY_CURRENT_CONFIG is used to modify HKEY_LOCAL_MACHINE\System\CurrentControlSet\Enum\Root, only items that must be changed on a temporary basis are included in HKEY_CURRENT_CONFIG.

Services   Services contains subkeys for each device changed from the default configuration. Every system has at least one entry in this subkey for the video card. For example, consider one computer that is running Windows XP Professional with an ARK chipset video adapter. This device's parameters are stored in a subkey called ark, at HKEY_CURRENT_CONFIG\System\CurrentControlSet\Services\ark.

Your computer will have a similar subkey for its video card with virtually identical entries. The name will be different. For example, if you have a Matrox Millennium video card, the subkey's name will be mga_mil, not ark.

For video (specifically VGA) subkeys, typical entries include:

DefaultSettings.BitsPerPel   Indicates the number of bits per pel (pixel); this will be a number between 1 (indicating a monochrome system) and 32 (true-color systems).

DefaultSettings.Xresolution   The resolution in the X plane (horizontal). Settings range from 640 to 1280 or more for very high resolution systems.

DefaultSettings.Yresolution   The resolution in the Y plane (vertical). Settings range from 480 to 1024 or more for very high resolution systems.

DefaultSettings.Vrefresh   The vertical refresh rate, which usually has a value between 20 and 100, with a typical value of about 70. This reflects the monitor's refresh rate, in Hz. If you change this value, make sure the video adapter at the specified resolution supports the value chosen. Oh, also realize that the Display Properties dialog box will probably change it back to whatever it wants.

DefaultSettings.Flags   This entry controls the specification of any device flags, as necessary.

DefaultSettings.Xpanning   If the device supports hardware panning, this specifies the default horizontal panning value.

DefaultSettings.YPanning   If the device supports hardware panning, this is the default vertical panning value.

Part **V**

Appendices

Appendix A

Common Hives and Keys

IN VIRTUALLY ALL REGISTRIES, there are a number of common entries. These entries, mostly for basic system components, usually have either the same values or predictable values. Table A.1 lists some common registry hives and keys.

TABLE A.1: COMMON REGISTRY HIVES AND KEYS

HIVE/KEY	SUBKEY	DESCRIPTION
HKEY_LOCAL_MACHINE\	All keys	The main system description hive. This hive is critical to the execution of Windows XP.
HKEY_LOCAL_MACHINE\Hardware\Description\	All keys	Contains information on installed hardware. This key is created at boot time, though some entries may be retained from previous executions.
HKEY_LOCAL_MACHINE\Hardware\Description\	System	Contains system device information, excluding NIC (network interface card) and video devices.
HKEY_LOCAL_MACHINE\Hardware\Description\	System\CentralProcessor	Contains CPU information, such as make, model, and version.
HKEY_LOCAL_MACHINE\Hardware\Description\	System\FloatingPoint Processor	Contains floating point processor data, such as make, model, and version.
HKEY_LOCAL_MACHINE\Hardware\Description\	System\Multifunction Adapter\2\DiskController\ 0\DiskPeripheral	Contains installed disk controller information. Systems may have one, two, or three controllers in a typical configuration: primary IDE, secondary IDE, and SCSI.
HKEY_LOCAL_MACHINE\Hardware\Description\	System\Multifunction Adapter\2\Keyboard Controller	Contains keyboard controller information at the hardware level.
HKEY_LOCAL_MACHINE\Hardware\Description\	System\Multifunction Adapter\2\Parallel Controller	Contains printer (parallel) port information.
HKEY_LOCAL_MACHINE\Hardware\Description\	System\Multifunction Adapter\2\Pointer Controller	Contains mouse port information.
HKEY_LOCAL_MACHINE\Hardware\Description\	System\Multifunction Adapter\2\Serial Controller	Contains information on installed serial ports.
HKEY_LOCAL_MACHINE\Hardware\Description\	System\Multifunction Adapter	Contains information on device classes, other than network and disk.
HKEY_LOCAL_MACHINE\Hardware\Description\	System\PCMCIA PCCARDs	Contains information on installed PCMCIA (PC Card) devices.

Continued on next page

TABLE A.1: COMMON REGISTRY HIVES AND KEYS *(continued)*

HIVE/KEY	SUBKEY	DESCRIPTION
HKEY_LOCAL_MACHINE\Hardware\DeviceMap\	All keys	Contains basic device-mapping and control information.
HKEY_LOCAL_MACHINE\Hardware\DeviceMap\	KeyboardClass	Contains keyboard device-mapping information.
HKEY_LOCAL_MACHINE\Hardware\DeviceMap\	KeyboardPort	Contains keyboard port configuration information.
HKEY_LOCAL_MACHINE\Hardware\DeviceMap\	PARALLEL PORTS	Contains printer (parallel) port configuration information.
HKEY_LOCAL_MACHINE\Hardware\DeviceMap\	PointerClass	Contains mouse information.
HKEY_LOCAL_MACHINE\Hardware\DeviceMap\	PointerPort	Contains information on the port (mouse port, PS/2 mouse port, serial port, and so on) the mouse (pointer) connects to.
HKEY_LOCAL_MACHINE\Hardware\DeviceMap\	Scsi	Contains general disk interface information on IDE and SCSI devices.
HKEY_LOCAL_MACHINE\Hardware\DeviceMap\	Scsi\Scsi Port 0	Contains information on the first disk drive interface adapter (although labeled as SCSI, this may be an IDE device).
HKEY_LOCAL_MACHINE\Hardware\DeviceMap\	Scsi\Scsi Port 1	Contains information on the second disk drive interface adapter (although labeled as SCSI, this may be an IDE device).
HKEY_LOCAL_MACHINE\Hardware\DeviceMap\	SERIALCOMM	Contains information on serial communications device configurations.
HKEY_LOCAL_MACHINE\Hardware\DeviceMap\	VIDEO	Contains video configuration information.
HKEY_LOCAL_MACHINE\Hardware\ResourceMap\	All keys	Contains information on (hardware) system mapping.
HKEY_LOCAL_MACHINE\Hardware\ResourceMap\	Hardware Abstraction Layer\ PC Compatible Eisa\Isa HAL	Describes the system configuration to Windows. HALs exist for generic systems and for computers that have special hardware configurations, such as multiple processors or special bus configurations.

Continued on next page

TABLE A.1: COMMON REGISTRY HIVES AND KEYS *(continued)*

HIVE/KEY	SUBKEY	DESCRIPTION
HKEY_LOCAL_MACHINE\Hardware\ResourceMap\	KeyboardPort\PointerPort	Contains general keyboard/mouse interface information.
HKEY_LOCAL_MACHINE\Hardware\ResourceMap\	KeyboardPort\PointerPort\msi8042prt	Contains mouse/keyboard interface information.
HKEY_LOCAL_MACHINE\Hardware\ResourceMap\	LOADED PARALLEL DRIVER RESOURCES	A description of currently loaded printer (parallel) port driver configurations.
HKEY_LOCAL_MACHINE\Hardware\ResourceMap\	LOADED SERIAL DRIVER RESOURCES	A description of currently loaded serial port driver configurations.
HKEY_LOCAL_MACHINE\Hardware\ResourceMap\	OtherDrivers	Contains general information on devices not otherwise classified.
HKEY_LOCAL_MACHINE\Hardware\ResourceMap\	OtherDrivers\<NIC>	A description of the NIC.
HKEY_LOCAL_MACHINE\Hardware\ResourceMap\	ScsiAdapter	Contains information about SCSI and IDE adapters.
HKEY_LOCAL_MACHINE\Hardware\ResourceMap\	ScsiAdapter\atapi	A description of the installed IDE (ATAPI) disk interface.
HKEY_LOCAL_MACHINE\Hardware\ResourceMap\	System Resources	Contains general information on system resources.
HKEY_LOCAL_MACHINE\Hardware\ResourceMap\	System Resources\Reserved	Contains reserved system resources information.
HKEY_LOCAL_MACHINE\Hardware\ResourceMap\	System Resources\Physical Memory	Contains system memory resources information.
HKEY_LOCAL_MACHINE\Hardware\ResourceMap\	VIDEO	Contains information on video configurations supported by the system.
HKEY_LOCAL_MACHINE\Hardware\ResourceMap\	VIDEO\chips	Contains information on the installed VGA adapter for the Chips & Technology VGA system.
HKEY_LOCAL_MACHINE\Hardware\ResourceMap\	VIDEO\VgaSave	Contains information on the originally installed VGA video system, generally a generic VGA system.
HKEY_LOCAL_MACHINE\Hardware\ResourceMap\	VIDEO\VgaStart	Contains information on the VGA driver used to start the system.

Continued on next page

TABLE A.1: COMMON REGISTRY HIVES AND KEYS *(continued)*

HIVE/KEY	SUBKEY	DESCRIPTION
HKEY_LOCAL_MACHINE\SAM\	SAM	The SAM subkey. Usually protected from user browsing and modification. (Yes, the key is named SAM\SAM.)
		In Windows 2000 and Windows XP domains using Active Directory, SAM is not used.
HKEY_LOCAL_MACHINE\SAM\	SAM\Domains\Account\ Aliases	Contains SAM alias information.
HKEY_LOCAL_MACHINE\SAM\	SAM\Domains\Account\ Aliases\Members	Contains member alias information.
HKEY_LOCAL_MACHINE\SAM\	SAM\Domains\Account\ Aliases\Names	Contains domain name alias information.
HKEY_LOCAL_MACHINE\SAM\	SAM\Domains\Account\ Groups	Contains Groups information.
HKEY_LOCAL_MACHINE\SAM\	SAM\Domains\Account\ Groups\ Names	Contains group name information.
HKEY_LOCAL_MACHINE\SAM\	SAM\Domains\Account\Users	Contains specific user information.
HKEY_LOCAL_MACHINE\SAM\	SAM\Domains\Account\ Users\Names	Contains user name information.
HKEY_LOCAL_MACHINE\SAM\	SAM\Domains\Account\Users \Names\Administrator	Contains user administrator information.
HKEY_LOCAL_MACHINE\SAM\	SAM\Domains\Account\Users \Names\Guest	Contains user guest information.
HKEY_LOCAL_MACHINE\SAM\	SAM\Domains\Builtin\ Aliases\Members\S-1-5-21- xxxxxxxxxx-xxxxxxxxxx- xxxxxxxxxx	Contains information on built-in users: Administrator and Guest.
HKEY_LOCAL_MACHINE\SAM\	SAM\Domains\Builtin\ Aliases\Members\S-1-5-21- xxxxxxxxxx-xxxxxxxxxx- xxxxxxxxxx\000001F4	Contains information on the built-in user: Administrator.
HKEY_LOCAL_MACHINE\SAM\	SAM\Domains\Builtin\ Aliases\Members\S-1-5-21- xxxxxxxxxx-xxxxxxxxxx- xxxxxxxxxx\000001F5	Contains built-in user information.

Continued on next page

TABLE A.1: COMMON REGISTRY HIVES AND KEYS *(continued)*

HIVE/KEY	SUBKEY	DESCRIPTION
HKEY_LOCAL_MACHINE\SAM\	SAM\Domains\Builtin\ Aliases\Members\S-1-5-21- xxxxxxxxxx-xxxxxxxxxx- xxxxxxxxxx	Contains Domain Groups information.
HKEY_LOCAL_MACHINE\SAM\	SAM\Domains\Builtin\ Aliases\Members\S-1-5-21- xxxxxxxxxx-xxxxxxxxxx- xxxxxxxxxx\00000200	Contains Domain Admins group information.
HKEY_LOCAL_MACHINE\SAM\	SAM\Domains\Builtin\ Aliases\Members\S-1-5-21- xxxxxxxxxx-xxxxxxxxxx- xxxxxxxxxx\00000201	Contains Domain Users group information.
HKEY_LOCAL_MACHINE\SAM\	SAM\Domains\Builtin\ Aliases\Members	Contains member alias information for user groups.
HKEY_LOCAL_MACHINE\SAM\	SAM\Domains\Builtin\ Aliases\Names\ Administrators	Contains member alias information for Administrators.
HKEY_LOCAL_MACHINE\SAM\	SAM\Domains\Builtin\ Aliases\Names\Backup Operators	Contains member alias information for Backup Operators (users who perform system backups).
HKEY_LOCAL_MACHINE\SAM\	SAM\Domains\Builtin\ Aliases\Names\Guests	Contains member alias information for Domain Guests.
HKEY_LOCAL_MACHINE\SAM\	SAM\Domains\Builtin\ Aliases\Names\Power Users	Contains member alias information for Power Users.
HKEY_LOCAL_MACHINE\SAM\	SAM\Domains\Builtin\ Aliases\Names\Replicator	Contains member alias information for the Replicator account.
HKEY_LOCAL_MACHINE\SAM\	SAM\Domains\Builtin\ Aliases\Names\Users	Contains member alias information for Domain Users.
HKEY_LOCAL_MACHINE\SAM\	SAM\RXACT	The SAM RXACT key. Used by the registry transaction package, there are a number of RXACT keys located in the registry. Typically these keys contain nothing.
HKEY_LOCAL_MACHINE\Security\	All keys	The protected Windows security key.
HKEY_LOCAL_MACHINE\Software\	All keys	Contains information about installed user and system software.

Continued on next page

TABLE A.1: COMMON REGISTRY HIVES AND KEYS *(continued)*

HIVE/KEY	SUBKEY	DESCRIPTION
HKEY_LOCAL_MACHINE\Software\	Classes	Contains information about extensions and the usage of file types.
HKEY_LOCAL_MACHINE\Software\	Classes*	Contains information about files in general—that is, files that are not otherwise classified.
HKEY_LOCAL_MACHINE\Software\	Classes\CLSID	Contains information about CLSID (class ID) assignments. Almost all applications, and those that support OLE, have a CLSID.
HKEY_LOCAL_MACHINE\Software\	Classes\Interface	Contains information about OLE interface assignments. Almost all applications that support OLE have an OLE interface.
HKEY_LOCAL_MACHINE\Software\	Description	Contains information about RPC objects and configurations.
HKEY_LOCAL_MACHINE\Software\	Windows NT\CurrentVersion	Contains information on the currently installed version of Windows.
HKEY_LOCAL_MACHINE\Software\	Program Groups	Contains information on program groups as used by Program Manager.
HKEY_LOCAL_MACHINE\Software\	Secure	Contains security information.
HKEY_LOCAL_MACHINE\Software\	Windows 3.1 Migration Status	Contains information on migration from Windows NT 3.*x* to Windows NT 4/2000/XP.
HKEY_LOCAL_MACHINE\System\ControlSet001\	All keys	The control set used to manage system resources.
HKEY_LOCAL_MACHINE\System\ControlSet002\	All keys	Backup control sets are numbered 002, 003, 004, and so on. Typically, there will only be two control sets.
HKEY_LOCAL_MACHINE\System\ControlSet003\	All keys	Backup control sets are numbered 002, 003, 004, and so on. Typically, there will only be two control sets.

Continued on next page

TABLE A.1: COMMON REGISTRY HIVES AND KEYS *(continued)*

HIVE/KEY	SUBKEY	DESCRIPTION
HKEY_LOCAL_MACHINE\System\ControlSet004\	All keys	Backup control sets are numbered 002, 003, 004, and so on. Typically, there will only be two control sets.
HKEY_LOCAL_MACHINE\System\CurrentControlSet\	All keys	The current control set is mapped to the control set used for starting the computer.
HKEY_LOCAL_MACHINE\System\CurrentControlSet\	Control\BootVerification Program	That program used to verify that the system booted correctly.
HKEY_LOCAL_MACHINE\System\CurrentControlSet\	Control\Class	Contains information about CLSIDs (OLE).
HKEY_LOCAL_MACHINE\System\CurrentControlSet\	Control\ComputerName\ ActiveComputerName	Holds the computer's current name.
HKEY_LOCAL_MACHINE\System\CurrentControlSet\	Control\ComputerName\ ComputerName	Holds the computer's name.
HKEY_LOCAL_MACHINE\System\CurrentControlSet\	Control\CrashControl	Determines events when/if the system fails.
HKEY_LOCAL_MACHINE\System\CurrentControlSet\	Control\FileSystem	A description of the system file system (FAT or NTFS).
HKEY_LOCAL_MACHINE\System\Disk\	All keys	A description of the system disk.
HKEY_LOCAL_MACHINE\System\Select\	All keys	A description of the control set used.
HKEY_LOCAL_MACHINE\System\Setup\	All keys	A description of the system setup state.
HKEY_LOCAL_MACHINE\System\	All keys	A description of the system.
HKEY_USERS\	All keys	Contains general user information.
HKEY_USERS\.DEFAULT\	All keys	The default user active when no other user is logged on. All information in .DEFAULT would also be found for specific users.
HKEY_USERS\.DEFAULT\	AppEvents\EventLabels	Event labels are used to notify users (with sound) when events happen.
HKEY_USERS\.DEFAULT\	AppEvents\Schemes	Schemes are used to apply which sounds are used for events.

Continued on next page

TABLE A.1: COMMON REGISTRY HIVES AND KEYS *(continued)*

HIVE/KEY	SUBKEY	DESCRIPTION
HKEY_USERS\.DEFAULT\	AppEvents	Contains application events, such as Startup, Document Open, and so on.
HKEY_USERS\.DEFAULT\	Console	The system's command prompt for Windows configuration.
HKEY_USERS\.DEFAULT\	Control Panel	The System Control Panel used to configure Windows.
HKEY_USERS\.DEFAULT\	Control Panel\ Accessibility	The Control Panel's Accessibility applet.
HKEY_USERS\.DEFAULT\	Control Panel\Appearance	The Control Panel's Appearance applet.
HKEY_USERS\.DEFAULT\	Control Panel\Colors	The Control Panel's Colors applet.
HKEY_USERS\.DEFAULT\	Control Panel\Current	The Control Panel's Current applet.
HKEY_USERS\.DEFAULT\	Control Panel\Custom Colors	The Control Panel's Custom Colors applet.
HKEY_USERS\.DEFAULT\	Control Panel\Desktop	The Control Panel's Desktop applet.
HKEY_USERS\.DEFAULT\	Control Panel\ International	The Control Panel's International applet.
HKEY_USERS\.DEFAULT\	Control Panel\IOProcs	The Control Panel's I/O Processes applet.
HKEY_USERS\.DEFAULT\	Control Panel\Keyboard	The Control Panel's Keyboard applet.
HKEY_USERS\.DEFAULT\	Control Panel\MMCPL	The Control Panel's MMCPL applet.
HKEY_USERS\.DEFAULT\	Control Panel\Mouse	The Control Panel's Mouse applet.
HKEY_USERS\.DEFAULT\	Control Panel\Patterns	The Control Panel's Patterns applet.
HKEY_USERS\.DEFAULT\	Control Panel\Screen Saver .3DFlyingObj	The Control Panel's Screen Saver.3DFlyingObj saved configuration.

Continued on next page

TABLE A.1: COMMON REGISTRY HIVES AND KEYS *(continued)*

HIVE/KEY	SUBKEY	DESCRIPTION
HKEY_USERS\.DEFAULT\	Control Panel\Screen Saver .3DPipes	The Control Panel's Screen Saver.3DPipes saved configuration.
HKEY_USERS\.DEFAULT\	Control Panel\Screen Saver .Bezier	The Control Panel's Screen Saver.Bezier saved configuration.
HKEY_USERS\.DEFAULT\	Control Panel\Screen Saver.Marquee	The Control Panel's Screen Saver.Marquee saved configuration.
HKEY_USERS\.DEFAULT\	Control Panel\Screen Saver.Mystify	The Control Panel's Screen Saver.Mystify saved configuration.
HKEY_USERS\.DEFAULT\	Control Panel\Screen Saver.Stars	The Control Panel's Screen Saver.Stars saved configuration.
HKEY_USERS\.DEFAULT\	Control Panel\Sound	The Control Panel's Sound applet.
HKEY_USERS\.DEFAULT\	Environment	Contains definitions of environment variables, used with both Windows and command prompts.
HKEY_USERS\.DEFAULT\	Keyboard Layout	The keyboard layouts for NLS (National Language Support).
HKEY_USERS\.DEFAULT\	Software\Microsoft\ Windows Help	Contains configurations for the Windows help system.
HKEY_USERS\.DEFAULT\	Software\Microsoft\ Windows NT\CurrentVersion	Contains the Windows current software configurations.
HKEY_USERS\.DEFAULT\	Software\Microsoft\ Windows NT\CurrentVersion\ Devices	Contains configurations of software drivers for hardware.
HKEY_USERS\.DEFAULT\	Software\Microsoft\ Windows NT	Contains Windows configuration items.
HKEY_USERS\.DEFAULT\	Software\Microsoft\ Windows\CurrentVersion	Contains Windows configuration items.
HKEY_USERS\.DEFAULT\	Software\Microsoft\ Windows	Contains general information about Windows.

Continued on next page

TABLE A.1: COMMON REGISTRY HIVES AND KEYS *(continued)*

HIVE/KEY	SUBKEY	DESCRIPTION
HKEY_USERS\.DEFAULT\	Software\Microsoft	Contains information about Microsoft components and software.
HKEY_USERS\.DEFAULT\	Software	Contains software configurations (as compared to hardware configurations).
HKEY_USERS\.DEFAULT\	UNICODE Program Groups	Unused on most systems.
HKEY_USERS\<SID>\	All keys	Contains information for specific users as identified by <SID>.
HKEY_USERS\<SID>\	AppEvents\EventLabels\ .Default	Contains information regarding application event labels, as in .DEFAULT.
HKEY_USERS\<SID>_Classes\	<None>	New as of Windows 2000, this key contains no usable information.

Appendix B

Registry Data Types

A VALUE ENTRY IN THE REGISTRY can contain data in different formats. All registry data is stored in binary format, along with a value indicating the data's actual type. There are potentially hundreds of types of data that can be stored in the registry; however, Windows only uses fewer than 20 of these types. These types are classed as:

Common data types   These are supported and edited by RegEdit and most other registry tools.

Windows XP–specific data types   These are supported and edited by RegEdit and some other registry tools.

Special and component/application-specific data types   These are both supported and unsupported by registry tools, but cannot usually be edited by users, except as binary data.

Keep in mind that registry editors actually allow the editing of all unsupported data types, including data types that display as REG_UNKNOWN. However, editing is done in binary mode, requiring the user to have intimate knowledge of the data object's contents.

The Data Types

If you find it necessary to modify the registry, it's important that you understand each data type, how data is stored for each data type, and so on. Much of the information about the default registry data types is contained in the file WinNT.h, as included in the Microsoft Windows SDK (Software Development Kit). The registry data types are described in Table B.1.

TABLE B.1: KNOWN REGISTRY DATA TYPES

TYPE	DATA TYPE INDEX (IF KNOWN)	SIZE	DESCRIPTION
REG_BINARY	3	0 or more bytes	A binary object that may contain any data
REG_COLOR_RGB	*	4 bytes	A color description

Continued on next page

TABLE B.1: KNOWN REGISTRY DATA TYPES *(continued)*

TYPE	DATA TYPE INDEX (IF KNOWN)	SIZE	DESCRIPTION
REG_DWORD	4	4 bytes	A DWORD (32-bit) value
REG_DWORD_BIG_ENDIAN	5	4 bytes	A 32-bit value stored in reverse order of a DWORD value
REG_DWORD_LITTLE_ENDIAN	4	4 bytes	A DWORD (32-bit) value
REG_EXPAND_SZ	2	0 or more bytes	A string with an optional environment substitution placeholder
REG_FILE_NAME	*	0 or more bytes	A filename
REG_FILE_TIME	*	Unknown	A file time
REG_FULL_RESOURCE_DESCRIPTOR	9	Varies with contents	A list of hardware resources
REG_LINK	6	0 or more bytes	A Unicode string naming a symbolic link
REG_MULTI_SZ	7	0 or more bytes	A collection of Unicode strings, each separated by a null character, with the final string terminated with two null characters
REG_NONE	0	Unknown	A data object with a defined type of REG_NONE for data that needn't be otherwise classified; different from REG_UNKNOWN
REG_QWORD	11	8 bytes	Twice the size of a REG _DWORD; a 64-bit integer variable
REG_QWORD_LITTLE_ENDIAN	11	8 bytes	The same as a REG_QWORD in size and format
REG_RESOURCE_LIST	8	Varies with contents	A list of resources used for a device
REG_RESOURCE_REQUIREMENTS_LIST	10	Varies with contents	A list of resources required by a driver
REG_SZ	1	0 or more bytes	A string terminated with a null
REG_UNKNOWN	(Undefined)	Unknown	An object whose type cannot be determined because the data type index is not valid

* At this time, these object types appear to be unsupported by Windows XP.

Now, to determine what type a particular object is, the registry stores a data type index value that indicates the data type of the object. For instance, a REG_SZ object has a data type index of 1. For those objects in Table B.1 without a data type index value, Windows will list them with a type that is equal to their hexadecimal value.

Oh, there is always the possibility that some additional data types will be added as Windows XP matures.

TIP   Look in a RegEdit .reg file, and you will see many instances of hex(n) where n is a number, typically between 0x0 and 0xFF. This number is the object's data type. This allows RegEdit to import (and export) registry data without having to know the data format.

The following sections describe the compatibility of each data type.

REG_BINARY

REG_BINARY holds binary data. It is compatible with RegEdit.

REG_BINARY is the most basic data type used in the registry. Windows is able to express every registry data type in REG_BINARY form, although this can be very inconvenient.

Windows saves a binary object in the registry as a length and a series of bytes. When a REG_BINARY object is stored in the registry, the length parameter is preserved. However, the user is unable to change the length parameter except by changing the object's actual size.

REG_COLOR_RGB

REG_COLOR_RGB holds color definition. It is compatible with RegEdt32 (from earlier versions of Windows).

REG_COLOR_RGB holds an RGB color index, which may be displayed by RegEdt32. None of the registry tools is able to create a REG_COLOR_RGB data object, and it cannot be determined whether Windows XP or any component supports this object type.

Future versions of Windows may support this object type. However, there is currently no support for the REG_COLOR_RGB object.

REG_DWORD

REG_DWORD holds a 32-bit number (that's 4 bytes, folks, no more, no fewer) expressed in either decimal or hexadecimal. REG_DWORD is compatible with all registry tools.

Like REG_BINARY, the REG_DWORD type is a basic data type for registry value entries.

REG_DWORD_BIG_ENDIAN

REG_DWORD_BIG_ENDIAN holds a DWORD value. REG_DWORD_BIG_ENDIAN is compatible with custom-written registry tools. The original Windows NT 4 Resource Kit's RegChg program worked with this registry data type.

Different computers store numbers in memory in different orders. Two orders are used: big endian and little endian. The Intel processor stores numbers in little endian format.

In the big endian format, the 4 bytes of a DWORD value are stored with the highest-order byte at the highest address and the lowest-order byte at the lowest address. See Table B.2 for an example of how the value 0x12345678 (in decimal that's 305419896) would be stored at memory address 0x5.

TABLE B.2: A DWORD VALUE STORED IN BIG ENDIAN FORMAT

ADDRESS	VALUE
0x5	12
0x6	34
0x7	56
0x8	78

REG_DWORD_LITTLE_ENDIAN

REG_DWORD_LITTLE_ENDIAN holds a DWORD value. REG_DWORD_LITTLE_ENDIAN is compatible with RegEdit. (Note that this data type is typically treated as REG_DWORD.)

In the little endian format, the 4 bytes of a DWORD value are stored with the highest-order byte at the lowest address and the lowest-order byte at the highest address. Table B.3 shows an example of the value 0x12345678 (in decimal that's 305419896) stored at memory address 0x5.

TABLE B.3: A DWORD VALUE STORED IN LITTLE ENDIAN FORMAT

ADDRESS	VALUE
0x5	78
0x6	56
0x7	34
0x8	12

Windows runs on computers that store numbers in little endian format. Some operating systems are designed for big endian computers. When an operating system is designed for a different endian than what the hardware supports, the operating system will convert as necessary.

TIP   Endian is a hardware issue, generally. The importance of knowing how numbers are stored in memory is usually only important when transferring data between two different types of computers. Therefore, it is generally unnecessary for users to consider endian issues. The only time that endian format becomes important is when you are transferring data between two dissimilar computer systems using raw binary transfer methods. Since virtually all transfer methods (including data transfers over the Internet) do not use raw binary transfers, it's rarely an issue.

In all cases, the Windows XP registry treats REG_DWORD_LITTLE_ENDIAN as a REG_DWORD type. There is no real difference between these two types in the Windows XP registry.

REG_EXPAND_SZ

The REG_EXPAND_SZ data object contains a single string terminated with a null; a null is a character whose value is zero. The REG_EXPAND_SZ data object is compatible with RegEdit and all other registry tools. This string may contain one or more unexpanded environment variables.

There are many examples of REG_EXPAND_SZ in the registry, most of which are references to files accessed from the environment variables %SystemRoot%, %SystemDrive%, and %Path%.

Windows substitutes environment variables when percent (%) signs surround the name. In a command-prompt window, the command SET displays a list of all the current environment variables. These environment variables (with surrounding percent signs) are also used from command prompts or in batch files. In the next example, lines that I typed are in bold; the lines starting with REM are comments:

```
Windows 18:05:31 C:\TEMP
REM-display the contents of the environment variable SystemRoot
Windows 18:05:32 C:\TEMP
set systemroot
SystemRoot=C:\WINNT40

Windows 18:05:34 C:\TEMP
REM-Use the environment variable SystemRoot
Windows 18:05:35 C:\TEMP
dir %SystemRoot%\*.bat
 Volume in drive C is (c) - Boot drive
 Volume Serial Number is CC56-5631

 Directory of C:\WINNT

02/10/98 03:55p            46        PB.BAT
        1 File(s)        46 bytes
            152,050,688 bytes free

Windows 18:05:40 C:\TEMP
```

REG_FILE_NAME

The REG_FILE_NAME object type is not currently used (or supported) other than in RegEdt32 display mode. The REG_FILE_NAME object type is compatible with early versions of RegEdt32. The Windows XP RegEdit manages this type as binary data.

None of the registry tools is able to create a REG_FILE_NAME data object, and it's unclear whether either Windows XP or any component supports this object type.

It is possible that future versions of Windows will support this object type. However, there is currently no support for the REG_FILE_NAME object.

REG_FILE_TIME

The REG_FILE_TIME object type is not currently used (or supported) other than in RegEdt32 display mode. The REG_FILE_TIME object type is compatible with earlier versions of RegEdt32. The Windows XP RegEdit manages this type as binary data.

None of the registry tools is able to create a REG_FILE_TIME data object, and it's unclear whether either Windows XP or any component supports this object type.

It is possible that future versions of Windows will support this object type. However, there is currently no support for the REG_FILE_TIME object.

REG_FULL_RESOURCE_DESCRIPTOR

The REG_FULL_RESOURCE_DESCRIPTOR object contains a list of hardware resources that a physical device is using. The REG_FULL_RESOURCE_DESCRIPTOR object is compatible with RegEdit.

This information is detected and written into the HKEY_LOCAL_MACHINE\ Hardware\Description key by the system at bootup time.

Generally, it would be very unwise to edit a REG_FULL_RESOURCE_ DESCRIPTOR object. RegChg allows the creation of a REG_FULL_ RESOURCE_DESCRIPTOR object if an edit is necessary.

Table B.4 shows the objects found in a REG_FULL_RESOURCE_DESCRIPTOR.

TABLE B.4: OBJECTS IN A REG_FULL_RESOURCE_DESCRIPTOR

OBJECT	SIZE	DETAILS
Interface Type	4 bytes	One of the following values:
		–1 = Interface Type Undefined
		0 = Internal
		1 = ISA
		2 = EISA
		3 = Micro Channel
		4 = Turbo Channel
		5 = PCI Bus
		6 = VME Bus
		7 = NuBus
		8 = PCMCIA Bus
		9 = Cbus
		10 = MPI Bus
		11 = MPSA Bus
		12 = Processor Internal

Continued on next page

TABLE B.4: OBJECTS IN A REG_FULL_RESOURCE_DESCRIPTOR *(continued)*

OBJECT	SIZE	DETAILS
Interface Type	4 bytes	13 = Internal Power Bus
		14 = PNP ISA Bus
		15 = Maximum Interface Type
Bus Number	4 bytes	Bus number for this resource
Type*	1 byte	Uses CM_RESOURCE_TYPE:
		0 = Null
		1 = Port
		2 = Interrupt
		3 = Memory
		4 = DMA
		5 = Device Specific
		6 = Maximum
Share Disposition*	1 byte	Uses CM_SHARE_DISPOSITION:
		0 = Undetermined
		1 = Device Exclusive
		2 = DriverExclusive2
		3 = Shared
Flags*	2 bytes	The resource flag values depend on the resource type (see Type):
		For an Interrupt resource type:
		0 = INTERRUPT_LEVEL_SENSITIVE
		1 = INTERRUPT_LATCHED
		For a Memory resource type:
		0x0000 = READ_WRITE
		0x0001 = READ_ONLY
		0x0002 = WRITE_ONLY
		0x0004 = PREFETCHABLE
		0x0008 = COMBINEDWRITE
		0x0010 = 24
		For a Port resource type:
		0 = PORT_MEMORY
		1 = PORT_IO

Continued on next page

TABLE B.4: OBJECTS IN A REG_FULL_RESOURCE_DESCRIPTOR *(continued)*

OBJECT	SIZE	DETAILS
Flags* (cont.)		For a DMA resource type:
		0x0000 = DMA_8
		0x0001 = DMA_16
		0x0002 = DMA_32
Start*	8 bytes	64 bit: 32 bits low, 32 bits high port address
Length*	4 bytes	Length of port address
Level*	4 bytes	Interrupt
Vector*	4 bytes	Interrupt
Affinity*	4 bytes	Interrupt
Start*	8 bytes	64-bit physical memory addresses
Length*	4 bytes	Length of memory
Channel*	4 bytes	DMA channel number
Port*	4 bytes	DMA port number
Reserved 1*	4 bytes	Reserved for future DMA use
Data Size*	4 bytes	Device-specific data size
Reserved 1*	4 bytes	Reserved for future use
Reserved 2*	4 bytes	Reserved for future use

* These objects, as a group, may be repeated as needed.

REG_LINK

REG_LINK is a Unicode string naming a symbolic link. REG_LINK is compatible with RegEdit.

This type is relevant to device and intermediate drivers only and should be of no interest to anyone except geeky programmers.

REG_MULTI_SZ

The REG_MULTI_SZ object consists of one or more strings. The REG_MULTI_SZ object is compatible with RegEdit.

Windows separates each string from the next using a null. The final string terminates with two nulls. For strings that are Unicode (all strings in the Windows registry are Unicode), the null shall be the same width as a Unicode character. For example (\0 indicates a null character):

```
String one\0
String two\0
String three\0
Last string\0\0
```

NOTE   *What the heck is a null? A null character has a numeric value of zero, irrespective of the character's width.*

REG_NONE

REG_NONE is data with no particular type. REG_NONE is compatible with RegEdit.

Notice that this type is different from REG_UNKNOWN. REG_NONE is data that is stored in binary format, with 0 or more bytes of information. Generally, REG_NONE objects are created by default, although some components and applications may create a REG_NONE object intentionally.

REG_QWORD

REG_QWORD holds a 64-bit number expressed in either decimal or hexadecimal. REG_QWORD is compatible with RegEdit.

Like REG_DWORD, the REG_QWORD type is a basic data type, containing a numeric value. This registry type will become more commonly used with future 64-bit versions of Windows.

REG_QWORD_LITTLE_ENDIAN

REG_QWORD_LITTLE_ENDIAN holds a 64-bit number expressed in either decimal or hexa-decimal. This type is identical to the REG_QWORD type. REG_QWORD_LITTLE_ENDIAN is compatible with RegEdit.

Like REG_DWORD, the REG_QWORD_LITTLE_ENDIAN type is a basic data type, con-taining a numeric value. This registry type will become more commonly used with future 64-bit ver-sions of Windows.

REG_RESOURCE_LIST

A REG_RESOURCE_LIST object describes information about resources used by a specific device. A REG_RESOURCE_LIST object is compatible with RegEdit.

Found primarily in `HKEY_LOCAL_MACHINE\Hardware\ResourceMap`, there are entries for each device installed in the system. REG_ RESOURCE_LIST information is organized by bus structure:

◆ Cbus

◆ EISA

- Internal
- ISA
- Micro Channel
- MPI Bus
- MPSA Bus
- NuBus
- PCI Bus
- PCMCIA Bus
- Turbo Channel
- VME Bus

Information stored in REG_RESOURCE_LIST may include:

- Device Specific Data Size
- Device Specific Data Reserved1
- Device Specific Data Reserved2
- DMA Channel
- DMA Port
- DMA Reserved1
- Interrupt Affinity
- Interrupt Level
- Interrupt Vector
- Memory Length
- Memory Physical Address
- Memory Start
- Port Length
- Port Physical Address
- Port Start

Table B.5 shows the arrangement of information that is stored in the REG_RESOURCE_LIST registry data type.

TABLE B.5: ARRANGEMENT OF ACTUAL VALUES IN THE REG_RESOURCE_LIST TYPE

OBJECT	SIZE	DETAILS
Version	2 bytes	Version number
Revision	2 bytes	Revision number
Count	4 bytes	Object count
Option*	1 byte	Undocumented
Type*	1 byte	Uses CM_RESOURCE_TYPE: 0 = Null 1 = Port 2 = Interrupt 3 = Memory 4 = DMA 5 = Device Specific 6 = Maximum
Share Disposition*	1 byte	Uses CM_SHARE_DISPOSITION: 0 = Undetermined 1 = Device Exclusive 2 = Driver Exclusive 3 = Shared
Spare1*	1 byte	Unused; it is present to force proper alignment.
Flags*	2 bytes	The resource flag values depend on the resource type (see Type near the beginning of this table): For an Interrupt resource type: 0 = INTERRUPT_LEVEL_SENSITIVE 1 = INTERRUPT_LATCHED For a Memory resource type: 0x0000 = READ_WRITE 0x0001 = READ_ONLY 0x0002 = WRITE_ONLY 0x0004 = PREFETCHABLE 0x0008 = COMBINEDWRITE 0x0010 = 24

Continued on next page

TABLE B.5: ARRANGEMENT OF ACTUAL VALUES IN THE REG_RESOURCE_LIST TYPE *(continued)*

OBJECT	SIZE	DETAILS
Flags* (cont.)	2 bytes	For a Port resource type:
		0 = PORT_MEMORY
		1 = PORT_IO
		For a DMA resource type:
		0x0000 = DMA_8
		0x0001 = DMA_16
		0x0002 = DMA_32
Spare2*	2 bytes	Align the remainder of the objects.
Length*	4 bytes	Only Port type resources use this variable.
Alignment*	4 bytes	Only Port type resources use this variable.
Minimum Address*	8 bytes	Only Port type resources use this variable.
Maximum Address*	8 bytes	Only Port type resources use this variable.
Length*	4 bytes	Only Memory type resources use this variable.
Alignment*	4 bytes	Only Memory type resources use this variable.
Minimum Address*	8 bytes	Only Memory type resources use this variable.
Maximum Address*	8 bytes	Only Memory type resources use this variable.
Minimum Vector*	4 bytes	Only Interrupt type resources use this variable.
Maximum Vector*	4 bytes	Only Interrupt type resources use this variable.
Minimum Channel*	4 bytes	Only DMA type resources use this variable.
Maximum Channel*	4 bytes	Only DMA type resources use this variable.

* These objects, as a group, may be repeated as needed.

REG_RESOURCE_REQUIREMENTS_LIST

REG_RESOURCE_REQUIREMENTS_LIST objects contain lists of hardware resources that a device driver would require. REG_RESOURCE_REQUIREMENTS_LIST objects are compatible with RegEdit.

This list of hardware resources is used to update the HKEY_LOCAL_MACHINE\Hardware\ResourceMap subkey.

Table B.6 shows the arrangement of objects in the REG_RESOURCE_REQUIREMENTS_LIST object.

TABLE B.6: OBJECTS IN A REG_RESOURCE_REQUIREMENTS_LIST

OBJECT	SIZE	DETAILS
List Size	4 bytes	
Interface Type	4 bytes	One of the following values:
		−1 = Interface Type Undefined
		0 = Internal
		1 = ISA
		2 = EISA
		3 = Micro Channel
		4 = Turbo Channel
		5 = PCI Bus
		6 = VME Bus
		7 = NuBus
		8 = PCMCIA Bus
		9 = Cbus
		10 = MPI Bus
		11 = MPSA Bus
		12 = Processor Internal
		13 = Internal Power Bus
		14 = PNP ISA Bus
		15 = Maximum Interface Type
Bus Number	4 bytes	
Slot Number	4 bytes	
Reserved[3]	12 bytes	
Alternative Lists	4 bytes	
Version*	2 bytes	
Revision*	2 bytes	
Count*	4 bytes	
Option*	1 byte	
Type*	1 byte	Uses CM_RESOURCE_TYPE:
		0 = Null
		1 = Port
		2 = Interrupt
		3 = Memory

Continued on next page

TABLE B.6: OBJECTS IN A REG_RESOURCE_REQUIREMENTS_LIST *(continued)*

OBJECT	SIZE	DETAILS
Type* (cont.)	1 byte	4 = DMA
		5 = Device Specific
		6 = Maximum
Share Disposition*	1 byte	Uses CM_SHARE_DISPOSITION:
		0 = Undetermined
		1 = Device Exclusive
		2 = DriverExclusive2
		3 = Shared
Spare1*	1 byte	Unused (typically used to force proper alignment).
Flags*	2 bytes	The resource flag values depend on the resource type (see Type near the beginning of this table):
		For an Interrupt resource type:
		0 = INTERRUPT_LEVEL_SENSITIVE
		1 = INTERRUPT_LATCHED
		For a Memory resource type:
		0x0000 = READ_WRITE
		0x0001 = READ_ONLY
		0x0002 = WRITE_ONLY
		0x0004 = PREFETCHABLE
		0x0008 = COMBINEDWRITE
		0x0010 = 24
		For a Port resource type:
		0 = PORT_MEMORY
		1 = PORT_IO
		For a DMA resource type:
		0x0000 = DMA_8
		0x0001 = DMA_16
		0x0002 = DMA_32
Spare2*	2 bytes	Unused.
Length*	4 bytes	Only Port type resources use this variable.
Alignment*	4 bytes	Only Port type resources use this variable.

Continued on next page

TABLE B.6: OBJECTS IN A REG_RESOURCE_REQUIREMENTS_LIST *(continued)*

OBJECT	SIZE	DETAILS
Minimum Address*	8 bytes	Only Port type resources use this variable.
Maximum Address*	8 bytes	Only Port type resources use this variable.
Length*	4 bytes	Only Memory type resources use this variable.
Alignment*	4 bytes	Only Memory type resources use this variable.
Minimum Address*	8 bytes	Only Memory type resources use this variable.
Maximum Address*	8 bytes	Only Memory type resources use this variable.
Minimum Vector*	4 bytes	Only Interrupt type resources use this variable.
Maximum Vector*	4 bytes	Only Interrupt type resources use this variable.
Minimum Channel*	4 bytes	Only DMA type resources use this variable.
Maximum Channel*	4 bytes	Only DMA type resources use this variable.

* These objects, as a group, may be repeated as needed.

REG_SZ

REG_SZ contains a single string terminated with a null. REG_SZ is compatible with all registry tool(s). The REG_SZ string will be in Unicode for Windows XP installations.

REG_UNKNOWN

If Windows encounters an undefined registry data type, the REG_UNKNOWN object type is used. The REG_UNKNOWN object type is compatible with RegEdit.

Windows permits system components and system applications to write their own types of data into the registry. Moreover, none of the registry tools, such as the registry editors, will know about these data types. Whenever a registry tool encounters a data type that it does not know about, the tool will display the data in binary format and flag it as REG_UNKNOWN.

Appendix C

Where Can I Get More Help?

MAYBE THIS BOOK DIDN'T have enough information for you, or more likely, you need some very specialized help. There are many sources of assistance. Many are free, and some are costly; but generally, we get what we pay for in life. As a rule, personalized, hand-holding assistance can be expensive—consultants typically cost between $100 and $350 an hour, and they usually charge for travel time and other expenses.

User groups and other self-help sources are cheaper, but you may not profit from assistance that is quickly shot out to you in an e-mail. You must determine if such help will work for you.

The Web

On the Internet's Web you'll find many sites that focus on the registry. Your first choice is to use one of the popular search engines to find a site. I've listed a number of sites below; however, even though these sites were current in early 2002, there is no guarantee that they will be valid as time goes on. Some sites (Microsoft's own website is an excellent example of this) change on an almost daily basis—it looks like the web developers are trying to prove their worth, perhaps? Regardless, if a specific page fails to load, consider looking at the site's root (or home) page—perhaps that will give you a clue where to actually search to find the needed information.

In Table C.1, I have tried to keep the URLs as simple as possible, but in one or two cases, that was not possible. Just be careful that you do not mistype these URLs as you use them! These sites may have information that you will find useful in your registry work. Visit these sites and see if you can find information that is appropriate to your needs.

TABLE C.1: VARIOUS INTERNET WEBSITES SHOWING REGISTRY-RELATED TOPICS

URL	DESCRIPTION
`http://66.34.160.192/spywareinfo/comdlg32.html`	This site describes how to clear/remove the MRU (most recently used) file list in Windows. This list contains a list of the files that you recently opened, and some users, on public computers, find allowing others to see what files they opened to be unacceptable.
`http://freepctech.com/pc/002/Windows_registry_faq.shtml`	This site is a general-purpose Windows registry site.
`http://msdn.microsoft.com/visualj/technical/tutorial/wfcregistry/default.asp`	This site is useful for Java programmers.
`http://newbieclub.com/rfncopy/`	This site is a basic, general-purpose Windows registry site.
`http://searchwin2000.techtarget.com/sDefinition/0,,sid1_gci212883,00.html`	This site is a general-purpose Windows registry site.
`http://service2.symantec.com/SUPPORT/tsgeninfo.nsf/docid/199762382617`	This site is a general-purpose Windows registry site. The page cited covers backing up the Windows registry.
`http://www.3dspotlight.com/tweaks/registry/index.shtml`	This site is a general-purpose Windows registry site and covers issues such as tweaking the registry for better performance.
`http://www.5star-shareware.com/Utilities/Registry/Registry1.html`	This site provides a list of registry-related software tools.
`http://www.5starsupport.com/resources/registry.htm`	This site is a general-purpose Windows registry resources site.
`http://www.activewin.com/tips/reg/index.shtml`	This site is an advanced Windows registry site. There are many tips arranged in a library.
`http://www.annoyances.org/exec/show/registry`	This site gives a listing of virtually all the registry settings.
`http://www.codebits.com/p5be/xp0d.cfm`	This site is a general-purpose Windows registry site.
`http://www.computerhelp.net/bookcat/windows_registry.html`	This site gives a listing of Windows registry books.
`http://www.computerhope.com/registry.htm`	This site contains extended information about the Windows registry and various settings contained in the registry.

Continued on next page

TABLE C.1: VARIOUS INTERNET WEBSITES SHOWING REGISTRY-RELATED TOPICS *(continued)*

URL	DESCRIPTION
http://www.dcsoft.com/prod01.htm	This site hosts a (freeware) program named RegEditX, a RegEdit extension program that provides additional information and power to the Windows RegEdit program. The status of RegEditX may change from freeware.
http://www.easydesksoftware.com/	This site is a general-purpose Windows registry site.
http://www.easydesksoftware.com/howto.htm	This site gives information about how to repair the Windows registry.
http://www.elementkjournals.com/w9p/0012/w9p00c4.htm	This site is gives information on how to compact the Windows registry.
http://www.fiveanddime.net/notes.html	This site has Windows registry and system file notes and tips.
http://www.glencove.com/95regedit.html	This site is a general-purpose Windows registry site.
http://www.gnusoftware.com/Emacs/Registry/	This site provides GNU Emacs patches for allowing registry access from within Emacs.
http://www.itp-journals.com/search/e1209.htm	This site offers a (free) tutorial to help you learn more about the Windows registry.
http://www.jsiinc.com/	This site is run by Jerold Schulman (JSI, Inc.). It is jam-packed with helpful tips and ideas. The registry section that Jerold has set up includes almost 500 different registry-related tips and techniques.
http://macspeedzone.com/archive/articles/macwindowsrossettastone/registry.shtml	This site is a general-purpose Windows registry site oriented toward those who use Macs.
http://www.mkssoftware.com/docs/man1/registry.1.asp	This site is a general-purpose Windows registry site.
http://www.ntutility.com/arm/	This site offers a utility named the Active Registry Monitor (ARM). This program monitors changes to the registry allowing the user to determine what has been changed.
http://www.onecomputerguy.com/app_info/regedit.htm	This site is a general-purpose Windows registry site.
http://www.pcmech.com/show/os/150/	This site is a general-purpose Windows registry site.

Continued on next page

TABLE C.1: VARIOUS INTERNET WEBSITES SHOWING REGISTRY-RELATED TOPICS *(continued)*

URL	DESCRIPTION
http://www.pcmech.com/show/os/156/	This site offers a product called the Shop Vac for the Windows Registry.
http://www.pconline.com/~erc/perlreg.htm	A Perl-like utility for the registry is offered by this site.
http://www.pcworld.com/hereshow/article/0,aid, 44044,pg,2,00.asp	This site offers methods to "clean up" the Windows registry.
http://www.regedit.com/	The Windows Registry Guide site provides an extensive range of registry tweaks, tricks, and hacks. With this site's resources optimizing, enhancing and securing the Windows registry is possible.
http://www.registrytool.com/	This site, named the Registry Tool, offers a Windows registry editor and registry utility. This product is claimed to be capable of remote registry administration, maintenance, analysis, compare, and recovery/restore operations
http://www.securityfriday.com/Topics/win_reg.html	This site is a general-purpose Windows registry site.
http://www.security-tips.com/001.htm	This site offers information about improving general registry security.
http://www.smartcomputing.com/editorial/article .asp?article=articles%2Farchive%2Fc0101%2F51c01% 2F51c01%2Easp	This site is a general-purpose Windows registry site, offering a number of useful Windows registry tweaks.
http://www.softricks.com/vb/registry/Registry.html	This site offers assistance for Visual Basic users accessing the Windows registry.
http://www.speedguide.net/Cable_modems/ cable_patches.shtml	This site is oriented toward higher-speed (cable modem, DSL, or other broadband connection) Windows registry tweaking, offering a number of useful tips.
http://www.vb-world.net/registry/registry2/	This site covers accessing the Windows registry with the Windows registry API.
http://www.webattack.com/Freeware/system/ fwregtools.shtml	This site provides some interesting registry utilities. Many of these utilities are freeware.
http://www.webattack.com/~get/winreg.shtml	This site is a general-purpose Windows registry site, offering a number of useful Windows registry tune-up techniques.

Continued on next page

TABLE C.1: VARIOUS INTERNET WEBSITES SHOWING REGISTRY-RELATED TOPICS *(continued)*

URL	DESCRIPTION
`http://www.webopedia.com/TERM/R/Registry.html`	This site is a general-purpose Windows registry site, offering a number of useful Windows registry tweaks.
`http://www.webtechgeek.com/center_Frame_Windows_Registry_Guide.htm`	This site offers the Windows Registry Guide.
`http://www.we-compute.com/registry.html`	This site is a general-purpose Windows registry site, offering a number of useful Windows registry tweaks.
`http://www.windowsgalore.com/windows.95/registry_edit.html`	This site is a general-purpose Windows registry site, offering a number of useful Windows registry tweaks.
`http://www.windowsitlibrary.com/`	This site is oriented toward Windows IT professionals. It offers a general Windows registry technical library.
`http://www.winguides.com/`	This site is a general-purpose Windows registry site, offering a number of useful Windows registry tweaks.
`http://www.winsite.com/tech/reg/`	This is the WinSite Windows Registry Tools website.
`http://www.woram.com/`	Though oriented toward the Windows 98 registry, this site can provide much useful information for a registry wannabe expert.
`http://www.zdnet.com/downloads/stories/info/0,10615,44197,.html`	This site is a general-purpose Windows registry site, offering a number of useful Windows registry tweaks.

There are many more sites on the World Wide Web that offer assistance to Windows users than I have listed above. Not all sites are specific to the registry, though many of these sites offer either a section for the registry or a general area that may be helpful to someone who has a registry problem.

The site at `http://www.jsiinc.com/reghack.htm` is run by Jerold Schulman (JSI, Inc.). It is jam-packed with helpful tips and ideas. The registry section that Jerold has set up includes almost 500 different registry-related tips and techniques.

The site at `http://www.ntfaq.com` is run by John Savill (SavillTech Ltd.). It has a number of very interesting features, including answers to over 1600 common questions, a Java and CGI search engine with a single-file version that can be downloaded, and several help file versions that can be used locally.

The site at `http://www.bhs.com` is run by Beverly Hills Software. It is one of the premier sites for users of Windows NT. A close alliance with Microsoft has allowed BHS to remain in the forefront of Windows NT support and technology.

The site at `http://www.sysinternals.com/` is run by Mark Russinovich and Bryce Cogswell. These two experts in the Windows NT field offer freeware utilities that they have written. (Freeware is software that is essentially free, though freeware authors may ask for a donation.)

At `http://www.winsupersite.com/`, you'll find Paul Thurrott's Super Site for Windows, a site dedicated to Windows. Paul is an expert who is well known for his expertise with Windows NT. This is Paul's main site for Windows, and it is well worth browsing.

The site `http://www.win2000security.com/` has lots of information about Windows security. This site emphasizes the server versions of Windows, but also has coverage of other products.

When looking for hardware drivers, the site `http://www.windrivers.com/` is a good place to start. Go there and do a search, and you will receive all relevant information about the driver. This site used to be free, but now requires a subscription. This is unfortunate...

The Interior Alaska Windows NT Users Group hosts the site `http://www.iawntug.org`. This site has a number of useful features and links.

At `http://support.microsoft.com/default.aspx?scid=fh;en-us;winxp`, you'll find Microsoft's online support for Windows XP. This site, along with other Microsoft sites, form Microsoft's online interactive support services.

The site at `http://www.microsoft.com/backofficeserver/default.asp` is Microsoft's site for information about Windows 2000 and the other members of the Microsoft BackOffice family. BackOffice is Microsoft's business-solutions offering for advanced users.

You can contact Microsoft's technical people by using Microsoft's sites at `http://support` `.microsoft.com/` and `http://www.microsoft.com/backofficeserver/support/newsgroups/` `default.asp`. The second URL allows access to the newsgroups described in the "Newsgroups" section later in this appendix.

Companies and Magazines

Many companies offer support, training, and other services. These companies are usually a combination of consultants and resellers. To find larger support companies, peruse magazines such as *PC Magazine*, *InfoWorld*, and *PC Week*.

Consultants

In virtually all locations, you will find independent consultants. They are sometimes difficult to find, and most consultants don't advertise. Consultants are often one- and two-person outfits, and they are typically expensive.

Similar to the procedure with stores (discussed next), always check references if possible. Check the consultant's areas of expertise. A consultant who is respected in the field and writes articles and books is probably qualified. Ask the consultant if they are using tools, such as Microsoft TechNet and MSDN. If not, the consultant is probably going to spend a lot of time reinventing the wheel by trying to solve problems that were solved and documented long ago.

Consultants' rates vary, with most requiring either a minimum charge of one to two hours, and/or a charge for travel time. Most consultants do not have a storefront, so walk-in business is not the norm. Hourly rates vary from a low of about $100 to a high of almost $350. Generally, the higher-priced service people are going to solve the problem more quickly than the lower-priced ones.

Computer Stores

Many computer stores offer services to users of Microsoft Windows. Start with local, nonchain computer stores. Most chain stores do not specialize in offering service, while nonchain stores usually excel in service. Ask for references.

Consider bringing in the computer if possible, to save on the cost of repair. Hourly rates vary from a low of about $50 to a high of almost $200.

NOTE   *No one has solved the problem of paying for incompetence! You hire someone to do a job and may actually end up paying for his or her learning experience. To avoid paying for work that is not solving the problem, be sure to check references.*

User Groups

User groups form a two-way street: if you get assistance from the group, you must support them as well. Most user groups are either not funded or are very limited financially—don't ask them to call you back long distance.

No user group list is ever up-to-date. That's life—things are always changing, especially with user groups. Table C.2 is a listing of some Windows NT user groups. For any group you might be interested in, please either check the group's web page or e-mail the contact at the address given for more information about such points as the group's meeting place, date, and time. Some user groups don't hold regular meetings, but there may be other assistance they can provide.

Sizes of groups range from small (perhaps fewer than 20 members), to medium (about 20 to 100 members), to large (generally more than 100 members).

Is there no user group in your area? Start one! Most newspapers will provide free publicity. Usually meetings can be at local libraries, schools, or at your business. You will meet new people, make friends, and become very popular. Oh, and if you didn't guess, starting a user group will take some time and effort—but it's worth it!

Due to the ever-changing nature of user groups, it is possible that a group listed in Table C.2 is no longer active. If this is the case, it may be possible to find another group that meets in the same geographical area.

NOTE   *Those groups that do not have a web page listed may no longer exist, or may be dedicated to other platforms than Windows. (Several groups have changed their focus from Windows platforms to Unix/Linux).*

TABLE C.2: WINDOWS NT USER GROUPS AROUND THE WORLD

USER GROUP	WEB PAGE ADDRESS	CITY, STATE, COUNTRY	GROUP SIZE	CONTACT NAME	CONTACT E-MAIL ADDRESS
Birmingham Windows NT User Group	http://www.bwntug.org/	Birmingham, Alabama	Small	Mike Chilson	mchilson@bwntug.org
Anchorage Windows NT Users Group	unknown	Anchorage, Alaska	Unknown	Jon Dawson	jdawson@anc.ak.net
Interior Alaska Windows NT Users Group	http://www.iawntug.org/	Fairbanks, Alaska	Small	Roger M. Marty	marty@rmm.com
Windows NT Group (Argentina)	unknown	Capital Federal, Argentina	Medium	Ricardo Fig	RFig@smart.com.ar
NT Users Group	None	San Miguel, Argentina	Unknown	Angulo	ANGULOA@TELEFONICA.COM.AR
Phoenix PCUG NT SIG	None	Phoenix, Arizona	Unknown	Ray Moore	nt-sig@phoenixpcug.org
Brisbane NT Users Group	http://www.humbug.org.au/	Brisbane, Australia	Unknown	Derek Kowald	dkowald@ozemail.com.au
Queensland NT Users Group	http://www.qntug.asn.au/	Brisbane, Australia	Medium	David Steadson	davids@ambience.com
Melbourne NT User Group	http://www.co.rmit.edu.au/ausnt	Melbourne, Australia	Small	Mark A Gregory	m.gregory@rmit.edu.au
Perth Users Group	http://plug.linux.org.au/	Perth, Australia	Small	Kevin Merritt	kevinm@acslink.aone.net.au
Sydney NT Users Group	None	Sydney, Australia	Unknown	J. Noiles	killara@hotmail.com
NT Users in Vienna	None	Vienna, Austria	Unknown	Gerhard Wenk	wenk@vienna.at

Continued on next page

TABLE C.2: WINDOWS NT USER GROUPS AROUND THE WORLD *(continued)*

USER GROUP	WEB PAGE ADDRESS	CITY, STATE, COUNTRY	GROUP SIZE	CONTACT NAME	CONTACT E-MAIL ADDRESS
Windows NT User Group of Austria	`http://www.wug.or.at`	Vienna, Austria	Medium	Sepp Reichholf	`josef.reichholf @reichholf.co.at`
MBS	None	Belgium	Small	Jose Gonzalez	`jgon@usa.net`
BeNTUG—Belgian NT User Group	`http://www.bentug.org`	Brussels, Belgium	Medium	Unknown	`info@bentug.org`
NTX—Belgian Windows NT Corporate Account Group	`http://www.econ .kuleuven.ac.be/ntx`	Leuven, Belgium	Medium	Wim Van Holder	`Wim.VanHolder @econ.kuleuven.ac.be`
DIN NT User Group	None	Curitiba, Brazil	Small	Wallace A.B.S. Macedo	`wallace@furukawa .com.br`
Exchange	None	Rio de Janeiro, Brazil	Unknown	Roberto Boclin	`boclin@unikey.com.br`
NT User Group Brazil—NT Brazil	None	Rio de Janeiro, Brazil	Unknown	Paul Smith	`psmith @centroin.com.br`
NT Services	None	Sao Paulo, Brazil	Unknown	Ana	`analucia@opus.com.br`
Fresno PC Users Group	None	Fresno, California	Large	Susy Ball or George Simpson	`susyball@aol.com or georgesi@cybergate .com`
Riverside NT User Group	None	Riverside, California	Unknown	Chris Navigato	`chris@navigato.com`
Sacramento NT Users Group	None	Sacramento, California	Unknown	Steven W. Linthicum	`slinthi@ns.net`
Southern California Exchange Users Group	None	Santa Monica, California	Medium	Ivan K. Nikkhoo	`ivann@vertexsystems .com`

Continued on next page

TABLE C.2: WINDOWS NT USER GROUPS AROUND THE WORLD *(continued)*

USER GROUP	WEB PAGE ADDRESS	CITY, STATE, COUNTRY	GROUP SIZE	CONTACT NAME	CONTACT E-MAIL ADDRESS
Quebec Windows NT Users Group	None	Montreal, Quebec, Canada	Unknown	Maxime Bombardier	maxime@4dm.com
Vancouver Island NT User Group	http://www.vintug.bc.ca	Victoria British Columbia, Canada	Large	Guy Gondor	webmaster@vintug.bc.ca or nancy@steeves.bc.ca
Windows NT Group, La Serena, Chile	None	La Serena, Chile	Small	Pablo Peña	win-nt@mercury.andesnet.cl
Download Center	None	Nj, China	Unknown	Ghost	Heaven_ghost@163.net
NT-Colombia-Cali	None	Cali, Colombia	Small	Guillermo Matiz	gmatizo@col2.telecom.com.co
GUNTCOL	None	Cartagena de Indias, Santafé de Bogotá, Colombia	Unknown	Tomas Mac Master	ima@axisgate.com
Rocky Mountain Windows NT User Group	http://www.rmwntug.org	Denver, Colorado	Unknown	Dennis Martin	76314.1441@compuserve.com
Northern Colorado Windows NT Users Group	None	Fort Collins, Colorado	Unknown	Eric Leftwich	ncwntug@ataman.com
Connecticut Area NT User Group	None	Farmington, Connecticut	Medium	Art Alexander	Arthur_Alexander@msn.com
Windows NT Group Consults	None	Costa Rica	Unknown	Alejandro Esquivel Rodriguez	aesquiv@irazu.una.ac.cr
Association of Windows NT Systems Professionals (NT*Pro)	http://www.ntpro.org	Washington, DC	Large	Charles Kelly	ckelly@msn.com

Continued on next page

TABLE C.2: Windows NT User Groups Around the World (*continued*)

User Group	Web Page Address	City, State, Country	Group Size	Contact Name	Contact E-Mail Address
S. Florida NT Group	None	Ft. Lauderdale, Florida	Unknown	Gabriel B.H. Polmar	mongo@netrox.net
Jacksonville BackOffice User Group	http://www.jbug.com	Jacksonville, Florida	Unknown	Kevin Haynes	jbug@tech-point.com
Jacksonville BackOffice Users Group	None	Jacksonville, Florida	Small	James Farhat	jbug@tech-point.com
NW Florida NT Users Group	None	Panama City, Florida	Small	Jeff Bankston	jeff@mail.bciassoc..com
Atlanta BackOffice User Group	None	Atlanta, Georgia	Large	Lisa Thomassie	mind_share@msn.com
Looking for One	None	Atlanta, Georgia	Unknown	Donameche Miller	Donameche@Tsi.Tsifax.Com
German NT User Group	None	Germany	Unknown	Paulette Feller	pfeler@skd.de
Manu	None	Essen, Germany	Unknown	Lars Hasshoff	lhasshof@manu.com
NT Guatemala Users Group	None	Guatemala City, Guatemala	Small	Jose A. Chajon	viacomp@guate.net
Big Island NT	http://bintug.org	Kamuela, Hawaii	Small	Matthew Pearce	sysop@bintug.org
infosys nt group	None	Bangalore, India	Unknown	Krishnakumar	krishnakumarc@inf.com
NT Developers Group, INDIA	None	Bangalore, India	Small	Nilendu Pal	nilendu@wipinfo.soft.net
Trigent-systems	None	Bangalore, India	Small	Saravana Bhavan	saravana_bk@trigent.com

Continued on next page

TABLE C.2: WINDOWS NT USER GROUPS AROUND THE WORLD (*continued*)

USER GROUP	WEB PAGE ADDRESS	CITY, STATE, COUNTRY	GROUP SIZE	CONTACT NAME	CONTACT E-MAIL ADDRESS
Migration from Novell Netware to Windows NT	None	Bombay, India	Medium	Manoj Rakheja	manoj.rakheja @owenscorning.com
KPMF NT User Group	None	Chennai, India	Small	Solomon Sagayaraj	solomonj@hotmail.com
NTGROUP	None	Chennai, India	Small	M. Subramonian	MSM24@HOTMAIL.COM
Welcome Group	None	Chennai, India	Unknown	Santhosh	santhosh@pentafour.com
Mavericks	None	Madras, India	Small	Ramesh Venkatraman	tnv1ramesh@hotmail.com
HAWKS	None	New Delhi, India	Small	Himanshu Sharma	himanshu@rsysi .stpn.soft.net
Aroostook NT User Group	http://www.aroostook.org	Huntington, Indiana	Unknown	Jerry Curtis	winnt_users @aroostook.org
gba c-250	None	Bandung, Indonesia	Unknown	Ipoel	ikocel@rocketmail.com
NT Blom Indonesia	None	Kemang Raya 24 Jakarta 12730, Indonesia	Unknown	Muhammad Abduh	ma@blom.co.id
IRELAND	None	Ireland	Unknown	John Doherty	doherty_mj@hotmail.com
Windows NT Italian User Group WNTIUG	None	Potenza, Italy	Medium	Enrico Fasulo	webmaster@powernet.it
WIN NT–BHS Gruppo Italia–Discussione	None	Rome, Italy	Unknown	Davide Rossi	rossi@ancitel.it
ClieNT & Servers	None	Ames, Iowa	Unknown	Rick Gammon	bulldog@netins.net
IOWA Windows NT User Group	None	Iowa City, Iowa	Unknown	Alex Postnikov	apostnik@blue.weeg .uiowa.edu

Continued on next page

TABLE C.2: WINDOWS NT USER GROUPS AROUND THE WORLD *(continued)*

USER GROUP	WEB PAGE ADDRESS	CITY, STATE, COUNTRY	GROUP SIZE	CONTACT NAME	CONTACT E-MAIL ADDRESS
MS Israel	None	Tel Aviv, Israel	Medium	Cohen Gal	root@widecom.sys.co.il
Japan Windows NT Users Group	http://www.jwntug.or.jp/	Tokyo, Japan	Large	Ryoji Kaneko	rkaneko@jwntug.or.jp
Tokyo English NT Users Group	http://www.tentug.org	Tokyo, Japan	Unknown	Administrator	admin@tentug.org
Kansas City Windows NT Users Group	None	Kansas City, Kansas	Unknown	Steve Rodgers	srodgers@kumc.edu
Northeast Kansas Windows NT Users Group	None	Unknown, somewhere in Kansas	Unknown	Lad	lad@tinman.dot.state.ks.us
JPA Communications	None	Elizabethtown, Kentucky	Small	June Mizoguchi	jpa@ekx.infi.net
NT-ISP-Support	None	Lexington, Kentucky	Unknown	Lee Murphy	web@chapel1.com
LitNT	None	Kaunas, Lithuania	Small	Ricardas Baltaduonis	baltad@soften.ktu.lt
Louisiana WinNT Users Group	None	Monroe, Louisiana	Small	Richard Driggers	richard@lawinntug.org
NT User Group	None	Unknown, somewhere in Louisiana	Unknown	Laird Goolsby	laird@addtech.com
PowerNT	None	Kuala Lumpur, Malaysia	Large	Ahmad Ridzuan Mohd Noor	ridzuan.mn@feldaprodata.com.my
New England Computer Society Windows 95/NT User Group	None	Springfield, Massachusetts	Small	Rene M. Laviolette	rene@costimator.com

Continued on next page

TABLE C.2: WINDOWS NT USER GROUPS AROUND THE WORLD *(continued)*

USER GROUP	WEB PAGE ADDRESS	CITY, STATE, COUNTRY	GROUP SIZE	CONTACT NAME	CONTACT E-MAIL ADDRESS
BWUG—Boston Windows User Group	http://www.bwug.org	Waltham, Massachusetts	Medium	Steve Allen	sallen@world.std.com
WinTech Group	http://www.bostonusergroups.com/	Boston/Waltham, Massachusetts	Small	Len Segal	lsegal@fcl.net
GUNT—Grupo de Usuarios de NT	None	Celaya, Mexico	Unknown	German Rodriguez	soporte@mail.mindvox.ciateq.mx
West Michigan NT User Group (WMNTUG)	http://www.wmntug.org	Grand Rapids, Michigan	Medium	Brett R. Mello	bmello@perrigo.com
Michigan Windows NT User Group	None	Southfield, Michigan	Unknown	Donald Barry	dbarry@wisne.com
CSP	None	Kishibeu, Moldova	Small	Timur Fbucashvili	tt97702@usm.md
Windows NT The Netherlands (TADIS)	None	Leusden, Netherlands	Small	A.P. Meeuwsen	tadis@Compuserve.com
NT Support	None	Las Vegas, Nevada	Unknown	Nigel Sampson	Nigel@therio.net
The Mad Scientist Club	None	Warren, New Jersey	Small	Frank A. Del Buono	fdelbuono@hiserv-na.com
New Jersey PC User Group—NT-SIG	http://www.njpcug.org	Wyckoff, New Jersey	Medium	Terry P. Gustafson	terryg@warwick.net
Developer SIG	None	Unknown, somewhere in New Jersey	Unknown	Unknown	djs@cnj.digex.net
Monkeys	None	Albuquerque, New Mexico	Small	Pedro Morales	Pmorales@bernco.gov

Continued on next page

TABLE C.2: WINDOWS NT USER GROUPS AROUND THE WORLD *(continued)*

USER GROUP	WEB PAGE ADDRESS	CITY, STATE, COUNTRY	GROUP SIZE	CONTACT NAME	CONTACT E-MAIL ADDRESS
Capital District NT/ Backoffice Users Group	None	Albany, New York	Small	Cindy Hermann	hermann@taconic.net
Westchester County NT User Group	None	Elmsford, New York	Unknown	Dinesh Ganesh	sherrydin@yahoo.com
New York Windows NT User Group	None	New York, New York	Large	Bill Zack	wzack@compuserve.com
New York City NT Developers SIG	None	New York, New York	Unknown	Unknown	lee_t@access.digex.net
New York City Windows NT Users Group	None	New York, New York	Large	John Rhodes	JRhodes@bbn.com
Rochester/ Monroe County Library User Group	None	Rochester, New York	Small	David Deaugustine	davidd@mcls.rochester.lib.ny.us
SI NT Admin	None	Staten Island, New York	Unknown	Craig Caggiano	crc61@bigfoot.com
Long Island NT Users Group	None	Uniondale, New York	Unknown	Gerald Shamberger	Gerald.Shamberger@uscoopers.com
NZNTUG	None	New Zealand	Unknown	Nathan Mercer	nathan@MCS.co.nz
Taranaki NT Users Group	None	New Plymouth, New Zealand	Unknown	Chris Sharpe	chris.sharpe@computerland.co.nz
NCNT	None	Charlotte, North Carolina	Unknown	Stephen Carabetta	vianet@ix.netcom.com
TNTUG— Triangle NT Users Group	None	Raleigh, North Carolina	Large	John Mcmains	tntug@networks.com

Continued on next page

TABLE C.2: WINDOWS NT USER GROUPS AROUND THE WORLD (*continued*)

USER GROUP	WEB PAGE ADDRESS	CITY, STATE, COUNTRY	GROUP SIZE	CONTACT NAME	CONTACT E-MAIL ADDRESS
Red River Windows NT Users Group	None	Grand Forks, North Dakota	Medium	Roy Beard	rbeard@plains .nodak.edu
MANUS—Microsoft Advanced Network Users Society	None	Norway	Large	Kay Seljeseth	Kay.Seljeseth @Cinet.No
COUNT, Central Ohio Users NT	None	Columbus, Ohio	Medium	Ed Zirkle	Zirkle.5@osu.edu
Dayton NT Users Group (DAYNTUG)	None	Dayton, Ohio	Medium	Chris T Haaker	chris.haaker @stdreg.com
NT in Manufacturing Automation Users	None	Findlay, Ohio	Unknown	Bill Wagner	BillW@FESTech.com
Philadelphia Back-Office Users Group (PBOG)	None	Philadelphia, Pennsylvania	Medium	Bill Wolff, Mike Ward	bill@wolffdata.com, Mike_Ward@on1c.com
Print & Publishing in Poland	http://arra.com.pl	Kalisz, Poland	Medium	Roman Lewicki	Webmaster@arra .com.pl
Media Print & Publishing in Poland—Inwestycje, Marketin, Media	http://www.arra.com.pl	Kalisz, Poland	Small	Roman Lewicki	Webmaster@arra .com.pl
Polish Users of Windows NT 4.0 Server	None	Poznan, Poland	Medium	Tomasz Waslowicz	tomaszwa@free .polbox.pl

Continued on next page

TABLE C.2: WINDOWS NT USER GROUPS AROUND THE WORLD *(continued)*

USER GROUP	WEB PAGE ADDRESS	CITY, STATE, COUNTRY	GROUP SIZE	CONTACT NAME	CONTACT E-MAIL ADDRESS
Windows NT Group, Portugal (WNTGP)	None	Portugal	Unknown	Luis Centeio	luisc@poboxes.com
PRUNT (Puerto Rico NT User Group)	None	Toa Alta, Puerto Rico	Unknown	Richard Arroyo	rarroyo@prtc.net
Rhode Island NT Users Group	None	Coventry, Rhode Island	Unknown	Ernie Quaglieri	celebty@concentric.net
SneNUG Southern New England Network Users Group	None	East Providence, Rhode Island	Large	Bill Dwyer	billd@loa.com
Russian Windows NT User Group	None	Moscow, Russian Federation	Unknown	Konstantin Gusev	gusevk@quarta.com
Cape Microsoft User Group	None	Cape Town, South Africa	Unknown	Gordon Thelander	enigmax@iafrica.com
grupo de ususarios de nt españoles	None	Valencia, Spain	Unknown	Isaac Jaramillo	ijs@mx3.redestb.es
NT Anvndargruppen	None	Stockholm, Sweden	Unknown	Friberg	iir@iir.telegate.se
Swiss NT Users Group	None	Switzerland	Unknown	Deffer@ Eunet.Ch	deffer@eunet.ch
CERN Windows NT Users Group	None	Geneva, Switzerland	Unknown	Alberto AlMAR	alberto.aimar@cern.ch
NT Syria by CompuCrest	None	Damascus, Syria	Small	A. Aziz	maziz@usa.net

Continued on next page

TABLE C.2: WINDOWS NT USER GROUPS AROUND THE WORLD (*continued*)

USER GROUP	WEB PAGE ADDRESS	CITY, STATE, COUNTRY	GROUP SIZE	CONTACT NAME	CONTACT E-MAIL ADDRESS
Chattanooga-River Valley NT Users Group	None	Chattanooga, Tennessee	Unknown	James	james@press.southern.edu
NT4_Users Group	None	Martin, Tennessee	Large	J. Garner	jgarner@utm.edu
Capital Area NT User Group	None	Austin, Texas	Unknown	Perry Stokes	stokes@jump.net
DFW NT Users Group	None	Dallas/ Ft. Worth, Texas	Unknown	Ralph Shumway	rshumway@swbell.net
Dallas BackOffice Users Group (DeBUG)	http://www.debug.org/	Dallas, Texas	Medium	Mark Saum	info@debug.org
North Texas NT Users Group (NTsquared)	None	Dallas, Texas	Large	Charles Reiss	charlier@unicomp.net
The El Paso & Las Cruces Windows NT User Group	None	El Paso, Texas	Medium	Shane A. Weddle	sweddle@worldnet.att.net
Fort Worth NT User Group	None	Fort Worth, Texas	Unknown	Paul Knox	paulk@netaci.com
Houston Area NT Users Group	None	Houston, Texas	Unknown	Arthur Kettelhut	atkette@ix.netcom.com
Houston Microsoft User Group	None	Houston, Texas	Medium	Alisa Wanger	alisaw@infotecweb.com
NT TECH PARTY	None	Houston, Texas	Unknown	Hiphop	hiphopluva@hotmail.com

Continued on next page

TABLE C.2: WINDOWS NT USER GROUPS AROUND THE WORLD *(continued)*

USER GROUP	WEB PAGE ADDRESS	CITY, STATE, COUNTRY	GROUP SIZE	CONTACT NAME	CONTACT E-MAIL ADDRESS
Plano BackOffice User Group (PBUG)	None	Plano, Texas	Medium	Marcia Loughry	`mloughry @cyberramp.net`
Alamo PC Organization Windows NT SIG	None	San Antonio, Texas	Medium	Larry Lentz	`Larry@LentzComputer .com`
Rio Grande Valley Area IT Group	None	Weslaco, Texas	Unknown	Cindy Barber	`cabarber@usa.net`
ThaiNTprimer	None	Bangkok, Thailand	Unknown	Siramet	`siramet@yth.co.th`
TURKEY NT USER GROUP	None	Istanbul, Turkey	Small	Ozan Zkara	`OZAN.OZKARA@USA.NET`
Wyndows NT GRUBU	None	Istanbul, Turkey	Small	Harun Aksoz	`harunaksoz @hotmail.com.tr`
Emirates NT User Group	None	Dubai, United Arab Emirates	Small	Rizwan Ahmed Khan	`rizwan@emirates .net.ae`
Microsoft Windows NT & BackOffice Forum	None	London, United Kingdom	Large	Tony Larks	`tony_larks @researchgroup.co.uk`
The Microsoft Windows (NT) & BackOffice Forum (UK)	`http://www .researchgroup.co.uk`	London, United Kingdom	Large	Simon Moores	`smoores@softech.co.uk`
Vermont NT Users Group (VTNTUG)	None	Burlington, Vermont	Medium	Michael Gambler	`mgambler@sover.net`
Central Virginia NT Users Group	`http://www.harbour.net/ ntgroup/`	Richmond, Virginia	Small	Anthony S. Harbour, Med	`aharbour@harbour.net`

Continued on next page

TABLE C.2: WINDOWS NT USER GROUPS AROUND THE WORLD *(continued)*

USER GROUP	WEB PAGE ADDRESS	CITY, STATE, COUNTRY	GROUP SIZE	CONTACT NAME	CONTACT E-MAIL ADDRESS
BackOffice Professionals Association	None	Seattle, Washington	Large	Marjorie James	backoffice @ariscorp.com
Wisconsin NT Users Group	None	Brookfield, Wisconsin	Medium	Bob Escher	bescher@wintug.org
NT User Group	None	Belgrade, Yugoslavia	Large	Milan Zivkovic	zivkovic @internetplus.ch

Virtual Support Groups: The ExpertZone

There are a number of organizations dedicated to assisting users of Microsoft products. ExpertZone is an important one of these. This group is part of Microsoft's marketing arm and is made up of volunteer, non-Microsoft users who have demonstrated a great deal of skill in their fields.

It is a self-organized group of computer professionals and advanced users from the U.S., Canada, and Europe, who have hundreds of thousands of hours of experience with Microsoft Windows 9*x*, Windows 2000, and Windows XP. The group is made up of hardware, software, applications, networking, and support professionals who have a commitment to providing information and support for others using Windows. ExpertZone has joined forces to cover major online services (such as MSN, CompuServe, America Online, and others) and the World Wide Web. The ExpertZone designation on a Web page, or in a tagline or signature, designates a person who has made a commitment to the organization.

I am a member of ExpertZone. The group is an excellent source of help and information. The ExpertZone web page is located at `http://www.microsoft.com/windowsxp/expertzone/default.asp`.

Training

Several companies offer training on registry-related maintenance. Contact Data-Tech Institute at `http://www.datatech.com` for more information on their courses.

Another source of training is your local college or university. For example, Boston University offers a number of excellent training courses for Windows professionals, mostly in the Boston, Massachusetts area. The college where I teach (Franklin Pierce College) offers both short courses and college credit courses in all aspects of Windows.

Generally, conferences offer some useful training opportunities. Most conferences advertise using direct mail.

Other Internet Information Sources

The Internet offers many areas of support and assistance, including newsgroups and chat (IRC) groups. Both of these resources can be unexpected sources of valuable advice and information.

Newsgroups

One source of information on the Internet is newsgroups. The `msnews.microsoft.com` site has all of the Microsoft-supported newsgroups. There are over 700 different groups on this news server, and between 40 and 50 groups are dedicated to various versions of Windows NT. In addition, there are a number of programming groups oriented toward Windows NT platforms from which valuable information may be gleaned.

If you are unfamiliar with using newsgroups, you need to have a newsgroup reader. There are many free or low-cost newsreaders. For example, Microsoft's Outlook Express has a built-in newsreader. In addition, Forté offers a product called FreeAgent; see their licensing agreement to know if you qualify for a free version. You can find Forté on the Web at `http://www.forteinc.com/agent/`. If you do not have a newsreader, you can use `www.groups.google.com` to search for a specific newsgroup.

There are well-established protocols for posting in a newsgroup. It is generally best if you simply read messages (lurk) for a few days to get the feel of things. *Lurking* is the term for a person who reads, but does not post, in a newsgroup. Then you will have a feel for how to ask questions. Follow these simple guidelines when posting:

♦   Don't post "off topic" messages. If you are in the Windows NT Setup group, don't post a message about Exchange.

♦   Never, ever post a "get rich quick" message.

♦   Make the title of your message or topic informative and catchy. You want the right people to read your question. Don't title your message "Help Me!" Say something like, "System Hangs with BSOD after Installing ASDF App."

♦   Though your message will contain your e-mail address (and you should include your name and e-mail in the message), don't expect anyone to e-mail you a solution. They will post the reply in the newsgroup, so check there. It's bad form to ask for e-mail replies.

♦   To avoid getting spam (unsolicited, mass e-mail marketing messages), it is acceptable to subtly change your e-mail address, both in the program and in the message signature. Many users add something to their e-mail address that somewhat obviously doesn't belong there; for example, newsgroup members would recognize that to send e-mail to me, they'd have to alter `phipson@nospam.acm.org` by deleting the `nospam.` part of the address.

♦   Last, but certainly not least, check the newsgroup's previous messages before posting your problem. It is quite possible that someone else has had the same problem recently and you can benefit from responses to that person. People get tired of answering the same question repeatedly.

Chat

Chat (IRC) is a well-used part of the Internet. Chat sessions can sometimes be useful, especially if you get onto the right chat server.

One interesting thing about chat servers is that if there is not a chat covering the topic you are interested in, you can start your own chat session. Microsoft also offers an ActiveX control to access chat groups. It is available at the Microsoft BackOffice website. The best chat client is Microsoft's Comic Chat. Go to Microsoft's website at `http://support.microsoft.com/default.aspx?scid=kb;en-us;Q166370` and download the latest version of Comic Chat, version 2.

NOTE   *Like those classy Comic Chat characters? If so, you can actually create a personalized character for your identity. Use the Comic Chat character editor, which is available at the same web address as Comic Chat.*

Appendix D

Performance Counters

TABLE D.1 SHOWS THE Performance Monitor counters for a typical Windows XP installation. Each counter is stored in two registry keys—one for the counter name, the other for the help description. Actually, Windows XP (and all versions of Windows NT after 3.51) stores all of the performance counters in two files, and the system accesses these files as if they were part of the registry. These two files are:

perfc009.dat Contains all the counter names. Items in this file display either as counters or as performance objects.

perfh009.dat Contains the corresponding help text (displayed when the user requests help) for each item in the list of counters and performance objects.

Figure D.1 shows the Add Counters dialog box with the System performance object selected and one of its counters highlighted. Help text for the highlighted counter is displayed in the bottom of the dialog box.

FIGURE D.1

The Add Counters dialog box allows the user to specify performance objects and counters.

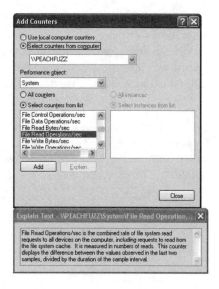

Counter names are stored in the REG_MULTI_SZ data object at `HKEY_LOCAL_MACHINE\`
`Software\Microsoft\Windows NT\CurrentVersion\Perflib\009\Counter`, which through the magic
of the registry is actually stored in the file `perfc009.dat`.

A help description has an index number that is one greater than the number for the counter, or
object, name. For example, for the `% Processor Time` counter (at index 6), the help text is at index 7.
(Even though the two lists are separate, Microsoft uses different numbers for the counter name and
the help text.) The counter descriptions are stored in the REG_MULTI_SZ data object at `HKEY_`
`LOCAL_MACHINE\Software\Microsoft\Windows NT\CurrentVersion\Perflib\009\Help`, which is
actually the file `perfh009.dat`.

NOTE *Why a subkey named* 009*? Why does the Performance Monitor support files (*`perfc009.dat` *and*
`perfh009.dat`*) have* 009 *in them? This is because the performance counters' names and descriptions are language spe-*
cific. If your installation is not U.S. English (language ID 009*), it is likely that your registry will have a different subkey*
containing counters and descriptions in your language.

Table D.1 lists the main performance monitoring objects and the counters that these objects use.
(Notice that though some counters seem to be reused, actually, it's only the descriptive text that is
reused; each actual counter is stored in a unique location.)

NOTE *Counters in Table D.1 are generally limited to those installed with a default (basic) installation of Windows XP.*
Virtually all installations will have more counters than those shown.

In Table D.1, the Object column shows the index number for the performance monitoring object.
For example, the first object, System, is at index 2. In the System object, there are an additional 17
counters, starting with index number 12. It is important to realize that counters are not stored consecutively. The Name column shows the text that the MMC Performance Monitor snap-in uses for
counters and objects.

The first object in the counters list, 1, is the number of the last object that is part of the Windows set of counters. All counters following this value (1847 in Windows XP) are for add-in
components.

Several notes about counters: Some counters (such as the counter that monitors disk performance,
which would have an instance for each drive) have multiple instances, while other counters (such as
Processes) have only a single instance. This table does not differentiate between single and multiple
instance counters. Additionally, some counters are "shared" between different objects, but will only
be listed one time.

NOTE *See Chapter 11 for more on using performance objects and counters, and for information on adding custom*
counters for your applications and systems. All of the object and counter index numbers mean little at this stage. The (hid-
den) registry hive `HKEY_PERFORMANCE_DATA` *contains the necessary information to allow an application to successfully*
interact with and display performance data.

TABLE D.1: PERFORMANCE COUNTERS ON A WINDOWS XP SERVER

OBJECT NUMBER	COUNTER NUMBER	OBJECT NAME	COUNTER*
1		Contains the value 1847 (though this value may vary with different installations and versions). This number is the object number of the last counter or object (numerically) in the Windows installation.	1847
2		**System**	
	4	**Memory**	
	6		% Processor Time
	10		File Read Operations/sec
	12		File Write Operations/sec
	14		File Control Operations/sec
	16		File Read Bytes/sec
	18		File Write Bytes/sec
	20		File Control Bytes/sec
	24		Available Bytes
	26		Committed Bytes
	28		Page Faults/sec
	30		Commit Limit
	32		Write Copies/sec
	34		Transition Faults/sec
	36		Cache Faults/sec
	38		Demand Zero Faults/sec
	40		Pages/sec
	42		Page Reads/sec
	44		Processor Queue Length
	46		Thread State
	48		Pages Output/sec
	50		Page Writes/sec

Continued on next page

TABLE D.1: PERFORMANCE COUNTERS ON A WINDOWS XP SERVER *(continued)*

OBJECT NUMBER	COUNTER NUMBER	OBJECT NAME	COUNTER*
52		Browser	
	54		Announcements Server/sec
	56		Pool Paged Bytes
	58		Pool Nonpaged Bytes
	60		Pool Paged Allocs
	64		Pool Nonpaged Allocs
	66		Pool Paged Resident Bytes
	68		System Code Total Bytes
	70		System Code Resident Bytes
	72		System Driver Total Bytes
	74		System Driver Resident Bytes
	76		System Cache Resident Bytes
	78		Announcements Domain/sec
	80		Election Packets/sec
	82		Mailslot Writes/sec
	84		Server List Requests/sec
86		Cache	
	88		Data Maps/sec
	90		Sync Data Maps/sec
	92		Async Data Maps/sec
	94		Data Map Hits %
	96		Data Map Pins/sec
	98		Pin Reads/sec
	100		Sync Pin Reads/sec
	102		Async Pin Reads/sec
	104		Pin Read Hits %
	106		Copy Reads/sec
	108		Sync Copy Reads/sec

Continued on next page

TABLE D.1: PERFORMANCE COUNTERS ON A WINDOWS XP SERVER *(continued)*

OBJECT NUMBER	COUNTER NUMBER	OBJECT NAME	COUNTER*
	110		Async Copy Reads/sec
	112		Copy Read Hits %
	114		MDL Reads/sec
	116		Sync MDL Reads/sec
	118		Async MDL Reads/sec
	120		MDL Read Hits %
	122		Read Aheads/sec
	124		Fast Reads/sec
	126		Sync Fast Reads/sec
	128		Async Fast Reads/sec
	130		Fast Read Resource Misses/sec
	132		Fast Read Not Possibles/sec
	134		Lazy Write Flushes/sec
	136		Lazy Write Pages/sec
	138		Data Flushes/sec
	140		Data Flush Pages/sec
	142		% User Time
	144		% Privileged Time
	146		Context Switches/sec
	148		Interrupts/sec
	150		System Calls/sec
	152		Level 1 TLB Fills/sec
	154		Level 2 TLB Fills/sec
	156		Enumerations Server/sec
	158		Enumerations Domain/sec
	160		Enumerations Other/sec
	162		Missed Server Announcements
	164		Missed Mailslot Datagrams

Continued on next page

TABLE D.1: PERFORMANCE COUNTERS ON A WINDOWS XP SERVER *(continued)*

OBJECT NUMBER	COUNTER NUMBER	OBJECT NAME	COUNTER*
	166		Missed Server List Requests
	168		Server Announce Allocations Failed/sec
	170		Mailslot Allocations Failed
	172		Virtual Bytes Peak
	174		Virtual Bytes
	178		Working Set Peak
	180		Working Set
	182		Page File Bytes Peak
	184		Page File Bytes
	186		Private Bytes
	188		Announcements Total/sec
	190		Enumerations Total/sec
	198		Current Disk Queue Length
	200		% Disk Time
	202		% Disk Read Time
	204		% Disk Write Time
	206		Avg. Disk sec/Transfer
	208		Avg. Disk sec/Read
	210		Avg. Disk sec/Write
	212		Disk Transfers/sec
	214		Disk Reads/sec
	216		Disk Writes/sec
	218		Disk Bytes/sec
	220		Disk Read Bytes/sec
	222		Disk Write Bytes/sec
	224		Avg. Disk Bytes/Transfer
	226		Avg. Disk Bytes/Read
	228		Avg. Disk Bytes/Write

Continued on next page

TABLE D.1: PERFORMANCE COUNTERS ON A WINDOWS XP SERVER *(continued)*

OBJECT NUMBER	COUNTER NUMBER	OBJECT NAME	COUNTER*
230		**Process**	
232		**Thread**	
234		**PhysicalDisk**	
236		**LogicalDisk**	
238		**Processor**	
	240		% Total Processor Time
	242		% Total User Time
	244		% Total Privileged Time
	246		Total Interrupts/sec
	248		Processes
	250		Threads
	252		Events
	254		Semaphores
	256		Mutexes
	258		Sections
260		**Objects**	
262		**Redirector**	
	264		Bytes Received/sec
	266		Packets Received/sec
	268		Read Bytes Paging/sec
	270		Read Bytes Nonpaging/sec
	272		Read Bytes Cache/sec
	274		Read Bytes Network/sec
	276		Bytes Transmitted/sec
	278		Packets Transmitted/sec
	280		Write Bytes Paging/sec
	282		Write Bytes Nonpaging/sec
	284		Write Bytes Cache/sec

Continued on next page

TABLE D.1: PERFORMANCE COUNTERS ON A WINDOWS XP SERVER *(continued)*

OBJECT NUMBER	COUNTER NUMBER	OBJECT NAME	COUNTER*
	286		Write Bytes Network/sec
	288		Read Operations/sec
	290		Read Operations Random/sec
	292		Read Packets/sec
	294		Reads Large/sec
	296		Read Packets Small/sec
	298		Write Operations/sec
	300		Write Operations Random/sec
	302		Write Packets/sec
	304		Writes Large/sec
	306		Write Packets Small/sec
	308		Reads Denied/sec
	310		Writes Denied/sec
	312		Network Errors/sec
	314		Server Sessions
	316		Server Reconnects
	318		Connects Core
	320		Connects Lan Manager 2.0
	322		Connects Lan Manager 2.1
	324		Connects Windows NT
	326		Server Disconnects
	328		Server Sessions Hung
330		**Server**	
	336		Thread Wait Reason
	340		Sessions Timed Out
	342		Sessions Errored Out
	344		Sessions Logged Off
	346		Sessions Forced Off

Continued on next page

TABLE D.1: PERFORMANCE COUNTERS ON A WINDOWS XP SERVER *(continued)*

OBJECT NUMBER	COUNTER NUMBER	OBJECT NAME	COUNTER*
	348		Errors Logon
	350		Errors Access Permissions
	352		Errors Granted Access
	354		Errors System
	356		Blocking Requests Rejected
	358		Work Item Shortages
	360		Files Opened Total
	362		Files Open
	366		File Directory Searches
	370		Pool Nonpaged Failures
	372		Pool Nonpaged Peak
	376		Pool Paged Failures
	378		Pool Paged Peak
	388		Bytes Total/sec
	392		Current Commands
	398		NWLink NetBIOS
	400		Packets/sec
	404		Context Blocks Queued/sec
	406		File Data Operations/sec
	408		% Free Space
	410		Free Megabytes
	412		Connections Open
	414		Connections No Retries
	416		Connections with Retries
	418		Disconnects Local
	420		Disconnects Remote
	422		Failures Link
	424		Failures Adapter

Continued on next page

TABLE D.1: PERFORMANCE COUNTERS ON A WINDOWS XP SERVER *(continued)*

OBJECT NUMBER	COUNTER NUMBER	OBJECT NAME	COUNTER*
	426		Connection Session Timeouts
	428		Connections Canceled
	430		Failures Resource Remote
	432		Failures Resource Local
	434		Failures Not Found
	436		Failures No Listen
	438		Datagrams/sec
	440		Datagram Bytes/sec
	442		Datagrams Sent/sec
	444		Datagram Bytes Sent/sec
	446		Datagrams Received/sec
	448		Datagram Bytes Received/sec
	452		Packets Sent/sec
	456		Frames/sec
	458		Frame Bytes/sec
	460		Frames Sent/sec
	462		Frame Bytes Sent/sec
	464		Frames Received/sec
	466		Frame Bytes Received/sec
	468		Frames Re-Sent/sec
	470		Frame Bytes Re-Sent/sec
	472		Frames Rejected/sec
	474		Frame Bytes Rejected/sec
	476		Expirations Response
	478		Expirations Ack
	480		Window Send Maximum
	482		Window Send Average
	484		Piggyback Ack Queued/sec

Continued on next page

TABLE D.1: PERFORMANCE COUNTERS ON A WINDOWS XP SERVER *(continued)*

OBJECT NUMBER	COUNTER NUMBER	OBJECT NAME	COUNTER*
	486		Piggyback Ack Timeouts
	488		NWLink IPX
	490		NWLink SPX
	492		NetBEUI
	494		NetBEUI Resource
	496		Used Maximum
	498		Used Average
	500		Times Exhausted
502		**NBT Connection**	
	506		Bytes Sent/sec
	508		Total Bytes/sec
510		**Network Interface**	
	512		Bytes/sec
	520		Current Bandwidth
	524		Packets Received Unicast/sec
	526		Packets Received Non-Unicast/sec
	528		Packets Received Discarded
	530		Packets Received Errors
	532		Packets Received Unknown
	536		Packets Sent Unicast/sec
	538		Packets Sent Non-Unicast/sec
	540		Packets Outbound Discarded
	542		Packets Outbound Errors
	544		Output Queue Length
546		**IP**	
	552		Datagrams Received Header Errors
	554		Datagrams Received Address Errors

Continued on next page

TABLE D.1: PERFORMANCE COUNTERS ON A WINDOWS XP SERVER *(continued)*

OBJECT NUMBER	COUNTER NUMBER	OBJECT NAME	COUNTER*
	556		Datagrams Forwarded/sec
	558		Datagrams Received Unknown Protocol
	560		Datagrams Received Discarded
	562		Datagrams Received Delivered/sec
	566		Datagrams Outbound Discarded
	568		Datagrams Outbound No Route
	570		Fragments Received/sec
	572		Fragments Re-assembled/sec
	574		Fragment Re-assembly Failures
	576		Fragmented Datagrams/sec
	578		Fragmentation Failures
	580		Fragments Created/sec
582		ICMP	
	584		Messages/sec
	586		Messages Received/sec
	588		Messages Received Errors
	590		Received Dest. Unreachable
	592		Received Time Exceeded
	594		Received Parameter Problem
	596		Received Source Quench
	598		Received Redirect/sec
	600		Received Echo/sec
	602		Received Echo Reply/sec
	604		Received Timestamp/sec
	606		Received Timestamp Reply/sec
	608		Received Address Mask

Continued on next page

TABLE D.1: PERFORMANCE COUNTERS ON A WINDOWS XP SERVER *(continued)*

OBJECT NUMBER	COUNTER NUMBER	OBJECT NAME	COUNTER*
	610		Received Address Mask Reply
	612		Messages Sent/sec
	614		Messages Outbound Errors
	616		Sent Destination Unreachable
	618		Sent Time Exceeded
	620		Sent Parameter Problem
	622		Sent Source Quench
	624		Sent Redirect/sec
	626		Sent Echo/sec
	628		Sent Echo Reply/sec
	630		Sent Timestamp/sec
	632		Sent Timestamp Reply/sec
	634		Sent Address Mask
	636		Sent Address Mask Reply
638		TCP	
	640		Segments/sec
	642		Connections Established
	644		Connections Active
	646		Connections Passive
	648		Connection Failures
	650		Connections Reset
	652		Segments Received/sec
	654		Segments Sent/sec
	656		Segments Retransmitted/sec
658		UDP	
	660		% Total DPC Time
	662		% Total Interrupt Time
	664		Datagrams No Port/sec

Continued on next page

TABLE D.1: PERFORMANCE COUNTERS ON A WINDOWS XP SERVER *(continued)*

OBJECT NUMBER	COUNTER NUMBER	OBJECT NAME	COUNTER*
	666		Datagrams Received Errors
	670		Disk Storage Unit
	672		Allocation Failures
	674		System Up Time
	676		System Handle Count
	678		Free System Page Table Entries
	680		Thread Count
	682		Priority Base
	684		Elapsed Time
	686		Alignment Fixups/sec
	688		Exception Dispatches/sec
	690		Floating Emulations/sec
	692		Logon/sec
	694		Priority Current
	696		% DPC Time
	698		% Interrupt Time
700		**Paging File**	
	702		% Usage
	704		% Usage Peak
	706		Start Address
	708		User PC
	710		Mapped Space No Access
	712		Mapped Space Read Only
	714		Mapped Space Read/Write
	716		Mapped Space Write Copy
	718		Mapped Space Executable
	720		Mapped Space Exec Read Only
	722		Mapped Space Exec Read/Write

Continued on next page

TABLE D.1: PERFORMANCE COUNTERS ON A WINDOWS XP SERVER *(continued)*

OBJECT NUMBER	COUNTER NUMBER	OBJECT NAME	COUNTER*
	724		Mapped Space Exec Write Copy
	726		Reserved Space No Access
	728		Reserved Space Read Only
	730		Reserved Space Read/Write
	732		Reserved Space Write Copy
	734		Reserved Space Executable
	736		Reserved Space Exec Read Only
	738		Reserved Space Exec Read/Write
	740		Image
	742		Reserved Space Exec Write Copy
	744		Unassigned Space No Access
	746		Unassigned Space Read Only
	748		Unassigned Space Read/Write
	750		Unassigned Space Write Copy
	752		Unassigned Space Executable
	754		Unassigned Space Exec Read Only
	756		Unassigned Space Exec Read/Write
	758		Unassigned Space Exec Write Copy
	760		Image Space No Access
	762		Image Space Read Only
	764		Image Space Read/Write
	766		Image Space Write Copy
	768		Image Space Executable
	770		Image Space Exec Read Only
	772		Image Space Exec Read/Write
	774		Image Space Exec Write Copy

Continued on next page

TABLE D.1: PERFORMANCE COUNTERS ON A WINDOWS XP SERVER *(continued)*

OBJECT NUMBER	COUNTER NUMBER	OBJECT NAME	COUNTER*
	776		Bytes Image Reserved
	778		Bytes Image Free
	780		Bytes Reserved
	782		Bytes Free
	784		ID Process
	786		Process Address Space
	788		No Access
	790		Read Only
	792		Read/Write
	794		Write Copy
	796		Executable
	798		Exec Read Only
	800		Exec Read/Write
	802		Exec Write Copy
	804		ID Thread
	806		Mailslot Receives Failed
	808		Mailslot Writes Failed
	810		Mailslot Opens Failed/sec
	812		Duplicate Master Announcements
	814		Illegal Datagrams/sec
	816		Thread Details
	818		Cache Bytes
	820		Cache Bytes Peak
	822		Pages Input/sec
	870		RAS Port
	872		Bytes Transmitted
	874		Bytes Received
	876		Frames Transmitted

Continued on next page

TABLE D.1: PERFORMANCE COUNTERS ON A WINDOWS XP SERVER *(continued)*

OBJECT NUMBER	COUNTER NUMBER	OBJECT NAME	COUNTER*
	878		Frames Received
	880		Percent Compression Out
	882		Percent Compression In
	884		CRC Errors
	886		Timeout Errors
	888		Serial Overrun Errors
	890		Alignment Errors
	892		Buffer Overrun Errors
	894		Total Errors
	896		Bytes Transmitted/sec
	898		Bytes Received/sec
	900		Frames Transmitted/sec
	902		Frames Received/sec
	904		Total Errors/sec
	906		RAS Total
	908		Total Connections
	920		WINS Server
	922		Unique Registrations/sec
	924		Group Registrations/sec
	926		Total Number of Registrations/sec
	928		Unique Renewals/sec
	930		Group Renewals/sec
	932		Total Number of Renewals/sec
	934		Releases/sec
	936		Queries/sec
	938		Unique Conflicts/sec
	940		Group Conflicts/sec
	942		Total Number of Conflicts/sec

Continued on next page

TABLE D.1: PERFORMANCE COUNTERS ON A WINDOWS XP SERVER *(continued)*

OBJECT NUMBER	COUNTER NUMBER	OBJECT NAME	COUNTER*
	944		Successful Releases/sec
	946		Failed Releases/sec
	948		Successful Queries/sec
	950		Failed Queries/sec
	952		Handle Count
	1000		MacFile Server
	1002		Max Paged Memory
	1004		Current Paged Memory
	1006		Max Nonpaged Memory
	1008		Current Nonpaged memory
	1010		Current Sessions
	1012		Maximum Sessions
	1014		Current Files Open
	1016		Maximum Files Open
	1018		Failed Logons
	1020		Data Read/sec
	1022		Data Written/sec
	1024		Data Received/sec
	1026		Data Transmitted/sec
	1028		Current Queue Length
	1030		Maximum Queue Length
	1032		Current Threads
	1034		Maximum Threads
	1050		AppleTalk
	1052		Packets In/sec
	1054		Packets Out/sec
	1056		Bytes In/sec
	1058		Bytes Out/sec

Continued on next page

TABLE D.1: PERFORMANCE COUNTERS ON A WINDOWS XP SERVER *(continued)*

OBJECT NUMBER	COUNTER NUMBER	OBJECT NAME	COUNTER*
	1060		Average Time/DDP Packet
	1062		DDP Packets/sec
	1064		Average Time/AARP Packet
	1066		AARP Packets/sec
	1068		Average Time/ATP Packet
	1070		ATP Packets/sec
	1072		Average Time/NBP Packet
	1074		NBP Packets/sec
	1076		Average Time/ZIP Packet
	1078		ZIP Packets/sec
	1080		Average Time/RTMP Packet
	1082		RTMP Packets/sec
	1084		ATP Retries Local
	1086		ATP Response Timeouts
	1088		ATP XO Response/sec
	1090		ATP ALO Response/sec
	1092		ATP Recvd Release/sec
	1094		Current Nonpaged Pool
	1096		Packets Routed In/sec
	1098		Packets Dropped
	1100		ATP Retries Remote
	1102		Packets Routed Out/sec
	1110		Network Segment
	1112		Total Frames Received/second
	1114		Total Bytes Received/second
	1116		Broadcast Frames Received/second
	1118		Multicast Frames Received/second

Continued on next page

TABLE D.1: PERFORMANCE COUNTERS ON A WINDOWS XP SERVER *(continued)*

OBJECT NUMBER	COUNTER NUMBER	OBJECT NAME	COUNTER*
	1120		% Network Utilization
	1124		% Broadcast Frames
	1126		% Multicast Frames
1150		**Telephony**	
	1152		Lines
	1154		Telephone Devices
	1156		Active Lines
	1158		Active Telephones
	1160		Outgoing Calls/sec
	1162		Incoming Calls/sec
	1164		Client Apps
	1166		Current Outgoing Calls
	1168		Current Incoming Calls
	1228		Gateway Service For NetWare
	1230		Client Service For NetWare
	1232		Packet Burst Read NCP Count/sec
	1234		Packet Burst Read Timeouts/sec
	1236		Packet Burst Write NCP Count/sec
	1238		Packet Burst Write Timeouts/sec
	1240		Packet Burst IO/sec
	1242		Connect NetWare 2.x
	1244		Connect NetWare 3.x
	1246		Connect NetWare 4.x
	1260		Logon Total
1300		**Server Work Queues**	
	1302		Queue Length

Continued on next page

TABLE D.1: PERFORMANCE COUNTERS ON A WINDOWS XP SERVER *(continued)*

OBJECT NUMBER	COUNTER NUMBER	OBJECT NAME	COUNTER*
	1304		Active Threads
	1306		Available Threads
	1308		Available Work Items
	1310		Borrowed Work Items
	1312		Work Item Shortages
	1314		Current Clients
	1320		Bytes Transferred/sec
	1324		Read Bytes/sec
	1328		Write Bytes/sec
	1332		Total Operations/sec
	1334		DPCs Queued/sec
	1336		DPC Rate
	1342		Total DPCs Queued/sec
	1344		Total DPC Rate
	1350		% Registry Quota in Use
	1360		VL Memory
	1362		VLM % Virtual Size in Use
	1364		VLM Virtual Size
	1366		VLM Virtual Size Peak
	1368		VLM Virtual Size Available
	1370		VLM Commit Charge
	1372		VLM Commit Charge Peak
	1374		System VLM Commit Charge
	1376		System VLM Commit Charge Peak
	1378		System VLM Shared Commit Charge
	1380		Available KBytes
	1382		Available MBytes

Continued on next page

Table D.1: Performance Counters on a Windows XP Server *(continued)*

Object Number	Counter Number	Object Name	Counter*
	1400		Avg. Disk Queue Length
	1402		Avg. Disk Read Queue Length
	1404		Avg. Disk Write Queue Length
	1406		% Committed Bytes in Use
	1408		Full Image
	1410		Creating Process ID
	1412		IO Read Operations/sec
	1414		IO Write Operations/sec
	1416		IO Data Operations/sec
	1418		IO Other Operations/sec
	1420		IO Read Bytes/sec
	1422		IO Write Bytes/sec
	1424		IO Data Bytes/sec
	1426		IO Other Bytes/sec
1450		**Print Queue**	
	1452		Total Jobs Printed
	1454		Bytes Printed/sec
	1456		Total Pages Printed
	1458		Jobs
	1460		References
	1462		Max References
	1464		Jobs Spooling
	1466		Max Jobs Spooling
	1468		Out of Paper Errors
	1470		Not Ready Errors
	1472		Job Errors
	1474		Enumerate Network Printer Calls
	1476		Add Network Printer Calls

Continued on next page

TABLE D.1: PERFORMANCE COUNTERS ON A WINDOWS XP SERVER *(continued)*

OBJECT NUMBER	COUNTER NUMBER	OBJECT NAME	COUNTER*
	1478		Working Set - Private
	1480		Working Set - Shared
	1482		% Idle Time
	1484		Split IO/sec
1500		**Job Object**	
	1502		Current % Processor Time
	1504		Current % User Mode Time
	1506		Current % Kernel Mode Time
	1508		This Period mSec - Processor
	1510		This Period mSec - User Mode
	1512		This Period mSec - Kernel Mode
	1514		Pages/sec
	1516		Process Count - Total
	1518		Process Count - Active
	1520		Process Count - Terminated
	1522		Total mSec - Processor
	1524		Total mSec - User Mode
	1526		Total mSec - Kernel Mode
1548		**Job Object Details**	
	1746		% Idle Time
	1748		% C1 Time
	1750		% C2 Time
	1752		% C3 Time
	1754		C1 Transitions/sec
	1756		C2 Transitions/sec
	1758		C3 Transitions/sec
	1760		Heap
	1762		Committed Bytes

Continued on next page

TABLE D.1: PERFORMANCE COUNTERS ON A WINDOWS XP SERVER *(continued)*

OBJECT NUMBER	COUNTER NUMBER	OBJECT NAME	COUNTER*
	1764		Reserved Bytes
	1766		Virtual Bytes
	1768		Free Bytes
	1770		Free List Length
	1772		Avg. Alloc Rate
	1774		Avg. Free Rate
	1776		Uncommitted Ranges Length
	1778		Allocs - Frees
	1780		Cached Allocs/sec
	1782		Cached Frees/sec
	1784		Allocs <1K/sec
	1786		Frees <1K/sec
	1788		Allocs 1-8K/sec
	1790		Frees 1-8K/sec
	1792		Allocs over 8K/sec
	1794		Frees over 8K/sec
	1796		Total Allocs/sec
	1798		Total Frees/sec
	1800		Blocks in Heap Cache
	1802		Largest Cache Depth
	1804		% Fragmentation
	1806		% VAFragmentation
	1808		Heap Lock contention
	1846		End Marker
1848		**RSVP Service**	
	1850		Network Interfaces
	1852		Network sockets
	1854		Timers

Continued on next page

TABLE D.1: PERFORMANCE COUNTERS ON A WINDOWS XP SERVER *(continued)*

OBJECT NUMBER	COUNTER NUMBER	OBJECT NAME	COUNTER*
	1856		RSVP Sessions
	1858		QoS Clients
	1860		QoS-Enabled Senders
	1862		QoS-Enabled Receivers
	1864		Failed QoS Requests
	1866		Failed QoS Sends
	1868		QoS Notifications
	1870		Bytes in QoS Notifications
1872		**RSVP Interfaces**	
	1874		Signaling Bytes Received
	1876		Signaling Bytes Sent
	1878		PATH Messages Received
	1880		RESV Messages Received
	1882		PATH ERR Messages Received
	1884		RESV ERR Messages Received
	1886		PATH TEAR Messages Received
	1888		RESV TEAR Messages Received
	1890		RESV CONFIRM Messages Received
	1892		PATH Messages Sent
	1894		RESV Messages Sent
	1896		PATH ERR Messages Sent
	1898		RESV ERR Messages Sent
	1900		PATH TEAR Messages Sent
	1902		RESV TEAR Messages Sent
	1904		RESV CONFIRM Messages Sent
	1906		Resource Control Failures
	1908		Policy Control Failures
	1910		General Failures

Continued on next page

TABLE D.1: PERFORMANCE COUNTERS ON A WINDOWS XP SERVER *(continued)*

OBJECT NUMBER	COUNTER NUMBER	OBJECT NAME	COUNTER*
	1912		Blocked RESVs
	1914		RESV State Block Timeouts
	1916		PATH State Block Timeouts
	1918		Send Messages Errors - Big Messages
	1920		Receive Messages Errors - Big Messages
	1922		Send Messages Errors - No Memory
	1924		Receive Messages Errors - No Memory
	1926		Number of Incoming Messages Dropped
	1928		Number of Outgoing Messages Dropped
	1930		Number of Active Flows
	1932		Reserved Bandwidth
	1934		Maximum Admitted Bandwidth
	1936		RAS Port
	1938		Bytes Transmitted
	1940		Bytes Received
	1942		Frames Transmitted
	1944		Frames Received
	1946		Percent Compression Out
	1948		Percent Compression In
	1950		CRC Errors
	1952		Timeout Errors
	1954		Serial Overrun Errors
	1956		Alignment Errors
	1958		Buffer Overrun Errors

Continued on next page

TABLE D.1: PERFORMANCE COUNTERS ON A WINDOWS XP SERVER *(continued)*

OBJECT NUMBER	COUNTER NUMBER	OBJECT NAME	COUNTER*
	1960		Total Errors
	1962		Bytes Transmitted/sec
	1964		Bytes Received/sec
	1966		Frames Transmitted/sec
	1968		Frames Received/sec
	1970		Total Errors/sec
	1972		RAS Total
	1974		Total Connections
	1976		Terminal Services Session
	1978		Input WdBytes
	1980		Input WdFrames
	1982		Input WaitForOutBuf
	1984		Input Frames
	1986		Input Bytes
	1988		Input Compressed Bytes
	1990		Input Compress Flushes
	1992		Input Errors
	1994		Input Timeouts
	1996		Input Async Frame Error
	1998		Input Async Overrun
	2000		Input Async Overflow
	2002		Input Async Parity Error
	2004		Input Transport Errors
	2006		Output WdBytes
	2008		Output WdFrames
	2010		Output WaitForOutBuf
	2012		Output Frames
	2014		Output Bytes

Continued on next page

TABLE D.1: PERFORMANCE COUNTERS ON A WINDOWS XP SERVER *(continued)*

OBJECT NUMBER	COUNTER NUMBER	OBJECT NAME	COUNTER*
	2016		Output Compressed Bytes
	2018		Output Compress Flushes
	2020		Output Errors
	2022		Output Timeouts
	2024		Output Async Frame Error
	2026		Output Async Overrun
	2028		Output Async Overflow
	2030		Output Async Parity Error
	2032		Output Transport Errors
	2034		Total WdBytes
	2036		Total WdFrames
	2038		Total WaitForOutBuf
	2040		Total Frames
	2042		Total Bytes
	2044		Total Compressed Bytes
	2046		Total Compress Flushes
	2048		Total Errors
	2050		Total Timeouts
	2052		Total Async Frame Error
	2054		Total Async Overrun
	2056		Total Async Overflow
	2058		Total Async Parity Error
	2060		Total Transport Errors
	2062		Total Protocol Cache Reads
	2064		Total Protocol Cache Hits
	2066		Total Protocol Cache Hit Ratio
	2068		Protocol Bitmap Cache Reads
	2070		Protocol Bitmap Cache Hits

Continued on next page

TABLE D.1: PERFORMANCE COUNTERS ON A WINDOWS XP SERVER *(continued)*

OBJECT NUMBER	COUNTER NUMBER	OBJECT NAME	COUNTER*
	2072		Protocol Bitmap Cache Hit Ratio
	2074		Protocol Glyph Cache Reads
	2076		Protocol Glyph Cache Hits
	2078		Protocol Glyph Cache Hit Ratio
	2080		Protocol Brush Cache Reads
	2082		Protocol Brush Cache Hits
	2084		Protocol Brush Cache Hit Ratio
	2086		Protocol Save Screen Bitmap Cache Reads
	2088		Protocol Save Screen Bitmap Cache Hits
	2090		Protocol Save Screen Bitmap Cache Hit Ratio
	2092		Input Compression Ratio
	2094		Output Compression Ratio
	2096		Total Compression Ratio
2098		**Terminal Services**	
	2100		Total Sessions
	2102		Active Sessions
	2104		Inactive Sessions
2112		**Internet Information Services Global**	
	2114		Total Allowed Async I/O Requests
	2116		Total Blocked Async I/O Requests
	2118		Total Rejected Async I/O Requests
	2120		Current Blocked Async I/O Requests

Continued on next page

TABLE D.1: PERFORMANCE COUNTERS ON A WINDOWS XP SERVER *(continued)*

OBJECT NUMBER	COUNTER NUMBER	OBJECT NAME	COUNTER*
	2122		Measured Async I/O Bandwidth Usage
	2124		Current Files Cached
	2126		Total Files Cached
	2128		File Cache Hits
	2130		File Cache Misses
	2132		File Cache Hits %
	2136		File Cache Flushes
	2138		Current File Cache Memory Usage
	2140		Maximum File Cache Memory Usage
	2142		Active Flushed Entries
	2144		Total Flushed Files
	2146		Current URIs Cached
	2148		Total URIs Cached
	2150		URI Cache Hits
	2152		URI Cache Misses
	2154		URI Cache Hits %
	2158		URI Cache Flushes
	2160		Total Flushed URIs
	2162		Current BLOBs Cached
	2164		Total BLOBs Cached
	2166		BLOB Cache Hits
	2168		BLOB Cache Misses
	2170		BLOB Cache Hits %
	2174		BLOB Cache Flushes
	2176		Total Flushed BLOBs
2178		**Distributed Transaction Coordinator**	

Continued on next page

TABLE D.1: PERFORMANCE COUNTERS ON A WINDOWS XP SERVER *(continued)*

OBJECT NUMBER	COUNTER NUMBER	OBJECT NAME	COUNTER*
	2180		Active Transactions
	2182		Committed Transactions
	2184		Aborted Transactions
	2186		In Doubt Transactions
	2188		Active Transactions Maximum
	2190		Force Committed Transactions
	2192		Force Aborted Transactions
	2194		Response Time — Minimum
	2196		Response Time — Average
	2198		Response Time — Maximum
	2200		Transactions/sec
	2202		Committed Transactions/sec
	2204		Aborted Transactions/sec
2206		**Web Service**	
	2208		Total Bytes Sent
	2210		Bytes Sent/sec
	2212		Total Bytes Received
	2214		Bytes Received/sec
	2216		Total Bytes Transferred
	2218		Bytes Total/sec
	2220		Total Files Sent
	2222		Files Sent/sec
	2224		Total Files Received
	2226		Files Received/sec
	2228		Total Files Transferred
	2230		Files/sec
	2232		Current Anonymous Users
	2234		Current Nonanonymous Users

Continued on next page

TABLE D.1: PERFORMANCE COUNTERS ON A WINDOWS XP SERVER *(continued)*

OBJECT NUMBER	COUNTER NUMBER	OBJECT NAME	COUNTER*
	2236		Total Anonymous Users
	2238		Anonymous Users/sec
	2240		Total Nonanonymous Users
	2242		Nonanonymous Users/sec
	2244		Maximum Anonymous Users
	2246		Maximum Nonanonymous Users
	2248		Current Connections
	2250		Maximum Connections
	2252		Total Connection Attempts (all instances)
	2254		Connection Attempts/sec
	2256		Total Logon Attempts
	2258		Logon Attempts/sec
	2260		Total Options Requests
	2262		Options Requests/sec
	2264		Total Get Requests
	2266		Get Requests/sec
	2268		Total Post Requests
	2270		Post Requests/sec
	2272		Total Head Requests
	2274		Head Requests/sec
	2276		Total Put Requests
	2278		Put Requests/sec
	2280		Total Delete Requests
	2282		Delete Requests/sec
	2284		Total Trace Requests
	2286		Trace Requests/sec
	2288		Total Move Requests
	2290		Move Requests/sec

Continued on next page

TABLE D.1: PERFORMANCE COUNTERS ON A WINDOWS XP SERVER *(continued)*

OBJECT NUMBER	COUNTER NUMBER	OBJECT NAME	COUNTER*
	2292		Total Copy Requests
	2294		Copy Requests/sec
	2296		Total Mkcol Requests
	2298		Mkcol Requests/sec
	2300		Total Propfind Requests
	2302		Propfind Requests/sec
	2304		Total Proppatch Requests
	2306		Proppatch Requests/sec
	2308		Total Search Requests
	2310		Search Requests/sec
	2312		Total Lock Requests
	2314		Lock Requests/sec
	2316		Total Unlock Requests
	2318		Unlock Requests/sec
	2320		Total Other Request Methods
	2322		Other Request Methods/sec
	2324		Total Method Requests
	2326		Total Method Requests/sec
	2328		Total CGI Requests
	2330		CGI Requests/sec
	2332		Total ISAPI Extension Requests
	2334		ISAPI Extension Requests/sec
	2336		Total Not Found Errors
	2338		Not Found Errors/sec
	2340		Total Locked Errors
	2342		Locked Errors/sec
	2344		Current CGI Requests
	2346		Current ISAPI Extension Requests

Continued on next page

TABLE D.1: PERFORMANCE COUNTERS ON A WINDOWS XP SERVER *(continued)*

OBJECT NUMBER	COUNTER NUMBER	OBJECT NAME	COUNTER*
	2348		Maximum CGI Requests
	2350		Maximum ISAPI Extension Requests
	2352		Current CAL Count for Authenticated Users
	2354		Maximum CAL Count for Authenticated Users
	2356		Total Count of Failed CAL Requests for Authenticated Users
	2358		Current CAL Count for SSL Connections
	2360		Maximum CAL Count for SSL Connections
	2362		Total Blocked Async I/O Requests
	2364		Total Allowed Async I/O Requests
	2366		Total Rejected Async I/O Requests
	2368		Current Blocked Async I/O Requests
	2370		Total Count of Failed CAL Requests for SSL Connections
	2372		Measured Async I/O Bandwidth Usage
	2374		Total Blocked Bandwidth Bytes
	2376		Current Blocked Bandwidth Bytes
	2378		Service Uptime
2380		**Web Service Cache**	
	2382		Current Files Cached
	2384		Total Files Cached
	2386		File Cache Hits

Continued on next page

TABLE D.1: PERFORMANCE COUNTERS ON A WINDOWS XP SERVER *(continued)*

OBJECT NUMBER	COUNTER NUMBER	OBJECT NAME	COUNTER*
	2388		File Cache Misses
	2390		File Cache Hits %
	2394		File Cache Flushes
	2396		Current File Cache Memory Usage
	2398		Maximum File Cache Memory Usage
	2400		Active Flushed Entries
	2402		Total Flushed Files
	2404		Current URIs Cached
	2406		Total URIs Cached
	2408		URI Cache Hits
	2410		URI Cache Misses
	2412		URI Cache Hits %
	2416		URI Cache Flushes
	2418		Total Flushed URIs
	2420		Current Metadata Cached
	2422		Total Metadata Cached
	2424		Metadata Cache Hits
	2426		Metadata Cache Misses
	2428		Metadata Cache Hits %
	2432		Metadata Cache Flushes
	2434		Total Flushed Metadata
	2436		Kernel: Current URIs Cached
	2438		Kernel: Total URIs Cached
	2440		Kernel: URI Cache Hits
	2442		Kernel: URI Cache Hits/sec
	2444		Kernel: URI Cache Misses
	2446		Kernel: URI Cache Hits %

Continued on next page

TABLE D.1: PERFORMANCE COUNTERS ON A WINDOWS XP SERVER *(continued)*

OBJECT NUMBER	COUNTER NUMBER	OBJECT NAME	COUNTER*
	2450		Kernel: URI Cache Flushes
	2452		Kernel: Total Flushed URIs
2454		**Active Server Pages**	
	2456		Debugging Requests
	2458		Errors during Script Runtime
	2460		Errors from ASP Preprocessor
	2462		Errors from Script Compilers
	2464		Errors/Sec
	2466		Request Bytes in Total
	2468		Request Bytes Out Total
	2470		Request Execution Time
	2472		Request Wait Time
	2474		Requests Disconnected
	2476		Requests Executing
	2478		Requests Failed Total
	2480		Requests Not Authorized
	2482		Requests Not Found
	2484		Requests Queued
	2486		Requests Rejected
	2488		Requests Succeeded
	2490		Requests Timed Out
	2492		Requests Total
	2494		Requests/sec
	2496		Script Engines Cached
	2498		Session Duration
	2500		Sessions Current
	2502		Sessions Timed Out
	2504		Sessions Total

Continued on next page

TABLE D.1: PERFORMANCE COUNTERS ON A WINDOWS XP SERVER *(continued)*

OBJECT NUMBER	COUNTER NUMBER	OBJECT NAME	COUNTER*
	2506		Templates Cached
	2508		Template Cache Hit Rate
	2512		Template Notifications
	2514		Transactions Aborted
	2516		Transactions Committed
	2518		Transactions Pending
	2520		Transactions Total
	2522		Transactions/sec
	2524		In Memory Templates Cached
	2526		In Memory Template Cache Hit Rate
2528		**SMTP Server**	
	2530		Bytes Sent Total
	2532		Bytes Sent/sec
	2534		Bytes Received Total
	2536		Bytes Received/sec
	2538		Bytes Total
	2540		Bytes Total/sec
	2542		Message Bytes Sent Total
	2544		Message Bytes Sent/sec
	2546		Message Bytes Received Total
	2548		Message Bytes Received/sec
	2550		Message Bytes Total
	2552		Message Bytes Total/sec
	2554		Messages Received Total
	2556		Messages Received/sec
	2558		Avg Recipients/msg Received
	2560		Base Avg Recipients/msg Received

Continued on next page

TABLE D.1: PERFORMANCE COUNTERS ON A WINDOWS XP SERVER *(continued)*

OBJECT NUMBER	COUNTER NUMBER	OBJECT NAME	COUNTER*
	2562		% Recipients Local
	2564		Base % Recipients Local
	2566		% Recipients Remote
	2568		Base % Recipients Remote
	2570		Messages Refused for Size
	2572		Messages Refused for Address Objects
	2574		Messages Refused for Mail Objects
	2576		Messages Delivered Total
	2578		Messages Delivered/sec
	2580		Message Delivery Retries
	2582		Avg Retries/msg Delivered
	2584		Base Avg Retries/msg Delivered
	2586		Pickup Directory Messages Retrieved Total
	2588		Pickup Directory Messages Retrieved/sec
	2590		NDRs Generated
	2592		Local Queue Length
	2594		Local Retry Queue Length
	2596		Number of MailFiles Open
	2598		Number of QueueFiles Open
	2600		Categorizer Queue Length
	2602		Messages Sent Total
	2604		Messages Sent/sec
	2606		Message Send Retries
	2608		Avg Retries/msg Sent
	2610		Base Avg Retries/msg Sent
	2612		Avg Recipients/msg Sent

Continued on next page

TABLE D.1: PERFORMANCE COUNTERS ON A WINDOWS XP SERVER *(continued)*

OBJECT NUMBER	COUNTER NUMBER	OBJECT NAME	COUNTER*
	2614		Base Avg Recipients/msg Sent
	2616		Remote Queue Length
	2618		DNS Queries Total
	2620		DNS Queries/sec
	2622		Remote Retry Queue Length
	2626		Inbound Connections Total
	2628		Inbound Connections Current
	2630		Outbound Connections Total
	2632		Outbound Connections Current
	2634		Outbound Connections Refused
	2636		Total Connection Errors
	2638		Connection Errors/sec
	2640		Directory Drops Total
	2642		Directory Drops/sec
	2644		Routing Table Lookups Total
	2646		Routing Table Lookups/sec
	2648		ETRN Messages Total
	2650		ETRN Messages/sec
	2652		Badmailed Messages (No Recipients)
	2654		Badmailed Messages (Hop Count Exceeded)
	2656		Badmailed Messages (General Failure)
	2658		Badmailed Messages (Bad Pickup File)
	2660		Badmailed Messages (Triggered via Event)
	2662		Badmailed Messages (NDR of DSN)

Continued on next page

TABLE D.1: PERFORMANCE COUNTERS ON A WINDOWS XP SERVER *(continued)*

OBJECT NUMBER	COUNTER NUMBER	OBJECT NAME	COUNTER*
	2664		Messages Pending Routing
	2666		Messages Currently Undeliverable
	2668		Total Messages Submitted
	2670		Total DSN Failures
	2672		Current Messages in Local Delivery
	2674		Cat: Messages Submitted
	2676		Cat: Messages Submitted/sec
	2678		Cat: Categorizations Completed
	2680		Cat: Categorizations Completed/sec
	2682		Cat: Categorizations in Progress
	2684		Cat: Categorizations Completed Successfully
	2686		Cat: Categorizations Failed (Nonretryable Error)
	2688		Cat: Categorizations Failed (Retryable Error)
	2690		Cat: Categorizations Failed (Out of Memory)
	2692		Cat: Categorizations Failed (DS Logon Failure)
	2694		Cat: Categorizations Failed (DS Connection Failure)
	2696		Cat: Categorizations Failed (Sink Retryable Error)
	2698		Cat: Messages Categorized
	2700		Cat: Messages Bifurcated
	2702		Cat: Messages Aborted
	2704		Cat: Recipients before Categorization

Continued on next page

TABLE D.1: PERFORMANCE COUNTERS ON A WINDOWS XP SERVER *(continued)*

OBJECT NUMBER	COUNTER NUMBER	OBJECT NAME	COUNTER*
	2706		Cat: Recipients after Categorization
	2708		Cat: Recipients NDRd by Categorizer
	2710		Cat: Recipients NDRd (Unresolved)
	2712		Cat: Recipients NDRd (Ambiguous Address)
	2714		Cat: Recipients NDRd (Illegal Address)
	2716		Cat: Recipients NDRd (Forwarding Loop)
	2718		Cat: Recipients NDRd (Sink Recip Errors)
	2720		Cat: Recipients in Categorization
	2722		Cat: Senders Unresolved
	2724		Cat: Senders with Ambiguous Addresses
	2726		Cat: Address Lookups
	2728		Cat: Address Lookups/sec
	2730		Cat: Address Lookup Completions
	2732		Cat: Address Lookup Completions/sec
	2734		Cat: Address Lookups Not Found
	2736		Cat: Mailmsg Duplicate Collisions
	2738		Cat: LDAP Connections
	2740		Cat: LDAP Connection Failures
	2742		Cat: LDAP Connections Currently Open
	2744		Cat: LDAP Binds

Continued on next page

TABLE D.1: PERFORMANCE COUNTERS ON A WINDOWS XP SERVER *(continued)*

OBJECT NUMBER	COUNTER NUMBER	OBJECT NAME	COUNTER*
	2746		Cat: LDAP Bind Failures
	2748		Cat: LDAP Searches
	2750		Cat: LDAP Searches/sec
	2752		Cat: LDAP Paged Searches
	2754		Cat: LDAP Search Failures
	2756		Cat: LDAP Paged Search Failures
	2758		Cat: LDAP Searches Completed
	2760		Cat: LDAP Searches Completed/sec
	2762		Cat: LDAP Paged Searches Completed
	2764		Cat: LDAP Search Completion Failures
	2766		Cat: LDAP Paged Search Completion Failures
	2768		Cat: LDAP General Completion Failures
	2770		Cat: LDAP Searches Abandoned
	2772		Cat: LDAP Searches Pending Completion
2774		**SMTP NTFS Store Driver**	
	2776		Messages in the Queue Directory
	2778		Messages Allocated
	2780		Messages Deleted
	2782		Messages Enumerated
	2784		Open Message Bodies
	2786		Open Message Streams
2788		**Indexing Service**	
	2790		Word Lists
	2792		Saved Indexes

Continued on next page

TABLE D.1: PERFORMANCE COUNTERS ON A WINDOWS XP SERVER *(continued)*

OBJECT NUMBER	COUNTER NUMBER	OBJECT NAME	COUNTER*
	2794		Index Size (MB)
	2796		Files to Be Indexed
	2798		Unique Keys
	2800		Running Queries
	2802		Merge Progress
	2804		# Documents Indexed
	2806		Total # Documents
	2808		Total # of Queries
	2810		Deferred for Indexing
2812		**Indexing Service Filter**	
	2814		Total Indexing Speed (MB/hr)
	2816		Binding Time (msec)
	2818		Indexing Speed (MB/hr)
2820		**Http Indexing Service**	
	2822		Cache Items
	2824		% Cache Hits
	2826		Total Cache Accesses 1
	2828		% Cache Misses
	2830		Total Cache Accesses 2
	2832		Active Queries
	2834		Total Queries
	2836		Queries per Minute
	2838		Current Requests Queued
	2840		Total Requests Rejected
2848		**DHCP Server**	
	2850		Packets Received/sec
	2852		Duplicates Dropped/sec
	2854		Packets Expired/sec

Continued on next page

TABLE D.1: PERFORMANCE COUNTERS ON A WINDOWS XP SERVER *(continued)*

OBJECT NUMBER	COUNTER NUMBER	OBJECT NAME	COUNTER*
	2856		Milliseconds per Packet (Avg).
	2858		Active Queue Length
	2860		Conflict Check Queue Length
	2862		Discovers/sec
	2864		Offers/sec
	2866		Requests/sec
	2868		Informs/sec
	2870		Acks/sec
	2872		Nacks/sec
	2874		Declines/sec
	2876		Releases/sec
2878		**WMI Objects**	
	2880		HiPerf Classes
	2882		HiPerf Validity

* Counter names may be shared between multiple Performance Monitor objects.

Appendix E

Plug and Play Identifiers

MICROSOFT, WHEN DEVELOPING THE specifications for Plug and Play (PnP), worked with an existing standard call EISA (Extended Industry Standard Architecture). EISA includes a methodology for identifying devices, assigning each device a three-character manufacturer identifier and a four-digit device identifier (expressed in hexadecimal).

The three-character manufacturer identifier "PNP" was acquired by Microsoft for use with devices that did not normally have identifiers. This allows Windows to use identifiers with devices such as hardware on the system board, I/O ports, keyboards, mice, and so forth.

NOTE *Plug and Play is often shown as PnP (note the lowercase n). Either PnP or PNP is acceptable in the registry.*

In the Windows registry (mostly in HKEY_LOCAL_MACHINE), there are five main classes of PNP numbers, as shown in Table E.1.

TABLE E.1: CLASSES OF PnP DEVICE IDENTIFIERS

CLASS	ID RANGE
System devices, I/O, timers, input, etc.	PNP0xxx
Network adapters	PNP8xxx
SCSI, proprietary CD adapters	PNPAxxx
Multimedia hardware	PNPBxxx
Modems	PNPCxxx–PNPDxxx

System Devices

System devices use identifiers from PNP0000 to PNP0FFF. Microsoft has subdivided the system class of devices into a number of subcategories (see Table E.2).

TABLE E.2: CATEGORIES OF SYSTEM DEVICES

TYPE OF SYSTEM DEVICE	DEVICE ID RANGE
Interrupt controllers	PNP0000–PNP00FF
Timers	PNP0100–PNP01FF
DMA	PNP0200–PNP02FF
Keyboards	PNP0300–PNP03FF
Parallel devices	PNP0400–PNP04FF
Serial devices	PNP0500–PNP05FF
Disk controllers	PNP0600–PNP06FF
Floppy disk controllers	PNP0700–PNP07FF
System speaker	PNP0800
Compatibility	PNP0802–PNP08FF
Display adapters	PNP0900–PNP09FF
Peripheral/expansion buses	PNP0A00–PNP0AFF
Real-time clock	PNP0B00
Unassigned	PNP0B01–PNP0BFF
BIOS and system motherboard devices	PNP0C00–PNP0CFF
PCMCIA controller	PNP0E00–PNP0EFF
Mice	PNP0F00–PNP0FFF
Network adapters	PNP8000–PNP8FFF
Mitsumi CD-ROM controller	PNPA030
Miscellaneous adapters	PNPB000–PNPB0FF

Table E.3 shows device IDs for some specific devices in the system class. There may be other devices, though the list does not change frequently.

TABLE E.3: THE SYSTEM DEVICES CLASS

DEVICE ID	DESCRIPTION
Interrupt Controlsers	
PNP0000	AT interrupt controller
PNP0001	EISA interrupt controller

Continued on next page

TABLE E.3: THE SYSTEM DEVICES CLASS *(continued)*

DEVICE ID	DESCRIPTION
Interrupt Controllers	
PNP0002	MCA interrupt controller
PNP0003	APIC
PNP0004	Cyrix SLiC MP interrupt controller
Timers	
PNP0100	AT timer
PNP0101	EISA timer
PNP0102	MCA timer
DMA	
PNP0200	AT DMA controller
PNP0201	EISA DMA controller
PNP0202	MCA DMA controller
Keyboards	
PNP0300	IBM PC/XT keyboard controller (83-key)
PNP0301	IBM PC/AT keyboard controller (86-key)
PNP0302	IBM PC/XT keyboard controller (84-key)
PNP0303	IBM Enhanced (101/102-key, PS/2 mouse support)
PNP0304	Olivetti keyboard (83-key)
PNP0305	Olivetti keyboard (102-key)
PNP0306	Olivetti keyboard (86-key)
PNP0307	Microsoft Windows keyboard
PNP0308	General Input Device Emulation Interface (GIDEI) legacy
PNP0309	Olivetti keyboard (101/102 key)
PNP030A	AT&T 302 keyboard
PNP030B	Reserved by Microsoft
PNP0320	Japanese 101-key keyboard
PNP0321	Japanese AX keyboard
PNP0322	Japanese 106-key keyboard A01

Continued on next page

TABLE E.3: THE SYSTEM DEVICES CLASS *(continued)*

DEVICE ID	DESCRIPTION
PNP0323	Japanese 106-key keyboard 002/003
PNP0324	Japanese 106-key keyboard 001
PNP0325	Japanese Toshiba Desktop keyboard
PNP0326	Japanese Toshiba Laptop keyboard
PNP0327	Japanese Toshiba Notebook keyboard
PNP0340	Korean 84-key keyboard
PNP0341	Korean 86-key keyboard
PNP0342	Korean Enhanced keyboard
PNP0343	Korean Enhanced keyboard 101b
PNP0343	Korean Enhanced keyboard 101c
PNP0344	Korean Enhanced keyboard 103
Parallel Devices	
PNP0400	Standard LPT printer port
PNP0401	ECP printer port
Serial Devices	
PNP0500	Standard PC COM port
PNP0501	16550A-compatible COM port
PNP0502	Non-16550A-compatible COM ports
PNP0510	IrDA-compatible device
PNP0511	IrDA-compatible device
Disk Controllers	
PNP0600	Generic ESDI-, IDE-, and ATA-compatible hard disk controllers
PNP0601	Plus Hardcard II
PNP0602	Plus Hardcard IIXL/EZ
PNP0603	Generic IDE that supports the Microsoft Device Bay specification
PNP0700	Standard PC floppy disk controller
PNP0701	Standard PC floppy disk controller that supports the Microsoft Device Bay specification

Continued on next page

TABLE E.3: THE SYSTEM DEVICES CLASS *(continued)*

DEVICE ID	DESCRIPTION
Compatibility	
PNP0800	AT-style speaker sound
PNP0802	Microsoft Sound System–compatible devices (obsolete; instead use PNPB0xx, multimedia devices)
Display Adapters	
PNP0900	VGA compatible
PNP0901	Video Seven VRAM/VRAM II/1024i
PNP0902	8514/A compatible
PNP0903	Trident VGA
PNP0904	Cirrus Logic Laptop VGA
PNP0905	Cirrus Logic VGA
PNP0906	Tseng ET4000
PNP0907	Western Digital VGA
PNP0908	Western Digital Laptop VGA
PNP0909	S3 Inc. 911/924
PNP090A	ATI Ultra Pro/Plus (Mach 32)
PNP090B	ATI Ultra (Mach 8)
PNP090C	XGA compatible
PNP090D	ATI VGA Wonder
PNP090E	Weitek P9000 graphics adapter
PNP090F	Oak Technology VGA
PNP0910	Compaq QVision
PNP0911	XGA/2
PNP0912	Tseng Labs W32/W32i/W32p
PNP0913	S3 Inc. 801/928/964
PNP0914	Cirrus Logic 5429/5434 (memory mapped)
PNP0915	Compaq Advanced VGA (AVGA)
PNP0916	ATI Ultra Pro Turbo (Mach64)
PNP0917	Reserved by Microsoft

Continued on next page

TABLE E.3: THE SYSTEM DEVICES CLASS *(continued)*

DEVICE ID	DESCRIPTION
Display Adapters	
PNP0918	Matrox MGA
PNP0919	Compaq QVision 2000
PNP091A	Tseng W128
PNP0930	Chips & Technologies Super VGA
PNP0931	Chips & Technologies Accelerator
PNP0940	NCR 77c22e Super VGA
PNP0941	NCR 77c32blt
PNP09FF	Plug and Play monitors (VESA DDC)
Peripheral Buses	
PNP0A00	ISA bus
PNP0A01	EISA bus
PNP0A02	MCA bus
PNP0A03	PCI bus
PNP0A04	VESA/VL bus
PNP0A05	Generic ACPI bus
PNP0A06	Generic ACPI Extended-IO bus (EIO bus)
Real-Time Clock	
PNP0B00	AT real-time clock
BIOS and System Motherboard Devices	
PNP0C00	Plug and Play BIOS (only created by the root enumerator)
PNP0C01	System board
PNP0C02	General ID for reserving resources required by Plug and Play motherboard registers (not specific to a particular device)
PNP0C03	Plug and Play BIOS event notification interrupt
PNP0C04	Math coprocessor
PNP0C05	APM (Advanced Power Management) BIOS (version independent)
PNP0C06	Reserved for identification of early Plug and Play BIOS implementations
PNP0C07	Reserved for identification of early Plug and Play BIOS implementations

Continued on next page

TABLE E.3: THE SYSTEM DEVICES CLASS *(continued)*

DEVICE ID	DESCRIPTION
BIOS and System Motherboard Devices	
PNP0C08	ACPI (Advanced Configuration and Power Interface) system board hardware
PNP0C09	ACPI embedded controller
PNP0C0A	ACPI control method battery
PNP0C0B	ACPI fan
PNP0C0C	ACPI power-button device
PNP0C0D	ACPI lid device
PNP0C0E	ACPI sleep-button device
PNP0C0F	PCI interrupt link device
PNP0C10	ACPI system indicator device
PNP0C11	ACPI thermal zone
PNP0C12	Device Bay Controller
PNP0C13	Plug and Play BIOS (for non-ACPI systems)
PCMCIA Controller	
PNP0E00	Intel 82365–compatible PCMCIA controller
PNP0E01	Cirrus Logic CL-PD6720 PCMCIA controller
PNP0E02	VLSI VL82C146 PCMCIA controller
PNP0E03	Intel 82365–compatible CardBus controller
Mice	
PNP0F00	Microsoft bus mouse
PNP0F01	Microsoft serial mouse
PNP0F02	Microsoft InPort mouse
PNP0F03	Microsoft PS/2-style mouse
PNP0F04	Mouse Systems mouse
PNP0F05	Mouse Systems three-button mouse (COM2)
PNP0F06	Genius mouse (COM1)
PNP0F07	Genius mouse (COM2)
PNP0F08	Logitech serial mouse

Continued on next page

TABLE E.3: THE SYSTEM DEVICES CLASS *(continued)*

DEVICE ID	DESCRIPTION
Mice	
PNP0F09	Microsoft BallPoint serial mouse
PNP0F0A	Microsoft Plug and Play mouse
PNP0F0B	Microsoft Plug and Play BallPoint mouse
PNP0F0C	Microsoft-compatible serial mouse
PNP0F0D	Microsoft InPort–compatible mouse
PNP0F0E	Microsoft-compatible PS/2-style mouse
PNP0F0F	Microsoft BallPoint–compatible serial mouse
PNP0F10	Texas Instruments QuickPort mouse
PNP0F11	Microsoft-compatible bus mouse
PNP0F12	Logitech PS/2-style mouse
PNP0F13	PS/2 port for PS/2-style mice
PNP0F14	Microsoft Kids mouse
PNP0F15	Logitech bus mouse
PNP0F16	Logitech SWIFT device
PNP0F17	Logitech-compatible serial mouse
PNP0F18	Logitech-compatible bus mouse
PNP0F19	Logitech-compatible PS/2-style mouse
PNP0F1A	Logitech-compatible SWIFT device
PNP0F1B	HP Omnibook mouse
PNP0F1C	Compaq LTE trackball PS/2-style mouse
PNP0F1D	Compaq LTE trackball serial mouse
PNP0F1E	Microsoft Kids trackball mouse
PNP0F1F	Reserved by Microsoft Input Device Group
PNP0F20	Reserved by Microsoft Input Device Group
PNP0F21	Reserved by Microsoft Input Device Group
PNP0F22	Reserved by Microsoft Input Device Group
PNP0F23	Reserved by Microsoft Input Device Group
PNP0FFF	Reserved by Microsoft Systems

NIC Devices

The next class of PnP devices includes NIC (network interface card) devices. NICs are found on virtually all computers. Table E.4 lists the NIC device IDs.

NOTE   *Do not confuse the NIC's MAC (Media Access Control) address with the NIC's PNP identifier. The MAC is unique to each NIC, and PNP does not consider the MAC when identifying a NIC.*

TABLE E.4: THE NETWORK INTERFACE CARDS CLASS

DEVICE ID	DESCRIPTION
PNP8001	Novell/Anthem NE3200
PNP8004	Compaq NE3200
PNP8006	Intel EtherExpress/32
PNP8008	HP EtherTwist EISA LAN Adapter/32 (HP27248A)
PNP8065	Ungermann-Bass NIUps or NIUps/EOTP
PNP8072	DEC (DE211) EtherWorks MC/TP
PNP8073	DEC (DE212) EtherWorks MC/TP_BNC
PNP8078	DCA 10 Mb MCA
PNP8074	HP MC LAN Adapter/16 TP (PC27246)
PNP80c9	IBM Token Ring
PNP80ca	IBM Token Ring II
PNP80cb	IBM Token Ring II/Short
PNP80cc	IBM Token Ring 4/16Mbps
PNP80d3	Novell/Anthem NE1000
PNP80d4	Novell/Anthem NE2000
PNP80d5	NE1000 compatible
PNP80d6	NE2000 compatible
PNP80d7	Novell/Anthem NE1500T
PNP80d8	Novell/Anthem NE2100
PNP80dd	SMC ARCNETPC
PNP80de	SMC ARCNET PC100, PC200
PNP80df	SMC ARCNET PC110, PC210, PC250
PNP80e0	SMC ARCNET PC130/E

Continued on next page

TABLE E.4: THE NETWORK INTERFACE CARDS CLASS *(continued)*

DEVICE ID	DESCRIPTION
PNP80e1	SMC ARCNET PC120, PC220, PC260
PNP80e2	SMC ARCNET PC270/E
PNP80e5	SMC ARCNET PC600W, PC650W
PNP80e7	DEC DEPCA
PNP80e8	DEC (DE100) EtherWorks LC
PNP80e9	DEC (DE200) EtherWorks Turbo
PNP80ea	DEC (DE101) EtherWorks LC/TP
PNP80eb	DEC (DE201) EtherWorks Turbo/TP
PNP80ec	DEC (DE202) EtherWorks Turbo/TP_BNC
PNP80ed	DEC (DE102) EtherWorks LC/TP_BNC
PNP80ee	DEC EE101 (built in)
PNP80ef	DEC pc 433 WS (built in)
PNP80f1	3Com Etherlink Plus
PNP80f3	3Com Etherlink II or IITP (8- or 16-bit)
PNP80f4	3Com TokenLink
PNP80f6	3Com Etherlink 16
PNP80f7	3Com Etherlink III
PNP80f8	3Com generic Etherlink Plug and Play device
PNP80fb	Thomas Conrad TC6045
PNP80fc	Thomas Conrad TC6042
PNP80fd	Thomas Conrad TC6142
PNP80fe	Thomas Conrad TC6145
PNP80ff	Thomas Conrad TC6242
PNP8100	Thomas Conrad TC6245
PNP8105	DCA 10 MB
PNP8106	DCA 10 MB fiber-optic
PNP8107	DCA 10 MB twisted-pair
PNP8113	Racal NI6510

Continued on next page

TABLE E.4: THE NETWORK INTERFACE CARDS CLASS *(continued)*

DEVICE ID	DESCRIPTION
PNP811C	Ungermann-Bass NIUpc
PNP8120	Ungermann-Bass NIUpc/EOTP
PNP8123	SMC StarCard PLUS (WD/8003S)
PNP8124	SMC StarCard PLUS with onboard hub (WD/8003SH)
PNP8125	SMC EtherCard PLUS (WD/8003E)
PNP8126	SMC EtherCard PLUS with boot ROM socket (WD/8003EBT)
PNP8127	SMC EtherCard PLUS with boot ROM socket (WD/8003EB)
PNP8128	SMC EtherCard PLUS TP (WD/8003WT)
PNP812a	SMC EtherCard PLUS 16 with boot ROM socket (WD/8013EBT)
PNP812d	Intel EtherExpress 16 or 16TP
PNP812f	Intel TokenExpress 16/4
PNP8130	Intel TokenExpress MCA 16/4
PNP8132	Intel EtherExpress 16 (MCA)
PNP8137	Artisoft AE-1
PNP8138	Artisoft AE-2 or AE-3
PNP8141	Amplicard AC 210/XT
PNP8142	Amplicard AC 210/AT
PNP814b	Everex SpeedLink /PC16 (EV2027)
PNP8155	HP PC LAN Adapter/8 TP (HP27245)
PNP8156	HP PC LAN Adapter/16 TP (HP27247A)
PNP8157	HP PC LAN Adapter/8 TL (HP27250)
PNP8158	HP PC LAN Adapter/16 TP Plus (HP27247B)
PNP8159	HP PC LAN Adapter/16 TL Plus (HP27252)
PNP815f	National Semiconductor EtherNODE *16AT
PNP8160	National Semiconductor AT/LANTIC EtherNODE 16-AT3
PNP816A	NCR Token Ring 4Mbps ISA
PNP816D	NCR Token Ring 16/4Mbps ISA
PNP8191	Olicom 16/4 Token Ring adapter

Continued on next page

TABLE E.4: THE NETWORK INTERFACE CARDS CLASS *(continued)*

DEVICE ID	DESCRIPTION
PNP81c3	SMC EtherCard PLUS Elite (WD/8003EP)
PNP81c4	SMC EtherCard PLUS 10T (WD/8003W)
PNP81c5	SMC EtherCard PLUS Elite 16 (WD/8013EP)
PNP81c6	SMC EtherCard PLUS Elite 16T (WD/8013W)
PNP81c7	SMC EtherCard PLUS Elite 16 Combo (WD/8013EW or 8013EWC)
PNP81c8	SMC EtherElite Ultra 16
PNP81e4	Pure Data PDI9025-32 (Token Ring)
PNP81e6	Pure Data PDI508+ (ARCNET)
PNP81e7	Pure Data PDI516+ (ARCNET)
PNP81eb	Proteon Token Ring (P1390)
PNP81ec	Proteon Token Ring (P1392)
PNP81ed	Proteon ISA Token Ring (1340)
PNP81ee	Proteon ISA Token Ring (1342)
PNP81ef	Proteon ISA Token Ring (1346)
PNP81f0	Proteon ISA Token Ring (1347)
PNP81ff	Cabletron E2000 Series DNI
PNP8200	Cabletron E2100 Series DNI
PNP8209	Zenith Data Systems Z-Note
PNP820a	Zenith Data Systems NE2000 compatible
PNP8213	Xircom Pocket Ethernet II
PNP8214	Xircom Pocket Ethernet I
PNP821d	RadiSys EXM-10
PNP8227	SMC 3000 Series
PNP8228	SMC 91C2 controller
PNP8231	Advanced Micro Devices AM2100/AM1500T
PNP8263	Tulip NCC-16
PNP8277	Exos 105
PNP828A	Intel '595–based Ethernet

Continued on next page

TABLE E.4: THE NETWORK INTERFACE CARDS CLASS *(continued)*

DEVICE ID	DESCRIPTION
PNP828B	Tl2000-style Token Ring
PNP828C	AMD PCNet Family cards
PNP828D	AMD PCNet32 (VL version)
PNP8294	IrDA infrared NDIS driver (Microsoft supplied)
PNP82bd	IBM PCMCIA-NIC
PNP82C2	Xircom CE10
PNP82C3	Xircom CEM2
PNP8321	DEC Ethernet (all types)
PNP8323	SMC EtherCard (all types except 8013/A)
PNP8324	ARCNET compatible
PNP8326	Thomas Conrad (all ARCNET Types)
PNP8327	IBM Token Ring (all types)
PNP8385	Remote network access driver
PNP8387	RNA Point-to-Point Protocol driver
PNP8388	Reserved for Microsoft Networking components
PNP8389	Peer IrLAN infrared driver (Microsoft supplied)
PNP8390	Generic NICs

SCSI and CD-ROM Devices

The next class of PnP devices includes the SCSI and CD-ROM devices. Most high-performance computers use SCSI to interface the disk storage with the system. In addition, virtually every computer today is equipped with at least one CD-ROM drive. Table E.5 lists the SCSI and CD-ROM device IDs.

TABLE E.5: THE SCSI AND CD-ROM CLASS

DEVICE ID	DESCRIPTION
PNPA002	Future Domain 16-700 compatible controller
PNPA003	Panasonic proprietary CD-ROM adapter (Sound Blaster Pro/Sound Blaster 16)
PNPA01B	Trantor 128 SCSI controller

Continued on next page

TABLE E.5: THE SCSI AND CD-ROM CLASS *(continued)*

DEVICE ID	DESCRIPTION
PNPA01D	Trantor T160 SCSI controller
PNPA01E	Trantor T338 Parallel SCSI controller
PNPA01F	Trantor T348 Parallel SCSI controller
PNPA020	Trantor Media Vision SCSI controller
PNPA022	Always IN-2000 SCSI controller
PNPA02B	Sony proprietary CD-ROM controller
PNPA02D	Trantor T13b 8-bit SCSI controller
PNPA02F	Trantor T358 Parallel SCSI controller
PNPA030	Mitsumi LU-005 Single Speed CD-ROM controller & drive
PNPA031	Mitsumi FX-001 Single Speed CD-ROM controller & drive
PNPA032	Mitsumi FX-001 Double Speed CD-ROM controller & drive

Multimedia Devices

The next class of PnP devices includes multimedia devices. Most computers have a sound card and many are video capable. Nearly all computers have a joystick port too, useful for games and other software. Table E.6 lists the multimedia device IDs.

TABLE E.6: THE MULTIMEDIA DEVICES CLASS

DEVICE ID	DESCRIPTION
PNPB000	Sound Blaster 1.5–compatible sound device
PNPB001	Sound Blaster 2.0–compatible sound device
PNPB002	Sound Blaster Pro–compatible sound device
PNPB003	Sound Blaster 16–compatible sound device
PNPB004	Thunderboard-compatible sound device
PNPB005	Adlib-compatible FM synthesizer device
PNPB006	MPU401 compatible
PNPB007	Microsoft Windows Sound System–compatible sound device
PNPB008	Compaq Business Audio

Continued on next page

TABLE E.6: THE MULTIMEDIA DEVICES CLASS *(continued)*

DEVICE ID	DESCRIPTION
PNPB009	Plug and Play Microsoft Windows Sound System device
PNPB00A	MediaVision Pro Audio Spectrum (Trantor SCSI enabled, Thunder Chip disabled)
PNPB00B	MediaVision Pro Audio 3D
PNPB00C	MusicQuest MQX-32M
PNPB00D	MediaVision Pro Audio Spectrum Basic (no Trantor SCSI, Thunder Chip enabled)
PNPB00E	MediaVision Pro Audio Spectrum (Trantor SCSI enabled, Thunder Chip disabled)
PNPB00F	MediaVision Jazz-16 chipset (OEM Versions)
PNPB010	Auravision VxP500 chipset - Orchid Videola
PNPB018	MediaVision Pro Audio Spectrum 8-bit
PNPB019	MediaVision Pro Audio Spectrum Basic (no Trantor SCSI, Thunder Chip enabled)
PNPB020	Yamaha OPL3–compatible FM synthesizer device
PNPB02F	Joystick/game port

Modem Devices

The final class of PnP devices includes modem devices, both internal and external. Most computers have a modem, used to connect to the Internet, other computers, or online services. Modem devices are assigned identifiers in the range PNPC000 to PNPC001. Table E.7 lists the modem device IDs.

TABLE E.7: THE MODEM DEVICES CLASS

DEVICE ID	DESCRIPTION
PNPC000	Compaq 14400 modem (TBD)
PNPC001	Compaq 2400/9600 modem (TBD)

Appendix F

Microsoft Office CLSIDs

OFFICE 2000 AND OFFICE XP BOTH install a number of CLSIDs in the registry. If you come across a CLSID that you don't recognize, check this list to see if the CLSID is from Microsoft Office. Keep in mind that CLSIDs are critical to the proper operation of Windows, so do not delete them unless you know what you are doing.

The Microsoft Office CLSIDs—including brief descriptions of their functionality and file, type, and ordinal information—are listed in Table F.1; not every installation will install all of these CLSIDs. The path to these CLSIDs is HKEY_CLASSES_ROOT\CLSID.

TABLE F.1: MICROSOFT OFFICE CLSIDS

CLSID	DESCRIPTION	FILE, ORDINAL, TYPE
0000002F-0000-0000-C000-000000000046	CLSID Record Info	oleaut32.REG, 10, CLSID
0000002F-0000-0000-C000-000000000046	Inproc Server32	oleaut32.REG, 20, CLSID
00020420-0000-0000-C000-000000000046	PS Dispatch	oleaut32.REG, 40, CLSID
00020420-0000-0000-C000-000000000046	Inproc Server	ole2disp.dll, 50StdPicture, CLSID
00020420-0000-0000-C000-000000000046	Inproc Server32	oleaut32.REG, 7, oleaut32.REG, 8, CLSID
00020421-0000-0000-C000-000000000046	Inproc Server32	oleaut32.REG, 11, oleaut32.REG, 12, CLSID
00020421-0000-0000-C000-000000000046	PS Enum Variant	oleaut32.REG, 9, CLSID
00020421-0000-0000-C000-000000000046	Inproc Server ORAPI	JETERR40.CHM
00020422-0000-0000-C000-000000000046	PS Type Info	oleaut32.REG, 13, CLSID
00020422-0000-0000-C000-000000000046	Inproc Server OLE2disp.DLL	oleaut32.REG, 14, CLSID
00020422-0000-0000-C000-000000000046	Inproc Server32	oleaut32.REG, 15, oleaut32.REG, 16, CLSID
00020423-0000-0000-C000-000000000046	PS Type Lib	oleaut32.REG, 17, CLSID
00020423-0000-0000-C000-000000000046	Inproc Server	oleaut32.REG, 18, CLSID
00020423-0000-0000-C000-000000000046	Inproc Server32	oleaut32.REG, 19, oleaut32.REG, 2, CLSID
00020424-0000-0000-C000-000000000046	PS OA Interface	oleaut32.REG, 21, CLSID
00020424-0000-0000-C000-000000000046	Inproc Server	oleaut32.REG, 22, CLSID
00020424-0000-0000-C000-000000000046	Inproc Server32	oleaut32.REG, 23, oleaut32.REG, 24, CLSID
00020425-0000-0000-C000-000000000046	PS Type Comp	oleaut32.REG, 25, CLSID
00020425-0000-0000-C000-000000000046	Inproc Server	oleaut32.REG, 26, CLSID
00020425-0000-0000-C000-000000000046	Inproc Server32	oleaut32.REG, 27, oleaut32.REG, 28, CLSID
00020430-0000-0000-C000-000000000046	OLE Automation Microsoft Office Web Components 9	Omsrtedit 1.0 Type Library
0002E500-0000-0000-C000-000000000046	Implemented Categories	<Unknown>
0002E500-0000-0000-C000-000000000046	Microsoft Office Chart 9.0	<Unknown>
0002E500-0000-0000-C000-000000000046	Programmable	<Unknown>

Continued on next page

TABLE F.1: MICROSOFT OFFICE CLSIDs *(continued)*

CLSID	DESCRIPTION	FILE, ORDINAL, TYPE
0002E500-0000-0000-C000-000000000046	ToolboxBitmap32	\<Unknown\>
0002E500-0000-0000-C000-000000000046	\<Unknown\>	\<Unknown\>
0002E500-0000-0000-C000-000000000046	TypeLib	\<Unknown\>
0002E500-0000-0000-C000-000000000046	Version1.0	msowcd.REG, 1300WC.FieldList.9, CLSID
0002E500-0000-0000-C000-000000000046	VersionIndependent ProgID	msowcd.REG, 1400WC.Record Navigation Control.9, CLSID
0002E500-0000-0000-C000-000000000046	Control	\<Unknown\>
0002E500-0000-0000-C000-000000000046	Implemented Categories	msowcd.REG, 30, CLSID
0002E500-0000-0000-C000-000000000046	Implemented Categories	\<Unknown\>
0002E500-0000-0000-C000-000000000046	Inproc Server32	msowcd.REG, 50, CLSID
0002E500-0000-0000-C000-000000000046	Miscellaneous Status	\<Unknown\>
0002E500-0000-0000-C000-000000000046	Miscellaneous Status 1	msowcd.REG, 80, CLSID
0002E500-0000-0000-C000-000000000046	ProgID	msowcd.REG, 90, CLSID
0002E510-0000-0000-C000-000000000046	\<Unknown\>	Microsoft Office Spreadsheet 9.0
0002E510-0000-0000-C000-000000000046	\<Unknown\>	msowcd.REG, 16, CLSID
0002E510-0000-0000-C000-000000000046	Control	msowcd.REG, 17, CLSID
0002E510-0000-0000-C000-000000000046	Implemented Categories	msowcd.REG, 18, CLSID
0002E510-0000-0000-C000-000000000046	Implemented Categories	\<Unknown\>
0002E510-0000-0000-C000-000000000046	Inproc Server32	msowcd.REG, 2, CLSID
0002E510-0000-0000-C000-000000000046	Miscellaneous Status	msowcd.REG, 22, CLSID
0002E510-0000-0000-C000-000000000046	Miscellaneous Status	msowcd.REG, 23, CLSID
0002E510-0000-0000-C000-000000000046	ProgID	OWC.Spreadsheet.9, 24, CLSID
0002E510-0000-0000-C000-000000000046	Programmable	msowcd.REG, 25, CLSID
0002E510-0000-0000-C000-000000000046	ToolboxBitmap32	msowcd.REG, 26, CLSID
0002E510-0000-0000-C000-000000000046	TypeLib	msowcd.REG, 27, CLSID
0002E510-0000-0000-C000-000000000046	Version	msowcd.REG, 28, CLSID
0002E510-0000-0000-C000-000000000046	Version-Independent ProgID	OWC.Spreadsheet, 29, CLSID
0002E520-0000-0000-C000-000000000046	\<Unknown\>	\<Unknown\>

Continued on next page

TABLE F.1: MICROSOFT OFFICE CLSIDs *(continued)*

CLSID	DESCRIPTION	FILE, ORDINAL, TYPE
0002E520-0000-0000-C000-000000000046	<Unknown>	msowcd.REG, 3, CLSID
0002E520-0000-0000-C000-000000000046	Control	msowcd.REG, 31, CLSID
0002E520-0000-0000-C000-000000000046	Implemented Categories	msowcd.REG, 32, CLSID
0002E520-0000-0000-C000-000000000046	Implemented Categories	<Unknown>
0002E520-0000-0000-C000-000000000046	InprocServer32	<Unknown>
0002E520-0000-0000-C000-000000000046	Miscellaneous Status	msowcd.REG, 36, CLSID
0002E520-0000-0000-C000-000000000046	Miscellaneous Status 1	msowcd.REG, 37, CLSID
0002E520-0000-0000-C000-000000000046	ProgID	OWC.PivotTable.9, 38, CLSID
0002E520-0000-0000-C000-000000000046	Programmable	msowcd.REG, 39, CLSID

Index

Note to the Reader: Throughout this index **boldfaced** page numbers indicate primary discussions of a topic. *Italicized* page numbers indicate illustrations.

TELL US WHAT YOU THINK!

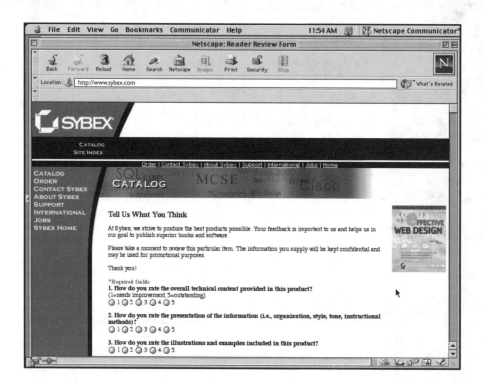

Your feedback is critical to our efforts to provide you with the best books and software on the market. Tell us what you think about the products you've purchased. It's simple:

1. Visit the Sybex website
2. Go to the product page
3. Click on **Submit a Review**
4. Fill out the questionnaire and comments
5. Click **Submit**

With your feedback, we can continue to publish the highest quality computer books and software products that today's busy IT professionals deserve.

www.sybex.com

SYBEX Inc. • 1151 Marina Village Parkway, Alameda, CA 94501 • 510-523-8233

A Quick Reference to Essential Registry Keys

Hive or Key	Subkey	Description
HKEY_LOCAL_MACHINE	All keys	This is the main system description hive. This hive is critical to the execution of Windows.
HKEY_LOCAL_MACHINE\Hardware\Description\	All keys	Contains information about the hardware installed in the computer. Much of this key is created at boot time, though some entries may be retained from previous executions.
HKEY_LOCAL_MACHINE\Hardware\Description\	System	Contains all system device information, excluding NIC and video devices.
HKEY_LOCAL_MACHINE\Hardware\Description\	System\Central Processor	Contains information about the actual CPU, such as make, model, and version information.
HKEY_LOCAL_MACHINE\Hardware\DeviceMap\	All keys	Contains basic device-mapping and control information.
HKEY_LOCAL_MACHINE\Hardware\DeviceMap\	KeyboardClass	Contains keyboard device-mapping information.
HKEY_LOCAL_MACHINE\Hardware\DeviceMap\	KeyboardPort	Contains information about the keyboard port configuration.
HKEY_LOCAL_MACHINE\Hardware\DeviceMap\	PARALLEL PORTS	Contains information about the printer (parallel) port configuration.
HKEY_LOCAL_MACHINE\Hardware\DeviceMap\	PointerClass	Contains information about the mouse.
HKEY_LOCAL_MACHINE\Hardware\DeviceMap\	PointerPort	Contains information about the port (mouse port, PS/2 mouse port, serial port, and so on) the mouse (pointer) is connected to.
HKEY_LOCAL_MACHINE\Hardware\DeviceMap\	Scsi	Contains general disk interface information for both IDE and SCSI devices.
HKEY_LOCAL_MACHINE\Hardware\DeviceMap\	SERIALCOMM	Contains serial communications device configurations.
HKEY_LOCAL_MACHINE\Hardware\DeviceMap\	VIDEO	Contains video configuration information.
HKEY_LOCAL_MACHINE\Hardware\ResourceMap\	All keys	Contains information about how resources (hardware) are mapped in the system.